SAP° Activate

SAP PRESS is a joint initiative of SAP and Rheinwerk Publishing. The know-how offered by SAP specialists combined with the expertise of Rheinwerk Publishing offers the reader expert books in the field. SAP PRESS features first-hand information and expert advice, and provides useful skills for professional decision-making.

SAP PRESS offers a variety of books on technical and business-related topics for the SAP user. For further information, please visit our website: *www.sap-press.com*.

Aditya Lal
SAP Activate Project Management Certification Guide: Certified Associate Exam
2021, 530 pages, paperback and e-book
www.sap-press.com/5194

Saueressig, Gilg, Grigoleit, Shah, Podbicanin, Homann
SAP S/4HANA Cloud: An Introduction (2nd Edition)
2022, approx. 465 pages, hardcover and e-book
www.sap-press.com/5457

Bardhan, Baumgartl, Choi, Dudgeon, Górecki, Lahiri, Meijerink, Worsley-Tonks
SAP S/4HANA: An Introduction (4th Edition)
2021, 648 pages, hardcover and e-book
www.sap-press.com/5232

Densborn, Finkbohner, Freudenberg, Höft, Mathäß, Rubarth
Migrating to SAP S/4HANA (2nd Edition)
2021, 606 pages, hardcover and e-book
www.sap-press.com/5279

Wolfgang Fitznar, Dennis Fitznar
Using SAP S/4HANA: An Introduction for Business Users
2022, 420 pages, paperback and e-book
www.sap-press.com/5065

Sven Denecken, Jan Musil, Srivatsan Santhanam

SAP® Activate

Project Management for SAP S/4HANA® and SAP S/4HANA® Cloud

Editor Megan Fuerst
Acquisitions Editor Emily Nicholls
Copyeditor Melinda Rankin
Cover Design Graham Geary
Photo Credit iStockphoto: 154957014/© ThomasVogel
Layout Design Vera Brauner
Production Kelly O'Callaghan
Typesetting SatzPro, Krefeld (Germany)
Printed and bound in Canada, on paper from sustainable sources

ISBN 978-1-4932-2213-1
© 2022 by Rheinwerk Publishing, Inc., Boston (MA)
2nd edition 2022

Library of Congress Cataloging-in-Publication:
Names: Denecken, Sven, author. | Musil, Jan (Program director), author. |
  Santhanam, Srivatsan, author.
Title: SAP activate : project management for SAP S/4HANA and SAP S/4HANA
  cloud / by Sven Denecken, Jan Musil, and Srivatsan Santhanam.
Description: 2nd edition. | Boston : Rheinwerk Publishing, [2022] |
  Includes index.
Identifiers: LCCN 2022002689 | ISBN 9781493222131 (hardcover) | ISBN
  9781493222148 (ebook)
Subjects: LCSH: Project management--Data processing. | SAP HANA (Electronic
  resource)
Classification: LCC HD69.P75 D46 2022 | DDC 658.4/04028553--dc23
LC record available at https://lccn.loc.gov/2022002689

Contents at a Glance

Dear Reader,

The other day, I got lost while driving in the city. I blame my GPS.

Trying to navigate downtown Boston on a rainy night, I followed my GPS app's guidance and took a sharp right turn—into a construction site. (In my defense, that road used to be an on-ramp to the highway.) In an attempt to course correct, I reversed and opted for the soft right turn, prompting my GPS to not-so-helpfully redirect me back to the closed road. I realized that I was going to need to puzzle out the route on my own.

It's difficult to keep up with change, whether you're heading across town or toward a new software implementation. Your transition path to SAP S/4HANA evolves with the changing SAP landscape (what's the buzz about RISE with SAP? What's available for hybrid landscapes? How has the product terminology changed?). To ensure a successful implementation project free of wrong turns and wasted time, you need an up-to-date map. This second edition includes the latest guidance for your SAP S/4HANA project, whether your journey is a new implementation or system conversion, and whether your destination is on-premise, public cloud, or private cloud.

What did you think about *SAP Activate: Project Management for SAP S/4HANA and SAP S/4HANA Cloud*? Your comments and suggestions are the most useful tools to help us make our books the best they can be. Please feel free to contact me and share any praise or criticism you may have.

Thank you for purchasing a book from SAP PRESS!

Megan Fuerst
Editor, SAP PRESS

meganf@rheinwerk-publishing.com
www.sap-press.com
Rheinwerk Publishing · Boston, MA

Contents

4   Starting with a Working System   121

5   Configuration, Data Migration, Extensibility, Integration, and Testing   139

6   Agile Project Delivery

7   New Implementation of SAP S/4HANA

8   System Conversion and Selective Data Transition to SAP S/4HANA

10   Organizational Change Management

Foreword

The past two years of the global pandemic, during which time we have experienced significant disruptions to the business environment, only underlined the need for businesses to rapidly respond to the pace of change in order to continue thriving. This accelerated the impact of the digital- and innovation-driven economy that is now the reality for us all.

The pace of change that businesses need to deal with will continue to accelerate throughout this new decade and can only be managed with the ability to modernize and evolve business processes utilizing agile and intelligent ERP platforms. With SAP S/4HANA Cloud, businesses are best placed to utilize the embedded intelligence and analytics to reimagine business processes and to make the right decision at the right time.

To maintain and build this agility, more and more businesses are quickly turning to cloud or hybrid deployment approaches for their ERP system. A cloud approach provides businesses with a much quicker time to value as they welcome a fit-to-standard approach to rapidly deploy. This approach provides the business with a more flexible IT strategy that can more effectively support the changing business strategies that the digital marketplace demands.

It has become clear that a prescriptive guidance that delivers pre-configured content is the key to ensure the aspirational benefits of a cloud approach to rapidly deploy solutions at a lower total cost of ownership (TCO)/total cost of implementation (TCI) for the business. This is something that I am proud to say confidently that SAP Activate delivers. The combination of SAP S/4HANA Cloud and SAP Activate is unique in the marketplace and demonstrates the thought leadership that SAP brings to the table based on its decades of experience delivering ERP solutions for customers across the world and in all industries.

As you'll read throughout this book, the broad span of SAP Activate not only covers the initial deployment, where the focus is on enabling and supporting a fit-to-standard approach, but also supports the customer running the solution to continuously adopt the innovations that SAP S/4HANA Cloud delivers through regular upgrades. The global pandemic also changed how we get work done. SAP Activate fully supports teams working in hybrid or fully remote setups with dedicated playbooks and tools that help project teams deliver on business values without missing a step.

Finally, I would like to thank the authors of this book for taking the time to constructively and concisely lay out all aspects of SAP Activate and its strategic importance for

SAP S/4HANA Cloud customers. The expertise of these authors is market leading. They have hands-on experience in many projects from around the world, and you can be confident that what follows in this book is the most up to date and relevant information about SAP Activate from the most trusted sources.

Jan Gilg
President and Chief Product Officer SAP S/4HANA, SAP SE

Preface

Welcome to the second edition of the most comprehensive book about SAP Activate for SAP S/4HANA Cloud and SAP S/4HANA, in which we'll take you on a journey of deploying and innovating your software environment in your organization.

In today's fast-changing business environment, companies face disruption everywhere, often described as *digital transformation*. But the challenges we're all facing are bigger than that, whether faced by new entrants or existing competitors who are faster and more agile in the adoption of new business models or the use of intelligent technologies. Businesses need to constantly innovate in how they create value through new ways to interact with customers and business partners, as well as how they compete with other companies. This need for fast and agile response was felt by many businesses and organizations even more significantly in the past few years during the global pandemic.

As we write this book, the world is facing an enormous crisis: the COVID-19 pandemic. The pandemic is far from over, but we are all hopeful that we are going to emerge strong and healthy on the other side. Still, its significant impact on business operations cannot be understated, and the need for adaptability and digital transformation is only increasing. Ultimately, a major challenge we face is determining how software can support this dramatic shift while allowing you to run your existing business processes more efficiently— business processes that your organization has built and fine-tuned over years. We believe every organization needs to address this challenge quickly to stay relevant.

Within this book, we'll provide information on how your organization can prepare for, plan, and adopt an SAP S/4HANA Cloud (or on-premise) solution that provides your organization with a flexible digital core for innovating your business processes rapidly and continuously. SAP has designed the SAP Activate approach to help organizations not only deploy their SAP S/4HANA Cloud and on-premise solutions fast, but also apply principles that enable them to adopt new capabilities and innovate their business processes as SAP delivers new functionality and as businesses and organizations evolve.

With the rapid innovation cycles of SAP S/4HANA Cloud, your business can take advantage of key innovations such as robotic process automation (RPA), artificial intelligence (AI), embedded analytics capabilities, machine learning scenarios, and key usability innovations in SAP Fiori to unlock the potential of this next-generation intelligent enterprise resource planning (ERP) system for your organization.

No matter which deployment strategy you choose, each is covered in its own chapter or unit in this book. This book takes you on a journey through SAP Activate, from introducing the key concepts and components through discussing the tools and applications you'll use during your deployment. We then provide comprehensive coverage of the deployment approaches: new implementation, system conversion, and selective data transition.

We truly hope you enjoy this book and wish you luck on your journey of transition to SAP S/4HANA Cloud or SAP S/4HANA.

Objective of This Book

Our goal in writing this book is to provide one comprehensive guide to SAP Activate for IT professionals, business users, and consultants who are planning or implementing SAP S/4HANA Cloud (or on-premise) in their organizations. This book aims to provide details about the implementation and operation of SAP S/4HANA Cloud, SAP S/4HANA (on-premise), and a hybrid environment combining both the cloud and on-premise solutions in a federated deployment model. You'll not only learn the fundamentals and principles of SAP Activate but also discover how to access SAP Activate content and methodology and utilize the expertise and knowledge of the SAP Activate community of experts. In addition, you'll learn about the subtle differences between using SAP Activate for implementation of cloud solutions and on-premise solutions. Finally, this book provides a set of practice questions that you can review as preparation for your SAP Activate certification exam.

Who This Book Is For

This book is targeted at a wide range of people in roles that plan, execute, contribute to, or influence deployment of SAP software solutions in their organizations or their client organizations. Specifically, the following roles will benefit from reading this book and following the SAP Activate approach during deployment of SAP S/4HANA Cloud and SAP S/4HANA in their organizations:

- Sponsors of transformation programs
- IT executives and managers
- Leaders of line of business (LoB) organizations, such as finance and logistics
- Program managers and project managers
- Agile coaches and agile practitioners
- Solution, application, and technology architects
- Application experts and consultants
- Technology experts and consultants
- Developers
- Students interested in a career in IT or consulting services

How This Book Is Organized

This book is structured into 11 chapters and an appendix:

- **Chapter 1: SAP S/4HANA Fundamentals**
  We begin with an introduction of SAP S/4HANA Cloud and SAP S/4HANA and a discussion of the deployment strategies customers can apply via SAP S/4HANA in their organizations to meet their goals by deploying the software in the cloud, on premise, or in a hybrid two-tier setup.

- **Chapter 2: Introduction to SAP Activate**
  This chapter takes you on a journey through SAP Activate, explaining the fundamentals of the approach; discussing the structure of the methodology; discussing the golden rules for implementation, including the recommended governance to follow the rules in your project; and covering the importance of the SAP Activate community on *sap.com*.

- **Chapter 3: Accessing SAP Activate**
  In this chapter, we'll dive into the details of the key tools to support users of SAP Activate in their journey, including SAP Cloud ALM, the SAP Activate Roadmap Viewer, SAP Best Practices Explorer, and SAP Solution Manager. You will learn what each of these tools does and how you can leverage them in your project.

- **Chapter 4: Starting with a Working System**
  In Chapter 4, we'll focus on the two key types of preconfiguration that customers will use in their deployment of SAP S/4HANA: SAP Best Practices and the enterprise management layer for SAP S/4HANA. We provide comprehensive descriptions of the business content and consumption of these assets in your project. We also discuss the importance of the business content for successfully running fit-to-standard workshops.

- **Chapter 5: Configuration, Data Migration, Extensibility, Integration, and Testing**
  In Chapter 5, we'll focus on the fundamentals of how the solution is configured, extended, integrated with other solutions, and tested. This chapter provides an overview of the concepts for these topics and sets the foundation for Chapters 7 and 8, in which we'll focus on deployment of SAP S/4HANA Cloud and SAP S/4HANA. In this edition, we have expanded the discussion to also include the new configuration framework for SAP S/4HANA Cloud provided by SAP Central Business Configuration.

- **Chapter 6: Agile Project Delivery**
  Before you get to the deployment processes, Chapter 6 offers a detailed explanation of how SAP Activate incorporates agile concepts in the approach and how agile can be scaled in large organizations and projects. We discuss the roles, organization, governance and processes agile teams apply in their implementation process.

- **Chapter 7: New Implementation of SAP S/4HANA**
  In Chapter 7, you'll learn how to perform a new implementation of all the SAP

S/4HANA Cloud and SAP S/4HANA solutions. We will discuss the new implementation of SAP S/4HANA Cloud in a three-system landscape; SAP S/4HANA Cloud, private edition; and the SAP S/4HANA (on-premise) solution. For each of the solutions, we will take you through all the phases of SAP Activate to help you understand the key steps for deployment of the solution and learn how to prepare for regular upgrades and innovation shipments from SAP.

- **Chapter 8: System Conversion and Selective Data Transition to SAP S/4HANA**
Chapter 8 will then discuss the strategies and steps for system conversion and selective data transition of SAP S/4HANA Cloud and SAP S/4HANA. For each of these deployment approaches, we'll take you on a journey through the key steps your project team will go through from the discover to the run phase of SAP Activate.

- **Chapter 9: Deploying Hybrid System Landscapes**
Chapter 9 will explore the deployment of SAP S/4HANA in hybrid landscapes and will explain the hybrid scenarios across finance, sales, procurement, manufacturing, and analytics. This section has also been significantly enhanced in this second edition as SAP has expanded the scope of the two-tier hybrid scenarios. We also cover recommendations for organizations deploying SAP S/4HANA Cloud in their existing environments while maximizing the use of their existing investment in their IT infrastructure.

- **Chapter 10: Organizational Change Management**
Everybody deploying SAP S/4HANA Cloud and SAP S/4HANA in their organizations needs to be familiar with critical concepts and approaches for organizational change management (OCM). These are fundamental for successful solution adoption and customer lifetime value realization. The topics of change management are often underestimated, and this negatively impacts the adoption of the solution in the business. This chapter is a must-read for all transformation managers.

- **Chapter 11: SAP Activate for Other SAP Products**
Finally, Chapter 11 provides several examples of SAP Activate assets for other SAP products, such as SAP SuccessFactors, and detailed guidance for implementation of multiple products in SAP Activate for the intelligent enterprise. We also discuss SAP Activate for SAP Analytics Cloud, which provides guidance for customers deploying analytics solutions in their organization, and we introduce the methodology for upgrading your SAP S/4HANA solution and for additional product integration. This chapter includes a complete list of SAP Activate roadmaps that are available at the time of writing this book (winter 2022). For additional assets, you can access the SAP Activate Roadmap Viewer and SAP Best Practices Explorer.

- **Appendix A: SAP Activate Certification Preparation**
In Appendix A, you'll find practice questions for your preparation for the SAP Activate certification exam. These questions are different from the actual certification exam questions but follow the same structure that you'll encounter while taking the SAP Activate certification exam. They cover the scope of topics this book addresses, with a focus on topics and categories listed in the certification exam.

Acknowledgments

We thank our families for their patience and support while we were working on this book. Your support and encouragement helped us get through long nights of writing and revising the text to make this book something we're all proud of.

We also thank all the contributors and reviewers who helped make this book a comprehensive compendium of SAP Activate approaches, content, tools, and methods. You'll find short biographies for all the contributors in Appendix B.

Chapter 1
SAP S/4HANA Fundamentals

*Planning and executing digital business transformation is essential
for the success of every business during this time of constantly changing
markets, customer needs, and competition. SAP S/4HANA provides
an intelligent, integrated ERP system that runs on the SAP HANA
in-memory database to help innovate processes across a wide range
of businesses and industries.

For today's businesses, success comes when you can work together across all domains and jointly focus on business outcomes. Having visibility of information across business domains and being able to perform periodic course corrections based on forecasting and reporting isn't enough.

Therefore, the new challenge for enterprise resource planning (ERP) systems is to overcome today's fragmentation of business decision-making and execution and to bring about truly integrated business management without the limitations and complexity of legacy environments. Informed decisions and agile simulations of alternative business scenarios will allow enterprises to adapt and continuously advance. Modern ERP systems need to help businesses evolve from reactive decision-making and partially informed execution to continuous and proactive simulation of possible business outcomes. Such outcomes will be executed by a fully informed workforce that can wholly focus on value-adding activities and off-loading low-value tasks to system-automated processes—all to the delight of customers at every touchpoint with the company.

SAP provides organizations with the foundation to become intelligent enterprises, enabling them to run business operations better, become more resilient to changes in the marketplace, increase profitability, and become more sustainable. At the core of the intelligent enterprise, SAP S/4HANA redefines enterprise management by exploiting modern technologies, such as integration of online analytical processing (OLAP) and online transactional processing (OLTP), artificial intelligence (AI), big data processing, and automation, while simultaneously applying them to new digital business practices. With such capabilities at play, enterprises will be able to consume new data streams from partners, consumers, and devices.

Enterprises will also be able to supplement these capabilities with automatically identified patterns and predicted data points, provide them as insights of previously unknown depth and breadth to all stakeholders of the enterprise, and effectively engage them in collaborative value creation and customer focus.

In this chapter, we'll establish the SAP S/4HANA basics, including key technologies such as SAP HANA and SAP Fiori, the available offerings and deployment models, and the transition options. To begin, we'll explore the context in which SAP S/4HANA is positioned: the intelligent enterprise.

1.1   Transition into an Intelligent Enterprise

Today's businesses are constantly tested with changing business environments, evolving customer needs, and evolving market situations. Over the past two years, the entire world experienced massive changes to the way consumers behave, employees work, supply chains behave, and governments respond to evolving health crises. If anything, the pace of change each business needs to respond to only accelerated. Many businesses are in the thick of the transition to the intelligent enterprise and need to develop business models resilient to disruption. Table 1.1 notes the differences between traditional enterprise management and enterprise management suited for the intelligent enterprise.

Traditional	Intelligent Enterprise
Focus on supply/demand matching and profitability	Focus on customer experience along the entire value chain
Bottom-up versus top-down (strategy, business plan, and directives)	Strategy execution at all levels of the corporate structure
Periodic planning of resources to meet time-bound profitability goals	Ongoing business optimization via simulation of scenarios and embedded valuation
Management process focused on forward projections and results review	Management exploiting strategic opportunities through organizational agility
Automation of simple recurring tasks only	Automation of comprehensive processes that used to require human intervention
Enterprise focuses on top line and bottom line	Social, sustainable enterprise focusing on top line, bottom line, and green line

Table 1.1 Differences between Enterprise Management Today and in the Future

The effectiveness of this new style of management hinges on the extent to which meaningful insights for game-changing outcomes can be generated fast enough to be ahead of competitive pressures. Therefore, we need to ensure that all relevant streams of information are brought together with the business information traditionally seen in the scope of ERP (operational data), such as relevant patterns emerging from big data pools (market and resource signals, device information) and customer experience feedback (experience data). Today's enterprise needs to drive business innovation to grow the top line, drive operational excellence to improve bottom line, and do all this in a sustainable and socially responsible way to sustain the green line. Figure 1.1 shows the components of the intelligent enterprise that runs business processes powered by applications across the intelligent suite and industry cloud to ensure an excellent customer experience and sustainable enterprise. All these components are built on top of SAP Business Technology Platform (SAP BTP) and infrastructure that enables scalable, sustainable, and resilient business execution.

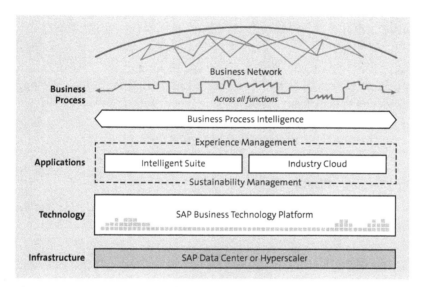

Figure 1.1 Components of Intelligent Enterprise

SAP Business Technology Platform

SAP BTP provides customers one platform that brings together intelligent enterprise applications, database and data management, analytics, and integration and extension capabilities. You can leverage SAP BTP for both cloud and hybrid environments. It provides access to hundreds of prebuilt integrations for SAP and third-party applications. You can learn more at *https://www.sap.com/products/business-technology-platform.html*.

Three overall market trends, as discussed in the following subsections, set the bar for differentiation, the rise of the intelligent enterprise, and the adoption of intelligent technology such as process automation, AI, and machine learning.

1.1.1 Preparing Businesses for a Fast-Changing Future

Uncertainty is among the biggest challenges businesses face today as the pace of change continues to accelerate. In this climate, most organizations must make the right decisions to ensure survival and growth. But they don't necessarily know how, when, and where change will happen; as we all experienced in the past two years, change can come rapidly and both accelerate business trends and impact consumer behaviors. For example, a significant shift in buying patterns to online shopping, increased use of delivery services, and much more strained supply chains. In other words, organizations must have the structural and financial flexibility to make swift decisions and grab opportunities as soon as they appear. In the same way, they need to reinvent the enterprise. But businesses focused on the existing digital landscape for predicting the future will find this landscape inappropriate to modernize their business into an intelligent enterprise.

One of the first steps is to update your digital landscape to support your organization in evolving its business processes, which requires a sequential path of technology adoption. This allows you to transform the business and connect the dots between current and future digital capabilities and thus enable new opportunities. You need agile IT solutions to be well prepared for an unpredictable future.

1.1.2   The Evolving Nature of Data

In the classical IT landscape, a separation exists between OLTP and OLAP systems. In general, OLTP systems provide source data to data warehouses, whereas OLAP systems help to analyze it.

Data-driven decision-making, which gives managers fact-based understanding beyond intuition when making decisions, is evolving into a vastly more sophisticated concept known as *big data*.

Companies must consider centralizing their data (with OLTP and OLAP no longer siloed) into one central place from which they can build and operate new and innovative processes, business models, and customer experiences. Handling data in one place is critical to becoming an intelligent enterprise.

1.1.3   Adoption of Intelligent Technology

It's all about using the new smart technologies—AI, machine learning, robotic process automation (RPA), blockchain, natural language processing, predictive analytics, and intelligent situation handling—in all business units of the company and everywhere in the software stack in such a way that they together exploit their potential to generate greater added value.

Within this framework of an intelligent enterprise, you can set the right foundation to embrace tomorrow's digital capabilities and make your core intelligent and extended technology a key part of your ERP platform.

Let's look at some examples of intelligent technology:

- **Machine learning**
  Machine learning can suggest data-driven improvements to optimize operational efficiency through insight based on evaluation of structured and unstructured data.

- **Artificial intelligence**
  AI can detect patterns in complex data sets at extreme speed and scale that help your organization understand the underlying trends and respond fast.

- **Predictive analytics**
  Predictive analytics can anticipate trends, take proactive action, or suggest actions to take to automate data-based decision-making and to respond to changing conditions in real time as a result of rapidly analyzing large amounts of data.

- **Robotic process automation**
  RPA is used to conduct rule-based processes that don't require human decisions and to automate individual tasks. This way you can redirect your human capital to value-adding processes while improving the employee experience.

- **Natural language processing engine**
  Natural language processing is used to enhance the user experience (UX) with a conversational interface that uses voice or text.

1.2   Key Technologies

Now let's take a look at the foundational technologies for delivering intelligent ERP in SAP S/4HANA. We'll detail the technologies of SAP HANA, the modern in-memory database that powers intelligent ERP. We'll also discuss the benefits of one UX across the entire application suite, powered by SAP Fiori, as well as the intelligent ERP applications in SAP S/4HANA.

1.2.1   SAP S/4HANA Cloud

SAP S/4HANA Cloud is an intelligent and integrated ERP solution that runs on SAP's in-memory database, SAP HANA (which we'll discuss in the next section). It provides organizations with software that addresses their business requirements across 26 verticals (i.e., niche markets) and enables organizations to evolve their business models as their industry changes over time. SAP S/4HANA Cloud provides organizations access to intelligent technologies for process automation supported by RPA and AI. Users and organizations are equipped for better and faster decision-making with embedded analytics and get faster answers with conversational interfaces and digital assistants. SAP S/4HANA Cloud provides organizations with a choice of deployment in hybrid, cloud, and on-premise scenarios to optimize their IT landscapes.

SAP S/4HANA Cloud provides organizations with a broad range of capabilities in the following areas (see Figure 1.2):

- **Asset management**
  Asset management capabilities help organizations achieve operational excellence through planning, scheduling, and executing asset maintenance activities.

- **Finance**
  These capabilities help organizations simplify accounting processes and the financial close, enable improvements to the treasury and financial risk processes, provide support for collaborative financial operations, help simplify real estate management, and more.

- **Manufacturing**
  The manufacturing capability helps organizations implement processes to support complex assembly execution, improve production planning, support seamless manufacturing engineering, and accelerate manufacturing operations, including enhanced quality management.

- **R&D and engineering**
  The R&D and engineering capabilities provide organizations with processes to improve product development and project control, as well as help achieve effective management of enterprise-wide projects, better product lifecycle management, and improved efficiency through requirement-driven processes.

- **Sales**
  The sales capability enables organizations to drive and manage sales force performance, supports your sales professionals and sales managers, maximizes your revenue with optimized sales processes for contract and order management, and more.

- **Service**
  The service capability provides organizations with processes to optimize engagement profitability, achieve better staffing levels, help capture time sheets faster with simplified time entry, streamline quote-to-cash processes, reimagine bid management processes, and more.

- **Sourcing and procurement**
  The sourcing and procurement capability helps organizations gain in-depth insight into their purchasing operations, streamlines their operational purchasing, automates contract management and sourcing, centralizes procurement processes, reduces supply chain risk, manages commodity procurement, and more.

- **Supply chain**
  The supply chain capability enables excellence in your supply processes to provide more accurate commitment dates, achieve more streamlined warehouse management, optimize inventory processes for optimal inventory levels, integrate transportation management, and more.

- **Industry capabilities**
  Industry capabilities are used across 31 industries, such as automotive, consumer,

chemicals, mill, mining, media, public services, retail, sports and entertainment, and wholesale distribution.

Finance	Procurement	Sales	Service	Cross Functions
• Accounting and financial close • Financial operations • Cost management • Treasury • Enterprise risk and compliance	• Procurement of direct materials and services • Supplier management • Central procurement	• Sell from stock • Sell services • Rebates and commissions • Convergent and external billing	• Sell, deliver, bill, and monitor a combination of physical goods and services as one solution offering	• Master data, data migration, data protection and privacy, information lifecycle management • Integration capabilities • Legal content management
SAP S/4HANA Cloud				
Asset Management	**Supply Chain**	**Manufacturing**	**R&D**	**Industry Capabilities**
• Resource scheduling for maintenance planner • Enhanced collaboration and review	• Warehouse outbound and inbound processing • Core inventory management • Advanced ATP processing	• Material requirements planning (MRP) with demand-driven and/or predictive MRP • Make-to-stock and make-to-order • Quality management	• Product compliance • Enterprise portfolio and project management • Variant configuration	• Professional services • Public sector • Higher education • Manufacturing • Mining services

Figure 1.2 SAP S/4HANA Cloud Scope Highlights

RISE with SAP

SAP introduced RISE with SAP in January of 2021 as a new commercial offering for customers adopting SAP S/4HANA Cloud. It is designed to support organizations transforming their business processes into the cloud. The offering includes the following components:

- **SAP S/4HANA Cloud**
  Cloud ERP solution to transform and innovate your organization with new industry business models and best practices, establish process excellence with built-in AI, and elevate sustainability standards end to end.

- **Business process intelligence**
  Help your organization continuously understand, innovate, and transform processes by providing a clear picture of how processes work end to end.

- **Business platform and analytics**
  Capabilities that enable you to complement, extend, and integrate with any other solution (SAP, partner, or third party) and use the data model and business services on SAP BTP to connect it all.

- **SAP Business Network starter pack**
  Create dynamic, digital connections with your trading partners and assets. As part of the RISE with SAP offering, you can apply network-wide intelligence to guide decisions with real-time data and visibility.

- **Outcome-driven services and tools**
  Drive accelerated business outcomes with the services and tools included in the RISE with SAP offering, providing access to products and services for lifecycle management, analytics, support, and more for the migration to SAP S/4HANA.

You can find more about the RISE with SAP offering on SAP website at *https://www.sap.com/products/rise.html*.

These capabilities enable organizations to achieve higher efficiency and better performance across a wide range of processes in their enterprise, such as the following:

- Engineer-to-order
- Invoice-to-pay
- Invoice-to-cash
- Produce-to-invoice
- Make-to-order
- Treasury management
- Sell-from-stock
- Financial planning and analysis

- Idea-to-product
- Engagement-to-cash
- Asset maintenance and operations
- Quote-to-order
- Managing real estate and facilities
- Record-to-report
- Return-to-restock

Further Resources

If you're interested in more detailed functional information about SAP S/4HANA, refer to *SAP S/4HANA: An Introduction* (SAP PRESS, 2021) at *sap-press.com/5232*. For information specific to SAP S/4HANA Cloud, refer to *SAP S/4HANA Cloud: An Introduction* (SAP PRESS, 2022) at *sap-press.com/5457*. You can also find additional information about SAP S/4HANA functions and capabilities on SAP's website at *http://s-prs.co/v502700*.

1.2.2   SAP HANA

In the SAP HANA Master Guide, used by IT professionals when planning an installation of SAP HANA system landscapes, SAP HANA is defined as "a modern, in-memory database and platform that is deployable on premise or in the cloud." Let's go a little deeper to evaluate why SAP HANA provides the next-generation data management foundation for all the industry-leading SAP solutions necessary to build an intelligent enterprise.

In-Memory Database

SAP HANA revolutionized the data management industry by delivering the first in-memory data platform to market in 2010 with its in-memory-first architecture. With SAP HANA, data is maintained in memory by default. Other storage media, such as SSDs or HDs, can also be used to manage larger data sets that don't fit in memory and data that is rarely accessed in order to lower storage costs.

This is fundamentally different from how traditional databases operate. They are designed to store data on disk and move data to memory only for processing. Even with the most recent introduction of in-memory extensions, these legacy databases carry the intrinsic complexity of having to manage all the data on disk and having to be told what data needs to be copied into memory and when. This translates into higher data latency, unnecessary data duplication, and higher administration costs. Instead,

SAP HANA's architecture supports true real-time performance without latency or data duplication, allowing you to support more diverse and complex workloads and applications.

Database and Platform

SAP HANA allows OLTP and OLAP on one system, without the need for redundant data storage or aggregates. The "online" in OLTP and OLAP once expressed the novelty that transactions occurred in real time, and not with punch cards updating the system overnight. But analytics still requires special processing to get the data out of the system of record and into multidimensional cubes. With SAP HANA, this special processing isn't required because it's a single database system with a single data copy.

SAP HANA is called a *platform* because different technologies are integrated with the database server. When you start up an SAP HANA system, you're also starting up an application server. This built-in functionality promotes the concept of in-database processing and keeping a single data copy. The application server, called SAP HANA extended application services (SAP HANA XS), provides both a runtime and a development environment.

Besides database and application services, the platform also includes a graph engine and a spatial engine; both are built into one system in real time without tuning and are accessible through the same SQL interface used for transactions and analytics. Other advanced analytics "capabilities" (features and functions) concern the execution of predictive analytics and business functions, and the manipulation of unstructured data (as opposed to structured relational data).

To connect SAP HANA with the outside world (and connect the outside world with SAP HANA), SAP HANA offers state-of-the-art data integration, visualization, and quality capabilities, allowing applications and dashboards to gain a logical view of all your enterprise data regardless of source (Hadoop, Spark, cloud, or third-party databases). These services provide connectivity to big data sources, Internet of Things (IoT) devices, and external R and machine learning engines, and they also address data replication, data quality, and data management needs in general.

SAP HANA in the Cloud or On-Premise

The term *on-premise* refers to running the system in your own corporate data center. In this case, you'll rely on certified hardware and certified engineers to install and operate the platform. Deploying *in the cloud* refers to running SAP HANA anywhere else. Many options are available (public and private cloud, managed services, pay as you go), with the latest offering being SAP HANA Cloud services.

With SAP HANA, you gain access to a modern data platform that can support all your data management needs and that works synergistically with your technology landscape, including Hadoop, Spark, and other data sources, to accelerate your ability to get value from your data by simplifying your application architectures and IT landscapes. As shown in Figure 1.3, the SAP HANA platform encompasses the following capabilities:

- **Application development**
  These tools simplify the application architecture, achieve optimal application performance, and reduce complexity in the IT environment.

- **Advanced analytical processing**
  Advanced analytics are processed natively on relational and nonrelational data by effectively managing multimodel data—for example, relational, JavaScript Object Notation (JSON), graph, and spatial data—and by applying specialized analytical processing, such as predictive analysis/machine learning, text mining, time series analysis, and more.

- **Data integration and quality**
  The runtime edition allows the use of SAP HANA smart data integration (SDI) and SAP HANA smart data quality (SDQ) software only to the extent that it's controlled by the licensed application. With the enterprise edition, the full capabilities of SDI and SDQ enable all types of data acquisition and transformation integrated into the licensed application.

- **Database management**
  Data of any size is managed efficiently to allow rarely accessed data to be moved from memory to more economical storage media with its policy-driven dynamic storage tiering capability.

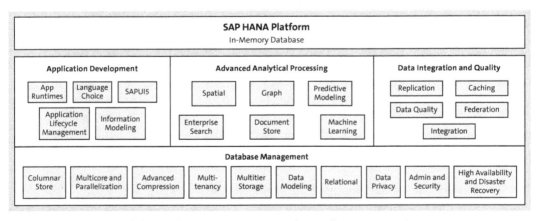

Figure 1.3 Capabilities of SAP HANA Powering the Intelligent Enterprise

1.2.3   SAP Fiori

As part of a digital transformation, the way users access ERP solutions is different than in the past. In recent years, there has been a massive change in the behavior of specific target groups, such as Generation Y or millennials; they're looking for a customized, personalized, responsive, and focused UX that's intuitive and easy to handle across all devices (e.g., mobile, desktop, and tablet). Based on changing requirements and the future of digitally enabled enterprises, SAP provided a new UX called SAP Fiori. SAP Fiori applies the following new design principles to reimagine the UX:

- **Role-based**
  SAP Fiori is designed to meet users' business needs and to support the way users work in the application. It draws from deep insight into today's workforce to provide users with the right information at the right time and to reflect how users work in their business roles.

- **Adaptive**
  SAP Fiori enables users to work from any place they want and to use any device they prefer to access their applications. Users gain instant insight by accessing relevant information at their fingertips.

- **Simple**
  Users can perform their jobs in an intuitive and simple environment that is responsive to their needs. SAP Fiori helps users focus on important functions via an easy-to-use environment that users can personalize to fit their needs.

- **Coherent**
  No matter your role and function in the organization, SAP Fiori will provide a consistent experience and unified visual design language. Users across the organization will enjoy the same consistent and intuitive experience whether they manage leave requests, analyze the latest sales performance metrics, or fulfill a sales order.

- **Delightful**
  SAP Fiori helps users work smarter by providing a rich UX that allows them to focus on their jobs and perform them more efficiently.

With usage of SAP Fiori, there is a significant shift from the purely functional view that was available in the old SAP ERP to a role-based UX with a single entry point and a common design in SAP S/4HANA (see Figure 1.4) across business applications, whether cloud or on-premise.

The changing UX strategy aims to support the simplification of the SAP S/4HANA Cloud solution, which is why SAP S/4HANA Cloud and SAP Fiori are tightly integrated. At present, not all SAP solutions are enabled fully with SAP Fiori, but solution development will continue. More SAP Fiori apps will be available in later releases that will simplify the overall solution. In addition, not all transactions are being replaced with SAP Fiori apps because there will be a move to a more role-based UX, and the processes will be streamlined and condensed to the necessary core functionality.

To identify currently available SAP Fiori apps, you can browse the SAP Fiori apps reference library (see Figure 1.5) at *http://s-prs.co/v502701*.

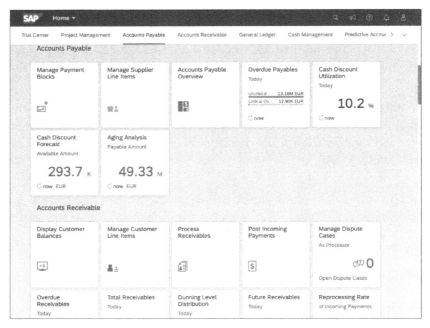

Figure 1.4 Role-Based View with SAP Fiori as Part of SAP S/4HANA Cloud

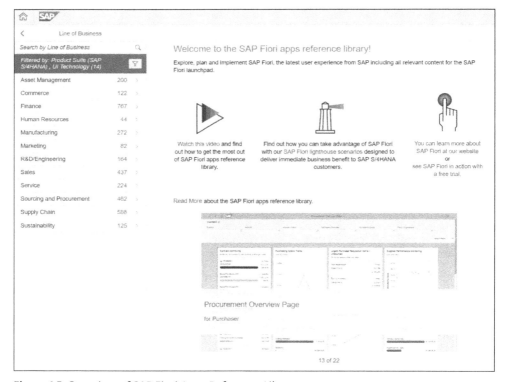

Figure 1.5 Overview of SAP Fiori Apps Reference Library

SAP Fiori 3

The focus of the SAP Fiori 3 UX design is to be adopted by all SAP products, resulting in consistency and integration across the portfolio. Therefore, SAP Fiori 3 provides a coherent UX across the various SAP products to facilitate seamless integration and promote the intelligent suite.

The following features are introduced with the SAP Fiori 3 UX to support this focus:

- **Quartz Light**
  The Quartz Light theme (sap_fiori_3) introduces a new, neutral gray, color scheme that blends with the background, giving focus to the application content.

- **Quartz Dark**
  Quartz Dark is an additional theme created for SAP Fiori applications to work in environments where low light is necessary or unavoidable.

- **Home page**
  To go to the home page at any time, you can now use the SAP logo at the left-hand side of the header bar. The logo is now an active button that replaces the previously available **Home** button.

- **App title button**
  The app title button was moved to the left-hand side of the header bar. You'll now find it to the right of the SAP logo. You can use it to access all your applications.

- **User actions**
  You'll find all personalization settings in a **User Actions** menu on the right-hand side of the header bar.

- **Notifications viewport**
  The **Notifications** viewport was moved to a dialog window at the right-hand side of the header bar.

- **Web assistant**
  Additional changes have been made to the design of the web assistant content. The horizontal bar (also called a carousel) and its content can be found in a vertical sidebar to the right. In addition, this content is no longer accessible via a question mark icon, but rather via a stylized i icon in the top-right corner of the screen. All pointing lines and overlay elements are now omitted to allow better visibility of the various app sections.

We encourage those interested in SAP Fiori to explore the SAP Fiori design guidelines at *https://experience.sap.com/fiori-design-web/*.

1.3   Deployment and Operating Models

SAP S/4HANA can be deployed in multiple deployment models to support your specific needs and to fit your IT architecture and strategy. We'll discuss the various deployment models in this section, and we'll outline how to deploy the SAP S/4HANA solution based on your needs and preferences later in the book.

The three key deployment models and respective operating models are as follows:

1. Cloud

2. On-premise

3. Hybrid

Let's discuss each in more detail.

1.3.1 Cloud

In cloud operating models, instead of you operating or managing the software, a service provider is engaged for this purpose. The software and the corresponding services are leased for a defined period of time in the cloud operating model. Hardware and operating system software aren't required on-premise. The enterprise's IT staff can thus focus on other tasks. Internet access is necessary to access the solution, and users can access the cloud software from anywhere and, in most cases, via mobile devices. One of the major benefits of the cloud operating model is the associated cost transparency.

SAP offers companies full flexibility in their choice of how the SAP S/4HANA Cloud is deployed. This choice is typically made by an organization after considering the available capabilities, localization needs, the deployment model needed for the business, and so on. Companies can choose from two primary landscape options in the cloud:

1. **Public cloud**

   In a public cloud scenario, the SAP S/4HANA Cloud application runs as a service provided to business users. In the public cloud, the infrastructure and software are shared by multiple businesses. The software is on the same release level for all customers. The operational model ensures that in this shared model, no changes made for one client impact another client, and the data is strictly separated. To ensure efficient operation, SAP sets the maintenance cycles and upgrade schedules of the cloud software. This ensures faster delivery of innovation, and customers running in the public cloud can activate new capabilities much faster than in any other landscape option or deployment model (e.g., faster than on-premise or private cloud offerings).

2. **Private cloud**

   In a private cloud scenario, the software and infrastructure are operated by SAP or a hyperscaler and provided to the company as a service. This landscape option provides companies with the full scope of SAP S/4HANA (comparable to on-premise scope), coverage of 25 industries, availability of a wide range of partner add-ons, and 64 country versions in 39 languages. One of the key differences of this landscape option as compared to the public cloud is that a company has more granular control over upgrades and software updates. As a result, the adoption of new capabilities is somewhat slower than in the public cloud.

For deployment of SAP S/4HANA Cloud in both landscape options, data security and cloud security are critical topics for every customer. SAP sets up the data center operations, security standards, and processes to provide the highest level of security and protection. These standards are detailed in the SAP Trust Center, and you can access them here: *https://www.sap.com/about/trust-center.html*. In general, the security provided by trustworthy cloud providers is higher than that of typical enterprise IT organizations. Cloud providers document their security and operational capabilities via Service Organization Controls (SOC) reports. You can access SAP's SOC reports in the SAP Trust Center.

Deploying SAP S/4HANA Cloud involves several characteristics, and many are related to the nature of the deploying software as a service (SaaS) solution. The key characteristics are as follows:

- **Ability to innovate rapidly by using standard functionality**
  Cloud solutions such as SAP S/4HANA Cloud allow you to adopt the solution quickly and continuously add new capabilities as SAP adds new capabilities into the solution. During the initial deployment, the objective is to implement the solution fast by staying close to the standard solution, which enables you to adopt the new capabilities SAP delivers in future releases much faster. We will dedicate a significant part of this book to this topic and will explore it in more details in later chapters. The speed of innovation will be generally fastest in the public cloud landscape option.

- **Stronger focus on organizational change management (OCM)**
  Adopting a cloud solution often requires companies to adjust their existing business processes, which increases the effort and focus that project teams need to spend on assisting business users with the changing environment. This also increases the need to plan, execute, and monitor implementation of the organizational change management activities in the project. We'll discuss this topic in more detail in Chapter 10.

- **Rapid deployment and innovation cycles**
  In general, SAP S/4HANA Cloud has much shorter deployment and innovation cycles than on-premise. This is especially true where when you apply the cloud mindset of minimizing the number of extensions and focusing on deploying the minimal viable solution in the first implementation cycle and then add to it in short innovation cycles. We've seen this approach applied more often with project teams deploying cloud solutions than with project teams deploying in on-premise environments.

These are just a few characteristics of deployment in the cloud. We'll discuss this deployment model in more detail in Chapter 7, where we'll go over the details of the cloud mindset, rapid innovation cycles, and how to use an agile approach during your deployment projects. We will also discuss how the deployment varies between the two landscape options for cloud (public cloud and private cloud).

1.3.2   On-Premise

Usually, the *on-premise operating model* refers to running and managing software you own on your own hardware. As a result, you're in full control of the hardware and software, mission-critical application data, and software maintenance schedules. Moreover, you have maximum flexibility when it comes to custom enhancements and integration with other systems (in-house solutions or external systems). However, you also are fully responsible for the availability of the software, as well as access, security, and system stability. In addition to the costs for hardware and software, powerful and complex ERP systems incur further costs for the IT experts needed to introduce, manage, and maintain the software.

In some cases, you may decide to subcontract the management of the hardware and software to a managed services provider or deploy the on-premise software on a hardware infrastructure provided in the cloud. In these cases, the operating and deployment model for the software follows the deployment of on-premise software detailed in SAP Activate.

Deployment of SAP S/4HANA in the on-premise model follows the same steps as SAP S/4HANA Cloud deployment, although there are several differences provided by the added flexibility of the solution and typically a larger number of requirements for extensibility of the solution driven by your users. We will discuss these topics in Chapter 7 and Chapter 8.

The on-premise deployment model is best for those who want to manage their entire IT stack or have requirements for keeping the business application close to other parts of their organization (e.g., manufacturing processes that are sensitive to latency) or for those who have strict rules governing access to their data that don't allow them to operate their systems outside of their premises.

1.3.3   Hybrid

The hybrid operating model enables you to combine the characteristics of the on-premise operating model and the cloud operating model. For example, core areas of your enterprise, where you want a high degree of control and a high level of flexibility, can be operated on-premise, while other enterprise areas can be operated in the cloud as common industry standards are sufficient. Many organizations are using this approach to evolve their IT infrastructure while maximizing their existing investment in it. Such companies have adopted public cloud solutions in their landscapes for specific subsidiaries or parts of their business in order to build the cloud skills in their organization that will support their ongoing journey to the cloud.

Two-Tier ERP Deployment of SAP S/4HANA Cloud

SAP published a white paper titled *Two-Tier ERP Deployment for SAP S/4HANA® Cloud: A Practical Guide for Senior Leadership* in December 2021 that details the part businesses could play to progressively shift their infrastructure into the cloud and benefit from the speed and agility of that deployment model while maximizing the benefits of their existing investment in their infrastructure. You can download the white paper from *http://s-prs.co/v546301*. If you have complex geographical structures or need distributed systems, you'll benefit from using a hybrid operating model powered by a two-tier ERP system. This model supports solutions in which some parts of the business scenario are operated on-premise (e.g., central ERP for headquarters, where the corporation consolidates and reports financial results), and some parts are operated in the cloud (e.g., smaller or dedicated units focusing on sales or exploration). It also caters to situations where some parts of your business are running in the cloud and others remain on the existing on-premise infrastructure. This deployment model offers maximum flexibility to enterprises transitioning their infrastructure to the cloud.

We'll discuss this deployment and operating model in Chapter 9, where we'll go over specific business scenarios that provide benefits for organizations running them in this decentralized federated deployment approach.

1.3.4   Deployment Considerations with SAP S/4HANA

SAP S/4HANA's simplified data model and modern UX are consistent for cloud, hybrid, and on-premise deployments. Designed for in-memory usage, SAP S/4HANA brings new business capabilities while simplifying the IT landscape.

When deciding which of the previously explained deployment and operating models for SAP S/4HANA is right for your company, you should consider the following:

- IT strategy
- Innovation cycles
- Adoption/upgrade efforts
- Total cost of ownership (TCO)
- Commercial models

- Business functionality
- Regulatory, industry, and regional requirements
- Data protection needs
- Localization
- Individualization options

The objective of this chapter is simply to introduce you to the options. We'll discuss all these topics in more detail in the appropriate chapters dedicated to each of the deployment models in the second half of this book.

1.4   Deployment Approaches

Now that we've discussed the various ways the SAP S/4HANA application can be deployed, let's go over the options you have for the *transition path*—that is, how the software will be deployed. SAP offers a wide range of options for each of the variants of the SAP S/4HANA deployment both to cater to companies who are new to SAP S/4HANA Cloud and to support existing businesses looking for the most efficient way to move their SAP ERP environments into SAP S/4HANA Cloud.

When determining the optimal path to SAP S/4HANA for your company, SAP recommends matching your business objectives with the available transition path and destination you're aiming for. Figure 1.6 shows the business objective categories, available transition paths, and destination options.

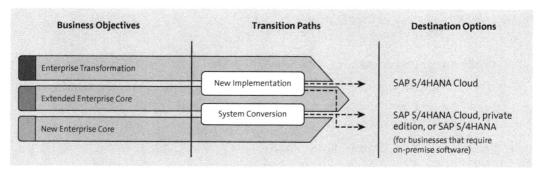

Figure 1.6 Considering Your Deployment Approach Options

Let's now discuss the business objective categories in more detail:

- **Enterprise transformation**
  This category fits companies that are in the middle of a comprehensive business transformation or companies that are implementing new business models in line with their digital transformation goals. Companies in this category typically plan

their transition to SAP S/4HANA Cloud or SAP S/4HANA via a multistage roadmap aligned with their business transformation goals, and a significant portion of the roadmap activity will be new implementations of new business processes to support their transformation goals. Sponsorship of such transformation typically comes directly from the chief executive officer (CEO). Companies in this category are focused on implementing new business processes that encourage new revenue models or organizations that are implementing intelligent technologies (e.g., IoT or RPA scenarios) or shared services models in their organization.

- **Extended enterprise core**
  Businesses that are looking not only to convert into the new technology but also to immediately benefit from extending their current ERP core solution fit into this category. The focus is on optimization and redesign of selected business processes based on best value or return on investment (ROI). This category also includes companies that are looking for simplification of their IT environment to optimize cost of operations and enable faster innovation. Companies in this category have a choice of converting their existing environment to SAP S/4HANA Cloud, private edition or SAP S/4HANA or implementing the solution from scratch. Selecting the appropriate approach is largely driven by the scope of "outdated" business processes that will need to be redesigned, the age of the existing solution, and its relative ability to support not only current processes but also future business models currently being implemented or anticipated for the future. Typical sponsorship for this category comes from the impacted line of business (LoB) or from the LoB lead cosponsorship with the CIO.

- **New enterprise core**
  This category fits businesses that are looking to build a foundation for innovation by introducing SAP S/4HANA Cloud, private edition or SAP S/4HANA as their digital core while minimizing the impact on existing business operations. The focus in this case is on converting the existing landscape and then evolving it along with the business. Typically, companies in this category operate SAP ERP and look for system conversion to SAP S/4HANA Cloud, private edition or SAP S/4HANA while considering implementation of innovations such as the Universal Journal, embedded analytics, or the new SAP Fiori UX for selected functions in the organization where this change allows for introducing innovation with minimal disruption. Initiatives in this category typically are sponsored by the chief information officer (CIO).

Now that we've defined the business context for the various transition paths, let's briefly define the characteristics of these paths to set the stage for detailed discussion in each of the chapters dedicated to deployment to cloud, on-premise, and hybrid environments. Table 1.2 offers an overview of the transition paths.

Type	Reusing via In-Place Conversion	Reengineering with Data Migration	
		Standardized	Customer-Tailored Based on Predefined Content and Scenario
Transition path	System conversion	New implementation	Selective data transition (customer-tailored service based on predefined content and scenario)
Available for	SAP ERP system to SAP S/4HANA Cloud, private edition or businesses that need to run on-premise SAP S/4HANA.	SAP ERP or third-party system(s) to SAP S/4HANA Cloud (public or private). Businesses that need to run on-premise can choose SAP S/4HANA.	SAP ERP or third-party system(s) to SAP S/4HANA Cloud or businesses that need to run on-premise SAP S/4HANA.
Purpose	Bringing your business processes to the new platform: ■ A complete technical in-place conversion of an existing ERP software system in SAP Business Suite to SAP S/4HANA ■ Adoption of new innovations at your speed	New implementation/ reimplementation: ■ Reengineering and process simplification based on latest innovations ■ Implementing innovative business processes with preconfigured content on a new platform ■ Performing initial data load	Enabling the right balance between process redesign and reuse with possibility of (selective) history migration: ■ You don't want to fully redesign or fully reuse your SAP ERP processes but rather reuse some parts and redesign some other parts—for example, reuse logistics, redesign finance. ■ Migrate a selection of data (such as by organizational units or time slices) or migrate application-related data into an SAP S/4HANA Cloud-based solution landscape. ■ For full migration-based approach, less business involvement is required.

Table 1.2 Overview of Transition Paths to SAP S/4HANA Cloud

Let's take a closer look at each path:

- **New implementation**

  This transition path allows companies to completely reinvent their ERP environment by implementing SAP S/4HANA Cloud as the new solution (or SAP S/4HANA, if the business needs to run on-premise) and at the same time migrating data from their existing SAP or legacy environment into this new solution. As we discussed earlier, this strategy is typically used by companies that have determined their existing ERP environment is no longer serving their current and/or future business and need to implement a new foundation for innovation that will do the job better.

- **System conversion**

  This transition path is favored by current businesses on SAP ERP 6.0 or newer that want to minimize the disruption to their existing business operations while updating their existing landscape for future innovations. Companies using this approach have kept their IT environment close to the latest release of SAP software, added custom code selectively, and planned to gradually introduce innovation brought by SAP S/4HANA Cloud, private edition or SAP S/4HANA to their business along a longer innovation path. Although they don't have a need for significant business process innovation at this time, they will benefit from new capabilities, such as the Universal Journal, embedded analytics, or SAP Fiori UX.

- **Selective data transition**

  This approach is used by companies that prefer a system conversion but also require sizable work in the standardization of their environment by using the new SAP S/4HANA Cloud, private edition or SAP S/4HANA capabilities (previously known as landscape transformation). For example, companies might want to innovate their financial processes while reusing their existing logistics functionality and porting it to the new platform. There are other scenarios where this approach is also applicable, such as when a company wants to migrate only a subset of data (e.g., organizational units or specific time slices) into its SAP S/4HANA environment. This approach is delivered as a tailored service based on the specific needs of the company. We'll briefly discuss this approach in Chapter 8, Section 8.4.

1.5   Summary

This chapter introduced the key concepts of SAP S/4HANA, including an overview of the technologies that companies will have access to in the solution. We also discussed, at least on a high level, the functional capabilities in the SAP S/4HANA system. We spent a bit of time covering the business content for selecting the appropriate deployment model and transition path to help you understand the approach before we get into the discussion of the version of SAP Activate that is appropriate for each transition path. Later, we'll review each of the SAP Activate versions (for new implementation in

Chapter 7 and for system conversion and selective data transition in Chapter 8) and discuss how each transition path is supported by the SAP Activate methodology, content, and tools.

In the next chapter, we'll introduce the principles and concepts of SAP Activate for SAP S/4HANA Cloud and SAP S/4HANA. We'll introduce the SAP Activate phases, hierarchy, and key preconfiguration assets, such as SAP Best Practices and the enterprise management layer for SAP S/4HANA. We'll also introduce the SAP Activate community, designed to provide users with a one-stop shop for information and news about SAP Activate.

Chapter 2

Introduction to SAP Activate

This chapter provides a fundamental understanding of the concepts and principles SAP has built into SAP Activate. This is an important chapter to read before you proceed to the later chapters in the book that detail the specific deployment strategies in SAP S/4HANA projects.

This chapter introduces SAP Activate as the innovation adoption framework that enables your business to deploy new capabilities fast and continue innovating. We'll start by discussing the nature of the SAP S/4HANA deployment project, where the project team needs to shift their focus to consistently apply the cloud mindset in order to maximize the value that the new solution creates for the organization. We'll then deep dive into the principles that SAP Activate follows and discuss each in more detail. After that, we'll introduce the SAP Activate phases, outline what happens in each phase, and describe how deliverables created in one phase relate to each other and together support project success. Before closing the chapter, we'll invite you to the SAP Activate community on SAP Community and discuss the available training, enablement, and certification offerings.

2.1 SAP Activate Key Concepts

Organizations that are starting or are in the middle of their SAP S/4HANA transition have questions that SAP Activate aims to answer throughout the entire transition process. SAP Activate's main focus is on addressing questions during the actual project, but it also offers guidance for the discovery activities in the discover phase and details how to run and operate the solution after the initial go-live in the run phase. Figure 2.1 shows a few sample questions the project team may have during their transition journey.

SAP introduced SAP Activate at SAPPHIRE in 2015, just as the SAP S/4HANA product was launched, and structured it around a major shift in the mindset that's applied to deployment, as shown in Figure 2.2.

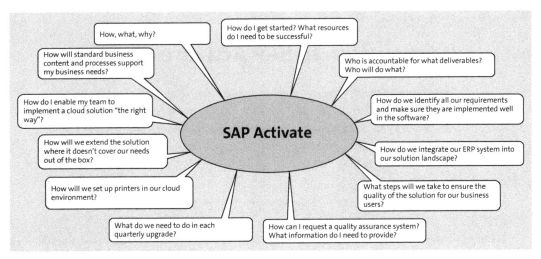

Figure 2.1 SAP Activate: Helping to Address Project Team Questions throughout Transition to SAP S/4HANA

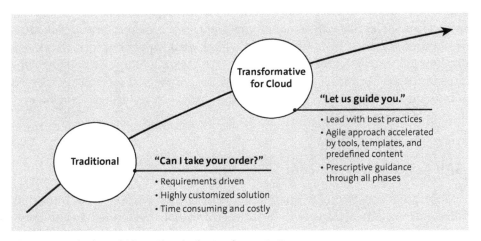

Figure 2.2 Mindset Shift to Cloud-Like Implementation

The shift is represented by the move from the traditional requirements-based approach—heavy on design work in an empty system, resulting in highly customized solutions that take a long time to implement—to an approach that leverages predelivered, ready-to-run best practices; aims to reuse much of the predelivered functionality and standard functions of the solution; and uses an agile approach to implement the identified delta requirements and extensions to meet an organization's needs. SAP Activate also adds prescriptive guidance that expands the traditional methodology with product-specific procedures and accelerators to help not only project managers and workstream leads but also business users, IT personnel, and application and technology consultants.

SAP Activate builds on SAP's previous methodologies: ASAP for on-premise projects and SAP Launch for cloud projects. It's designed around the following key principles:

- **Start with ready-to-run business processes**

  The methodology is structured around using a working system that is built on ready-to-run business processes delivered by SAP or an SAP partner. In Chapter 4, we'll discuss two key assets that SAP delivers: SAP Best Practices (available to all customers) and the enterprise management layer for SAP S/4HANA. Both of these packages offer a starting point for implementing SAP S/4HANA Cloud and SAP S/4HANA and enable organizations to get started fast with a working system.

- **Confirm solution fit**

  This is done using a working system built on the ready-to-run business processes we discussed in the previous point. Project teams use a fit-to-standard approach to both confirm the fit of the standard predelivered business processes and identify the delta requirements needed to make the solution fit the organization. These delta requirements typically fit into categories of configuration, extensibility, analytics, integration, data, security and access, and so on. The delta requirements are stored in the backlog that the project team uses to capture the work required to deliver the solution to the organization.

Fit-to-Standard or Fit-Gap?

In earlier versions of SAP Activate, on-premise deployments utilized the fit-gap approach, which was considered better suited to the implementation of on-premise solutions. But in the last few years, as more organizations have embraced the principles of keeping the core clean, project teams have shifted to using the fit-to-standard approach because it is more suitable for keeping close to the standard. There are a few main differences between the fit-to-standard and fit-gap approaches:

- **Fit-to-standard**

  This approach is used in implementations that are applying a cloud mindset—that is, staying close to the standard and keeping the core clean—or where a product has defined boundaries, such as SAP S/4HANA Cloud and SAP SuccessFactors. The approach emphasizes maximizing the use of standard functionality over unnecessary tailoring or extending the solution. This approach still allows for the use of extensibility (key user, developer, and side by side) where needed to address critical business requirements that the solution needs to provide to the organization in order to realize the desired business benefit and value.

- **Fit-gap**

  This approach was traditionally used in on-premise implementations where the project team has wider ability or desire to extend the solution with custom code or via the extensibility framework. The focus in this approach is again on adoption of standard functionality first, but the desire is to allow the project team to use broader options for extending the functionality, including custom code, significant configuration, and so on. This approach has been used in SAP S/4HANA (on-premise) projects where the project team has decided to use the full development environment inside the application to modify SAP code or develop significant extensions inside the application.

In both approaches, the project team must strive to avoid modifications of SAP-delivered code; when this is unavoidable, the team must ensure that the changes are properly documented. We will discuss this in more detail in Section 2.4.

- **Modular, scalable, and agile**
  This principle encompasses three aspects: First, the modularity of the approach allows companies and implementation partners to swap out specific SAP Activate modules as needed. For example, solution adoption activities that include organizational change management (OCM) deliverables and tasks can be swapped with company or partner activities for OCM. Second, scalability is demonstrated by the ability to use the same approach to implement SAP S/4HANA Cloud for growing organizations in a rapid cycle of just a few weeks and to deploy SAP S/4HANA in large multinational companies across a broad number of countries and geographies. SAP Activate can be scaled up or down depending on the needs of the project (influencing factors are project scope, geographical or organizational footprint, number of integrated systems, etc.). Third, the agile approach is used to structure a project into multiple releases built via increments and sprints that allow the team to focus on building the higher-value and higher-priority features first. This approach is embedded in SAP Activate and can be tailored to a company's situation by choosing the desired duration of sprints and structuring the releases according to the company's plans to introduce the solution to the organization. We'll discuss the agile approach in more detail in Chapter 6.

What Is Agile?

The term *agile* is used to describe a new approach to working in organizations and businesses. It focuses on a change in mindset that individuals and organizations need to apply in the way they approach their work. The key principles are captured in the *agile manifesto*, introduced in 2001 as a means to change the approach to software development. You can find the complete text of the agile manifesto at *https://agile-manifesto.org*.

The key principles stated in the agile manifesto are as follows:

- Individuals and interactions over processes and tools
- Working software over comprehensive documentation
- Customer collaboration over contract negotiation
- Responding to change over following a plan

As the manifesto states, agile practitioners value the items on the left side of the points we've listed more than the items on the right side (e.g., customer collaboration is valued more highly than contract negotiation). This statement doesn't mean that items on the right side are unimportant; instead, it means that agile practitioners prioritize the items on the left. In essence, that approach reflects the change in mindset of increased collaboration, communication, and adaptability.

The agile principles are coded in multiple methods for software development. The most popular among agile practitioners is Scrum, which is also used as the foundation for the agile approach in the SAP Activate.

- **Cloud-ready**
  This principle is not only applicable for companies implementing their solution in the cloud but also can be used by project teams implementing SAP S/4HANA in on-premise deployments. In such situations, the cloud technology can be used to access the trial environment or to provide the project team with a working sandbox environment based on SAP Cloud Appliance Library, which offers a broad selection of predefined systems that companies can use in the early stages of their project. Organizations deploying their solution in the cloud will benefit from the cloud mindset embedded into the methodology and the detailed information about how to request provisioning of the cloud solution and how to access it, activate it, and use it during implementation.

- **Premium engagement–ready**
  We discussed earlier that SAP Activate has been built as a modular methodology that enables companies, partners, and SAP to bring in specific modules. SAP has incorporated links to support and implementation services through SAP Activate where appropriate. This is the most visible for the premium engagement services, such as SAP MaxAttention or SAP ActiveAttention, that are layered onto SAP Activate to provide companies and partners information about how to best leverage SAP Services and Support offerings in their implementation projects. The use of these services is recommended, but customers that do not opt to use them will still benefit from using SAP Activate as it provides instructions for completing the tasks and deliverables regardless of whether SAP Services and Support offerings are used or not.

  As a specific example, inside the Transition to SAP S/4HANA implementation roadmap in the SAP Activate Roadmap Viewer (see Chapter 3, Section 3.1), you'll find "How SAP Can Support" sections that detail which services from SAP are applicable in the context of a specific deliverable or task. The description text provides more details about the service scope, how to order, and the outcomes the service delivers. See Figure 2.3 for how this text is incorporated into the task description in the methodology.

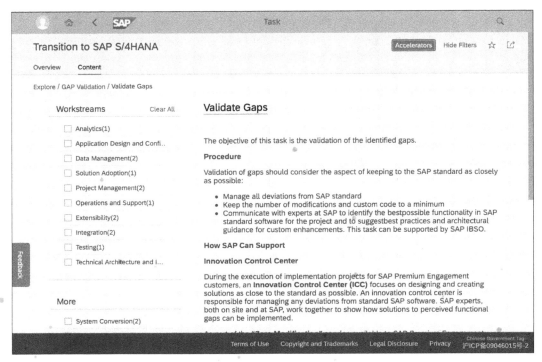

Figure 2.3 SAP Activate for Transition to SAP S/4HANA: How SAP Can Support Section

Premium Engagement Services from SAP

SAP Services and Support offers a portfolio of services under the umbrella of premium engagement services that are designed to safeguard company implementations, optimize operations, maximize the value of existing investments, and build new capabilities for your organization to become an intelligent enterprise.

The services are structured into a few categories, but these are the primary offerings:

- **SAP MaxAttention**
  This provides a holistic engagement between the company and SAP that aims to cover the company's business and IT needs. The engagement is managed jointly by the company and SAP to plan and execute a portfolio of initiatives, from innovation to optimization of existing solutions and operations, in order to drive predictable outcomes for the company in a coordinated manner. You can find more details about this service offering at *http://s-prs.co/v502702*.

- **SAP ActiveAttention**
  This service offering focuses on enabling companies to successfully deploy programs and run operations. It's designed to plan and safeguard the portfolio of a

company's landscapes, implementation and innovation projects, and operations. SAP offers different levels of services and a portfolio of predefined services that a company can consume to achieve the desired business outcomes. You can find more about these services at *http://s-prs.co/v502703*.

- **Quality built-in**

  Planning and managing quality during the implementation project is one of the critical factors for delivering a successful implementation. SAP Activate provides structured guidance for planning quality in the prepare phase, starting with developing quality management plans for the implementation project, then monitoring and controlling activities throughout the entire project, and finally executing predefined quality gates in each SAP Activate phase. Quality is also targeted in the detailed guidance for planning, execution, and resolution of various testing activities during the course of the project, including unit testing performed early in the realize phase, string testing that ties together multiple unit tests to ensure the data flow through the business process and system, and the ultimate end-to-end integration testing and user acceptance testing (UAT) in later stages or the realize phase. We'll discuss the details of testing in Chapter 5, Section 5.5.

2.2   Components of SAP Activate

The SAP Activate *innovation as a service* is a unique combination of the SAP Best Practices preconfigured business processes, guided and clear methodology, and tools for adoption and extensibility that helps companies and partners implement SAP S/4HANA solutions. Designed for IT and business professionals involved in the implementation, configuration, integration, or extension of SAP S/4HANA solutions, SAP Activate covers new implementations, system conversions, and selective data transition projects.

Figure 2.4 shows the key components of SAP Activate on the left side, which we'll cover in more detail as we progress in this book. The right side provides a summary of the benefits SAP Activate delivers, including increased speed of innovation, greater productivity for both the project team and the business, and a scalable environment that supports projects from small to large multinational rollouts (growth and scalability), ultimately driving positive business impact for organizations using SAP Activate to implement SAP solutions.

In this section, we'll walk through the key components of SAP Activate: ready-to-run business processes, clear and guided methodology, and applications and tools for adoption and extensibility.

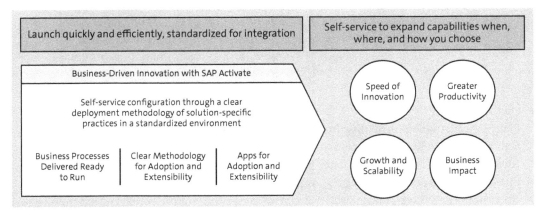

Figure 2.4 SAP Activate: Business Process Preconfiguration, Guided Methodology, and Applications for Adoption and Extensibility

2.2.1   Ready-to-Run Business Processes

Earlier in this chapter, we introduced the foundational principles of SAP Activate, one of which is *start with ready-to-run business processes*. This principle helps project teams set up the initial system that is then used in the explore phase for fit-to-standard analysis workshops. The current SAP Best Practices packages fall into two categories that are distinguished by branding and offered coverage. The first is the SAP Best Practices packages that companies and partners can access and download from SAP Best Practices Explorer (available at *https://rapid.sap.com/bp/*).

The SAP Best Practices packages are structured into logical groups of scope items. Scope items have a wide range of granularity and each represent a business process or end-to-end scenario that is configured inside the SAP Best Practice package. For example, scope item 19O is Automated Dynamic Discounts with SAP Ariba Discount Management. The scope item delivers ready-to-run business processes that can be activated with SAP Best Practices in a company's system. These packages include all the necessary configuration, organizational setting (sample), master data (sample), business roles, and—for some scope items—transactional data so that after the scope item is activated, the company can perform the process in the system. Thus, SAP refers to these packages as *ready-to-run business processes* or sometimes as *preconfigured packages*. Figure 2.5 shows the **Solution Packages** tab within SAP Best Practices Explorer.

The second variant of the ready-to-run business processes for use with your SAP S/4HANA implementation is the enterprise management layer for SAP S/4HANA (available for both on-premise and private cloud deployments). Just like SAP Best Practices, it provides a preconfigured package that can be deployed into a company's environment to start fit-to-standard workshops.

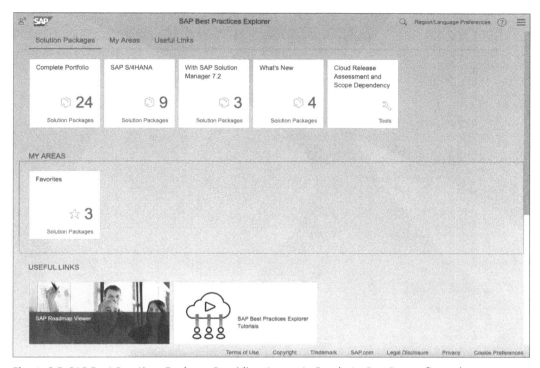

Figure 2.5 SAP Best Practices Explorer, Providing Access to Ready-to-Run Preconfigured Packages from SAP

The difference between the two is that the enterprise management layer for SAP S/4HANA provides specific business processes for multicountry deployment (optionally, upon request, it can be also deployed for a single country). The enterprise management layer covers all major end-to-end business processes by default in both deployment options. Additional scope options can be selected based on each customer's functional requirements. The multicountry deployment option comes preconfigured and localized for up to 43 countries, with a corporate financial template allowing for parallel accounting according to group and local requirements, based on three accounting principles (group/local/tax) and a total of five ledgers. The single-country version comes with one single country and this country's Generally Accepted Accounting Principles (GAAP) as the leading accounting principle (and ledger). A second accounting principle (and ledger) allows for International Financial Reporting Standards (IFRS) reporting. In both versions, the group currency and the fiscal year variant can be adapted to customer requirements.

The second difference is the commercial model under which SAP offers these packages. SAP Best Practices are available to all companies and partners with no additional fee. Alternatively, the enterprise management layer for SAP S/4HANA is offered as a service offering for a fee (unless otherwise stated in a company's subscription agreement). You can learn more about the enterprise management layer for SAP S/4HANA via the SAP Best Practices Explorer at *http://s-prs.co/v546300*. The enterprise management layer for SAP S/4HANA overview page from SAP Best Practices Explorer is shown in Figure 2.6.

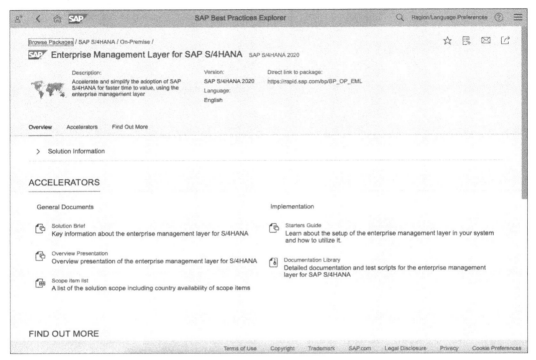

Figure 2.6 SAP Best Practices Explorer Overview Page: Enterprise Management Layer for SAP S/4HANA

We'll deep dive into the preconfigured packages and ready-to-run processes in Chapter 4, where we'll discuss their taxonomy, provisioning, and activation processes, as well as show you examples of content that is available in each.

2.2.2 Methodology

As an implementation or migration methodology for SAP S/4HANA and other SAP solutions, the SAP Activate methodology is a modular and agile framework that builds on its predecessors: the ASAP methodology (for on-premise implementations) and the SAP Launch methodology (for cloud deployments). You can use the SAP Activate methodology on your own, with SAP Services and Support, or with an SAP implementation partner company.

With SAP Activate, you'll follow a disciplined project management approach for your SAP S/4HANA implementation project. The methodology aligns with the industry's best practices documented by the Project Management Institute in the *PMBOK Guide*, helping you minimize risk, streamline and accelerate your implementation project, and reduce the total cost of implementation. A standardized work breakdown structure (WBS) helps project managers define and manage project tasks and focus on the deliverables and outcomes that are important for project success.

The traditional project management concepts in SAP Activate are matched with the project team's agile practices based on the Scrum agile framework, which prescribes roles, processes, and ceremonies the team executes during the project. For example, the users of SAP Activate will find a clear explanation of how to create the initial backlog and use it for planning and executing sprints. SAP Activate doesn't stop there: the methodology provides accelerators that explain how to apply agile techniques in the context of an SAP S/4HANA implementation project.

In addition to proper project management techniques and an agile approach, the SAP Activate methodology provides detailed SAP product- and solution-specific guidance for a broad range of project team roles in the SAP project, from application consultants to business users to architects and trainers. SAP Activate significantly expanded the range of users who can benefit by providing prescriptive tasks that detail the procedure for completing work in the project. For example, one task in SAP Activate for SAP S/4HANA Cloud details how companies receive the starter environment and how to set up project team users in the system. Consultants will find detailed guides and accelerators explaining how to prepare for, execute, and capture the findings from fit-to-standard workshops. And the team responsible for implementation of organizational change management will find OCM documents and guidance in the solution adoption workstream.

All SAP customers and partners can access the SAP Activate methodology in the SAP Activate Roadmap Viewer tool (accessible at *http://s-prs.co/v502705*). We'll explain how to use the tool in Chapter 3, Section 3.1. Companies implementing SAP S/4HANA Cloud will get access to the SAP Activate methodology tasks directly in the SAP Cloud ALM application when they use the environment for their SAP S/4HANA Cloud implementation project (see Figure 2.7 for an example of a methodology task screen). Companies with on-premise projects that use SAP Solution Manager can load the SAP Activate WBS to their cProjects system in SAP Solution Manager using the WBS provided on the Roadmap Viewer site. They can also use the agile techniques inside Focused Build for SAP Solution Manager. We'll explain SAP Cloud ALM in Chapter 3, Section 3.3.

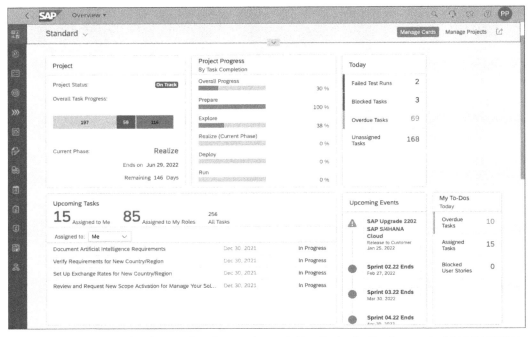

Figure 2.7 SAP Cloud ALM, Showing Implementation Tasks for Deployment of SAP S/4HANA Cloud

2.2.3   Tools for Adoption and Extensibility

SAP Activate users will use various tools during the project to implement the solution. SAP Activate recommends the use of specific tools for specific purposes, such as configuration, extensibility, integration, testing, data loads, and so on. We'll introduce some of the tools in this chapter, but the main discussion of the specific tooling required for implementing the different versions of SAP S/4HANA will be provided in each implementation's chapter because different tools are used when implementing SAP S/4HANA Cloud than when implementing on-premise SAP S/4HANA.

Now let's outline the key capabilities that the project team needs during the delivery of the project. While the title of this section mentions configuration and extensibility, the scope of these tools is broader and covers at least the following capabilities:

- Configuration
- Documenting the solution, including business process models
- System change management and transport management
- Data loads and data migration
- Testing
- Delivery of training and enablement

- Managing the project work
- Extending the solution
- Integration
- Access and identity management

The topic of tools is so broad that it could fill another book this size, especially if we were to go into the details of how to use each tool. Instead, we'll focus on the key capabilities that project teams need and talk about the tools that provide those capabilities.

Many of these capabilities can be provided by one tool, while other capabilities require a different, dedicated tool. Here, we'll use the implementation of SAP S/4HANA in the on-premise deployment model as an example. The key tool for project teams in this situation is SAP Solution Manager, which provides coverage for capabilities such as solution documentation, business process modeling, change request management, testing, and managing project work, as well as additional capabilities that are necessary for not only implementing but also running the implemented solution productively.

In addition to SAP Solution Manager, the project team will use specialized tools such as the Implementation Guide (IMG) in SAP S/4HANA to configure the application settings in order to tailor the solution to a company's requirements. The project team will use in-app extensibility and open application programming interfaces (APIs) along with SAP Business Technology Platform (SAP BTP) to extend the delivered solution capabilities. For migrating data into SAP S/4HANA, the project team will use the SAP S/4HANA migration cockpit. The cockpit provides predefined data load templates the customer team will use for data load, avoiding the need to build the data load templates and routines from scratch. And, finally, for delivery of enablement and training, the project team will use SAP Enable Now to create end user training and simulations. This is just one example of the tooling that the on-premise project teams can use to get all the work done.

We'll highlight the tools that deliver the SAP Activate content to users in Chapter 5 and discuss the use of tools for specific use cases in the detailed chapters in the later part of this book, starting with Chapter 7.

2.3   SAP Activate Phases and Project Management

The SAP Activate methodology provides guidance over the six phases that support your team throughout the project lifecycle of an SAP S/4HANA solution. Underlying these phases is a series of deliverables, tasks, and quality checks to ensure that the solution, as implemented, delivers the expected value. Figure 2.8 illustrates the phases of the SAP Activate methodology for SAP S/4HANA solutions, which we'll discuss in this chapter.

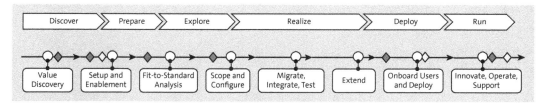

Figure 2.8 SAP Activate Phases and Key Activities in Project Lifecycle

SAP Activate Methodology Deliverables

During each project phase, your project team will produce a prescribed set of deliverables to serve as inputs to subsequent phases. The SAP Activate methodology provides a detailed list of project deliverables, including procedural descriptions explaining how to prepare and complete the deliverable. The methodology also provides accelerators for each phase and workstream, which may include files and assets such as templates, questionnaires, checklists, how-to documents, and guidebooks. Remember, the objective is to facilitate the efficient, consistent, and repeatable delivery of an SAP S/4HANA implementation.

Let's now review the work, deliverables, and activities that the project team performs during each phase of SAP Activate. In this section, we'll provide examples of deliverables that are created in each phase, talk about the work that is done in each phase, and examine how the work from one phase flows into the next one to progressively build the solution.

2.3.1   Discover

The purpose of the discover phase is to find the solution's capabilities, to understand its business value and its benefits for your business, and to determine an adoption strategy and roadmap in alignment with the solution's capabilities and product roadmap. During this phase, users often access trial environments to get hands-on experience with the application and aid in the selection process.

Example deliverables in the discover phase are as follows:

- Strategic planning
- Application value and scoping
- Trial system access
- Discovery assessment

2.3.2   Prepare

The prepare phase kicks off the initial planning and preparation for the project. At this time, the project is started, plans are finalized, project team resources are assigned, and work is underway to start the project. In addition, the initial technical and application environment is provisioned or set up during this stage of the project (this is different from previous methodologies that instructed users to set up the initial environment much later in the project as they didn't use the working system during the solution fit confirmation and requirements definition stage).

Example deliverables in the prepare phase are as follows:

- Project team (self-)enablement
- Project initiation
- Project governance
- Plan project, schedule, and budget
- Project kickoff
- Project standards and infrastructure
- Initial environment provisioning/setup and activation of best practices
- OCM roadmap
- Access to implementation-supporting tools
- Fit-to-standard preparation, including system preparation (functionality/data/authorizations)
- Data migration strategy
- Testing strategy and approach
- End-user learning strategy
- Phase closure and sign-off

2.3.3   Explore

The purpose of the explore phase is to perform a fit-to-standard analysis to confirm the fit of the solution's standard functionality to your company's needs and to determine configuration values, necessary extensions, and analytics requirements. The explore phase also involves identifying required integrations, establishing data requirements, and designing identity and access management. Identified delta requirements and configuration values are added to the backlog to be addressed during the realize phase. During the explore phase, the project team also prepares for execution of data migration activities, makes plans for testing (including selecting the appropriate testing tools to ensure the quality of the delivered solution), and begins putting together a learning team as part of the adoption workstream that manages the OCM and end user enablement activities.

Example deliverables in this phase are as follows:

- Execution and monitoring of the project
- Fit-to-standard analysis
- Company execution of standard processes
- Solution definition
- Integration planning and design
- Extensions planning and design
- Analytics planning and design
- Identity and access management planning and design
- Data load preparation
- Test planning
- Mobilization of the learning team
- Phase closure and sign-off

2.3.4   Realize

During the realize phase, you'll use a series of agile iterations to incrementally build, test, and validate an integrated business and system environment based on the business scenarios and process requirements identified during the fit-to-standard analysis workshops in the explore phase. This phase includes loading company data, performing adoption activities, and planning operations in the new environment.

Example deliverables in this phase are as follows:

- Execution and monitoring of the project
- OCM alignment activities
- Initial access and setup of the development environment (SAP S/4HANA Cloud)
- Initial access and setup of the test environment (SAP S/4HANA Cloud)
- Configuration and solution documentation
- Setup of integrations
- Development and setup of solution extensibility
- Setup of output management and printing
- Legacy data migration activities
- Execution of unit and string testing in sprints
- Solution walkthrough in each sprint
- Technical operations and handover plan
- Planning of Center of Expertise (COE) for operational support
- Development of key user enablement materials

- Development of end user training and documentation
- Preparation and execution of integration testing
- Preparation and execution of UAT
- Cutover planning
- Phase closure and sign-off
- Optional activation of additional scope items (when needed)
- System upgrade (optional and relevant especially for planning for cloud solution deployment)

Upgrade during the Implementation Project

The upgrade of your current release could occur during the implementation project, especially when deploying SAP S/4HANA Cloud (or other public cloud solutions), where you'll receive regular upgrades per a published schedule. These upgrades can't be delayed or skipped. Project teams need to plan sufficient time and capacity to perform preupgrade preparation activities, regression testing, and other postupgrade actions.

An SAP S/4HANA Cloud upgrade takes place in a three-week window where first the test environment is upgraded, and then the development environment and production environment are upgraded simultaneously three weeks later. This time allows for a customer project team to perform regression testing.

During the time between the test environment upgrade and the end of the upgrade window, some activities in the system may be restricted. For example, importing configuration and development objects from development to a test system is not possible after the test system has been upgraded to the new release. Thus project teams need to exercise extreme caution when releasing emergency fixes into production during the upgrade window. Note that in critical situations project teams can propagate emergency fixes to the production environment using the transport system but must skip testing in a dedicated test environment. This increases the risk of potentially introducing untested and disruptive changes into the production environment.

2.3.5   Deploy

The purpose of the deploy phase is to set up the production environment, to confirm organizational readiness, and to switch business operations to run in the new environment.

Example deliverables in this phase are as follows:

- Execution and monitoring of the project
- Execution of OCM activities
- End user learning delivery
- Dress rehearsal

- Production cutover
- Operation readiness
- Hypercare support
- Stabilization of the production environment after cutover
- Handover to support organization

2.3.6   Run

The run phase is the open-ended phase after go-live. Its purpose is to ensure that the solution is running at peak performance and to take advantage of the regular innovations that SAP releases for the SAP S/4HANA Cloud environment. This phase also focuses on the continuous adoption of the solution by new users per your organization's needs.

Example deliverables in this phase are as follows:

- Ongoing system operations
- Continuous OCM activities
- Continuous learning
- Continuous business process and system improvements
- New scope activation
- New country/countries activation
- Setup and onboarding of new users
- System upgrade

2.3.7   Project Management

The project management deliverables and tasks are comprehensively covered in the SAP Activate methodology. The process follows the standard defined in the Project Management Institute's *PMBOK Guide*. The general flow of the project management activities starts in the prepare phase of the methodology with activities for initiation and planning of the project. Figure 2.9 shows an example of the project management workstream deliverables from SAP Activate for the **Transition to SAP S/4HANA** implementation roadmap.

During the prepare phase, the project team completes the following artifacts and events:

- Project charter
- Project WBS
- Project budget

- Project management plans to manage the schedule, resources, risk, quality, contracts, and other aspects of project delivery
- Project schedule that will be progressively detailed during the course of the project
- Definition of project team roles and responsibilities
- Establishment of governance for the project
- Identification of stakeholders and creation of the stakeholder management plan
- The kickoff of the project in a formal session
- Onboarding of project team members through self-enablement or training sessions
- Provisioning of the environment for application lifecycle management (ALM), such as SAP Solution Manager or SAP Cloud ALM applications
- Project team infrastructure and workspace, including physical facilities, collaboration space, and the document management environment for project documents

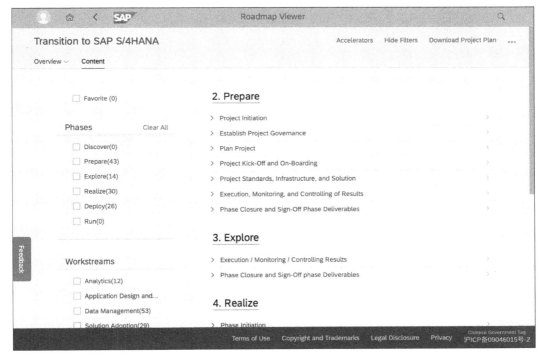

Figure 2.9 Project Management Workstream in SAP Activate for Transition to SAP S/4HANA

The project team also starts to execute the project activities, such as managing the project, right from the prepare phase. This is indicated in the SAP Activate methodology by the execute/monitor and control deliverables and tasks that occur in every phase (refer to Figure 2.9). The following is a summary of activities that happen in each phase during the execution, monitoring, and controlling of the project:

- **Updates to project schedule**
  This may include updates to the project timeline, including detailing and refining the high-level timeline for upcoming phases. There is progressive planning of detailed steps in each phase.

- **Directing and managing project execution activities**
  The tasks in this area focus on executing the project activities per the plan defined during the project. The helps the project manager oversee the progress and direct the team to deliver on planned results.

- **Monitoring and controlling the project activities**
  This also includes a regular review of progress, assessment of risks and issues, and management of project quality.

- **Manage issues, risks, and changes**
  This area is very important for the project manager to keep under control per defined management plans that the team created in the beginning of the project based on predelivered templates from SAP Activate.

- **Communicate status and progress to project stakeholders**
  This includes regular updates to project stakeholders about progress, risks, issues, and deliverables.

Each phase is also formally closed per guidance in phase closure and sign-off phase deliverables. The steps in this stage cover the activities of formally closing the phase by conducting a formal quality gate review to assess the completeness of deliverables from the current phase and readiness to start the next phase of the project. SAP provides a template for conducting the quality gates in the form of quality gate templates and guides. SAP Activate prescribes one quality gate in each phase to close the phase. Other activities during the phase closure may include collecting lessons learned in a formal knowledge gate, conducting project review activities (e.g., review of project management service), and managing fulfilled contracts.

2.4   Golden Rules for Implementing SAP S/4HANA

Organizations deploying SAP S/4HANA in their business will benefit from keeping the solution as close to standard as possible, which allows for faster adoption of innovations that SAP delivers both for cloud and on-premise systems. SAP experts often refer to this as a *cloud mindset* or *keeping the core clean*. To help customers execute this approach, SAP Activate includes guidance and governance for application of the so-called golden rules for implementing SAP S/4HANA. In this section, we will review the approach and rules in more detail. It will set foundation for later chapters in this book, including Chapter 7 on deployment of SAP S/4HANA Cloud and SAP S/4HANA.

SAP S/4HANA offers a high level of flexibility and extensibility options that are embedded in the solution and enabled with the full ABAP development environment. Some choices that the implementation team makes during the project could lead to increased total cost of ownership during the regular operations and upgrades of the environment later. As you implement the solution, SAP recommends project teams to stay close to the standard functionality and limit the use of some extensibility and custom coding techniques to absolutely critical cases where the solution needs to be adapted to support the business objectives.

SAP has published five golden rules for implementing SAP S/4HANA that provide project teams, architects, technical and functional consultants, and key users with guidelines to implement the solution in a way to make it easier to upgrade and continuously enhance.

We'll walk through each of the golden rules in the following sections and explain how to apply it in your SAP S/4HANA project. First, let's look at the rules at a high level and discuss their business benefits.

2.4.1   Rules and Benefits

Let's begin with a high-level overview of the five golden rules and consider their business benefits. The five golden rules are as follows:

1. **Foster a cloud mindset by adhering to fit-to-standard and agile deployment, as detailed in SAP Activate**
   The following activities fall under this rule:
   - Leverage SAP standard processes where possible.
   - Deploy your solution incrementally with short releases and sprints.

2. **Use preconfigured solutions with predefined processes and leverage the SAP Fiori UX**
   The preconfigured solution options are as follows:
   - SAP Best Practices for SAP S/4HANA Cloud and SAP S/4HANA (on-premise)
   - Enterprise management layer for SAP S/4HANA
   - SAP-qualified partner package
   - Modern SAP Fiori UX

3. **Ensure the use of modern integration technologies**
   To use modern integration technologies, follow these guidelines:
   - Use public APIs (also known as allow-listed APIs).
   - Provide no native access to APIs that aren't public.
   - Follow the given SAP Activate guidance for integration.
   - Use SAP BTP functionality for cloud integration.

4. **Ensure use of modern extensibility technologies**
   To use modern extensibility technologies, follow these guidelines:
   - Develop company extensions in a side-by-side approach using SAP BTP.
   - Leverage key user extensibility for no-code extensions.
   - Use developer extensibility to create custom code where needed.
   - Avoid backend enhancements.
   - Don't modify SAP source code.

5. **Ensure transparency on deviations**
   You can ensure transparency via the following methods:
   - Clearly document any deviations as part of the implementation; this will help the company replace these with standard capabilities if they are offered in the future.
   - Use the standard capabilities of ALM tools like SAP Solution Manager or SAP Cloud ALM to document the solution.

Companies that adhere to these rules realize the following benefits:

- **Faster time to value**
  Adopting standard processes reduces the number of decisions and effort to configure, tailor, and test the solution, thus resulting in faster time and lower effort for implementation. This approach also allows for tailoring the solution when an organization will gain value from using a customized solution rather than the standard. In many ways, this is a balancing act of implementing the solution close to standard and maximizing the benefits the organization can extract from the solution.

- **Lower cost of initial deployment and ongoing cost of running the solution**
  Reducing the number of changes in the solution leads to cleaner software that is easier to upgrade and continuously enhance, thus leading to lower overall cost of initial implementation and ongoing upgrades.

- **Ability to absorb innovations delivered by SAP at a faster rate**
  A clean core allows your organization to innovate at a faster rate as you're ready to leverage the regular innovations SAP delivers in your system.

- **Lower risk during the deployment of the solution**
  Adopting standard software exposes your organization to less risk that could be introduced in custom code during the project, including potential security gaps.

- **Higher flexibility and lower reliance on one system integrator**
  Rule 5 stipulates the need to document the key configuration decisions and any deviation from the golden rules. Having clear documentation of the decisions used to design the solution allows organizations to be less dependent on one system integrator and provides them with choice in the market.

- **Deployment of future-proof solutions using modern technologies**
  Using modern technologies, such as open APIs for extensibility and integration, sets

up the system for the future and allows organizations to benefit from the well-designed system longer as the technologies evolve. Using old technology will lead to them becoming obsolete, and organizations will need to invest in redesigning and rebuilding specific parts of the system that use old technology after they become obsolete or get phased out.

2.4.2 Rule 1: Foster a Cloud Mindset

One of the key principles in implementation of the cloud solutions is to stay close to standard capabilities of the software and to either fully avoid or at least minimize customization of the software. The fit-to-standard approach in your project will help you structure workshops around reviewing the standard functionality delivered in SAP software, whether you're building your solution around SAP Best Practices, the enterprise management layer for SAP S/4HANA, or an SAP-qualified partner package. With all these packages, the project team starts with a set of predelivered processes that are shown to the business users to secure buy-in and to define delta requirements for capabilities that need to be configured or created during the implementation of the software.

Figure 2.10 shows the application of the fit-to-standard approach in the flow of the project from the prepare phase through the explore phase.

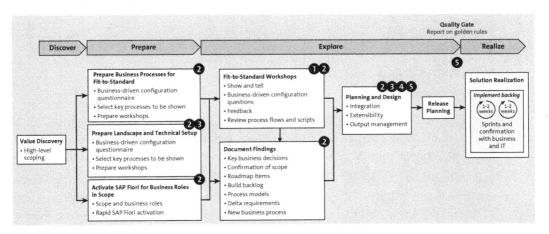

Figure 2.10 Golden Rules 1 and 2 Applied in SAP Activate Methodology

The key steps in each phase that pertain to the rules are referenced with the rule number in the circle. While the focus is on the first two rules in Figure 2.10, all five rules work in conjunction and build on each other. You can see that in cases where the box referencing an activity is linked to multiple rules. For example, the Prepare Landscape and Technical Setup activity links to both rule 2 and rule 3 as integrations are a key part of the technical setup.

The second part of the first golden rule is to apply agile techniques in deployment of the software, which enables your organization to clearly set the focus on the most valuable capabilities first and deliver the software to the business via incremental deployments to maximize the value you're getting from the solution. Refer to the agile techniques discussed in Chapter 6 for more details.

2.4.3   Rule 2: Use Preconfigured Solutions and Leverage SAP Fiori

This second golden rule goes hand in hand with the first one that we discussed in the previous section. We will provide more details on the structure and components of SAP Best Practices and the enterprise management layer for SAP S/4HANA in Chapter 4, when we discuss how to get started with a working system. The principle we discuss here is to use preconfigured and ready-to-use standard business processes and thus adopt the standard functionality where these processes are a good fit for your business. In many cases, this will require driving strong change management to the organization to adopt the new standard instead of tailoring the predelivered processes. This is especially the case with business processes that don't bring differentiation to your business but are necessary to run your organization. In this case, it makes sense to adopt standard processes and rely on SAP for delivery of innovation. Some examples of these processes are as follows:

- Accounting and financial close
- Asset accounting
- Purchase order accruals
- Preventive maintenance
- Emergency maintenance

Even processes for which you adopt the standard may bring significant innovation into your organization through an ability to use innovation technologies like machine learning, artificial intelligence (AI), and robotic processing automation (RPA).

The second part of the rule refers to leveraging the SAP Fiori UX to take advantage of the innovation SAP is building into the software with a new UX that helps process business transactions more efficiently by exposing business information to the user in new way. SAP Fiori can expose both the analytical data and transactional data in one screen, thus allowing you to analyze the situation and take action.

Figure 2.11 shows the **Sales Order Fulfillment Issues** screen designed in SAP Fiori, which provides a combined set of information with the analytical view at the top of the screen and the individual sales documents in the bottom part of the screen. With this UI, you can quickly zoom in and act on the orders that need attention. Many SAP Fiori screens also include additional intelligent technologies that help you identify and perform the action based on analysis of previous situations using machine learning and AI.

Figure 2.11 Order Fulfillment Monitor in SAP S/4HANA Combining Analytics and Transactional Data in One View

2.4.4   Rule 3: Use Modern Integration Technologies

SAP provides several predefined integrations for SAP-to-SAP integration scenarios as the recommended ways to integrate your SAP S/4HANA solution with other SAP software in your landscape—for example, SAP SuccessFactors Employee Central or SAP Ariba. For such situations, we recommend using the predelivered integration scenarios you can find in SAP Best Practices Explorer (see Chapter 3, Section 3.2).

For integration of homegrown systems or systems from other vendors, SAP recommends using SAP's Cloud Integration capability, available with SAP Integration Suite. This applies to both cloud-to-cloud and cloud-to-on-premise integration scenarios.

SAP Activate provides specific steps for project teams to follow during the design of integrations. The tasks guide project teams to identify the integration needs, define the integration scenario, and create detailed functional and technical designs for integrations that aren't delivered out of the box. Then in the realize phase, you can implement the integration using available APIs on SAP API Business Hub (you can learn more at *http://api.sap.com*).

Figure 2.12 shows the flow of these steps in SAP Activate. At the top, you can see items from the integration scenario and interface list, which is used to collect a list of integrations. The steps below that show the flow of activities driving the definition and design of integrations. The integration scenario and interface list accelerator are used to detail the functional and technical aspects of the integration, including the API and details of the data the interface uses (including information such as data type and field length that are important for technical realization).

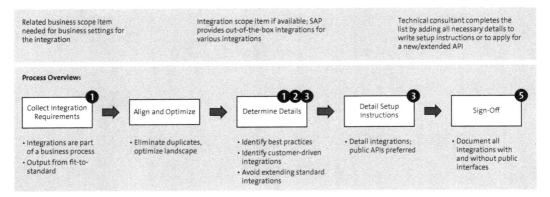

Figure 2.12 How to Handle Integrations during SAP Activate Projects

2.4.5   Rule 4: Use Modern Extensibility Technologies

SAP S/4HANA supports a wide range of extensibility options that allow businesses to tailor solutions to their needs. The following extensibility options are recommended (introduced in Chapter 5, Section 5.3):

- **Key user extensibility**
  This allows users to adapt standard functionality to meet their requirements without the need for any external tools. It can be used both for applying small changes, such as hiding standard fields for specific user groups, or for including additional business logic. SAP S/4HANA Cloud offers tools that cover diverse extensibility needs. The following is a list of in-app extensibility actions:
  - Change and adapt the UI layout and context
  - Create a new custom UI
  - Create custom fields
  - Create custom business objects
  - Create and extend forms and email templates
  - Create custom-specific CDS views
  - Enhance the current business process by creating custom business logic

- **Developer extensibility**
  This type of extensibility is possible through the integrated development tools in SAP S/4HANA Cloud and SAP S/4HANA, like the full ABAP development environment in SAP S/4HANA Cloud, private edition or the ABAP environment for SAP S/4HANA Cloud (note that at the time of writing, this capability was in early adopter stage with select customers).

- **Managed extensibility using SAP BTP**

  This extensibility approach uses SAP BTP (a platform as a service [PaaS]) to extend the application by using the capabilities exposed via services on SAP BTP. The applications built on the platform are then integrated with SAP S/4HANA Cloud and SAP S/4HANA and extend the standard functionality in one of many areas. You can develop applications such as the following:

  - Proxy applications
  - Convenience applications
  - Substitute applications
  - Preprocessing applications
  - Postprocessing applications
  - Analytical applications

  The applications developed on SAP BTP use the following integration contexts to integrate the application with SAP S/4HANA Cloud and SAP S/4HANA:

  - UI integration
  - User integration
  - Rules and workflow integration
  - Process integration
  - Events integration
  - Data integration

Figure 2.13 shows the flow of steps in the context of a project, where the project team needs to identify the need for extensibility, capture the requirements, detail the design for specific extensibility, and develop and test the extensibility. Figure 2.13 depicts the key sources of information that help you work on extensibility, such as SAP Extensibility Explorer and business process flows from standard SAP Best Practices processes used to indicate the extensibility requirements. In the lower portion of Figure 2.13, you can see the process steps that project team experts follow to define and design extensions in the system. The numbers above the boxes indicate the golden rule(s) applicable in each box.

Further Resources

If you're interested in extensibility, review the details provided via SAP Extensibility Explorer at *http://s-prs.co/v502725* and review the example extensibility samples provided there.

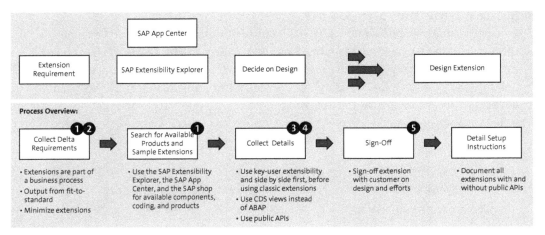

Figure 2.13 How to Handle Extensibility during SAP Activate Projects

2.4.6   Rule 5: Ensure Transparency on Deviations

The fifth rule is aimed at ensuring that any deviations from rules 1–4 are clearly documented so they can be accessible to the company during future solution upgrades or application of system patches by the service center. This rule has several purposes, the main one being the ability to understand the design decisions that were made during the implementation of the software.

This is especially important during upgrades that may introduce new capabilities requiring reconfiguration of the existing features to work with new software. For example, new functionality introduced in release X+1 may change the way the application runs and may require new configuration. In such cases, access to comprehensive documentation and decision rationales is important. This applies not only to configuration but also to integrations and extensions that have been introduced in the system.

SAP recommends that companies use ALM tools such as SAP Solution Manager or SAP Cloud ALM to keep track of key design decisions for configuration, extensions, and integrations. The ALM tools provide capabilities to document the process flow decisions, document the design rationale, and capture the key design decisions for the future. It's also important to keep this documentation up to date in the release upgrades as the system gets new release functionality and the design is updated.

2.4.7   Governance to Keep the Core Clean

As we stated at the beginning of this section, the goal of these five golden rules is to help the customer project team keep the core clean and maximize the reuse of standard functionality instead of customizing the system functionality to cater to every single requirement raised by the business users. While this may sound counterintuitive, the experience in many projects has been that a large number of the requirements raised during the project are not in use either from the beginning of productive use of the system or shortly after use. SAP Activate recommends applying the lens of value to the business during the approval process before a requirement is added to the backlog.

To implement such governance, the SAP Activate team has added the Solution Standardization Board (SSB) to the prepare phase. Figure 2.14 shows the Establish Solution Standardization Board task as part of the activities in the prepare phase, related to project initiation and governance (see the starred task in the expanded deliverable).

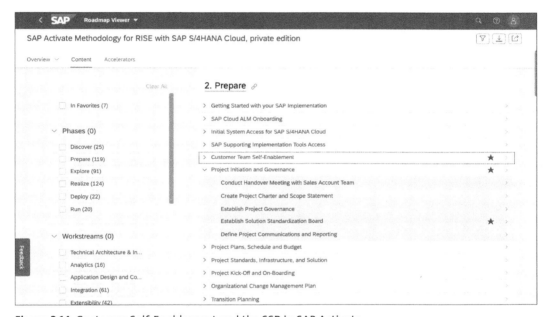

Figure 2.14 Customer Self-Enablement and the SSB in SAP Activate

Figure 2.14 also points to the self-enablement activities (see the star next to **Customer Team Self-Enablement**) that all project teams implementing SAP S/4HANA Cloud should go through (note that this also applies to project teams implementing on-premise SAP S/4HANA that aim to keep the ERP core clean). The key self-enablement activities prior to fit-to-standard workshops should focus on understanding the cloud mindset and learning the principles of the fit-to-standard approach. There are additional self-enablement activities done during the prepare phase, but the absolute minimum for the business users and project team members participating in the fit-to-standard workshops is to understand the cloud mindset, fit-to-standard, and the product capabilities in their area of responsibility.

Let's now talk about the role and scope of work of the SSB. The project team establishes this governance function very early in the implementation project and its role is to ensure that the project standardizes business processes and complies with the five golden rules. This means that the SSB evaluates, reviews, approves, or rejects the following requirements and requests from the individual functional project work streams:

- Delta requirements addressed through in-app and side-by-side extensions, especially ones in amber and red categories per the extensibility guide for SAP S/4HANA Cloud
- Required integrations with emphasis on use of allow-listed APIs and compliance with golden rules
- Architectural and cross team design decisions that deviate from the golden rules

Essentially, the SSB functions as the gatekeeper to keep the project team and solution design in line with the five golden rules and guidance in the extensibility guide. The role of the SSB is to review all the noncompliant requests and decide whether they are going to be implemented. The board meets weekly to review all the submitted requests and make a decision on each. If a request is rejected and the project workstream wants to escalate this decision, they can trigger escalation to the project steering group, as shown in Figure 2.15. Note that Figure 2.15 depicts one page from the SAP Activate SSB template that you can download from the accelerator list in the task shown in Figure 2.14.

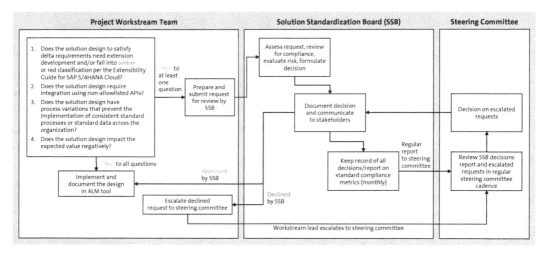

Figure 2.15 SSB Design Review Process to Ensure Compliance with Golden Rules

The SSB includes representatives from the company and the system integrator. On specific occasions, it also may include additional participants from project workstreams requesting the change or workstreams that are impacted by the request. The standing participants are as follows:

- SSB chair from the company and system integrator
- Company and system integration project managers

- Chief SAP solution architect (system integrator)
- Lead SAP technical architect (system integrator)
- Company enterprise IT architect
- Development leads responsible for SAP development (company and system integrator)

The role of the SSB is important during the implementation project, but it should not cease to exist after the first go-live. It is important to transition the function of the SSB into a permanent role in the IT organization to continue supporting future projects and point enhancements of the implemented system. Figure 2.16 shows the recommended steps for using SSB during the project and transition of the function into a permanent role after the initial go-live.

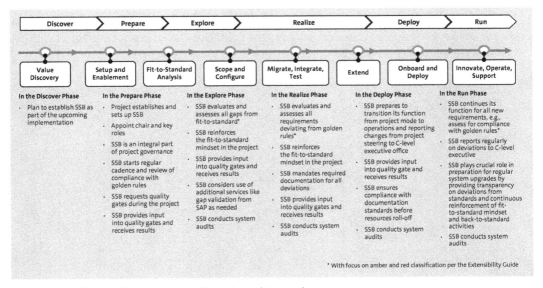

Figure 2.16 SSB Activities in Project Lifecycle and Beyond

The role and importance of SSB continues after the initial go-live to ensure continuous focus on implementing the new functionality in a manner compliant with the golden rules and a cloud mindset. Companies with multiple ERP projects could consider establishing an SSB function on the corporate IT level to provide oversight across all projects to monitor compliance with golden rules.

Practical Experience with the SSB

We encourage our readers to review additional resources about SSB in the SAP Activate community blogs. In particular, the following two blog posts provide (1) more details on the function and role of the governance board and (2) the practical experience of a project manager that established the SSB in their project:

- Practical governance to drive fit-to-standard mindset in your SAP S/4HANA implementation: *http://s-prs.co/v546302*
- The value of an SSB as part of implementing SAP S/4HANA Cloud: *http://s-prs.co/v546303*

2.5   SAP Activate Methodology Taxonomy

In addition to the traditional lifecycle-based hierarchy we've outlined in the previous sections, users can view the content of the SAP Activate methodology by a specific workstream and use tags for filtering and navigation.

Figure 2.17 shows the structure of the methodology along the six phases (shown at the top of the image: discover to run), and the rows represent the workstreams of related deliverables and tasks that are shown in the grid. This figure is available for download at *www.sap-press.com/5463*.

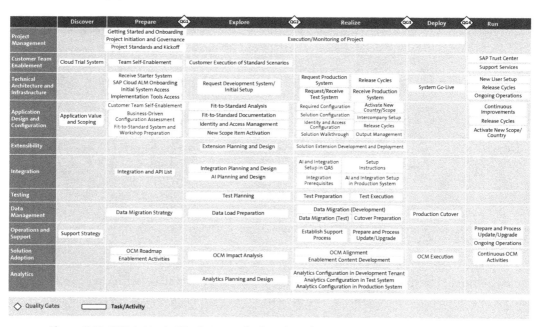

Figure 2.17 SAP Activate Workstream (Left Column), Showing Related Deliverables across Phases (Top Row) in End-to-End Lifecycle

In this section, we'll dig deeper into the structure of the SAP Activate methodology and provide additional details about how SAP structured the content and how to best use it in implementation projects.

2.5.1   Workstreams

As shown in Figure 2.17, *workstreams* represent groupings of related deliverables from specific areas, such as project management, solution design, or adoption. Each deliverable and task in the methodology is assigned to a workstream.

The following is a brief description of workstreams in SAP Activate:

- **Project management workstream**
  This workstream covers planning, scheduling, project governance, controlling, project standards, and monitoring activities for the execution of the project. Project leadership, such as project managers, team leads, or program managers, comprise the audience for this workstream.

- **Solution adoption workstream**
  This workstream covers OCM activities such as stakeholder management, change management planning and execution, and value management (VM) in context of the SAP implementation, where the stream focuses on realization of expected value from the implementation of the new system. This workstream closely interacts with the application design and configuration workstream we discuss later in this list. This workstream also includes deliverables and tasks related to planning, preparation, and delivery of end user training. Organizational change managers, business readiness leads, and trainers comprise the audience for this workstream.

- **Customer team enablement workstream**
  This workstream is related to solution adoption and covers the enablement activities for the customer project team, which also includes enablement activities for key users. The critical enablement activities must occur before the majority of work starts in the explore phase, especially the fit-to-standard workshops, where customer key users should already be enabled on the application functionality using the sandbox environment. In addition, key users and administrators (as applicable in specific deployments) must be trained to prepare for execution of their duties during the project. For example, they must be enabled on the ALM tool used for capturing requirements, creating solution documentation, and testing. Enablement leads and trainers who are driving the enablement and training activities in the project comprise the audience for this workstream.

- **Application design and configuration workstream**
  This is one of the anchoring workstreams that deals with all aspects of application requirements and design and configuration activities. The main activities during the project are setting and confirming the solution scope; planning, conducting, and documenting the fit-to-standard analysis workshops; identifying and capturing the delta business process requirements; and creating the solution functional design and technical design documents. This workstream is interconnected with other workstreams for extensibility (including development of reports, conversion routines, enhancements, forms, and workflows) and integration. Functional consultants, key users, and business process experts comprise the target audience for this workstream.

- **Data management workstream**

  This workstream provides guidance required for the discovery, planning, and execution of moving data from the legacy environment to the new system. It also covers the topics of data archiving and data volume management, data migration activities for cutover planning and execution, and managing the data volumes during the run phase. Data migration experts, system administrators, and system architects comprise the target audience for this workstream.

- **Testing workstream**

  This workstream is related to all the application and technical testing activities that the project team will conduct during the project. The work starts early in the project when the team defines the test strategy that drives the test-planning activities. The testing is conducted repeatedly during the entire project to drive continuous integration of the solution: for example, the project team conducts unit and string testing in delivery of sprints, and integration testing and UAT are done for each release. To complement the functional testing, SAP Activate guides technical teams to plan and conduct performance, load, and system testing at specific times during the project to mitigate risk to the go-live activities. The work done in this workstream directly contributes to the principle we introduced in Section 2.1: quality built-in. Test managers, testing team leads, testing experts, and technical and functional consultants comprise the target audience for this workstream.

- **Technical architecture and infrastructure workstream**

  This workstream covers topics related to architecting and setting up the solution from a technical standpoint. This workstream deals with consultants defining the system architecture; receiving the provisioned environment, whether it's in the public cloud, a hybrid deployment, or on-premise; designing the system landscape; designing and setting up the technical system (primarily for on-premise and managed cloud projects); and handling technical operations standards and processes. System architects, administrators, and technical users comprise the target audience for this workstream.

- **Extensibility workstream**

  This workstream covers the requirements definition, design, development, and deployment of system functionality that can't be provided by the standard product and needs to be custom-developed. Note that extensibility goes beyond the traditional topics of custom development of Workflows, Reports, Interfaces, Data Conversions, Enhancements, and Forms (WRICEF) objects. Application and technology developers comprise the target audience for this workstream.

- **Integration workstream**

  This workstream covers the activities needed to complete to plan, design, and set up (or develop) integrations between SAP S/4HANA and other applications. The topics included in this workstream are integration requirements identification, integration approach, integration solution design, and integration environment and middleware setup between the solution and external systems. Integration implementation experts and technical users comprise the target audience for this workstream.

- **Analytics workstream**
  This workstream discusses the key activities the project team needs to complete to establish a strong analytical solution for the business. The topics covered in this workstream include design, creation, and testing of the reporting and analytics inside the implemented solution; data modeling; data connections and integration for analytics; creation of stories through analytics; and predictive analysis. Analytics report developers and analytics experts comprise the target audience for this workstream. Note that for some dedicated analytical solutions, like SAP Analytics Cloud, SAP Activate provides a dedicated implementation roadmap with all the workstreams discussed in this section.

- **Operations and support workstream**
  This workstream is established to guide the project team in defining proper standards and policies for running the solution productively. These standards and policies need to be put in place during the implementation project. The company also needs to create an organization that will be responsible for running the environment.

  There is a difference in deliverables for on-premise and public cloud guidance that is given by the scope of services that SAP or other application management service providers cover. In general, in on-premise projects, the work in this workstream is much more involved than in public cloud implementations; but it's important to set up such an operational organization, even for cloud solutions, to take care of activities such as adding new users, adding new scope, coordinating regular solution upgrades, or expanding the geographical footprint of the solution after the initial go-live. Sample deliverables in this workstream are the definition and setup of the help desk process and organization; the definition, handling, and management of incidents; the post go-live change management process; and user-related operations standards and processes. Support agents, power users, and IT organization staff comprise the target audience for this workstream.

2.5.2 Deliverables

A *deliverable* is an entity in the methodology that resides directly underneath the phase. In addition, the deliverable is assigned to a workstream where the work occurs; the two assignments are clearly shown in Figure 2.17 as boxes assigned to a phase and a workstream. Every deliverable contains a title and textual description in the body of the deliverable, as shown in Figure 2.18. The deliverable represents an outcome from tasks performed in the project. These tasks are assigned to the deliverable and shown as a dynamic list in the SAP Activate Roadmap Viewer. Some deliverables have additional links to accelerators that help project team members complete the work on a specific deliverable.

The following is true for deliverables:

- A deliverable is an outcome of performing one or multiple tasks during a specific phase.
- A deliverable represents a basis for execution of project quality gates and often represents an element for customer acceptance/sign-off of the project outcomes.
- Each deliverable has at least one task, although often more than one task must be completed to create a deliverable.
- Each deliverable is assigned to a methodology workstream as defined in the previous section.

Figure 2.18 Example of Deliverable in SAP Activate for SAP S/4HANA Cloud

2.5.3   Tasks

Tasks in the SAP Activate methodology represent the lowest level of the hierarchy, detailing the work procedure each project team member needs to complete to contribute to creating the deliverable. Tasks generally contain additional links to accelerators that support the owner of the task in completing the task. Accelerators are defined in the next section.

The following is true for tasks:

- Tasks describe the work that needs to be done to complete a deliverable; for example, multiple tasks represent the sequence of work on the deliverable.
- The description of the task is more granular than in previous SAP methodologies (like ASAP) and provides guided details for those assigned to execute the task. For example, a description expands on the how-to guidance outlined in the deliverable and provides detailed steps describing how to execute the task.
- Each task is assigned to one accountable project role that will complete the task.

Figure 2.19 shows an example of a task from SAP Activate for the SAP S/4HANA Cloud implementation methodology. Notice the structure of the description, which provides a bulleted list detailing the procedure for completing the task.

Figure 2.19 Example of Task in SAP Activate for SAP S/4HANA Cloud

2.5.4   Accelerators

SAP Activate provides a rich repository of *accelerators* that are attached to the tasks and deliverables described in the previous sections. The accelerators provide additional documents, templates, links to tools, and descriptions that help project teams complete the tasks and deliverables faster. For example, one accelerator in SAP Activate for SAP S/4HANA Cloud provides project teams with a detailed guide for planning, scheduling, running, and documenting the results of fit-to-standard workshops.

2.6   SAP Activate Community

SAP encourages users of SAP Activate to follow and actively participate in the SAP Activate community space on SAP Community, which is open to all customers, partners, prospects, and SAP internal users. The community provides users access to the latest news, hot topics, and materials from using SAP Activate in company projects. It's a great place to find answers to your pressing questions. SAP also encourages users of SAP Activate to share their experience with using the approach in customer projects via blog posts, to share examples of how they applied the concepts, and to discuss their experiences.

The SAP Activate community is the place to stay up to date on new content, learn about the best way to apply the approach in your next project, and find information about your area of interest.

In this section, we'll review the key activities that community users can be involved in to maximize the benefit of being part of the community. Note that because SAP continues to evolve the community structure and content, some of the steps outlined here may change over time.

2.6.1   Register and Follow the SAP Activate Community

The first step in getting into the SAP Community is to register for SAP ID by clicking on the person icon in the top-right side of your screen at *https://community.sap.com/*. On the next screen, select the **Register** button and proceed with the guided registration steps as shown in Figure 2.20.

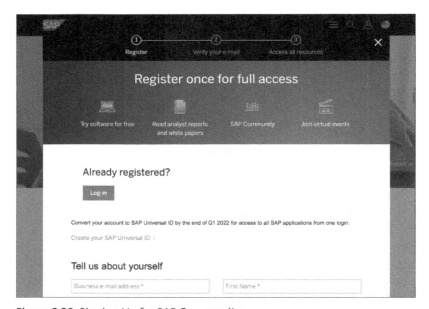

Figure 2.20 Signing Up for SAP Community

Once registered, you will be able to log on directly to the community by clicking the same person icon the next time you access the page. If you already have an SAP ID, you can use it to log into the SAP Community without needing to register.

Once you are registered for SAP Community, you can access the SAP Activate community page at *https://community.sap.com/topics/activate* and bookmark it in your preferred browser. We also recommend that you follow the SAP Activate community. You can do that by clicking on the **Follow SAP Activate Tag** on the right side of the main SAP Activate community page under the **Get Started with SAP Activate** section. Then, click on the blue **Follow** button under the community name.

2.6.2 Find Your Way in the SAP Activate Community

The SAP Activate community offers a simple structure that is represented on the main page and provides users with easy access to relevant SAP Activate resources. At the top of the main page, you will find a rotating carousel with the most recent updates and blogs. When you scroll a little more down the page, you will find a streamlined overview of the SAP Activate phases with key activities and highlighted accelerators. The page also provides access to additional resources on the right side of the page, where you can find links to topics and areas of the community that help you find relevant information, post blogs, or questions and engage with other users.

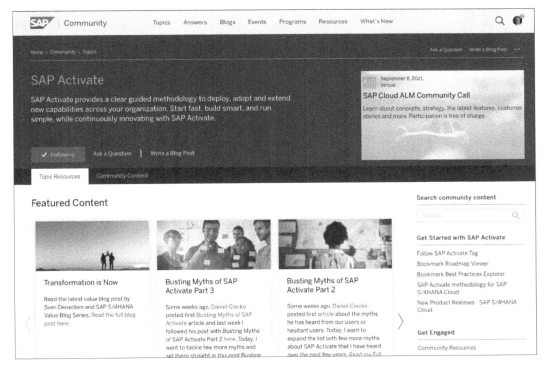

Figure 2.21 Main SAP Activate Community Space

Figure 2.21 shows the home page of the SAP Activate community. You can use the **Community Content** tab to access all blog posts and questions posted with the SAP Activate managed tag. There you can apply additional filters to narrow down the type of asset you are looking for—for example **Q&A**, **Blog Posts**, or **Documents**.

We'll explain key activities, such as posting a question, adding a blog, or adjusting your notifications, next.

2.6.3   Ask Questions and Find Answers

Users accessing SAP Community often come with specific questions or topics they need to research. The SAP Activate community provides search functionality that will help them find answers quickly.

There are multiple ways to search SAP Community. We recommend accessing the **Community Content** tab from the SAP Activate community main page. Then select the content type you want to locate (in the **CONTENT TYPES** selection on the right side of the screen), type a search phrase in the **Search community content** field, and press ⌷Enter⌷.

You can see an example of searching for "fit-to-standard" in the SAP Activate space in Figure 2.22.

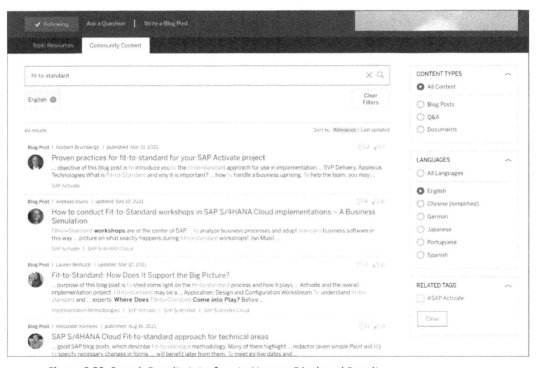

Figure 2.22 Search Results Interface to Narrow Displayed Results

Users of the community also can ask questions directly from any page in the community. In general, before raising a question, you should first search the community for answers. Over the life of this community, many questions have already been answered, and you may locate an existing answer faster than you could get a response to your own question. If you can't find the answer in the community, you can post your question using the **Ask a Question** link on the SAP Activate community main page; alternatively, you can select **Answers** at the top of the SAP Community navigation and select the **Ask a Question** menu item. Don't forget to assign the SAP-managed SAP Activate tag to your question to make sure it is correctly associated with the SAP Activate community space.

Efficient Questions

Make your question as specific as possible while omitting any details that could identify the project or customer you're working with. Remember that SAP Community is open to various types of users and freely searchable by search engines like Google or Bing.

2.6.4   How to Contribute Blog Posts

If you have examples from your project to share with the community or you have an experience with SAP Activate you want to discuss, you should post directly to the site as a blog post. The process is similar to posting the question as just described. You'll need to select **Write a Blog Post** from the SAP Activate community space.

This will open a new page where you'll input your blog post title, the text of the blog post, and tags that will help users find the content easier. Be sure to use a descriptive title and always assign the SAP Activate managed tag to help users find your blog post in the future. Just like questions, the blog posts are moderated by community moderators before they are posted. If you are contributing your very first blog post, it will be likely tagged for moderator review before it is approved for publication. A moderator may reach out to you if the text needs to be adjusted before it is ready to be posted.

You'll receive email notifications from the SAP Activate community when other users post new content (blog posts or questions), comment on your blog post, or provide feedback as a response to your question.

2.7   SAP Activate Training and Certification

If you want to learn more about the SAP Activate approach, SAP offers a comprehensive training curriculum consisting of classes offered either on the SAP Learning Hub or in an SAP training facility. The courses SAP offers are structured into a logical flow, from overview courses through courses that help attendees become proficient in the SAP

Activate approach to courses that help participants stay current. The entire training curriculum is shown in the learning journey for SAP S/4HANA—Implementation Tools and Methodology at *http://s-prs.co/v502707*.

The learning journey (shown in Figure 2.23) also offers the SAP Activate certification exam for consultants, project managers, and users of SAP Activate who want to demonstrate their understanding of the approach and obtain certification from SAP. You can take the certification exam on the SAP Learning Hub (allow about three hours to complete the exam). We'll share practice certification questions with you in Appendix A to support you in preparation for the exam and provide a review of the materials we cover in this book. We'll provide a more detailed breakdown of the exam topics in Appendix A and offer a series of practice questions for each topic.

Figure 2.23 SAP S/4HANA Implementation Tools and Methodology Learning Journey: SAP Activate Methodology

SAP Activate Certification Guide

For a complete guide to the SAP Activate certification, check out *SAP Activate Project Management Certification Guide: Certified Associate Exam* by Aditya Lal (SAP PRESS, 2021, *www.sap-press.com/5194*).

SAP Activate Courses on openSAP

SAP Activate courses also can be found on the openSAP enterprise massive open online courses (MOOC) platform at *http://open.sap.com*, where you can learn together with others studying the same course. You can go through the courses during the active period, or you can request reactivation of archived courses for a handling fee. You're eligible to receive a Record of Achievement upon completion of multiweek course materials. Details of this process are explained on the openSAP platform in the FAQ section. As of the time of writing, the Agile Project Delivery with Focused Build for SAP Solution Manager (Update Q3/2021) course covers using the build tools through the SAP Activate project lifecycle, focusing on agile project management and project delivery.

2.8   Summary

This chapter introduced the SAP Activate approach and its principles, including the use of SAP Best Practices and the application of the agile approach in the course of the project. We also introduced the six phases of the SAP Activate approach and discussed how the process flows through the phases. We have discussed the five golden rules for implementation of SAP S/4HANA that help organizations live the cloud mindset.

Later in the chapter, you learned about the workstreams that group related deliverables and tasks in the methodology. In addition, we looked at the accelerators that provide you with access to easy-to-use templates, examples, and other tools to accomplish the deliverables faster and with less effort. You've also seen that SAP Activate provides a guided journey to SAP S/4HANA (and other SAP products).

This chapter also introduced you to the SAP Activate community, including the key actions you can take in the community to engage with other SAP Activate experts and the SAP Activate team in SAP. In the last section, we provided an overview of the training and certification offerings from SAP that will help you learn more about SAP Activate and stay current on its continuous improvements.

In the next chapter, we'll introduce tools for accessing the SAP Activate methodology and preconfiguration assets, as well as discuss tools that project teams use to consume SAP Activate during the course of an implementation or upgrade project.

Chapter 3
Accessing SAP Activate

To implement both cloud and on-premise projects, project team members need the support of key tools when accessing and using SAP Activate. We'll provide an overview of these tools for both deployment options in this chapter.

In this chapter, we'll discuss the key tools that you'll use to access the SAP Activate components: methodology, SAP Best Practices, and tools for application lifecycle management (ALM).

We'll start by introducing the Roadmap Viewer tool that you can use to view and navigate the SAP Activate methodology content. Then we'll discuss the SAP Best Practices Explorer environment, in which you can access detailed information about the ready-to-use business process content delivered in SAP Best Practices and the enterprise management layer for SAP S/4HANA. In the second half of this chapter, we'll focus on the two key ALM tools: SAP Cloud ALM to support deploying and running cloud applications and the SAP Solution Manager standard toolset for managing on-premise and hybrid environments. These tools provide capabilities for creating solution documentation, managing requirements, planning and monitoring the project, and running and operating the solution.

Project teams use many other tools to leverage SAP Activate as well, and we'll discuss those in the specific chapters about deployment of SAP S/4HANA and SAP S/4HANA Cloud solutions. This chapter will focus on dedicated tools that allow the project team to access the methodology or ready-to-run business processes.

3.1 Roadmap Viewer

You can access the full content of the SAP Activate methodology in the Roadmap Viewer either via *https://go.support.sap.com/roadmapviewer/* or from the tile in SAP Solution Manager. The Roadmap Viewer provides an easy-to-navigate way to access SAP Activate methodology guidance for your specific solution—or, if a solution-specific roadmap isn't available, you can use the generic SAP Activate methodology for the cloud or on-premise solution.

The **Roadmap Viewer** entry screen presents you with several tiles that help you understand the role and functionality of the tool, as shown in Figure 3.1. The content behind these tiles helps first time users explore the key functionality of the Roadmap Viewer and learn how to use it most efficiently. The information includes an explanation of the content provided in the Roadmap Viewer in the **1. Overview** tile, navigational instructions with short video showing how to get around in the tool in the **2. How to Use** tile, and the **3. Learn More** tile offers a list of additional resources and links. The **4. SAP Cloud ALM** tile teaches how to access and use SAP Cloud ALM (we will cover this tool in Section 3.3). You can click the blue **Explore All Roadmaps** button to navigate to a list of available SAP Activate methodology roadmaps.

Figure 3.1 Roadmap Viewer Entry Screen

The list is grouped into following categories, as shown in Figure 3.2:

- Cloud Specific Methodology
- On-Premise Specific Methodology
- Upgrade Methodology
- General Methodology

You can click on the star in front of one or more methodology roadmaps to favorite specific instances of SAP Activate. Once they are favorited, the tool will show them automatically on the home page when you enter the Roadmap Viewer tool. You can arrange the tiles on the home page in any sequence by simply dragging the tiles to the desired spots. You can open a methodology roadmap either directly from the categorized list or from the home page if you select a favorite roadmap; simply click on the tile on the home page or click on the name of the roadmap.

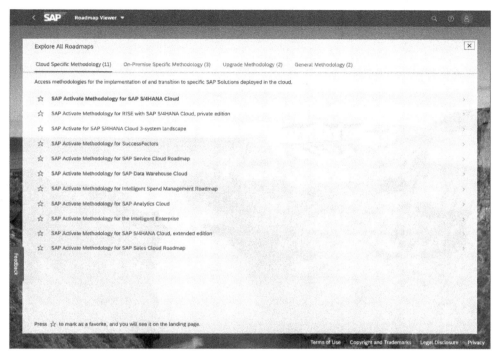

Figure 3.2 Navigation in All SAP Activate Roadmaps

After you pick a specific roadmap and open it, the screen will show the roadmap overview information that provides the description of the roadmap's purpose, the solution supported by the roadmap, and an overview of the approach and key deliverables in each phase, as shown in Figure 3.3. This page offers additional details as well, including the following:

- A link to the release blog that provides information about the latest updates to the methodology content
- A link to the overview presentation that helps you understand the overall flow of the methodology for your selected implementation roadmap
- Additional links to additional important assets that are available to the users of this roadmap

After reviewing the roadmap **Overview** section, you should navigate to the work breakdown structure (WBS) of the methodology to access all the details of the methodology content. In the **Content** tab, you can then browse the methodology hierarchy by phases and access specific descriptions and accelerators attached to the deliverables or tasks in the methodology hierarchy, as shown in Figure 3.4.

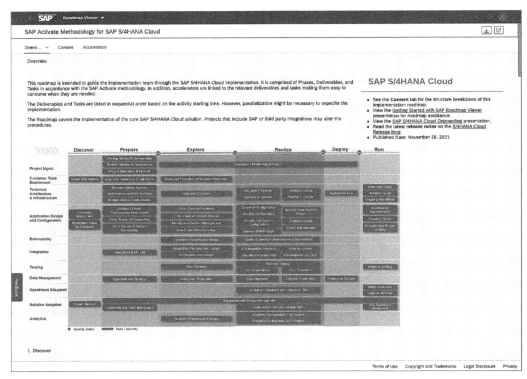

Figure 3.3 Overview Page for the SAP Activate Methodology for SAP S/4HANA Cloud

Figure 3.4 Content Navigation Screen for Browsing SAP Activate Methodology Content

You can either click on a specific deliverable to see its description and associated accelerators or expand the deliverable to show the tasks that are contributing to completion of that deliverable. Use the > sign on the left side of the deliverable to expand it and see the tasks, as shown in Figure 3.5. You can also use the up- and down-pointing arrows on the top right of the screen to expand all or collapse all items in the list. This way, you can quickly expand or collapse the entire methodology hierarchy with just one click.

In addition, you can filter the hierarchy by selecting specific (or multiple) phases, workstreams, assigned products, or additional roadmap-specific tags available in the **More** section; you will find these items on the left side of the screen.

Figure 3.5 Expanded Task List under Roadmap Viewer Deliverable

If you're looking for a specific accelerator you need at the moment, you can navigate directly to the complete list of accelerators assigned to the roadmap by clicking on the **Accelerators** tab at the top of the screen. This will bring you to a page with all accelerators sorted by phase. This page provides similar navigation and filtering capabilities as those for the WBS navigation, shown in the previously discussed figures. You can use these filters to narrow the search for an accelerator by phase and workstream to locate the specific accelerator or template you need.

In addition, on the **Overview** page, **Content** page, or **Accelerators** page, you can download the project WBS using the down-arrow icon in the top right. The WBS can be used in your preferred project scheduling tool or can be directly loaded into the SAP Solution Manager tool that we'll cover in Section 3.4.

After you navigate to the deliverable or task description, you'll learn about its purpose/process, and the Roadmap Viewer will provide access to accelerators and additional web links that support you in completing the task or deliverable. Figure 3.6 provides an example of one task from the SAP Activate Methodology for SAP S/4HANA Cloud and shows the structure of the task description and additional accelerators and links at the bottom of the description.

You can also make favorites of your frequently used tasks and deliverables by clicking the star icon in the top-right corner of the task description in the deliverable (see Figure 3.6). This information can later be used for filtering the content in the WBS.

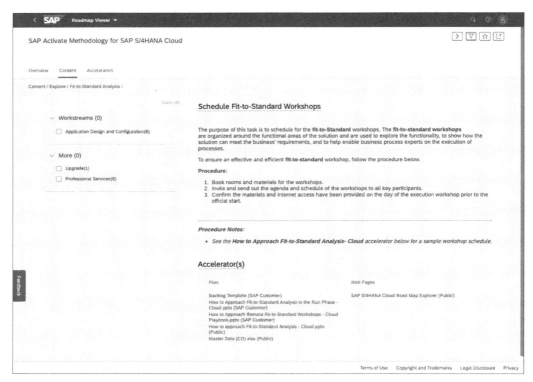

Figure 3.6 Example of Task Description in Roadmap Viewer

When you want to navigate between tasks under the same deliverable, you can use the **< >** arrows at the top right of the screen to navigate back and forth in the list of tasks without needing to exit the task. In addition, you can use the breadcrumb links at the top-left side of the screen to navigate back up to the deliverable, the phase, or the list of all deliverables and tasks (note that the filters you select on the complete task list are persistent throughout all navigation).

The Roadmap Viewer offers additional capabilities that help you locate specific assets, such as accelerators, tasks, or deliverables, very quickly. You can use the **Search** function (magnifying glass icon) at the top right of every screen to either search all roadmaps in the Roadmap Viewer or search for a specific roadmap or group of roadmaps.

We'll refer to the Roadmap Viewer in the remainder of this book when we point out specific accelerators, tasks, or deliverables as we discuss the deployment of SAP S/4HANA solutions in your environment.

3.2   SAP Best Practices Explorer

The SAP Best Practices Explorer provides descriptive information to prospects, customers, partners, presales, and consultants about the preconfigured solutions and their business processes delivered for SAP Best Practices for SAP S/4HANA Cloud, SAP Best Practices for SAP S/4HANA, and rapid-deployment solutions (see Figure 3.7).

Figure 3.7 SAP Best Practices Explorer

In SAP Best Practices Explorer, you'll find accelerators such as process flows, test scripts, setup instructions, and other documents to help you understand the scope of the preconfigured solutions.

In this section, we'll walk through the SAP Best Practices Explorer content positioning for both SAP S/4HANA and SAP S/4HANA Cloud, take a closer look at the content for SAP S/4HANA Cloud, and discuss localization, language, and tool features.

3.2.1   Positioning of Content

SAP Best Practices Explorer provides information about preconfigured localized solutions for SAP S/4HANA Cloud. This includes information about the preconfigured business processes in the form of downloadable process flows and test scripts, as well as details of key information about the solution, such as organization structure, sample financial master data, and detailed explanations of delivered content that are needed to understand the solution before system provisioning and during fit-to-standard workshops. In the SAP Best Practices Explorer user interface (UI), you'll find factsheet descriptions of localized processes in all languages supported by SAP S/4HANA Cloud.

Alternatively, for SAP S/4HANA and for rapid-deployment solutions, SAP Best Practices Explorer provides descriptions of the preconfigured localized solutions, including descriptions of how to manually configure the solution. Furthermore, a predefined structure is provided for use in your SAP Solution Manager system.

Getting Started

To get started with SAP Best Practices Explorer, see the following resources:

- Introduction Tutorial for SAP Best Practices Explorer at *http://s-prs.co/v502744*. (You can access the tutorials from the main page of SAP Best Practices Explorer by clicking on the **SAP Best Practices Tutorials** tile.)
- Online help documentation for SAP Best Practices Explorer at *http://s-prs.co/v502709*.

3.2.2   SAP S/4HANA Content Structure

In this section, we'll provide more details about the structure of the SAP S/4HANA content in SAP Best Practices Explorer by using SAP S/4HANA Cloud content as an example. The content for the on-premise SAP S/4HANA solution follows the same structure, with the only difference being that you would select the release version for the on-premise content, whereas the cloud content is available for the current release of cloud software (as all SAP S/4HANA Cloud customers are on the same release of the software).

SAP S/4HANA content is structured into two versions, as shown in Figure 3.8:

1. **Package version**

   A selection of scope items that cover the scope of preconfigured ready-to-run business processes for SAP S/4HANA cloud localizations are structured by line of business (LoB) to business area.

   Accelerators on the package level, such as availability and dependency matrix, scope presentation, and organization overview, provide overviews of key information about the scope of the solutions.

2. **Scope item versions**

   A scope item version has a specific product, release, and localization. It's typically a predefined business process, such as sales order processing, which represents a best practice implementation choice. Each scope item has a set of accelerators with detailed delivery documentation that is used during the implementation project.

Accelerators on the scope item version level, such as process diagrams, help you understand the implementable scope items.

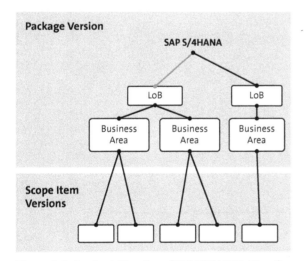

Figure 3.8 Content Structure (SAP S/4HANA Cloud)

For SAP S/4HANA Cloud scope items, the scope item pages in SAP Best Practices Explorer show whether an additional SAP S/4HANA Cloud license is required to use the scope item. This information will be displayed in SAP Best Practices Explorer (see Figure 3.9) when you navigate to the specific scope item screen in the drilldown or you search for it. In addition, the scope item pages show whether a scope item is excluded from the default activation (nonstandard) and, if so, the details about why the scope item is excluded from the default activation.

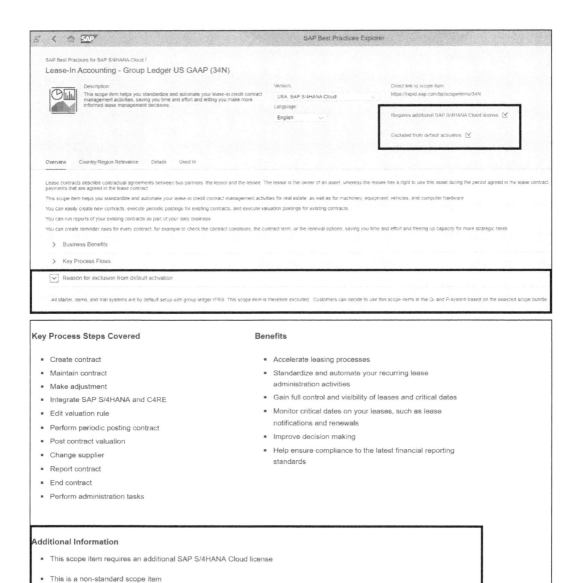

Figure 3.9 SAP S/4HANA Cloud Additional License

Links to the SAP Training and Adoption task tutorials are provided on the scope item version pages if a task tutorial exists for the scope item, as shown in Figure 3.10. You'll need to scroll to the **DETAILS** section in the scope item screen and then click on **Task tutorials**.

Figure 3.10 Task Tutorials

An offline package containing accelerators from the package version is provided in the SAP Software Download Center (see Figure 3.11). You can select and download a package for one country version. After a package is downloaded offline, a ZIP archive is provided with the content library that contains links to accelerators (see Figure 3.12). The content library is also available online from the package pages in SAP Best Practices Explorer. It enables a user to access all accelerators of a package from a single entry page.

In a new release of SAP S/4HANA Cloud, new scope items and versions might be introduced, and existing scope items might be changed or upgraded.

Figure 3.11 Offline Package Downloads

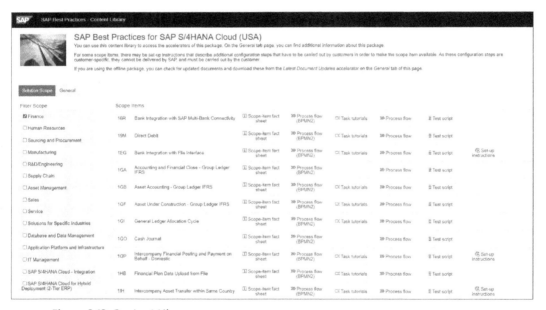

Figure 3.12 Content Library

You can find the first release with which a scope item was introduced for a particular localization in the Availability & Dependencies Overview accelerator on the package page, as shown in Figure 3.13. You can see the lists of new scope items in the current release in the Scope Presentation accelerator on the package page (see Figure 3.14).

Scope Item ID	Description	AU	BE	BR	CA	CH	CN	CZ	DE	DK	ES	FI	FR
2QU	Analytics - Purchase Order Visibility and Procurement Spend	1802	1802	1802	1802	1802	1802	1802	1802	1802	1802	1802	1802
2QW	Analytics for Production Unit - Plan/Actual Production Cost	1802	1802	1802	1802	1802	1802	1802	1802	1802	1802	1802	1802
1NN	Business Event Handling	1708	1708	1708	1708	1708	1708	1708	1708	1708	1708	1708	1708
30K	Predictive Analytics Model Training - Finance	1905	1905	1905	1905	1905	1905	1905	1905	1905	1905	1905	1905
1NJ	Responsibility Management	1705	1705	1705	1705	1705	1705	1705	1705	1705	1705	1705	1705
31N	Situation Handling	1808	1808	1808	1808	1808	1808	1808	1808	1808	1808	1808	1808
43R	Maintenance Resource Scheduling	2005	2005	2005	2005	2005	2005	2005	2002	2005	2005	2005	2005
8H1	Corrective Maintenance	1605	1605	1805	1605	1608	1605	1908	1605	1711	1705	1808	1605
8H2	Emergency Maintenance	1605	1605	1805	1605	1608	1605	1908	1605	1711	1705	1808	1605
4VT	Improvement Maintenance	2102	2102	2102	2102	2102	2102	2102	3011	2102	2102	2102	2102
3YE	Integration with Asset Central Foundation	1905	1905	No	1905	1905	1905	1905	1905	1905	1905	1905	1905
4WM	Operational and Overhead Maintenance	2102	2102	2102	2102	2102	2102	2102	3011	2102	2102	2102	2102
8J2	Preventive Maintenance	1605	1605	1805	1605	1608	1605	1908	1605	1711	1705	1808	1605
4HI	Proactive Maintenance	2102	2102	2102	2102	2102	2102	2102	3011	2102	2102	2102	2102
4HH	Reactive Maintenance	2102	2102	2102	2102	2102	2102	2102	2011	2102	2102	2102	2102
4RV	SAP Maintenance Assistant	2105	2105	2105	2105	2105	2105	2105	2105	2105	2105	2105	2105
53M	ABAP core data services extraction for SAP Data Intelligence	2102	2102	2102	2102	2102	2102	2102	2102	2102	2102	2102	2102
53L	ABAP core data services extraction for SAP Data Warehouse Cloud	2102	2102	2102	2102	2102	2102	2102	2102	2102	2102	2102	2102
3AB	Automated Provisioning via SAP Cloud Identity Access Governance	1808	1808	1808	1808	1808	1808	1808	1808	1808	1808	1808	1808
55F	Automotive Supply To Customer - Inventory Management	2108	2108	No	2108	2108	2108	2108	2105	2108	2108	2108	2108
1NX	Collaborative Manufacturing with SAP Digital Manufacturing Cloud	1705	1705	1705	1705	1705	1705	1705	1705	1705	1705	1705	1705
35D	Core Data Services-Based Extraction with SAP S/4HANA Cloud	1811	1811	1811	1811	1811	1811	1811	1811	1811	1811	1811	1811
J81	Core HR with SAP SuccessFactors Employee Central	1511	1511	1711	1511	1608	1511	1908	1511	1711	1705	1808	1603
5I9	Customer Data Return	2105	2105	No	2105	2105	2105	2105	2105	2105	2105	2105	2105
8H3	Data Migration to SAP S/4HANA from SAP	1603	1603	1605	1603	1605	1603	1605	1511	1605	1605	1605	1603
2Q2	Data Migration to SAP S/4HANA from Staging	1805	1805	1805	1805	1805	1805	1805	1805	1805	1805	1805	1805
5LE	Data Protection and Privacy	2105	2105	2105	2105	2105	2105	2105	2105	2105	2105	2105	2105
4AP	Data Quality Management for Business Partner	1911	1911	1911	1911	1911	1911	1911	1911	1911	1911	1911	1911
4AQ	Data Quality Management for Product	1911	1911	1911	1911	1911	1911	1911	1911	1911	1911	1911	1911

Figure 3.13 Availability & Dependency Matrix

Finance

Business Area	Scope Item	SID	Short Description
Advanced Accounting and Financial Close	Compliance Formats - Support Preparation for Czech Republic	5ZZ	Advance Compliance Reporting for Czech Republic enables you to configure, generate, analyze, and electronically submit statutory reports that contain indirect taxes, such as value-added tax for Czech Republic.
Advanced Accounting and Financial Close	Compliance Formats - Support Preparation for South Africa	5Z5	Advance Compliance Reporting for South Africa enables you to configure, generate, analyze, and electronically submit statutory reports that contain indirect taxes, such as value-added tax for South Africa.
Advanced Accounting and Financial Close	Compliance Formats - Support Preparation for Sweden	5Z6	Advance Compliance Reporting for Sweden enables you to configure, generate, analyze, and electronically submit statutory reports that contain indirect taxes, such as value-added tax for Sweden.
Advanced Accounting and Financial Close	Group Reporting Planning	5PU	This scope item delivers group reporting planning functions to support balance sheet planning and P&L planning.
Advanced Accounting and Financial Close	SAP Document and Reporting Compliance	5KU	SAP Document and Reporting Compliance allows a customer to comply with e-Invoicing, e-Reporting, and statutory reporting obligations. This scope item allows you to activate and control the visibility of advanced features on a country level.
Advanced Financial Operations	Tax Posting Proposal	5ZB	This scope item manages taxes in cross border goods movements related to intracompany stock transfer and customer consignment.
Advanced Financial Operations	VAT Tax Calculation and Reporting for Czech Republic	5Z2	This scope item provides information on calculating and reporting taxes in Czech Republic. This covers companies based in Czech Republic and foreign companies that do business in Czech Republic.
Advanced Financial Operations	VAT Tax Calculation and Reporting for South Africa	5Z0	This scope item provides information on calculating and reporting taxes in South Africa. This covers companies based in South Africa and foreign companies that do business in South Africa.
Advanced Financial Operations	VAT Tax Calculation and Reporting for Sweden	5Z3	This scope item provides information on calculating and reporting taxes in Sweden. This covers companies based in Sweden and foreign companies that do business in Sweden.
Cost Management and Profitability Analysis	Group Valuation	5W2	For steering purposes, international organizations need a management view of their operations where intercompany profits between trading partners are eliminated in real-time.
Treasury Management	Shareholding Management	5WE	With Shareholding Management, you can manage the whole business process from purchasing and selling of a Shareholding to financial accounting.
Treasury Management	Shareholding Management - Group Ledger IFRS	5WG	The parallel valuation process enables you to post the values calculated in Shareholding Management according to IFRS 9 phase I (Classification and Measurement).
Treasury Management	Shareholding Management - Group Ledger US GAAP	5WH	The parallel valuation process enables you to post the values calculated in Debt and Investment Management according to US GAAP.
Enterprise Risk and Compliance	Intrastat Processing for Czech Republic	5Z4	This scope item provides system-generated intrastat declarations.
Enterprise Risk and Compliance	Intrastat Processing for Sweden	5Z3	This scope item provides system-generated intrastat declarations.

Figure 3.14 Scope Presentation

3.2.3 Localizations and Languages

In this section, we'll go into the details of the localization (e.g., tailoring the scope items for a specific country or region) and language translation (e.g., availability of the content in specific languages). These two terms aren't interchangeable as they refer to different capabilities, as we'll discuss.

Localizations

SAP Best Practices for SAP S/4HANA Cloud provides information about the preconfigured localized solutions for SAP S/4HANA Cloud. Figure 3.15 shows the field in which you can select which localization you want to display when you browse the SAP Best Practices content in SAP Best Practices Explorer.

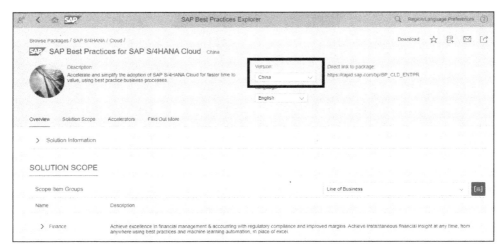

Figure 3.15 Selecting Localization from Package Home Page

A scope item version may itself be localized to a specific country, or it may be relevant for multiple country versions. The availability of a specific scope item version for a given localization of the solution is indicated in the **COUNTRY RELEVANCE** section of the scope items, as shown in Figure 3.16.

Languages

The SAP Best Practices Explorer UI is provided in the languages defined by the SAP S/4HANA Cloud product language scope. The following content for SAP S/4HANA Cloud is provided in multiple languages:

- Factsheet descriptions in the SAP Best Practices Explorer UI
- Accelerators (test scripts, process flows, and content library)

Scope item factsheet information is provided for SAP S/4HANA Cloud scope items in all SAP S/4HANA Cloud product languages in the SAP Best Practices UI.

Translated accelerators (where available) can be accessed directly in the SAP Best Practices Explorer UI when displaying the scope item pages for a particular localization in the corresponding language. If a translated accelerator isn't available, the English accelerator is provided. For example, Figure 3.17 shows the SAP Best Practices for SAP S/4HANA Cloud entry page in Mandarin.

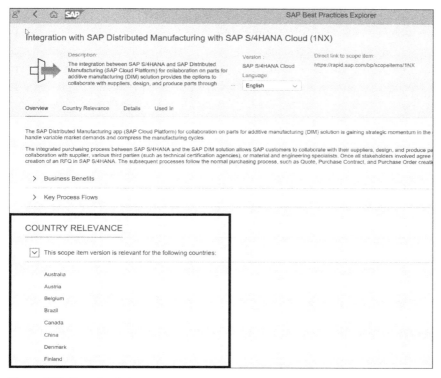

Figure 3.16 Country Relevance

Figure 3.17 Translated Content

Preferences

The SAP Best Practices Explorer UI is provided in the languages defined by the SAP S/4HANA Cloud product language strategy. You can save your own localization and language preferences in the UI, as shown in Figure 3.18, and the SAP Best Practices Explorer UI will be opened in your preferred language whenever you log on. If content pages (e.g., package or scope item versions) are available in your preferred localization and language, these will be opened by default when you navigate to a content page; otherwise, the pages will default to German/English.

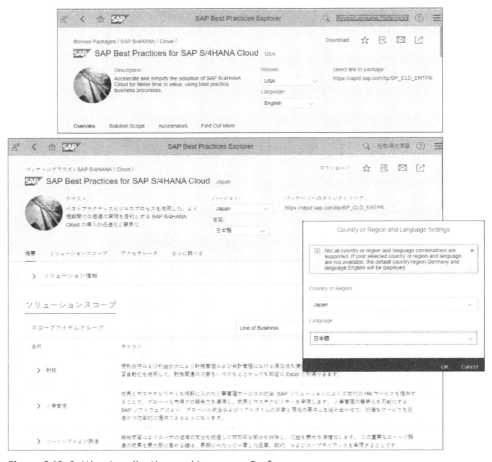

Figure 3.18 Setting Localization and Language Preferences

3.2.4   Tool Features

In the following sections, we'll discuss some useful tool features. First, to navigate to the scope items through the hierarchy in SAP Best Practices Explorer, you can use functions for searching the content. You can also report any issues with the content using the functionality in SAP Best Practices Explorer. Finally, we'll show you how to derive stable URLs for specific SAP Best Practices documents that will help you find the content faster.

Search Features

You can search for scope items in SAP Best Practices Explorer (see Figure 3.19). As you can see here, searching for a keyword such as "tax" produces results across all the SAP Best Practices packages that refer to tax and that offer tax-processing functionality.

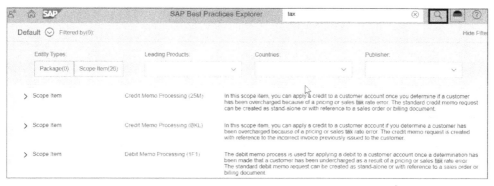

Figure 3.19 Scope Item Search in SAP Best Practices Explorer

You can also search for scope items in a specific package version, as shown in Figure 3.20. The search triggered from within the SAP Best Practices package will limit the scope of the search to only scope items and documents included in that package.

Figure 3.20 Scope Item Search in Package Version

Report an Issue with Documentation

You can report an issue in the following ways:

- Use the SAP Support Portal at *http://support.sap.com* (a trackable incident is needed).

- Use the **Contact Us** form at the top right of the SAP Best Practices Explorer window (envelope icon), which will send the information to the publishing team (without a trackable incident ID; see Figure 3.21). This can be used to report broken links or nonurgent documentation errors and to give feedback on specific documents. The feedback is sent to the publishing team to investigate. If necessary, the publishing team will report an internal incident to the relevant content component.

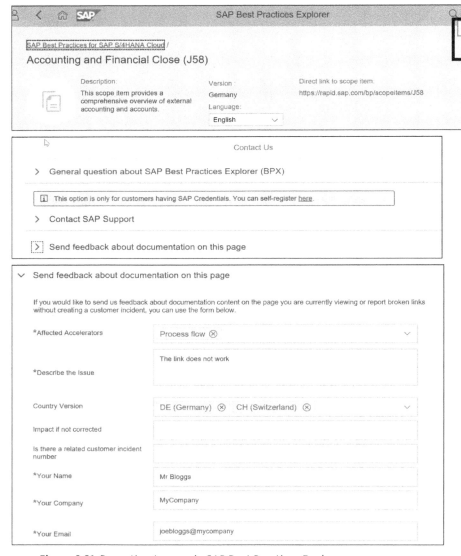

Figure 3.21 Reporting Issues via SAP Best Practices Explorer

Stable URLs

Stable URLs provide a way for other applications to link to specific pages for SAP Best Practices Explorer that will continue to work with new releases of the content. The following stable URLs are available:

- SAP Best Practices Explorer home page: *https://rapid.sap.com*
- SAP Best Practices for SAP S/4HANA Cloud: *http://s-prs.co/v502745*
- SAP Best Practices for SAP S/4HANA on-premise: *http://s-prs.co/v502746*
- Package versions (localized, independent link):
  - URL pattern: *https://rapid.sap.com/bp/<Package ID>/*
  - Example: *https://rapid.sap.com/bp/BP_CLD_ENTPR/*
- Package versions (localized, specific link):
  - URL pattern: *https://rapid.sap.com/bp/#/<Package ID>?country=<Two-digit country ID>/*
  - Example: *https://rapid.sap.com/bp/#/BP_CLD_ENTPR?country=CN/*
- Scope items:
  - URL pattern: *https://rapid.sap.com/bp/scopeitems/<Scope item ID>/*
  - Example: *https://rapid.sap.com/bp/scopeitems/BKP*

3.3   SAP Cloud ALM

SAP Cloud ALM is a tool designed to offer a working environment to help with implementation and postimplementation activities. It has two main pillars: SAP Cloud ALM for implementation and SAP Cloud ALM for operations. Next, we'll discuss why you need this tool to implement SAP S/4HANA and what it can offer.

3.3.1   Why SAP Cloud ALM?

SAP Cloud ALM for implementation is designed to offer a ready-to-run working environment that brings the SAP Activate methodology to life. When you sign an SAP S/4HANA Cloud contract, you automatically get an entitlement enabling you to request SAP Cloud ALM. The ptool is designed to offer you a seamless implementation and operations experience and continues to help you even during upgrade cycles and postimplementation activities. Figure 3.22 shows the entry screen to the SAP Cloud ALM toolset that provides all the information about the project in one easy-to-read view.

As you learned in Chapter 2, SAP Activate provides instructions that help project managers, business experts, and consultants understand what to do and when; however, tracking project completion still remains a tedious task.

Figure 3.22 SAP Cloud ALM for Implementation Entry Screen

SAP Cloud ALM comes preloaded with SAP Activate content and offers you an intuitive UI in which you can set a timeline for project phases, set statuses for SAP Activate tasks, and track project completion. SAP Cloud ALM also allows creation of a sprint schedule or custom milestones for planning your project.

On top of that, because SAP Activate content is regularly updated, you always get the latest content with a detailed change log and a notification when any change demands your attention. This is helpful in case some SAP S/4HANA capabilities change with an upgrade or some SAP Activate tasks are updated and need immediate attention.

3.3.2 SAP Cloud ALM for Implementation

SAP Cloud ALM offers a plethora of features designed to simplify the life of the project team. Let's walk through them:

- **Easy setup and onboarding**
  SAP Cloud ALM comes preloaded with SAP Activate and SAP Best Practice content. It also knows your landscape and the status of your systems. The tool comes preloaded with a list of roles delivered by SAP Activate; the project lead can assign the team members to the different roles by simply entering their email addresses. The project lead can also add custom roles in SAP Cloud ALM based on project needs. The onboarded team members need to be approved by the administrator after specific procedures are completed. This means you can start using the tool productively in as little as 20 minutes.

- **Business scoping**
  This tool helps you understand the business process hierarchy that SAP delivers in the form of best practices.

- **Supporting fit-to-standard workshops**
  As a business process expert, you may want to understand a process in greater detail before deciding if it should be scoped or not. Even though your project may be based on SAP S/4HANA Cloud, you may want to understand how it's relevant in intelligent enterprise end-to-end processes. SAP Cloud ALM shows the business process flows (see Figure 3.23) and detailed information about the process steps in one screen. The project team can use this environment to directly capture requirements and notes during the fit-to-standard workshops.

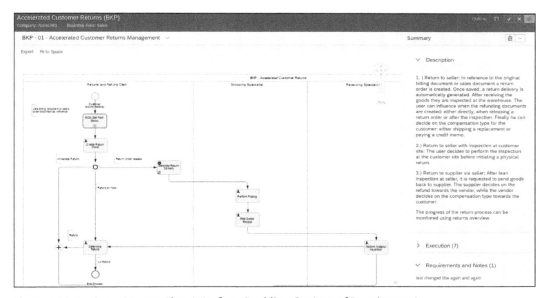

Figure 3.23 Business Process Flow Interface, Enabling Capture of Requirements

Another useful feature is that you can track the requirements discovered during the workshop directly in the business context in which they were discovered. When the requirements are created in the business process flow by clicking on the process flow, you can categorize them to specify how they should be addressed (via configuration, integration, extensibility, etc.), as shown in Figure 3.24.

- **Offering a task-driven environment**
  SAP Cloud ALM guides users via the tasks assigned to them. As you scope the business processes, some tasks are generated just in time to offer you precise guidance and automatically disappear if you descope something. The requirements captured earlier can be refined, approved, and broken down into user stories and project tasks so that they can be tracked to completion. Multiple analytical applications such as

Requirement Traceability and Process Traceability help different stakeholders at multiple stages in the project.

If you need to capture some tasks that don't come predelivered, such as testing tasks for your custom extensions after every upgrade, you can enhance the task list by creating manual tasks or via mass upload of tasks. The **Open Tasks** screen is shown in Figure 3.25. Note that SAP Cloud ALM shows tasks grouped via deliverables as default. You have an option to see a Gantt view in addition to the list view.

- **Testing and deployment**
  SAP Cloud ALM also offers creation of test cases and track test execution. Both manual and automated testing is supported. SAP customers using the SAP S/4HANA Cloud test automation tool have the ability to review the test results from the SAP S/4HANA Cloud system in SAP Cloud ALM. This is done through close integration of the SAP S/4HANA Cloud system and SAP Cloud ALM. This allows you to use SAP Cloud ALM as a centralized reporting option for both manual and automated testing.

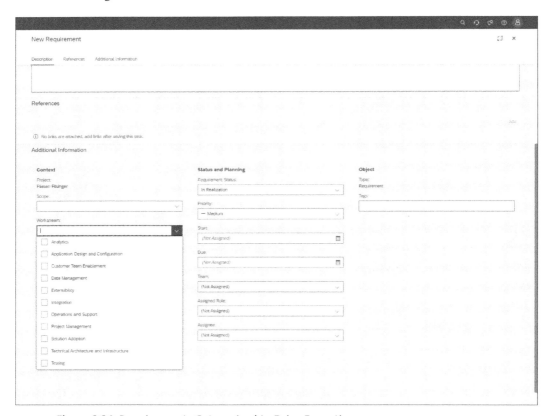

Figure 3.24 Requirements Categorized to Drive Execution

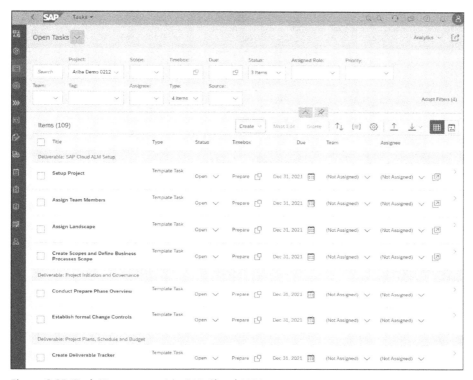

Figure 3.25 Task Management in SAP Cloud ALM

3.3.3   SAP Cloud ALM for Operations

After implementing the customer solution, it is usually handed over to operations. Today, many challenges are found in solution landscapes, and a company's solution landscape is subject to transformation, including transformation from a monolithic to a multisystem landscape. The complexity in end-to-end monitoring is also increasing. Therefore, transparency into the communication between the different services and the execution of end-to-end businesses processes of the intelligent suite is required. SAP Cloud ALM for operations is the latest cloud-based ALM solution and therefore the ideal solution for cloud-centric companies. Figure 3.26 shows SAP Cloud ALM for available operations and planned scope.

SAP Cloud ALM for operations covers the following use cases:

- **Business service management**
  Business service management includes a business event calendar and business service availability management. In this application, SAP Cloud ALM consolidates the information derived from single technical services to business services. The target group of business service management is business and IT, so the relevant information is maintained and visualized at the business service level as a kind of common language between business and IT.

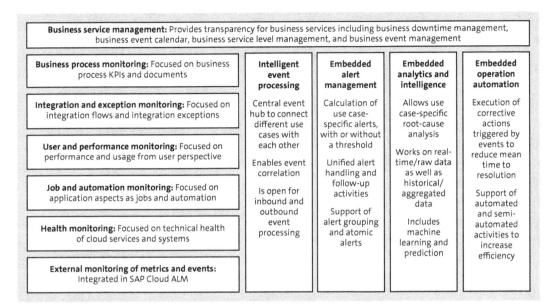

Business service management: Provides transparency for business services including business downtime management, business event calendar, business service level management, and business event management				
Business process monitoring: Focused on business process KPIs and documents	**Intelligent event processing**	**Embedded alert management**	**Embedded analytics and intelligence**	**Embedded operation automation**
Integration and exception monitoring: Focused on integration flows and integration exceptions	Central event hub to connect different use cases with each other	Calculation of use case-specific alerts, with or without a threshold	Allows use case-specific root-cause analysis	Execution of corrective actions triggered by events to reduce mean time to resolution
User and performance monitoring: Focused on performance and usage from user perspective	Enables event correlation	Unified alert handling and follow-up activities	Works on real-time/raw data as well as historical/aggregated data	
Job and automation monitoring: Focused on application aspects as jobs and automation	Is open for inbound and outbound event processing	Support of alert grouping and atomic alerts	Includes machine learning and prediction	Support of automated and semi-automated activities to increase efficiency
Health monitoring: Focused on technical health of cloud services and systems				
External monitoring of metrics and events: Integrated in SAP Cloud ALM				

Figure 3.26 SAP Cloud ALM for Operations: Available and Planned Scope

- **Business process monitoring**
  By focusing on business process key performance indicators (KPIs) and documents, business process monitoring provides transparency into the end-to-end processes of the entire intelligent suite. Business process monitoring monitors the processes' health, detects anomalies during process execution, and enables LoB users—but also IT users—to directly identify process disruptions and react to them.

- **Integration and exception monitoring**
  Integration and exception monitoring ensures reliable data exchange processes at the application level in cloud-only and hybrid scenarios. It provides end-to-end monitoring across different SAP cloud services and applications based on the SAP passport mechanism. Integration and exception monitoring closes the gap between business and IT during the issue-resolution process (technical issue versus business issue).

- **User and performance monitoring**
  User and performance monitoring allows you to monitor end user requests across components and technologies. This type of monitoring is based on synthetic probes (synthetic user monitoring) or real user load (real user monitoring). With real user monitoring, you will get visibility into the frontends and into the involved cloud services and systems. Synthetic user monitoring provides a simulation of end user behavior based on scenarios that are scripted and deployed as robots. Figure 3.27 shows the user interface of SAP Cloud ALM for real user monitoring.

Figure 3.27 SAP Cloud ALM for Operations: Real User Monitoring

- **Job and automation monitoring**
  Besides monitoring of classical jobs, as used in ABAP-based components, the monitoring of automation environments like SAP Intelligent Robotic Process Automation (SAP Intelligent RPA) and SAP Workflow Management also becomes more and more relevant. Job and automation monitoring addresses mainly IT users, but business users also may be interested in information for business-critical jobs.

- **Health monitoring**
  In contrast to system monitoring, SAP Cloud ALM for operations offers health monitoring to monitor components without a dedicated landscape model and autodiscovery. Attributes describing the managed cloud service or system are sent together with the monitoring information. Heath monitoring is offered for non-SAP on-premise components and for cloud services.

- **External monitoring of metrics and events**
  SAP Cloud ALM for operations will be able to retrieve metrics and events from external monitoring and alerting tools (third-party or open source). This can be relevant to get the complete picture for a solution landscape to cover IT infrastructure aspects or non-SAP components.

- **Intelligent event processing**
  With intelligent event processing, SAP Cloud ALM introduced dedicated event management that can handle events independently on alerts. This is the foundation for correlating manually generated events (e.g., end user tickets) with automatically generated events (e.g., alerts).

- **Embedded alert management**
  Alerts are calculated per monitoring use case and are visualized in the use case-specific alert inboxes, which are directly embedded into the monitoring applications.

- **Embedded analytics and intelligence**
  Embedded analytics enables use-case specific root-cause analyses and works with raw data as it is collected, as well as with historical data that is aggregated.

- **Embedded operation automation**
  SAP Cloud ALM for operations provides a built-in integration to SAP Workflow Management, SAP Intelligent RPA, and SAP Automation Pilot. The goal is to use the content already provided by these three platforms for cloud-centric landscapes.

SAP Cloud ALM Product Roadmap

SAP Cloud ALM will continue to evolve in the future. You can review the current state of planning for SAP Cloud ALM in the product roadmap, which provides an overview of planned capabilities for the next few rolling quarters. You can find it at *http://s-prs.co/v546304*.

Further Resources

For more information about SAP Cloud ALM, check out *Introducing SAP Cloud ALM for Implementations* by Jagmohan Singh Chawla, Wulff-Heinrich Knapp, and Nicolas Alech (SAP PRESS, 2022, *sap-press.com/5477*).

3.4   SAP Solution Manager

The SAP Solution Manager 7.2 toolset provides capabilities that support you across the entire application lifecycle of IT solutions running on-premise, in the cloud, or in a hybrid deployment. SAP Solution Manager 7.2 provides a wide range of functionality, supporting the following ALM processes:

- Application operations
- Business process operations
- Change control management
- Custom code management
- Data volume management
- IT service management
- Landscape management
- Process management

- Project management
- Test suite

Using SAP Solution Manager 7.2 in your organization allows you to leverage the preceding functionality to implement, maintain, run, and drive adoption of your IT solutions in your business operations. SAP Solution Manager helps to manage SAP and non-SAP solutions while allowing for continuous adoption of innovation, supporting business continuity and efficient operational processes.

We'll now look briefly at each of the previously listed ALM processes.

> **Further Resources**
>
> You can find more detailed information about SAP Solution Manager 7.2 on the SAP Support Portal (*http://s-prs.co/v502711*), including guided tours, videos, and additional practice documents that go into specifics for each of the ALM processes.

3.4.1   Application and Business Process Operations

Applications operations provide capabilities to establish and run strong practices for operating your IT applications. Application operations rely on the following functionalities:

- System monitoring
- Integration monitoring
- Business intelligence monitoring
- Hybrid operations
- Job monitoring
- User experience monitoring
- Analytics and dashboarding
- Technical administration and guided procedures
- Root cause analysis
- Exception management

SAP Solution Manager also supports business process operations with a dedicated set of tools that help you ensure support for productive operations of your business solution across your systems and components. The key areas of SAP Solution Manager supporting operations are as follows:

- Business process and interface monitoring
- Business process improvement
- Data consistency management
- Job scheduling management

3.4.2   Data Volume Management

Managing data volumes in your IT environment is an important process to ensure that your system operates at peak performance and at an optimal operating cost. The data volume management capabilities help organizations not only monitor the data volumes but also reduce the amount of data in the landscape, leading to better costs for operating the solution. The Data Volume Management work center allows you to display details of data movements within a single landscape or over multiple system landscapes.

3.4.3   Change Control Management

SAP Solution Manager provides IT teams with a powerful and comprehensive workflow that helps control changes in your system environment. The environment supports creation and management of change control requests in tight integration with the requirements management process. This allows organizations to establish a tight process to assess requested changes and manage their implementation, testing, and, ultimately, deployment into the productive system.

SAP Solution Manager provides capabilities for the following areas in its Change Control Management functionality:

- Change and Transport System (CTS; also enhanced variant)
- Transport analytics
- Change diagnostics
- Dual landscape synchronization
- Quality gate management
- Change request management
- Release management

3.4.4   Custom Code Management

Custom code can be a significant cost factor, especially in upgrade projects or during transitions to SAP S/4HANA. You'll benefit from using the SAP Solution Manager Custom Code Management functionality that provides support for the complete lifecycle of custom code—from capturing and clarifying requirements through code development, management, and ultimately retirement.

Having a good grasp of your custom code is important for continuous optimization and elimination of unused or no longer needed code that could drive up the cost of operations and management of your SAP solution. Custom Code Management in SAP Solution Manager provides you with capabilities to optimize custom code development and monitor use and quality.

> **Custom Code Management and the Five Golden Rules**
>
> Note that this functionality is critical for project teams following the five golden rules for implementation of SAP S/4HANA to keep their ERP core clean and extend the solution using the modern technologies that we discussed in Chapter 2, Section 2.4. The Solution Standardization Board (SSB) should use this feature set to monitor all new custom code introduced into the quality and production systems in order to prevent unwanted introduction of unapproved modifications and custom code.

3.4.5   IT Service Management

All IT organizations need to have reliable and scalable processes and environments for management and processing of user messages. SAP Solution Manager integrates with SAP Customer Relationship Management (SAP CRM) to enable organizations to coordinate work via messages between multiple parties, whether they are internal IT personnel, consultants, or support staff. IT Service Management (ITSM) can be integrated with an external help desk solution, allows you to set up service connections, and provides access to SAP Services and Support. The following capabilities are delivered with ITSM:

- Change request management
- Interfaces for third-party help desks
- Global SAP support backbone

3.4.6   Landscape Management

Managing and evolving the system landscape is a critical function of every SAP IT organization. It allows organizations to introduce business process innovations and optimize operational costs. SAP Solution Manager provides landscape management tools in the cloud-based maintenance planner that enables IT personnel plan changes to your SAP landscape. These changes may include installation of new systems, application of support packages and enhancement packages in your existing systems, performing upgrades, or system conversion to SAP S/4HANA and SAP BW/4HANA.

3.4.7   Process Management

SAP Solution Manager provides holistic support for always keeping the system and solution documentation synchronized. This way, the IT organization keeps the solution documentation (business process descriptions, process models, documentation of interfaces, custom code, integrations) in sync with the functionality in the system. There are two applications inside SAP Solution Manager that assist the organization in this effort:

1. **Solution Administration**
   This application shows an overview of the existing solutions, allows creation of new solutions, displays existing solutions, and is used by administrators to set up the environment for Solution Documentation.

2. **Solution Documentation**
   This application provides an environment to capture business processes and related documentation in a structured way. This environment is primarily used by business analysts, consultants, business process owners, and process modelers, and it's where the project teams store documents for key configuration decisions, functional and technical design documents, and other key artifacts.

3.4.8   Project Management

SAP Solution Manager supports project teams with sophisticated project management capabilities based on SAP Portfolio and Project Management, which allows project teams to create project schedules based on WBSs, assign project resources, manage time and capacities, and track progress and statuses. Project management capabilities are integrated in the following areas:

- Change request management
- Solution documentation
- Requirements management

3.4.9   Focused Build and Focused Insight

You can also take advantage of focused offerings built on top of SAP Solution Manager that are designed to be turnkey solutions for specific ALM areas. The following solutions are available in SAP Solution Manager 7.2:

- **Focused Build for SAP Solution Manager**
  This solution delivers a ready-to-use environment for management of requirements and software development projects using the agile approach to help implement innovation in your business. It comes with predefined standards, processes, and enablement that helps you get started and use the capabilities fast.

SAP Activate with Focused Build for SAP Solution Manager

SAP provides a detailed guide for how to use SAP Activate and Focused Build for SAP Solution Manager in the form of a presentation. It provides a detailed explanation of how to implement agile design and build processes using SAP Solution Manager while adhering to SAP Activate. You can download a copy at *http://s-prs.co/v546305*.

- **Focused Insights for SAP Solution Manager**
  This solution helps you create powerful dashboards to show unified and aggregated

information to the right people in real time. The solution allows you to reuse prede-livered dashboards and tailor them to your needs. It is built on top of experiences and learnings from customer projects that are delivered in the solution in the form of best practices for analytics and dashboards.

You can learn more about Focused Build for SAP Solution Manager at *https://support.sap.com/en/alm/focused-build.html* and about Focused Insights for SAP Solution Manager at *https://support.sap.com/en/alm/focused-insights.html*.

3.4.10   Test Suite

SAP Solution Manager includes a comprehensive test management suite built into the tool. The Test Suite supports project teams in defining their testing scope, executing testing cycles (including close integration with ITSM for defects reporting and resolution), and evaluating testing results. The Test Suite can be used for planning and execution of tests during the implementation project or during continuous improvements of the running solution. It supports a wide range of tests, from string tests to integration tests to user acceptance testing (UAT).

SAP Activate leverages SAP Solution Manager as the execution environment to perform critical activities during the project and during operational (running) use of your SAP solution. During the project execution, the key capabilities that support the project team include the following:

- Project Management
- Process Management, including Solution Documentation
- Landscape Management
- Test Suite

SAP Activate directs project team members to use SAP Solution Manager and provides procedures to follow, for example, for loading the SAP Activate WBS into the Project Management functionality in SAP Solution Manager 7.2. You can see the project schedule based on the SAP Activate WBS in Figure 3.28.

> **Further Resources**
>
> The explanation of SAP Solution Manager's capabilities in this section was meant as an introduction and overview of the key features. If you're interested in more comprehensive coverage of SAP Solution Manager's capabilities and functionality, explore the SAP PRESS titles that discuss the functionality of SAP Solution Manager in detail here: *http://s-prs.co/v502713*.
>
> You can also access detailed documentation and guides for SAP Solution Manager in the SAP Support Portal here: *http://s-prs.co/v502714*.

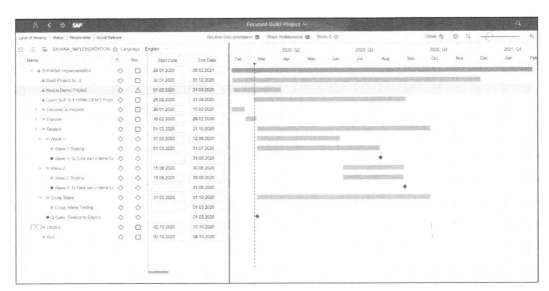

Figure 3.28 SAP Activate WBS in Gantt Chart Form in SAP Solution Manager

3.5   Summary

This chapter introduced the key tools for accessing SAP Activate content: the Roadmap Viewer that you can use to access the SAP Activate methodology, its descriptions, and accelerators, and the SAP Best Practices Explorer that provides you with easy access to the documentation of the ready-to-run business processes delivered in SAP Best Practices and the enterprise management layer for SAP S/4HANA documentation.

We also introduced the concept of ALM and explained how project teams can use tools such as SAP Cloud ALM and SAP Solution Manager to control and manage implementation projects and their system environments. We'll use this information in later chapters when we dive into the details of the deployment strategies for SAP S/4HANA.

In the next chapter, we'll talk about how project teams gain speed when they start with a working system based on SAP Best Practices or the enterprise management layer for SAP S/4HANA.

Chapter 4

Starting with a Working System

SAP Activate uses the principle of "showing and telling" over just telling to help business users understand the capabilities of the solution that's being implemented. Teams should prepare a working system for their show-and-tell sessions during the fit-to-standard workshops. Now, let's discuss the business process content project teams can use to set up the system.

One of the foundations of SAP Activate is to start with a working system based on ready-to-use business processes in SAP S/4HANA. While we often emphasize the use of SAP Best Practices for setting up the working system in some sections of the book, there are other packages that can be used to set up the working environment in SAP S/4HANA as well. This chapter focuses on introducing the two main sets of packages that SAP delivers for your use: SAP Best Practices and the enterprise management layer for SAP S/4HANA. We introduced the tools that you can use to access this content in the previous chapter, so here we'll drill down into the structure of the content and ways to activate it in your environment.

4.1 SAP Best Practices for SAP S/4HANA

SAP delivers regular updates for SAP Best Practices for SAP S/4HANA and SAP Best Practices for SAP S/4HANA Cloud. In this section, we'll discuss the content available in both of these packages and provide examples of assets that you can access in the SAP Best Practices Explorer and in application lifecycle management (ALM) tools such as SAP Solution Manager or SAP Cloud ALM.

4.1.1 SAP S/4HANA Cloud

SAP Best Practices for SAP S/4HANA Cloud provides ready-to-use business process content for core business processes in finance, sourcing and procurement, manufacturing, sales, and the supply chain, as shown in Figure 4.1.

These processes are supported by SAP Fiori for a role-specific, intuitive, and simple user experience. In addition, SAP S/4HANA Cloud offers SAP Best Practices for integration with other cloud solutions, such as SAP SuccessFactors Employee Central, SAP Concur,

SAP Fieldglass, and SAP Ariba. The SAP Best Practices for Data Migration package complements the foundation of business processes and offers a nondisruptive, simplified transition of your data to SAP S/4HANA Cloud. In the following sections, you'll see how you can access all these assets in SAP Best Practices Explorer.

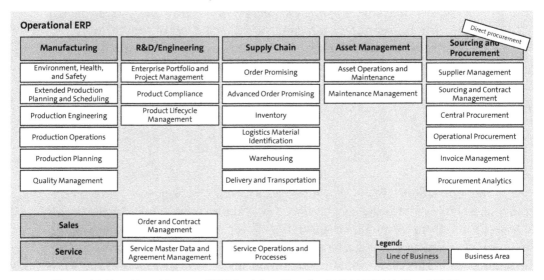

Figure 4.1 Functional Scope of SAP Best Practices for SAP S/4HANA Cloud 2202

SAP Best Practices Scope

We won't list the current scope of the SAP Best Practices content in this book; by the time it reaches you, the content will have been updated a few times by SAP as the SAP S/4HANA Cloud content gets updated several times a year. We recommend that you access the content in SAP Best Practices Explorer at *http://s-prs.co/v502715*.

Structure of the Content

The hierarchical structure of the SAP Best Practices content starts with the *package*, which serves as the entity that groups together all relevant scope items into logical groups, such as finance, sourcing and procurement, and manufacturing. Each of these groups is then split into subgroups that correspond to business functions; for example, the finance group contains subgroups for accounting and financial close, financial operations, enterprise risk and compliance, and so on.

You can navigate the content in SAP Best Practices Explorer by expanding the selected group and subgroups in the **SOLUTION SCOPE** section to access a specific scope item (you can also think about a scope item as a process). In addition, the package information contains the description of the package in the **Solution Information** section within the **Overview** tab, as shown in Figure 4.2.

Figure 4.2 Package Page for SAP Best Practices for SAP S/4HANA Cloud

The package also has several key pieces of information available that help you understand the solution scope, organizational structure, chart of accounts, key master data that is delivered in the package, and additional package-wide preconfiguration details. You can find these assets in the **Accelerators** tab in SAP Best Practices Explorer (see Figure 4.3).

The key assets in this area are the following:

- Scope presentation
- Availability and dependencies of scope items
- What's new
- Task tutorials
- Organizational data overview
- Master data overview, financial accounting master data, and controlling master data
- Chart of accounts
- Preconfigured tax codes
- Account determination (global and local)
- Fiscal year variants
- Forms

- Configuration apps
- Application programming interfaces (APIs)

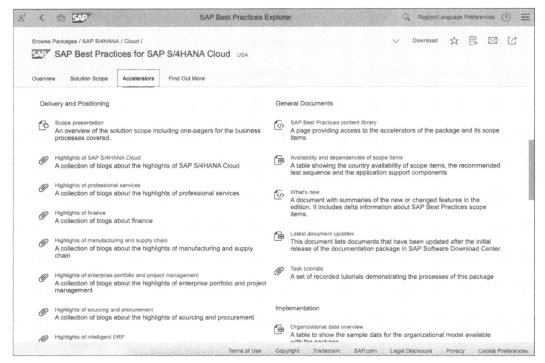

Figure 4.3 SAP Best Practices Accelerators for Implementation of SAP S/4HANA Cloud

Now let's take a look at the scope item information and assets that are available to you in SAP Best Practices Explorer. Each *scope item* comes with a **Description** of the functionality the scope item delivers, **Business Benefits**, and the **Key Process Flows** in the **Overview** tab; localization information in the **Country/Region Relevance** section; and detailed assets describing the functionality and capabilities of the scope item in the **Details** section. The key assets are the following:

- **Task tutorials**
  These guided enablement materials for business users show the functionality in easy-to-follow tutorials. The task tutorials are available for many scope items, and the coverage continues to grow.

- **Test script**
  Detailed scripts are provided for executing the processes in the scope item with business roles, sample data, and step-by-step execution details.

- **Process flow**
  Business process flows show the process steps in swim lanes by business process

participants. We showed examples of process flows in Chapter 3 when we introduced SAP Best Practices Explorer.

- **Set-up instructions**
  Additional setup of integration settings and other setup instructions are provided here for scope items that that require these instructions.

Figure 4.4 shows an example of one scope item, **Requisitioning (18J)**, with the previously described assets. You also can choose to view the description in other languages by using the **Language** field selection on the screen. Note that some assets may only be available in English.

Figure 4.4 Scope Item Requisitioning (18J) Showing Key Assets in SAP Best Practices Content

If you're familiar with SAP Best Practices content and structure, you can use the compact view of all the assets included in the package by clicking on the **SAP Best Practices Content Library** link (not shown) in the **Accelerators** section of the package. This view allows you to access any of the SAP Best Practices content from one screen, eliminating the clicks required to navigate the hierarchical structure in SAP Best Practices Explorer. Figure 4.5 shows the **SAP Best Practices—Content Library** screen for the SAP S/4HANA Cloud package.

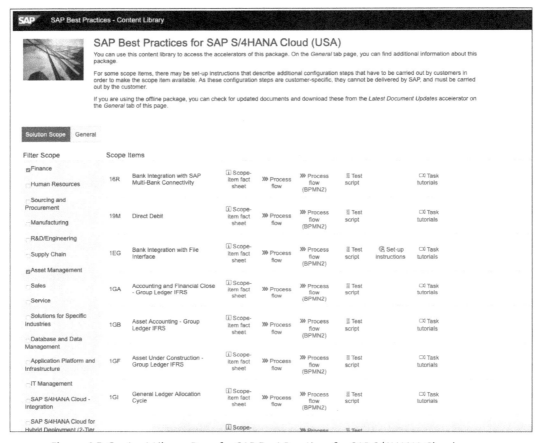

Figure 4.5 Content Library Page for SAP Best Practices for SAP S/4HANA Cloud

SAP Best Practices for SAP S/4HANA Cloud are available in multiple languages and localizations for many markets. At the time of writing this book, the package is available in 43 local versions in 27 languages, as follows:

- **Local versions**

  Australia, Austria, Belgium, Brazil, Canada, China, Czechia, Denmark, Finland, France, Germany, Hong Kong (China), Hungary, India, Indonesia, Ireland, Italy, Japan, Luxembourg, Malaysia, Mexico, Netherlands, New Zealand, Norway, Philippines, Poland, Portugal, Romania, Russia, Saudi Arabia, Singapore, South Africa, South Korea, Slovakia, Spain, Sweden, Switzerland, Taiwan (China), Thailand, Turkey, United Arab Emirates, United Kingdom, United States.

- **Available languages**
  Arabic, Bahasa (Malaysia), Chinese (simplified), Chinese (traditional), Czech, Danish, Dutch, English, Finnish, French, German, Greek, Hebrew, Hungarian, Italian, Japanese, Korean, Norwegian, Polish, Portuguese, Romanian, Russian, Slovak, Spanish, Swedish, Thai, Turkish.

Always check for current coverage in the SAP Best Practices Explorer in the Scope presentation, which you can find under **Accelerators** in the **Delivery and Positioning** subsection.

Best Practices for Integration, Extensibility, and Hybrid Deployment

In addition to the business process–based SAP Best Practices, you can also access content for integration, extensibility, and hybrid (or two-tier) deployment. You can find these scope items by selecting the appropriate group in the selection box in the **SOLUTION SCOPE** section of the package in the **Overview** tab, as shown in Figure 4.6 (note the selection was made to display content for **SAP S/4HANA Cloud – Integration**). You also can use this selector to access the content for extensibility and hybrid deployment. (We'll discuss the hybrid deployment topic in more detail in Chapter 9.)

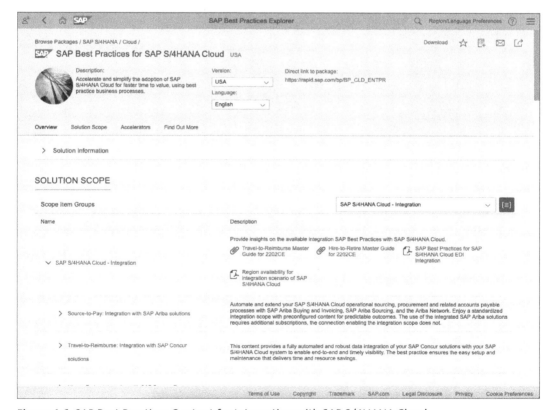

Figure 4.6 SAP Best Practices Content for Integration with SAP S/4HANA Cloud

What's New Viewer

You should also frequently review the information about new, updated, and deprecated scope items in SAP S/4HANA Cloud in the What's New Viewer that you can find in the SAP Help Portal at *http://help.sap.com*. Enter "SAP S/4HANA Cloud" into the **Search** field, select the **SAP S/4HANA Cloud** entry on the right, select the **What's New** tab on the next screen, and then click on the **What's New Viewer** link. You can then use the search capabilities or filters to identify changed and updated scope items in the viewer (see Figure 4.7).

Figure 4.7 What's New Viewer for SAP S/4HANA Cloud

Release Assessment and Scope Dependency Application

If you're using SAP S/4HANA Cloud, SAP recommends that you use the Release Assessment and Scope Dependency application to learn about new functionality and changed functionality in each release of the product. The application provides insights and recommendations that are specific to your scope. The application provides the following information:

- Tailored scope analysis based on your activated or implemented scope
- Categorization of changes as functional, API, deprecated, core data services (CDS) views, authorizations, and Self-Service Configuration UIs (SSCUIs) for quick analysis of the impact on your existing scope
- Testing recommendations based on the degree of change and impact of change to the scope items
- Information on new scope items that you can potentially activate based on the dependencies among scope items

Figure 4.8 shows a landing page of the tool that helps you better understand the impact of the new functionality on your activated scope and assess the potential new capabilities you can activate in your solution. You can access the Release Assessment and Scope Dependency application directly from the SAP Best Practices Explorer entry screen.

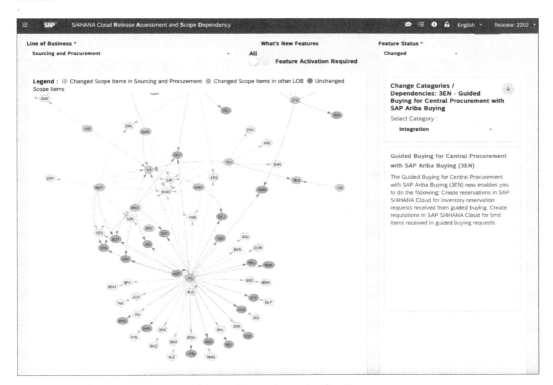

Figure 4.8 Release Assessment and Scope Dependency Application

Further Resources

You can review a blog post about the application at *http://s-prs.co/v502716*.

Activating SAP Best Practices for SAP S/4HANA Cloud

SAP Best Practices for SAP S/4HANA Cloud are delivered preactivated in the SAP S/4HANA Cloud solution. The starter system will contain preactivated SAP Best Practices for the entire solution, whereas the quality assurance system and production system activation will happen based on your selection of scope items after the fit-to-standard workshops. We'll discuss these processes in detail in Chapter 7.

4.1.2   SAP S/4HANA

Now that you have a good understanding of the content in SAP Best Practices for SAP S/4HANA Cloud, let's take a look at the content in SAP Best Practices for SAP S/4HANA. The content structure of this package mirrors the structure of what you've seen in Section 4.1.1. The SAP Best Practices content is delivered in the package with a similar structure and scope items. The scope and coverage of SAP Best Practices differ, though. As of the time of writing, the latest SAP S/4HANA release is SAP S/4HANA 2021. The SAP Best Practices for this release provide the scope of functionality shown in Figure 4.9.

> **SAP Best Practices Scope**
> Note that the scope of SAP Best Practices for SAP S/4HANA doesn't have full coverage of all configuration and industry capabilities available in the SAP S/4HANA solution. We'll discuss this in more detail in Section 4.2.

The assets on the package level provide the same information that we've discussed for SAP S/4HANA Cloud. For example, the package contains description and key assets such as overviews of the scope, organizational data, and master data; availability and dependencies of the scope items matrix; and a chart of accounts. On the scope item level, the information is structured in a similar way as for the cloud package; for example, the scope item provides a description of the functionality contained in the scope item and access to the test script and business process flow in a viewable and downloadable format (in the BPMN2 file format).

The SAP Best Practices for SAP S/4HANA 2021 are available in 43 local versions and support 25 languages, as follows:

- **Local versions**
  Australia, Austria, Belgium, Brazil, Canada, China, Czechia, Denmark, Finland, France, Germany, Hong Kong, Hungary, India, Indonesia, Ireland, Italy, Japan, Luxembourg, Malaysia, Mexico, Netherlands, New Zealand, Norway, Philippines, Poland, Portugal, Romania, Russia, Saudi Arabia, Singapore, Slovakia, South Africa, South Korea, Spain, Sweden, Switzerland, Taiwan, Thailand, Turkey, United Arab Emirates, United Kingdom, United States.

- **Languages available**

   Arabic, Chinese (simplified), Chinese (traditional), Czech, Danish, Dutch, English, Finnish, French, German, Hungarian, Italian, Japanese, Korean, Malay, Norwegian, Polish, Portuguese, Romanian, Russian, Slovak, Spanish, Swedish, Thai, Turkish.

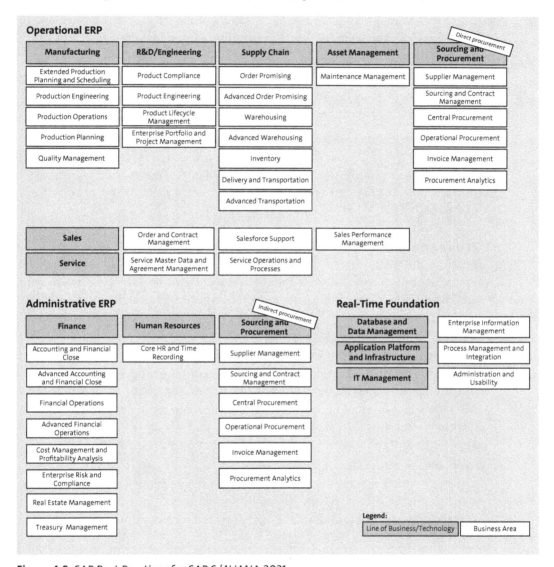

Figure 4.9 SAP Best Practices for SAP S/4HANA 2021

We'll now look at where the two packages differ, which is in the way they are activated.

Activation of SAP Best Practices for SAP S/4HANA

If you're using the SAP Best Practices for SAP S/4HANA in your solution, you'll need to import the package into your system and then use the SAP solution builder tool to activate it.

Let's first walk through an overview of the prerequisite settings that are needed to import, prepare, and activate SAP Best Practices for SAP S/4HANA:

1. **Activate the required business functions**
   During this step, you'll activate the required business functions in your SAP S/4HANA system using the Switch Framework (Transaction SWF5) that allows selective activation of business functions using switches to keep the core solution lean.

> **Further Resources**
>
> For more details on the Switch Framework capabilities and functionality, refer to the SAP Help Portal at *http://s-prs.co/v502717*. These business functions are required for successful activation of the SAP Best Practices content.

2. **Set up a new target client for SAP Best Practices**
   There are different variants for setting up the target client. The recommended approach for most users is to use the client copy of allowlisted settings from client 000. In addition, make sure to complete the import of required languages before copying the client.

3. **Carry out the technical setup steps**
   During this step, you'll download the SAP Best Practices content, apply the required SAP Notes, execute the SAP Fiori configuration, configure the system to connect to the System Landscape Directory (SLD) of SAP NetWeaver, create settings in the SAP S/4HANA backend, create basic settings in SAP Fiori launchpad, set up SAP S/4HANA attachment services (backend and frontend), and set up the email exchange between the SAP system and Simple Mail Transfer Protocol (SMTP) mail server.

4. **Carry out the settings for implementation**
   In this step, you'll ensure that activation can be executed. You'll provide (or create) users for content activation with the appropriate authorizations, create a dialog user for activation, and adjust system settings to prevent memory dumps or timeouts.

> **Further Resources**
>
> The detailed steps are provided in the administration guide for the implementation of SAP S/4HANA, which you can find in the SAP Best Practices Explorer at *http://s-prs.co/ v502718* under **Accelerators** in the **Implementation** subsection.

Next, to activate SAP Best Practices, you can follow these high-level implementation steps:

1. Download the SAP Best Practices content.
2. Import the content to your system.
3. Define the scope of the solution by selecting the desired scope items from the package. (Note that some scope items may require additional licenses, so review the list of specially priced scope items in the administration guide.)
4. Activate your solution.
5. Execute manual activities.
6. Delete the metadata cache.
7. Check and release transports with configuration settings.
8. Execute data migration activities.

Further Resources

Note that the preceding procedure explains activation of SAP Best Practices for SAP S/4HANA 2021, and the steps can change. Always refer to the detailed guidance in the administration guide on SAP Help Portal pages.

Fully Activated Appliance in SAP Cloud Appliance Library

You can also use the fully activated appliance with preactivated SAP Best Practices content that is available in SAP Cloud Appliance Library as a 30-day trial environment that can be deployed on Microsoft Azure, Amazon Web Services (AWS), or Google Cloud Platform. This package can be used for demos, proofs of concept, or sandbox environments for fit-to-standard workshops. The preactivated appliance can be started up in a cloud hyperscaler environment in a matter of about 60–90 minutes, compared to a much longer process for the manual activation of SAP Best Practices. At the time of writing, the fully activated appliance is available for SAP S/4HANA release 2021.

The appliance is built on top of the SAP S/4HANA solution. Users of the appliance don't have to worry about the technical details as SAP Cloud Appliance Library provides predefined appliance sizing and guides for deployment to the desired cloud infrastructure. The appliance can also be deployed in your own data center.

Figure 4.10 shows the structure of the fully activated SAP S/4HANA appliance for release 2021 that you can access on SAP Cloud Appliance Library and deploy to the desired environment, such as AWS, Microsoft Azure, or Google Cloud Platform (or alternatively in your data center).

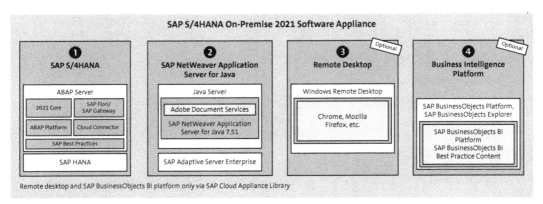

Figure 4.10 Fully Activated Appliance with SAP Best Practices for SAP S/4HANA 2021

> **Note**
>
> The business intelligence platform and remote desktop are only available when using the SAP Cloud Appliance Library and are not for download/Blu-ray shipment.
>
> The business intelligence platform and remote desktop are optional in the SAP Cloud Appliance Library (the hosting fee will decrease if you opt out). Both are included by default, but you can opt out in the advanced mode of instance creation. This cannot be undone unless you create a new instance that include these options.

4.2   Enterprise Management Layer for SAP S/4HANA

The enterprise management layer for SAP S/4HANA is a prepackaged, ready-to-use, end-to-end solution template that is tailored to multinational corporations. It is not specific to an industry and covers most lines of business (LoBs) for up to 46 countries. It provides an extra layer of configuration and content on top of SAP Best Practices and captures the experience from successful, real-life projects. Sold and delivered as a service, a template-driven approach enables any suitable project to increase quality, accelerate adoption, reduce cost, and decrease risk.

The enterprise management layer for SAP S/4HANA can be used during new implementations or to drive innovation of existing SAP implementations. It can be used in SAP-led or individual company/partner-led projects. It can be deployed on-premise or with a cloud provider. Once deployed, the system can be used, configured, enhanced, extended, and connected to other SAP solutions just like any other system. The enterprise management layer for SAP S/4HANA is used to jump-start a project and is ideally suited to drive a fit-to-standard analysis during the explore phase. In addition, the enterprise management layer for SAP S/4HANA can also be deployed in the customer's productive landscape and provide SAP Best Practices for the implementation. This leads to faster deployment, faster decision-making, and a higher adoption of standard SAP functionality.

In this section, we'll discuss the structure of the enterprise management layer for SAP S/4HANA by explaining the content structure and discussing updates and deployment options.

4.2.1   Structure of Content

The content in the enterprise management layer for SAP S/4HANA is based on SAP Best Practices for 43 countries. However, the content has been enhanced and adapted for multinational corporations with their complex business and reporting requirements across a multitude of countries. It includes a preconfigured solution, test scripts, process diagrams, and sample organization structures and master data. Whereas SAP Best Practice content for SAP S/4HANA is free of charge but must be activated, the enterprise management layer for SAP S/4HANA is sold and delivered by SAP. The service includes the appliance (in technical terms, a database backup) containing the enterprise management layer for SAP S/4HANA, documentation, and a handover session to the customer's project team.

The enterprise management layer for SAP S/4HANA provides SAP Best Practices for multiple countries in one SAP instance. Simply select which countries you need out of the 46 countries currently available (more are planned), and you'll get multiple company codes with a harmonized SAP Best Practices chart of accounts and harmonized business processes for multiple LoBs across all countries. Each country is preconfigured with localized business processes to comply with local tax and statutory requirements, hence ensuring document and reporting compliance for the individual countries. Parallel accounting and reporting capabilities according to your group accounting principles as well as local and tax accounting principles are the cornerstone of the enterprise management layer for SAP S/4HANA: in technical terms, three accounting principles linked to five ledgers are preconfigured.

The enterprise management layer for SAP S/4HANA is configured with 25 languages. End users can work in any of these languages, and all data and print forms are translated to ensure that correspondence with business partners abroad is possible in their local languages.

The content of the enterprise management layer for SAP S/4HANA is structured into three layers:

1. A *standard scope* that consists of close to 200 business processes (or scope items) that are always included and only require the SAP S/4HANA Enterprise Management license.

2. *Scope options* allow you to select the additional scope that you want and to exclude scope options for which you don't have the required software licenses—for example, scope options for group reporting, cash management, advanced available-to-promise (ATP), or advanced variant configuration, just to name a few.

3. *Service options* can be added on customer request and provide additional business processes that are not offered by SAP Best Practices: intercompany processes between two countries, the Project System module for accounting or for engineering projects, and more.

Further Resources

The latest information can be found in the SAP Best Practices Explorer at *https://rapid.sap.com/bp/BP_OP_EML*, as well as in the blog series at *http://s-prs.co/v546306*.

Among other documents, a one-page service summary is available, as shown in Figure 4.11. This lists the applications required, the scope options available, and the business processes and capabilities.

Business Process Coverage

Supply Chain
- Inventory
- Warehousing

R&D and Engineering
- Product engineering

Database and Data Management
- Enterprise informationmanagement

Manufacturing
- Production engineering
- Production operations
- Production planning
- Quality management

Sourcing and Procurement
- Invoice management
- Operational procurement
- Procurement analytics
- Sourcing and contract management
- Supplier management

Finance
- Accounting and financial close
- Cost management and profitability analysis
- Enterprise risk and compliance
- Financial operations
- Treasury management (basic)

Asset Management
- Maintenance management

Sales
- Order and contract management
- Salesforce Support

Service
- Service operations and processes
- Service master data and agreement management

Service Scope

Service Scope Options
- Actual costing
- Advanced cash management
- Advanced compliance reporting
- Advanced receivables management
- Contract and lease management
- Group reporting
- Warehouse management
- Advanced ATP
- Advanced variant configuration
- Extended production planning and scheduling
- Contract management

Service Scope Enhancements
- Parallel accounting
- Localization
- Intercompany sales and returns
- Cross-plant stock transfer
- Project System for accounting and for engineering project
- Letter of credit management

Figure 4.11 Enterprise Management Layer for SAP S/4HANA Summary

4.2.2   Updates

A new version of the enterprise management layer for SAP S/4HANA content is provided for each software release and becomes available roughly one quarter after the new SAP S/4HANA software is released. Regular updates of the functional and localization content, as well as additional content such as new business processes, become available throughout the year and can be downloaded from the SAP Best Practices Explorer. This distinguishes the enterprise management layer for SAP S/4HANA from other template solutions, such as those offered by partners.

Once deployed in the customer landscape, there is no process to upgrade the enterprise management layer content when a new version is released. A software upgrade can be performed in the normal way. Required changes, such as those due to changing legal requirements in some countries, need to be performed by the project team.

4.2.3   Deployment Options

SAP can set up the enterprise management layer for SAP S/4HANA quickly. This means that your organization doesn't need to activate SAP Best Practices and upskill people on how to do this.

There are two main ways to consume the enterprise management layer for SAP S/4HANA:

1. **Trial edition with a fixed scope**
   A 30-day trial edition is available for the enterprise management layer for SAP S/4HANA. This is typically used during the discover phase and requires no licenses. The solution is made available through the SAP Cloud Appliance Library. In this case, the enterprise management layer for SAP S/4HANA is not tailored to individual customer requirements and does not exclude business processes that require additional software licenses.

2. **Custom edition**
   The enterprise management layer for SAP S/4HANA can be adapted to each customer's requirements. Based on a questionnaire, you can choose which countries are needed (countries where you have legal entities), which scope options are needed, but also your group currency and your fiscal year variant. In addition, the local currency and the usual fiscal year variant are preconfigured for each country.

The custom edition requires a signed order form for the enterprise management layer service. The enterprise management layer custom edition can be deployed in the following ways:

- **SAP S/4HANA Cloud, private edition**
  SAP sets up the enterprise management layer for SAP S/4HANA and hosts and manages the solution.

- **On-premise**
  You get a custom edition built by SAP and you deploy the database backup that SAP provides in your on-premise landscape.
- **Cloud provider (e.g., Microsoft Azure, AWS, or Google Cloud Platform)**
  As with the on-premise deployment, you can download the enterprise management layer database backup files and use the cloud provider of your choice.

The enterprise management layer for SAP S/4HANA is most frequently used to set up the full productive landscape, the development, quality, and production systems. Having the preconfigured content already deployed helps to accelerate the explore phase and the realize phase. Sometimes the enterprise management layer for SAP S/4HANA will also be deployed in a dedicated sandbox system. The sandbox system is typically used for the explore workshops but can also be used as a reference system for copying configuration into a development system where the enterprise management layer for SAP S/4HANA cannot be deployed—for example, in a customer's legacy system.

The system landscape may require multiple servers: an SAP S/4HANA server and an Adobe Document Services (ADS) server. SAP Fiori apps are embedded in SAP S/4HANA and do not require a separate server.

To deploy on-premise or with a cloud provider, the installation of the server hardware and operating systems is the customer's responsibility. The solution is deployed via a database backup that needs to be downloaded and restored. The accelerators (documentation) can be downloaded in SAP Best Practices Explorer at *https://rapid.sap.com/bp/BP_OP_EML*.

4.3   Summary

This chapter provided an in-depth understanding of the ready-to-use preconfiguration SAP provides in SAP Best Practices and the enterprise management layer for SAP S/4HANA. These packages and related documentation are major accelerators for any implementation project deploying SAP S/4HANA software in an organization and should be used to accelerate time to value and leverage the investment SAP makes in building and delivering these packages. They provide significant acceleration not only through the preconfiguration but also in the business user's understanding of the solution capabilities by being able to execute business processes in a running system.

In the next chapter, we'll review the key capabilities and processes that are critical in all implementation projects, such as collecting requirements, configuring the solution, extending and integrating systems, and testing.

Chapter 5

Configuration, Data Migration, Extensibility, Integration, and Testing

Now that we've established the importance of working with running systems for the solution requirements and design, we'll cover the configuration, migration, integration, extensibility, and testing, which are all critical for planning and executing a successful solution implementation.

In this chapter, we'll walk through several key processes related to planning and executing an SAP S/4HANA Cloud or SAP S/4HANA implementation. For configuration of these solutions, a fit-to-standard analysis is performed to validate the solution functionality included in the project scope and to confirm that the business requirements can be satisfied. Identified delta requirements and configuration values are added to the backlog for use in the next phase. Industry and solution experts from SAP lead a series of structured solution demos and solution design workshops.

Next, we incrementally build and test an integrated business and system environment that is based on the business processes and process requirements identified previously and captured in the backlog. The project team loads customer data into the system, plans adoption activities, and prepares cutover plans and plans for operationally running the solution.

Finally, the project team uses a series of iterations to incrementally configure, test, confirm, and document the entire end-to-end solution and to load data. The project team actively works with business representatives to ensure a good fit of the built solution.

Let's dive into these core processes in the following sections, starting with configuration.

5.1 Business-Driven Configuration

In this section, we'll discuss how the configuration process—from planning and designing to realizing the planned value—is supported by SAP Activate for the various SAP S/4HANA solutions: SAP S/4HANA Cloud; SAP S/4HANA Cloud, private edition; and SAP S/4HANA.

> **SAP S/4HANA Cloud in a Three-System Landscape**
>
> When we discuss SAP S/4HANA Cloud, we're specifically discussing the new SAP S/4HANA Cloud three-system landscape roadmap. This innovation provides companies with three systems to deploy the solution into—staring with a development system that is used for configuration, extensibility, and integration; followed by a test system predominantly used as a preproduction test and validation environment; and ending with a production system that the company uses for productive operation of its business. We will discuss the details of this deployment option in Chapter 7.

The configuration process, in all solutions, is supported by the application design and configuration workstream. The purpose of the application design and configuration workstream is to help you plan, prepare, and realize the planned value-add of the SAP solution for your business. This workstream covers the confirmation of scope, fit-to-standard, identification of delta business process requirements, and functional design of the solution. Topics such as integration, extensibility, and testing, which are covered in more detail in other workstreams and later in this chapter, are supported by the application design and configuration workstream.

The configuration process during an implementation project is often compared to the building of a house. If the correct preparation and planning is done up front, and the correct amount of time is spent performing these activities, the configuring or building of the house is more efficient as all major decisions, and the risk of rework, is mitigated at the beginning. The goal is to ensure that the actual configuration of the system is as efficient as possible to help the business realize the planned value-add sooner. Deliberate time spent up front enabling, preparing, and planning helps ensure an effective and efficient project with a lower cost of implementation.

Regardless of the SAP solution, the configuration process can be broken down into three major sections:

- Preparation for planning configuration
- Planning configuration
- Configuration

Up-front enablement, as mentioned, is a key driver and enabler for ensuring a seamless, end-to-end configuration process during an implementation. Therefore, it's important for the business process experts to start and continue their self-enablement in parallel with the configuration process.

> **Further Resources**
>
> Further details on self-enablement activities for project members can be found in the customer team enablement workstream in the Roadmap Viewer (see Chapter 3, Section 3.1).

5.1.1   SAP Central Business Configuration

Before doing a deep dive into the configuration process within the application design and configuration workstream, it is first important to understand the configuration tool available to configure specific SAP products.

SAP Central Business Configuration is a new tool used when configuring the end-to-end business processes that span various SAP products from one central place. The vision for SAP Central Business Configuration is to allow the configuration of end-to-end processes across the intelligent enterprise. Although SAP S/4HANA Cloud is one of the first solutions to be integrated with SAP Central Business Configuration, additional cloud solutions are planned for the future.

As a configuration tool, SAP Central Business Configuration includes all the configuration activities that take place during an implementation project while not containing any duplicate content from SAP Activate. Instead, the SAP Activate implementation methodology provides the guidance on the right points in time when the configuration tool is needed and allows the tool to take over and guide users through the configuration process.

Much like the configuration process can be broken down into major sections, SAP Central Business Configuration is structured around three different phases within the configuration process:

1. Scope and organizational structure
2. Product-specific configuration
3. Production system settings

As part of the scope and organizational structure phase, users will select the scope and countries and regions; settings that are required before solution configuration, such as the standard fiscal variant or group currency; and the definition of the organization structure of your company. Note that future activities follow the selection of the scope chosen during the scope and organization structure phase. This functionality means that what you select during the scope and organization structure phase is automatically considered by SAP Central Business Configuration later within the implementation project and matches the decisions needed with the scope chosen. Once these settings are chosen, the initial deployment takes place.

For the product-specific configuration phase, which takes place during the realize phase in SAP Activate, the preconfigured settings are adjusted to better fit the needs of the business.

Finally, the cutover activities, such as the migration of the business's productive data, are carried out in the production system settings phase.

Now that we've covered the overall configuration process and the configuration tool used when configuring SAP S/4HANA Cloud, we can dive deeper into how the configuration process works within each SAP product at a high level.

5.1.2   SAP S/4HANA Cloud

Within the SAP S/4HANA Cloud three-system landscape implementation roadmap, the application design and configuration workstream covers the end-to-end configuration process by taking project teams through the preparation for planning configuration (with the business-driven configuration assessment, fit-to-standard preparation, and fit-to-standard system preparation), planning configuration (with fit-to-standard analysis, solution definition, and planning and design workshops), and configuration. We'll walk through each phase in the following sections.

Preparing for Planning Configuration in SAP S/4HANA Cloud

The configuration process starts in the prepare phase with the business-driven configuration assessment. The purpose of this assessment is to discuss a company's current business processes and gain a foundational understanding of the business that can be leveraged during the fit-to-standard workshops. The business-driven configuration questionnaires can be leveraged by the configuration expert as a tool to help drive and document these discussions. When leveraging these assessments, the configuration expert will download the project-relevant line of business (LoB) configuration questionnaires and refine each so that only the relevant scope for the project is shown. Once completed, the refined questionnaires are provided to the company's business process experts to answer the questions.

Note that in these questionnaires, there are two levels of questions: level 2 and level 3 questions (level 1 questions have already been asked during the presales and sales discussions in the discover phase). Level 2 questions should be answered during the prepare phase and are geared toward collecting information prior to the execution of the fit-to-standard workshops. The goal is to prevent stop/go execution of the fit-to-standard workshops due to missing information. These questions also help the configuration expert determine the topics that will need to be further discussed and captured during the fit-to-standard workshops. The goal of level 3 questions is to provide more detailed information on what is needed to make a business decision and to define specific configuration values that will be captured in the backlog. These questions should be discussed and documented in the fit-to-standard workshop during the explore phase.

After the business process experts have responded to the level 2 questions and provided the filled-out questionnaires to the configuration expert, the preparation for the fit-to-standard workshops can begin.

Self-enablement is a key component for executing an effective and efficient fit-to-standard workshop that fosters rich discussions. Thus, it's important for all business process owners to start preparing for the fit-to-standard workshops by reviewing key assets such as the SAP Best Practices test scripts, process flows in SAP Cloud ALM, and other self-enablement accelerators for topics such as analytics, data protection, and chart of accounts. In addition, all the business process experts participating in the fit-to-standard workshops should verify access to the SAP S/4HANA Cloud starter system. Then, after access to the system is confirmed, business process experts should continue with self-enablement by executing some of the test scripts for the project scope. The purpose of this activity is for the business process expert to gain hands-on experience in the system, which will help drive fit-to-standard discussions with the configuration experts on the business's processes.

While the business process experts are pursuing self-enablement with the solution, the various technical experts begin to create initial requirements lists that will later be used as capturing requirements for specific topics during the fit-to-standard workshops, such as analytics, identity and access management, extensibility, and integration. These initial lists are created from the results of the digital discovery assessment from the discover phase, or from executive decisions from meetings that took place after the contract was signed.

The final step for preparing for the fit-to-standard workshops is to prepare the starter system that will be used to demonstrate the functionality of the solution during the fit-to-standard workshops (refer to Chapter 3) with any additional project-specific data needed. Although the starter system does come with predelivered SAP Best Practices master data, you can create more project-specific data. During the fit-to-standard workshops, the system will be used as a focal point for facilitating discussion; thus, any additional project-specific data that can help aid this discussion is encouraged.

Planning Configuration in SAP S/4HANA Cloud

Following the preparation for planning configuration in the prepare phase, the planning of configuration takes place during the explore phase. This phase, for the application design and configuration workstream, includes the fit-to-standard workshops, the documentation of the requirements and backlog items, and the planning and designing workshops for technical topics.

Each of the fit-to-standard workshops are organized around the functional areas of the solution and follow an iterative approach, as shown in Figure 5.1. The focus of these workshops is on the business and its requirements. They don't deep-dive into technical topics; rather, the technical discussions are handled during the planning and design workshops. Let's explore the fit-to-standard steps in a bit more detail:

❶ **Review SAP Best Practices process flow**
The configuration expert explains a scope item using the SAP Best Practices process flow and responses from the business-driven configuration questionnaires.

❷ **Demonstrate scope item and concepts**
The configuration expert demonstrates the scope item using the starter system and delivered master data and then highlights the areas that require configuration decisions. The process flow is used as a point of reference when transitioning in the system.

❸ Discuss how the processes fit with the company's requirements

The team fosters discussion to better understand the company's business require-ments, referencing the business-driven configuration questionnaire, and explains how the solution meets these requirements.

❹ Identify delta requirements

The team identifies and catalogs the delta requirements in the backlog for further analysis and closure. Delta requirements are business requirements that can't be satisfied with the standard scenarios.

❺ Identify the required configuration

The team leverages the business-driven configuration questionnaires to arrive at critical configuration decisions. All configuration values required and any needed in-app extensions are determined and documented in the backlog. The company is responsible for providing value lists (i.e., product group definition).

❻ Enable company execution of standard scenarios

The configuration expert enables the business process expert to execute the process on his or her own in the starter system.

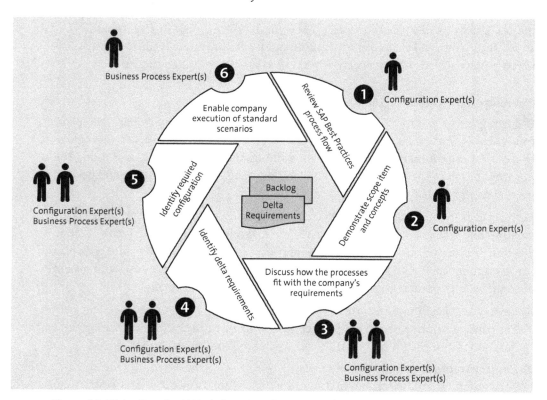

Figure 5.1 Fit-to-Standard Workshop Iterative Approach

During the fit-to-standard workshops, the configuration expert demonstrates the solution using the starter system and facilitates discussions of some of the key areas identified in the initial business assessment, or the answers for the level 2 questions in the business-driven configuration questionnaires from the prepare phase. In addition, to help continue discussion of the configuration values, the configuration expert will also ask the workshop participants the level 3 questions from the business-driven configuration questionnaires.

The goal of these workshops, overall, is to validate the predefined processes of the standard solution with the company requirements and identify any delta requirements that need further refinement by technical experts during the planning and design workshops. Any delta requirements identified (for analytics, integration, output management, identity and access management, etc.) are then captured in the initial lists that were created in the prepare phase by the technical experts. Prior to the handover of all these backlog items and delta requirements for the planning and design workshops, the configuration experts validate that all the configuration values and requirements have been captured, and they document any additional outcomes that were discussed after the fit-to-standard workshops.

After all backlog items and delta requirements have been handed over to the corresponding technical experts, the further refinement of the delta requirements takes place during a set of planning and designing workshops, in which the technical experts take the businesses requirements and map them to the technical feasibility of the solution. The details of the planning and design workshops, while part of the fit-to-standard process, are located in SAP Cloud ALM in the workstreams in which the technical experts are focused.

The goal of these planning and design workshops is to further refine the delta requirements brought up by the business during the fit-to-standard workshops into backlog items that can be easily configured during the realize phase. If the fit-to-standard workshops were executed well—with the necessary self-enablement completed prior to each of the workshops to help foster rich discussions with the business—and provide the planning and design workshops with good inputs, the configuration for the solution, based on the backlog in SAP Cloud ALM at the end of the explore phase, will be effective and efficient.

Configuration in SAP S/4HANA Cloud

As we've discussed, the efficiency of configuring the solution is directly correlated to the quality and time spent by the business process experts for self-enablement; that is, quality inputs help create quality outputs. With all the planning completed during the explore phase, the actual configuration of the solution takes place during the realize phase. Ideally, this portion of the configuration process should be one of the shortest, as all the heavy work has been completed up front with only the execution step remaining.

For SAP S/4HANA Cloud, the configuration process follows two-week sprint cycles, or iterations, where the configuration experts configure the solution in SAP Central Business Configuration and then transport the configuration from the development system to the test system, where the configuration is validated and then forwarded to the production system. Note that the planning of these sprints is determined at the end of the explore phase in the project management workstream, where the backlog is consolidated after all the planning and design workshops and is signed off on by the company.

Each of the configuration sprints follows this iterative configuration approach:

1. Configure
2. Track changes in configuration
3. Execute test
4. Transport configuration
5. Verify with the business

Some required configuration must take place before system use, so the first sprints should focus on this configuration prior to the configuration of the functional areas. Some of the required configuration before system use includes tax solution, profit center, cost center master data, house bank, and customer-specific fiscal year variant. In addition, during the configuration sprints, additional countries may be added; this additional country activation must be taken into consideration during the planning and the execution of the sprints.

After the configuration sprints are completed, the configured solution is demonstrated to the business for solution acceptance prior to company testing.

Even after the solution is deployed to the company, the solution and company will continuously improve their organizational efficiencies and adopt further innovations through the expanded use of the system's functionality in the run phase. Any new solution scope and additional countries needed for expansion will be executed as the company continues to add further value via the solution.

5.1.3   SAP S/4HANA Cloud, Private Edition

Like SAP S/4HANA Cloud, SAP S/4HANA Cloud, private edition, follows a fit-to-standard planning configuration approach. For this solution, the preparation for the planning of configuration is covered by a business-driven configuration assessment, fit-to-standard preparation, fit-to-standard system preparation, transition planning and preparation, and user strategy workshops. The planning of configuration follows, and is covered by, the fit-to-standard analysis, solution definition, and planning and design workshops. Finally, the solution is configured before being deployed. We'll walk through these steps in the following sections.

Prepare for Planning Configuration in SAP S/4HANA Cloud, Private Edition

The preparation for planning configuration in SAP S/4HANA Cloud, private edition begins with the configuration expert performing an initial process assessment using the business-driven configuration assessment questionnaires as one of the tools to gain a foundational understanding of the customer's current business processes. These questionnaires, the LoB questionnaires relevant to the project scope, can be given to the business process experts to review and answer the level 2 questions. The answers to these level 2 questions will be reviewed and analyzed by the configuration expert prior to the fit-to-standard workshops as they will help the configuration expert understand which topics need further clarification or discussion.

To help drive an efficient and effective fit-to-standard workshop, all the business process experts should review the necessary SAP Best Practices material (test scripts and process flows) for the related scope items that will be demonstrated during the fit-to-standard workshops in the Processes app within SAP Cloud ALM. This hands-on experience allows the business process experts to become familiar with the tools that will used during the fit-to-standard workshops and to help guide and contribute to the configuration discussions more effectively.

In addition, business process experts should also make themselves familiar with the golden rules for implementing SAP S/4HANA Cloud, private edition (discussed previously in Chapter 2, Section 2.4):

1. Foster a cloud mindset by adhering to fit-to-standard and agile deployment, as detailed in SAP Activate.
2. Use preconfigured solutions with predefined processes and leverage the SAP Fiori user experience (UX).
3. Ensure use of modern integration technologies. Use public application programming interfaces (APIs), and provide no native access to APIs that aren't public.
4. Ensure use of modern extensibility technologies. Develop company extensions in a side-by-side approach using SAP Business Technology Platform (SAP BTP).
5. Ensure transparency on deviations. Any deviation has to be clearly documented as part of the SAP S/4HANA Cloud, private edition implementation.

These rules help to foster a cloud mindset and are referenced throughout the application design and configuration workstream. We discussed the golden rules and Solution Standardization Board (SSB; for governance of the golden rules) in Chapter 2, Section 2.4.7.

In parallel to the self-enablement of the business process experts, the configuration experts prepare the system that will be used to demonstrate the solution during the fit-to-standard workshops. The configuration expert will prepare the system by enhancing it with additional configuration. Because some of the processes might not fully fit the expected business scope, it's important to have a predefined and system-based solution before you start the fit-to-standard workshops as it will help foster configuration discussions during the workshops.

In addition, it's important to verify the data in the system that will be used during the fit-to-standard workshops, which help to demonstrate the business process in a way that is relevant to the project. If the standard predelivered sample and transactional data isn't enough for demonstration purposes, additional sample data can be created in the system to further enhance the business processes to be demonstrated. Finally, for the last system preparation step, it's recommended to execute transactions in the system to populate data in the analytical reports because it will allow the reporting functionality to be demonstrated during the fit-to-standard workshops.

Prior to moving into the next phase, and all throughout the prepare phase, the planning and the objectives of the transition should be defined. The planning of this action plan takes place in the project management workstream; however, the outcome of this action plan has an impact on the configuration process as the requirements for adaptation of existing custom code and the development of custom code are clarified.

In addition, the UX/UI strategy should be defined and updated before continuing to the explore phase. SAP Fiori is the UX of the intelligent enterprise and changes the way that businesses work. Thus, having a strategy based on the collected requirements within SAP Fiori allows the project to have an aligned vision of what the future SAP Fiori front-end service architecture will be. Often this strategy will help provide a focus on what UX should be explored for each business role prior to the fit-to-standard workshops and supports the second golden rule: use preconfigured solutions with predefined processes, and leverage the SAP Fiori UX.

Planning Configuration in SAP S/4HANA Cloud, Private Edition

When the preparation is complete, the project team will move into the explore phase to start planning the configuration. The planning, designing, and documentation of the configuration for the solution in the explore phase will serve as a reference during the execution of the configuration of the solution in the realize phase.

Keeping in line with the fit-to-standard approach, each of the workshops should be executed in an iterative manner: the solution is demonstrated, how the business process matches the predelivered solution is discussed, and any of the configuration values and delta requirements are documented. The first golden rule, foster a cloud mindset, and the second golden rule, use SAP Best Practices, should act as guidance for fostering discussions during the workshops.

After the business has completed and documented the backlog items and delta requirements from the fit-to-standard workshops in SAP Cloud ALM, any further refinement of requirements for technical configuration then go through a planning and designing process. For this round of workshops, the requirements documented are refined further by technical experts. Some examples of requirements that go through this secondary refinement process are analytics, output management, extensibility, integration, and UI design. These requirements are refined during the workshops and converted to backlog items that will be planned into sprints during the release planning prior to the end of the explore phase.

Configuration in SAP S/4HANA Cloud, Private Edition

After determining what will be included in the initial release, as dictated by the release plan created in the explore phase, the execution of the configuration can take place during the realize phase.

For the configuration of SAP S/4HANA Cloud, private edition, the execution of configuration follows a series of iterations that incrementally build and test the integrated business and system environment. Typically, configuration takes place in sprints that are time-boxed into two-week cycles. During each of these sprints, the configuration expert considers the system configuration, documentation, and unit testing based on the backlog that was planned during the explore phase. This configuration activity is executed per LoB or end-to-end solution.

Following the completion of unit testing, a string test is run within the sprint to test initial solution integration with the business priorities or end-to-end solutions in scope. Note, however, this isn't a fully loaded integration test and doesn't replace the text execution that takes place in the testing workstream later in the phase.

What Is a String Test?

A string test is performed when more than one related unit test, which is a test intended to isolate and test a single piece of functionality, is performed one after another to form a string. Rather than test the functionality of a single application, for example, a string test may check the flow of data from one application to another. Further information on testing and different testing types will be discussed later in this chapter. (See also Chapter 7, Section 7.3.5.)

Documentation of configuration is key for change management and is also in line with the five golden rules; as a result, it should take place in parallel with the configuration of the solution. Any changes to the configuration that take place after the solution walkthrough and during the bug-fixing portion should be amended or added to the original configuration documentation.

After the solution has been fully configured and deployed to the business, to realize the planned value, improvements to the solution may be made as the business periodically updates the system and imitates an innovation cycle in the run phase. In addition, new functionality may be released that might cause the creation of a strategic roadmap for continuous improvement.

5.1.4   SAP S/4HANA

Following the same fit-to-standard mindset as the SAP S/4HANA Cloud solutions, the implementation of SAP S/4HANA uses a fit-to-standard configuration approach for planning configuration. For the application design and configuration workstream of this solution, the preparation for planning begins with prototyping, planning the transition, and preparing for the transition. The planning of the configuration then follows with a series of fi-to-standard and design workshops that allow the company to identify the deltas between the solution and the company's business process and to design, verify, and accept any planned custom configuration. Finally, the system is configured similarly to SAP S/4HANA Cloud, private edition, with iterations that have the main configuration, a unit test, and a string test that a configuration will walk through for the business. Any bugs or additional feedback taken from this walkthrough session will be addressed and the documentation updated.

We'll walk through the core phases in this section.

Prepare for Planning Configuration in SAP S/4HANA

SAP S/4HANA has a wider ability to extend the solution with custom code or with various extensibility options. Therefore, to properly plan and prepare for the transition, it's key for the business to understand the value of the innovations to be delivered with the new system. The prepare phase, and start of the configuration process, begins with prototyping, which is a small optional project on its own. Prototyping helps to enable the business to evaluate the value-add of the solution with real business scenarios and data. It's one way the business can start to enable itself on the solution prior to the fit-to-standard workshops.

To help with the transition and the future value that is to come with this new solution, a first version of an action plan, or transition plan, should be created to serve as the basis for the project plan. This transition plan will constantly be refined throughout the project in the project management workstream; however, this plan impacts the application design and configuration workstream by helping to clarify the adaptation of custom code or the development of new custom code, if required. In addition, topics such as UX and UI strategy are discussed and defined earlier on in the implementation to allow for more efficient and effective design workshops later in the explore phase.

Any of the preparation activities discussed during the transition planning that must take place before the transition project starts should be executed prior to the end of the prepare phase so that the planning for configuration can start.

Planning for Configuration in SAP S/4HANA

For SAP S/4HANA, the preparation of the system for the fit-to-standard workshops takes place at the start of the explore phase. The activation of this system is essential to the overall implementation strategy as it's the foundation for demonstrating the pre-configured solution during the explore phase.

The activation activities for the sandbox system may vary, however, depending on which of the three implementation scenarios is relevant for the implementation (system conversion, new implementation, or selective data transition).

After the sandbox system to be used for demonstration purposes is prepared, the fit-to-standard workshops with the business process experts can take place. The purpose of the fit-to-standard workshops is to validate the predefined scenarios and enhancements in scope for the implementation and to identify potential gaps between the pre-delivered product and the customer's requirements following a particular structure (see Chapter 7, Section 7.3.4 for new implementations, and see Chapter 8, Section 8.3.2 for system conversions).

The fit-to-standard workshops and documentation, once completed, are then followed by a series of design workshops. During these workshops, the solutions for the prioritized deltas identified are documented and detailed. These delta design documents are in a format that is suitable for communication and that allows for a formal sign-off by the company, after being reviewed by an independent instance. The signed-off designs are then added to the configuration backlog for execution in the realize phase.

Additional workshops, for topics such as UX/UI, security, and data volume, will be executed even after the review and sign off on the delta design documents but prior to the end of the explore phase.

Configuration in SAP S/4HANA

After all the design workshops are completed and the design documents have been confirmed and signed off on by the company, the execution of the designs that were discussed and determined in the explore phase takes place during the realize phase.

Like the configuration of SAP S/4HANA Cloud, private edition, the execution of configuration for SAP S/4HANA follows a series of iterations, typically executed through sprints, which incrementally build the system environment. Within each of these sprints, the configuration expert configures, documents, and performs a unit test based on the backlog that was planned during the explore phase.

Prior to the completion of each sprint, a string test is run to test an initial solution integration within the business priorities, or end-to-end solutions, in scope. A fully loaded integration will take place in the testing workstream later in the phase, and thus this string test isn't a fully loaded integration test.

Documentation is important throughout the configuration process as it's used as a reference later in the implementation for key user enablement. Therefore, any changes to configuration that take place after the solution walkthrough and for bug fixing should be captured in the original configuration documentation.

Finally, after the solution has been fully configured and deployed to the business to realize the planned value, additional improvements and innovations may take place as the system is being periodically updated during the run phase.

5.2   Data Migration

All SAP ERP systems require customer-specific master data objects to run the business processes configured in the system. To facilitate the entering of potentially very large volumes during the initial implementation, SAP has developed the SAP S/4HANA migration cockpit, along with processes to support the tool; it is available for both SAP S/4HANA and SAP S/4HANA Cloud implementations.

The SAP S/4HANA migration cockpit assists in transferring business data from a source legacy system to a new implementation of SAP S/4HANA or SAP S/4HANA Cloud either through direct transfer from another SAP ERP solution or through the use of staging tables. Migration objects within the migration cockpit are used to identify and transfer the relevant business object data. The migration objects contain information about the source and target structures, as well as the relationships between these structures. Object mapping information for the relevant fields is also stored, as well as any mappings that are required to convert values from the source value to the target value. SAP provides predefined migration templates that are used to structure and load your data. The SAP S/4HANA migration cockpit can be accessed by opening the Migrate Your Data app.

The migration cockpit supports two different methods of transfer:

- **Migrate data using staging tables**
  The system automatically creates a database table for each migration object. These tables can be populated from an XML file or from other tools.

- **Migrate data directly from SAP system**
  SAP S/4HANA is connected directly to a supported SAP ERP system and the table system within that system. Only SAP S/4HANA and SAP S/4HANA Cloud, private edition support direct data migration.

The process of data migration can be broken down into the planning and execution of data migration. In planning, the following tasks are performed:

- Selecting the required master and transactional data objects
- Determining the migration cockpit field structures
- Defining specifications for data extraction from the legacy system (staging tables only)
- Performing data cleansing activities

For execution, the following tasks are performed, as shown in Figure 5.2:

- Creating the migration project and selecting migration objects (staging tables only)
- Populating data into the migration template (staging tables only)
- Loading the data into staging tables (staging tables only)
- Validating data and performing value mapping
- Simulating the data migration
- Executing the data migration

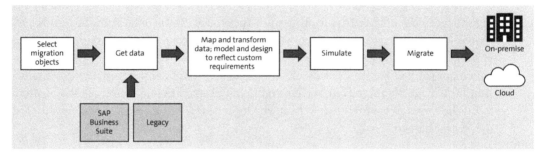

Figure 5.2 Data Migration Process

The process of preparing and executing data migration is detailed in the following sections.

5.2.1 Data Migration Preparation

Data migration is a process that can take longer than expected. It's important to begin preparation shortly after the project start and in parallel with the fit-to-standard workshop. Let's walk through the key tasks.

Selecting Master and Transactional Data Objects

The purpose of the first task is to determine the master data and transactional data along with the data sources required for the scope of your implementation. Start by determining all master and transactional data objects needed to support the processes detailed in the fit-to-standard workshops. After the list of required objects is determined, the data sources can be mapped to them. In many cases, a legacy equivalent won't be available, and the field data will need to be created or derived.

> **Migration Objects**
>
> Note that the coverage and functionality for data migration objects expands with each quarterly release of SAP S/4HANA Cloud. A complete list of objects is available via the

> SAP Help Portal in the **SAP S/4HANA Migration Cockpit** topic area and in the SAP S/4HANA migration cockpit. Templates should always be checked after an upgrade as they may have changed. If coverage is not available and you are implementing SAP S/4HANA or SAP S/4HANA Cloud, private edition, then SAP provides the SAP S/4HANA migration object modeler, which allows for modeling custom objects.

Determining the SAP S/4HANA Migration Cockpit Field Structures

The purpose of the next task is to view the SAP S/4HANA data structures by downloading the template files and associating the structures with the data from the legacy system(s). The templates can be downloaded from your project in the Migrate Your Data app and contains the metadata (fields, data type, mandatory fields, etc.) to help with the data mapping (see Figure 5.3). Downloading the files at this early stage helps you understand the available migration objects and fields, prepare the data, and determine how to fill the templates with the data from the legacy system. Open the downloaded XML files with Microsoft Excel.

The downloaded templates contain an introduction with instructions, a field list, and data sheets per structure. The data sheet contains at least one mandatory structure and additional optional structures depending on the complexity of the migration object. Only mandatory sheets need to be filled; however, after an optional sheet is populated, all the mandatory fields for that structure must be filled.

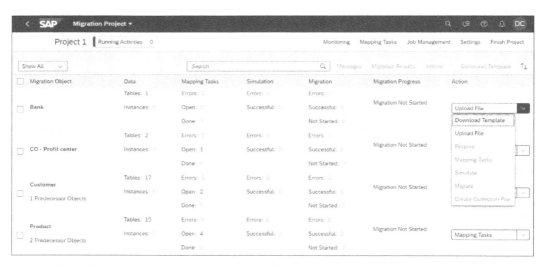

Figure 5.3 Data Migration Template Download

Defining Specifications for Data Extraction from Legacy Systems

The next step is not relevant if direct transfer for another SAP ERP system is used. Extracting data from the legacy systems to populate into the new system simplifies the manual effort required for starting productive use of a new system. In this task, the specifications for extraction of data from the legacy system are created, and any related legacy system reporting/development is initiated. Because master data and transaction data can change frequently, the process must be created so that it can be efficiently executed during the cutover to production. Data that will be manually entered also requires a specification so that it can also be efficiently executed during the cutover.

Performing Data Cleansing Activities

Prior to converting data from the legacy system to SAP S/4HANA, you have a good opportunity to remove or update records that are obsolete or don't meet current standards. By doing this, the data load volume will be less and the user experience better in the new system. This process can be time-consuming, so it should be started as soon as possible.

5.2.2   Data Migration Execution with Staging Tables

Data migration execution takes place during the realize phase. Solution configuration usually uses manually created sample data, but for user acceptance testing (UAT), the final data should be loaded via the processes that will be used during the production cutover. This will allow both business processes and data to be tested together. Let's walk through the key tasks related to the staging tables migration approach.

Creating the Migration Project and Selecting Migration Objects

The migration project is the framework used to manage the data migration process and is the first step in the transfer process. In the development tenant, a project is created, and objects are assigned to begin the process. The scope of the objects and data should be limited at first and then expanded after each successful load. The migration project can be copied once a successful test has been executed.

Populating Data into the Migration Template

In this task, the project team will populate the data extracted from your legacy system into the migration templates available from within the migration project. Figure 5.4 shows the structure of the load template, including descriptions of all fields. Always use the latest templates provided by the SAP S/4HANA migration cockpit for your release and version. Note that the default size limit for each upload file is 100 MB. Multiple files can be added to a ZIP file, but the combined size cannot exceed 100 MB.

Field List for Migration Object: Bank						
Version SAPSCORE 126 - Standard Scope - 12.07.2021 © Copyright SAP SE. All rights reserved.						
Sheet Name	Group Name	Field Description	Importance	Type	Length	Decimal
Bank Master (mandatory)						
	Key	Bank Country/Region Key	mandatory for sheet	Text	80	
		Bank Key	mandatory for sheet	Text	80	
	Address	Name of Bank	mandatory for sheet	Text	60	
		Region (State, Province, Country)		Text	80	
		House Number and Street		Text	35	
		City		Text	35	
		Bank Branch		Text	40	
	Control Data	SWIFT Code for International		Text	11	
		Bank Number		Text	15	
		Bank Group (Bank Network)		Text	2	
	Control Indicator	Do Not Overwrite Existing Data		Text	1	

Figure 5.4 Data Migration Template: Field List

Uploading Data into SAP S/4HANA

In the realize phase, iterations of data loads are performed to perfect the data and process. One or more filled-out template files for each migration object are loaded via the project and stored in the staging area of the SAP S/4HANA migration cockpit. The uploaded files can be viewed, deleted, and uploaded again if you encounter errors. For every object in the project, you can find online documentation on how to test and validate the migrated data.

Validating Data and Performing Value Mapping

After the data is loaded into the system, the system validates the data and outputs the errors warnings. After processing the output, value mapping is performed. Value mapping allows for data transformation to occur based on mappings that are proposed, manually entered, or uploaded. The system will, by default, propose mapping values for required objects, but each must be confirmed before proceeding.

Simulating the Data Migration

We recommend that the project team execute a simulation of the data load using the SAP S/4HANA migration cockpit. This activity will simulate the migration of your data through the relevant application interfaces without committing the data to your actual database tables. The team should resolve any issues resulting from the simulation process, which may require adjusting configuration or data.

Executing the Data Migration

After all the steps have been performed, and the project team is confident in the data quality, you can proceed with loading the legacy data into the system. See Figure 5.5 for an example data migration project in the SAP S/4HANA migration cockpit.

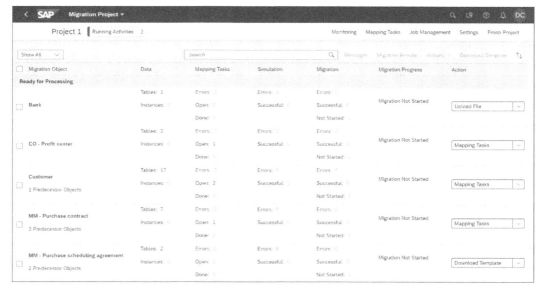

Figure 5.5 Data Migration Project

This migration can be performed directly or via background processing. By completing this step, the project team delivers the master and transactional data required by SAP S/4HANA Cloud to run transactions and complete the testing cycles to determine production readiness.

The cutover sequence is maintained and verified so that the process can be repeated in the production environment as part of the production cutover.

5.2.3   Data Migration Execution Using Direct Transfer

As an alternative to data migration using staging tables, the SAP S/4HANA migration cockpit can be connected directly to a supported SAP ERP system. By connecting directly to another SAP ERP system, the staging tables are eliminated, simplifying the process and reducing the overall throughput time. At the time of writing, direct transfer is only supported by SAP S/4HANA and SAP S/4HANA Cloud, private edition.

Further Resources

For more information, see SAP Note 2747566.

5.3   Extensibility

Most SAP S/4HANA and SAP S/4HANA Cloud systems can be extended to fulfill companies' needs. Therefore, extensibility includes changes to software behavior that go beyond the capabilities of business configuration, data model extensions, data exposure and integration, layout changes to UIs or forms and reports, and creation of new UIs and a business's own applications.

Figure 5.6 shows the big picture of SAP S/4HANA Cloud extensibility options.

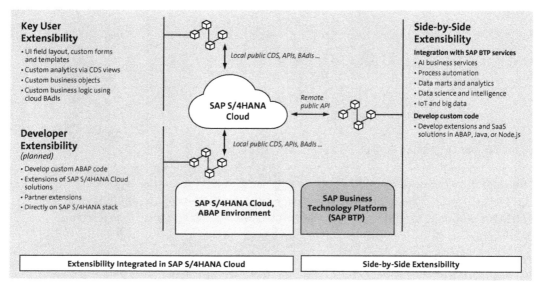

Figure 5.6   SAP S/4HANA Cloud Extensibility: Big Picture

As you can see, there are three approaches to extensibility, which we'll discuss in the following sections.

5.3.1   Key User Extensibility

This approach is taken directly within the software stack and allows for extensibility directly in the application—for example, field extensibility or application logic extensibility. This allows standard functionalities to be adapted to user requirements without the need for any external tools. Some key features of key user extensibility are as follows (see Figure 5.7):

- Adapts standard functionalities to user and business requirements
- Ranges from small UI adaptations to complex custom business logic
- Suited for technical and nontechnical users
- Update-proof changes

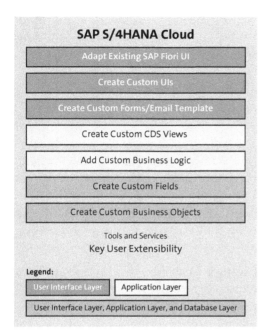

Figure 5.7 Key User Extensibility

5.3.2   Developer Extensibility

Developer extensibility is available to users in SAP S/4HANA Cloud and SAP S/4HANA. Users of SAP S/4HANA Cloud in a three-system landscape have access to SAP S/4HANA Cloud, ABAP environment inside the application stack, as shown previously in Figure 5.6. Users of SAP S/4HANA Cloud, private edition and SAP S/4HANA have access to the full ABAP environment inside their solution, which can be used for extending the application. We will continue to focus on developer extensibility in the context of SAP S/4HANA Cloud as that is a newly introduced capability available to SAP S/4HANA Cloud users.

SAP S/4HANA Cloud, ABAP environment allows you to create development projects in the SAP S/4HANA Cloud system. It gives you the opportunity to develop cloud-ready and upgrade-stable custom ABAP code on SAP S/4HANA Cloud, combining the benefits of custom ABAP code with the required restrictions for cloud readiness and with the SAP S/4HANA programming model to build SAP Fiori apps. Some key features of developer extensibility are as follows:

- Develop custom ABAP code inside SAP S/4HANA Cloud
- Extensions of SAP S/4HANA Cloud solutions
- Partner extensions
- Directly on SAP S/4HANA stack

This additional capability now allows organizations and individuals with existing ABAP knowledge to continue developing applications and extensions for SAP S/4HANA Cloud. For more details about development in the ABAP environment, visit *http://s-prs.co/v546307*.

5.3.3   Side-by-Side Extensibility

In addition to key user extensibility and developer extensibility, you can use side-by-side extensibility to create large extensions and standalone applications that integrate with your SAP S/4HANA solution. This approach uses all the capabilities of SAP BTP as a platform as a service (PaaS) environment to create the required capabilities in a dedicated application running on SAP BTP. This application is then integrated with the SAP S/4HANA Cloud or SAP S/4HANA solution using published APIs that you can access on the SAP Business API Hub at *http://api.sap.com*.

This approach is used for extensions of application capabilities that can't be achieved with key user extensibility or developer extensibility and that are better stored in separate applications for purposes of upgradability or maintenance. This includes the following and can integrate with both cloud and on-premise versions:

- Developing dependent extensions
- Developing your own custom application
- Consuming existing apps
- Partner-delivered applications extending SAP solution capabilities

5.3.4   Artificial Intelligence Technologies

Organizations should explore the use of artificial intelligence technologies such as robotic process automation (RPA), artificial intelligence (AI), and machine learning in their implementation of SAP S/4HANA Cloud to identify and implement intelligent business processes in their business. SAP Activate includes exploration, identification and use of intelligent technologies as part of the extensibility workstream. They are closely linked with the application design and configuration workstream as they extend the capabilities of the solution and can significantly improve the speed of decision-making, as well as automate processes that are executed manually.

SAP added dedicated deliverables and tasks into the methodology to emphasize the need to explore this area with more focus even in your initial implementation of an SAP S/4HANA solution. Figure 5.8 shows a view of these dedicated deliverables and tasks in the SAP Activate methodology for SAP S/4HANA Cloud.

Figure 5.8 AI-Specific Deliverables through Lifecycle

In addition to the inclusion of the deliverables and tasks, you can find a dedicated set of accelerators for handling this topic during the implementation project. Project teams should use the business-driven configuration questionnaire for AI automation early in the project to start exploring the intelligent technology scenarios for their organizations. This accelerator provides questions to ask during the fit-to-standard workshop and should be used to start surfacing opportunities to use intelligent technology in the business processes in the organization prior to and during the workshops. Users of SAP Activate will find additional accelerators in AI-related tasks. The accelerators provide access to AI technologies–related documents and templates through their implementation journey. An example of a task for reviewing RPA is shown in Figure 5.9. It includes accelerators to help capture the requirements and understand the RPA capabilities, plus links to additional knowledge base articles outlining a release strategy for RPA.

SAP Activate for SAP S/4HANA Cloud includes a dedicated tag for identification of these AI-related deliverables, tasks, and accelerators that you can find in the Roadmap Viewer in the **More** filter area under the title **Artificial Intelligence Technology**.

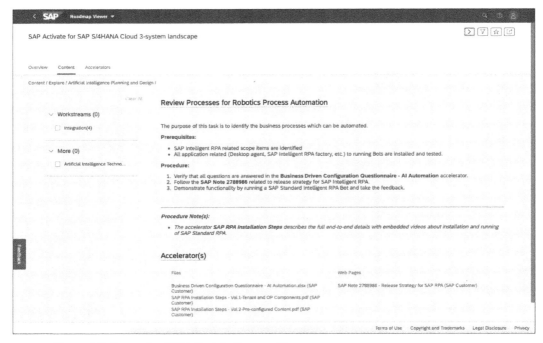

Figure 5.9 Example of RPA Task in Prepare Phase

5.3.5   Tools and Implementation

The following resources are used for learning about extending the SAP S/4HANA Cloud and SAP S/4HANA applications:

- **SAP Extensibility Explorer**
  The SAP Extensibility Explorer provides a comprehensive overview of extension options for SAP S/4HANA Cloud. You can explore a range of extensibility patterns using different sample scenarios.

> **Further Resources**
>
> For more information about SAP Extensibility Explorer, see *http://s-prs.co/v502719*.

- **SAP API Business Hub**
  SAP API Business Hub is a central, publicly available overview of APIs on SAP **BTP**. It includes API design and API documentation for each API or service. You can access it at *https://api.sap.com*. You can also connect your SAP S/4HANA Cloud application to this service in order to test the APIs live.

The extensibility tools are designed for the cloud but are also made available in the on-premise solution. Both cloud and on-premise have some differences with respect to transport setup and gateway setup. In the on-premise version, the key user extensibility and classical ABAP development tools can be used in parallel.

The various phases of implementation related to extensibility in cloud and on-premise solutions are shown in Figure 5.10:

1. **Prepare phase**

   During the prepare phase of the implementation, the project team will prepare a list of all the extensions required for smooth running of the company's business. The result of these discussions will be a Microsoft Excel file with a consolidated list of extensions. Alternatively, the initial list of extensions can be captured in SAP Cloud ALM as the basis for the detailed design activities during the fit-to-standard workshop in the explore phase.

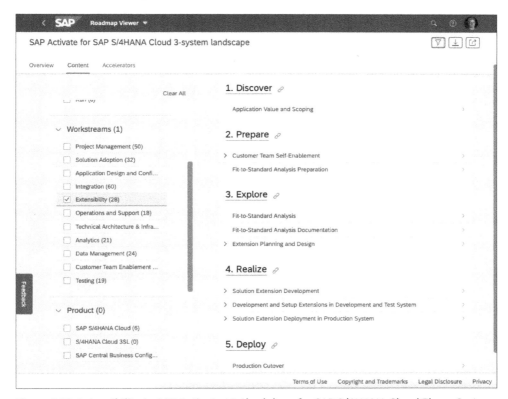

Figure 5.10 Extensibility in SAP Activate Methodology for SAP S/4HANA Cloud Three-System Landscape

2. **Explore phase**

   During this phase, the project team should check for available products and review the details for the extensions collected in the prepare phase. After dividing the extensions among key user extensibility, developer extensibility, and side-by-side extensibility, the company does a thorough review and sign-off of each extension.

The various workshops are conducted by each LoB to identify the list of extensions after reviewing the existing processes in SAP Best Practices flows. The extensions should be reviewed and validated against the golden rules we introduced in Chapter 2, Section 2.4.

3. **Realize phase**
   During this phase, all the approved extensions are developed and tested in the development system and test system. Once passed in the testing, all extensions are transported to the production system and are deployed to productive use.

5.4   Integration

An intelligent enterprise is an integrated enterprise. All enterprises are looking to achieve three main scenarios using integration platforms: real-time digital interactions, simplified connected experiences, and process excellence. To do so, the organizations aim to integrate the various systems in their business and IT environments. SAP provides a means to do that in the SAP Integration Suite on SAP BTP, which helps you do the following:

- Integrate anything (people, things, processes, data, and applications), anywhere (on-premise, in the cloud, using edge computing), with versatile cloud integration.
- Share real-time data with your supply chain, business networks, and customers with well-managed APIs.
- Orchestrate people, processes, events, and things with process and data integration.
- Automate decision-making with dynamic business rules.
- Enable omnichannel experiences across devices and channels with well-managed APIs.
- Streamline workflows.

The various integration options for SAP S/4HANA are as follows:

- **SAP APIs**
  SAP releases APIs to enable companies digitizing their business to securely connect apps to other systems. The published SAP APIs can be found at *http://s-prs.co/v502720* (cloud) and *http://s-prs.co/v502721* (on-premise).
- **Core data service (CDS) views**
  SAP releases CDS views to read data from the SAP S/4HANA system as OData services.
- **Traditional APIs**
  Business Application Programming Interfaces (BAPIs)/IDocs can be used to connect SAP S/4HANA Cloud with SAP on-premise applications.

The SAP Activate methodology implementation roadmaps help by providing a recommendation list of deliverables in each phase and a process description in the form of tasks and accelerators (templates, examples, guides, and web links) in a user-friendly format to a project team. Whatever SAP S/4HANA solution you're implementing—SAP S/4HANA Cloud, SAP S/4HANA Cloud, private edition, or SAP S/4HANA—SAP Activate offers a wide range of accelerators and step-by-step processes for implementing any solution.

Figure 5.11 shows the integration-relevant deliverables and tasks in the SAP Activate methodology for SAP S/4HANA Cloud implementation.

Figure 5.11 Integration Workstream in SAP Activate Methodology for SAP S/4HANA Cloud

The various phases of the SAP Activate methodology for any SAP S/4HANA solution for integration are discussed in the following sections.

5.4.1   Prepare

In the prepare phase, the project team is formed, the scope is refined, and the project gets underway. From the integration standpoint, there are several key decisions and steps that the team needs to walk through that we'll explain in this section.

Let's examine the key deliverables:

- **SAP supporting implementation tools access**
  To begin, we start with accessing the supporting implementation tools. In this deliverable, the company gets access to various tools available in SAP S/4HANA Cloud, such as the following:
  - Request for access to SAP Integration Suite on SAP BTP
  - Request for Cloud Integration Automation service

- **Company team self-enablement**
  Next, the company moves on to team self-enablement. The company team will read all the help related to various tools, which will be helpful in the implementation process. Some of these tools are as follows:
  - **Cloud Integration Automation service**
    This is a cloud service that allows users to create their own guided, partially automated procedures for the integration of scenarios. After a procedure is defined and is available, the service can help companies do the following:
    - Role-based execution: Tasks are assigned to the right person based on role assignments.
    - Integrated parameter management: Data can be entered once and reused throughout the workflow.
    - System landscape information: This information is available as a dropdown list from known company SAP systems.
    - Traceability of activity: Information is provided on who did which steps in the integration.
  - **Open connectors**
    The various accelerators provided in the SAP Activate methodology will help users familiarize themselves with open connectors on SAP BTP for customer-driven integration and side-by-side extensions.
  - **Business-to-business (B2B) integrations using Electronic Data Interchange (EDI)**
    This provides information about integration between SAP S/4HANA and third-party systems (e.g., suppliers and buyers) leveraging API-enabled EDI integration. There are various scope items available under EDI integration.
  - **Project plans, schedule, and budget**
    All the planning activities related to the early stages of a project and its schedule and budget are completed in the next deliverable. The alignment of project schedules and key milestones as follows are considered:

- Different system landscape provisioning
- System landscape configuration start date
- System landscape configuration completion date
- Testing in the quality system landscape and the production system landscape
- System operations related to the software update schedule

- **Business-driven configuration assessment**
  In the business-driven configuration assessment deliverable, various accelerators are provided in the SAP Activate methodology related to questionnaires for each LoB and including questions related to integration considerations.

- **Fit-to-standard analysis preparation**
  Finally, for fit-to-standard analysis preparation, the company will download the SAP Best Practices content and select the various scope items corresponding to their business needs. A list of initial integrations and APIs is provided as an accelerator for preparing the list of the company's current integrations.

5.4.2   Explore

In this phase, the project scope is validated, and it's confirmed that the business requirements can be satisfied by selecting the SAP Best Practices scope items. Any gaps and configuration values are added to the backlog for use in the next phase.

Let's walk through the key deliverables:

- **Fit-to-standard analysis**
  The various LoB-specific workshops are conducted, and SAP Best Practices flows are reviewed. The various accelerators are provided in each roadmap. During the fit-to-standard workshops, the project team identifies the required integration requirements and captures them in SAP Cloud ALM.

- **Solution definition**
  All the documentation captured in each workshop is complete. This includes the detailing of the integration requirements into a formalized set of documented requirements.

- **Integration planning and design**
  The optimized list of integrations is planned and designed, which will be tested in the realize phase of the implementation. The various integrations listed are delegated to the integration expert team that will plan, map, and draft the step-by-step process for each integration. The various tasks involved in this deliverable are as follows:
  - Scenario options for integration
  - Customer-driven integrations

- Customer-driven integrations using open connectors
- B2B integrations using EDI
- Customer-driven integrations with SAP Integration Suite iFlows

5.4.3   Realize

During this phase, both functional and technical implementation takes place. All required interfaces are implemented as designed in the explore phase. All integrations are set up and tested in the test system.

In SAP S/4HANA Cloud, the integrations with SAP SuccessFactors Employee Central are set up in the development and test system landscape, where various users with SAP SuccessFactors Employee Central integrations are created. After it's successfully tested in the quality assurance system landscape, SAP SuccessFactors Employee Central is integrated in the production system by configuring the integration with SAP Success-Factors Employee Central and creating the users for SAP SuccessFactors Employee Central.

In all the various solutions, the setup instructions for customer-driven integrations are written up and reviewed. An accelerator is already available in the explore phase to consolidate all the integration scenarios in the scope of the company's project.

After all the integrations are set up and approved in the quality system landscape, the setup is completed in the production system landscape.

5.5   Testing

SAP Activate covers a range of testing processes and activities across the many SAP solutions, including SAP S/4HANA, SAP S/4HANA Cloud, and SAP S/4HANA Cloud, private edition. This section will guide you on how the testing workstream activities are executed and how the upgrade testing activities are run.

5.5.1   SAP S/4HANA Cloud

The SAP S/4HANA Cloud three-system landscape implementation roadmap starts project teams with self-enablement on test management and tools to guide them related to SAP Cloud ALM and the test automation tool for SAP S/4HANA Cloud. The project team during this time should be reviewing the test management tool and application lifecycle management (ALM) tool to understand the foundational concepts and tutorials for self-enablement. Enablement of the testing processes should be understood and learned by all testing members.

The next activity includes configuring the test automation tool for SAP S/4HANA Cloud. The tool is connected to the SAP S/4HANA Cloud quality assurance system, which is where the business/test users are added and maintained with their respective roles to launch the solution applications. Following the configuring of the test automation tool for SAP S/4HANA Cloud, the team needs to define the details of the test case. SAP Best Practices Explorer has all the predelivered scope items, process flows, test scripts, and additional documentation needed for the testing team to understand the business processes and how they are connected. The test case is a combination of a test process and test data. A test process can be tested with several test data variants. Where possible, we recommend that the master data within your test data be data sets that are also available in your productive environment (e.g., material master).

As with other solutions as well, test planning activities are performed in the explore phase to set the stage for the remainder of the testing workstream for the project deployment. Paying extra attention to details in the beginning stages of planning will minimize the risk of gaps, rework, setbacks, and additional changes. This is where the test strategy is outlined that covers the testing objectives and assumptions, scope, testing cycles, approach, tools, defect management, and roles and responsibilities.

The test scope needs to be determined early for a project, regardless of whether the project is executed independently or as part of a release, to ensure the testing environments and materials are available for execution. With such a variety of testing cycles available (e.g., unit, string, business process test, user acceptance, regression test, and postupgrade test), it's important to define the cycles that are required to support the planned conversion event.

After the explore phase testing activities have concluded, the realize phase begins. In this phase, test preparation and execution are the main activities the team executes. Test preparation includes setting up the users in the test automation tool with the appropriate roles. Then, the test cases are defined for end-to-end business processes (SAP Best Practices Explorer provides predelivered process flows and test scripts), and the team defines the test data for the test case, which is a combination of a test process with test data. It is recommended to reuse test cases as much as possible, or to copy them and adapt them by adding/removing steps or changing steps. In addition, your own test cases can be created via the recording functionality. You can create custom test processes by copying standard test processes and/or by creating a new custom test process. The same goes for editing custom test processes: you can adjust test process steps and/or edit the action data in the test process steps.

Following defining the test case, the project team prepares the automated test scripts in the test automation tool for SAP S/4HANA Cloud, which covers individual business scenarios and test data. With the solution, standard test automations are delivered as mentioned previously with the SAP Best Practices Explorer content and test scripts. The team should allow for automated testing via automated test scripts that are delivered by SAP, adapted, or created by the company. Some business processes can't be automated via the test automation tool for SAP S/4HANA Cloud, such as integration processes, analytics, or output documents. For such processes or process steps, a manual test needs to be considered.

Test Automation Tool

SAP S/4HANA Cloud offers an excellent suite for testing deliverables for project teams and companies alike. The built-in testing platform in the test automation tool gives you the ability to create manual and customized test cases for more unique business processes, along with the option to leverage predelivered test scripts that are more streamlined and are ready immediately for testing activities.

Per industry standards, we strongly recommend project teams use the test automation tool for SAP S/4HANA Cloud within the solution due to its many advantages.

In addition, the SAP S/4HANA Cloud testing environment offers the benefit of having the SAP team run the predelivered test scripts—after upgrade—to ensure the upgrade updates run smoothly (with the consent of the company/project team to allow SAP to run this in the backend). This adds an extra benefit layer of confirming that the test scripts don't have any bugs, defects, or failures so that the company can have peace of mind. Letting SAP take on this action versus the company executing these processes saves time.

The option of adding manual test cases and customized test cases is also available if additional test scripts beyond the predelivered ones are needed. SAP encourages the company/project team to minimize the use of custom and manual test scripts because as each upgrade release occurs, the test scripts need to be evaluated to ensure they are still running smoothly and accurately. This is required because the automated test tool doesn't test these types of custom scripts, adding additional time and effort to confirm that the steps in these cases were run successfully.

To create and schedule the test plan in the test automation tool for SAP S/4HANA Cloud, you include standard and/or custom test processes in the sequence that defines the end-to-end business flow. Data should be reviewed and/or modified using data variants. In addition, the team will modify action data in customer-specific automated test scripts and change the visibility of the test process in the Manage Your Test Processes app.

Next, the test plan is executed. With the test automation tool for SAP S/4HANA Cloud, test scripts can be easily run in the solution and give you status updates during the test execution process, including screenshots, status progress (i.e., **Pass, Failed, In Progress**), and the ability to run test scripts with execution schedules that can be run in the background. Figure 5.12 shows an example of one test plan that can be scheduled to execute and one test plan that has failed.

Figure 5.12 Test Your Processes App with Test Plan Execution Details

After the test plan has been executed, identified errors must be resolved and rerun to ensure accuracy. After all errors have been resolved, the team generates, views, and analyzes the report of the test results shown under **Test Processes**, for either **Post-Upgrade Tests** or **Customer Tests** in the **Test Plan Details** dashboard available in SAP S/4HANA Cloud.

The last set of activities of the realize phase are performed under the automated test execution for SAP S/4HANA Cloud deliverable: execute the test plan, correct and rerun the test plan, and perform test execution analysis and reporting.

After the test planning, the test execution is performed to execute the testing cycles. The chosen test suite is utilized (e.g., SAP Cloud ALM and test automation tool), and the outcomes of the analysis and reporting are documented.

The test case and incident message(s) within the test tool(s) are linked to each other and can be called directly from status reporting for further analysis. After all activities in the realize phase are executed and completed, the next set of testing activities need to be considered; these are available in the SAP Activate for Upgrade of SAP S/4HANA Cloud Three-System Landscape implementation roadmap.

Project teams will utilize the direction for the testing workstream in this implementation roadmap for regression tests and regression test execution. This upgrade roadmap will bring us to regression testing first. Within the regression test deliverable, we will ensure we are prepared for the postupgrade testing by SAP for live customers (this is done for a limited set of SAP S/4HANA Cloud applications, and only for productive customers). The test plans are generated by SAP and then executed in the customer's test system. Keep in mind that the team must consent for this activity to occur; this consent can be given directly in the test automation tool. If consent is not given, the postupgrade test execution activities will not be performed (consent needs to be given at least two weeks prior to the start of the upgrade). Reviewing the postupgrade test accelerators is strongly recommended to ensure a smooth upgrade process. The team will analyze the postupgrade test results via the test automation tool to review the statuses and successful execution of the test results. In addition, under the regression test deliverable, preparation of test cases that need to be executed by the customer is performed.

To close out the final set of testing activities, regression test execution is done. This is where the regression tests are executed in the solution to validate functionalities that were previously tested to ensure they are still working as designed after the changes are made (such as an upgrade, ongoing enhancements, and additional improvements). Re-execution of failed test plans will need to be done after errors have been corrected.

5.5.2   SAP S/4HANA Cloud, Private Edition

The testing workstream in the SAP S/4HANA Cloud, private edition implementation roadmap guides project teams through the test planning, preparation, execution, and quarterly release activities for a successful testing outcome. The SAP Activate Roadmap Viewer includes the entire SAP Activate workstream suite and can be filtered on workstreams, such as testing, for a more focused view of the upcoming testing activities and milestones.

The first step in the testing workstream starts in the prepare phase to enable the team in the testing tools being used for the project as they relate to testing to maximize enablement and learning, create efficiencies in later deliverables (i.e., SAP Cloud ALM and SAP Solution Manager), and set foundational knowledge for the project.

In the explore phase, we focus on test planning activities, including test strategy creation, determining the test scope, and creating and scheduling an overall test plan. When creating the test strategy, the elements of the test strategy and documentation are agreed upon prior to starting testing and signed off on by the team (typically the customer and implementation partner) to define how testing will be performed and completed in the project. Next, the determination of the test scope and creation and scheduling the overall test plan occurs. The test scope needs to be determined early for a project, regardless of whether the project is executed independently or as part of a release, to ensure the testing environments and materials are available for execution. With such a variety of testing cycles available (e.g., integration, regression, performance, cutover, and UAT), it's important to define the cycles that are required to support the planned conversion event. Detailed test planning will cover the dependencies, tasks, criteria, resources, and duration of testing timeframes to outline the end-to-end testing activities during the project implementation. To close out the explore phase, the creation and scheduling of a detailed test plan is performed by the team. This will allow for all scenarios that may occur to optimally have the schedule documented to cover tasks, dependencies, and durations and thus mitigate risk.

At the start of the realize phase, the project team starts the testing preparation activities, which include prerequisites such as preparing for the continuous releases that occur mid-project, identifying the availability of the testers, using a test management system, or ensuring the availability and accessibility of selected test automation tools and chosen test management tools (such as SAP Solution Manager and SAP Cloud ALM).

The project team must understand the changes that have occurred at the mid-implementation point of the project (where an upgrade has occurred) to ensure that the impact of the project has been addressed, understood, and adapted. The project kickoff meeting occurs, and the team is onboarded with the necessary tool setup, knowledge transfers, and user IDs for the systems needed for the project implementation.

Next, the creation of manual test cases occurs to define the manual test cases and supporting test data to be used for customer solution testing. It is strongly recommended to limit the amount of manual test cases where possible. For automated test cases, the team will utilize the selected test automation tools to create them in the tool directly.

Project teams can edit the action data and change the visibility of the test processes to modify actions in company-specific automated test scripts and to manage the visibility of test cases.

The final set of testing activities in the realize phase is test execution, which includes executing the test plan, correcting and rerunning the test plan to remove any errors or messages, and then analyzing and reporting the testing outcomes. These tasks are based on the previous planning the project team has done in subsequent phases to ensure the most successful execution of testing activities.

5.5.3   SAP S/4HANA

SAP S/4HANA testing is based on on-premise activities and testing tools that are different from the two cloud solutions. With the Transition to SAP S/4HANA implementation roadmap, there are three scenarios that can occur for a project deployment: new implementation, system conversion, and selective data transition (see Chapter 8). We'll focus on the on-premise guidance in this section and walk you through the testing workstream in the explore and realize phases.

The testing workstream begins with the test planning activities that occur in the explore phase. The main activities include the following:

- Familiarizing yourself with the tools in test management
- Setting up test management in SAP Solution Manager
- Determining the test scope
- Performing detailed test planning

It's strongly encouraged to finalize the planning for testing as early as possible and out-line and identify the project scope, testing objectives and assumptions, types of testing, approach, tools, defect management, and roles and responsibilities of the testing team to minimize the number of risks and issues going forward. Having a solid ground for these key elements sets the road for smoother testing activities and milestones for the project deployment.

Teams must understand the test tools in test management and the setup of SAP Solu-tion Manager as these will be used heavily during multiple key events. Multiple resources are available to the project team to fully familiarize themselves with the test-ing learning journey (see Figure 5.13).

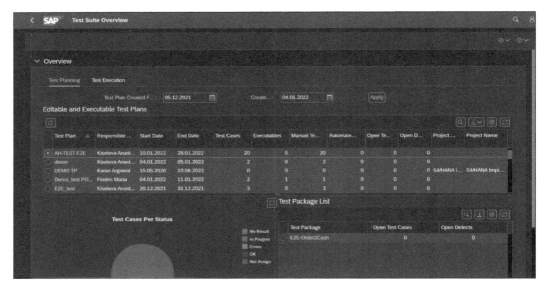

Figure 5.13 SAP Solution Manager Test Suite Overview

Next, the scope of testing for a project, regardless of whether the project is executed independently or as part of a release, needs to be determined early to ensure the testing environments and materials are available for execution. With such a variety of testing cycles available (e.g., integration, regression, performance, cutover, and UAT), it's important to define the cycles that are required to support the planned conversion event.

The last activity, which closes out the explore phase, is detailed test planning. This is where the scoping and planning of the test is required for the transition project to determine which testing cycles are required to meet the quality gate conditions for entering the realize phase. This includes evaluating and enabling test management and the test automation tools to support the testing activities across milestones, as well as executing tasks using ALM best practices for test management and tailoring the tem-plates for the test strategy and functional test plan to meet the project team needs. In addition, the detailed testing plan should support the need to mitigate risks that may arise for the end-state solution and during cutover activities.

The last phase in the testing workstream for the Transition to SAP S/4HANA implementation roadmap encompasses the following:

- Execution plan for the realize phase
- Test preparation
- Test execution

Let's take a dive into these last three key components of the testing workstream.

The purpose of the execution plan for the realize phase is to execute the work defined, manage the sprints/testing as defined previously, log all issues, and document them in the system for traceability. Furthermore, the project team manages the integration, security, and UAT.

Next, the test preparation task and objective is to prepare all business process-related tests according to customer-specific configurations. Preparing the tests is based on determining the evaluation of the existing test materials, which were identified in the explore phase (i.e., testing plan), and other assets for execution of the testing cycles. Any missed test materials and test scripts that are realized must be developed in accordance with the detailed test plan to capture all testing-critical materials and documentation. Testing teams can leverage the fully ready and detailed test scripts, process flows, and other documentation via SAP Best Practices Explorer. SAP Best Practices Explorer provides scope item content and documentation for project teams to leverage and use ready-to-access content and assets easily and quickly with the ease of the tool navigation and the added benefits it provides.

Finally, test execution occurs by performing integration, regression, and UAT testing activities. The testing team prepares a test environment with the required test data as defined previously in the testing workstream. After all criteria have been collected and defined, test execution can begin.

Typical testing processes for the realize phase are as follows:

- Software developers perform unit tests in the development systems. Depending on the type and scope of the test cycle, various functional tests are performed.
- Manual testers are provided with the tester handout document and receive details regarding their test package by email.
- Automated tests are scheduled or started directly.
- Every test that is executed is logged and documented with test notes, and a test status is set manually or automatically.
- If the system responds in an unexpected way during manual testing—for example, if an error message appears—the tester records the incident in the corresponding

ITSM system, attaching screenshots, log messages, and so on. Usually, this also must be done manually, even for automated tests.

- The incident is sent to the persons responsible for the analysis and categorization of defects, who then correct the defect in the development system.
- The correction is transported to the test system according to the existing arrangements and timelines, where it's then retested.

Further Resources

For additional details, see the Test Execution deliverable in the realize phase in the Transition to SAP S/4HANA implementation roadmap in the SAP Activate Roadmap Viewer.

The objective of integration testing is to perform the end-to-end process integration between all SAP and non-SAP components of the solution landscape and validate that all application systems are functioning properly as intended. Integration testing in combination with regression testing ensures that all business scenarios have been tested prior to UAT. UAT is then performed by the users who will be using the solution after the project team is finished with the implementation to ensure the solution is working as it should with the company's various end-to-end business processes. During the test execution in the various testing cycles, defects and bugs should be logged in SAP Solution Manager for defect resolution and tracking. In addition, all testing details are tracked in SAP Solution Manager, as well as in a central tool location. After these two phases are executed and completed, the testing workstream concludes.

5.6   Summary

This chapter introduced the key topic areas of fit-to-standard, configuration, data migration, extensibility, and testing across the solutions. It's important to recall that these and previous activities require added attention to ensure that the planning and execution performed in previous phases was captured correctly and thus avoid any unforeseen setbacks during the project implementation.

Then, configuration was performed to meet the business processes, data migration and extensibility were executed, and test cases and plans were tested to ensure that all the previous workstream activities are in alignment and passed successfully to meet the project standards with the solution capabilities.

In the next chapter, we'll discuss how to apply agile techniques and processes in the content of an SAP S/4HANA Cloud project. We'll describe the agile project team roles, governance, and key agile processes, from release planning through the execution of the sprints that form the foundation for the agile approach.

Chapter 6
Agile Project Delivery

In today's rapidly changing business environment, it's critical for IT organizations to embrace new ways of working to allow for quicker response to changing needs of their business users. An agile way of working empowers project teams to adjust priorities quickly, allowing them to focus on the highest importance items and thus respond to evolving business needs rapidly.

We introduced the SAP Activate approach and key tools in the previous chapters. Now, let's dive into the details of using the agile mindset during the deployment of your SAP S/4HANA-based solution.

Agile has gained traction over the past several years and has become an accepted way of working for IT organizations. While the concepts started with software development, they have been adopted also in other areas of IT and business. SAP Activate was designed as a hybrid approach that leverages the accelerators we talked about in the previous chapters—for example, SAP Best Practices—to set up the ready-to-use system the project team uses for fit-to-standard and ultimately to surface the delta requirements and potential gaps to address throughout the realize phase. SAP has incorporated agile project delivery into the SAP Activate flow to take advantage of the initial backlog coming from fit-to-standard as a basis for agile planning and execution. It allows the team to set a focus for each short time box, called a *sprint*, and deliver value in the form of realized requirements. Sprints are used in the realize phase to work on the highest priority items from the backlog to progressively configure, extend, integrate, and test the system.

In this chapter, we'll go over the details of governance in agile projects, which sets the way team the works in each release and sprint. In addition, we'll discuss the more advanced topic of scaling agile to larger complexity projects with scaling frameworks.

6.1 Roles, Responsibilities, and Governance

SAP Activate leverages the Scrum agile framework for team-level and project-level implementation of agile values, roles, events, and artifacts. The Scrum approach is built around a defined set of values, predefined roles, prescribed processes, and artifacts we'll outline here.

The Scrum framework values are as follows:

- **Courage**
  The teams using the Scrum framework must have courage to do the right thing and work on challenging problems. The team members who follow the Scrum approach will champion the user's point of view in their work and strive to deliver the best solution for the user and business.

- **Focus**
  All people working in the Scrum framework focus on delivering the stated objectives of the sprint and release. This is one of the aligning principles to set the focus for every sprint by committing to the delivery of a specified subset of items from the backlog.

- **Commitment**
  All team members are personally committed to delivering value and agreed-upon deliverables and capabilities.

- **Respect**
  Scrum members have respect for each other and for the users they are working to deliver the solution to.

- **Openness**
  One of the key principles is the openness and transparency that are critical for the agile way of working to function. All Scrum members agree to be open about their challenges and the work they are doing to deliver the goals of the Scrum.

SAP Activate builds on these values and formulates them into principles that are tailored to the context of an SAP project. We reviewed these principles in Chapter 2. In the following sections, we'll take a closer look at the roles, events, and artifacts involved in the Scrum agile framework.

6.1.1   Roles

The Scrum framework defines several key roles, which we'll discuss in the following sections. SAP Activate uses them in addition to SAP project roles, which provide a more detailed profile of the role in the context of SAP project.

Product Owner

The *product owner* is the person responsible for maximizing the value that the Scrum team delivers. The product owner must clearly define the backlog items (e.g., capabilities, key functionality, attributes of the solution) and prioritize the items to give the team direction regarding what is more important to deliver the maximal value.

In SAP projects, the product owner role is played by representatives of the business users. This way, the person in this role can best represent the business user needs and identify the backlog items that help maximize the business value of the solution for the specific group of business users.

Scrum Master

The *Scrum master* role helps the team and product owner follow the Scrum processes and helps with delivery of Scrum artifacts throughout the project. Their responsibility is to educate all team members on principles, procedures, rules, and values. They also often are responsible for scheduling the Scrum events, such as planning meetings, daily standups, or retrospectives.

The Scrum master is typically a team member that takes on the responsibility for educating the team and directing the Scrum events during the project. We've also seen situations where the Scrum master is a dedicated role in the project; such Scrum masters typically serve multiple teams. In our experience, the dedicated Scrum master can serve up to three teams, but not more, as the teams work on a synchronized Scrum heartbeat; this means that the Scrum events are occurring in the same timeframe, limiting the Scrum master's ability to serve more teams.

Team

The Scrum *team* consists of cross-functional experts and professionals brought together to deliver the capabilities stated in the backlog to realize value for the users or business. The team works in an iterative mode, following the sprint model, to deliver increments of work defined in the backlog. Their responsibility is to understand the backlog items and deliver them during the duration of the sprint to reach the definition of done so that the items can be deployed.

Teams in SAP projects consists of cross-functional experts that work on a specific functional or line of business (LoB) area. Each team has a product owner and Scrum master, as well as a group of expert resources, such as business process experts and functional experts. Figure 6.1 shows an example of the team composition in the SAP Activate methodology. However, this isn't the only way the team can be composed.

There are many ways to set up the teams to support the objectives of your project. Some roles and skills may not be available to each Scrum team via a dedicated resource (e.g., user experience [UX] expert or operational support), and multiple Scrum teams share the capacity of the expert in each sprint. In such cases, it's important that each Scrum team plans for the required capacity of such shared resources in the sprint planning session to ensure they have all the resources needed to deliver the backlogged items the team is committing to complete in a particular sprint.

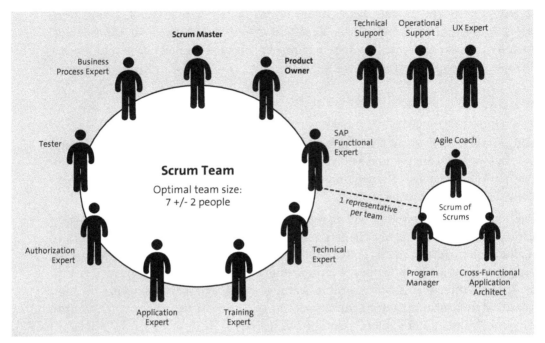

Figure 6.1 Example Setup for Agile Project Team in SAP Project

The second consideration for Scrum team composition is the use of development factories, centralized data management teams, or central organizational change management (OCM)/training teams (centralized function teams). In such cases, the Scrum team also needs to create respective backlog items for such dedicated teams to ensure the centralized function teams deliver what the Scrum team needs and in the agreed-upon timeframe. Think, for example, about the delivery of test data for sprint testing activities that is supported by a centralized data migration team. A similar situation may apply for specific data that Scrum teams need for running a sprint review session to demonstrate the delivered functionality on data like that of the company to gain buy-in from business users and product owners.

In addition, note the circle on the right side of Figure 6.1, which shows the regular (typically weekly) meeting between all Scrum team representatives (finance, sales and distribution, etc.) to work on cross-Scrum team topics. This is extremely important for highly integrated solutions such as SAP where many configuration and setup decisions in one area have an impact on other areas, such as the definition of an organizational structure or setup of the chart of accounts.

In the context of SAP S/4HANA projects, the project team typically consists of multiple Scrum teams with dedicated product owners responsible for specific functional or business areas and an assigned Scrum master, as shown in Figure 6.2.

For example, the project may consist of the following Scrum teams structured around the key functional areas of the company's solution:

- Finance
- Sales and distribution
- Procurement
- Manufacturing

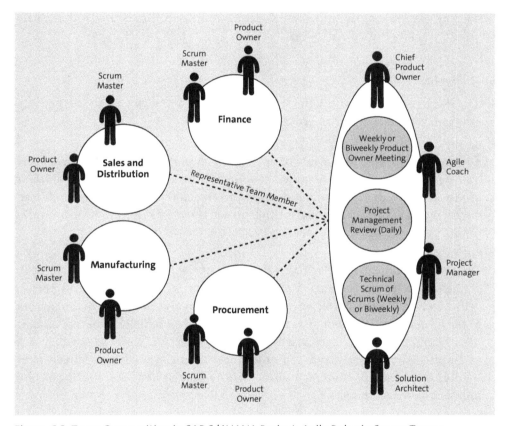

Figure 6.2 Team Composition in SAP S/4HANA Project: Agile Roles in Scrum Teams

It's important to coordinate among these Scrum teams, and the Scrum approach is extended by having the following coordination meetings:

- Weekly (or biweekly) meetings of all product owners to ensure consistent definition of the product in the backlog, including the key integrations
- Daily project reviews to identify and address any challenges or issues that the individual Scrum team can't address on its own and that need support from the project manager or project leadership

- Weekly (or biweekly) Scrum of Scrums meetings to coordinate work on cross-team topics related to configuration and setup that impacts multiple Scrum teams

The composition of the Scrum teams often needs to reflect specific situations. For example, organizations using remote development factories or centralized data management functions will impact the composition of your Scrum teams. In such cases, the project team may have two layers of Scrum team dependencies; for example, the development objects (requiring coding and testing) defined in the finance Scrum team are fulfilled by the dedicated development factory Scrum team. This is similar to the data preparation example we discussed earlier.

6.1.2 Events

Several events also occur within the Scrum framework, and teams using SAP Activate use the same events to run their project:

- **Sprint**
  A sprint is a predefined time box of up to a month during which the team delivers backlog items to satisfy the definition of done. A sprint is an entity that Scrum teams use to structure the incremental delivery of value and it has a defined and fixed duration that doesn't change during the project. During the sprint, the team works toward delivery of the sprint goal that has been set in the beginning.

- **Sprint planning**
  The team performs this collaborative exercise at the beginning of each sprint to define the sprint goal and agree on the backlog items that the team commits to deliver during the sprint. During this event, the team also details the required work to the level that helps them assess feasibility and effort to deliver specific backlog items, including the resources that are required to reach the sprint goal (going back to the discussion about shared teams for data or coding). The team effectively pulls selected backlog items from the backlog to the sprint backlog, thus making a commitment to deliver them.

- **Daily Scrum**
  Also called the daily standup meeting, the purpose of this meeting is to share information among the team members about the work they are doing, what they plan to do next, and whether they are facing any challenges or blockers. The meeting is set up by the Scrum master, but it isn't a status report to the Scrum master; instead, the team communicates to each other in short sessions every day (about 15 minutes long). The goal is to identify points of synergy where team members can help each other and surface challenges and blockers that the team members need help with (it's the role of the Scrum master to support resolution of these challenges if team members are unable to resolve them on their own).

- **Sprint review**
  During this event that is scheduled at the end of the sprint, the team demonstrates

the delivered backlog items to the product owner and interested stakeholders. The backlog items are either accepted as delivered and then marked appropriately in the backlog, or they remain in the backlog if there are gaps between what was delivered and the acceptance criteria according to the definition of done. During this event, the product owner and team work jointly to realign the backlog items to ensure that the backlog still reflects the priorities and maximizes value delivery.

- **Sprint retrospective**
The team holds a retrospective at the end of each sprint to identify what to keep, what to drop, and what to change or add to their execution of the Scrum process. This event is one of the most critical ones for adapting the approach to the team and to mature the agile practices. Teams often identify sources of waste and are able to optimize them very quickly by agreeing to work on that particular improvement in the next sprint.

We'll review the use of Scrum events in the course of delivering SAP projects in Section 6.3.2.

The SAP Activate methodology provides additional details about how to implement these events in the context of the SAP project. They are embedded in the specific deliverables and tasks in the methodology. You'll find them in the project management workstream as defined tasks with additional guides attached as accelerators. Figure 6.3 shows an example of the **Plan and Execute Agile Sprints** task in the **SAP Activate Methodology for SAP S/4HANA Cloud** implementation roadmap in the Roadmap Viewer.

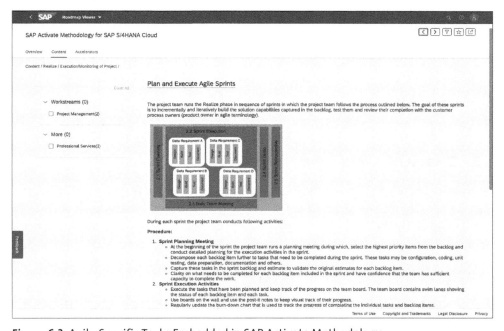

Figure 6.3 Agile-Specific Tasks Embedded in SAP Activate Methodology

6.1.3   Artifacts

During the execution of agile processes, the team will produce a number of artifacts. Scrum defines three key artifacts:

1. **Product backlog (or backlog, in short)**
   The backlog is a place that contains an ordered (prioritized) list of backlog items that reflect everything that needs to be delivered in the product. As we mentioned in Section 6.1.1, the product owner is responsible for maintaining the backlog, including the contents, prioritization, and sequencing.

> **Product Backlog versus ASAP Blueprint**
>
> The product backlog is a living document that continues to evolve during the course of the project, unlike an ASAP blueprint, which used to be created in the ASAP methodology and was defined early in the project and frozen by a formal sign-off. The project team will continue to adjust the product backlog during the sprint review. In addition, product owners will continue to groom the backlog during the project execution as preparation for the next sprint to provide the Scrum team with detailed backlog items that can be planned into the sprint.

2. **Sprint backlog**
   The Scrum team commits to deliver this subset of backlog items during the sprint time box. This sets the focus for the team for the duration of the sprint. Typically, the teams detail the work required during the sprint planning discussed in Section 6.1.2.

3. **Increment**
   Increments represent all the backlog items that are delivered during the sprint and meet the definition of done. The team and product owner jointly decide whether to deploy the increment into productive use by users.

We'll discuss the use of these artifacts throughout the rest of this chapter.

6.2   Creating and Managing the Backlog

Fit-to-standard workshops are the mechanism that the project team uses to create the backlog to reflect all the capabilities that the solution needs to deliver to maximize its value to the business. During the solution demo and delta design workshops, the team defines and agrees on the required product capabilities and whether they require additional configuration, extension, or integration. These workshops run in parallel, and the process owners define the initial backlog.

The situation may look something like what is shown in Figure 6.4, where you can see the initial product backlogs defined by product owners in individual workshops (first box at the top-left side). Then the backlog gets consolidated and aligned on the program level. During this exercise, the centralized product backlog reflects the requirements of all teams for feature A in one large backlog item (Scrum teams refer to it as an *epic*) that has subitems from all the teams harmonized so that they can be delivered to the dedicated team during the project. After the central product backlog has been created and the team proceeds to the realize phase, the individual teams will pull backlog items from the central backlog to their team sprint backlogs to drive execution of the requirements.

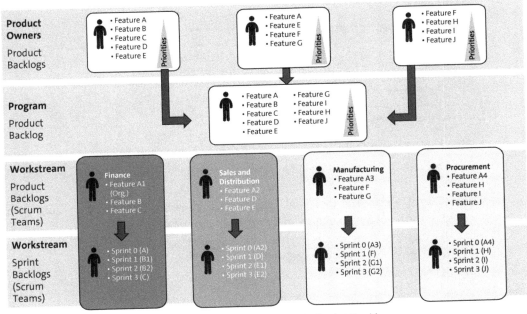

Figure 6.4 Definition of Product Backlog and Realization in Sprint Backlogs

We talked about product ownership in Scrum in Section 6.1.1. In most organizations, the business process ownership is too complex for one central product owner to be defined. This is the case in global organizations that have a multilayered process ownership model that establishes the chief product owner at the top of the hierarchy, with dedicated product owners for each area of the solution that is being implemented. This model allows for the product owners to work directly with their dedicated Scrum team while ensuring the consistent definition of the product along the aligned vision and objectives. Figure 6.5 shows an example of such a setup. Product ownership can be complex in large organizations, and it's important to establish a product ownership hierarchy to involve all key stakeholders in the right stages of the project. Be sure to align the Scrum teams with the product owners for maximum impact.

Another concept for backlog definition is that not all the backlog items are fully detailed right from the beginning. The product owners work through the backlog to help the team understand the backlog items and detail them prior to key activities such as release planning or sprint planning, during which the team needs to have enough information about the backlog item to estimate the effort to complete it and to identify the skills and resources needed for its completion.

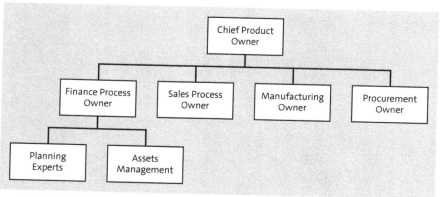

Figure 6.5 Product Ownership Hierarchy Setup along Process Ownership in Organizations

Backlog items are typically created initially in the format of user stories and then detailed to the level that the team members can understand and decide how to implement the required functionality. This detailing process consists of producing more detailed design documents or mock-ups of the desired capabilities. In SAP S/4HANA projects, these additional details could be one or more of the following artifacts:

- Business scenario description or process description document
- Updates to business process flows/process models
- Functional specifications for extensions or custom objects
- Technical integration design document
- Data requirements document
- Authorization concept or requirement document

Teams also will create more technical realization–specific documents in the realize phase during the sprints to detail technical implementation aspects of the capability being implemented. Typically, more documentation is created in projects that use dedicated development factories where the functional and technical teams aren't colocated. The additional documentation is required to ensure that the development factory understands the requirements in detail and can implement them to meet the user needs.

Backlog Management Tools

While SAP Activate comes with a template for backlog that is based on Microsoft Excel, this solution will only work for small teams with a small number of requirements. Larger project teams should consider using Focused Build for SAP Solution Manager for backlog management or SAP Cloud ALM requirement management capabilities. Organizations that already have access to a dedicated backlog management tool such as Jira, VersionOne, or any of the many backlog management tools on the market can use these dedicated tools to manage their backlogs. Both SAP Solution Manager and SAP Cloud ALM allow for linking the requirements with external tools via URLs to keep a connection between the requirement and solution documentation.

We'll now talk about what the team does with the backlog during the realize phase and how they work on the backlog items in the sprint cadence to build up a release.

6.3   Agile Realization

As we outlined in the previous section, the project team and business users jointly define the backlog and prioritize it by business value to establish an agreement between the product owner and the team on what are the highest value (and thus highest priority) capabilities that the system should provide. This prioritization and list of features in the backlog isn't fixed and can change during the course of the project. The backlog serves as the input into the team's planning activities.

In this section, we'll dive deeper into the concepts of releases and sprints. We'll start with the definitions of release and sprint before going into the details of how sprints are planned, executed, and formally closed.

6.3.1   Defining Release and Sprint

Typically, agile projects define the number of releases and at which times these releases will occur; that is, the team defines how they will deliver the product to the business on a product roadmap. The term *release* typically indicates a shipment of working software to the business for its use. Each release is then structured into multiple sprints that allow the team to set a focus for a time-boxed amount of time to deliver the backlog items the team commits to work on. There is no single number of releases and sprints for a typical SAP project, and the duration of releases are a function of the scope, complexity, and team ability to deliver the capabilities in the solution being deployed. The duration of the sprint should be fixed for the project and should be between one week and a maximum of four weeks. Longer sprints lead to issues in maintaining the team's focus and cadence for delivery of the selected features.

Figure 6.6 shows a schematic of how the backlog initially defined, prioritized, and estimated in the explore phase is used to drive the realization of the requirements during the course of the realize phase. One agile release of working software is shown here, but note that in projects there may be multiple releases of working software to the business. In such cases, the project team may go through an abbreviated set of activities from the explore phase to reconfirm the backlog, including prioritization, before starting the next release cycle.

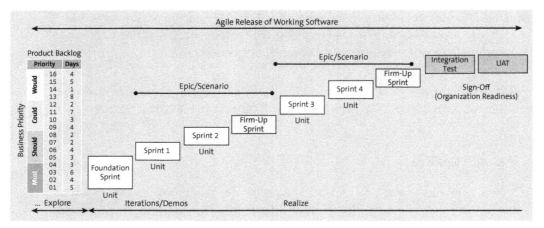

Figure 6.6 Structure of Agile Release in SAP Activate Methodology

The second item shown in Figure 6.6 is the series of sprints in a typical SAP project. The design of the sprints is based on experience from SAP projects using agile and consists of the following types of sprints:

- **Foundation sprint**
  During this very first sprint, the project team focuses on setting up the foundational configuration in the SAP system that will allow the project team to proceed into more complex configuration settings. Typical activities in this sprint in the SAP S/4HANA project include setting up charts of accounts, organizational structures, units of measure, and other general settings for the application.

- **Sprint (also called build sprint)**
  In this traditional sprint, the project team delivers committed features from the backlog and plays them back to the product owners (and business users) at the end of the sprint. We'll cover this further in Section 6.3.2, where we'll explain the activities the project team follows during the time-boxed sprint. During this sprint, the project team conducts unit testing of the features delivered in the sprint. In later sprints, the project team also does string testing, during which they "string together" multiple unit tests to continuously test integration between the components of the system.

- **Firm-up sprint**

  Sometimes these sprints are referred to as *hardening sprints*, and their purpose is to ensure the team continuously integrates the solution and doesn't leave any technical debt in the solution. Traditionally in the SAP S/4HANA environment during this sprint, the finished features are moved from the development system to the quality assurance system using the transport management functionality and are then tested in the quality assurance system. The teams will also finish the solution documentation to capture the rationale for configuration or extensibility decisions. In some cases, the project team may also create end user documentation for the features delivered in the previous sprint to ensure readiness for key user and end user training.

In the next section, we'll go deeper into the concept of the sprint and decompose the activities that the project team does in each of the agile sprint cycles.

6.3.2   Anatomy of a Sprint

The sprint is a time-boxed segment of a project during which the project team follows a set of activities to plan, execute, and deliver the committed functionality; confirm that the features meet the customer needs; and conduct activities to continuously improve execution of the agile process. The objective of the sprint is to deliver working software that is ready to be deployed into production. This doesn't mean that the result of the sprint must be deployed to production, however. As SAP environments are usually highly controlled systems in a company's environment, it's typical to only deploy into the production environment at the end of each agile release, when the features committed for release are ready for deployment.

All the sprint activities are detailed in the following sections, and they follow the structure of the sprint as it's defined in the agile Scrum framework. We'll go over each of the steps in a little more detail and follow the structure shown in Figure 6.7.

Sprint Planning

During the sprint planning, the project team reviews the backlog for stories that are ready to be included in the sprint (some teams refer to these as *sprintable stories*). The project team then takes the highest-value stories from the backlog into the planning meeting. During this meeting, the project team assesses if they understand the story and its acceptance criteria. The project team also discusses what tasks or steps they need to do to complete the story; for example, the story may require configuration, test data, or a special skillset that the team needs to procure from other teams or shared resources. If there is architectural work that needs to be done, for instance, the team will need to secure some capacity of the architect during the course of the sprint to make sure they can deliver the capability in the sprint.

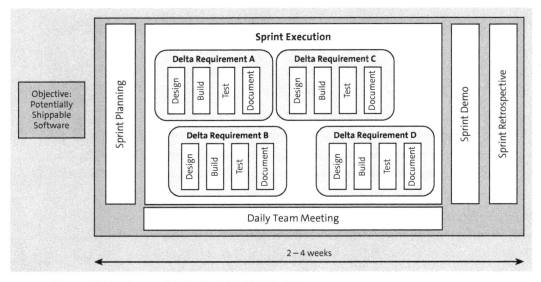

Figure 6.7 Anatomy of Agile Sprint in SAP Activate

During this process, the team also refines the story estimates to make sure the story hasn't been underestimated in the first pass of estimations that happened before the story was decomposed into individual tasks and activities the team will perform. The team then decides whether the story becomes part of the next sprint (and will be included in the sprint backlog for the team).

Typically, sprint planning is conducted as a workshop, with all Scrum team members participating in the process. The workshop duration should be kept to a maximum of one day, but experienced agile project teams may need much less time—from a few hours to half a day—for the sprint planning activities.

Sprint Execution

Execution activities cover a majority of the sprint after the team completes the sprint planning. During execution, the sprint team members select the tasks or stories they will work on and move them to their lane on the Scrum board. They perform the required work, whether it's to configure and test the solution, develop custom code, or set up integration communications arrangements.

The key for the sprint execution is to keep the work visible by using Kanban boards. The objective of making the work visible to everybody in the team and outside the team is to minimize the typical overhead for traditional projects with elaborate reporting processes and meetings. The project team also keeps track of the work spent on each of the stories and estimates the work remaining on each story that has been worked on. The Scrum master is responsible for monitoring the progress with burn-down charts to ensure the team is on track and no backlog items are blocked. The team also communicates regularly in daily team meetings, which we'll discuss next.

Daily Team Meetings

These daily meetings are also called standup meetings and are very short compared to what many consider a meeting. A typical daily standup meeting is between 15 and 20 minutes long, with the objective of exchanging information about what the team needs to work on and whether they have encountered any blockers they need help to resolve. Standup meetings are usually structured as a team standing up in circle, facing each other. Each team member then answers the following three questions:

1. What have I accomplished since the last meeting?

2. What will I work on next?

3. Is there anything blocking my progress?

Some teams also include a fourth question in their daily standup: What is my level of confidence that we'll deliver the sprint as planned? This question is helpful in gauging the confidence level of each team member in delivery of the sprint and assessing if there are hidden challenges that could potentially derail the delivery.

Sprint Demo

Toward the end of the time box, the team schedules a sprint demo session with the product owners (and business key users). The goal of this session is to demonstrate the completed functionality to the business users to gain acceptance and confirm that they meet the user requirements.

The demo is set up as a walkthrough of the backlog items with a live demo of the functionality in the system. It's recommended to minimize the use of tools such as PowerPoint in favor of showing the actual capabilities directly in the system. We also recommend that business users are given the opportunity to try the functionality firsthand after the demo. This will help drive adoption of the new capabilities into the organization. Capabilities that aren't considered complete will remain in the backlog, and the respective backlog items will be updated to indicate the required functional changes and adjustments to the acceptance criteria (for minor fine-tuning of the backlog item).

If the requirement is significantly changed, the product owner needs to create a new backlog item that is then estimated, prioritized, and—in some projects—may need to go through an additional change request process (for fixed price projects, fixed scope projects, or projects that specify this process in the project governance documents).

Sprint Retrospective

The last activity that the team conducts is the retrospective session to identify potential improvements to the agile process, tools, and interaction for the team. Because this session is internally focused on the team, only the team and Scrum master attend this session (product owners and business users are not invited). The session is structured into three steps:

1. **Brainstorm and capture**
   During this stage, the project team discusses how the sprint went, including the high points, what should be kept unchanged, opportunities to improve the process, and potential for eliminating waste. The team members capture their thoughts and input on sticky notes and place them in the collection space on a whiteboard. After enough input has been collected, the Scrum master stops the activity and proceeds to the next step.

2. **Sort and group**
   During this activity, the team groups related input and structures the input into a smaller number of themes that the team can work on in the next step. In some cases, when the team is large, this step is done by the Scrum master and selected team members while others take a short break.

3. **Prioritize and select improvements**
   The last step is to jointly prioritize the improvements that the team wants to drive into the next sprint and select one or, at most, two improvements they will work on in the next sprint.

Retrospectives are critical for all agile project teams because they help teams continuously improve the agile process and tailor it to optimize the throughput and eliminate wasteful activities. In our experience, this is often an underestimated part of the process, and teams that skip this step aren't fully realizing their agile potential as they get stuck executing their agile sprints with no consideration for how the team is evolving and maturing.

6.4   Definition of Ready and Done

The *agile backlog* is a living document that the project team uses to capture all the work that needs to be done during the course of the project to deliver the desired outcome. The backlog typically contains pools of items that are in different states. Agile refers to these as *flow regions* inside the backlog. The typical flow regions in the backlog are items that are in the following states:

- **In sprint**
  These backlog items are currently being worked on in a sprint.

- **Ready to be sprinted**
  These backlog items have yet to be assigned to the sprint; these items are cleared to the team and are then prioritized and estimated.

- **In preparation**
  The team works on clarifying these items with the business users, detailing them, or breaking larger stories into smaller ones that can be done in a sprint (see the Backlog Grooming note box).

- **New**
  These are newly added stories that may not have sufficient detail and need to be clarified with the business users before the team can work on them.

In each flow region, the granularity of the backlog items is different; that is, the backlog stories in the new flow region may be much too large to fit into one sprint or may not be detailed enough for the project team to be able to estimate the effort. The project team regularly does backlog grooming to ensure there are enough stories to be added to the upcoming sprint.

Backlog Grooming

Agile teams need to continuously review the backlog and prepare the backlog items for the next sprint. This exercise is either done as an ongoing process in each sprint, or the team dedicates a time block for this activity to ensure the backlog always has stories ready to be brought into the next sprint or next few sprints. During the grooming, the project team members may break larger backlog items (i.e., epics) into smaller stories that can be inserted into the sprint. The goal of breaking the larger story into smaller ones is to ensure that the sprintable story can be completed during the course of a sprint. During backlog grooming, the team also works with business users to clarify any story that isn't understood by the team or that may need additional detail.

The project team uses the *ready* and *done* states to identify the status of each of the stories. For each story, the project team applies a set of clearly defined criteria to define whether the backlog item (or story) is ready and whether it's completed or done. Project teams can apply this set of criteria on different levels. Traditionally, the criteria are applied for the sprint, and the definition of ready specifies when the team understands the backlog item so they can include it in the scope of the sprint. These criteria generally focus on the following:

- **Understanding why**
  Why is this capability important, what business value does the capability deliver, and who will benefit from this new capability?

- **Understanding what needs to be delivered**
  Sometimes this is also referred to as *acceptance criteria*. In other words, how will the business users judge that the software does what they expect? For example, for a credit card payment on a website, the user can supply a credit card issued by Visa, Mastercard, or American Express or pay with Apple Pay. In such a definition of acceptance criteria, the user can't issue payment via other providers, such as Discover or the Google Pay service.

- **Being able to determine how the story needs to be realized**
  These criteria allow the team to determine the specific tasks and skills needed to

deliver the story. The team needs to be able to determine if the story requires them to do technical design, import specific data, or create a prototype to deliver the capability to the user in the sprint.

Upon satisfying these items, the team can plan the story into an upcoming sprint. You can think of the definition of ready as the contract the team has with the product owner on the minimal required detail for the story to be ready for the sprint.

You can use following definition of ready for stories in the backlog in your SAP S/4HANA project:

- The story is recorded in the backlog.
- The team understands the problem.
- The team understands why this is important.
- This story has been estimated by the team.
- The team knows how to demo this story to the product owner.
- The team has insight into the context of the story.
- Acceptance criteria for the product owner are clear and agreed upon.
- Acceptance criteria for operations are clear and agreed upon.

The definition of done is used in the context of sprints to determine if the backlog items are completely done. Sometimes, the agile teams will refer to the story as "done, done." In other words, the story is completely implemented, and the other supporting items (e.g., documentation and training materials) have been completed. You'll hear project teams also refer to the story as being done without any outstanding technical debt.

The typical definition of done for the sprint in SAP projects has the following characteristics:

- The functionality is configured or built in the system.
- The functionality is unit-tested.
- The functionality is tested by the product owner.
- The functionality is documented; that is, solution documentation exists.
- All outstanding bugs found in testing are fixed.
- The sprint demo has been completed.
- The functionality has been transported to the quality system and is ready for integration and acceptance testing (this may be delayed until the firm-up sprints).

Project teams also apply the definition of done for each release to complete the remaining activities that are needed to be done to deliver an integrated system supporting the business requirements. Here is an example of the definition of done for release in the context of an SAP project:

- The scope of the release is integration tested.
- The scope of the release is user acceptance tested.
- The end user documentation is completed.
- The training material is completed.
- No technical debt remains—that is, no unfinished work or compromises ("We'll get to this later").
- The functionality is ready for release to the business.

The definitions of ready and done serve as gates. They help the team assess whether the backlog story is ready to be worked on (definition of ready), whether the backlog item has been completed (definition of done for a sprint), and whether it's ready to be delivered to the business users (definition of done for the release). SAP Activate provides an explanation of the concept in the accelerator assigned to the agile deliverables and tasks in the methodology and also shows the typical definitions of ready and done that we encourage teams to adapt to their needs.

6.5   SAP Activate in a Scaled Agile Environment

The agile process we've discussed in this chapter is based on the use of Scrum, the agile framework that is most used across various agile teams and industries. In some situations, when the project team size grows, companies use scaling concepts for scaling the execution of agile processes for a large number of project or program team members. One of the best-known scaling frameworks is Scaled Agile Framework (SAFe) maintained by Scaled Agile, Inc. SAFe is designed to scale agile processes for large teams and organizations. It provides a way for organizations to establish a structure for management of portfolios, programs, projects, and deployments. The framework itself is comprehensive and complex, and it caters especially to large programs and organizations.

In our work with SAP clients that adopted SAFe in their IT organizations, we've designed an approach to benefit from the use of the SAP Activate methodology for deployment of SAP solutions while retaining the benefits of SAFe for the organization. In this section, we'll discuss how the two work together and outline the key common principles that SAFe and SAP Activate follow. The model described here will be applicable in other scaling frameworks that extend the core Scrum approach for large teams and organizations.

Further Resources

In this chapter, we won't go into the details of SAFe. To explore SAFe in detail, we recommend readers to review available documentation at *www.scaledagileframework.com*.

6.5.1   Common Principles in SAFe and SAP Activate

Before we discuss the alignment points and mechanics, let's discuss the common principles that both SAFe practitioners and teams using SAP Activate need to keep in mind.

As we've outlined in this chapter, the SAP Activate agile process is built on the roles, processes, and principles defined in the Scrum agile framework. This includes the execution of agile activities, backlog management, sprint cadence, team structure, and ceremonies during the project. The Scrum framework works well for teams following agile in small or mid-size projects. It has limits, however, in providing guidance for large programs and organizations when it comes to cross-team coordination, management of enterprise backlog, and so on. Scaling frameworks such as SAFe help with the necessary structure, governance, and transparency for large teams. Both SAFe and SAP Activate are built on the following principles that help to show how SAP Activate can be incorporated into the environment that uses SAFe:

- **Deliver value incrementally**
  The concept of incremental value delivery is at the heart of agile thinking and is embedded into both approaches, which helps line them up conceptually. SAFe uses terms of program increments and solution trains to reflect this approach. SAP Activate uses terms of releases that represent the incremental deliveries to production. Both aim to shorten the time to value and deliver value incrementally.

- **Time-boxing and focusing the team in each iteration**
  The SAFe project team plans each increment by selecting capabilities and enablers from the appropriate backlog, and then the team works throughout the program increment timeline in iterations to deliver the selected backlog items. Similarly, SAP Activate uses the fit-to-standard workshops to create the initial backlog for the scope of the release and then iterates in time-boxed sprints on selected backlog items that are completed.

- **Close involvement of business users**
  SAP Activate emphasizes close involvement of business users in the project by making them an integral part of the project team and bringing them to strategic points in the project, such as fit-to-standard or sprint demos. SAFe uses a plan, do, check, adjust cycle common to agile projects, and the team plays back the results of the iteration in the iteration review event.

- **Use of common language and terms**
  SAFe and SAP Activate use common terms such as backlog, sprint/iteration, continuous delivery, built-in quality, product owner, Scrum master, team, product owner, business owners, and many others. These are terms commonly used in agile and have the same meaning in both.

6.5.2   Alignment Points for Each Level of SAFe

In this section, we'll discuss how SAP Activate lines up with SAFe, which is the higher-level framework managing the execution of the program or realization of a portfolio. We'll focus on the three most important layers of SAFe—team level, program level, and large solution level—that have the most touchpoints for SAP Activate.

Team Level

On this level, you'll find the most commonality in the deliverables, procedures, processes, and artifacts. The team structure and roles in both SAP Activate and SAFe include Scrum master, product owner, and team members. SAP Activate nicely extends the guidance for how to structure the project team with the relevant experts for SAP solutions, such as solution architects, key users, application consultants, data migration specialists, and so on. The second area for alignment is the actual execution process for running the sprints/iterations. Both frameworks use planning activities, execution activities, inspection activities with sprint review, and adjustment activities with retrospective. In terms of artifacts, the alignment is done through the use of the backlog for managing the scope of work and what gets included in each iteration or release (or as SAFe calls it, *program increment*). Both approaches build on common agile practices of working as a cross-functional team to deliver value.

Program Level

The notion of continuous delivery via the release train from SAFe is represented in SAP Activate with the ability to split a larger project into multiple releases, as introduced earlier in this chapter. This concept of grouping deliverables from individual sprints and storing them in the quality system environment until the team is ready to deploy into the production environment is embedded in the SAP Activate methodology. The second key element that ties to the continuous delivery is the execution of the program in increments: SAP Activate refers to them as *releases*, whereas SAFe uses the term *program increment*. Conceptually these are very similar as both aim to deliver working, tested software that is ready to deploy.

So, how do you use the SAP Activate approach in SAFe on the program level? Conceptually, the program will execute the fit-to-standard workshops for the scope of the program increment in the beginning of each program increment (during planning and early stages of the increment) and then deliver the backlog items that have been included in the increment. This occurs regardless of whether the backlog items are configuration, data migration, extensibility, or integration requirements.

Large Solution Level

In SAP Activate, the solution adoption workstream includes the value management (VM) framework, OCM activities, and project team onboarding, as well as business user training. The VM framework in SAP Activate provides the *economic framework* (in SAFe terms) for the program to deliver value. In addition, the management of the overall program scope, standards, policies, and governance will be largely represented on this level of SAFe. The program management, including the key program milestones, high-level schedule, and objectives of the program from the SAP Activate project management workstream will support SAFe deliverables on this level. The solution architecture work represented in SAP Activate in the technical solution management workstream will also support deliverables in this area of SAFe.

SAFe and SAP

The key reason for the use of SAP Activate in organizations that implemented SAFe is that SAP Activate provides an SAP-specific flavor to solution-agnostic frameworks such as SAFe. Thus, companies using SAP Activate inside SAFe will benefit both from the SAP-specific guidance and the scaling framework for their organization and team.

6.6   Summary

In this chapter, we elaborated on the agile implementation approach concepts that we introduced in Chapter 2. You learned how the project team roles are defined in an agile project and the responsibilities of each role. We then reviewed the anatomy of the releases and sprints with all their activities, such as release planning, sprint planning, daily standup meetings, and the actual execution of the sprint activities that lead to reviewing and confirming that the delivered work meets the business users' requirements. Finally, we covered the feedback loop and improvement process that the team creates with the use of regular retrospectives to not only capture the lessons learned but also act on the highest-priority improvement to the way the team works in the upcoming sprints. This is one of the most important parts of the agile process that allows teams to evolve and improve the way they work while adhering to simple agile processes. And in the last part of this chapter, we provided guidance for organizations that use SAFe on how to incorporate SAP Activate into their working setup.

In the next chapter, we'll dive into the details of new implementations of SAP S/4HANA–based solutions. We'll cover the details of the implementation process in the context of SAP Activate for SAP S/4HANA Cloud and discuss the key content, guidance, and tools project teams use during the implementation.

Chapter 7

New Implementation of SAP S/4HANA

In this chapter, we'll provide detailed explanations of the new imple-mentation process of three SAP S/4HANA deployment versions: public cloud, private cloud, and on-premise. The new implementation approach is used to introduce SAP S/4HANA in organizations imple-menting an SAP solution for the first time in their business or for existing SAP customers that want to reimplement their ERP system and adopt the innovation introduced in SAP S/4HANA Cloud or SAP S/4HANA.

This chapter focuses on explaining how to use SAP Activate for new implementations of SAP S/4HANA Cloud, SAP S/4HANA Cloud, private edition, and on-premise SAP S/4HANA. SAP S/4HANA Cloud allows you to benefit from the software as a service (SaaS) consumption model and receive more frequent innovations, among other characteristics, as discussed earlier in Chapter 1.

During the software selection process, before subscribing, the company preferences, geographical footprint, industry, functional requirements, preference for higher level of standardization, or preference for more flexibility help SAP determine which version of SAP S/4HANA software will be deployed to meet your needs.

The SAP Activate roadmaps for different options of SAP S/4HANA follow the same phases and key deliverables, but the technical and functional details differ in specific areas we'll discuss in this chapter. We'll begin with the deployment process for SAP Activate for SAP S/4HANA Cloud. Then we'll discuss the implementation of SAP S/4HANA Cloud, private edition before we conclude with SAP S/4HANA (on-premise). We'll emphasize the differences between implementing each of these solutions, especially in the solution landscape, and cover capabilities such as configuration, application lifecycle management (ALM), and testing.

7.1 New Implementation of SAP S/4HANA Cloud

SAP S/4HANA Cloud provides a solid SAP-engineered cloud solution delivered via a SaaS delivery model that includes rapid innovation cycles. The technology behind SAP S/4HANA Cloud not only brings a lower cost of ownership but also enables, along with SAP Activate, a more efficient and fast deployment.

In this section, we'll examine the key aspects of the SAP S/4HANA Cloud implementation by following the SAP Activate phases as detailed in Chapter 2 and summarized in Figure 7.1.

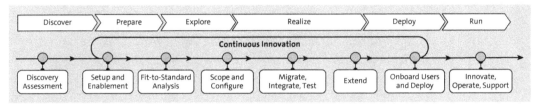

Figure 7.1 SAP Activate Phases and Key Activities

7.1.1 Deployment Approach Overview

Before we start, it's important to note both the landscape of the implementation and the upgrade cycles as these require consideration across the entire project.

SAP S/4HANA Cloud leverages a three-system landscape, with an additional starter system to accelerate learning the standard functionality, as shown in Figure 7.2. The starter system is the first system provided at the time of the subscription start and contains preconfiguration and master data based on SAP Best Practices. Test scripts are provided that allow for immediate execution of business processes in the explore phase. The development system will be used in the realize phase to configure the solution based on the output of the fit-to-standard analysis workshops and to conduct unit testing. The business processes are then tested in the test system, verifying that the master data and configuration setup in the development system can meet the business needs. The starter system will be decommissioned approximately a month after the quality assurance system is provisioned.

In addition to the SAP S/4HANA systems, three other cloud applications support the implementation:

1. **SAP for Me**

   The hub for self-service provisioning of the SAP S/4HANA Cloud tenants when they are needed.

2. **SAP Central Business Configuration**

   The configuration engine for SAP S/4HANA Cloud and other solutions. We discussed SAP Central Business Configuration in Chapter 5, Section 5.1.1.

3. **SAP Cloud ALM**

   The implementation manager loaded with SAP Activate methodology. We discussed SAP Cloud ALM in Chapter 3, Section 3.3.

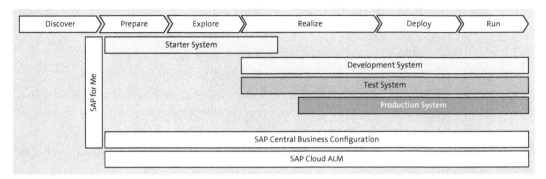

Figure 7.2 SAP Activate Phases and System Landscape

Periodic release updates are applied to SAP S/4HANA Cloud to keep the system current and to support continuous innovations. Standard automated tests are executed by SAP, and companies should plan additional custom regression tests. In between releases, corrections are seamlessly applied approximately every other week, with minimized downtime for the productive system. SAP also implements a continuous feature delivery monthly in which companies can adopt needed innovations earlier than the standard upgrade cycle.

> **Further Resources**
>
> See the SAP Activate for Upgrade of SAP S/4HANA Cloud Three-System Landscape roadmap in the Roadmap Viewer for more guidance related to the upgrade.
>
> See the Release and Update Cycles for SAP S/4HANA Cloud deliverable in the SAP Activate for Upgrade of SAP S/4HANA Cloud Three-System Landscape roadmap for more information on the release upgrade of SAP S/4HANA Cloud.

With that foundation, let's start with the discover phase of SAP Activate.

7.1.2   Discover Your Solution

In this section, we'll discuss how you can test-drive SAP S/4HANA Cloud in the trial environment. SAP offers the SAP S/4HANA Cloud trial environment for anyone who wants to experience the solution in a real running system that is activated with SAP Best Practices scenarios. The trial system is available for 14 days, but you can reregister as often as you need to. While using the trial, you can navigate in a functional system with end-to-end business scenarios for project management, finance, cash management, purchasing, sales, and supply chain.

This system is like the system you'll receive during the implementation project, but you'll need to consider the following limitations while using it:

- The trial is available in a limited number of languages.
- The trial is active for 14 days, but it can be reregistered after the expiration.
- Only a subset of predefined scenarios is activated in the trial system; in other words, the complete scope of SAP Best Practices for SAP S/4HANA Cloud is much broader than what is available in the trial system.
- Only predefined demo data is available in the system; you can't upload your company data.
- Keep in mind that other trial users have access to the data you input into the trial system.

Let's now go over the steps you can take to discover SAP S/4HANA Cloud's capabilities after signing up for the trial environment.

Sign Up for SAP S/4HANA Cloud Trial

To start your own trial, access the SAP S/4HANA trial pages at *http://s-prs.co/v502722*. Select **Start your 14-day trial** (see Figure 7.3) and fill out the registration form as prompted.

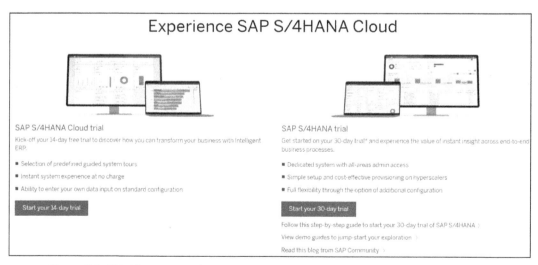

Figure 7.3 SAP S/4HANA Trial Pages

Access Your SAP S/4HANA Cloud Environment

After you've completed the registration process, SAP will send you an email with a link to activate your account. After clicking the link, you'll be directed to a welcome screen that includes your user ID and a link to start the trial. Save the user ID and the link for the SAP S/4HANA Cloud trial in a safe place.

The SAP S/4HANA Cloud trial environment provides access to detailed guided tours in which you'll assume the role of a specific business user, such as a general ledger accountant, accounts receivable accountant, and others. As shown in Figure 7.4, each business area contains several guided tours. By selecting the tour, you'll be launched into the SAP S/4HANA Cloud solution and a guide process that will walk you through the transaction steps in the live system.

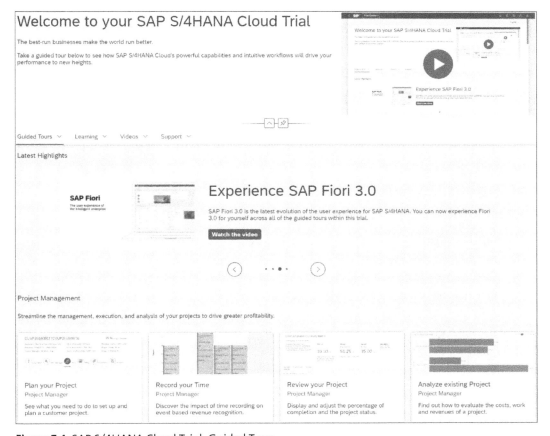

Figure 7.4 SAP S/4HANA Cloud Trial: Guided Tour

The on-screen guidance will tell you which SAP Fiori app tile to select, which buttons to click, and what information you need to input into the application. If you need to get back to the list of guided tours, return to the home screen by clicking **Home** in the drop-down next to the SAP logo and selecting the **Guided Tours** tile.

If you're doing freestyle exploration, you can always activate the help function with the **Open Help** button to learn more about the application. As shown in Figure 7.5, this help function will provide more detailed guidance about the purposes and roles of key screen elements.

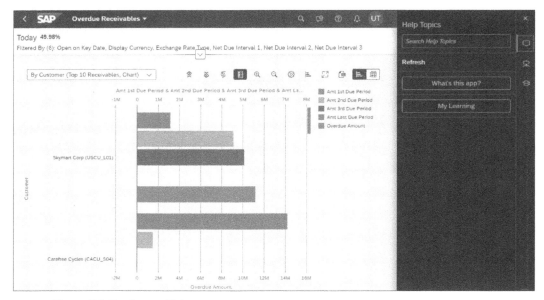

Figure 7.5 On-Screen Help

In addition to the guided tours, select **Getting Started Guides** in the **Learning** area for guides to help you understand how to work with SAP Fiori launchpad, including how to personalize the apps shown in your launchpad; how to work with SAP Fiori apps; and how to configure your solution. The **Learning Center** link provides access to numerous tutorials on different SAP S/4HANA Cloud processes.

Now that you've taken a test-drive with the SAP S/4HANA Cloud trial system, let's examine the next SAP Activate project phase: prepare.

7.1.3   Prepare Your Project

This section will cover the activities the project team needs to complete in the prepare phase of an SAP S/4HANA Cloud implementation project. We'll focus on activities supporting project initiation and planning, activities related to the provisioning of SAP S/4HANA Cloud, and team self-enablement tasks. Taken together, these activities prepare business users for the fit-to-standard analysis workshops that the team will later conduct in the explore phase.

After an overview of this phase, the information in this section is structured into several topics that go over the key activities in the prepare phase.

Phase Overview

The purpose of the prepare phase is to provide the initial planning and preparation for the project. In this phase, the project is started, plans are finalized, the project team is

204

assigned, and work gets underway to start the project. The SAP S/4HANA Cloud environment is provisioned, and the project team gains access to the starter system and is ready to start planning for the fit-to-standard analysis workshops in the explore phase. Figure 7.6 provides an overview of the deliverables the project team will complete during the prepare phase.

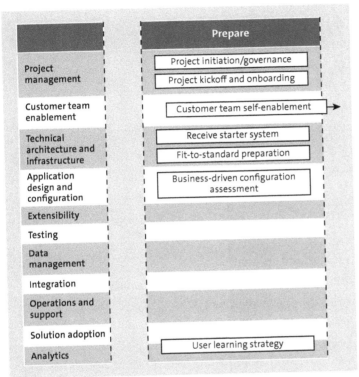

Figure 7.6 SAP Activate Prepare Phase Deliverables for SAP S/4HANA Cloud

The prepare phase includes the following activities:

- Defining project goals, a high-level scope, and a project plan
- Securing executive sponsorship
- Establishing project standards, organization, and governance
- Defining roles and responsibilities for the project team
- Validating the project's objectives
- Establishing project management, tracking, and reporting mechanisms for value delivery
- Developing a company project team enablement strategy and starting company project team enablement
- Documenting all initiation activities in the project charter

- Requesting provisioning of SAP Cloud ALM
- Requesting initial access to applicable SAP systems
- Preparing for fit-to-standard workshops, including self-enablement activities
- Closing the phase

Typically, the prepare phase creates the following deliverables:

- Project scope document
- Project organization and governance
- Project schedule, budget, and management plans
- Project standards and policies
- Project risk documentation
- Solution adoption approach, including the organizational change
- Fit-to-standard preparation
- Data migration approach and strategy
- Project quality gate

The prepare phase includes the following typical project milestones and key decisions:

- Project scope validated
- Company project team staffed and enabled
- Project team organization, responsibilities, and location established
- Key stakeholders for communications identified
- Implementation plan defined
- Project environment provisioned

Let's now go over the key activities the project team will perform during the prepare phase of implementing SAP S/4HANA Cloud.

Setting Up the Project

Every SAP S/4HANA Cloud implementation project needs to establish a game plan and rules of engagement to keep all project team members moving toward the common goal. The project management workstream in the SAP Activate methodology covers most of the necessary deliverables and tasks that the project manager and project team need to provide as a game plan for everyone involved in the project.

Typical project management deliverables in the prepare phase include the following:

- Project initiation and governance
- Project plans, schedule, and budget
- Project kickoff and project team onboarding materials
- Project standards and project infrastructure

Putting these fundamentals in place will help the project team focus on reaching the project's objectives and enable your business to realize the goals stated in the business case. Let's look at each of these deliverables closely.

Project Initiation and Governance

The purpose of the project initiation and governance deliverable is to formally recognize that a new project exists and to initiate work on the project. During this time, the project sponsor and project manager work to align stakeholders around the project and its scope, provide updated information for planning, and obtain a commitment to proceed.

As part of the initiation activities, the project manager conducts a handover from the discover phase, creates a project charter document and scope statement document, and establishes the project governance to ensure a proper management process for the project. These activities achieve alignment between the SAP system integrator, the company's project team, the company's strategic direction, and the satisfaction of operational requirements for the solution.

Project governance is a critical management framework for the project to ensure that decisions are made in a structured manner. It establishes a policy for the project team, project stakeholders, executives, and system integrators that clearly specifies roles, responsibilities, accountability, and organizational setup. As shown in Figure 7.7, project governance provides a decision-making framework that is robust and logical to ensure that decisions are timely and approved by the authorized personnel.

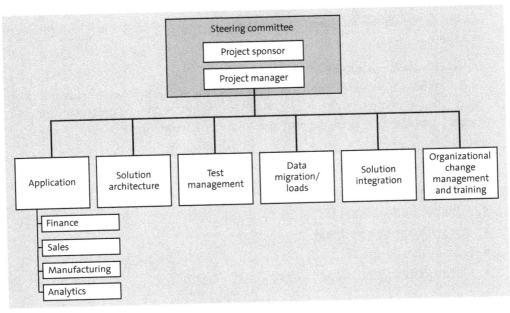

Figure 7.7 Project Organization and Governance

> **Governance Caution**
>
> If you skip this key deliverable, the project isn't formally approved by the company sponsor, and the project manager isn't authorized to apply organizational resources to project activities. You also risk having the scope of the project be misunderstood and project governance processes remain undefined.

Project Plans, Schedule, and Budget

Planning activities during the early stages of the project include developing a project management plan, preparing the project's work breakdown structure (WBS), and defining the project's schedule and budget.

The project management plan is a comprehensive document that details the plans for managing schedules, budgets, issues, risks, project changes, and so on. The SAP Activate methodology provides you with guidance and templates for creating a management plan for your SAP S/4HANA Cloud project. Further, the SAP Activate methodology gives you a detailed WBS in the Roadmap Viewer that your project manager can use to define and sequence required tasks within the scope of the project.

Project Kickoff and Onboarding

To formally start the project, the project manager schedules a project kickoff meeting. This kickoff meeting includes discussion of project objectives, organizational structure, roles and responsibilities, project governance, schedule, scope, communication standards, change request processes, and decision-making processes. The kickoff meeting is attended by the project team, key stakeholders, the project sponsor, and company executives.

Project Standards and Infrastructure

Project standards provide a consistent means of executing and governing project work in an efficient and effective manner. You'll elaborate on these standards throughout the prepare phase, although you can fine-tune some standards later in the project.

The project team must establish minimum project standards for the following areas:

- Requirements management
- Configuration and documentation
- Authorizations and security
- Test planning and execution
- Change management
- Postimplementation support and new user onboarding

To support adherence to project standards, the project team also sets up the project team environment and ensures that project team members have the appropriate level of access to the company facility, project room, and project systems.

This activity also involves IT support to set up project team workstations, including installing and updating the required software, such as internet browsers, communication tools (e.g., Zoom, Microsoft Teams), or collaboration environments (e.g., SAP Community, MURAL).

Provisioning and Setup

SAP Cloud ALM is an essential solution for managing all aspects of any SAP cloud solution's implementation and operations. We covered SAP Cloud ALM capabilities in Chapter 3, Section 3.3. SAP S/4HANA Cloud customers should follow the guidance in the Request SAP Cloud ALM Tenant task to request provisioning and access to SAP Cloud ALM. As of the time of writing, this provisioning is done via the SAP Cloud ALM Access Management app in SAP ONE Support Launchpad. Detailed instructions can be found in the SAP Activate Roadmap Viewer.

Users can request access to SAP Central Business Configuration, the configuration environment designed for SAP S/4HANA Cloud, via SAP for Me at *https://me.sap.com*. We covered the SAP Central Business Configuration capabilities in Chapter 5, Section 5.1.1. SAP for Me is the central place designed to improve the experience throughout all touchpoints with SAP, including requesting provisioning of cloud systems and tenants. The request for provisioning of SAP Central Business Configuration can be found under **Systems and Provisioning** in SAP for Me. Click on the **Start Provisioning** button to trigger the provisioning process. Once provisioned, an email with instructions for access will be sent to the IT contact. The Request SAP Central Business Configuration task in the Roadmap Viewer provides detailed guidance.

Next you will need to request provisioning of an SAP S/4HANA Cloud starter system. The provisioning process is similar to the steps taken to request provisioning of SAP Central Business Configuration that we covered earlier. The IT contact will request the SAP S/4HANA Cloud starter system in SAP for Me. The SAP S/4HANA Cloud starter system contains two tenants: the *starter customizing* tenant and *starter development* tenant. After your starter environment is ready, the IT contact will receive provisioning emails providing details for access and setup of the systems. Note that the IT contact will receive one email for each tenant and instructions for accessing the administration console for the Identity Authentication service. Detailed guidance can be found in the Request Initial System Access and Initial System Access for SAP S/4HANA Cloud Starter System deliverables in the Roadmap Viewer.

> **Note**
>
> SAP S/4HANA Cloud comes predelivered with initial business role templates that you can use to set up business roles to assign to your users.

Team Self-Enablement

During the prepare phase, the company project team learns about different aspects of SAP S/4HANA Cloud and the SAP Activate methodology via self-enablement materials such as e-learning, documentation, and self-paced training.

Cloud projects are intended to be implemented over a shorter time, which requires more focus on learning tools. It's important that self-enablement begins prior to project kickoff to maximize the time for learning and to create efficiencies in later deliverables. SAP offers a range of structured training options to learn about the scope and functionality of the solution and to understand the structure and flow of the work in the implementation project. SAP has prepared learning journeys to provide a structured way to enable the various users involved in the project.

Figure 7.8 shows an example of the **RISE with SAP S/4HANA Cloud (Public)—Onboarding Fundamentals** learning journey. The learning journey directs learners to enablement and training resources in SAP Learning Hub, at openSAP, and with other resources such as blogs or e-learning courses. One of the first steps on this journey is to join the SAP S/4HANA Cloud implementation learning room, where you can access a range of materials providing information about implementation approaches, methodologies, and tools. You can find the links to learning journeys in the Roadmap Viewer in tasks under the Customer Team Self-Enablement deliverable.

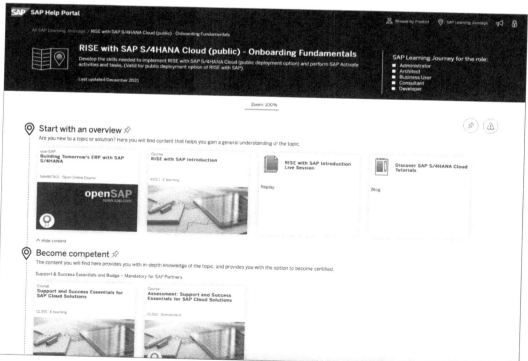

Figure 7.8 Example of Learning Journey for SAP S/4HANA Cloud

Key learning tutorials also are available inside SAP S/4HANA Cloud in the My Learning app.

SAP Support Portal

SAP recommends that all project team members have access to SAP Support Portal, where the project team can communicate directly with SAP support and service centers. User details for accessing SAP Support Portal enable each customer to access the SAP Best Practices Explorer and Roadmap Viewer applications and be recognized as a customer, thus getting access to additional documents and templates needed during the implementation project.

Project team members are encouraged to request access and follow the SAP Activate community on sap.com to find additional resources and to engage directly with SAP Activate experts. You can register and follow the community at *https://community.sap.com/topics/activate*. Use the **Login/Sign-up** button in the top right of your screen to register.

Organizational Change Management

The purpose of this task is to set up the organizational change management (OCM) team and agree on an OCM concept, which includes the following:

- OCM network concept
- Stakeholder engagement concept
- Communication concept
- Organizational transition concept
- Learning concept
- Change effectiveness concept
- OCM sustainability concept

The change readiness of the organization is assessed by participating in the Cloud Mindset Assessment accelerator and leveraging the results to create awareness for OCM-related topics among the stakeholders. See Chapter 10 for additional details.

Analysis and Planning of End User Learning Needs

The project team needs to start preparing the end users to use the new application early in the project because, as we discussed previously, cloud implementation projects generally have a compressed schedule compared to on-premise deployments. Therefore, one goal in the prepare phase is to develop a high-level learning plan that provides the recommended approach and activities to prepare end users for using the new system.

The project team executes the following activities to prepare the high-level learning plan:

■ **Conduct learning needs identification**
The project team performs an end user analysis with a specific focus on determining the current skill levels, knowledge gaps, and training requirements per user group. This activity provides a thorough analysis of required training and helps determine the appropriate learning mechanism for each user group.

■ **Develop a detailed end user learning curriculum**
Based on the outcome of the learning needs analysis, the project team will develop a working document to formulate an end user learning curriculum structured by user groups and learning needs identified in the previous step. The team should consider all available options to train users, including formal training, shadowing, and the use of social training such as SAP Learning Hub.

In SAP S/4HANA Cloud implementations, the teams prepare learning experiences for key users and end users based primarily on self-enablement using e-learning and easy-to-consume materials online. Additional details are covered in Chapter 10.

Fit-to-Standard Preparation

Preparation for running the fit-to-standard workshop is essential for an effective experience for both the business experts and configuration experts. It includes the following activities:

■ Determine the workshop scope based on the project scope statement.

■ Review the How to Approach Fit to Standard Analysis presentation in the Roadmap Viewer, which provides detailed guidance for running the fit-to-standard analysis workshops.

■ Download the scope documentation of the business processes covered in the workshop from SAP Best Practices Explorer.

■ Walk through the SAP Best Practices test scripts in the starter system.

■ Adjust the sample data in the system to fit your business. Although the starter system is delivered with master data, some company-specific data can be created to help facilitate understanding by the business experts.

■ Review the Expert Configuration and SSCUI Reference.xlsm accelerator in the Roadmap Viewer to help map the configuration required to the scope of the solution. You must understand both the solution abilities and the boundaries of the configuration.

■ Anticipate requirements for extensibility and integration that may come up during the workshop.

■ Identify the required participants for your workshop and schedule sufficient time to conduct the workshop.

With the prepare phase complete, it's time for the explore phase.

7.1.4   Explore the Solution

This section will provide details about the activities that project team members will execute during the explore phase. The focus will be on planning and running the fit-to-standard analysis workshops that help the project team determine how the SAP Best Practices processes fit your business needs and whether adjustments are needed. We will also outline how the project team determines configuration values and identifies the necessary extensions and integration points for the solution.

After an overview of this phase, this section is structured into several subsections that cover the key activities of the explore phase.

Phase Overview

In the explore phase, industry and solution experts from SAP or SAP partners lead a series of structured fit-to-standard workshops. The purpose of the fit-to-standard workshops is to validate the solution functionality included in the project scope and to confirm that business requirements will be satisfied. During the workshops, the project team identifies and documents the necessary configuration values, extensions, integration points, and gaps for the end-to-end solution, as shown in Figure 7.9.

The following activities are key to the explore phase:

- Managing the project with a strong focus on executing, monitoring, and controlling the results
- Preparing and running company project team enablement activities
- Planning and executing fit-to-standard workshops
- Capturing configuration values to personalize the solution for your business
- Identifying and documenting required integration and solution extensions
- Preparing for data migration
- Designing interfaces, analytics, access management, and enhancements

The following deliverables are typical of the explore phase:

- Fit-to-standard workshops
- Prioritized and documented configuration values in a backlog
- List of required extensions
- Change impact analysis and communication plan
- Integration prerequisites confirmed and resolved
- Data load strategy
- Test strategy
- Inventory of standard and nonstandard interfaces
- Release plan, including confirmation of planned go-live date
- Designs for interfaces, analytics, access management, and enhancements

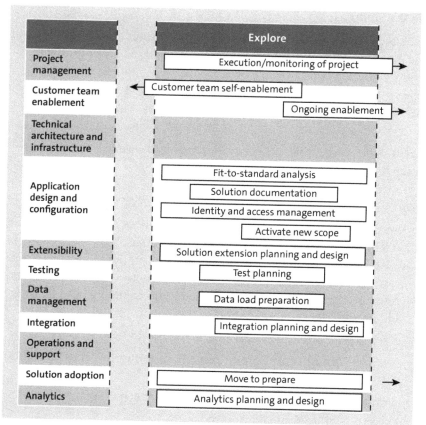

Figure 7.9 SAP Activate Explore Phase Deliverables for SAP S/4HANA Cloud

Finally, the following are typical milestones and key decisions that occur during the explore phase:

- Fit-to-standard workshops for full scope of the implementation completed
- Configuration values captured
- Extensions defined and documented
- Integrations defined and documented
- Project team enabled
- Phase quality assessment conducted

First, let's look at the fit-to-standard analysis workshops.

Fit-to-Standard Workshops

The purpose of fit-to-standard workshops is to validate the predefined SAP Best Practices scenarios delivered in the system with your business requirements. Multiple outcomes can occur from the fit-to-standard workshops, including the confirmation of solution fit; the definition of required configuration values; a list of needed extensions to forms, reports, fields, or business logic; the identification of required integrations; and a list of gaps.

7

Workshop Tips

At the start of the workshop, we recommend that project teams set rules of engagement during the workshop.

■ **Dos**
  - Contribute to the discussion.
  - Ask questions if you don't understand something.
  - Be concise in the interest of time.
  - Understand the SAP-delivered best practices.
■ **Don'ts**
  - Use your cell phone, laptop, or tablet.
  - Be afraid to speak up.
  - Forget that you're all on the same team!

Workshops can be conducted remotely. For additional information, see the How to Approach Remote Fit-to-Standard Workshops—Cloud Playbook accelerator in the Roadmap Viewer.

The focused scope of SAP S/4HANA Cloud allows for a more efficient approach to validating the fit of the standard solution against your requirements. Fit-to-standard workshops organized around the functional areas of the solution are used to explore the functionality and confirm that the solution can meet your requirements. Gaps are identified and added to the backlog list (gap list). The validation process uses an iterative approach to ensure that integrated dependencies are addressed, including integration requirements and extensibility requirements. In addition, configuration changes are determined and cataloged.

Each fit-to-standard analysis workshop includes the process outlined in Figure 7.10, which is repeated for each business process and process variant. Follow-up workshops may be required if business process requirements are difficult to identify and satisfy.

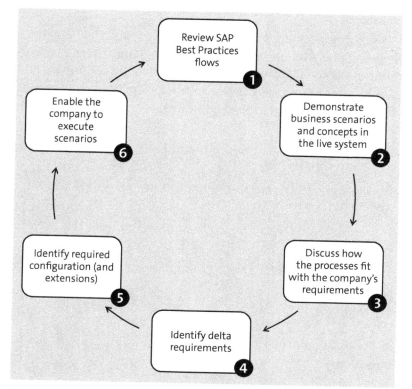

Figure 7.10 Fit-to-Standard Iterative Process

Let's take a closer look at each step:

❶ Review SAP Best Practices flows

The configuration expert explains the process using the SAP Best Practices process flows, which are available in SAP Cloud ALM.

❷ Demonstrate business scenarios and concepts in the live system

The configuration expert leverages the configured system and delivered data to demonstrate the SAP Best Practices process in the starter system and highlight areas that likely require configuration decisions or may vary for current business processes. The test script documents provided with SAP Best Practices are used to drive the execution of the demonstration in the system.

❸ Discuss how the processes fit with the company's requirements

The team engages in discussions to better understand the company's business requirements and to provide understanding of how the solution meets these requirements.

❹ Identify delta requirements
The team identifies and catalogs the delta requirements in SAP Cloud ALM for further analysis and closure. The project team will need to validate identified delta requirements against the product roadmap (*www.sap.com/roadmaps*) to make qualified decisions about whether the gap requires development of extensions or whether the gap can be satisfied with an interim solution until the functionality is delivered in a future quarterly update.

❺ Identify required configuration (and extensions)
The team determines and documents the configuration values required. The company is responsible for providing value lists such as product group definitions. The team also captures all required in-app extensions that can be satisfied in the product, items such as adjusting forms, adding business logic, or extending fields. This category also includes standard integrations, where the team can leverage predelivered setup guides for integrating SAP S/4HANA Cloud with other systems. Custom integrations are handled as gaps if they require the development of extensions.

❻ Enable the company to execute scenarios
The process flows and test scripts are available in SAP Cloud ALM so that key users can execute the scenarios on their own. If necessary, sample company data can be created to improve learning using more customer-centric examples.

Let's briefly consider the typical workshops conducted when implementing SAP S/4HANA Cloud. Note that the list of workshops will vary from company to company, depending on the scope of the solution, and our list is based on selected current capabilities of SAP S/4HANA Cloud. Based on the size of the project, many workshops can occur in parallel.

First comes the chart of accounts workshop, which is used to define how the company's chart of accounts can be reflected in the solution. During the workshop, the project team reviews the predelivered chart of accounts, maps the company's chart of accounts against the predelivered one, and makes the appropriate adjustments needed to reflect the company's business in the solution.

This is followed by the organizational structure workshop, which defines how the company's organizational structure will be reflected in the solution. During the workshop, the project team reviews the predelivered organizational structure, maps the company's organizational structure against it, and makes the appropriate adjustments to accommodate the company's organizational needs.

From here, the functional workshops begin. Each functional team separately conducts the fit-to-standard analysis for the corresponding functionality. Table 7.1 lists lines of business (LoBs) and topics that are typically covered in each workshop.

Workshop	Typical Topics Discussed
Finance	■ Accounting and financial close ■ Advanced accounting and financial close ■ Financial operations ■ Advanced financial operations ■ Cost management and profitability analysis ■ Enterprise risk and compliance ■ Real estate management ■ Subscription billing and revenue management ■ Treasury management
Human resources	■ Core human resources
Sourcing and procurement	■ Central procurement ■ Invoice management ■ Operational procurement ■ Procurement analytics ■ Sourcing and contract management ■ Supplier management
Supply chain	■ Order promising ■ Advanced order promising ■ Inventory ■ Delivery and transportation ■ Warehousing
Manufacturing	■ Environment, health, and safety ■ Production planning ■ Extended production planning and scheduling ■ Production engineering ■ Production operations ■ Quality management
Sales	■ Sales rebate processing ■ Accelerated company returns ■ Credit and debit memo processing ■ Company consignment ■ Company returns ■ Free delivery ■ Intrastat processing ■ Intercompany sales order processing (domestic/international) ■ Sales inquiry ■ Sales quotation ■ Sell from stock

Table 7.1 Functional Fit-to-Standard Analysis Workshops

Workshop	Typical Topics Discussed
Sales (Cont.)	■ Scheduling agreements ■ Sales contract management ■ Order fulfillment
Asset management	■ Asset operations and maintenance ■ Maintenance management
Professional services	■ Controlling and accounting ■ Projects and engagements ■ Resource management ■ Service-centric billing
Service	■ Service master data and agreement management ■ Service operations and processes
R&D and engineering	■ Enterprise portfolio and project management ■ Product compliance ■ Product lifecycle management

Table 7.1 Functional Fit-to-Standard Analysis Workshops (Cont.)

Determining Configuration Values and Extensions

One of the outputs of the fit-to-standard workshops is documentation of the necessary configuration changes for the team to implement during the realize phase. A blueprint document isn't produced in the SAP Activate approach; however, the project team will record the required configuration and extensions in SAP Cloud ALM that will support the planning and execution of the configuration process in the realize phase.

In each fit-to-standard workshop, the project team determines the following requirements: configuration, master data, forms and reports, identity and access management, extensibility, and integration.

Let's examine these critical decisions in more detail:

■ **Defining the organizational structure**
The team defines the required organizational structure using the Org. Structure Definition Template available in SAP Cloud ALM or the Roadmap Viewer as a starting point or by adopting the standard organizational structure delivered with the starter system. Figure 7.11 shows the default organizational structure delivered with SAP Best Practices for SAP S/4HANA Cloud. The definition will be configured in SAP Central Business Configuration during the initial set up of the development tenant.

■ **Defining the chart of accounts**
The project team can review the delivered chart of accounts in the starter system using the Manage Chart of Accounts app in SAP S/4HANA Cloud. These accounts can be used as is or as the starting point for a company-specific chart of accounts. Also, three different chart of accounts type should be considered in the definition:

- *Operating chart of accounts*: Mandatory to perform financial postings and used for daily postings to company codes

- *Group chart of accounts:* Only necessary if a corporate group exists and financial consolidation is needed

- *Alternative (local) chart of accounts:* Required if the customer has any specific local legal requirements

Unneeded accounts can be marked as **Not Used** and blocked from posting. Don't reuse accounts for purposes other than what is defined in the original description because automatic postings may occur to these accounts.

- **Defining configuration values**
  During the fit-to-standard analysis, the business scenarios are demonstrated and validated using the starter system and SAP Best Practices documentation (process flows, test scripts). In addition, relevant configuration settings are explored and the needed changes are determined. These changes are documented as requirements in SAP Cloud ALM and used by the project team in the realize phase. Some configuration lists may contain only a few items, while others will be longer. The company is responsible for providing the values that are appropriate to their business processes.

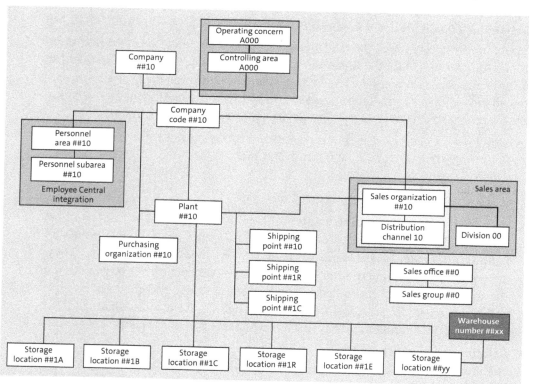

Figure 7.11 Default Organizational Structure Delivered with SAP Best Practices for SAP S/4HANA Cloud

- **Defining expert configuration**
  In exceptional circumstances, expert configuration is required and executed by SAP via the service center (SAP support). The Expert Configuration and SSCUI Reference accelerator in the SAP Activate implementation roadmap lists the approved expert configuration available, and once completed it is submitted to the service center via a support ticket with the title Expert Configuration Request and component XX-S4C-OPR-SRV in the realize phase.

- **Defining master data requirements**
  The required master data is identified and defined. The data requirements are used for master data creation for testing end-to-end scenarios, as well as data migration design and planning.

- **Documenting business process flows**
  As the business processes are tailored to meet the business requirements, they are updated to reflect the new process. The updated flows provide documentation on new processes and are used to support change management and training. Companies can use SAP Cloud ALM to capture the required changes to the process flow.

- **Documenting analytics requirements**
  The standard reports are reviewed during the fit-to-standard analysis workshops. Requirements are added to SAP Cloud ALM or, alternatively, in the Analytics List Template for later review with the analytics experts.

- **Documenting output management requirements**
  Communications channels and the format of output documents are determined. SAP provides form templates that can be used as a starting point to create new templates. The company's current output documents can also be used as documentation of the requirements.

- **Documenting extensibility requirements**
  All extensibility requirements are captured, including business scenarios, user stories, and sources of data. This information will be handed over to the extensibility experts who will develop the detailed designs.

- **Documenting integration requirements**
  All standard and company integrations requirements are documented and cataloged in SAP Cloud ALM as requirements. The Integration Scenario and API List.xlsx template is available in the Roadmap Viewer and can also be used to track required integration.

- **Documenting identity and access management**
  Special authorization requirements, such as segregation of duties and data visibility, are identified and documented.

The work in fit-to-standard analysis workshops covers the end-to-end solution comprehensively—in other words, both the configuration set directly in the system and also the configuration set via forms, integrations, and extensions. The team needs to determine the scope of the functionality for the initial go-live as a basis for the planning work in the realize phase.

Planning and Design Elements

Areas such as extensibility, integration, analytics, and access management require additional planning and design based on the requirements gathered in the fit-to-standard workshops. The requirements are handed over to the experts in these areas who can develop detailed designs and implementation plans. Because these areas are typically nonstandard items, they often represent the bottleneck in the implementation and should be monitored closely. The output is detailed implementation plans and specifications that can be executed in the realize phase.

Data Load Preparation

Data load preparation is the process of taking existing data from a legacy system and preparing it for use in a new SAP system. As of the time of writing, only the staging tables method is supported for SAP S/4HANA Cloud, but direct transfer from another SAP ERP system is being planned. The staging tables method allows a company to load data from load templates into the staging tables in the SAP S/4HANA Cloud application nondestructively. After the load, the data sits in the staging tables, where it is reviewed for quality. Only after the review is it approved for load into the actual application. This allows the project team to repeat the loads multiple times to ensure the data load templates are accurate without impacting data in the application. This way, the data migration team can resolve any data load issues before the final load to the system and prepare a smooth cutover.

The preparation consists of four tasks:

1. Determining the required master data and transactional data
2. Determining SAP S/4HANA migration cockpit field structures
3. Defining the specification for data extraction from your legacy systems
4. Performing data cleansing activities

It's important that this process begins early in the project because the data extraction and data cleansing activities are typically on the critical path for a successful go-live.

We'll take a closer look at each activity in the following sections.

Determining the Required Master Data and Transactional Data

The purpose of this task is to determine the master data and transactional data required for the scope of your SAP S/4HANA Cloud implementation project and to determine the data sources for these objects. A list of the available migration objects for your SAP S/4HANA Cloud system is available in the solution or in the SAP Help Portal for SAP S/4HANA Cloud under **Migration Objects for SAP S/4HANA Cloud.**

Start by determining all master and transactional data objects needed to support the processes detailed in the fit-to-standard workshops. After the list of required objects is determined, the data sources can be mapped to them. In some cases, a legacy equivalent won't be available, and the field data will need to be created or derived.

Historical transaction objects such as completed sales orders and completed purchase orders are not migrated to the new system. They are typically available via reporting or other archival retrieval tools.

Migration Objects

Note that the coverage and functionality for data migration objects expands with each quarterly release of SAP S/4HANA Cloud. A complete list of objects is available via the SAP Help Portal under **Data Migration** and in the SAP S/4HANA migration cockpit itself. Templates should always be checked after an upgrade as they may have changed.

Determining SAP S/4HANA Migration Cockpit Field Structures

The purpose of this task is to view the SAP S/4HANA Cloud data structures by downloading the template files and associating the structures with the data from the legacy system(s).The specific templates can be downloaded in a Microsoft Excel 2003 XML spreadsheet file using the **Download Template** button in the Migrate Your Data app (see Figure 7.12). These files contain the metadata (fields, data type, mandatory fields, etc.) and can help with the data mapping. Downloading the files at this early stage helps you understand the available migration objects and fields, prepare the data, and determine how to fill the templates with the data from the legacy system. Additional information about migration templates can be found in under **Data Migration** in the SAP Help Portal.

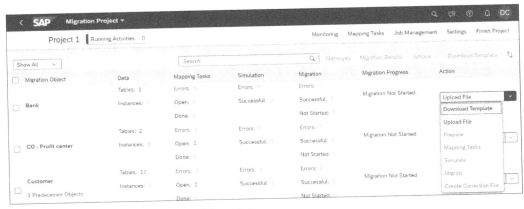

Figure 7.12 Data Migration Download Template

The downloaded templates contain an introduction with instructions, a field list, and data sheets per structure. The data sheet contains at least one mandatory structure and additional optional structures depending on the complexity of the migration object. Only mandatory sheets need to be filled in; however, after an optional sheet is populated, all the mandatory fields for that structure must be filled.

Defining Specifications for Data Extraction from Legacy System

The purpose of this task is to develop the specifications for extraction of data from the legacy system, where necessary, and to initiate the development of the extraction processes. Master and transactional data can change frequently, so a process must be created to assure efficient execution during the cutover to production. Data that will be manually entered also requires a specification so that it can also be created for the cutover.

Performing Data Cleansing Activities

The purpose of this activity is to cleanse the data and eliminate unnecessary legacy data. In addition, the data should be verified to be complete. Unnecessary data should be removed from the legacy data source to reduce the volume of data to load and keep the new system free from extraneous data.

Test Planning

During the explore phase, the project team will start preparing for testing. While most test activities don't start until the realize phase, it's important to prepare not only the testing activities performed during the project but also the regression tests that will be required with each quarterly upgrade.

Scoping and planning the tests for the implementation project are required to ensure that the right tests are planned and executed before bringing the system into productive use. Not only is it important to define what types of tests are to be done, but you should also determine who will be accountable for preparing the test plans, executing the tests, and signing off on the results of the testing.

In SAP S/4HANA Cloud implementation projects, the project team will need to capture the following testing approach elements in the test strategy document:

- Statement of the project testing objectives and assumptions
- High-level testing schedule to frame what is needed to be completed and when
- Scope of the test to clarify what is to be tested and not to be tested
- Types of testing, including unit testing, business process (string) testing, integration testing, data load testing, and user acceptance testing (UAT)
- Testing approach, including design, construction, and execution of the tests, along with the environments
- Defects management to track and resolve issues encountered
- Governance, roles, and responsibilities to outline the operating model

Along with preparing the testing strategy, the team members responsible for testing should enable and evaluate the test management capabilities in SAP Cloud ALM and the test automation tool in SAP S/4HANA Cloud, both of which can support the testing cycles.

7.1.5   Realize Your Requirements

In the previous section, you learned about the steps the project team takes to determine the configuration values and required extensions to the predelivered SAP Best Practices solution. Let's now shift our attention to how the project team can tailor the predelivered system with company-specific configuration and how the solution can be extended to cover your unique requirements beyond configuration.

After an overview of this phase, this section is structured into several subsections that go over the key activities in the realize phase.

Phase Overview

The purpose of the realize phase is to receive the SAP S/4HANA Cloud systems (development, test, and production) and to incrementally configure, extend, and test the preconfigured solution to reflect your integrated business based on requirements you defined in the explore phase and captured in the backlog. During this phase, the project team also loads company data into the system, plans adoption activities, and prepares cutover plans and plans for operationally running the solution, as shown in Figure 7.13.

The following activities are key to the realize phase:

- Request provisioning of SAP Cloud ALM
- Requesting and initial setup of SAP S/4HANA systems (development, test, production)
- Configuring the company solution in the development environment using agile iterations and the backlog
- Testing the solution in the development environment (unit tests) and test system (string, integration, and UAT)
- Walking through solution processes with stakeholders to confirm that the solution has been configured to meet their requirements
- Executing data migration loads into the development and test environments
- Integrating with other SAP systems and company legacy systems as required
- Developing side-by-side extensions and using developer extensibility (on stack) to extend the capabilities of the solution
- Conducting overall testing of the solution

- Continuing with project team enablement on key concepts and system operations
- Preparing the cutover plan, planning and running change management activities, and getting ready to deliver end user training

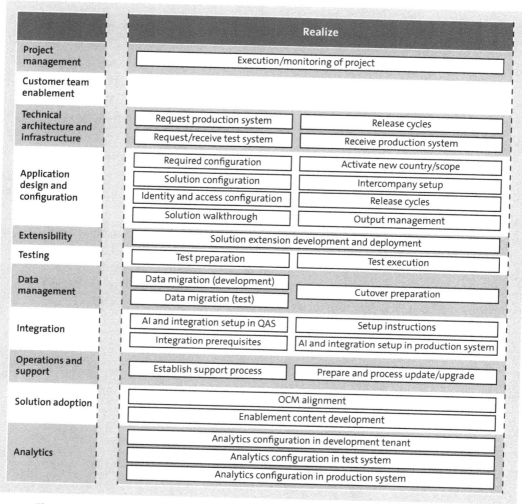

Figure 7.13 SAP Activate Realize Phase Deliverables for SAP S/4HANA Cloud

During the realize phase, the project team uses a series of agile sprints to incrementally configure, test, and confirm the entire end-to-end solution and to perform legacy data uploads. The project team should actively work with business representatives to ensure a good fit between the built solution and the requirements from the backlog. The project team releases the results of multiple agile sprints to business users in a release to production to accelerate time to value and provide early access to the finalized functionality.

Typically, the realize phase creates the following deliverables:

- Request and setup the development, test, and production systems
- Initial preset configuration and system activation using SAP Central Business Configuration
- Organization alignment and user enablement approach
- Solution configuration and solution extensions
- Evaluation and enhancement of security and access controls
- Analytics configuration and artificial intelligence (AI) setup
- Validation of integration points
- Executed data loads
- UAT
- Enablement delivery
- Support operations and handover plan
- Cutover and transition plan

The realize phase includes the following typical project milestones and key decisions:

- System activation
- Solution configuration and extensibility completed in each sprint
- Moving configuration and extensions from development to test environment
- Functionality reviewed and accepted by business users
- Integration testing complete
- Data migration testing conducted
- UAT completed
- Phase quality assessment conducted
- End user training
- Readiness for production release confirmed
- Defined support and operation processes

Let's begin with provisioning of the infrastructure, starting with the provisioning of and access to the development, test, and production systems.

Development System Provisioning

At the beginning of the realize phase, the company requests provisioning of a development system from the SAP for Me application. You can find detailed steps in the Request the SAP S/4HANA Cloud Development System/Initial Setup task in SAP Activate. This action will trigger provisioning of two tenants: one will be used by the project team for configuration activities (customizing tenant) and the second will be used for developer extensibility (development tenant). SAP Central Business Configuration will also be provisioned to assist with the activation and configuration steps during the realize phase.

When the provisioning process is finalized, the company will receive instructions for access to and setup of these tenants, including the steps to set up workspaces for activation and configuration activities through SAP Central Business Configuration. We will briefly outline these steps next.

Development System Access and Initial Setup

In this section, we'll discuss the first steps that the project team takes after receiving the instructions for access to and setup of the development system. As we mentioned earlier, the development system consists of a customizing tenant and development tenant. A company needs to perform activities to set up and activate each tenant.

The project team will perform the following key activities:

- **Set up the customizing tenant in SAP Central Business Configuration**
  As the project team will be using SAP Central Business Configuration to perform the initial confirmation, the system must be properly activated. The first step is to log into the Project Experience app in SAP Central Business Configuration and create a new project for a customizing tenant (look ahead to Figure 7.15). The details of these steps are covered in the Set Up Customizing Tenant in SAP Central Business Configuration task in SAP Activate. Then the configuration experts perform the following activities in SAP Central Business Configuration as they are guided through the implementation project for the customizing tenant. The following activities must be performed:
  - Scoping
  - Assign a deployment target
  - Milestone confirming scoping is completed
  - Set up org structure
  - Primary finance settings
  - Milestone completing the scope and organizational structure phase
- **Set up the development tenant in SAP Central Business Configuration**
  Next the configuration expert follows the same steps as in the previous section to set up the development tenant. This way the customizing tenant and development tenant have the same scope and setup to ensure that the developer extensibility, once tested in development tenant, will also work when transported into the test system. You will find details of this step in SAP Activate in the Set Up Development Tenant in SAP Central Business Configuration task.
- **Initial system access for the SAP S/4HANA Cloud development system**
  During the process, the company will also need to initially access the development

system, prepare it for the project team access, and adapt the chart of accounts prior to requesting provisioning of a test system. The detailed steps are provided in the Initial System Access for SAP S/4HANA Cloud Development System task in SAP Activate. The following tasks are performed during this process (once for each tenant in development system):

- Initial access to the system (first admin user)
- Adaptation and confirmation of chart of accounts
- Create users for project team
- Self-activation of project team members in the Identity Authentication service

After the development system is set up, the test and production systems can be requested from SAP for Me as detailed in the Request the SAP S/4HANA Cloud Test System and Request the SAP S/4HANA Cloud Production System deliverables in SAP Activate. Next, we will briefly cover steps to follow when receiving these systems.

Initial Access and Setup of Test System

After the test system access email has been received, the test system is set up using an initial transport from the development system. This transport content is released via the Export Customizing Transports app in the development system. On the receiving side in the test system, use the Import Collection app to import the transport into the test system. Note that the detailed description of the steps is covered in the Transport Configuration from Development System to Test System task in SAP Activate. Like in the development system, you will create users and perform self-activation of the project team members in the Identity Authentication service.

Initial Access and Setup of Production System

After the production system access email has been received and the test system has been set up as outlined in the previous sections, the production system is set up using an initial transport from the development system (the same transport used to set up the test system). This transport content is forwarded to the production system from the test system via the Import Collection app shown in Figure 7.14. The application is used to export, import, and forward the transports between the development, test, and production systems in the landscape.

Here are the steps to follow:

1. In the test system, identify the transport request and make sure it shows the **Imported** status.
2. Click on **Forward** to initiate transport to the production system.
3. Switch to the production system and, in the Import Collection app, select the transport once it shows **Ready for Import** and import it.

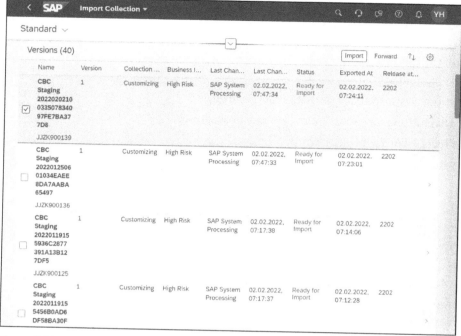

Figure 7.14 Import Collection App in SAP S/4HANA Cloud

The detailed process is available in SAP Activate in the Initial System Access for SAP S/4HANA Cloud Production System deliverable and Forward Configuration from Test System to Production System task. Like in the development and test systems, you will create users and perform self-activation of the productive environment for team members through the dedicated Identity Authentication service for production.

Note that the starter system will remain available to the project as a sandbox environment until 30 calendar days after the production system handover email is sent.

Solution Configuration and Walkthrough

The main purpose of the realize phase is to tailor the system to fit your business needs and confirm that the business process will meet the needs of the company.

The configuration in SAP S/4HANA Cloud is supported by the following processes:

- Guided configuration through SAP Central Business Configuration using easy-to-use configuration activities available to consultants and key users
- Configuration sprints where processes are configured, tested, and moved to the test system
- Solution walkthrough where the processes are demonstrated to the stakeholders for approval

Let's take a closer look at each one.

Guided Configuration with SAP Central Business Configuration

For most configuration tasks, such as setting up blocking reasons for billing or adjusting approval limits for purchase orders in your organizational unit, the project team will access the configuration activities in the SAP Central Business Configuration implementation project that is set up during the initial setup of the system after it has been received.

Figure 7.15 shows the Project Experience app, where configuration experts will find relevant configuration activities for their scope. This application provides a step-by-step view of the required configuration activities and is responsive to the scope selected for the implementation project defined in SAP Central Business Configuration. Consultants and configuration experts use this environment to access the configuration activities and realize the delta requirements and configuration values identified during the fit-to-standard in the explore phase and captured in the backlog.

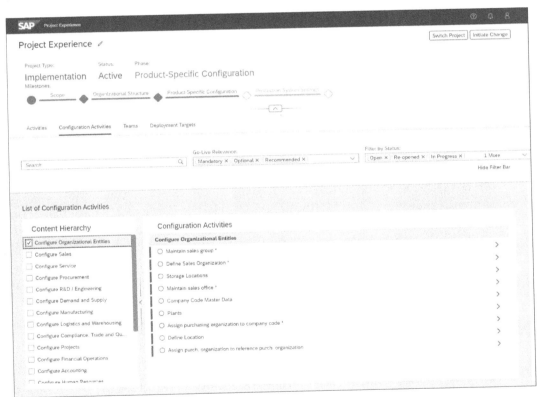

Figure 7.15 SAP Central Business Configuration: Project Experience

Configuration activities are structured into a hierarchy where each hierarchy item provides access to specific configuration activities relevant for the selected scope. The configuration is performed and unit-tested in the SAP S/4HANA Cloud development system, then transported to the test system for further testing (string and integration tests). The transports to the test system happen at least once every one or two weeks as part of the sprinting process. We will cover this topic in the next section.

The SAP Activate methodology recommends completing the following configuration activities before opening the system to general configuration and executing of the business processes (even for testing):

- Configuring the tax solution (as applicable)
- Maintaining profit center configuration
- Maintaining cost center master data
- Maintaining takeover date information for asset accounting
- Configuring customer-specific fiscal year variants

We recommend always referring to the latest information in the SAP Activate methodology in the Required Configuration Before System Use—SAP S/4HANA Cloud deliverable. After these topics are configured, multiple teams can start parallel configuration of finance, sales, sourcing and procurement, supply chain, manufacturing, asset management, and professional services as needed per the scope of the project.

The project team will also need to create sample master data for the purpose of unit-testing the configuration during the short configuration cycles. The sample data should be jointly determined by both consultants and business users so that the data can also be used for business process testing scenarios later. The data should be indicative of your typical data so that it can be used in the solution walkthrough sessions.

Configuration Sprints

Project teams execute configuration in short, one- to two-week agile sprints. In each sprint, as shown in Figure 7.16, the project team performs the required configuration and unit tests the business scenario in the development system. Then the completed configuration is transported into the test system, string testing is conducted, and the completed functionality is reviewed with business users in the test system. The configuration experts and business users follow this sequence of steps during the configuration sprints:

- Short configuration cycles including testing, reviewing, and transporting
- Configuration based on the configuration backlog created during fit-to-standard
- Complete testing of each sprint outcome
- Sprint reviews of what has been configured in the system to verify that business needs are satisfied
- Weekly transports from development system to test system via transport management
- Management of solution configuration tasks and user stories maintained in the SAP Cloud ALM system

In this way, the development system and test system are kept synchronized throughout the implementation project. The vehicle to move the configuration between the systems is called a *transport request*, and it enables the project team to move configuration (and extensibility) from the development system through the test system and all the way into the production system. A project team typically doesn't forward the transports from test to production immediately after testing, but rather prior to the cutover to productive use of the features.

Let's now discuss the flow of the configuration shown in Figure 7.16. The process starts with the definition of scope and setup activities in an SAP Central Business Configuration implementation project ❶. Next the activation of the business content ❷ creates an initial transport that is then used in the setup of the test and production systems, as we discussed earlier in this chapter. In addition, the configuration experts fine-tune the configuration ❸ in the development system to reflect the delta requirements and configuration settings captured in the fit-to-standard. The completed configuration is exported from the development system and imported into the test system, where it is further tested ❹. After successful testing, the transport can be forwarded from the test system to production and later imported into the production system ❺.

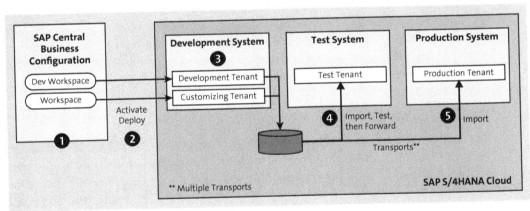

Figure 7.16 Transporting Configuration between Development, Test, and Production Systems

The strategy of employing configuration sprints that each last one or two weeks ensures that the team stays focused on completing the configuration of the business processes and testing and that the size and scope of the configuration stays manageable. In addition to the configuration, forms, extensions, and other related nonconfiguration items are moved via the Export Software Collection app and imported to production using the Import Collection app.

The following is an outline of the steps executed in each configuration sprint:

1. Plan the functionality that will be implemented in the sprint through configuration, key user extensions, developer extensions, output management, master data, and so on.

2. Configure in development system and perform unit and string testing. All configuration is automatically recorded for transport. Any dependent master data (e.g., general ledger accounts) must be manually recreated in the test and production systems before the changes are transported.

3. Using the Export Software Collection app in the development system, export the forms, extensions, or other objects associated with the current transport. A complete list of the objects moved via the Export Software Collection app is available in the application.

4. Use the Export Customizing Transports app in the development system to release the customizing transport with all the configuration changes.

5. In the test system, use the Import Collection app to import the queued changes.

6. After an end-to-end test, system integration test (SIT), and UAT in the test system, click on the **Forward** button in the Import Collection app to send all the changes (configuration and extensibility) to the production system.

7. In the production system, use the Import Collection app to import the queued changes.

Repeat the process for each configuration sprint. Note that the transports to the production environment can be done independently from the sprinting process (they do not need to be forwarded to production in each sprint) and instead can be buffered until the complete functionality is ready for release to the production system. This is especially relevant for customers executing subsequent implementation waves after the initial go-live.

Solution Walkthrough

The purpose of a solution walkthrough is to demonstrate to the stakeholders that the configured solution meets the organization's business needs. The first step of any solution walkthrough is to prepare the key business scenarios and data needed to demonstrate the functionality to the company's project team. Typically, the company representative presents the functionality to the stakeholders to demonstrate an understanding of the solution and how it will be used to run the business.

The second step is to demonstrate the configured solution to project stakeholders and gain initial approval and confirmation that the solution satisfies the business needs. The initial approval also triggers the beginning of a more comprehensive testing stream.

Data Migration

The purpose of data migration activities is to develop, test, and execute the data migration processes for all the data objects identified in the explore phase.

This activity consists of iterative cycles to analyze data quality, refine business rules, and run the migration processes that move, transform, and enrich the company data required to support project test cycles and, ultimately, production. The test cycles enable the migration team to improve data quality, develop a detailed cutover sequencing plan, and exercise the data reconciliation and validation processes required to support the production cutover.

Let's break the data migration process into steps:

1. **Creating the migration project and selecting migration objects**
   A migration project is created to specify the data objects that you want to transfer and to monitor the status of the migration. For each test transfer, a new migration project is created that includes any corrections or refinements identified in the previous test.

2. **Populating the staging tables with the files or preferred tool**
   In this step, the data migration experts will populate the data extracted from your legacy system into the migration template files. The migration template may change with each release, so it is important to always use the latest templates provided by the SAP S/4HANA migration cockpit. The project team will then upload data files for each migration object into the tenant via the Migrate Your Data app (see Chapter 5, Section 5.2). The data is then stored in the staging area, where the uploaded files can be reviewed, deleted, and uploaded again if errors are encountered. For every object in the tool, you can also find documentation on how to test and validate the migrated data from within the migration cockpit itself.

3. **Performing value mapping**
   After the data is loaded into the staging tables, the migration experts map the required field values of the staging table to fields in the tenant. Once all mapping tasks have been confirmed, the mapping process is complete.

4. **Simulating the data migration**
   This activity will simulate the migration of your data through the relevant application interfaces without committing the data to your actual database tables. The team should resolve any issues resulting from the simulation process, which may require adjusting configuration or business logic.

5. **Executing the data migration**
   After all the steps have been performed and the project team is confident in the source data quality, the data migration experts can proceed with loading the legacy data into the system (see Figure 7.17 for an example data migration project). This migration can be performed directly or via background processing. By completing this step, the project team delivers the master data and transactional data required by the SAP S/4HANA Cloud application. Populating master and transactional data enables the project team to complete the testing cycles and determine production readiness.

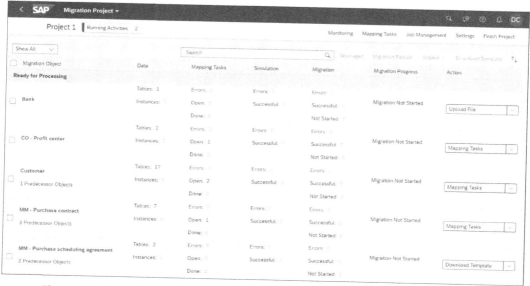

Figure 7.17 Data Migration Project with Included Data Objects

Testing

Progressive testing of the functionality as the system is configured during the realize phase is critical for any project, and this is no different when implementing SAP S/4HANA Cloud. As we mentioned earlier, SAP provides strong built-in testing automation capabilities in SAP S/4HANA Cloud and additional capabilities for test planning and orchestration powered by SAP Cloud ALM. (We introduced SAP Cloud ALM in Chapter 4 and discussed the testing topics in Chapter 5, Section 5.5.1.)

As shown in Figure 7.18, during the implementation, the project team will conduct several types of tests to ensure that the solution is configured properly and performs to the required specification level:

- **Unit test**

  This testing is performed by the configuration expert to ensure that specific units of a solution's functionality (configuration, output, etc.) work as required. This testing is done in each of the one- to two-week-long configuration sprints.

- **String test**

  Think of a string test as a string of unit tests, in which several units of functionality are combined to confirm that the collective functionality works as desired (e.g., creating an order and checking the approval levels for both the order item values and the value of the entire order). This type of testing is done during the one- to two-week-long configuration sprints, though in early sprints the project team may be limited in its scope of testing.

- **Business process test**
  A business process test covers an end-to-end flow with multiple units or strings within a single system.
  It focuses on testing the ability of the configured, extended, and integrated solution to meet the business requirements using migrated data and real business processes. It may be executed in additional cycles of testing based on the size of the project.

- **User acceptance test**
  The final testing is performed by the user or a subset of users to ensure that all job functions can be executed successfully in the new system. Using test scripts, training materials, and real experiences, day-to-day operations are simulated by job role to verify that the business can successfully operate after go-live. Successful completion indicates that the system is ready for productive use.

- **Postupgrade test**
  A standard list of tests defined by SAP is executed by SAP after the cloud system is upgraded. The company must give consent for these tests to be run by SAP in the solution. All postupgrade test plans are executed once by SAP, and the test results are available in the solution in the Analyze Your Test Result app, along with all applicable screenshots and statuses.

- **Regression test**
  The company validates that the business processes work as expected after changes are made that may impact the system, such as upgrades, extensions, and configuration changes. A company can leverage existing standard automated tests that are applicable to their processes with customer-specific test data and/or create their own processes.

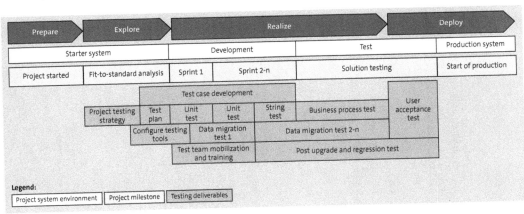

Figure 7.18 Test Activities and Deliverables

The SAP S/4HANA Cloud automated testing can be accessed via SAP Cloud ALM or the Manage Your Test Processes app in SAP S/4HANA Cloud. Custom test cases will be done within the test automation tool for SAP S/4HANA Cloud directly. If you are using a third-party testing tool, SAP Cloud ALM can be connected to supported tools to provide a central access point. We recommend that all the project team members involved in testing review the in-application help, user guides, and video recordings demonstrating how to use the tool. The SAP_BR_ADMIN_TEST_AUTOMATION SAP S/4HANA business role is required for access.

Before the tool can be used, the testing team creates the testing users that will be used during the automated test execution.

Further Resources

Step-by-step instructions are included in the Test Management Guide accelerator in the SAP Activate for SAP S/4HANA Cloud Three-System Landscape roadmap in the SAP Activate Roadmap Viewer.

The testing tool comes with predelivered test scripts for coverage of the SAP Best Practices functionality delivered in the system that can be modified or copied to create a new custom test process. SAP recommends using standard test process steps because these processes are updated automatically during the system upgrade. Custom-created process steps require manual updates by the company after a release upgrade, which can cause a delay in executing the tests. The testing will be run in the background, and the system will notify you about the results of the test has been executed. After the test is completed, you can view details and a log with applicable screenshots of the execution and review the results of every test step in detail, as shown in Figure 7.19.

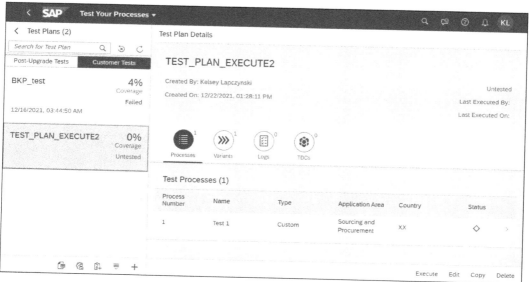

Figure 7.19 Testing Results in Testing Application

Adapting Forms and Configuring Output Management

Output management is an important part of getting the system ready for company use in the realize phase. During this stage, the project team will configure the output management in their SAP S/4HANA Cloud system and adjust the predelivered forms to meet company requirements. The output channels possible are print, email, and Electronic Data Interchange (EDI).

Printing and Form Adjustment Prerequisites

The project team will need to install both Cloud Print Manager and Adobe LiveCycle Designer. Both tools are available for download via the Install Additional Software app.

Additional documentation is available in the Output Management Set-Up Instructions (1LQ) SAP Best Practices scope item.

Let's take a closer look at these key activities for adaptation of forms and output management.

Adapting Forms in the Application

SAP S/4HANA Cloud contains SAP-delivered form templates. Simple changes can be completed using the Manage Logos app or the Manage Texts app. More significant changes can be made by downloading the templates from the Maintain Form Templates app and using Adobe LiveCycle Designer.

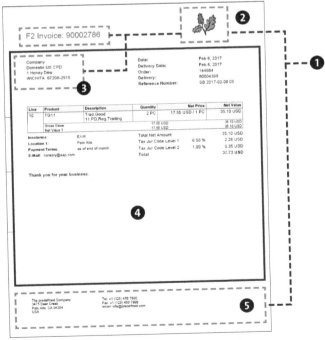

Figure 7.20 Master and Content Form Templates

Print forms use a two-tier concept, as shown in Figure 7.20: the *master* ❶ contains the header information, such as logo ❷ and address ❸, and the *content* ❹ contains the body details. Also note the footer block(s) at the bottom of the template form ❺. The email templates are edited directly in the solution via the Maintain Email Templates app.

Enabling Output Management

The purpose of enabling output management is to ensure that forms can be printed, emailed, or sent through an EDI channel. During this step, the project team configures the system through both SAP Central Business Configuration and SAP S/4HANA Cloud apps to support the required output destination.

Figure 7.21 shows the relevant tiles on your home screen for accessing these apps. Follow these steps to set up output management to a printer or set of printers:

1. Set up output channels via the Maintain Print Queues app.
2. Install the Cloud Print Manager for Pull Integration on a local server or PC.
3. Connect print queues and printers via Cloud Print Manager for Pull Integration.
4. Maintain the default print queue in the Output Parameter Determination app, and define the rules that determine which form will be used for each business scenario.

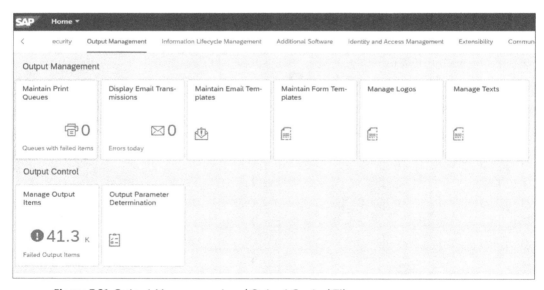

Figure 7.21 Output Management and Output Control Tiles

Application documents in PDF format can be automatically sent to business partners via email. In addition, the output can be configured to send transaction data via EDI.

> **Further Resources**
>
> For complete step-by-step documentation on setting up output management, see the documentation related to the Setting Up Output Management (1LQ) SAP Best Practices scope item.

Extensibility

SAP S/4HANA Cloud provides a range of options to extend the standard capabilities of the application. You can utilize key user extensibility, developer extensibility, and side-by-side extensibility. We discussed these in more detail in Chapter 5, Section 5.3. Now, we'll go over the key types of extensibility work performed in this phase.

Key User Extensions

Key user extensibility is one part of SAP S/4HANA Cloud's in-app extensibility capabilities that enable your key users to extend the standard functionality without modifying the code. These extensions are only applicable within a restricted organizational context, meaning that key users in this scenario can perform simple extensions of the application. SAP S/4HANA Cloud supports key user extensions to the UI, including the ability to add new custom fields to the UI and associated logic.

These extensions are created with a web-based key user tool, which provides easy-to-use access to customize the software without making code changes. A key user can make the following modifications on the fly:

- Adapt the UI to your company's naming terminologies by changing the field labels.
- Adapt and simplify the UI by hiding fields that aren't required.
- Organize the layout of fields in the UI to make it more accessible to your organization's needs.

To make changes to key user extensions, the key user must be assigned an appropriate business role that includes the SAP_CORE_BC_EXT business catalog. This assignment will make the key user tools accessible to the user and must be done through the Maintain Business User app in the SAP S/4HANA Cloud launchpad.

The key users will then be able to make the following changes in their SAP S/4HANA Cloud system:

- Make general UI adaptions for forms, tables, or filters, including hiding fields, removing fields, moving fields or UI blocks, creating a new group, adding a new field from the field repository, renaming labels, and so on.
- Add new custom fields to standard existing UIs.
- Add new custom business logic for standard existing UIs.

- Create new custom business objects, allowing data analysis of the underlying database tables.
- Create custom CDS views.

The built-in key user extensibility in SAP S/4HANA Cloud provides a wide range of extensibility options for your key users, as we've just outlined. The goal of this stage of the project is to implement the most critical extensions in the system and properly test them before they are transported to the production system.

Further Resources

Refer to the SAP Activate methodology and consult the relevant accelerators in the Roadmap Viewer for the latest guidance on key user extensibility.

Developer (On-Stack) Extensibility

Starting in 2021, SAP offers an additional extensibility option as part of SAP S/4HANA and SAP S/4HANA Cloud to complement current key user (in-app) extensibility capabilities. The developer (on-stack) extensibility option empowers ABAP developers to extend standard SAP processes with custom extensions that require tighter integration with the SAP S/4HANA backend while keeping the digital core isolated from the custom code. This will help minimize the efforts of regression testing during SAP S/4HANA upgrades. We introduced the developer extensibility topic in Chapter 5, Section 5.3.2.

Further Resources

Refer to the Developer Extensibility document in the SAP Help Portal at *http://s-prs.co/ v546312*.

Side-by-Side Extensibility

You also have option to use side-by-side extensibility, which utilizes SAP Business Technology Platform (SAP BTP) to build larger extensions or dedicated applications that are then integrated with SAP S/4HANA Cloud using the application programming interfaces (APIs) published on SAP API Business Hub. We discussed this type of extensibility in Chapter 5, Section 5.3.3.

Integration

For integrations included in the scope of the project, the team sets up the various integrations during the realize phase, following the guidance provided in the SAP Activate framework. SAP provides standard integrations for solutions such as SAP SuccessFactors Employee Central, SAP Fieldglass, SAP Ariba, SAP Concur, or SAP Customer

Experience, to list a few examples. Always refer to the latest information about available standard interfaces for SAP S/4HANA Cloud published in SAP Best Practices Explorer under the relevant business area in the **Line of Business** scope item group or the **SAP S/4HANA Cloud – Integration** scope item group, as shown in Figure 7.22. SAP Best Practices Explorer provides details about the integration, including setup instructions, process flows, task tutorials, test scripts, and links to the Cloud Integration Automation service.

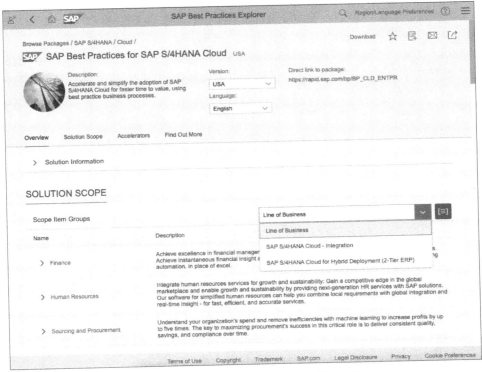

Figure 7.22 How to Access SAP S/4HANA Cloud Integration Scope Items

The Cloud Integration Automation service is available to provide workflow guidance to set up the standard integration in both systems. The steps in the service are from the SAP Best Practices setup guides and are presented in an interactive and guided way to allow quicker execution. The Cloud Integration Automation service subaccount must be created in SAP BTP to access the workflows.

In addition to standard integrations, you can integrate your custom applications with SAP S/4HANA Cloud using published APIs. SAP API Business Hub provides comprehensive documentation of all the available APIs for SAP S/4HANA Cloud. The SAP Activate methodology in the Roadmap Viewer provides a framework of tasks for project teams building custom interfaces.

Planning Cutover, End User Enablement, and User Support

During the realize phase, the project team needs to start detailed planning for the steps they will take to bring the solution into the production environment. These activities are documented in a *cutover plan* that captures the strategy, scope, and timelines for moving from the existing solution to the new solution and into the vulnerable period immediately after go-live.

We'll walk through each activity in the following sections.

Cutover Planning Workshop and Documentation

The purpose of the planning workshop is to document the strategy, scope, and time-lines for moving from the "as-is" solution to the "to-be" solution and the post-go-live support period immediately following go-live. This includes a workshop to document activities such as the following:

- Setting up and initializing the production system
- Setting up and verifying interface connections
- Migration or creation of master data manually, via a data migration tool, and/or via an interfaced system
- Migration of transactional data objects (e.g., purchase orders, sales orders)
- Testing of the complete data migration, at least once
- Validation of the migrated data
- User creation
- Notification of impacted third parties
- Go/no-go decision points
- Closing the legacy systems
- Completing all required documentation for regulatory purposes
- Planning timeline and meeting schedule for completing, sequencing, and simulating the cutover schedule

It is important that each team begin the development of the cutover list when starting the configuration and maintain the list throughout the implementation to avoid missing critical details. Estimated durations should also be kept and refined so that the final schedule can calculated down to the minute.

Remote Cutover Playbook

The SAP Activate team has introduced new remote playbooks for activities and tasks that were traditionally done on site. These playbooks support project teams in a shift to fully remote or hybrid execution of these project tasks. One such playbook is the

---

Remote Cutover Playbook, which has been added to SAP Activate. You can find it in the SAP Activate Roadmap Viewer under the relevant cutover planning and execution tasks. For example, in the task at *http://s-prs.co/v546313*, click on the **How to Approach Remote Cutover** accelerator to access the playbook.

End User Enablement

During the realize phase, the project team will prepare for user enablement to get new business users started in the system. One key aspect is the development of the learning and training materials for bringing new users into the system. In SAP S/4HANA Cloud implementations, project teams can leverage self-enablement materials such as videos, easy-to-access documentation, and recordings that users can consume at their own pace.

End user learning content must be designed to encourage effective user adoption and must complement the built-in functionalities of SAP S/4HANA Cloud, including the self-enablement content inside the product. The newly developed learning content must be employee-centric and business process–relevant. Learning experience design considers the type of material needed to target specific groups of end users. Learning content should also reflect the business's priorities in terms of process areas and subjects covered, while focusing on the user experience (UX; i.e., how and when employees will consume learning content). Learning experience design and development work will be undertaken within a clearly defined project plan and quality assurance process.

User Support

Before taking the system live, you'll need to establish a process for supporting your employees in using the new solution. It's critical for end users to know whom they can contact if issues arise and how they can escalate their support requests. Most organizations have existing IT policies and processes in place, and the goal of this activity in the realize phase is to ensure that user support for SAP S/4HANA Cloud is included in support handling and that the IT team can provide such support.

Your support organization must be able to communicate problems internally, troubleshoot data issues or improper system setup (configuration, printing, etc.), research issues, and escalate to SAP support when needed.

7.1.6   Deploy Your Solution

This section will explain how your project team can conduct the final validation of the solution prior to running the cutover activities that will bring the solution into live use by your end users. We'll also discuss end user enablement capabilities that simplify new user onboarding to SAP S/4HANA Cloud and discuss the salient differences in production support between a cloud environment and the on-premise systems that you're probably more familiar with.

After an overview of this phase, the information in this section is broken into two halves: the cutover to the production process and solution adoption and support.

Phase Overview

The purpose of this phase is to set up the production system, confirm organizational readiness, and switch business operations to the new system. Initiating the deploy phase means that the project team has already completed integration testing in the realize phase and has confirmed that all processes are functioning correctly and no issues remain that would hold back the transition to production. Thus, the team prepares for the transition to live business operations in the new environment, switches on the new solution, and conducts solution adoption and post-go-live support activities.

The following activities are key to the deploy phase:

- Preparing the organization for adoption of the new solution
- Executing cutover plans, including OCM plans
- Monitoring business process results in the production environment
- Establishing solution adoption support processes (e.g., onboarding new users, answering end user questions, and resolving user issues)

As shown in Figure 7.23, the deploy phase typically creates the following deliverables:

- Organizational and production environment readiness confirmation
- Completion of user enablement
- Results of integration and output management testing in production, as necessary
- Setup processes for adoption of the new live solution
- Cutover to production
- Post-go-live end user support
- Project closing

The deploy phase includes the following typical project milestones and key decisions:

- Data loads into production completed
- Production environment fully set up and verified
- Organization readiness for transition to production confirmed
- Go-live activities conducted
- Project formally closed

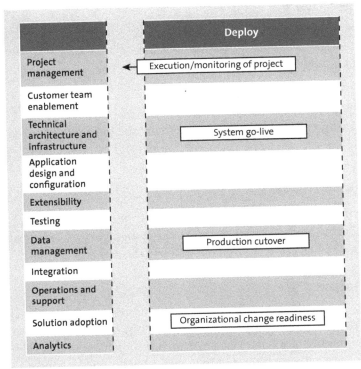

Figure 7.23 SAP Activate Deploy Phase Deliverables for SAP S/4HANA Cloud

Cutover to Production

The main activity during the deploy phase is to perform the cutover of the business to the new production software and to go-live. At this point, the organizational, business, functional, technical, and system aspects of the project are ready to be used in production. We'll walk through two key deliverables in the following sections.

Confirming Organizational Readiness for Cutover

Before you can proceed with the cutover activities outlined in the cutover plan, your project team needs to reconfirm that the business is ready to receive the new solution. This step includes confirmation of the following:

- Key users have been identified and trained and are ready to support the solution.
- End users have been enabled on the new solution.
- The production environment has been provisioned and is ready for cutover activities.
- Any business transactions in the legacy system have been stopped per the cutover plan, and contingency plans have been put in place (e.g., manual processing for the duration of cutover).

Now, it's time to perform the cutover.

Performing Cutover per the Cutover Plan

During the realize phase, the project team prepared a cutover plan that details the sequence, duration, and responsibilities for performing the cutover activities. The cutover plan includes but is not limited to the following:

- Closing the legacy system
- Setting up required integrations in the production environment
- Performing master data and transactional data loads to production per the cutover plan
- Setting up user accounts, including assignment of authorization profiles
- Setting up extensibility in production

After these cutover activities are completed, the project team confirms with the stakeholders the successful conclusion of the cutover before the system goes live for business users and before the company runs business activities in the new environment.

Solution Adoption and Support

The support processes for cloud solutions differ from the traditional on-premise model in several critical ways. You don't need a dedicated IT support organization to support the solution because the environment is managed by SAP; this support includes applying the quarterly releases of updates, applying hot fixes and patches, and resolving support tickets.

However, you'll need to establish an organization or appoint a responsible person to ensure the effective onboarding of new users, to drive the use of the solution, and to provide end user assistance not handled by the SAP support processes. In other words, support must be provided to answer procedural questions that users can't resolve on their own using in-application help functions or questions about company-specific processes and policies.

We'll discuss the key deliverables for solution adoption and support next.

Handover Onboarding and Adoption Support to the Company

The purpose of this activity is to transition from *project*-supported processes and organizational structures to *production*-supported processes and organizational structures. You'll need to set up sufficient support for end users to ensure that new users can be efficiently onboarded into the system (including creating users, assigning authorizations, and enablement to make end users proficient in using the environment). Such a support organization can also raise support tickets with SAP to resolve any production issues or can create service requests with the service center or other SAP support teams.

The project team will schedule a dedicated handover meeting to formally transition from the project support environment to the company onboarding and adoption environment. Because the new system is a cloud system, the responsible personnel must know how SAP will support the system and the proper methods of engaging with SAP when concerns, questions, or problems arise. The support organization will schedule and conduct the meeting prior to the go-live.

SAP Support Offerings for SAP S/4HANA Cloud Customers

To help SAP S/4HANA Cloud customers meet the needs of their new SAP solution, SAP provides different levels of proactive support, built on four pillars:

1. **Collaboration**
   SAP offers direct access to SAP support experts for best practice guidance on implementing, configuring, integrating, and adopting SAP S/4HANA Cloud.

2. **Empowerment**
   SAP Enterprise Support Academy offers guidance for the best practices, knowledge, and skills to quickly adopt SAP solutions.

3. **Innovation and value realization**
   SAP provides tools and proactive services to help companies identify and realize business value when using SAP cloud solutions, including the introduction of new innovations via quarterly updates.

4. **Mission-critical support**
   This support covers incident handling for both mission-critical and non-mission-critical applications.

As an SAP S/4HANA Cloud customer, you have access to the cloud edition of SAP Enterprise Support Academy, which provides ongoing support for the cloud solution starting on the first day of your subscription contract. In line with the SAP ONE Support principle, the cloud editions of SAP Enterprise Support Academy focus on collaboration, empowerment, innovation and value realization, and mission-critical support.

To support companies moving to cloud solutions, SAP Preferred Care offers personalized support and services at various milestones in your solution, help with nonstandard and new functionality, and a guided innovation process. Through ongoing and proactive advisory assistance and support from the company success manager and SAP's global network of experts, SAP Preferred Care allows you to do the following:

- Plot your business goals, projects, and release cycles on a support engagement plan, which includes applicable SAP Preferred Care deliverables.

- Leverage one-on-one empowerment sessions on specific topic areas to provide your team with the technical and functional best practices for operational excellence.

- Work closely with SAP support and implementation teams to ensure that open issues are documented and can be resolved before and after go-live.

- Access customized release notes based on your environment, provide support for the adoption of new features, and provide guidance related to key milestones.

- Reflect on successes and learn from challenges by leveraging the SAP Preferred Care scorecard, which quantifies business value and tracks performance.
- Analyze incident trends and monitor top issues to identify areas for improvement and to collect data for service improvement action planning.

The end is in sight! Let's look at the final stage of SAP S/4HANA Cloud implementation with SAP Activate.

7.1.7   Run Your Solution

The final phase of the SAP Activate methodology is the run phase, as shown in Figure 7.24. During this open-ended phase, companies and project teams further optimize the operability of SAP S/4HANA Cloud to maintain the IT systems in operating condition and guarantee system availability to execute business operations. In principle, productive use starts at the company's request right after the deployment of SAP S/4HANA Cloud to production and includes operational maintenance and support. In this phase, the operations team must ensure that the system is running as intended and be able to onboard new users. This phase also addresses the process of updates and upgrades that support the continuous adoption of new innovations.

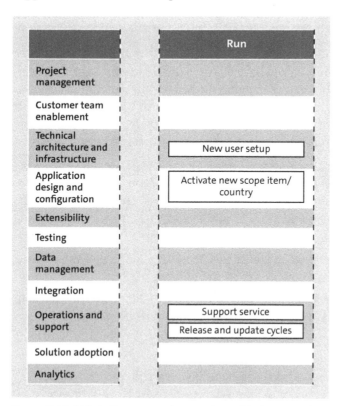

Figure 7.24 SAP Activate Run Phase Deliverable for SAP S/4HANA Cloud

We'll break up the important topics in the run phase into those that operate and support the implemented solution, and those that continuously improve and innovate.

Solution Operation and Support

Like previous SAP Activate implementation phases, the run phase breaks down into workstreams, deliverables, and tasks for end users as they begin to use their new cloud system.

In general, company roles are distinguished between business users (who basically work with the provided solution in their daily business) and key users (who have additional tasks to ensure that end users can fulfill their daily tasks with as few interruptions as possible). In detail, a key user needs to perform the following functions:

- Support business users
- Search for solutions (knowledge database, SAP community, and SAP Help Portal)
- Escalate incidents if necessary, as required per documented procedures and recommended criteria
- Track incident resolution progress
- Communicate provided solutions and timeframes to business users
- Sign off on solutions and confirm incidents (together with business users, if necessary)

We'll walk through key activities for solution operation and support in the following sections.

Onboarding New Users

The purpose of the onboarding and setup task is to determine the appropriate access, security, and authorizations for end users. Authorizations are broken down into simple user categories and are assigned to end users based on their job functions. After the appropriate and applicable roles and authorizations have been assigned, all business users must be authenticated through the Identity Authentication service. Users must then be uploaded into the system and given the necessary access and security authorizations.

> **Application Administrators**
> One key role is the company administrator, who serves as the main contact for any provisioning and system access topics. At least one primary and one backup contact should be application administrators.

Resolving Questions

Starting on the effective date of your subscription agreement for SAP S/4HANA Cloud, you may contact the SAP support organization for support services using one of following methods.

You can contact SAP support through the Customer Interaction Center (e.g., by phone, as described on the SAP Support Portal). The Customer Interaction Center will respond to your phone inquiries, create incidents on your behalf, and dispatch the incident to match the priority level. The preferred contact channel for SAP S/4HANA Cloud is through SAP Support Portal, which is available at *support.sap.com*. The SAP ONE Support Launchpad uses customizable role profiles and displays relevant applications that are task-driven support resources.

You can also gain direct access to the entire portfolio of SAP Activate implementation roadmaps through the SAP Activate community, available at *community.sap.com/topics/activate*. You can get answers in real time directly from SAP Activate experts who can guide you through the SAP Activate methodology phase by phase. We covered the SAP Activate community in more detail in Chapter 2.

On-Demand Support Requests

Recall from Section 7.1.6 that companies need to set up sufficient support for end users to ensure that the new users can be efficiently onboarded into the system. This support organization can raise support tickets with SAP to resolve any production issues or service requests to the service center or support teams.

SAP Trust Center

SAP provides transparent information about the cloud infrastructure and services in the SAP Trust Center. You can access the SAP Trust Center at *http://s-prs.co/v502724*, where you'll see the following information areas: **Cloud Status**, **Security**, **Privacy**, **Compliance**, **Cloud Operations**, **Data Center**, and **Agreements**.

Security and trust form the core of any project, especially for cloud projects. SAP offers transparency by releasing current and past reports for companies running live, companies experiencing interruptions, and companies in a maintenance window. The **Cloud Status** area shows details from the past four weeks and can be filtered using SAP S/4HANA Cloud. SAP S/4HANA Cloud companies logged into the SAP Trust Center with their user IDs also will see information about the data center that hosts their solution. In addition to the status of the infrastructure, the SAP Trust Center provides detailed information about cloud services, security, privacy, and available support services.

Continuously Improve and Innovate

With a cloud solution, you'll benefit from frequent updates and periodic upgrades that SAP deploys to the system, which give you the latest improvements and innovations. The upgrade and maintenance release schedule can be found in the Roadmap Viewer.

We'll walk through the key activities in the following sections.

Fast and Continuous Access to Innovation

SAP starts implementing continuous feature delivery via monthly shipments and is working toward reducing the number of system upgrades in a year. This means that companies can decrease the effort to enact release upgrades substantially, while still being able to adopt desired innovation and have access to new capabilities in a nondisruptive manner.

The upgrade process occurs over three weeks, but preparations should be made prior to the start. In addition, it's recommended that no new configuration is added until after the production system is upgraded. Software upgrades are executed by SAP and will start with the test system. The starter (if still available), development, and production systems will be completed afterward. Business content upgrades are deployed and executed at a company's discretion. The upgraded system is tested manually and with the automated testing tool to ensure that business processes can be executed as before. If a defect is found, an incident is entered immediately so that the issue can be resolved prior to the production upgrade.

An upgrade doesn't automatically activate new scope functionality and should not impact existing processes. The enhancements to existing functions can be viewed by scope item using SAP S/4HANA Cloud's Release Assessment and Scope Dependency tool. After the production system is upgraded, additional scopes can be activated.

Product Roadmap

SAP S/4HANA Cloud users receive regular innovations in their environments. SAP provides visibility into planned innovations in the SAP S/4HANA Cloud product roadmap, which is available at *www.sap.com/roadmaps/*. The SAP S/4HANA Cloud product roadmaps for various business areas can be accessed in the **Featured Road Maps** area of the site and offer lists of planned innovations in each functional area of SAP S/4HANA Cloud, as well as interrelated topics and planned localizations. SAP product roadmaps are updated regularly, and you're encouraged to check this site frequently to determine how you can benefit from innovations to be introduced in the upcoming releases for SAP S/4HANA Cloud. To view innovation available in current release, the What's New Viewer from the SAP Help Portal gives you a complete overview of new, changed, and deleted features and functions.

Biweekly Patches and Hot Fixes

The blue-green deployment model for the biweekly hotfix collection maintenance procedure means that new corrections are seamlessly deployed in the "green" version, while business users are working in the source release "blue" version. With this model, downtime for the productive system of SAP S/4HANA Cloud is minimized and can be further optimized.

7.2   New Implementation of SAP S/4HANA Cloud, Private Edition

We've detailed the deployment of SAP S/4HANA Cloud in Section 7.1. The SAP S/4HANA Cloud, private edition deployment follows the same flow and uses the same fit-to-standard techniques we detailed previously (and also discussed in more detail in Chapter 4 and Chapter 5). In this section, we'll focus on explaining the key differences in the preconfiguration content, implementation process, and tools that the project team will use to deploy the solution. We'll also discuss the differences in the system landscape, configuration capabilities, extensibility, and integration that are available in SAP S/4HANA Cloud, private edition.

This section will follow a similar outline to Section 7.1, where we provided an overview of the deployment before going into specific details for each SAP Activate phase. Let's start with the overview of SAP S/4HANA Cloud, private edition deployment.

7.2.1   Deployment Approach Overview

SAP S/4HANA Cloud, private edition provides companies with a highly flexible environment that follows the standardized deployment approach guided by the five golden rules we discussed in Chapter 2. The golden rules have been established to help companies running SAP systems to deploy the solution in such a way that it allows for frequent upgrades with lower effort than is typically needed for on-premise deployments. They also aim to help companies increase the frequency of consuming innovations SAP delivers with the SaaS model with SAP S/4HANA Cloud. The deployment follows the standard six phases of SAP Activate you learned about in Chapter 2 and, on a high level, mirrors the key activities we introduced earlier in this chapter. Figure 7.25 shows a detailed list of deliverables in each phase of SAP Activate for RISE with SAP S/4HANA Cloud, private edition. This figure is available for download at *www.sap-press.com/5463*.

We'll dive into more details in the following sections to discuss the key activities that the project teams complete in each of the phases. Before we do that, we also need to discuss the solution landscape that is typical for deployment of SAP S/4HANA Cloud, private edition.

The solution is provisioned with three default systems: development, quality, and production. The solution provides a full transport management system (TMS) for transporting configuration and custom code between the three systems in the landscape. Companies can also elect to add an optional sandbox system to the landscape for additional safety and for evaluation of functionality before they activate the business functions or bring the configuration into their productive landscape (e.g., bring the configuration into the development system and transport it up the transport path to quality and production systems). Note that there is no transport path set up between the sandbox system and any of the systems in the production landscape.

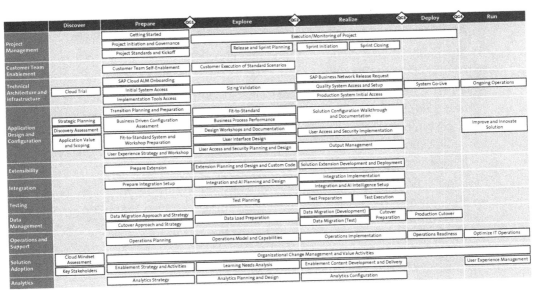

Figure 7.25 SAP Activate for RISE with SAP S/4HANA Cloud, Private Edition

The high-level depiction of the SAP S/4HANA Cloud, private edition system landscape is shown in Figure 7.26.

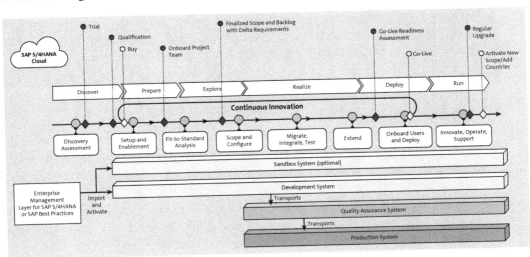

Figure 7.26 Example System Landscape of SAP S/4HANA Cloud, Private Edition

In this setup, the development system is used for exploration of the solution, after the preconfiguration content has been deployed into the system. The fit-to-standard approach, which we introduced in Chapter 2 and have seen throughout the book, is used for this solution to confirm the fit of the preconfigured solution, to determine the configuration values for using standard functionality and requirements for extensibility and integration, to define system authentication and security, and to determine data migration requirements.

Note that companies can also opt for a smaller footprint that combines the functions of the development and quality systems into one combined system along with the production system in the landscape. In such a setup, the solution is run in a two-tier system environment that uses the quality system for configuration and testing before changes are transported to the production system for productive use.

We'll discuss additional details about the landscape in the relevant subsections when we cover the details of the deployment approach. Let's now look at the key project team activities during the discover phase.

7.2.2 Discover Your Solution

During this phase, the project team performs several critical activities that help determine the value and define the high-level scope and approach for transition to SAP S/4HANA Cloud, private edition. The key activities include value discovery activities during which the team defines the business case for transition to the SAP S/4HANA solution, along with one or more value drivers discussed in Chapter 1 when we introduced the transition paths and deployment strategies. The value discovery from the application perspective is detailed in the application and value-scoping deliverable in the SAP Activate methodology for SAP S/4HANA Cloud, private edition.

Let's now outline the key steps in this deliverable that the project team performs for creating input into the business case:

1. **Strategic planning**

   The aim of strategic planning is to define an innovation strategy and high-level multiyear roadmap for all SAP solutions, including SAP Customer Experience, SAP Business Network, SAP SuccessFactors, and SAP BTP, and including analytics and intelligent technologies. To do so, start with an identification of strategic business and IT objectives, including current pain points. Cluster the objectives into benefit areas and for each benefit area, identify and prioritize the SAP solution enablers. These solutions provide the target enterprise architecture.

2. **Discover the value of the new functionality in SAP S/4HANA Cloud for your company**

   During this activity, the project team reviews the new capabilities of SAP S/4HANA Cloud for their business. The objective is to thoroughly evaluate the new standard functionality and capabilities that the solution delivers and that the business users can benefit from adopting. The key for this evaluation is access to the SAP S/4HANA Cloud, private edition trial that we'll discuss later in this section.

3. **Identify the impact of SAP S/4HANA Cloud on existing business processes**

   Along with the evaluation of the new functionality and capabilities, the project team needs to determine the impact of adopting the new standard functionality on the business processes currently in place in the company. This is very important information for understanding the scope and breath of the change management activities that will be required during the implementation project and to adopt the new functionality in the business by the end users. This is a key touchpoint with the OCM and solution adoption activities we'll detail later in Chapter 10.

4. **Perform a business scenario and solution mapping**

   SAP Activate offers an interactive workshop approach for teams looking to gamify the identification of the most impactful opportunities to adopt new standard capabilities using a card game and workshop format. During the workshop, the team performs the SAP S/4HANA board game to select the most desirable capabilities for the organization, ultimately building the value map for adoption of new capabilities. This workshop can be used not only during the initial implementation but also after the release upgrade to determine a set of priority capabilities that are to be adopted after the solution upgrade. SAP Activate provides a description of the game and instructions for ordering the game in the form of a workshop. See Figure 7.27 for overview of the board game accelerator in SAP Activate.

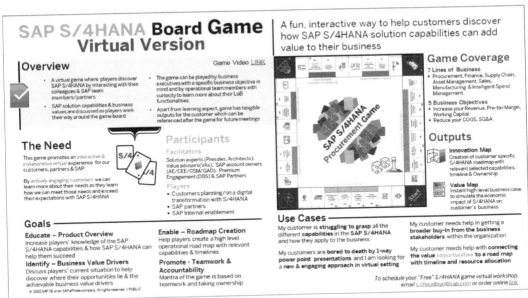

Figure 7.27 Accelerator for SAP S/4HANA Discovery Game

5. **Define the implementation strategy**

   During this activity, the project team will determine the overall implementation strategy, including the selection of the most appropriate preconfiguration package, whether SAP Best Practices, the enterprise management layer for SAP S/4HANA, or SAP-qualified partner packages. We introduced SAP Best Practices in Chapter 4 in detail as the standard preconfigured, ready-to-use set of processes that are used in fit-to-standard workshops during the project. The project team will also look at the results of the previous activities we outlined in this section and determine where the organization will follow the back-to-standard approach and drive change management activities.

6. **Create a strategic roadmap and value case**
   At the end of the execution of this deliverable, the team compiles the results of all activities into a formal strategic roadmap that shows the planned adoption of the solution along with a value case (sometimes referred to as business case) to present the value of the transition to SAP S/4HANA Cloud, private edition for the organization.

7. **Stakeholder identification**
   Identify executive sponsors, keys users, the extended project team, end users, and the implementation project team.

During the execution of these steps, the project team will need access to a trial environment to evaluate the functionality and determine where to stay with standard and SAP Best Practices processes and where it's warranted to deploy their own practices to preserve the business value of the differentiating processes and practices for the organization. We'll now take a look at how project teams can create the trial environment using SAP Cloud Appliance Library (access it at *http://cal.sap.com*).

SAP provides companies with access to an SAP S/4HANA fully activated appliance that can be used for trying out the software capabilities before obtaining a subscription. You can access the SAP S/4HANA fully activated appliance at *http://s-prs.co/v502726*. The appliance provides access to a system with preactivated SAP Best Practices configuration, ready-to-use business processes, and sample data.

The detailed documentation of the business process content is available on SAP Best Practices Explorer, which we discussed earlier in Chapter 3 and Chapter 4. Existing customers with a subscription to SAP Cloud Appliance Library also can access the appliance directly in the SAP Cloud Appliance Library environment and deploy it to their preferred cloud provider environment, whether Amazon Web Services (AWS), Google Cloud Platform, or Microsoft Azure. The appliance comes with a detailed Getting Started Guide, an Architecture and Design document, and predefined sizing for each cloud environment, shown in the **Recommended VM Sizes** section of the website. Figure 7.28 shows the SAP Cloud Appliance Library page for SAP S/4HANA as a fully activated appliance.

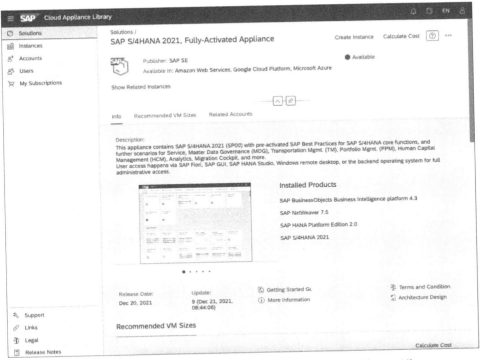

Figure 7.28 SAP S/4HANA Fully Activated Appliance in SAP Cloud Appliance Library

Further Resources

To understand how to deploy SAP S/4HANA as a fully activated appliance and what functionality is delivered, review the following blog post on the SAP website, which was updated for the current release of the software in December 2021: *http://s-prs.co/ v502727.*

Note that the SAP S/4HANA fully activated appliance is continually updated to keep pace with the latest software releases. You can check the list of available appliances when you access the SAP Cloud Appliance Library and use the latest release relevant for your project.

7.2.3   Prepare Your Project

Now we'll briefly review the activities the project team executes in the prepare phase. Note that we'll focus on the activities that significantly differ for deployment of SAP S/4HANA Cloud, private edition; we won't repeat all the activities from workstreams such as project management, project team onboarding, and so on that are common for deployment of SAP S/4HANA Cloud and were covered earlier in Section 7.1.3.

Phase Overview

The key deliverables in the prepare phase of the SAP Activate methodology for SAP S/4HANA Cloud, private edition, are shown in Figure 7.29. They help the project team set up, plan, and get the project underway. They also support the project team in self-enablement, setup of the system, and preparation for fit-to-standard.

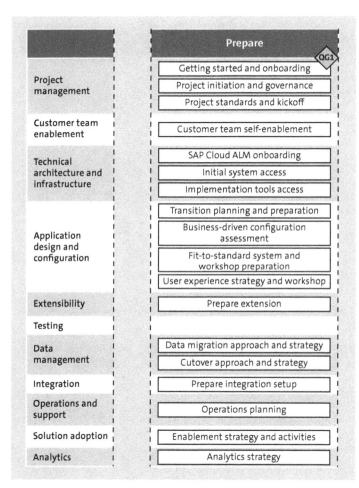

Figure 7.29 Prepare Phase of SAP Activate for RISE with SAP S/4HANA Cloud, Private Edition

We'll only focus on activities that are different because of the landscape setup for SAP S/4HANA Cloud, private edition. We recommend reviewing the following activities in Section 7.1 if you'd like a refresher:

- Setting up the project, including the setup of governance; definition of roles and responsibilities; preparation of the budget, project plan, and schedule; project kick-off; definition of project standards; and setup of project team environment

- Project team self-enablement on the solution capabilities, project approach, and use of standard tools and applications during the project
- Execution of OCM activities, such as setup of the OCM team and definition of the OCM concept, refinement of stakeholder lists, and initial stakeholder analysis

Next, we'll review the deliverables for which there are differences in SAP S/4HANA Cloud, private edition.

System Provisioning

We've discussed that the system landscape for SAP S/4HANA Cloud, private edition consists of three systems that are connected with a TMS. In this section, we'll look deeper into the setup of these systems and explain their role during the implementation and ongoing enhancements process (after initial go-live).

When the landscape is provided, it contains the following three systems (plus one optional system) that are interconnected via a TMS:

- **Development system**
  This system's main purpose is to serve as the environment where the team receives the preconfigured ready-to-use processes. During the discover phase, the determination was made as to which preconfiguration assets were best suited for particular companies. During this phase, the landscape is provisioned and the preconfiguration is installed. The preconfiguration package can be the SAP Best Practices package, the enterprise management layer for SAP S/4HANA, or an SAP-qualified partner package. Depending on the package chosen, the methodology provides detailed guidance about steps that are required to be done by the company to receive the system and activate the appropriate package.

- **Quality system**
  The purpose of the quality system is to serve as an environment for testing the configuration, extensibility, integration, and data loads before these are either transported or performed in the production system. There is a transport path between development system and quality system to move the configuration settings and other objects from the development system to the quality system for testing and confirmation before these objects get promoted to the production system. The quality system is also used in later stages of the project for cutover simulation, and some companies may use it as the environment for end user training and enablement as part of the initial implementation or in subsequent upgrades and continuous enhancements. The quality system will primarily contain the client for integration testing, but some companies may also have dedicated clients for end user training. In such cases, companies should consider using one client as the golden client for training that will contain the functionality and sample data and one client for execution of training that gets regularly refreshed for repeat training session runs.

- **Production system**

  This environment is dedicated to productive execution of business processes by the company. This is the environment that the business users access in their daily routine to execute business processes, such as asset management, financial accounting, and logistics. Companies should only import transports to the production system environment after they have been configured in the development system and tested in the quality system. There should be no direct configuration performed in the production system environment. The production environment will contain one productive client where the company performs its daily business. There may be additional optional clients set up during the cutover simulation to ensure the productive client isn't negatively impacted during the cutover simulation weekends in the deploy phase.

- **Sandbox system**

  This is an optional environment. While available to anyone, it's expected that midsize and larger companies are more likely to use this environment than are smaller companies. The sandbox environment provides additional safety and a place to prototype functionality that the project team isn't sure if they will use in production. For example, some activation of business functions that can't be reverted should be done in the sandbox environment before it's done in the development/quality/production landscape. The sandbox environment will be also important for execution of release upgrades, as an environment where the new business content for release +1 business content can be evaluated after release upgrade and considered for use in the productive landscape (through the standard path via the development system to the quality system and then to the production system).

The development system and optional sandbox are provisioned in the prepare phase. The quality and production systems are provisioned in the realize phase.

Nonreversible Enterprise Extension Activation without Sandbox

For companies that haven't purchased the sandbox environment, the activation of nonreversible enterprise extensions can be done in the development environment with the following considerations:

- A backup needs be made of the development system prior to activation of any nonreversible enterprise extensions that are being evaluated.

- After the evaluation is complete, if the company doesn't want the nonreversible enterprise extensions, then the development environment will need to be restored from the backup.

When this evaluation is taking place, the development environment can't be used to mitigate any production landscape defects because the development environment is technically different from the production environment and quality environment.

SAP recommends all customers use a dedicated environment for ALM. Currently, customers of SAP S/4HANA Cloud, private edition, use SAP Solution Manager 7.2 for solution documentation, testing, system change management, proactive monitoring, and operations. We covered these functions in Chapter 3, Section 3.4. The use of SAP Solution Manager is also important for compliance with the five golden rules discussed in Chapter 2, Section 2.4. Customers with a cloud-first environment should consider using SAP Cloud ALM for ALM in their environment, including customers using SAP S/4HANA Cloud, private edition.

The system landscape is provisioned and given to the companies during the prepare phase to ensure the environment can be set up and prepared for fit-to-standard.

Fit-To-Standard System and Workshop Preparation

Let's now focus on the activities that the project team needs to do to prepare for the fit-to-standard workshops. We've covered the provisioning of the system, including the activation of the preconfigured business processes, in the previous section. We'll now focus on what the team needs to do with the system before the workshops and how to prepare for the execution of the workshops. The following are the key steps that the project team executes during the prepare phase:

1. **Access initial system for fit-to-standard workshops**
   During this stage, the project team will set up users with appropriate authorizations to aid in the execution of fit-to-standard processes. The team will also perform the activation of the SAP Fiori UX for the business users.

2. **Enhance setup and additional configuration**
   The functional and technical consultants identify the additional configuration that will need to be set up before the execution of the workshops. The focus should be on quick wins of functionality that can be configured fast before the start of the workshops so that the participants can see the functionality in a live system. This is one of the principles discussed in Chapter 2 that helps accelerate learning about the solution with the key business users and is preferred to reviewing documentation or help documents.

3. **Activate SAP Fiori in the initial system**
   SAP Activate provides clear guidance about the use of the SAP Fiori rapid content activation functionality in SAP S/4HANA Cloud, private edition to prepare the SAP Fiori UX for fit-to-standard for the business roles that are in the project scope. Refer to the SAP Activate task Learn about SAP Fiori UX (either in SAP Cloud ALM or the SAP Activate Roadmap Viewer) that explains the process and provides references to related blog posts and SAP Help Portal documentation.

4. **Prepare and schedule fit-to-standard workshops**
   This activity includes a review of the fit-to-standard workshop guide accelerator that helps consultants and key users understand the flow of the workshop. They also gain

an understanding of the required inputs for the workshops and the output that gets created during the workshop. In addition, the technical consultants together with integration experts prepare an initial list of integrations that will be used during the fit-to-standard process.

Prepare Integration Setup

The project team verifies access to all the systems originally ordered in addition to SAP S/4HANA (e.g., SAP Business Network). They must then decide which integrations should be working for the fit-to-standard workshops and set these up.

Operations Planning

Plan the transition of the new solution to the operations team. With the introduction of the new solution, your current IT support framework will change. SAP provides guidance on the target IT support process activities, tools, and resources required for you to safely and efficiently operate the new SAP solutions in your environment.

7.2.4   Explore the Solution

Next, we'll review the key deliverables and activities that are done during the explore phase.

Phase Overview

During the explore phase, the project team will engage with business users to conduct the fit-to-standard workshops with the objective to confirm the fit of the standard solution; determine additional configuration, requirements for extensibility, and integration; and determine the data migration plans for loading master data, organizational data, and open balances. The team also focuses on executing OCM planning activities, preparing the testing, planning the strategy for delivery of end user enablement, and training. These are a few highlights of activities that are done during the explore phase. You can see a complete list of deliverables in the explore phase in Figure 7.30.

We covered these deliverables in detail in the description of SAP S/4HANA Cloud in Section 7.1.4. In this section, we'll focus on the deliverables that are approached completed differently for SAP S/4HANA Cloud, private edition, as we did for the prepare phase. We'll pay special attention to the following deliverables in the explore phase:

- Additional considerations for fit-to-standard analysis and design
- Analytics planning and design
- Additional capabilities for data load preparation
- Test planning review
- Operations models and capabilities

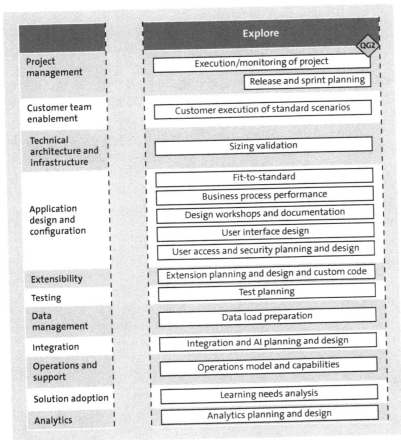

Figure 7.30 Explore Phase of SAP Activate for RISE with SAP S/4HANA Cloud, Private Edition

Let's start with the fit-to-standard analysis and design activities.

Fit-to-Standard Analysis and Design

The general approach and flow of steps in fit-to-standard analysis and design in SAP S/4HANA Cloud, private edition is the same as in SAP S/4HANA Cloud, as discussed in Section 7.1. You'll find the overall flow shown in Figure 7.31, where you can see that the tasks and activities follow the same steps as for SAP S/4HANA Cloud:

1. In the discover phase, the value discovery activities define the value of the solution for the business and set the initial scope for implementation.

2. In the prepare phase, the project team details the scope in the project charter and scope statement, and then uses that information to prepare for fit-to-standard (both system and logistics/processes). In parallel, the company project team goes through self-enablement activities to get familiar with the solution capabilities and implementation approach before the fit-to-standard workshops.

3. In the explore phase, the project team conducts the fit-to-standard workshops to confirm the fit of the solution to company needs and to capture any additional configuration values or delta requirements that will be designed during the design workshops, with a focus on integration requirements, extensibility needs, UI design, analytics, master data, and user access and security. SAP S/4HANA Cloud, private edition provides more options for extending the solution, which means that the design phase is typically longer than for SAP S/4HANA Cloud. All this information is stored in a backlog and used toward the end of the explore phase for release and for planning the initial few sprints. Note that the sprints are planned progressively and not all planned at the end of the explore phase. Project teams typically plan the next one or two sprints and primarily focus on making sure the desired high-priority backlog items are ready to be inserted into the sprint (we discussed this in detail in Chapter 6 when we reviewed the agile approach).

4. All this work is done as preparation for agile execution during the realize phase, as shown in the solution realization box in Figure 7.31.

You'll find this schema and all the steps of fit-to-standard analysis and design detailed in the How to Approach the Fit-to-Standard Analysis/Design in the Cloud accelerator in the SAP Activate methodology. You can download it from the Roadmap Viewer (refer to Chapter 3, Section 3.1, for how to access accelerators in the Roadmap Viewer).

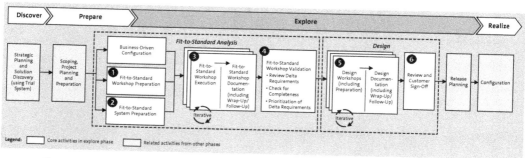

Figure 7.31 Fit-to-Standard for SAP S/4HANA Cloud, Private Edition

Use of SAP Solution Manager for Requirements Capture

As we mentioned, SAP recommends that companies implementing SAP S/4HANA Cloud, private edition use Focused Build for SAP Solution Manager 7.2 for capturing the solution documentation and requirements, which typically includes following:

- Key business decisions impacting the scope or design of the solution
- Confirmation of fit
- Scope information
- Business process models/process flows

- Design documents (scenario and, optionally, process level)
- Requirements for items covered by the design (e.g., integration, extensibility, analytics, master data, user access, and security)

This documentation should continue to be managed and updated even after the initial go-live to allow the company to manage the upgrade activities. The solution documentation will be critical for any work that will be done after the release upgrade to adjust the system for the new release (e.g., adjust the code in extensions or integrations for the new release level of the software).

Analytics Planning and Design

The project should evaluate the analytics solutions available for SAP S/4HANA. The explore phase should build on the work already done during the discover and prepare phases to document an analytics architecture, landscape, and design. The main SAP solutions in focus are as follows:

- **SAP S/4HANA embedded analytics**
  Includes LoB-specific prebuilt solutions. New real-time reports can also be produced based on the SAP HANA core data services (CDS) views.

- **SAP Analytics Cloud**
  Cloud-based analytics solution that can operate across all SAP solutions and non-SAP solutions.

Further Resources

SAP Analytics Cloud has its own separate SAP Activate roadmap in the Roadmap Viewer that follows the SAP Activate project phases. The on-premise roadmap covers additional solutions, such as SAP Digital Boardroom.

Analytics design covers analytics (e.g., reports, tables, charts, graphs, and geographic analysis), predictive analytics, and planning requirements. Analytics workshops are conducted for LoB-specific processes and requirements. The standard analytics apps and standard business content are reviewed, and a fit-to-standard analysis and design are performed.

Data Load Preparation

We discussed the data load process and capabilities in Chapter 5 and then covered the steps project teams follow in Section 7.1.4. The same process is used for data loads into SAP S/4HANA Cloud, private edition, but there are additional capabilities that are available for loading data into the system that we'll discuss here.

Further Resources

All these capabilities are detailed in the SAP Best Practices Explorer package for rapid data migration that you can find at *http://s-prs.co/v502729* once you are logged in with your customer or partner user ID. Specifically, review the SME vs LE Deployment Scenarios for SAP Best Practices for Data Migration document, which you'll find linked in the **Accelerators** section under **General Documents**.

There are two major models for data preparation for loading into the SAP S/4HANA Cloud, private edition environment:

1. **Small and medium enterprise (SME) model**
   In this model, there is a single local repository for the ERP data migration, and all the staging database data is stored from that local repository point to the same physical database. This model is used when there is a smaller amount of data to prepare for data loads or when there is one central coordinator for data preparation.

2. **Large enterprise (LE) model**
   In this model, there are multiple local repositories for ERP data migration content. It also consists of multiple staging databases and is typically used when multiple individuals work in the data migration environment in SAP Data Services. The setup of the LE model requires additional changes that are detailed in the guide and go beyond the scope of this book.

The actual load of data into the system follows the same process we outlined in Section 7.1.4.

Further Resources

You can find more details in *Migrating to SAP S/4HANA* (SAP PRESS, 2021).

Test Planning

Test planning is another critical activity that is completed during the explore phase. For SAP S/4HANA Cloud, private edition, it's recommended to use the SAP Solution Manager 7.2 Test Management capabilities to prepare and run testing of the functionality. During the explore phase, the project team needs to ensure that SAP Solution Manager is available and that it's set up to support the testing requirements. The project team also starts planning the structure of the tests that will be done during the realize phase, whether these are unit tests, string tests bringing together multiple units of testing, or preparations of larger tests for release—that is, integration tests and UAT.

Operations Models and Capabilities

The aim is to build on the work done in the prepare phase. All the relevant support areas need to be analyzed and defined in detail: roles and skills, processes/procedures, operations documentation, and enabling support tools.

Then a target model is defined that covers the key activities for a Center of Excellence (COE) and potential use of an external service provider. This will include establishing resources; setting up tools; documenting procedures, knowledge transfer, and operations cutover; and retiring parts of the old framework. Information is available on the typical roles and responsibilities for SAP S/4HANA Cloud, private edition, with details of what aspects of operations and support are covered by SAP.

Later, during the realize phase, the target model is put in place with knowledge transfer from the project team to the COE and any external service provider.

7.2.5   Realize Your Requirements

Now that we've covered the key aspects in the explore phase, we'll focus on the key differences in the realize phase that companies implementing SAP S/4HANA Cloud, private edition should be aware of.

Phase Overview

The overall picture of the deliverables completed during the realize phase is shown in Figure 7.32. The execution of these steps follows the same flow as explained for SAP S/4HANA Cloud earlier in this chapter. We'll focus on specific considerations that companies implementing SAP S/4HANA Cloud, private edition should be aware of as the solution offers a broader set of capabilities for configuration and extensibility, which increases the flexibility available to companies in this environment. We'll specifically discuss the considerations for system access and setup, solution configuration, analytics configuration, extensibility and integration, and testing execution.

Let's start with considerations for system access.

System Access and Setup

The system access and setup approach are different for SAP S/4HANA Cloud, private edition. Depending on the company's contract, all system access and provisioning emails are often shared with the company during the prepare phase. It's important for the company's IT contact/administrator to check all communication emails to get access to the right systems provisioning emails. If it has not been done already, the administrator will access the quality system and reset the password and create users for the project team. SAP delivers the system with the same SAP Best Practices or enterprise management layer for SAP S/4HANA as the development system.

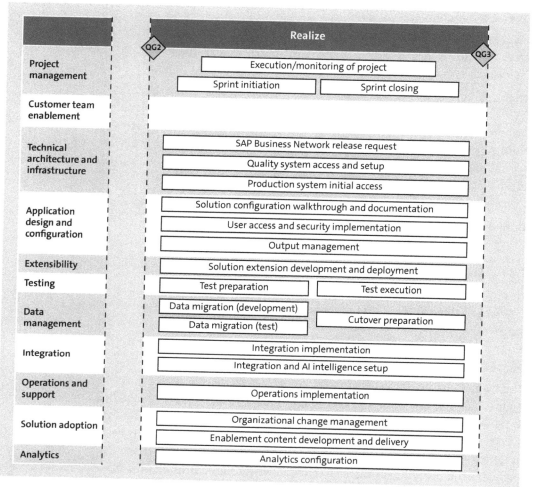

Figure 7.32 Realize Phase in SAP Activate for RISE with SAP S/4HANA Cloud, Private Edition

The SAP Fiori rapid activation is transported from the development system to the quality system. Existing configuration and development transports are run into the quality system, and manual rework activities (e.g., nontransportable configuration) are done.

If the project plans to use SAP Business Network included in the RISE with SAP contract, a release request form is completed. Once the scope is confirmed, SAP connects the SAP Business Network to the SAP S/4HANA quality system, and the integration is acceptance-tested.

The production system is accessed later in the realize phase and follows a similar process as the quality system.

Solution Configuration

As stated at the beginning of Section 7.2, companies implementing SAP S/4HANA Cloud, private edition have access to a broad set of configuration settings in the Implementation Guide (IMG; Transaction SPRO) in their SAP S/4HANA solutions. This environment provides companies with thousands of possible configuration options, significantly extending the configuration flexibility to reflect company needs with configuration using standard software. The environment for configuring the solution is very similar in scope and functionality to the one used for configuring the SAP S/4HANA solution in an on-premise or hosted setup. Refer to Section 7.3.5 for more detail on how configuration is done. The configuration decisions made to extend the scope of preconfigured content that the company or system integrator performs in this environment should be captured as part of the solution documentation, as discussed in Section 7.2.4, using SAP Solution Manager. In addition, refer to Chapter 2, Section 2.4.6, where we discussed the need for documentation in rule 5.

Analytics Configuration

The analytics solutions are configured based on the design and guidelines documented in the explore phase. The scope may cover analytics, predictive analytics, and planning requirements. The design will typically be based on embedded analytics in SAP S/4HANA and SAP Analytics Cloud to define the UX for analytics and planning.

Examples of the activities to be undertaken in SAP S/4HANA include the following:

- Configure the SAP Fiori launchpad.
- Perform the technical setup of SAP S/4HANA CDS views and SAP S/4HANA embedded analytical apps based on CDS views.
- Customize prebuilt SAP S/4HANA embedded analytics.
- Create custom CDS views for custom SAP S/4HANA embedded analytics.

Examples of the activities to be undertaken in SAP Analytics Cloud include the following:

- Configure general settings such as import functionality, database connector, and cloud connector.
- Import and enable prebuilt content for SAP Analytics Cloud.
- Configure the underlying SAP Analytics Cloud data models, planning models, and predictive models.
- Import data into the data models and perform data preparation for analytics, with persistent data in the cloud.
- Configure SAP Analytics Cloud stories for reports, tables, charts, graphs, and geographic analysis.

Integration and Extensibility

In Chapter 2, Section 2.4, we highlighted the need to use modern technologies for integration (rule 3) and extensibility (rule 4). One of the key principles for extensibility and integration in SAP S/4HANA Cloud, private edition is that SAP code must remain intact. This is to prevent modification of SAP-standard code that would impact the effort and duration of subsequent system release upgrades. We'll now review the options companies should consider for integration and extensibility while implementing SAP S/4HANA Cloud, private edition.

Integration

When it comes to defining and designing for integration, there is a set of principles to apply:

1. Companies should use the standard predelivered integration scenarios for integrating cloud and on-premise products that SAP delivers.
2. Companies should prioritize the use of open APIs published on SAP API Business Hub at *http://api.sap.com* before considering other options. The use of open APIs and SAP BTP for integration allows you to build a future-proof solution that uses modern technology. You'll find both the open APIs and the standard predefined integration scenario for SAP API Business Hub at *http://s-prs.co/v502730*.
3. The use of SAP Integration Suite is the preferred way to integrate with other cloud or on-premise applications. SAP Integration Suite offers a set of predelivered integration content, published as OData and Simple Object Access Protocol (SOAP) service APIs.

Further Resources

You can learn more about the capabilities of SAP Integration Suite at *http://s-prs.co/v502731*.

The SAP Activate methodology provides guidance on how to approach the integration topics throughout the flow of the SAP Activate phases. When it comes to the specific steps for definition and design of integration, technical experts will follow the steps outlined in Figure 7.33.

The first steps are to identify the appropriate API on SAP API Business Hub, set up the communication scenario and communication arrangement with the predetermined user and between the integrated systems, and then implement the integration using SAP Integration Suite.

There are additional options for integration that are available for companies integrating hybrid environments (e.g., on-premise and cloud applications). We'll cover the two-tier hybrid integration scenarios in detail in Chapter 9.

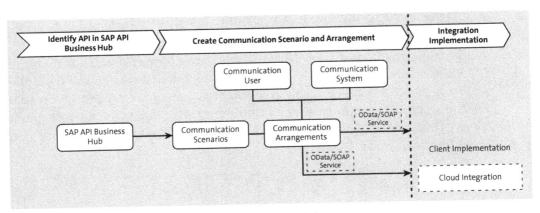

Figure 7.33 Steps to Consume APIs on SAP API Business Hub

But before we do that, consider the high-level overview of the integration options available in such situations shown in Figure 7.34.

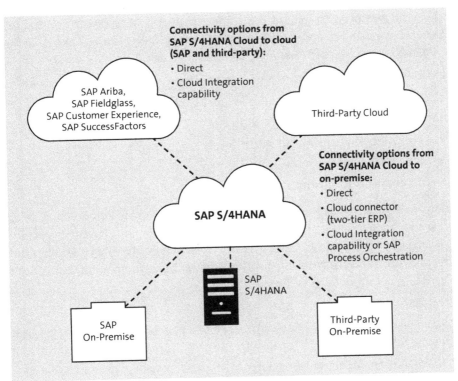

Figure 7.34 Integration Options for Hybrid Landscapes

You can see the options for connecting the cloud-to-cloud applications with SAP Integration Suite, as discussed in this section, and the options for integration of cloud and on-premise products with the cloud connector for two-tier ERP setup and with SAP Integration Suite (preferred) or SAP Process Orchestration.

SAP recommends the Integration Validation service to mitigate risk based on the use of SAP Value Assurance services. The aim is to ensure technical readiness of the entire solution for go-live. It includes analysis of critical business processes and interfaces to validate scalability, performance, data consistency, and exception management. A comprehensive monthly status of technical go-live readiness for core business processes is recommended.

> **Further Resources**
>
> A detailed discussion of integration technologies goes beyond the scope of this book, but if you're interested in these topics, review SAP documentation, or one of the SAP PRESS books on integration technologies available at *http://s-prs.co/v502732*.

Extensibility

Companies with the need to extend the standard functionality of the application should use the extensibility apps and side-by-side extensibility options available for the SAP S/4HANA stack (refer to Chapter 5, Section 5.3 for details).

The extensibility apps allow companies to accomplish actions such as the following:

- Adapting a new UI using the capabilities in SAP Fiori UX and applications
- Creating their own analytics reports and stories
- Creating email templates and print forms
- Adding application logic
- Adding custom fields to existing database structures

In addition to the extensibility apps, SAP S/4HANA Cloud, private edition companies have access to so-called classic extensibility, which allows companies to create custom code. SAP strongly recommends using classic extensibility only when the other options aren't possible, and always using it with a stable enhancement point that doesn't require a modification key, such as the following:

- ABAP business add-in (BAdIs)
- ABAP-Managed Database Procedures (AMDP) BAdIs to enhance standard SQL script procedures
- SMOD/CMOD user exit enhancements
- Business transaction events (BTEs) for finance

Companies using classic extensibility must avoid the following situations, as detailed in the Guidance on Rule 4 accelerator document in the implementation roadmap for SAP S/4HANA Cloud, private edition in the Roadmap Viewer:

- **Implicit enhancements, or enhancement spots**
  These don't require a modification key but otherwise are much like modifications. They enable companies to change any SAP code at the start or end of any coding block. In an upgrade, these would need to be processed in Transaction SPAU_ENH. The risk is that the enhancement point may no longer exist or may no longer have access to the same data.

- **Modifications of standard code**
  While technically possible, this should be avoided as a practice in all SAP S/4HANA Cloud, private edition systems. A company has the ability to modify standard SAP code, but this should only be done in exceptional cases that are reviewed and approved by a Solution Standardization Board (SSB; discussed in Chapter 2 along with the golden rules for implementation of SAP S/4HANA). In an upgrade, these modifications will need to be processed in Transaction SPAU. The risk is that the enhancement point may no longer exist or may no longer have access to the same data.

Testing

We discussed in Section 7.2.4 the preparation activities for testing, and we highlighted the need to install and set up SAP Solution Manager for testing. In the realize phase, the project team will use the SAP Solution Manager Test Management capabilities to plan, structure, execute, and evaluate the various tests that will be done during implementation. These tests include the unit testing that is usually done during each sprint and the string tests that are done in later sprints to progressively test the integration of various process steps.

> **String Testing**
> String testing doesn't replace end-to-end integration testing; instead, the purpose of the string test is to continuously test integration points and avoid finding all the integration issues during the integration test (e.g., shifting the error finding and correction to the left in the timeline, thus reducing the cost of fixing such errors).

The team will also run a full end-to-end integration test and UAT before planning a go-live release to the production system.

7.2.6   Deploy Your Solution

Now that we have completed configuration, extensibility, integration, and testing in the realize phase, we will proceed to bringing the solution to live use and deploy it to production. The goal is to ensure a smooth transition to using the new solution and successfully go live with the new system. We will now discuss the key activities that are done in this phase. Let's start with the phase overview.

Phase Overview

We covered the deliverables and activities the project team performs in the deploy phase for SAP S/4HANA Cloud in Section 7.1.6. The flow of activities for SAP S/4HANA Cloud, private edition is the same as covered previously (see Figure 7.35 for an overview of the deliverables).

In this section, we'll only focus on specific considerations companies implementing SAP S/4HANA Cloud, private edition should keep in mind in their project due to the different system landscape of this solution and additional ability to create dedicated clients for specific purposes such as cutover simulation and end user training. We'll focus on two areas:

- Production cutover considerations
- End user learning considerations

Let's now talk about cutover activities but focus specifically on how the flexibility of SAP S/4HANA Cloud, private edition can be used to structure the cutover activities.

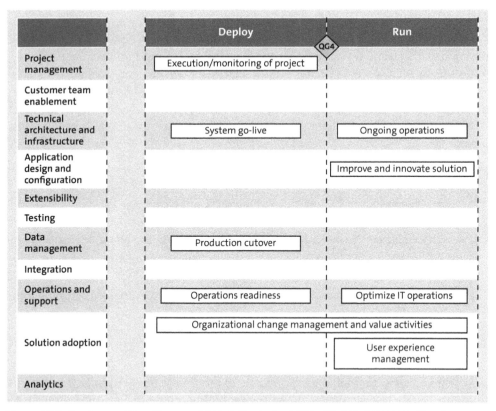

Figure 7.35 Deploy and Run Phases of SAP Activate for RISE with SAP S/4HANA Cloud, Private Edition

Production Cutover

We discussed earlier in this chapter the typical landscape for SAP S/4HANA Cloud with development, quality, and production systems interconnected with a TMS. During the production cutover, it's common to plan one or multiple cutover rehearsals during which the mock cutover activities are performed to make sure all the steps for final cutover have been performed at least once and that the team understands and has optimized the effort and duration of each step to make the cutover process optimal. During these mock cutover runs, the project team will release transports, set up the solution, and load data into the system. After the cutover, the production system should be brought back to the original state. With SAP S/4HANA Cloud, private edition, companies can request the setup of additional clients dedicated for mock cutovers that will be available temporarily to support the mock cutover process, after which these clients can be removed as they are no longer used.

End User Learning

During the end user enablement and learning activities, it's common to set up dedicated clients for delivery of the end user learning and practice in the system. Typically, these clients are created temporarily in the quality system, and it's good practice to have two clients:

1. **Golden master client**
   This client is for delivery of training that is accessible for trainers and is kept in its original state as a source for creating the training delivery client. The trainers and project team may make changes to the golden master client when the training exercises and practice are enhanced, but this client isn't accessible to end users.

2. **Training delivery client**
   This is the environment where the end users practice the use of the system functionality. This client gets regularly refreshed with fresh copies of the golden master client for delivery of training.

7.2.7   Run Your Solution

We have now successfully launched the productive use of the new solution in the business. The run phase provides guidance on key activities that continue to be done to bring new capabilities to the environment during the upgrades and implementation of continuous improvements/enhancements as the system is in use. Let's now look at this area of running the solution.

Phase Overview

We covered the deliverables and activities the project team performs in the run phase for SAP S/4HANA Cloud in Section 7.1.7. The flow of activities for SAP S/4HANA Cloud, private edition is the same as covered previously (see Figure 7.35 for an overview of the deliverables).

In this section, we'll only focus on specific considerations for companies implementing SAP S/4HANA Cloud, private edition.

Release Upgrade and Continuous Enhancements

SAP S/4HANA Cloud companies expect frequent releases of new capabilities and the ability to upgrade their software to take advantage of these innovations. SAP delivers one major release and two minor ones each year. Minor releases are the first two support package stacks (SPS), known as feature package stacks (FPS; i.e., FPS 01 and FPS 02). Support package stacks numbered three and later (SPS 03, SPS 04, etc.) are corrections only for mainstream maintenance and will last for five years for the respective major release.

The release upgrade for SAP S/4HANA Cloud, private edition is run as a project during which the development, quality, and production systems are upgraded gradually. After the development system upgrade, the project team works on resolution of all integration, extensibility, and configuration topics introduced by the new release. We've mentioned often in this book the need to stay close to the standard and to follow the five golden rules that aim to simplify and optimize the execution of upgrades by limiting the deviation from standard software and thus minimizing the number of topics that need to be addressed after each release upgrade. This portion of the project activities focuses on the technical aspect of the software update, with minimum mandatory updates in configuration and custom code.

After the release upgrade of SAP S/4HANA Cloud, private edition, companies can use the optional sandbox environment to install the upgraded version of the preconfiguration to evaluate additional functionality that they want to bring into their use in production. SAP S/4HANA Cloud, private edition doesn't have the content lifecycle management capabilities and doesn't allow direct load of the release +1 preconfiguration directly into the development system. The selected functionality either needs to be configured manually, following documentation such as the configuration guides in SAP Best Practices, or the configuration experts can package up the selected configuration and data into Business Configuration (BC) Sets to bring them into the development environment. After the configuration is finished and tested in the development environment, the standard TMS will be used to promote it to quality and production systems, just like any other configuration.

With SAP S/4HANA Cloud, private edition, a company can take advantage of the once-a-year entitlement of the software upgrade offered by SAP and do the minimum changes required in configuration and custom code without introducing new features and functions. This helps the company stay current as dictated by the SAP S/4HANA maintenance schedule, and offers corrections and improvements that stabilize the system, improve performance, and ensure the security of the system.

7.3 New Implementation of SAP S/4HANA

In this section, we will cover the new implementation of SAP S/4HANA, the on-premise version of the software. The phases and deliverables flow will be the same as in the other new implementations for public and private cloud options, but there will be some differences that customers implementing in an on-premise environment need to consider. Most of these differences will be in the area of installation and setup, as well as in the operations and support activities that are customer-managed (as compared to cloud delivery, where they are covered in full or to a large degree as a service).

We'll discuss the new implementation of an on-premise SAP S/4HANA solution with perpetual licenses in a company or third-party data center, including hyperscalers. In the new implementation approach, a new instance of SAP S/4HANA is implemented to replace a non-SAP legacy system or reimplement and replace an existing SAP solution. There are two business contexts in which companies prefer new implementations. The first is a change in the business model that implies a reevaluation of the way an organization operates. This will mean new demands on the capabilities and agility of an ERP solution. The second context is full business process reengineering, such as consolidating numerous order-to-cash process variants. Regardless of the case, a new implementation enables you to do the following:

- Start with a preconfigured new system that you can build with SAP Best Practices.
- Build a new system with a "clean core."
- Roll out the solution on a country-by-country basis to worldwide locations rather than use a big bang approach.
- Adopt innovations rapidly.

SAP S/4HANA Releases

SAP plans to release a new updated version of SAP S/4HANA once a year. Feature packs include enhancement updates shipped between the core version updates. You'll need to decide on the correct release level of your SAP S/4HANA solution-to-be and select the appropriate release-dependent information accordingly.

Figure 7.36 provides an overview of the new implementation approach. This section is organized by SAP Activate phase: discover, prepare, explore, realize, deploy, and run. Some of the activities documented in the prepare phase are often executed earlier in the project in the discover phase.

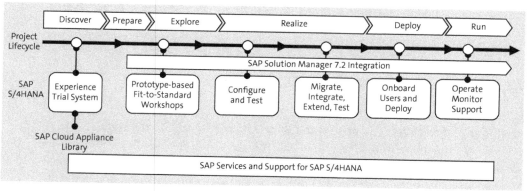

Figure 7.36 New Implementation Approach

7.3.1   Deployment Approach Overview

Your transition to SAP S/4HANA involves many activities throughout the key SAP Activate phases introduced in Chapter 2. Figure 7.37 illustrates the activities within the workstreams and phases. This figure is available for download at *www.sap-press.com/5463*.

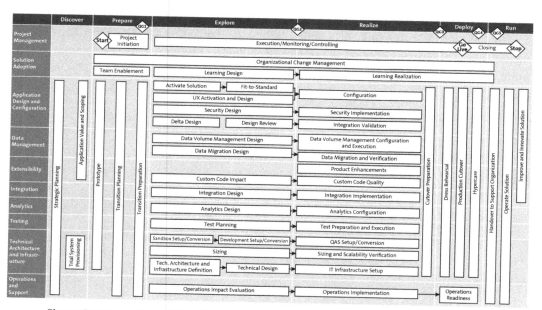

Figure 7.37 Overview of Transition to SAP S/4HANA Roadmap

There are three implementation approaches for SAP S/4HANA, which we introduced in Chapter 1:

1. **New implementation**
   Implement a new instance of SAP S/4HANA by moving either from a non-SAP legacy system or from an old SAP solution.

2. **System conversion**
   Convert an existing SAP ERP solution to SAP S/4HANA, including business data and configuration. We'll discuss this further in Chapter 8.

3. **Selective data transition**
   Consolidate an existing SAP software landscape or carve out selected entities or processes as part of a move to SAP S/4HANA. We'll discuss this further in Chapter 8.

For existing SAP customers, the choice of approach is driven by the following business and IT objectives:

- **New implementation**
  You want to maximize innovation, overhaul business processes, and perhaps adopt new cloud solutions. You may only want essential master data and transactional data from the existing solution.

- **System conversion**
  You don't want to merge or split ERP instances, and you want to keep your existing data and go live with a big bang. You may want to minimize change initially and then innovate selectively afterward.

- **Selective data transition**
  You want to merge or split existing ERP instances or have phased go-lives. You want to reuse only certain parts of the existing configuration, master data, and transaction data.

If you have multiple SAP ERP instances and other connected SAP solutions, you may want to use a combination of the approaches in a phased program. For example, you could do a system conversion of one lead SAP ERP development system, use selective data transition to merge in another SAP ERP system, and do a new implementation for certain parts of the solution.

Let's walk through the SAP Activate phases, in terms of these on-premise deployment options:

- **Discover phase**
  You should create an overall strategy for digital transformation by recognizing the benefits and value of SAP S/4HANA. This is then turned into a roadmap or implementation plan that includes a choice of implementation approach. Finally, you should evaluate the impact on the technical architecture and IT infrastructure, which, together with the implementation strategy, serve as the foundation of the business case.

- **Prepare phase**
  After the business case has been approved, the project is officially initiated in the

prepare phase. A first version of an implementation plan includes the findings from the discover phase and sets the stage for the entire project.

- **Explore phase**

  The design-to-be of the SAP S/4HANA solution is defined and documented in the explore phase. In a new implementation, fit-to-standard workshops are performed with the help of a preconfigured sandbox system that represents SAP Best Practices solutions. For a system conversion, a converted version of the existing system is used and existing custom code is analyzed. By the end of the explore phase, all technical and functional aspects of the implementation project are fully planned, documented in detail, and ready to be executed.

- **Realize phase**

  In a new implementation, you prepare the new technical architecture and infrastructure. In system conversion, the landscape is sequentially converted to SAP S/4HANA. Some of the existing custom code is adjusted. Application and analytics functions are implemented, configured, integrated, and tested. In parallel, IT can adjust operational tools and procedures to prepare for SAP S/4HANA. Finally, end user training, including project-specific training materials and team setup, is prepared.

- **Deploy phase**

  Finalize the business processes and solution for production go-live. This includes final testing, rehearsing the cutover, and finalizing the IT infrastructure and operations. End user training sessions are delivered. Finally, the productive instance of SAP S/4HANA is set up or converted on the go-live weekend. IT operations are further optimized with the help of the project team and SAP. This phase is referred to as *hypercare* and occurs before operational responsibility is fully transferred to the production support team.

- **Run phase**

  Operations are further stabilized and optimized in the run phase. The new SAP system is continuously updated, making the latest innovations from SAP available to the business. Then the innovation cycle starts again.

To support companies in executing the SAP S/4HANA transition successfully, SAP has several service offerings that provide different levels of engagement and advice:

- **SAP Enterprise Support**

  Proactive remote support for accelerated problem resolution, fewer business disruptions, and less unforeseen downtime. Access to tools, reports, and services to accelerate innovation.

- **SAP Value Assurance**

  Supports customers on their own or partner-led projects with dedicated planning, design support, and functional and technical safeguarding services throughout the project. Doesn't provide any implementation or delivery services.

- **SAP Advanced Deployment**
  SAP Services and Support provides end-to-end implementation and delivery services, collaborating with partners as required. Relevant SAP Value Assurance services are integrated into the delivery.

- **Premium engagements**
  Provides on-site, premium access to trusted SAP experts and tools that include and go beyond the SAP Value Assurance service portfolio. For example, SAP ActiveAttention and SAP MaxAttention build a long-term relationship with SAP through the project and beyond.

Throughout this chapter, there are notes that highlight the specific SAP service components that can be consumed to reduce risk, provide the best advice, and check the decisions being made. Most of these service components are common to SAP Value Assurance, SAP Advanced Deployment, and premium engagements.

Further Resources
Always refer to the online Roadmap Viewer for more complete descriptions of the service components and the latest links.

7.3.2   Discover Your Solution

The discover phase covers everything done leading up to the decision to proceed with an SAP S/4HANA project. On leaving the discover phase, an organization will have defined its digital transformation strategy and have an SAP S/4HANA roadmap or plan backed up by a business case. The company will have selected its delivery partners and delivery approach: new implementation, system conversion, or selective data transition. The activities in the discover phase are independent of the delivery approach. Some organizations may push some of the activities described in this section into the prepare phase.

This section begins with strategic planning, where you develop an innovation strategy and high-level roadmap based on SAP S/4HANA and intelligent technology innovations, and you also make early decisions on security and analytics. Then, we'll move on to trial system provisioning and application value and scoping, where you'll assess the value and impact of SAP S/4HANA and check your readiness.

Strategic Planning

SAP's intelligent enterprise features the following key components:

- **Intelligent suite**
  This integrated suite retains the modularity and flexibility of independent solutions, such as SAP S/4HANA, SAP Customer Experience, SAP Business Network, and SAP SuccessFactors.

- **Digital platform**
  With SAP BTP and data management in SAP HANA, SAP can facilitate the collection, connection, and orchestration of data, as well as the integration and extension of processes within the intelligent suite.

- **Intelligent technologies**
  Intelligent technologies enable companies to leverage their data to detect patterns, predict outcomes, and suggest actions with the help of advanced technologies such as machine learning and the Internet of Things (IoT).

The aim of strategic planning is to define an innovation strategy and high-level multi-year roadmap for these three key components. The roadmap should include, but isn't limited to, SAP S/4HANA and analytics.

Start with an identification of strategic business and IT objectives, including current pain points. Cluster the objectives into benefit areas, and for each benefit area, identify and prioritize the SAP solution enablers. These solutions provide the target enterprise architecture.

SAP provides some tools that can assist in the strategy definition:

- **SAP Transformation Navigator**
  Determines a high-level future SAP product map based on your current product map and your current and planned business capabilities.

- **Process Discovery for SAP S/4HANA transformation**
  For companies with existing SAP ERP systems, this identifies which new SAP S/4HANA functionalities are most relevant for each LoB. The output is generated by a free report that runs in your existing production system.

- **SAP Innovation and Optimization Pathfinder**
  A free tool from SAP that identifies which innovations are relevant based on system usage statistics.

The introduction of SAP S/4HANA into the solution landscape is an ideal opportunity to review and adjust the organization's analytics architecture. It's worth doing this early in the discover phase because there are many changes and new products and capabilities relevant for SAP S/4HANA. Refer to our discussion of analytics design in the explore phase in Section 7.3.4 for more details.

Another area worth visiting early is your security strategy, including topics such as data protection regulations. SAP offers a security strategy advisory service to help determine where security issues exist and how SAP can assist.

Further Resources

SAP offers the Innovation Strategy and Roadmap service component and the Analytics Strategy Workshop service component through SAP Value Assurance to help companies develop a multiyear strategic roadmap for digital transformation.

Innovation services for intelligent technologies are available through SAP MaxAttention and SAP Advanced Deployment.

The SAP S/4HANA Movement webpages (*http://s-prs.co/v502747*) provide information on moving from SAP ERP to SAP S/4HANA. Companies with a valid support agreement can check if they can participate in an SAP Adoption Starter program. This 90-day program helps companies create an SAP S/4HANA–centric transformation plan by using tools such as SAP Transformation Navigator.

Trial System Provisioning

To support the value identification and the impact evaluation in the discover phase, it may be beneficial to have access to an SAP S/4HANA system. You can deploy a system within hours or days using an SAP cloud appliance via SAP Cloud Appliance Library (*http://cal.sap.com*). The system is hosted on Microsoft Azure, AWS, or Google Cloud Platform. The provider will charge for hosting, and a user account at the cloud provider is required. SAP Cloud Appliance Library provides a detailed step-by-step guide for setup of the appliance that you'll follow during the installation and setup. Companies with an existing license can deploy an unrestricted SAP S/4HANA sandbox solution directly from SAP Cloud Appliance Library.

A cloud trial system is the fastest option for companies without a license and will provide up to 30 days of access. The trial solution can't be configured and is restricted to a certain number of users (*http://s-prs.co/v502734*).

In addition, the SAP Best Practices processes are ready to run immediately as documented in the SAP Best Practices Explorer (refer to Chapter 4, Section 4.1). This allows the team to get hands-on access to the solution and investigate the new features in detail.

Application Value and Scoping

Application value and scoping contains the following tasks, which we'll walk through in this section:

- Discovering the value of SAP S/4HANA
- Performing SAP Readiness Check for SAP S/4HANA for an existing SAP ERP solution
- Performing a business scenario and solution mapping
- Defining the implementation strategy
- Creating a strategic roadmap and value case

Service Components

SAP offers the Value and Implementation Strategy service component through SAP Value Assurance that provides a comprehensive migration analysis, including business scenario and value mapping, proposed implementation strategy and supporting road-map, and value case.

Discover the Value of SAP S/4HANA

Value and benefits drive all projects and must be understood early. The following resources can be used:

- Public webpages such as the SAP Help Portal, What's New Viewer, and SAP Fiori apps reference library
- SAP S/4HANA training, including openSAP training on integrations and extensions with SAP BTP
- Learning rooms in SAP Learning Hub
- SAP S/4HANA trial system (refer to our earlier discussion of trial system provisioning)
- Process Discovery for SAP S/4HANA transformation for existing SAP ERP solutions
- SAP S/4HANA Discovery Workshop, available from SAP Services and Support

For organizations new to SAP, the impact of SAP S/4HANA on existing business processes will be evaluated in the explore phase. For organizations moving from an existing SAP ERP solution, the impact is evaluated in SAP Readiness Check for SAP S/4HANA, as described in the next section.

Readiness Check of an Existing ERP Solution

SAP S/4HANA is the result of SAP rearchitecting the SAP ERP suite for modern business processes and the ever-increasing digitization of the world. This means that parts of SAP ERP have been improved, simplified, replaced, removed, or categorized as not strategic. All these changes are documented in the simplification list for SAP S/4HANA, which you can find on the SAP Help Portal.

If you have an existing SAP ERP solution, understanding the simplification items that impact the system is a key activity in the discover phase. SAP Readiness Check for SAP S/4HANA is a report run in your existing system that identifies the relevant simplification items. It analyzes many other aspects as well, including custom code, add-ons, active business functions, recommended SAP Fiori apps, and sizing.

There could be showstoppers or requirements that need to be addressed before the project starts. SAP Readiness Check for SAP S/4HANA provides a dashboard (see Figure 7.38) that addresses these questions:

- Is functionality used that will need to be replaced or changed? Are the simplification items mandatory, conditional, or optional? Should the work be done in the current SAP ERP system or in the new SAP S/4HANA system?

- Are there incompatible add-ons (e.g., third-party add-ons) or incompatible business functions?
- Are there custom solutions or add-ons delivered by SAP Innovation Services that must be investigated by SAP before a project starts?
- Are all technical system requirements fulfilled (e.g., software levels, single stack system, Unicode)?
- Are all dependent SAP hub systems (e.g., SAP Customer Relationship Management [SAP CRM] or SAP Extended Warehouse Management [SAP EWM]) on the required release?
- How many custom objects are impacted by the data model and software changes?
- Which business-critical reports and transactions will be replaced or removed?
- What SAP Fiori apps are relevant for your current scope?
- What configuration needs to be adjusted?
- What is the estimated SAP S/4HANA system size? Are there options to reduce the size before the conversion?
- Are there live SAP Business Warehouse (SAP BW) extractors that will be impacted?

Figure 7.38 SAP Readiness Check for SAP S/4HANA Dashboard

Perform a Business Scenario and Solution Mapping

Strategic planning provides a set of SAP solutions and a target architecture. Business process experts from each LoB should now produce a more detailed solution mapping at a business scenario level. Business scenarios are a level above scope items.

For a new implementation, refer to the structure of SAP Best Practices content in SAP Best Practices Explorer (refer to Chapter 3, Section 3.2, and Chapter 4, Section 4.1).

For existing SAP ERP solutions, you may choose to use Process Discovery for SAP S/4HANA transformation. We introduced Process Discovery during our earlier discussion of strategic planning. The report compares business key figures with industry benchmarks, illustrates opportunities to improve, and highlights relevant SAP S/4HANA innovations. You must run a report in your production system and upload the files to an SAP website. SAP will email you the results in a PDF file. Figure 7.39 shows a page from the Process Discovery for SAP S/4HANA transformation with a list of business scenarios that are used in the organization.

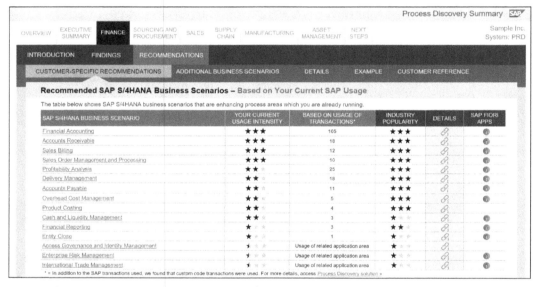

Figure 7.39 Process Discovery for SAP S/4HANA Transformation

Define the Implementation Strategy

The next step is to define your implementation strategy. Your strategy should cover the following aspects:

- What is the productive system strategy—that is, one single global instance or regional instances?
- Will the business go live in one big bang or with a multistage transition by country or business unit?
- What are the dependencies and the best sequence for the release plan?
- When will integration between SAP S/4HANA and other SAP and non-SAP solutions go live?
- What are the intermediate architectures in a staged approach?

- Will SAP S/4HANA Cloud, private edition or an on-premise data center or a cloud hyperscaler be used?
- Will a global template solution be adopted, and how will deviations from the template be managed?
- Will SAP Best Practices content be used and how?
- What is the strategy for custom development? What development will occur in SAP S/4HANA, and what will SAP BTP be used for?

Organizations moving to SAP S/4HANA from an existing SAP solution need to choose between the three transition approaches described in Section 7.3.1 (new implementation, system conversion, or selective data transition). The team must come to a decision to either reuse existing configuration or reengineer business processes with a reimplementation. For SAP S/4HANA Cloud, private edition, seek SAP's advice because the conversion of certain source ERP releases may not be supported yet.

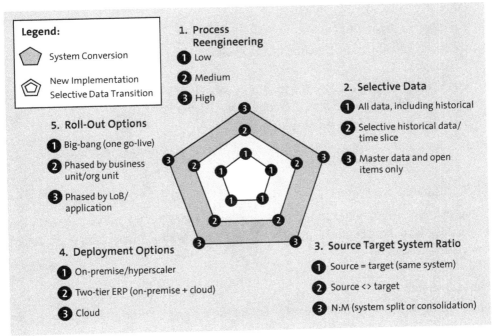

Figure 7.40 Factors Influencing the SAP S/4HANA Transition Approach

The main aspects to consider are as follows, and their impact is shown in Figure 7.40:

- How much process reengineering is required?
- Is implementing SAP S/4HANA a good opportunity to go back to the SAP standard? And should this be done based on a new implementation or incrementally after a technical conversion to SAP S/4HANA?
- How much of the historical transaction data needs to be retained?

- Will SAP ERP instances be consolidated or split?
- Will SAP S/4HANA or SAP S/4HANA Cloud, private edition be implemented?
- Does the roll-out have to be phased to reduce risk, or can each instance go live with a big bang approach?

Create a Strategic Roadmap and Value Case

A value (or business) case for the project is built based on quantified costs and benefits. The following approach may be used:

1. Define discrete scope blocks required to reach the defined target architecture. Each block will have an organizational, functional, and technical element—for example, the SAP S/4HANA Finance scope for Malaysia.
2. Agree on business transformation objectives, and map value drivers to the scope blocks.
3. Define and link key performance indicators (KPIs) to the value drivers. Use KPIs and value drivers to quantify benefits.
4. Identify cost drivers and quantify costs.
5. Compose a roadmap or timeline of scope blocks to implement the target solution landscape.
6. Assess the ability to execute the roadmap, considering organizational change, budget, technical capabilities, and previous project experience.
7. Determine the risks of transformation.
8. Summarize the alternative approaches and drive decision-making.

7.3.3 Prepare Your Project

The prepare phase provides initial planning and preparation for the implementation project. We'll walk through the prepare phase for a new implementation deployment project in this section.

Phase Overview

The purpose of the prepare phase is to kick off the initial planning and preparation for the project. The project officially starts, the team resources are assigned, and the preliminary system setup is done. Although each project has its unique objectives, scope, and priorities, the primary output documents of the prepare phase include the following:

- **Scope document**
  Defines the starting point, goals, target solution, and transition approach.
- **Project charter**
  Includes goals, scope, organization structure, roles and responsibilities, and governance.

- **Project plan**
  Includes a work breakdown structure (WBS), schedule, and budget.

- **UX/UI strategy**
  How SAP Fiori apps will be adopted and used.

- **Technical architecture**
  Defines the technical components, architecture, and infrastructure for the solution.

- **Interface register**
  Identifies the external systems, applications, and required interfaces.

- **Project standards**
  Defines the approach for requirements management, configuration, and custom code.

- **Operational standards**
  Includes test management and change control.

The rest of this section is organized into topics that appear in the roadmap. SAP Solution Manager is the recommended solution to support your new implementation of SAP S/4HANA.

Transition Planning

Transition planning defines the scope and execution plan for the upcoming SAP S/4HANA implementation project. The project plan will be continuously refined throughout the project as part of the project management workstream. SAP can assist with all transition planning topics through SAP Value Assurance or SAP MaxAttention.

> **Service Components**
> Refer to the Transition Planning for New Implementation service component within the Roadmap Viewer.

Let's walk through these steps in detail.

Define the Scope and the Objectives of the Transition

The first step is to create a scope document that defines the following:

- **IT and business objectives**
  Success criteria for the implementation project.

- **Starting point**
  SAP and/or non-SAP solutions to be replaced or remain the same.

- **Target solution**
  Target releases, scope, and related SAP systems.

Define Cutover Approach

The purpose of this activity is to determine and document the strategy for the cutover to the new SAP S/4HANA solution and the hypercare period immediately following the go-live. It's crucial to start the planning of the cutover approach early in the project. A cutover action list should be created and maintained by each responsible team throughout the explore and realize phases to avoid missing critical details.

The main cutover approach should cover the following topics:

- Sequence of go-lives
- Permitted business downtime
- Interim states
- Data load approach
- Reconciliation processes

Operational Readiness

The introduction of a new SAP S/4HANA solution will cause your current IT support framework to change. SAP provides guidance on the target IT support process activities, tools, and resources required for you to safely and efficiently operate the new SAP solutions in your environment.

Customer Center of Expertise

Companies that are new to SAP should look at SAP's general recommendations to set up a Customer COE. At least one primary Customer COE certification should be gained. The Customer COE acts as a collaboration hub across IT and LoBs in an organization. Its mission is to provide transparency and efficiency of implementation, innovation, operation, and quality of business processes and systems related to the SAP software solutions and services. See Chapter 10, Section 10.3 for more details.

Define the Technical Architecture and Security

The SAP S/4HANA solution will either require a new IT architecture or significant changes. The term *technical architecture and infrastructure* denotes the layout of SAP software solutions on technical infrastructures and covers data centers, hardware, virtualizations, high availability (HA), and disaster recovery (DR) solutions. Technical architecture information will be collected to create a sketch of a technical deployment plan by mapping the technical components to the hardware. This deployment plan is the basis for ordering the hardware at your hardware provider and is continuously refined throughout the project. Security should be planned, designed, and implemented during the SAP S/4HANA project. Specific roadmaps and documentation for the security topics must be covered.

Service Components

SAP offers a Technical Architecture and Infrastructure service component through SAP Value Assurance that supports companies in the creation of a technical architecture. A Security Design service is also available.

Define the Data Migration Architecture

Companies using SAP S/4HANA have choices to make about how to do the data migration. This activity is necessary to prepare a high-level assessment of the source systems, necessary data objects, and the methods to extract, transform, and load (ETL) the source data from legacy systems and or SAP systems. It's important to determine the approach and start work early. Influencing factors that may drive the approach include the following:

- The level of effort
- Amount of business data to be transferred and converted
- Permitted business downtime
- Business data quality of the original system

SAP provides two solutions to import data into the new SAP S/4HANA solution:

1. **SAP S/4HANA migration cockpit**
   Migrate master data and business data using one of three approaches: XML files, staging tables in an SAP HANA database, or direct API transfer from an existing SAP ERP solution. The SAP S/4HANA migration cockpit uses predefined migration content and mappings—that is, standard migration objects such as customers, suppliers, or purchase orders—to identify and transfer the relevant data.

2. **SAP Data Services**
   This software requires a separate license and provides additional transformation features such as matching, consolidation, address correction, and cleansing. You can leverage prebuilt SAP Best Practices content for more than 50 critical master and transactional data objects. The software can be used without the SAP S/4HANA migration cockpit, or it can be used to feed the staging tables for upload using the SAP S/4HANA migration cockpit.

Define the User Experience/User Interface Strategy

SAP S/4HANA comes with a new UI called SAP Fiori. The project team should learn about SAP Fiori, including the technical architecture, role model, and SAP Fiori apps reference library. The SAP Fiori apps reference library provides a set of lighthouse scenarios that offer immediate business benefits to the users of SAP S/4HANA. For existing SAP customers, the SAP Fiori apps recommendation report provides recommendations on apps to use based on your current system usage. This can be used by the LoB teams to understand the scope of UI change. To obtain this, you must run a report in your production system and upload the results to an SAP website. SAP will email you a PDF report.

Assess Interfaces and Integration

The purpose of this task is to identify and document the external systems, applications, and business objects or transactions that must be integrated with the SAP S/4HANA system to realize the objectives of the project. After they have been identified, an assessment of the impact on interfaces when moving to SAP S/4HANA is necessary. You'll document necessary interface adjustments in the backlog as gaps.

Transition Preparation

This activity covers the preparation work, which starts before the SAP S/4HANA explore phase. Preparation mainly concerns SAP Solution Manager, which you must prepare and set up.

SAP Solution Manager supports the implementation by providing a comprehensive set of processes, tools, and services to manage the solution throughout the project lifecycle and beyond. It offers specific functionality for project management activities and supports the project start, team setup, solution documentation, testing, and go-live.

You must prepare SAP Solution Manager to ensure that it's available, up to date with the latest support pack, and properly set up to support the implementation project. The following components may be used:

- Project Management
- Process Management
- Requirements Management
- Solution Documentation
- Test Management
- Release Management
- Change Control Management

Next, it's important to import the most recent SAP Best Practices content into SAP Solution Manager. This includes project management and business process and configuration content. The scope must be finalized at the start of the prepare phase when you decide which SAP Best Practices scope items to import.

Project Initiation, Governance, and Plan

The project is formally initiated and setup, including the setup of governance for all involved parties (e.g., the company, the system integrator, and any subcontractors). Key activities include the following:

- Hand over meetings from the previous discover phase.
- Review the commercial contract and resolve any issues.
- Identify stakeholders and confirm their requirements, expectations, and acceptance criteria.
- Create a project charter based on the scope document.
- Establish baselines for scope, schedule, cost, and quality.
- Create a project management plan.

The project management plan defines the timeline and structure of tasks. It includes the following:

- WBS
- Schedule
- Budget
- Quality standards
- Communications
- Risks and procurement

Prototype

Prototypes enable companies to evaluate specific innovations in a short period using real business scenarios and company data to validate the value of a new solution quickly.

Prototyping is an optional small project on its own. It requires dedicated planning, execution, and evaluation and is always driven by business or IT requirements. The main steps of a prototype are shown in Figure 7.41.

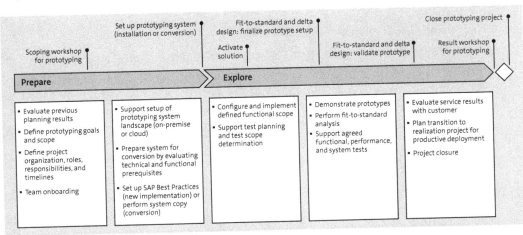

Figure 7.41 Prototyping Framework

> **SAP Value Assurance**
>
> SAP supports this activity with an SAP Value Assurance service that delivers a scoping workshop for prototyping.

Project Team Enablement

This activity ensures that the project team has the necessary knowledge to execute the work during the SAP S/4HANA implementation. Enablement may include different elements of the SAP system, SAP Activate methodology, SAP Solution Manager, agile principles and techniques, access to SAP Best Practices Explorer, and other supporting tools. Self-enablement must begin before the project kickoff to maximize the time for learning and create efficiencies in later deliverables.

Project Standards and Infrastructure

SAP S/4HANA implementation projects need a robust means of executing and governing project work and deliverables. Project standards include requirements management, process modeling, configuration and documentation, custom code, authorizations, agile processes, and use of SAP Solution Manager. Operational standards include test management, change control, incident management, and technical operations.

Project Kickoff and Onboarding

The goal of the project kickoff meeting is to ensure that everybody involved in the project understands its setup. Your project kickoff meeting should cover goals, objectives, scope, organization structure, decision-making process, roles and responsibilities, governance, regular meetings, project standards, infrastructure, schedule, and milestones.

Organizational Change Management Plan

Organizational change management (OCM) planning prepares an overview of all planned change management activities and ensures that all activities are related to each other. It also ensures consistency in the overall project plan and provides traceability of OCM activities. In the prepare phase, it's crucial for the success of the project to set up the OCM team and agree on its concept. See Chapter 10 for more information.

7.3.4   Explore the Solution

In the explore phase, a backlog of requirements and a design is created based on a fit-to-standard analysis of the solution. A sandbox environment based on the standard functionality of SAP Best Practices is used to drive the explore phase workshops. We'll walk through the explore phase for a new implementation deployment project in this section.

Phase Overview

As described in Chapter 2, Section 2.3.3, the purpose of the explore phase is to perform a fit-to-standard analysis to validate the solution functionality included in the project scope and to confirm that the business requirements can be satisfied. Identified gaps are designed and configuration decisions made. These are added to the backlog for use in the realize phase. In addition, decisions are made on the approach to analytics, integration, security, testing, architecture, infrastructure and data volume design, and data migration. During the explore phase, an end user training strategy is defined and change impact analysis is performed.

The main output documents of the explore phase include the following:

- **Design document**
  Overall design documents for business scenarios and end-to-end processes include the scope, objectives, benefits, requirements, KPIs, data requirements, and design.

- **Backlog of requirements**
  Detailed catalog of requirements by business process.

- **Workflows, Reports, Interfaces, Data Conversions, Enhancements, and Forms (WRICEF) list**
  Tracked status, complexity, and progress of WRICEFs.

- **Functional specifications**
  Detailed functional designs for the approved WRICEFs.

- **Data migration approach and strategy**
  Agreed-upon data migration scope and approach to quality, cleansing, ETL, and reconciliation.

- **Technical design document**
  Definition of architecture and infrastructure for productive and nonproductive systems.

- **Test strategy document**
  Definition of the testing scope, approach, deliverables, and tools.

Further Resources

The SAP Activate Roadmap Viewer (see Chapter 3, Section 3.1) contains templates for these project documents.

The rest of this section on the explore phase is organized into topics that appear in the roadmap. The use of SAP Solution Manager during the explore phase is covered in the last section.

Set Up Sandbox and Activate Solution

As the start of the explore phase, it's essential that a working functional SAP S/4HANA system is used to drive the fit-to-standard workshops. This is done by activating SAP Best Practices and SAP Fiori apps in a sandbox system. There are four approaches:

1. **Enterprise management layer for SAP S/4HANA**
   Set up a fresh SAP S/4HANA sandbox system. Engage SAP to activate the enterprise management layer for SAP S/4HANA to maximize speed of deployment of SAP Best Practices. SAP also activates the SAP Fiori apps.

2. **SAP S/4HANA fully activated appliance**
   Use this accelerator to speed up the provision of a hosted cloud or on-premise sandbox system with SAP Best Practices.

3. **Manual setup and activation of SAP Best Practices**
   Set up a fresh SAP S/4HANA sandbox system. Create a new client by selectively copying Customizing content from client 000. Import and activate selected SAP Best Practices using the SAP solution builder tool. Activate the required SAP Fiori apps.

4. **Manual setup without SAP Best Practices**
   If the functional fit of the enterprise management layer for SAP S/4HANA and SAP Best Practices is low, set up and configure the sandbox system from scratch. Then activate the required SAP Fiori apps. This should be done in the prepare phase because it may delay the start of the workshops.

The enterprise management layer for SAP S/4HANA approach is generally the best choice (refer to Chapter 4, Section 4.2) as it has several advantages. It is the fastest approach and, once done, can be reused to set up the development system. Companies with multiple countries in scope will get a baseline solution for all the countries, including business processes localized for statutory requirements. It includes a financial chart of accounts for each country that is aligned at the group level.

The scope to activate is selected from the SAP Best Practices scope options and/or items. SAP Solution Manager or SAP Best Practices Explorer can be used to examine the scope as described in Chapter 3.

Finally, you can integrate the sandbox system with other SAP systems as identified in the prepare phase. This must be done to support workshops and design cross-system business processes. In many cases, SAP Best Practices scope items are available to accelerate the integration between SAP S/4HANA and SAP cloud solutions such as SAP SuccessFactors and SAP Business Network.

Fit-to-Standard Analysis and Design

The purpose of the fit-to-standard analysis and design process is to approve a scope baseline and design to move into the realize phase. The company validates the activated SAP Best Practices processes and identifies potential gaps between the standard product and business requirements. These delta requirements are prioritized and a design is verified and accepted by the business owners. Prior to acceptance, SAP can check that there is no standard way of delivering the delta requirements and can review the overall design. A successful explore phase will provide a comprehensive design, minimizing customizations and preventing the need for rework in the realize phase.

The fit-to-standard analysis and design process consists of the following activities (refer back to Figure 7.31):

- **Fit-to-standard workshop preparation**
  Plan workshops and check that the project team has done training and workshop participants have done self-enablement.

- **Fit-to-standard system preparation**
  Check that the SAP S/4HANA sandbox system is ready to demonstrate the processes during the workshops.

- **Fit-to-standard workshops and documentation**
  Present and validate the business processes in workshops and identify potential delta requirements.

- **Fit-to-standard workshop validation**
  Classify, define, check, document, and prioritize the backlog of delta requirements. Decide which need to be discussed in a design workshop.

- **Design workshops and documentation**
  Define the design during a workshop and document this afterward.

- **Review and customer sign-off**
  Project architects review and adjust the design. SAP offers services that will make recommendations on potential design improvements and check whether the design is appropriate. Business and IT stakeholders give formal approval.

In the following sections, we'll take a closer look at the sequential activities in fit-to-standard analysis and design.

Fit-to-Standard Workshop Preparation

The workshops are organized by LoB areas (e.g., finance) and end-to-end solutions (e.g., accounting and financial close). This structure matches the hierarchy of content in SAP Best Practices Explorer. There are typically five or six LoB teams running in parallel. Each team has a series of end-to-end solution workshops, and each workshop covers a set of scope items (or processes).

The project manager will organize the workshop schedule and check that the boundaries and integration points between the workshops are clear. A standard set of workshop input and output template documents are defined. Before LoB-specific workshops start, the team will establish a working model of the SAP enterprise/organization structure and financial chart of accounts.

Fit-to-Standard System Preparation

Key business users will run through the business processes in the sandbox system using SAP Best Practices test scripts. The team will prepare sample master data so that the processes seem familiar during the workshops. Some additional configuration may be done for important requirements that aren't in the processes—for example, a specific type of commonly used sales order discount.

Fit-to-Standard Workshops and Documentation

Each workshop is jointly owned and delivered by an experienced SAP consultant and a business process owner from the business. They should work together closely to prepare a detailed agenda, agree on attendees, distribute prereading, prepare slides, practice the demonstrations, and develop a checklist of questions and required decisions. The SAP consultant needs to understand the as-is business, processes and systems. The business process owner needs to be able to execute the standard SAP processes and use the transaction apps. Both need to review all the content produced before the project started. This may include a business case, value drivers, and an initial fit-to-standard analysis.

The SAP Best Practices test scripts, process diagrams, and master data scripts are key inputs to the workshops.

The workshop uses a show-and-tell demonstration to validate the solution, process, organization units, and business roles. The stakeholders are challenged to see if the business can adapt to the standard SAP processes, and any business change impacts are recorded.

The workshop then validates detailed process steps and functionality and defines delta requirements. These are immediately recorded in the backlog. This Microsoft Excel spreadsheet is shown in Figure 7.42.

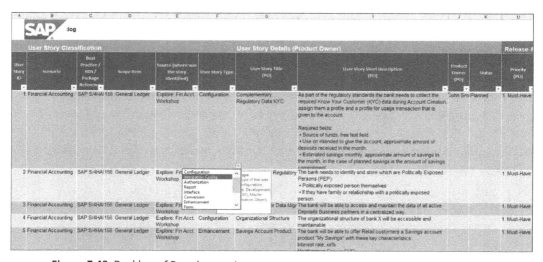

Figure 7.42 Backlog of Requirements

Requirements that are met by the standard SAP Best Practices solution don't need to be documented. This saves time compared to the traditional blueprint approach that was used in early SAP ERP implementations.

The following are the different types of delta requirements:

- **Configuration requirements (and values)**
  Specify the requirements for business processes, UIs, and SAP-to-SAP integration scenarios.

- **Authorizations**
  Specify how the standard authorizations are used and identify delta requirements.

- **Master data**
  Specify how the solution is to be used and identify delta requirements.

- **WRICEF**
  Identify WRICEF requirements. Enhancements include changes to the UIs and missing functionality.

- **Organization structure requirements**
  Create revisions to the centrally managed enterprise/organization structure, which is revised as each workshop delivers results.

Fit-to-Standard Workshop Validation

The teams research, document, and classify potential delta requirements. This may require discussion between the LoB teams. Some delta requirements may be met using configuration. Each WRICEF item is cataloged in a WRICEF list (Microsoft Excel) and assigned a scope item, initial priority, complexity, owner, and type. Large delta requirements map be treated as custom developments rather than enhancements. These will typically include new custom data objects with new business functionality. A custom development is managed as a mini project.

Before moving ahead with specifying the solution within design documents, it's important to sort out which delta requirements are relevant to fulfill the project objectives. The backlog of requirements is reviewed by the solution architects and project managers. Every item is challenged: Is it vital to meet the business requirement? If so, can it be delivered through standard configuration? A complexity rating can be used to provide a rough-cut estimate. Delta requirements are assigned to sprints considering dependencies, effort, and priorities. This will simplify any future rescoping. Some decisions may need to be escalated to the project steering committee

Companies with SAP Value Assurance or premium engagement can get a second opinion from SAP when it comes to validating delta requirements. SAP experts, both on-site and at SAP, work together to select the best solutions for functional gaps identified in the project. They look to minimize enhancements and avoid modifications (changes to the standard code outside designated APIs and exits).

Design Workshops and Documentation

The purpose is to design and document functional solutions for the delta requirements. The outputs are as follows:

- Design document
- Configuration requirements updated with outline configuration values
- Functional specifications for each WRICEF item
- Master data design documents
- Business user role documents

The design document summarizes the design for a set of scope items. Each one relates to a business scenario or end-to-end solution. The detailed requirements and WRICEFs relate to the scope items in these documents. Each document includes the following information:

- Process description
- Business objectives and benefits
- Pain points
- Key business requirements
- KPIs
- Organizational change impacts (see Chapter 10 on how these are used)
- Organization structure in SAP
- Process scope by scope item
- Process flow diagrams for scope items (referencing SAP Best Practices process diagrams that are adjusted to reflect the company processes)
- Systems (to be replaced or interfaced with)
- Master data used
- Summary of main delta requirements

Up to this point, the configuration requirements are high level. During design, the team drills down into the detail and, in some cases, defines specific configuration activities and values. This additional information is recorded in the configuration requirements. Configuration in the development system should be able to start at the beginning of the realize phase.

Functional specifications are written to define what is required for each WRICEF item. In some cases, depending on partner contracts and when estimates are required, functional specifications are prepared in the realize phase. How the WRICEF item will be technically delivered is defined in the technical specification written in the realize phase. Data conversions and interface specifications are produced as part of the data management workstream and the integration workstream. For forms, SAP Best Practices contains an accelerator that lists the predefined forms provided.

A master data design document is often created for each master data object. It defines the proposed design and controls. These documents will help drive the data volume design and data migration design later in the explore phase. SAP Best Practices contains master data scripts that show how to create the master data.

A business user role document is created for each role in the organization and defines how the role will operate. A matrix is often used to relate the user role to specific SAP authorization roles. SAP Best Practices contains an accelerator that lists the standard SAP Best Practices roles and their scope items and transaction apps.

User Experience Design

The project team needs to maximize the value of the SAP Fiori apps that provide an enhanced UX in SAP S/4HANA. SAP recommends that a UX lead work across the LoB teams. UX-specific working sessions are required after the fit-to-standard workshops. The lead can define, estimate, and prioritize UI configuration and delta requirements.

A process to look at UX requirements is shown in Figure 7.43. The UX lead will decide how to use the following:

- Theming, branding, and personalization
- UI enhancements (with key user tools) and UI extensibility (with SAP Web IDE)
- SAP Screen Personas for "classic" non–SAP Fiori apps: SAP GUI for HTML and Web Dynpro for ABAP
- New SAP Fiori apps

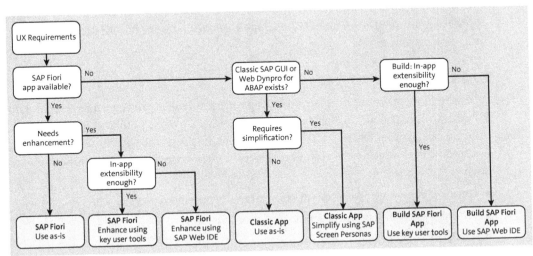

Figure 7.43 Design Options for UX Requirements

The UX lead will assist in the definition of business user roles and design the SAP Fiori launchpad experience and SAP Fiori tile setup. In some cases, low-fidelity UX mock-ups may be produced.

> **Further Resources**
>
> Refer to the Roadmap Viewer for details about how SAP can support UX work in the project.

Review and Customer Sign-Off

The project architects review and adjust the end-to-end design. SAP offers services that will make recommendations on potential design improvements and check whether the design is appropriate. Companies with SAP Value Assurance can use the Design Evaluation service. If there is uncertainty on the design of complex processes or concerns about robustness, operability, and sustainability of a process and solution design, premium engagements offer the Application Architecture Evaluation service.

The project obtains formal approval of the fit-to-standard analysis and design by business and IT stakeholders. This is done toward the end of the explore phase and incorporates all the design documents produced. It's important that the stakeholders genuinely understand the documents. They should be written in clear business language with SAP terminology clearly explained. Successful demonstrations and workshops are the key to truly informed approval.

With the sign-off, all stakeholders agree that the design is complete and the solution proposals for requirements are understood and accepted. Issues identified during acceptance need to be documented and classified.

The backlog is updated and now represents the backlog for the realize phase. If an agile approach is adopted (see Chapter 6), the updated backlog is the baseline for sprint planning in the realize phase.

Data Volume Design

After the fit-to-standard analysis and design is complete, it's time to move on to data volume design. The purpose of data volume design is to document and agree on a data volume management strategy. It will define what data is stored where and for how long (i.e., defining the residence and retention time). This considers and includes aspects such as the following:

- External reporting requirements (tax audits, product liability)
- Internal reporting requirements (i.e., fraud detection)
- Business process requirements
- Data privacy
- Dependencies between data archiving and document management

It defines the infrastructure (e.g., content servers), use of data aging and operation, sequencing and monitoring of data archiving, and data deletion jobs.

The following techniques are used to manage data volume:

- **Data aging**
  An SAP HANA database allows data to be divided into current/hot data (stored in main memory) and historical/cold data (primarily stored on disk).

- **Data archiving**
  Data with a long retention period (legal compliance, product liability data, etc.) is transferred from the online database to an alternative storage medium, which provides display access to the transferred data.

- **Data deletion**
  Out-of-date records that are no longer used by the business nor required for legal compliance are deleted from the online database.

> **Service Components**
> In SAP Value Assurance, you can use the Data Volume Design service to assist in this task.

Data Migration Design

Effective data migration from legacy systems to the new SAP S/4HANA solution is a critical success factor for new implementations. This will include automated processes and manual data migration through keying. It covers master data (e.g., customers, banks, and cost centers) and open transaction data (e.g., open sales or service orders). In many cases, legacy data may include sensitive or classified information that requires special handling procedures.

The steps in the explore phase are as follows:

1. **Prepare and conduct the data migration assessment**
   Finalize the list of data objects to be migrated based on the design. Consider the alternative data migration approaches and tools that can be used and learn how to use them.

2. **Perform the data audit**
   Identify the legacy systems that will supply data, and use data profiling to assess the quality of the legacy data.

3. **Prepare the data migration scope and requirements document**
   Use SAP's questionnaire to drive the requirements document that covers each data object in detail. This includes data volumes and the criteria for selecting the data records to be migrated. It also covers any special security requirements for classified information.

4. **Create the data migration approach and strategy document**

   Define the approach and tools to be used in the realize phase. This includes production of a data dictionary/catalog, data cleansing, ETL, testing, and reconciliation. It also defines the infrastructure requirements, use of data migration pilots and rehearsals, and the ultimate sign-off process.

5. **Manage test data**

   The realize phase will require many sets of data to execute testing. This includes system, integration, performance, and regression testing. This activity defines the data to be migrated or created in the development and systems.

6. **Define specifications for data migration**

   Define the functional specifications required for data migration requirements not delivered through the toolset. These include extract (e.g., legacy data extraction programs), transform, validate, load (e.g., APIs for custom objects), and reconcile (e.g., reports to compare source and loaded data).

The most commonly used tools are the following:

- **SAP S/4HANA migration cockpit**

  Provides predefined Microsoft Excel XML file upload templates that are mapped to standard load APIs in SAP S/4HANA. It provides tools to validate, convert, and load data, including reworking and loading incorrect data that fails. For larger data volumes, it can work with SAP HANA staging tables instead of Microsoft Excel templates. The staging table approaches are covered in SAP Best Practices scope item Data Migration to SAP S/4HANA from Staging (2Q2).

- **SAP S/4HANA migration object modeler**

  Used in on-premise projects to adjust or create migration objects and mappings for the SAP S/4HANA migration cockpit.

- **SAP Data Services**

  ETL software that can be used as an alternative to the SAP S/4HANA migration cockpit or alongside through the filling of SAP HANA staging tables. It's used to cleanse, standardize, de-duplicate, enrich, and load legacy data. It can also connect directly to legacy systems to extract data. Rapid Data Migration to SAP S/4HANA in SAP Best Practices offers out-of-the-box SAP Data Services content for 40-plus data objects.

Data migration is often on the critical path of the overall project timeline. For this reason, some of the realize phase activities may be started before the explore phase is complete. This may include data cleansing and pilot data migrations for the high-volume or complex data objects.

See Chapter 5, Section 5.2, for more about the SAP S/4HANA tools for data migration.

Further Resources

See the Roadmap Viewer for online resources and the range of services that SAP offers to assist companies with data migration.

Technical Architecture and Infrastructure Design

A target technical architecture and infrastructure is defined in a technical design document. The technical architects need to create a detailed infrastructure design that includes the selection of hardware vendors for servers and storage, mapping of technical components, network design, and definition of cloud integration options.

The approach in the explore phase is as follows:

1. **Discover technical boundary conditions**
   These include technical solutions required, size and purpose of nonproduction systems, data center strategy, system availability requirements, service-level agreements (SLAs) for planned and unplanned downtime, HA, and DR.

2. **Create a technical solution map**
   Collect detail information on each technical component, for example, deployment model, nonfunctional requirements, integration requirements, minimum releases, and release dependencies.

3. **Decide on integration with cloud applications**
   Define integration by considering available bandwidth, peak times, availability requirements, and recovery procedures.

4. **Select hardware and perform hardware sizing**
   Work with the hardware supplier to undertake hardware sizing.

5. **Develop the virtualization strategy**
   Determine how a virtualization platform will fit into the design to use virtual servers rather than dedicated hardware per server.

6. **Design the network**
   Consider data center interconnectivity, network zones, and local area network (LAN)/wide area network (WAN) bandwidth and latency.

7. **Prepare testing**
   Prepare meaningful test cases for flexibility, workload management, HA, DR, backup, and restore.

8. **Document the technical design**
   Technical design is developed and documented in a series of workshops. This includes technical components, scalability, load balancing, backup, HA, DR, architecture, infrastructure, deployment plan, and data center and third-party integration.

The SAP Activate Roadmap Viewer provides accelerators such as white papers, check-lists, and a Technical Solution Map template and Technical Design Document template.

Service Components

SAP can assist through the Technical Platform Definition service component and the Advanced Sizing service component.

Integration Design

The purpose of this activity is to define the architecture and design required for inter-faces between all systems. This activity is executed in close cooperation with the work on interfaces in the WRICEF list and design. The integration requirements between SAP systems are documented in the configuration requirements.

The interface architecture identifies all the systems-to-be and interfaces. An interface register lists the middleware technology, protocol type, frequency, and directions of communication of each interface.

After the architecture and scope are agreed upon, an integration design document is produced. The following aspects should be described for each integration aspect or interface:

- Short description of the integration aspect
- General business requirements (e.g., frequency and required fields)
- IT systems interfaced to SAP S/4HANA
- Identification of integration requirements (referencing the backlog)
- Solution for requirements (middleware, field mapping, or configuration)
- Important customizing
- Developments
- Organizational aspects
- Process quantification (i.e., expected data volume)

Functional specifications for interfaces between SAP and non-SAP systems are pro-duced during the explore or realize phase depending on the milestone definitions of the project.

The SAP middleware solutions to manage the operation of end-to-end integration pro-cesses are either SAP Process Integration (on-premise) or SAP Integration Suite. You can find APIs and predefined integrations scenarios online on SAP API Business Hub.

Service Components

SAP offers the Integration Validation service component to companies using SAP Value Assurance and premium engagements.

Analytics Design

The project should evaluate the strategic and business value of all the analytics solutions available for SAP S/4HANA. The explore phase should build on the work already done during the discover and prepare phases to document an analytics architecture, landscape, and design. The following SAP solutions may be considered:

- **SAP S/4HANA embedded analytics**
  Includes LoB-specific prebuilt solutions. New real-time reports can also be produced based on the SAP HANA CDS views.
- **SAP BW/4HANA**
  SAP's second-generation data warehousing solution for SAP and non-SAP data.
- **SAP Analytics Cloud**
  Cloud-based analytics solution that can operate across all SAP on-premise and SAP cloud solutions, SAP BW/4HANA, and non-SAP solutions.
- **SAP Digital Boardroom**
  An add-on to SAP Analytics Cloud to provide real-time analysis and decision support for C-level leadership.
- **SAP BusinessObjects Business Intelligence**
  On-premise alternative to SAP Analytics Cloud.

Further Resources

SAP Analytics Cloud and SAP BW/4HANA have their own separate SAP Activate roadmaps in the Roadmap Viewer that follow the SAP Activate project phases.

Analytics design covers analytics (e.g., reports, tables, charts, graphs, and geographic analysis), predictive analytics, and planning requirements. Analytics workshops are conducted for LoB-specific processes and requirements. The standard analytics apps and standard business content are reviewed, and a fit-to-standard analysis and design are performed. Note that the SAP Best Practices for analytics are currently for SAP S/4HANA Cloud and aren't yet available for SAP S/4HANA.

Analytics design guidelines are produced that define the following:

- When and how to use the different analytics solutions
- When to use the different connection types between the solutions

- Data modeling guidelines
- User access and security concepts

Service Components

SAP can assist through SAP Value Assurance with the Analytics Design service component.

Security Design

The purpose of the security design deliverable is to scope security and design user management. The security topics include infrastructure, network, operating system, database, and frontend access. User management topics cover roles, authorizations, user maintenance, and segregation of duties.

Security activities are prioritized (mandatory/recommended/optional) to create a detailed security roadmap for implementation in the realize phase and beyond. The required security topics are as follows:

- Planning SAP HANA security following the SAP HANA Security Guide
- Defining communication security
- Defining authentication mechanisms

There are also topics that are recommended but may not be required or prioritized by all companies:

- Planning the implementation of single sign-on (SSO)
- Defining processes for SAP auditing, logging, and monitoring
- Planning the security of the IT infrastructure
- Planning remote function call (RFC) connections and gateway security
- Patching SAP Notes for security
- Creating custom code security

The business roles and authorization requirements determined during the design drive the user management design.

Segregation of duties is the assignment of steps in a process to different people to avoid fraud through individuals having excessive control. The management of access risks is supported by SAP Access Control, which is part of SAP governance, risk, and compliance solutions.

Service Components

SAP can assist through SAP Value Assurance with the Security Design service component.

Test Planning

The purpose of this critical deliverable is to manage the quality of the solution and to minimize issues during and after go-live. A risk-based approach should be used to define test planning. This means that the testing effort is high for high-risk topics and low for low-risk topics.

The test strategy document covers the following topics:

- **Project testing**
  Determine project testing objectives and assumptions.
- **Test scope**
  Results from the design drive the scope. Compile a list of test cases and test scripts focusing on the business-critical and frequently used business processes.
- **Types of testing**
  Select test cycles, including unit testing, business process (string) testing, integration testing, data conversion testing, performance testing, UAT, and regression testing.
- **Testing approach**
  Determine how different test types relate to each other; for example, a successful unit test is a prerequisite for doing a string test.
- **Testing deliverables**
  Define test processes per project phase, test environments, and test data (aligned with the data migration design).
- **Testing tools**
  Determine which tools will be used to perform different tests.
- **Test automation**
  Decide whether automation will be used and evaluate and select the appropriate tools.
- **Defect management**
  Describe how defects will be documented.
- **Roles and responsibilities**
  Describe the test lead and the responsibilities of individual project team members.

Detailed test planning should be done to plan the timing, duration, criteria, dependencies, and resources for each of the test cycles.

You may use SAP Solution Manager as the central platform for test management of SAP-centric solutions. It can be used in combination with other test solutions if the company has other standards or tools.

Service Components

SAP can assist through SAP Value Assurance with the Test Planning service component.

Set Up Development Environment

Before configuration and development work starts in the realize phase, the development environment needs to be set up. There are three main approaches:

1. **Enterprise management layer for SAP S/4HANA**
   Set up a fresh development system by reusing the enterprise management layer for SAP S/4HANA originally created for the sandbox.

2. **Manual setup and activation of SAP Best Practices**
   Set up a fresh SAP S/4HANA development system. Create a new client and then import and activate selected SAP Best Practices using the SAP solution builder tool. The SAP S/4HANA fully activated appliance cannot be used to create a development system.

3. **Empty development system**
   This approach provides complete flexibility and control. After the new client is available, configuration is entered from scratch manually using the SAP Best Practices in the sandbox system as a reference.

Service Components

SAP can provision the development environment through the Platform Execution Enablement service component.

End User Learning and Change Impact Analysis

During the explore phase, the training requirements for key users and end users are analyzed and documented. A learning needs analysis identifies the skill levels, knowledge gaps, and training requirements. Based on the analysis, a training strategy and plan is designed. See Chapter 10 for more information.

After the fit-to-standard workshops are complete, a change impact analysis is done. An OCM expert will usually join the project team. The OCM expert will gather the organizational and technical changes identified in the workshops and refine these through comparing the business processes and solutions as is and to be. See Chapter 10 for more information.

Operations Impact Evaluation

An operations impact evaluation is undertaken. With the introduction of a new solution such as SAP S/4HANA, the current IT support framework will change.

The deliverables from the explore phase, such as the technical design document and other design documents, are important sources of information on what needs to be supported by IT after the new solution is live and how.

The aim is to identify new operational activities, modifications to existing activities, and activities that can be retired. All the relevant support areas need to be analyzed: roles and skills, processes/procedures, operations documentation, and enabling support tools. Then a roadmap is defined that includes the key activities for IT to fill the gaps and prepare the future IT support framework. This will include establishing resources; setting up tools; documenting procedures, knowledge transfer, and operations cutover; and retiring parts of the old framework.

Service Components
SAP can support this task with the Operations Impact Evaluation service component.

SAP Solution Manager in the Explore Phase

Nearly all on-premise customers use SAP Solution Manager to manage operations after the solution is live. SAP also recommends the use of SAP Solution Manager in all phases of an on-premise implementation project. Some companies and partners have their own standards for project tools and choose not to use some of the features we'll discuss in this section.

During the explore phase, SAP Solution Manager can be used for the following tasks:

- **Process management**
  The SAP Best Practices scope items, building blocks, and process diagrams are imported and then managed, adjusted, and annotated, as shown in Figure 7.44.

- **Document management**
  Project documents, such as design documents and WRICEF specifications, are stored with document versioning.

- **Requirements**
  The backlog of business requirements is transferred from a Microsoft Excel spreadsheet into SAP Solution Manager. This allows configuration and developments done in the realize phase to be linked back to specific requirements.

- **Project management**
  The project deliverables and tasks can be managed and tracked in SAP Solution Manager, which contains the SAP Activate roadmap content.

- **Change and release management**
  Configuration and delta requirements are allocated to releases with full change control.

The approach to using SAP Solution Manager is agreed upon and documented in an SAP Solution Manager guideline document. The approach is used to manage the build, test, and deployment in SAP Solution Manager during the realize phase.

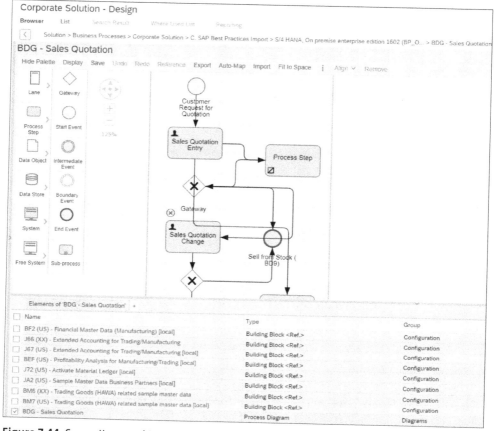

Figure 7.44 Scope Item and Process Diagram in SAP Solution Manager

The project may choose to adopt an SAP project-delivery approach called Focused Build for SAP Solution Manager that applies to all project phases. This agile approach uses SAP Solution Manager more rigorously and comprehensively and requires an add-on to the SAP Solution Manager system. It allows work and resources to be assigned to work packages and work items. Resources and costs can be planned and time recorded, and actual progress can be monitored against the plan. Focused Build for SAP Solution Manager is often used when SAP works with companies on custom developments through SAP Innovation Services. We briefly discussed the capabilities of Focused Build for SAP Solution Manager in Chapter 3, Section 3.4.9.

7.3.5   Realize Your Requirements

In the realize phase, business process requirements are implemented based on the design. Testing is done in the quality assurance system before deploying the SAP S/4HANA production system in the deploy phase. We'll walk through the realize phase for a new implementation project in this section.

Phase Overview

During the realize phase, a series of cycles are used to incrementally build, test, and validate an integrated business and system environment based on the business scenarios and process requirements identified during the explore phase. Configuration, extensions, integration, security, and analytics are implemented. The technical infrastructure is commissioned, including the quality assurance and production environments. Company legacy data is migrated or ready to migrate, and data volume management is set up. Adoption activities occur, and the operations support framework is prepared. The phase ends with preparation for the cutover.

The main outputs of the realize phase in a new implementation include the following:

- The system is configured and configuration documentation exists.
- Technical specifications, test cases, and custom code for WRICEFs are completed.
- Infrastructure, integration, security, and operational procedures are in place and tested.
- Quality assurance and production environments are set up with transports from the development system.
- Data migration processes are tested, and a data quality assessment report is delivered.
- Data aging, data archiving, and data deletion are ready.
- Tests, including UAT, are complete based on a test plan, test cases, and test scripts.
- The support operations framework and procedures are ready.
- Cutover from legacy systems to SAP S/4HANA has been planned and rehearsed.

The realize phase must be planned in detail with dependencies coming together in the plan for testing. Carefully defined entry and exit criteria must be transparent to the whole team to ensure that the workstreams remain coordinated. The plan must be frequently updated to reflect progress and changes in scope and timescales.

The LoB teams (e.g., finance or manufacturing) from the explore phase continue to operate through the realize phase. The project will have iterative build cycles with a specific set of user stories and scope assigned to each cycle. If an agile delivery approach is being used, the build cycles are called *sprints* and have a much shorter duration than in a traditional waterfall approach. Refer to Chapter 6 for more details about agile delivery and planning and managing sprints.

The following sections on the realize phase are organized into topics that appear in the roadmap. The use of SAP Solution Manager during the realize phase is covered in the last section.

Configuration

The purpose of this activity is to configure the solution settings according to the design defined and agreed upon during the explore phase. Configuration is done in the development environment, and steps are executed in cycles (or agile sprints). SAP Best Practices provide the baseline configuration in the development system, or configuration is done from scratch referring to the SAP Best Practices in the sandbox. A configuration guideline is produced to document the approach and define the standards to be used.

The configuration sequence depends on the business scope but typically follows this order:

1. Organizational unit settings
2. General settings for each LoB
3. Master data settings
4. Processes within each LoB for high-volume process variants (e.g., procurement of direct materials)
5. Processes that span LoB teams, which are done in one company code for high-volume process variants (e.g., sales orders to payment receipt or goods receipt with warehouse management)
6. Functions that cross processes and have a high impact (e.g., available-to-promise [ATP], pricing, or credit management)
7. Medium-volume process variants (e.g., production subcontracting or customer returns)
8. Replication and process testing in different company codes and countries
9. Complex cross-LoB functions (e.g., intercompany transfers and batch management)
10. Low-volume process variants (e.g., purchasing rebate processing or dangerous goods)
11. Country-specific localizations for statutory requirements or process variants

Each configuration cycle consists of the following stages:

1. **Handover session**
   Handover occurs from the design team to the configuration team.
2. **Perform configuration**
   Configure settings in the development system by LoB and end-to-end process.
3. **Unit test**
   Test the newly configured functions.
4. **String test**
   Test the end-to-end process or solution impacted by the configuration change.
5. **Solution walkthrough**
   Present the new capability to the project team.

6. **Bug fixing**
   Resolve issues identified in the unit test, string test, and solution walkthrough.

7. **Documentation**
   Document the configuration settings and any impacts on the design.

Much of the configuration is done using the IMG in Transaction SPRO. SAP Fiori apps are configured using adaptation at runtime. Configuration of integration between SAP products and configuration of analytics are covered later.

The following sections cover the sequential stages of configuration in detail.

Handover Session

The handover is done from the design team (in charge of the design documents) to the configuration team. The configuration team may be offshore or split across multiple physical locations. This is a good time to check the completeness and detail of the documentation.

Documents to handover may include the following:

- Design documents
- Organizational structure design
- Master data design
- Roles and security
- Configuration requirements
- Functional specifications for WRICEF objects
- UX design documentation
- SAP Best Practices configuration and documentation
- SAP Solution Manager guidelines
- Configuration guidelines

Perform Configuration

Configuration settings are made in the development system. Some are manually entered, some may be copied and pasted from the sandbox system, and some might be activated using the SAP solution builder tool. As this is a development system, all changes are recorded in transport requests. These will be used later to transfer configuration from the development system to the quality assurance and production systems.

Most of the configuration is done using the IMG in Transaction SPRO. This consists of a hierarchy of individual IMG activities, as shown in Figure 7.45. Help documentation is available within the IMG and under **Product Assistance** in the SAP Help Portal. The team should follow the configuration guidelines that govern the naming and numbering of new configuration records.

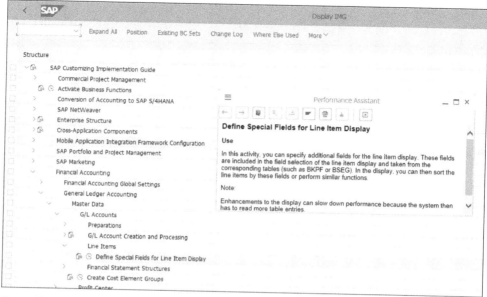

Figure 7.45 SAP Implementation Guide

Examples of IMG configuration settings include the following:

- **Organization structure**
  Company codes and plants
- **General settings**
  Chart of accounts and value-added tax (VAT) numbers
- **Master data**
  Settings for cost centers and business partners
- **LoB**
  Document types and correspondence

To understand what configuration is delivered for each SAP Best Practices scope item, use the Prerequisite Matrix accelerator in SAP Best Practices Explorer, as shown in Figure 7.46. A link for this can be found on the **Accelerators** tab under **SAP Best Practices for SAP S/4HANA (On-Premise)**. The SAP Best Practices IMG configuration is organized into building blocks. Each SAP Best Practices scope item is shown as a row (e.g., **US_16R**) and has several prerequisite building blocks shown in columns (e.g., **3Y5**, **J90**). Each building block contains configuration for several IMG activities.

SAP Best Practices content is also made available in SAP Solution Manager configuration library. Choose the **Solution Documentation** tile, select a solution, and then browse in the **Business Processes** section. You'll find links to the configuration activities organized by scope items and building blocks, as shown in Figure 7.47.

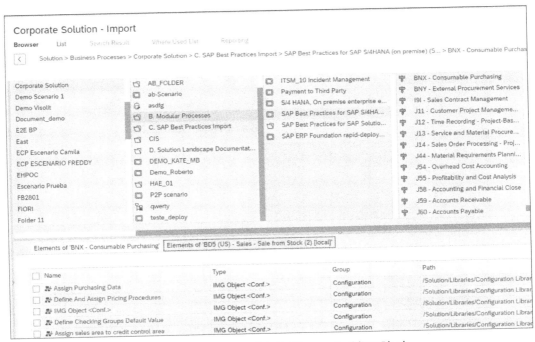

Figure 7.46 SAP Best Practices Accelerator: Prerequisite Matrix

The prerequisite matrix shown in Figure 7.46 contains the following columns:

Scope item/ Process	Scope item/ Process Description	You have to activate first														
		1	2	3	4	5	6	7	8	9	10	11	12	13	14	15
US_16R	Bank Integration with SAP Multi-Bank Connectivity	3Y5(XX)	J90(XX)	4M6(XX)	4C7(XX)	2MZ(XX)	J19(XX)	4NC(XX)	4NX(XX)	4RL(XX)	4RM(XX)	BN4(XX)	J98(XX)	2B9(XX)	4M4(XX)	4NE(XX)
US_18I	Requisitioning	3Y5(XX)	J90(XX)	4M6(XX)	4C7(XX)	2MZ(XX)	J19(XX)	4NC(XX)	4NX(XX)	4RL(XX)	4RM(XX)	BN4(XX)	J98(XX)	2B9(XX)	4M4(XX)	4NE(XX)
US_19C	Activity Management in Procurement	3Y5(XX)	J90(XX)	4M6(XX)	4C7(XX)	2MZ(XX)	J19(XX)	4NC(XX)	4NX(XX)	4RL(XX)	4RM(XX)	BN4(XX)	J98(XX)	2B9(XX)	4M4(XX)	4NE(XX)
US_19E	Supplier Classification and Segmentation	3Y5(XX)	J90(XX)	4M6(XX)	4C7(XX)	2MZ(XX)	J19(XX)	4NC(XX)	4NX(XX)	4RL(XX)	4RM(XX)	BN4(XX)	J98(XX)	2B9(XX)	4M4(XX)	4NE(XX)
US_19M	Direct Debit	3Y5(XX)	J90(XX)	4M6(XX)	4C7(XX)	2MZ(XX)	J19(XX)	4NC(XX)	4NX(XX)	4RL(XX)	4RM(XX)	BN4(XX)	J98(XX)	2B9(XX)	4M4(XX)	4NE(XX)
US_1B6	Sales Rebate Processing	3Y5(XX)	J90(XX)	4M6(XX)	4C7(XX)	2MZ(XX)	J19(XX)	4NC(XX)	4NX(XX)	4RL(XX)	4RM(XX)	BN4(XX)	J98(XX)	2B9(XX)	4M4(XX)	4NE(XX)
US_1BM	Make-to-Order Production - Semifinished Goods Planning and Assembly	3Y5(XX)	J90(XX)	4M6(XX)	4C7(XX)	2MZ(XX)	J19(XX)	4NC(XX)	4NX(XX)	4RL(XX)	4RM(XX)	BN4(XX)	J98(XX)	2B9(XX)	4M4(XX)	4NE(XX)
XX_1BS	SAP Fiori Analytical Apps for Sales	HB1(XX)														
US_1E1	Quality Management in Discrete Manufacturing	3Y5(XX)	J90(XX)	4M6(XX)	4C7(XX)	2MZ(XX)	J19(XX)	4NC(XX)	4NX(XX)	4RL(XX)	4RM(XX)	BN4(XX)	J98(XX)	2B9(XX)	4M4(XX)	4NE(XX)
US_1E3	Material Replenishment with Kanban - External Procurement	3Y5(XX)	J90(XX)	4M6(XX)	4C7(XX)	2MZ(XX)	J19(XX)	4NC(XX)	4NX(XX)	4RL(XX)	4RM(XX)	BN4(XX)	J98(XX)	2B9(XX)	4M4(XX)	4NE(XX)
US_1EG	Bank Integration with File Interface	3Y5(XX)	J90(XX)	4M6(XX)	4C7(XX)	2MZ(XX)	J19(XX)	4NC(XX)	4NX(XX)	4RL(XX)	4RM(XX)	BN4(XX)	J98(XX)	2B9(XX)	4M4(XX)	4NE(XX)
US_1EZ	Credit Memo Processing	3Y5(XX)	J90(XX)	4M6(XX)	4C7(XX)	2MZ(XX)	J19(XX)	4NC(XX)	4NX(XX)	4RL(XX)	4RM(XX)	BN4(XX)	J98(XX)	2B9(XX)	4M4(XX)	4NE(XX)
US_1F1	Debit Memo Processing	3Y5(XX)	J90(XX)	4M6(XX)	4C7(XX)	2MZ(XX)	J19(XX)	4NC(XX)	4NX(XX)	4RL(XX)	4RM(XX)	BN4(XX)	J98(XX)	2B9(XX)	4M4(XX)	4NE(XX)
US_1FD	Employee Integration - SAP S/4HANA Enablement	3Y5(XX)	J90(XX)	4M6(XX)	4C7(XX)	2MZ(XX)	J19(XX)	4NC(XX)	4NX(XX)	4RL(XX)	4RM(XX)	BN4(XX)	J98(XX)	2B9(XX)	4M4(XX)	4NE(XX)
US_1FM	Quality Management in Procurement	3Y5(XX)	J90(XX)	4M6(XX)	4C7(XX)	2MZ(XX)	J19(XX)	4NC(XX)	4NX(XX)	4RL(XX)	4RM(XX)	BN4(XX)	J98(XX)	2B9(XX)	4M4(XX)	4NE(XX)
US_1FS	Basic Warehouse Inbound Processing from Supplier	3Y5(XX)	J90(XX)	4M6(XX)	4C7(XX)	2MZ(XX)	J19(XX)	4NC(XX)	4NX(XX)	4RL(XX)	4RM(XX)	BN4(XX)	J98(XX)	2B9(XX)	4M4(XX)	4NE(XX)
US_1FU	Initial Stock Upload for Warehouse	3Y5(XX)	J90(XX)	4M6(XX)	4C7(XX)	2MZ(XX)	J19(XX)	4NC(XX)	4NX(XX)	4RL(XX)	4RM(XX)	BN4(XX)	J98(XX)	2B9(XX)	4M4(XX)	4NE(XX)
US_1FW	Physical Inventory in Warehouse	3Y5(XX)	J90(XX)	4M6(XX)	4C7(XX)	2MZ(XX)	J19(XX)	4NC(XX)	4NX(XX)	4RL(XX)	4RM(XX)	BN4(XX)	J98(XX)	2B9(XX)	4M4(XX)	4NE(XX)

Figure 7.47 SAP Solution Manager Showing IMG Activities per Building Block

It's possible to generate a configuration guide of the SAP Best Practices configuration in a building block, as shown in Figure 7.48. You can access the configuration report via the SAP solution builder tool. Use the Building Block Builder (for a selected configuration level) or Transaction /SMB/CONFIG_GUIDE_UI.

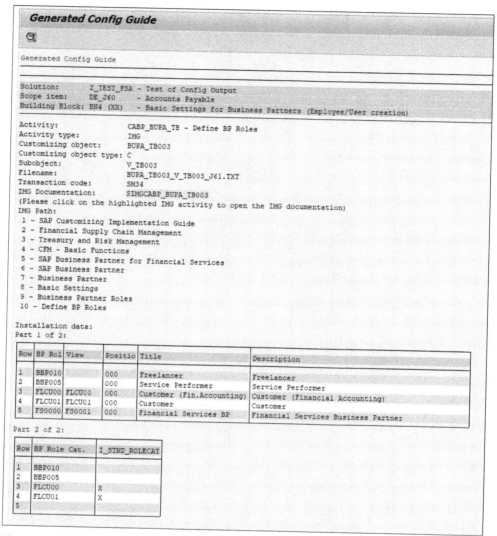

Figure 7.48 Generated SAP Best Practices Configuration Guide

Further Resources

Detailed instructions are provided in the SAP Help Portal, in the Administration Guide to Implementation of SAP S/4HANA with SAP Best Practices.

Configuration of the SAP Fiori UI is done with UI adaptation at runtime. It's possible to move, rename, and remove sections, groups, and fields, as shown in Figure 7.49. You can also combine fields or add standard fields or custom fields. Classic non–SAP Fiori apps (SAP GUI for HTML and Web Dynpro for ABAP) can be configured using SAP Screen Personas.

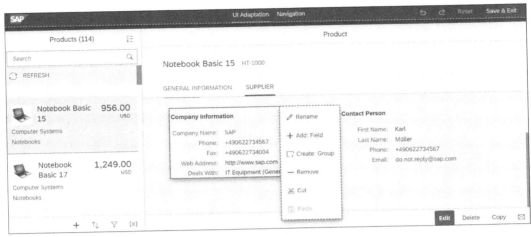

Figure 7.49 Configuring SAP Fiori App with UI Adaption

Unit Test

The objective of this task is to properly unit test the newly implemented functions in the development system and to log and fix issues. Each of the LoB teams create and manage a list of unit tests to cover all their processes. Each unit test has a test script that documents the precise steps to be followed in the system, the data to use, and the expected results. The SAP Best Practices test scripts can be extended to reflect the solution-specific scope.

String Test

A test is done for an end-to-end process by stringing together unit tests. The string test will often cross multiple LoB teams. Tests may be done in the development or quality assurance systems.

Because a full integration test is executed later in the realize phase, the recommendation is to test with manually created test data rather than migrated data. The focus should be on SAP processes and functionality. This can include standard integration between SAP products, such as SAP S/4HANA and SAP Business Network. Testing of company-specific WRICEF objects and interfaces with non-SAP systems is done during integration testing.

Test execution and results should be documented and stored in SAP Solution Manager. Issues should be logged and fixed.

Solution Walkthrough

The aim of this task is to present the solution capability and business process to business process owners in the LoB teams via live demonstration. Their early feedback is incorporated into the solution. If open questions can't be resolved within the project, the business process owner takes the queries to the business for resolution. Changes to the scope or design must be managed through the change request process (see Chapter 6, Section 6.3.2).

Bug Fixing

Issues and bugs identified during tests and the solution walkthrough should be resolved directly within the current build cycle or logged in the project issue list. The string test should be repeated to check that changes haven't produced any unwanted side effects.

Documentation

The LoB teams document the configuration settings and impacts on the design. The SAP Solution Manager configuration library can be used to capture a record of the settings made, including the reason for each decision.

Product Enhancements

In a new implementation, product enhancement covers the development of custom code for the WRICEFs defined during the explore phase. It may also include larger custom developments that may be executed by the company, a partner, or SAP Innovation Services. If a new implementation is being done in SAP S/4HANA to replace an old SAP ERP solution, the team may decide to reuse some of the old custom code. Refer to Chapter 8, Section 8.3.3, on system conversion guidance.

The following sections cover the product enhancement activities during the realize phase.

Select Development Technologies

Before developing new code in SAP S/4HANA, developers should be aware of the latest technical options available—for example, using extensibility apps within SAP S/4HANA or side-by-side extensibility with SAP Extension Suite.

Extensibility apps provide a more readily maintainable alternative to classic extensibility for a growing list of objects and enhancements. This includes adapting SAP Fiori UIs, adding custom fields, adding application logic, and creating reports, email templates, and forms.

SAP Extension Suite allows development to be done in parallel with the SAP S/4HANA implementation to keep the core clean and make software upgrades faster. It also allows the team to consume the latest technology platform for innovation use cases such as mobile, machine learning, big data, and IoT.

Developers should also be aware of the latest SAP Best Practices associated with the newest techniques. Where possible, these approaches should be considered before classic extensibility such as ABAP BAdIs and user exits. As always, modifications outside stable enhancement points should always be avoided. The golden rule for modern extensibility technologies in the cloud can also be applied on-premise. Decisions on the approach should be documented in a project-specific development guideline and reviews put in place to check that approaches are adopted.

Technical Design

Detailed technical specifications are produced for all WRICEFs based on the functional specifications prepared earlier. The technical specifications will include details such as entry point in the system, enhancement logic, process flow diagram, data model, and required authorizations. Template documents are available in the Roadmap Viewer. Unit test case documents are prepared. All documents are stored in SAP Solution Manager and reviewed by the application design team to check that they fit with the evolving design.

Develop and Test WRICEFs

The developers build, unit test, and document the WRICEFs. After development is complete, they're tested and retested by the application design team until all issues are resolved.

Enhancements may be required to UIs if requirements can't be met through configuration alone. Examples include the following:

- Enhancements through SAP Fiori extension points—that is, specific types of extension available in SAP Fiori screens (e.g., adding custom columns and filters to an SAP Fiori list report or worklist)
- Backend extensions (e.g., addition of new custom fields)
- Full-screen modifications
- Development of new SAP Fiori apps

Service Components

SAP Value Assurance offers the Technical Performance Optimization service component for WRICEFs.

Custom Developments

It's recommended to manage development requirements that are critical or exceed a certain threshold as custom developments. These are typically managed as small standalone agile projects. The functional specification, technical specification, development, and testing are managed through agile sprints (refer to Chapter 6, Section 6.3.2).

SAP Innovation Services can develop one-of-a-kind solutions through company-specific custom developments. Using this service maximizes supportability and operability.

Data Volume Management

Data volume management is configured based on the design from the explore phase. This includes data aging and processes to delete and archive data.

In data aging, an SAP HANA database allows data to be divided into current/hot data (stored in main memory) and historical/cold data (primarily stored on disk). Data aging is available for the following objects:

- Finance documents
- Unified journal entry
- Material documents
- Purchase orders
- Sales documents
- Deliveries
- Sales invoices
- Application logs
- Intermediate documents (IDocs)
- Change documents
- Workflow documents

Further Resources

Refer to the SAP Help Portal for documentation on how to do the configuration (design time) and test the solution (runtime).

Data Migration

For a new implementation, this activity develops, implements, and tests the data migration processes defined in the explore phase. This activity consists of iterative development and testing cycles focused on the analysis of data, refinement of business rules, and deployment of migration processes and programs. The test cycles enable the migration team to improve data quality to an acceptable production level, develop a detailed cutover sequencing plan, and exercise data reconciliation and validation processes required to support the cutover.

The project team develops the specific architecture, processes, and programs that support the extraction, validation, harmonization, enrichment, and cleansing of the legacy data. This is done based on the data migration approach and strategy document and data migration functional specifications developed in the explore phase. The processes depend directly on the tools and utilities selected in the explore phase (refer to Section 7.3.4). These deliverables can range from fully automated programs based on an ETL software platform to a series of manual processes based on tools such as Microsoft

Excel and Microsoft SQL Server. SAP supports data migration with the SAP S/4HANA migration cockpit and/or SAP Data Services.

The data migration approach for each data object may vary. Whatever the approach, multiple test rounds are executed. The results are recorded, and the defects are eliminated. The data migration test results are statistics that provide a detailed account of data load issues and successfully loaded data.

If data volumes are very large, the initial test cycles may need to use samples of representative data. Data profiling should be done to ensure representative variations are used; otherwise, defects and unique mappings and requirements may remain hidden. Runtimes for the production cutover process may need to be optimized. Master data that is likely to be static may be migrated early with delta updates run during the cutover.

A final data quality assessment report is produced at the end of the realize phase. This summarizes the results and assesses the overall data migration quality. This is reviewed with the project stakeholders. At the end of this task, the data migration team can move into the deploy phase with the confidence that a majority of data quality issues and migration issues have been resolved and mitigated.

> **Note**
>
> For more information on the data migration process, refer to Chapter 5, Section 5.2.

Set Up Infrastructure and Security

In the realize phase, the technical infrastructure must be installed and configured as defined in the technical design document created in the explore phase.

The IT infrastructure setup work includes the following:

- Server hardware, operating system, and virtualization platform
- Storage solution—that is, the physical setup of the storage infrastructure usually done by the storage supplier
- Integration of the new components into the existing IT environment—for example, integration into the existing network and backup solution
- HA, DR, and backup

The company-specific results from the security design phase are also implemented, including the following:

- User management, including roles, authorizations, and user maintenance
- Infrastructure and network security
- Operating system and database security
- Frontend access and authentication

The team must execute infrastructure tests based on the test cases and test plan. This will measure the performance against the defined KPIs to ensure the infrastructure operates within the boundary conditions of the business. The team resolves, documents, and retests issues and defects. Tests should include the following scenarios:

- Performance, as issues may require changes to the functional design in addition to infrastructure changes
- Flexibility procedures (e.g., by moving system load to other hosts, adding instances, or changing instances)
- HA
- DR
- Backup and restore
- Infrastructure security

If already available, the productive hardware is tested to validate the configuration. Otherwise, the productive hardware is tested in the deploy phase (see Section 7.3.6).

Service Components

SAP can assist through SAP Value Assurance with the Technical Feasibility Check, Business Process Performance Optimization, Technical Performance Optimization, and Volume Test Optimization service components. These may lead to changes in the functional design, configuration, and tuning for optimum performance, elimination of bottlenecks, and SAP Fiori-specific performance improvements.

Integration Implementation and Validation

During integration implementation, the customer-specific design from the explore phase is implemented. This activity should be executed in close cooperation with the configuration and product enhancement activities. The project team should do the following:

- Implement standard SAP Best Practices scope items for specific integration scenarios, such as Automated Purchase-to-Pay with SAP Ariba Commerce Automation (J82).
- Configure and customize SAP-to-SAP integration scenarios not covered by SAP Best Practices.
- Implement interfaces between SAP and non-SAP solutions based on interfaces built and unit tested in the product enhancement activities.

When implementing and running landscapes that drive mission-critical business processes, the integration of solutions can be complex and challenging. The implementation work is typically distributed across many teams and many stakeholders, including custom-built and third-party software.

SAP recommends the Integration Validation service to mitigate risk based on the use of SAP Value Assurance services. The aim is to ensure technical readiness of the entire solution for go-live. It includes analysis of critical business processes and interfaces to validate scalability, performance, data consistency, and exception management. A comprehensive monthly status of technical go-live readiness for core business processes is recommended. It includes these aspects:

- **Data consistency**
  In distributed solution landscapes, the consistency of the data across software systems must be subject to checks and validations. This requires transactional security, and all integration queues and interfaces must be monitored.

- **Business process monitoring and exception management**
  There must be 100 percent transparency into the status and completion of business processes. The flow of documents must be monitored.

- **Performance and scalability**
  Response time for critical transactions and runtime for batch jobs should meet business requirements. Adequate load balancing must be in place.

Service Components

SAP recommends the use of the following service components through SAP Value Assurance: Integration Validation, Interface Management, and Technical Integration Check. These tried-and-tested processes, provided by SAP Services and Support, give you access to lessons learned from hundreds of other live SAP implementations. See the Roadmap Viewer for more details.

Analytics Configuration

The analytics solutions are configured based on the design and guidelines documented in the explore phase. The scope may cover analytics, predictive analytics, and planning requirements. The design will typically be based on embedded analytics in SAP S/4HANA and SAP Analytics Cloud to define the UX for analytics and planning. SAP BW/4HANA provides a data warehouse for structured and unstructured data from SAP on-premise, SAP cloud, and third-party solutions.

Further Resources

Refer to the SAP Analytics Cloud and SAP BW/4HANA SAP Activate roadmaps in the Roadmap Viewer for more details.

Examples of the activities to be undertaken in SAP S/4HANA include the following:

- Configure the SAP Fiori launchpad.
- Perform the technical setup of SAP S/4HANA CDS views and SAP S/4HANA embedded analytical apps based on CDS views.
- Customize prebuilt SAP S/4HANA embedded analytics.
- Create custom CDS views for custom SAP S/4HANA embedded analytics.

Examples of the activities to be undertaken in SAP BW/4HANA include the following:

- Install the SAP BW/4HANA content add-ons, and activate the required content areas.
- Establish the system connection between SAP S/4HANA and SAP BW/4HANA.
- Set up a live data connection between SAP S/4HANA and SAP BW/4HANA to enable analytics without persistent data in SAP BW/4HANA.
- Build SAP BW/4HANA models, extract SAP S/4HANA data, and configure queries.
- Work with third-party data in SAP BW/4HANA.

Examples of the activities to be undertaken in SAP Analytics Cloud include the following:

- Configure general settings such as the import functionality, database connector, and cloud connector.
- Import and enable prebuilt content for SAP Analytics Cloud.
- Configure the underlying SAP Analytics Cloud data models, planning models, and predictive models.
- Set up a live data connection between SAP Analytics Cloud and SAP S/4HANA and SAP BW/4HANA to enable analytics without persistent data in the cloud.
- Import data into the data models and perform data preparation for analytics with persistent data in the cloud.
- Configure SAP Analytics Cloud stories for reports, tables, charts, graphs, and geographic analysis.

Service Components

SAP Services and Support can provide consulting enablement or implementation for SAP Analytics Cloud and SAP Digital Boardroom.

Testing

In this deliverable, the test strategy and test plan produced in the explore phase is put into action. Figure 7.50 provides an overview of the testing approach, which illustrates what systems are used and the sequence of test cycles. You can also refer to Chapter 5, Section 5.5 for more information on testing.

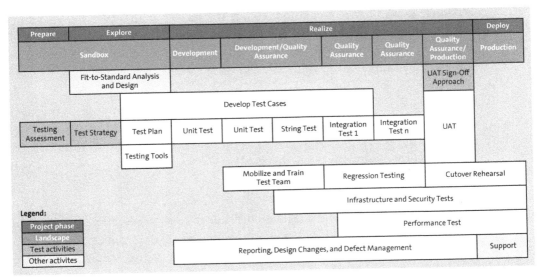

Figure 7.50 Overview of Testing Approach

Test cases and test scripts with expected results are produced for all the test cycles. Process flow diagrams and test scripts from SAP Best Practices scope items serve as accelerators. Testing tools are set up, and the testing teams are trained. A combination of manual testing and automated testing is used. The scope and source of the required test data is agreed upon. The details of the approval procedure for UAT are finalized, and the test plan is turned into a detailed schedule of activity.

During all test execution, defects are formally logged for traceability, fixes are applied and transported, and the process is retested until the issue is resolved. Errors can hide in the variants of processes, so ensure that test scripts mix these up well—for example, a foreign currency order with batch management.

All the different workstreams come together in the test process. As we've seen throughout our discussion of the realize phase, unit tests and string tests are part of configuration, for example.

The following tests are available:

- **Integration tests**
  Integration testing is performed to verify proper execution of the entire application, including all WRICEFs, integration between SAP solutions, and interfaces to external applications. Integration testing is conducted in the quality assurance system using migrated data. Integration testing is approved after all tests have passed.

- **Regression tests**
  During integration tests, many fixes are transported into the quality assurance system. Later fixes may break processes that had already passed their tests. To mitigate risk, regression tests are executed alongside the cutover rehearsals. The scope and

approach are similar to integration testing. The quality assurance system is monitored as if it were the production system, as this will provide an indication of end state operations. For example, errors in the system log, which may not be noticed by testers, could cause instability in the production system.

- **UAT**
  UAT provides formal approval from actual users that the solution works as specified and meets the business requirements. The scope and approach are similar to integration testing. The UAT team is guided by the project team and starts with the integration test cases and scripts and then adds real-world scenarios.

Set Up Quality Assurance and Production

A quality assurance environment is made available to test configuration and development in an environment sized like the production system to be as similar as possible to the existing solution. This must be done early enough in the realize phase to enable data migration and integration tests. Refer to the technical design document produced in the explore phase. Steps include the following:

1. Execute the technical installation of the required SAP products.
2. Run the technical system setup.
3. Set up the transports from the development system to the quality assurance system.
4. Transport development and configuration.
5. Perform manual rework activities for configuration that isn't transported.
6. Execute integration set up between the SAP S/4HANA solution and SAP and non-SAP solutions.
7. Document the detailed procedure to streamline the process for production.

Further Resources

For detailed information, refer to the Administration Guide for the Implementation of SAP S/4HANA on the SAP Help Portal.

Before the cutover activities start, a production environment is made available to execute final go-live simulations and cutover. This environment will be used as the future production system on go-live.

Operations Implementation

Changes to the support operations are implemented following the operations roadmap defined in the explore phase. The following areas are covered:

- **Detailed operations**
  The changes to the support framework are implemented. This is often managed through detailed IT change requests.

- **Roles and responsibilities**
  Changes to resources and their roles and responsibilities are implemented.

- **Support processes and procedures**
  Changed IT support processes are documented and tested. This includes incident management, problem management, access management, change management, test management, job management, and system recovery.

- **Operations support tools**
  Tools are adjusted or newly set up. Old operational tools are turned off.

- **Operations documentation**
  An operations handbook is produced, and all documentation is updated and stored in a central repository.

- **Knowledge transfer**
  The IT support resources prepare to run the new solution. Knowledge transfer is done through a combination of activities, including formal training, self-study, shadowing, and on-the-job training.

Cutover Preparation

Now, it's time to prepare for cutover with the following tasks:

- Create a detailed hour-by-hour cutover plan to mitigate risk.
- Plan the rehearsal and simulation of cutover activities in legacy and SAP systems.
- Define contingency processes for problem scenarios.
- Get approval from informed stakeholders.

During simulation, the tasks, sequence, and duration are optimized, and the responsibilities in the project team and business are finalized. Rehearsals are repeated until the go-live risk is mitigated to an acceptable degree.

The scope of rehearsals will include work in the legacy systems—for example, parking of logistics and warehouse processes, financial closing, blocking access to users, and stopping operational jobs. The cutover rehearsal will include backups, transports, manual configuration steps, data migration, data reconciliation, testing, business acceptance of the cutover, and contingency processes. The overall communication approach may include coordination with the company, suppliers, and other third parties.

A new implementation may require the following three or more simulations:

- **Technical**
  Definition and validation of the steps with the project team.

- **Dry run**
  Full execution of the cutover schedule with the entire team to validate steps, sequence, and data.

- **Final**
  Full execution of the entire cutover schedule to streamline execution and obtain exact timings.

Prepare Training and Organizational Change Management Alignment

Training material is created for end users. SAP recommends the SAP Enable Now tool for creating the training material, supporting translations, and developing e-learning (see Chapter 10, Section 10.5). It can be used for SAP and non-SAP applications. Possible training documents include the following:

- **Course concept**
  Goal and structure of each training event
- **Training manual**
  Instructions for the trainers
- **Work instructions**
  Step-by-step explanations of each process and transaction
- **Exercises**
  Instructions and data for hands-on use of the solution
- **Simulations**
  Recorded walkthroughs of processes and transactions with guidance
- **E-learning**
  Self-learning for less complex topics
- **Web-based training**
  Alternative to classroom training providing communication with the trainer via video, chat, and phone

Organizational change impacts were identified in the explore phase and help drive OCM activities. During the realize phase, these are reassessed with a focus on changes in the project scope, design, and assumptions. In particular, the alignment of OCM with the test, data migration, and cutover processes is checked. See Chapter 10 for more information.

SAP Solution Manager in the Realize Phase

During the realize phase, SAP Solution Manager can be used for the following:

- **Document management**
  Project documents such as configuration documentation, technical specifications, and test results are stored and linked back to requirements.
- **Configuration**
  The IMG configuration activities used are logged against processes and requirements.

- **Project management**
  The project deliverables and tasks can be managed and tracked.

- **Change management**
  Configuration and developments in SAP S/4HANA are recorded in SAP S/4HANA transport requests. These transport requests can be linked to SAP Solution Manager change documents that collect all related system and documentation changes into groups that can be released together.

- **Manage transports into quality assurance**
  Use SAP Solution Manager change documents to trigger transports from the development system to the quality assurance system.

7.3.6   Deploy Your Solution

During the deploy phase, the solution, supporting tools, and processes are made ready for the SAP S/4HANA production system go-live. We'll walk through the tasks in the deploy phase for a new implementation project in this section.

Phase Overview

At this point in the project, a production environment is already available. All configuration, enhancements, and UAT are complete. Final go-live simulations and cutover are executed. This phase includes a go or no-go decision and ensures that the organization is ready to run in the new environment.

The primary activities of the deploy phase in a new implementation include the following:

- End user learning and organizational change readiness
- Finalize testing
- Final production data load
- Operation and infrastructure readiness
- Cutover rehearsal
- Production cutover
- System go-live and hypercare support
- Handover to support organization

End User Learning and Organizational Change Readiness

In the deploy phase, the OCM activities ensure all relevant stakeholders are ready to go live. Monitoring of OCM activities, including the communication plan, is crucial to ensure end user adoption. See Chapter 10 for more information.

The learning plan developed in the previous phases is delivered. The training is necessary to ensure that end users are prepared for the new solution. The steps may include the following:

- Finalize a detailed training schedule.
- Deliver end user training.
- Collect training evaluations feedback.
- Perform people readiness assessment.

After the go-live, it's vital to ensure end users have adopted the solution and knowledge resources are maintained.

Finalize Testing

The testing activities initiated in the realize phase are finalized. The following testing activities must be closed and confirmed before cutover to production:

- Integration validation
- Infrastructure and security tests
- Performance tests

Final Production Data Load

After all preparations and configuration on both the technical and application levels are complete, data can be loaded from the legacy systems into the production environment of SAP S/4HANA. Static master data may be migrated before the cutover and more dynamic data during the cutover. This approach can be used to reduce the work and duration of data migration in the cutover.

Operation and Infrastructure Readiness

The technical infrastructure and SAP S/4HANA production environment must be ready. Ensure the operations and support organization is prepared to run the new solution. The activity provides a defined support approach for monitoring and measuring the day-to-day support operations. The following topics need to be covered:

- Roles and responsibilities
- Support processes, governance, and procedures
- Operations support tools and documentation
- Knowledge transfer

Service Components

SAP can support this activity with the Operations Readiness service component. It includes a status review of the IT operation changes defined during the operations impact evaluation. Ideally, the check is performed a couple of weeks before go-live.

Dress Rehearsal

Before performing the cutover to production, it's important to rehearse the cutover plan entirely in a test system that reflects the future state of the production system. The rehearsal is intended to confirm the ownership, sequence, and duration of the cutover activities to production. There may be a need to postpone the go-live date if significant changes and critical items are raised as a result of this rehearsal. The cutover schedule is likely to be complex, with many dependencies and owners from the business and IT. Therefore, communication plays a crucial role in ensuring a successful production cutover.

Production Cutover

The purpose of the cutover is to execute the cutover plan and get the solution ready for productive use and operation. The main activities in the cutover are the following:

- Execute the cutover, following the tasks defined in the cutover plan.
- Complete the final production data load if needed (e.g., open items).
- Document the actual duration of each step to support future projects.
- Capture any variances to the plan, along with decision makers who approved the change.
- The cutover managers should proactively notify task owners of upcoming tasks to ensure their availability.
- Regularly communicate the status to stakeholders.
- After the data is loaded, testing and data reconciliation must be completed.
- Complete all required documentation for regulatory purposes.
- Obtain system sign-off.

> **Service Components**
>
> SAP offers the production installation as part of the Platform Execution service component. The service provides a variety of predefined packages that are highly standardized, cost-effective, and scalable.

System Go-Live and Hypercare Support

The system go-live is the final milestone of a successful SAP S/4HANA implementation project. The solution is now running live in the production environment, and the hypercare period follows to ensure seamless adoption of the new system.

Hypercare is the period that comes directly after the go-live. Its purpose is to support questions and issues that might arise. During this period, predefined checks will be executed daily to closely monitor adoption of the new solution. It's essential to verify how the new system behaves and improve system performance if needed.

The main activities in the hypercare period should include the following:

- Monitor resource consumption.
- Analyze workload.
- Do a system health check.
- Verify sizing.
- Perform security monitoring.

Service Components

The following SAP Value Assurance services are provided during the hypercare period: SAP GoingLive Check, technical performance optimization, and business process improvement.

Handover to Support Organization

After the hypercare phase ends, it's crucial to fully enable the regular support organization to safely and securely operate the new SAP system. The following activities are covered:

- Finalize system documentation.
- Complete operational procedures as part of the operations handbook.
- Check the customer support organization.
- Resolve and close open issues.
- Perform the handover from the project team to operations.

SAP Solution Manager in the Deploy Phase

SAP Solution Manager is used to manage the transition to production. Solution documentation in the development branch of SAP Solution Manager is transported to the production branch in SAP Solution Manager. An SAP Solution Manager *branch* represents a version of the solution containing processes, libraries, applications, and systems. It provides a staging area for the business-processes-to-be.

SAP Solution Manager can be used to trigger transport requests from the quality assurance system to the production system. Figure 7.51 illustrates how to access Transportation Management in Change Request Management and Release Management in SAP Solution Manager 7.2. As you can see, various types of change can be created, managed, and released.

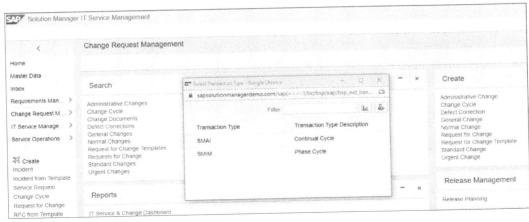

Figure 7.51 Move Transport to SAP S/4HANA Production System

7.3.7   Run Your Solution

The final phase of the SAP Activate methodology is the run phase. After the successful completion of the implementation project, companies and project teams further optimize the operability of the new SAP S/4HANA solution. In this open-ended phase, the operations team must ensure that the system is running as intended. This phase also supports the continuous adoption of the solution by new users.

The main topics in the run phase include the following:

- Ongoing system operations
- Continuous OCM
- Continuous end user learning activities
- Continuous improvement and innovation
- System upgrade

We'll walk through each in the following sections.

Ongoing System Operations

It's essential to perform routine actions to ensure that the system is running as expected. For example, this is necessary to maintain the systems in a functioning and operating condition, guaranteeing systems availability and required performance levels. With the project end, the customer support organization is responsible for operating the new solution, encompassing IT support people, processes, and tools.

The customer support organization should continuously improve and optimize the IT operations. This may include implementing automation and shifting from reactive to proactive approaches.

SAP MaxAttention

SAP has a large set of offerings for SAP MaxAttention customers for safe and efficient operations. For example, SAP can configure application operations in your environment and train your IT support experts in using the tools. If you want SAP to execute IT operational tasks, then SAP application management services can help you.

Continuous Organizational Change Management

The purpose of this activity is to continue the OCM tasks post-go-live to ensure continuous solution adoption by relevant stakeholder groups. The change management team regularly measures end user adoption and then plans and implements OCM activities by leveraging the lessons learned. See Chapter 10 for more information.

Continuous End User Learning Activities

In the run phase, it's good practice to monitor the users after the training has been completed and regularly update the training materials to ensure that they stay relevant. Processes must be in place to enable new users and upskill current users. Based on many years of experience with global software deployments, the SAP Training and Adoption organization has developed a continuous learning framework with clearly defined steps and training activities.

Further Resources

For more information on implementing the continuous learning framework from SAP, visit *http://s-prs.co/v546314*.

Continuous Improvement and Innovation

To support the business and end users, IT maintenance processes must be set in place to continuously improve the solution. It requires periodic updates, by implementing feature and support packs, to bring the latest software updates from SAP into the solution. A planning cycle involving business and IT should identify innovations to be deployed.

Service Components

SAP offers various service components to support the improvement and innovation cycle, including business transformation services, business process improvement for SAP solutions, and planning and execution of SAP maintenance.

SAP S/4HANA provides visibility into planned innovations in the SAP S/4HANA product roadmap, which is available at *www.sap.com/roadmaps/*. The roadmap describes how the product capabilities are planned to progress over time. It provides information on recent innovations, as well as planned innovations, and a summary of the future direction for the product.

System Upgrade

Companies that want to implement significant business change should revisit the overall strategy developed at the start of the project. This may drive an upgrade focused on business change. Upgrades focused on technical goals should be planned in parallel because technical upgrades keep the SAP system current by implementing corrections and selected innovations.

An upgrade is managed as a project. The upgrade project, including tools, phases, and activities, is covered as a separate roadmap in the Roadmap Viewer. You can access it at *http://s-prs.co/v546315*. A first check of the upgrade readiness of SAP S/4HANA is usually performed before the new upgrade project starts. This will reveal what administration activities must be done before the upgrade can start. The maintenance planner can be used to plan the change event, as we'll discuss in the next section.

SAP Solution Manager in the Run Phase

The following components of SAP Solution Manager 7.2 can be used to operate and upgrade the SAP S/4HANA solution:

- **Application Operations**
  Provides central monitoring, alerting, analytics, and administration of SAP solutions.

- **Business Process Operations**
  Supports the productive operation of the core business processes across the SAP S/4HANA system and components.

- **Change Control Management**
  Controls change in system landscapes in a comprehensive workflow.

- **IT Service Management**
  Provides central message management and processing.

- **Landscape Management**
  Provides information on IT landscapes as a basis for landscape operation and change planning of SAP-centric solutions. Helps companies to best manage and use the existing landscape and evolve it through new installations, support package and enhancement package updates, and system upgrades.

SAP Solution Manager's cloud-based maintenance planner, as shown in Figure 7.52, enables easy and efficient planning of these changes in your SAP system landscape. The maintenance planner is a cloud solution hosted by SAP that simplifies landscape maintenance processes when the company upgrades the existing system, updates it, or installs a new one.

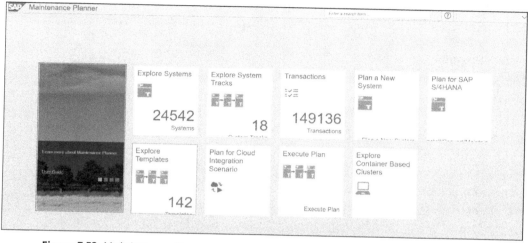

Figure 7.52 Maintenance Planner

Further Resources

Review the following blog about the maintenance planner to understand its capabilities: *http://s-prs.co/v502735*.

7.4   Summary

This chapter comprehensively covered the new implementation of SAP S/4HANA Cloud and SAP S/4HANA in your environment. We recommend all teams deploying SAP S/4HANA solutions to always check for the latest and most up-to-date guidance and content for their implementation in the SAP Activate Roadmap Viewer (guidance) and SAP Best Practices Explorer (preconfigured, ready-to-use business processes). While we made every effort to represent the current state of the solution as of the time of writing, the software continues to evolve, as do some processes for provisioning, configuration, extensibility, and testing. We've covered three versions of the SAP S/4HANA solution deployment to highlight some of the differences in capabilities that provide a higher level of standardization, in the case of SAP S/4HANA Cloud, and some of the extended flexibility options offered by SAP S/4HANA Cloud, private edition.

In the next chapter, we'll review how existing SAP ERP customers can transition to SAP S/4HANA (on-premise) or SAP S/4HANA Cloud, private edition. We'll discuss the system conversion and selective data transition scenarios in detail.

Chapter 8

System Conversion and Selective Data Transition to SAP S/4HANA

This chapter covers the transition to on-premise SAP S/4HANA or SAP S/4HANA Cloud, private edition for organizations that want to move from an existing SAP ERP solution to an SAP S/4HANA-based solution.

This chapter covers the transition project required to move to an SAP S/4HANA solution. It's relevant for organizations that want to move their old SAP ERP solution to on-premise SAP S/4HANA or SAP S/4HANA Cloud, private edition. The content applies if you have your own data center or if you use a cloud hyperscaler with an infrastructure as a service (IaaS) contract. Note that the transition scenario for new implementation of SAP S/4HANA is covered in Chapter 7.

In this chapter, we'll walk through an overview of the transition project, discovering the new solution and planning your journey. We'll then walk step by step through the SAP Activate phases for a system conversion. We'll conclude with a look at another deployment option, selective data transition. The text in this chapter applies both for SAP S/4HANA Cloud, private edition and on-premise SAP S/4HANA products, even if we use only one of the product names for brevity in the text. In cases where there are differences between the two products, we will point them out.

> **Roadmap Viewer**
>
> For additional information, you can refer to the SAP Activate Transition to SAP S/4HANA and SAP Activate Methodology for RISE with SAP S/4HANA Cloud, private edition roadmaps. The purpose of the roadmaps is to support transition projects and to help you with the following:
>
> - Creating a foundation through transparency of all activities and tasks
> - Making implementation and transition projects predictable
> - Managing risk proactively
>
> The content of this chapter is structured to mirror the roadmap in the Roadmap Viewer. For more details, accelerators, and the latest links, refer to the Roadmap Viewer at *http://s-prs.co/v502733*.

8.1   Deployment Project Overview

Your transition to SAP S/4HANA involves many activities throughout the key SAP Activate phases introduced in Chapter 2. Figure 8.1 illustrates the activities within the workstreams and phases. This figure is available for download at *www.sap-press.com/5463*.

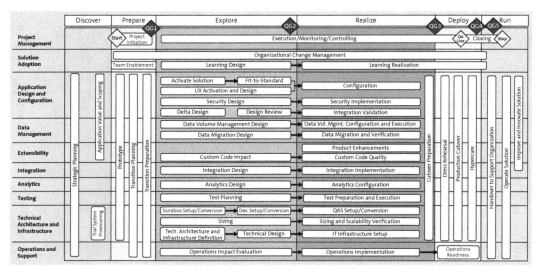

Figure 8.1 Overview of the Transition to SAP S/4HANA Roadmap

> **Note**
>
> The deployment project overview in this section and the discover phase discussion in Section 8.2 will be very similar to our coverage in Chapter 7, Section 7.3.1 and Section 7.3.2. We've included this discussion for both new implementations and system conversions of SAP S/4HANA for the sake of completeness. If you've already read Chapter 7, Section 7.3, feel free to skip to Section 8.3.

There are three implementation approaches for SAP S/4HANA, which we introduced in Chapter 1:

1. **New implementation**
   Implement a new instance of SAP S/4HANA by moving either from a non-SAP legacy system or from an old SAP solution. This is covered in Chapter 7.

2. **System conversion**
   Convert an existing SAP ERP solution to SAP S/4HANA, including business data and configuration.

3. **Selective data transition**
   Consolidate an existing SAP software landscape or carve out selected entities or processes as part of a move to SAP S/4HANA.

For existing SAP customers, the choice of approach is driven by the following business and IT objectives:

- **New implementation**
  You want to maximize innovation, overhaul business processes, and perhaps adopt new cloud solutions. You may only want essential master data and transactional data from the existing solution.

- **System conversion**
  You don't want to merge or split ERP instances, and you want to keep your existing data and go live with a big bang. You may want to minimize change initially and then innovate selectively afterward.

- **Selective data transition**
  You want to merge or split existing ERP instances or have phased go-lives. You want to reuse only certain parts of the existing configuration, master data, and transaction data.

If you have multiple SAP ERP instances and other connected SAP solutions, you may want to use a combination of the approaches in a phased program. For example, you could do a system conversion of one lead SAP ERP development system, use selective data transition to merge in another SAP ERP system, and do a new implementation for certain parts of the solution.

Let's walk through the SAP Activate phases, in terms of these deployment options:

- **Discover phase**
  You should create an overall strategy for digital transformation by recognizing the benefits and value of SAP S/4HANA. This is then turned into a roadmap or implementation plan that includes a choice of transition approach. Finally, you should evaluate the impact on the technical architecture and IT infrastructure, which, together with the implementation strategy, serve as the foundation of the business case.

- **Prepare phase**
  After the business case has been approved, the project is officially initiated in the prepare phase. A first version of an implementation plan includes the findings from the discover phase and sets the stage for the entire project.

- **Explore phase**
  The design-to-be of the SAP S/4HANA solution is defined and documented in the explore phase. For a system conversion, a converted version of the existing system is used, and existing custom code is analyzed. By the end of the explore phase, all technical and functional aspects of the implementation project are fully planned, documented in detail, and ready to be executed.

- **Realize phase**
  In system conversion, the landscape is sequentially converted to SAP S/4HANA. Some of the existing custom code is adjusted. Application and analytics functions

are implemented, configured, integrated, and tested. In parallel, IT can adjust operational tools and procedures to prepare for SAP S/4HANA. Finally, end user training, including project-specific training materials and team setup, is prepared.

- **Deploy phase**
  Finalize the business processes and solution for production go-live. This includes final testing, rehearsing the cutover, and finalizing the IT infrastructure and operations. End user training sessions are delivered. Finally, the productive instance of SAP S/4HANA is set up or converted on the go-live weekend. IT operations are further optimized with the help of the project team and SAP. This phase is referred to as *hypercare* and occurs before operational responsibility is fully transferred to the production support team.

- **Run phase**
  Operations are further stabilized and optimized in the run phase. The new SAP system is continuously updated, making the latest innovations from SAP available to the business. Then the innovation cycle starts again.

To support companies in executing the SAP S/4HANA transition successfully, SAP has several service offerings that provide different levels of engagement and advice:

- **SAP Enterprise Support**
  Proactive remote support for accelerated problem resolution, fewer business disruptions, and less unforeseen downtime. Access to tools, reports, and services to accelerate innovation.

- **SAP Value Assurance**
  Supports companies on their own or partner-led projects with dedicated planning, design support, and functional and technical safeguarding services throughout the project. Doesn't provide any implementation or delivery services.

- **SAP Advanced Deployment**
  SAP Services provides end-to-end implementation and delivery services, collaborating with partners as required. Relevant SAP Value Assurance services are integrated into the delivery.

- **Premium engagements**
  Provide on-site, premium access to trusted SAP experts and tools that include and go beyond the SAP Value Assurance service portfolio. For example, SAP ActiveAttention and SAP MaxAttention build a long-term relationship with SAP through the project and beyond.

Throughout this chapter, there are notes that highlight the specific SAP service components that can be consumed to reduce risk, provide the best advice, and check the decisions being made. Most of these service components are common to SAP Value Assurance, SAP Advanced Deployment, and premium engagements.

8.2   Discover Your Solution

The discover phase covers everything done leading up to the decision to proceed with an SAP S/4HANA project. On leaving the discover phase, an organization will have defined its digital transformation strategy and have an SAP S/4HANA roadmap or plan backed up by a business case. The company will have selected its delivery partners and delivery approach: new implementation, system conversion, or selective data transition. The activities in the discover phase are independent of the delivery approach. Some organizations may push some of the activities described in this section into the prepare phase.

This section begins with strategic planning, where you develop an innovation strategy and high-level roadmap based on SAP S/4HANA and intelligent technology innovations, and you also make early decisions on security and analytics. Then, we'll move on to trial system provisioning and application value and scoping, where you'll assess the value and impact of SAP S/4HANA and check your readiness.

8.2.1   Strategic Planning

SAP's intelligent enterprise features the following key components:

- **Intelligent suite**
  This integrated suite retains the modularity and flexibility of independent solutions, such as SAP S/4HANA, SAP Customer Experience, SAP Ariba, and SAP SuccessFactors.

- **Digital platform**
  With SAP Business Technology Platform (SAP BTP), SAP can facilitate the collection, connection, and orchestration of data, as well as the integration and extension of processes within the intelligent suite.

- **Intelligent technologies**
  SAP BTP enables companies to leverage their data to detect patterns, predict outcomes, and suggest actions with the help of advanced technologies such as machine learning, artificial intelligence (AI), and robotic process automation (RPA).

The aim of strategic planning is to define an innovation strategy and high-level multiyear roadmap for these three key components. The roadmap should include, but isn't limited to, SAP S/4HANA and analytics.

Start with an identification of strategic business and IT objectives, including current pain points. Cluster the objectives into benefit areas, and for each benefit area, identify and prioritize the SAP solution enablers. These solutions provide the target enterprise architecture.

SAP provides some tools that can assist in the strategy definition:

- **SAP Transformation Navigator**
  Determines a high-level future SAP product map based on your current product map and your current and planned business capabilities.

- **Process Discovery for SAP S/4HANA Transformation**
  Identifies which new SAP S/4HANA functionalities are most relevant for each line of business (LoB) based on the current use of SAP ERP. The output is generated by a free report that runs in your existing production system.

- **SAP Innovation and Optimization Pathfinder**
  A free tool from SAP that identifies which innovations are relevant based on system usage statistics.

The introduction of SAP S/4HANA into the solution landscape is an ideal opportunity to review and adjust the organization's analytics architecture. It's worth doing this early in the discover phase because there are many changes and new products and capabilities relevant for SAP S/4HANA. Refer to our discussion of analytics design in the explore phase in Chapter 7, Section 7.3.4 (new implementation) and Section 8.3.2 (system conversion) for more details.

Another area worth visiting early is your security strategy, including topics such as data protection regulations. SAP offers a security strategy advisory service to help determine where security issues exist and how SAP can assist.

Further Resources

SAP offers the Innovation Strategy and Roadmap service component and the Analytics Strategy Workshop service component through SAP Value Assurance to help companies develop a multiyear strategic roadmap for digital transformation.

Innovation services for intelligent technologies are available through SAP MaxAttention and SAP Advanced Deployment.

The SAP S/4HANA Movement webpages (*http://s-prs.co/v502747*) provide information on moving from SAP ERP to SAP S/4HANA. Companies with a valid support agreement can check if they can participate in an SAP Adoption Starter program. This 90-day program helps companies create an SAP S/4HANA–centric transformation plan by using tools such as SAP Transformation Navigator.

8.2.2 Trial System Provisioning

To support the value identification and the impact evaluation in the discover phase, it may be beneficial to have access to an SAP S/4HANA system. You can deploy a system within hours or days using an SAP cloud appliance via SAP Cloud Appliance Library (*http://cal.sap.com*). The system is hosted on Microsoft Azure, Amazon Web Services (AWS), or Google Cloud Platform. The provider will charge for hosting, and a user account at the cloud provider is required. SAP Cloud Appliance Library provides a detailed step-by-step guide for setup of the appliance that you'll follow during the installation and setup. Companies with an existing license can deploy an unrestricted SAP S/4HANA sandbox solution directly from SAP Cloud Appliance Library.

A cloud trial system is the fastest option for companies without a license and will provide up to 30 days access. The trial solution can't be configured and is restricted to a certain number of users (*http://s-prs.co/v502734*).

In addition, the SAP Best Practices processes are ready to run immediately as documented in SAP Best Practices Explorer (refer to Chapter 4, Section 4.1). This allows the team to get hands-on access to the solution and investigate the new features in detail.

8.2.3 Application Value and Scoping

Application value and scoping contains the following tasks, which we'll walk through in this section:

- Discovering the value of SAP S/4HANA
- Performing SAP Readiness Check for SAP S/4HANA for the existing ERP solution
- Performing a business scenario and solution mapping
- Defining the implementation strategy
- Creating a strategic roadmap and value case

Service Components

SAP offers the Value and Implementation Strategy service component through SAP Value Assurance that provides a comprehensive migration analysis, including business scenario and value mapping, proposed implementation strategy and supporting roadmap, and value case.

Discover the Value of SAP S/4HANA

Value and benefits drive all projects and must be understood early. The following resources can be used:

- Public webpages such as the SAP Help Portal, What's New Viewer, and SAP Fiori apps reference library

- SAP S/4HANA training, including openSAP training on integration and extensions with SAP BTP
- Learning rooms in SAP Learning Hub
- SAP S/4HANA trial system (refer to Section 8.2.2)
- Process Discovery for SAP S/4HANA transformation
- SAP S/4HANA Discovery Workshop, available from SAP Services and Support

For organizations moving from an existing SAP ERP solution, the impact of SAP S/4HANA is evaluated in SAP Readiness Check for SAP S/4HANA, as described in the next section.

Readiness Check of the Existing ERP Solution

SAP S/4HANA is the result of SAP rearchitecting the SAP ERP suite for modern business processes and the ever-increasing digitization of the world. This means that parts of SAP ERP have been improved, simplified, replaced, removed, or categorized as not strategic. All these changes are documented in the simplification list for SAP S/4HANA, which you can find on the SAP Help Portal.

If you have an existing SAP ERP solution, understanding the simplification items that impact the system is a key activity in the discover phase. SAP Readiness Check for SAP S/4HANA is a report run in your existing system that identifies the relevant simplification items. It analyzes many other aspects as well, including custom code, add-ons, active business functions, recommended SAP Fiori apps, and sizing.

There could be showstoppers or requirements that need to be addressed before the project starts. SAP Readiness Check for SAP S/4HANA provides a dashboard (see Figure 8.2) that addresses these questions:

- Is functionality used that will need to be replaced or changed? Are the simplification items mandatory, conditional, or optional? Should the work be done in the current SAP ERP system or in the new SAP S/4HANA system?
- Are there incompatible add-ons (e.g., third-party add-ons) or incompatible business functions?
- Are there custom solutions or add-ons delivered by SAP Innovation Services that must be investigated by SAP before a project starts?
- Are all technical system requirements fulfilled (e.g., software levels, single stack system, Unicode)?
- Are all dependent SAP hub systems (e.g., SAP Customer Relationship Management [SAP CRM] or SAP Extended Warehouse Management [SAP EWM]) on the required release?
- How many custom objects are impacted by the data model and software changes?

- Which business critical reports and transactions will be replaced or removed?
- What SAP Fiori apps are relevant for your current scope?
- What configuration needs to be adjusted?
- What is the estimated SAP S/4HANA system size? Are there options to reduce the size before the conversion?
- Are there live SAP Business Warehouse (SAP BW) extractors that will be impacted?

Figure 8.2 SAP Readiness Check for SAP S/4HANA Dashboard

Perform a Business Scenario and Solution Mapping

Strategic planning provides a set of SAP solutions and a target architecture. Business process experts from each LoB should now produce a more detailed solution mapping at a business scenario level. Business scenarios are a level above scope items.

For existing customers, you may choose to use the SAP S/4HANA business scenarios from the Process Discovery for SAP S/4HANA Transformation report. We introduced this report in Section 8.2.1. The report compares business key figures with industry benchmarks, illustrates opportunities to improve, and highlights relevant SAP S/4HANA innovations. You must run a report in your production system and upload the files to an SAP website. You can access the results from a dashboard or in a PDF file. Figure 8.3 shows a page from the Process Discovery report that includes a list of business scenarios used in the organization.

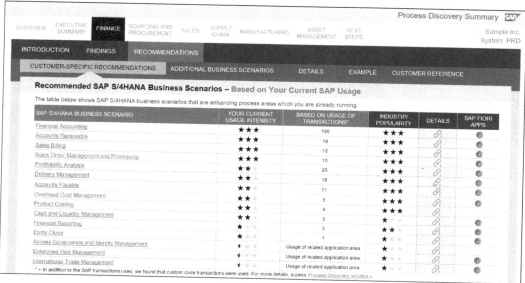

Figure 8.3 Process Discovery for SAP S/4HANA Transformation

Define the Implementation Strategy

The next step is to define your implementation strategy. Your strategy should address the following questions:

- What is the productive system strategy? That is, one single global instance or regional instances?
- Will the business go live in one big bang or with a multistage transition by country or business unit?
- What are the dependencies and the best sequence for the release plan?
- When will integration between SAP S/4HANA and other SAP and non-SAP solutions go live?
- What are the intermediate architectures in a staged approach?
- Will SAP S/4HANA Cloud, private edition or an on-premise data center or a cloud hyperscaler be used?
- Will a global template solution be adopted? And how will deviations from the template be managed?
- Will SAP Best Practices content be used, and how?
- What is the strategy for custom development? What development will occur in SAP S/4HANA and what will SAP BTP be used for?

Organizations moving to SAP S/4HANA from an existing SAP solution need to choose from among the three transition approaches described in Section 8.1 (new implementation, system conversion, or selective data transition). The team must come to a decision to either reuse existing configuration or reengineer business processes with a reimplementation. For SAP S/4HANA Cloud, private edition, seek SAP's advice because the conversion of certain source ERP releases may not be supported yet.

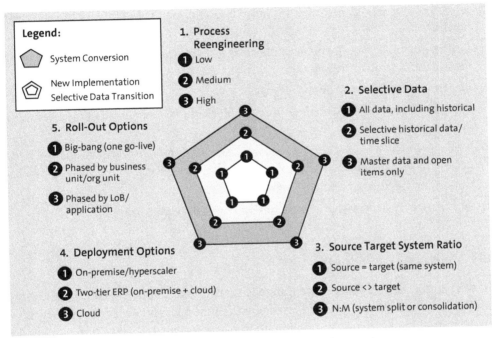

Legend:

System Conversion

New Implementation
Selective Data Transition

1. Process Reengineering
1 Low
2 Medium
3 High

2. Selective Data
1 All data, including historical
2 Selective historical data/ time slice
3 Master data and open items only

5. Roll-Out Options
1 Big-bang (one go-live)
2 Phased by business unit/org unit
3 Phased by LoB/ application

4. Deployment Options
1 On-premise/hyperscaler
2 Two-tier ERP (on-premise + cloud)
3 Cloud

3. Source Target System Ratio
1 Source = target (same system)
2 Source <> target
3 N:M (system split or consolidation)

Figure 8.4 Factors Influencing Each SAP S/4HANA Transition Approach

The main aspects to consider are as follows, and their impact is shown in Figure 8.4:

- How much process reengineering is required?
- Is SAP S/4HANA a good opportunity to go back to the SAP standard, and should this be done based on a new implementation or incrementally after a technical conversion to SAP S/4HANA?
- How much of the historical transaction data needs to be retained?
- Will SAP ERP instances be consolidated or split?
- Will SAP S/4HANA or SAP S/4HANA Cloud, private edition be implemented?
- Does the roll-out have to be phased to reduce risk, or can each instance go live with a big bang approach?

Create a Strategic Roadmap and Value Case

A value (or business) case for the project is built based on quantified costs and benefits. The following approach may be used:

1. Define discrete scope blocks required to reach the defined target architecture. Each block will have an organizational, functional, and technical element—for example, the SAP S/4HANA Finance scope for Malaysia.

2. Agree on business transformation objectives and map value drivers to the scope blocks.

3. Define and link key performance indicators (KPIs) to the value drivers. Use KPIs and value drivers to quantify benefits.

4. Identify cost drivers and quantify costs.

5. Compose a roadmap or timeline of scope blocks to implement the target solution landscape.

6. Assess the ability to execute the roadmap, considering organizational change, budget, technical capabilities, and previous project experience.

7. Determine the risks of transformation.

8. Summarize the alternative approaches and drive decision-making.

8.3   System Conversion

In the system conversion approach, an existing SAP ERP solution is converted to SAP S/4HANA or SAP S/4HANA Cloud, private edition and taken live. System conversion may be combined with a new implementation or selective data transition in a hybrid approach (see Section 8.4). This might be relevant where multiple SAP ERP instances are to be merged. For example, one development instance might be converted to SAP S/4HANA to form a baseline. Then parts of another instance might be added with selective data transition while a third is added with a new implementation.

Figure 8.5 illustrates the sequence of some of the main activities in the system conversion approach.

The SAP Readiness Check for SAP S/4HANA and identification of SAP S/4HANA simplification items are normally undertaken in the discover phase (refer to Section 8.2.3).

Some simplification item activities are best undertaken in the current SAP ERP system before the main project starts. Then in the explore phase, the production system is copied to a sandbox system, and a full conversion is done. This is used to drive a light fit-to-standard workshop focusing on any new SAP solutions or new business requirements. In the realize phase, new scope and simplification items are implemented and custom code is adjusted. Testing is done in a converted quality assurance system before deploying to a conversion of the production system.

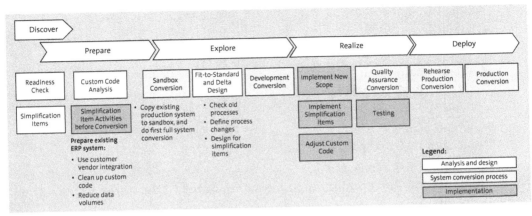

Figure 8.5 Overview of System Conversion Approach

This section is organized by the SAP Activate phases: prepare, explore, realize, and deploy. We'll walk through the key deliverables for a system conversion in each of the following sections. Note that some of the activities documented in the prepare phase are often executed earlier in the discover phase before the project starts. There are some differences in the names and sequence of deliverables in the SAP S/4HANA and SAP S/4HANA Cloud, private edition roadmaps. We'll provide examples of these differences throughout the chapter.

System Conversion versus New Implementation

System conversion projects have similar deliverables and activities as new implementation projects. Therefore, they share a common roadmap in SAP Activate. For this reason, some parts of this section share similar content from the new implementation section, especially for integration, analytics, and security topics.

8.3.1 Prepare Your Project

The prepare phase provides initial planning and preparation for the implementation project. We'll walk through the prepare phase for a system conversion project in this section.

Phase Overview

The purpose of the prepare phase is to kick off the initial planning and preparation for the project. The project starts, and the scope, approach, and plans are finalized. The project team resources are also assigned.

The main output documents of the prepare phase include the following:

- **Scope document**
  Defines the starting point, objectives, target solution, and transition approach

- **Project charter**
  Includes goals, scope, organization structure, roles and responsibilities, and governance

- **Project plan**
  Includes a WBS, schedule, and budget

- **System transition roadmap**
  Defines how systems will be used and the sequence of conversion

- **UX/UI strategy**
  Defines how SAP Fiori apps will be adopted and used

- **Technical architecture**
  Revised to show the impact of the move to SAP S/4HANA

- **Interface register**
  Revised to show the impact of the move to SAP S/4HANA

- **Project standards**
  Includes requirements management, configuration, and custom code

- **Operational standards**
  Includes test management and change control

The rest of this section on the prepare phase is organized into topics that appear in the roadmaps.

Transition Planning

In this deliverable, the team defines the scope and high-level execution plan for the SAP S/4HANA transition project. The tasks are as follows:

1. Perform the SAP Readiness Check for SAP S/4HANA for the current SAP ERP solution.

2. Define the scope and the objectives of the transition.

3. Define the cutover approach.

4. Clarify the custom code adaption.

5. Revise the technical architecture and security.

6. Perform data volume planning.

7. Define the UX/UI strategy.

8. Assess interfaces and integration.

9. Assess output management.

The following sections cover each of these tasks in more detail.

Service Components

SAP can assist with all transition planning topics through SAP Value Assurance or SAP MaxAttention. The Migration Planning Workshop (MPW) service component helps to define the scope and execution plan for the customer's conversion project to SAP S/4HANA.

SAP Readiness Check for SAP S/4HANA

SAP Readiness Check for SAP S/4HANA is usually run in the discover phase when the decision to start a system conversion project is made (refer to Section 8.2.3).

Define the Scope and the Objectives of the Transition

A scope document is produced that defines the following:

- **IT and business objectives**
  Success criteria for the transition project
- **Starting point**
  SAP solutions to be converted, replaced, or remain the same
- **Target solution**
  New target releases, new scope, quick wins, and related SAP systems
- **Transition approach**
  Preparation activities, infrastructure changes, landscape changes (e.g., system splits of consolidations), and maintenance windows

Define Cutover Approach

Cutover planning starts with a system transition roadmap that documents the conversion sequence and the creation of temporary systems for production support.

SAP S/4HANA Cloud, Private Edition

There are some differences between working with SAP S/4HANA Cloud, private edition and on-premise SAP S/4HANA. SAP S/4HANA Cloud, private edition requires some extra steps to move into a private cloud. The main differences that the project teams need to consider are driven by the operating model: subscription and services delivery for private cloud versus owning and running the software with full access to the entire stack on-premise. Always refer to the most recent content in the SAP Activate methodology for RISE with SAP S/4HANA Cloud, private edition for details. And remember to set the **System Conversion** view using the **More** filter section on the left side of the Roadmap Viewer tool, as shown in Figure 8.6.

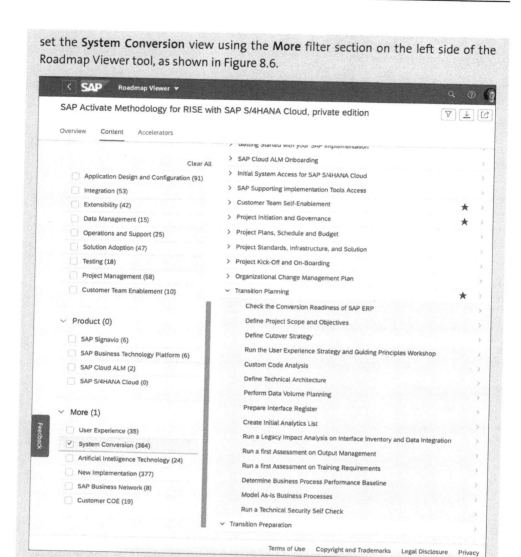

Figure 8.6 Set Filter to Show Only System Conversion Content in Roadmap Viewer

An on-premise example is shown in Figure 8.7. The dashed arrows show system copies, and the thick arrows are technical system conversions. Follow the sequence shown by the numbers. The first stage is to copy the production system to a sandbox system (PRD copy) in step **1a**, followed by a system conversion **1b**. Then a copy of the development system is made **2a** for ongoing production support followed by a system conversion **2b**. Next, the quality assurance system is copied **3a**, followed by another system conversion **3b**. Additional copies and conversions of the production system (**4a**, **4b**, **5a**, **5b**) are done, followed by the final system conversion **6**.

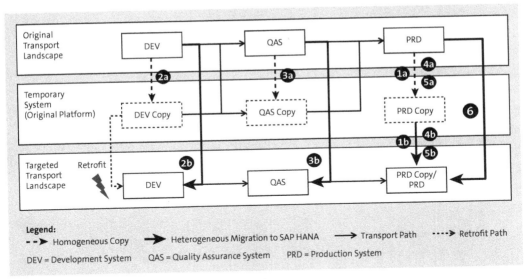

Legend:
- - ➤ Homogeneous Copy   ➡ Heterogeneous Migration to SAP HANA   ➝ Transport Path   ····➤ Retrofit Path

DEV = Development System   QAS = Quality Assurance System   PRD = Production System

Figure 8.7 Example On-Premise Cutover Approach

Note

The development copy and quality assurance copy systems are built in order to provide a temporary production support landscape tier while the original development and quality assurance systems are being migrated. The changes managed via the development system copy and the quality assurance system copy should be limited to standard (noninvasive) and urgent corrections for the duration of the project.

The technical conversion process and custom code work are illustrated in Figure 8.8. You can see the following main tools, which are used in the conversion process (custom code is covered in the next section):

- **Maintenance planner**
  Retrieves information about your SAP landscape via SAP Solution Manager, plans the change event, and generates the required stack XML and packages.

- **Prechecks**
  Repeats elements of the SAP Readiness Check for SAP S/4HANA and other final checks.

- **Software Update Manager (SUM)**
  Executes migration of the database to SAP HANA 2.0, applies a software update from SAP ERP to SAP S/4HANA, and converts from the old data model to the new SAP S/4HANA data model.

- **Finance follow-up activities**
  Undertakes essential finance configuration before doing the last part of the data model conversion.

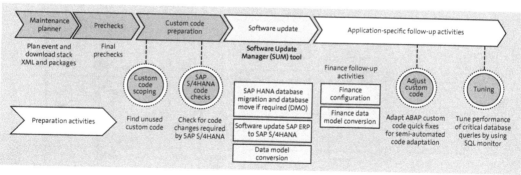

Figure 8.8 Overview of Technical Conversion Process

Further Resources

The conversion process and tools are documented in the Conversion Guide for SAP S/4HANA, available in the SAP S/4HANA Help Portal.

Clarify Custom Code Adaption

A considerable amount of SAP standard ABAP code from the SAP ERP solution has been simplified in SAP S/4HANA. Measures were taken to make the solution as compatible with custom code as possible. For example, core data services (CDS) compatibility views are available that provide an old view of new data models, and many APIs will work unchanged. Therefore, companies can assume that a large proportion of their custom code will work without any (or with only a few) changes.

During the prepare phase, the project team should do the following custom code activities:

- Learn how custom code adaption is managed and executed.
- Use SAP tools to identify unused code that can be retired.
- Use SAP tools to identify custom ABAP source code that must and should be adjusted.
- Prepare a rough-cut estimate of the work required, assuming the use of semiautomated quick fixes where possible.

Revise Technical Architecture and Security

The existing technical architecture is revised to reflect the changes defined in the scope document. It may also include the switch to an SAP HANA database and the introduction of SAP Fiori frontend components.

You also must document the new technical and functional security requirements related to SAP S/4HANA. These will include security role changes documented in simplification items and the introduction of SAP Fiori. A technical security self-check can be executed using SAP tools.

> **SAP S/4HANA Cloud, Private Edition**
>
> This may change considerably if you're moving to SAP S/4HANA Cloud, private edition. For example, you should consider the scope of services provided by SAP or a hyperscaler partner to operate and secure the environment that you don't need to plan to cover with your own resources. For an overview of technical operations and security for data centers, visit the SAP Trust Center at *https://www.sap.com/about/trust-center.html*.

Perform Data Volume Planning

Data volume management should be considered prior to a system conversion to reduce the amount of data to be converted (this has implications for the duration and downtime of the cutover) and to reduce the amount of data in memory (this has implications on hardware costs). The team must define the scope of cleanup work in the prepare phase and the scope of data volume work to be done in the explore and realize phases.

Define the User Experience/User Interface Strategy

The project team should learn about SAP Fiori, including the technical architecture, role model, and SAP Fiori apps reference library. The SAP Fiori apps recommendation report provides recommendations on apps to use based on your current system usage. This can be used by the LoB teams to understand the scope of UI changes. Finally, document any special requirements, such as simplified UIs for tablet and mobile scenarios.

Assess Interfaces and Integration

Check existing documentation and identify the external systems, applications, and business objects that must be integrated with SAP S/4HANA. These should be captured in an interface register (e.g., a Microsoft Excel spreadsheet). Then assess the impact of moving from SAP ERP to SAP S/4HANA on interfaces. SAP has kept most of the official interfaces to and from SAP ERP stable in SAP S/4HANA. This isn't necessarily the case for nonofficial interfaces (e.g., the use of Open Database Connectivity [ODBC] on the database level).

Assess Output Management

SAP S/4HANA introduces a new harmonized approach to output management. The new output management will be the successor of all other output management frameworks (sales and distribution output control, financial accounting correspondence, FI-CA print workbench, customer relationship management postprocessing). However, all other frameworks are still available and can be used, and it isn't mandatory to use the new output management framework.

Make yourself familiar with the new output management in SAP S/4HANA. By looking at the simplification list, determine and document how your existing output management is impacted by a system conversion. Develop a general strategy of how to adopt the new output management in the midterm and long term.

Transition Preparation

This deliverable covers all the preparation tasks that occur in the current SAP ERP solution before the main SAP S/4HANA project starts. The scope will have been defined during transition planning. The following sections cover the key tasks.

Simplification Items

A subset of the many SAP S/4HANA simplification items will be relevant for your project. The following list shows example tasks done in the current SAP ERP system, each driven by one or more simplification items:

- Integrate customer and vendor masters to become business partners
- New asset accounting (available in SAP ERP EHP 7)
- New cash management
- Financial supply chain management (FSCM) credit management replaces FI-AR credit management
- Trade finance replaces SD foreign trade
- Settlement management replaces rebate management
- Revenue accounting replace SD revenue management

Some business processes may remain open incorrectly. Analyze and close open business to make the documents available for archiving.

Service Components

SAP offers the Mandatory Preparation for System Conversion service component to support necessary preparation work.

Clean Up and Archive Data

Next, you must clean up and archive data in the productive SAP ERP system. Based on the residence time definition (i.e., when the business data can either be deleted or moved to an archive file), the deletion and archive jobs are scheduled to remove data from the database before the conversion starts.

Clean Up Unused Custom Code

The objective of this optional task is to decommission custom ABAP code that is no longer used. The SAP Solution Manager decommissioning cockpit is recommended.

> **Further Resources**
>
> You can find more details about the decommissioning cockpit in the SAP Solution Manager help, under **Custom Code**, at *http://help.sap.com*.

Alternatively, you may remove unused custom code from your system after it's converted by using the Custom Code Migration SAP Fiori app.

Improve Custom Code Quality

The objective of this optional task is to improve the software quality of your custom code. The work can be assisted by using software quality check tools, such as the ABAP test cockpit or code inspector.

The code inspector is a tool that helps developers check individual dictionary objects or sets of them for performance, security, syntax, and adherence to naming conventions. It's part of the ABAP Workbench in SAP software.

> **Further Resources**
>
> You can find more details about use of the ABAP test cockpit in the SAP Help Portal at *http://s-prs.co/v502736*.

Prepare SAP Solution Manager

Ensure SAP Solution Manager is available and up to date with the latest support pack. Section 8.3.2 on the explore phase describes how SAP Solution Manager is used.

Project Initiation, Governance and Plan

The project is formally initiated. Refer to Chapter 6 for project management topics, including project governance. Activities include the following:

- Hold handover meetings from the previous discover phase.
- Review the commercial contract and resolve any issues.
- Identify stakeholders and confirm their requirements, expectations, and acceptance criteria.
- Create a project charter based on the scope document.
- Establish baselines for scope, schedule, cost, and quality.
- Create a project management plan.

The project management plan includes the following:

- WBS
- Schedule

- Budget
- Quality standards
- Communications
- Risks
- Procurement

Project Standards and Infrastructure

SAP S/4HANA implementation projects need a robust means of executing and governing project work and deliverables. You should revise, approve, and communicate project standards and operational standards. The infrastructure should be ready for the project team, including computers, software and licenses, security, phones, meeting rooms, email, and remote access.

Project standards include requirements management, process modeling, configuration and documentation, custom code, authorizations, agile processes, and use of tools. Operational standards include test management, change control, incident management, and technical operations.

Project Team Enablement

Enable the project team on the project scope, system conversion approach, simplification items, and related SAP topics. Enablement may include different elements of the SAP system, SAP Activate methodology, SAP Solution Manager, agile principles, and techniques and other supporting tools. It's important that self-enablement begins prior to the project kickoff to maximize the time for learning and to create efficiencies in later deliverables. The System Conversion to SAP S/4HANA and Gain Experience with a System Conversion to SAP S/4HANA openSAP training courses are good resources.

Project Kickoff and Onboarding

The kickoff provides the project team, key stakeholders, and anybody else involved in the project with the information they need. Everybody involved in the project should understand the project charter, which includes goals, objectives, scope, organization structure, decision-making process, roles and responsibilities, governance, regular meetings, project standards, infrastructure, schedule, and milestones.

Organizational Change Management Plan

All change management activities are planned in a roadmap. The roadmap ensures that all activities align with each other and the project plan. In the prepare phase, it's important for the success of the project to set up the OCM team to agree on its concept. See Chapter 10 for more information.

8.3.2   Explore the Solution

In the explore phase, a light fit-to-standard analysis is done, focusing on any new SAP solutions and new business requirements. A sandbox environment based on a system conversion of the production system is used to drive the workshops. We'll walk through the explore phase for a system conversion project in this section.

Phase Overview

A system conversion project may include business transformation changes to deliver benefits by adopting new processes and features in the SAP S/4HANA solution. The greater the business transformation ambition, the higher the number of new business requirements when compared to the old SAP ERP solution. Often, a two-stage approach is taken with two go-lives: stage 1 is a technical conversion to SAP S/4HANA, which is followed by stage 2 for business transformation.

The purpose of the explore phase is to execute a full end-to-end conversion of the old SAP ERP system to SAP S/4HANA in a sandbox system. Much of the existing configuration will work unchanged. The project team performs a fit-to-standard analysis to validate the solution functionality and to confirm that the existing and new business requirements can be satisfied. Some new requirements will be driven by the SAP S/4HANA simplification items. The fit-to-standard analysis will check that old processes continue to work and identify changes caused by or enabled by the system conversion.

Identified requirements are designed and configuration decisions are made. These are added to the backlog to be used in the realize phase. Changes are assessed and made to the design of analytics, integration, security, testing, architecture, infrastructure, and data volume design. During the explore phase, an end user training strategy is defined and a change impact analysis is done.

The main output documents of the explore phase include the following:

- **Detailed conversion cookbook**
  Covers the end-to-end migration and conversion process and is specific to the company environment.

- **Custom code worklist**
  Prioritized list of custom objects and code that need to be adapted because of the system conversion.

- **Design document**
  Design documents for new business scenarios that include the scope, objectives, benefits, SAP S/4HANA conversion impacts, requirements, KPIs, data requirements, and design.

- **Backlog of requirements**
  Detailed catalog of requirements by business process. Also covers the relevant SAP S/4HANA simplification items.

- **WRICEF list**
  Track the status, complexity, and progress of Workflows, Reports, Interfaces, Data Conversions, Enhancements, and Forms (WRICEF).

- **Functional specifications**
  Detailed functional designs for new or changed WRICEFs.

- **Technical design document**
  Updates existing documentation to reflect the architecture and infrastructure for SAP S/4HANA.

- **Test strategy document**
  Updates existing documentation to define the testing scope, approach, deliverables, and tools.

Further Resources

The SAP Activate Roadmap Viewer (see Chapter 3, Section 3.1) contains templates for these project documents.

This section on the explore phase is organized into topics that appear in the roadmap. The use of SAP Solution Manager during the explore phase is covered in the last section.

Sandbox Conversion

In system conversion, an SAP S/4HANA sandbox system is created at the start of the project by copying the existing SAP ERP production system to a sandbox and doing an end-to-end SAP S/4HANA migration and conversion.

SAP S/4HANA Cloud, Private Edition

There are some additional steps with SAP S/4HANA Cloud, private edition that you will find in the Roadmap Viewer (refer to *http://s-prs.co/v546316*). For example, the Review and Prepare Conversion Activities task in the prepare phase lists preconversion steps to review before staring the conversion process. These activities include steps like reviewing the migration of customers and vendors to business partners and reviewing the conversion of accounting to SAP S/4HANA. You also need to consider the impact of your subscription contract, which may not include access to a dedicated sandbox environment. In such a case, you must plan your conversion strategy so that you run the sandbox system conversion towards the target in the quality system. You also must subsequently refresh the quality system before the conversion of the quality system. In

---

this situation, the quality system will be used temporarily to conduct the sandbox conversion. Your subscription contract will specify the maximum number of nonproductive and productive conversion runs you can do. You can refer to the RISE with SAP S/4HANA Cloud, private edition Roles and Responsibilities document on *sap.com* at *http://s-prs.co/v546317*.

The deliverables of this activity are a successfully converted sandbox system and a check of whether the process is feasible for the business, including the estimated business downtime. The development system can't be set up until after the sandbox conversion is successful, and the realize phase can't start until the development system is available.

The following sections cover the sandbox conversion activities in sequence.

Prerequisites to Conversion

Before you begin your sandbox conversion, you must complete the following prerequisites:

- Fulfill all application prerequisites from SAP Readiness Check for SAP S/4HANA (e.g., software releases).
- Attain an agreed-upon conversion scope.
- Set up the technical infrastructure.

Some SAP S/4HANA simplification items are best addressed by implementation work in the existing SAP ERP solution before the transition project starts. If these steps haven't been done, they must be executed in the sandbox before the conversion can start.

Examples of these simplification item activities were listed in Section 8.3.1. They may require significant time and work. For example, they include the migration of customer and vendor masters to business partners. Another example is the deletion or archiving of unwanted data. Document every step in the activities to build a cookbook specific to the environment.

Checks executed by SUM will report issues that need to be addressed before the system conversion can start.

Conversion

The migration and conversion of the sandbox systems will provide valuable insights, including confirmation of the planned conversion approach, potential business downtime, required prerequisites, and experience in the nuances and the functionality of each system.

Dependent on the scope of the project, the system sequence, and the high-level plan, the initial sandbox migration could include the full scope or just the first system planned for migration.

Execute the conversion of the sandbox system using the Conversion Guide for SAP S/4HANA document available in the SAP Help Portal. Establish a file server to create a central location for all the files used in the migration process. Document every step of the conversion to build a cookbook specific to the environment. The intent of such a document is to make the process resource-independent. For contingency purposes, all knowledge required for the conversion should be captured in the cookbook. The document will be validated and extended in further test conversions. The cookbook should include every step in the process, including prerequisites, application-specific steps, file names, patch levels, parameters, inputs to selection screens, and the duration for each step. The cookbook should contain data consistency checks (reconciliation reports run before and after conversion to compare, for example, a summary of ledgers and checks for duplicate records).

A conversion run may identify business data inconsistencies that need to be corrected. The sandbox conversion run needs to be repeated until all business data inconsistencies have been cleaned up.

Follow-On Activities

There are mandatory postprocessing activities detailed in the Conversion Guide for SAP S/4HANA. For example, in the finance area, these consist of updates to configuration, data migration of financial accounting, and additional activities after the data migration.

When the sandbox is converted, it's recommended to run the data consistency check reports listed in the Conversion Guide for SAP S/4HANA to identify data inconsistencies that need to be tackled in production.

User Experience Activation

An initial UI scoping is obtained from an analysis of SAP Fiori apps based on the usage of the existing system. Using a list of transaction codes uploaded to the SAP Fiori apps reference library, the Relevance and Readiness Analysis feature in the SAP Fiori apps reference library provides a list of SAP Fiori apps that fit the business processes in scope.

Integration with Other Test Systems

Integrate the sandbox with other SAP and non-SAP test systems that form part of the old landscape. This must be done to support workshops and design cross-system business processes. Some of the other SAP systems may need to have been upgraded to the minimum release required to integrate with SAP S/4HANA. It's important to adjust integration settings to remove integration with other production systems.

Business Downtime Optimization

Here you record the anticipated business downtimes for the overall migration and conversion process. You also utilize prior maintenance activities to estimate the ramp-down and ramp-up activities that would precede and follow the conversion.

Depending on the downtime requirements of the business and the downtimes already achieved during the test migrations, iterative testing cycles may be needed to optimize the migration and conversion procedures. Use production-like hardware and full copies of productive databases. The more important the business downtime and overall performance aspects are for a customer, the more times the sandbox conversion should be executed. The time required for this task should be planned for as a contingency when building the project plan, but in a best case, it's never utilized.

Because the overall duration has many influencing factors (e.g., database size, network throughput, CPU speed, and disk input output), there are some constraints on what can be done to reduce downtime. Therefore, it's important to manage the expectations of the downtime with the business early in the project.

To optimize migration and conversion downtime, follow these steps:

1. Analyze the conversion logs (e.g., from sandbox migration and conversion) to determine the long-running phases.

2. Identify bottlenecks and evaluate opportunities to reduce the runtime of the long-running phases.

3. Engage SAP to provide expert analysis of the end-to-end business downtime.

4. Execute the conversion following the adoption of the recommendations.

Service Components

SAP can assist through SAP Value Assurance via the Mandatory Preparation for System Conversion, System Conversion to SAP S/4HANA, and Business Downtime Optimization service components.

Fit-to-Standard Analysis and Design

The purpose of the fit-to-standard analysis and design is to approve changes to scope and design to move into the realize phase. As part of system conversion, the fit-to-standard is generally light, with some processes changing and some of the old SAP ERP transactions being replaced with SAP Fiori apps. New scope items may be added to the solution, and existing WRICEFs may be eliminated by adopting standard features.

There are SAP S/4HANA simplification items for all LoBs (e.g., finance). Some are minor, whereas others may impact larger parts of the existing solution. Their impact must be recorded as requirements and be addressed in the design.

The company checks the processes, and identifies new delta requirements, and defines whether old WRICEFs must be kept or replaced. The delta requirements are prioritized, and a design is verified and accepted by the business owners. Prior to acceptance, SAP can check that there is no standard way of delivering the gaps and can review the overall design. A successful explore phase will provide a design that minimizes customizations and prevents the need for rework in the realize phase.

Fit-to-standard analysis and design in the explore phase consists of the following activities, as illustrated in Figure 8.9:

❶ Fit-to-standard workshop preparation
Plan workshops and check that the project team has done training and workshop participants have done self-enablement.

❷ Fit-to-standard system preparation
Check that the SAP S/4HANA sandbox system is ready to demonstrate the processes during the workshops.

❸ Fit-to-standard workshops and documentation
Present and validate the business processes in workshops and identify potential delta requirements.

❹ Fit-to-standard workshop validation
Classify, define, check, document, and prioritize the backlog of delta requirements. Decide which need to be discussed in a design workshop.

❺ Design workshops and documentation
Define the design during a workshop and document it afterward.

❻ Review and customer sign-off
Project architects review and adjust the design. SAP offers services that will make recommendations on potential design improvements and check whether the design is appropriate. Business and IT stakeholders give formal approval.

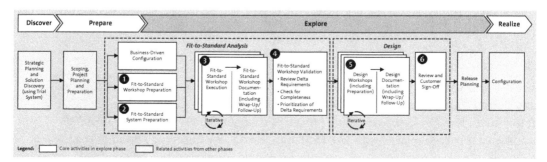

Figure 8.9 Fit-to-Standard Analysis and Design for System Conversion

The following sections cover the fit-to-standard analysis and design activities in sequence.

Fit-to-Standard Workshop Preparation

The workshops are organized by LoB areas (e.g., finance) and end-to-end solution (e.g., accounting and financial close). In a system conversion, the workshops focus on where the solution changes. There is an initial fit-to-standard workshop, which is followed by a design workshop where required. The project manager will organize the workshop schedule and check that the boundaries and integration points between the workshops are clear. A standard set of workshop input and output template documents are defined.

Fit-to-Standard System Preparation

Key business users will run through the existing business processes in the newly converted sandbox. The amount of change in each area will govern the scope of the workshops. SAP Best Practices test scripts may be helpful for setting up new processes. Some additional configuration may be done for new requirements.

Fit-to-Standard Workshops and Documentation

Each workshop is jointly owned and delivered by an experienced SAP consultant and a business process owner from the business. They should work together closely to prepare a detailed agenda, agree on attendees, distribute prereading, prepare slides, practice the demonstrations, and develop a checklist of questions and required decisions.

Documentation from the old SAP ERP solution will be an input to the workshops. This might include process diagrams, regression test cases, test scripts, and the original WRICEF list.

The fit-to-standard workshop uses a show-and-tell demonstration to validate changes to the existing solution, process, organization units, or business roles. The stakeholders focus on the actual and potential changes between the old SAP ERP solution and the new SAP S/4HANA solution. Any business change impacts are recorded.

The workshop defines requirements, including changes to the existing WRICEF items. The scope includes how simplification items are addressed and whether new features can eliminate existing WRICEF items. The delta requirements are immediately recorded in a backlog. The Microsoft Excel spreadsheet shown in Figure 8.10 may be used.

The following are the different types of delta requirements:

- **Configuration requirements**
  Most of the configuration from the old SAP ERP solution will remain unchanged. Requirements to change the configuration may relate to simplification items, business processes, UIs, and SAP-to-SAP integration scenarios.

- **Authorizations**
  Specify changes to how authorizations are used.

- **Master data**
  Specify changes in how the solution will be used.

- **WRICEFs**

  Changes may be required to existing WRICEFs, or new WRICEFs may be required. Enhancements include changes to the UI and missing functionality. Data conversions aren't required unless there is a new solution scope in the project.

- **Organization structure requirements**

  Identify any changes to the centrally managed enterprise/organization structure.

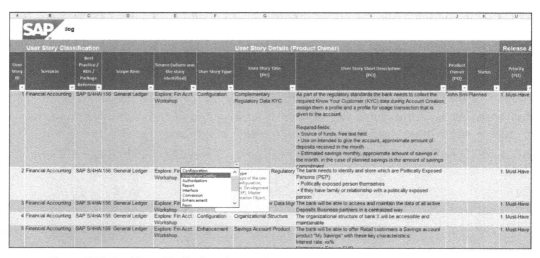

Figure 8.10 Backlog of Delta Requirements

Fit-to-Standard Workshop Validation

The teams research, document, and classify requirements. This may require discussion between the LoB teams. Each WRICEF is cataloged in the WRICEF list (Microsoft Excel) and assigned a scope item, initial priority, complexity, owner, and type.

SAP S/4HANA provides new, improved solutions for some workflows, forms, and reports. A decision needs to be made about whether these new solutions are to be adopted. If the old solutions are kept, they need to be tested and, in some cases, reworked.

Before moving ahead with designing the solution, it's important to sort out which requirements are relevant to fulfill the project objectives. The backlog of requirements is reviewed by the solution architects and project managers. Every item is challenged: Is it vital to meet the business requirement, and, if so, can it be delivered through standard configuration?

Design Workshops and Documentation

The purpose is to design and document functional solutions for the delta requirements.

Design documents may be available from the original ERP implementation. The project can rework these or choose to create new documents that summarize the design. Each one relates to a business scenario or end-to-end solution. The detailed requirements and WRICEFs relate to the scope items in these documents. Each document includes the following information:

- Process description
- Business objectives and benefits
- SAP S/4HANA conversion impacts
- Pain points
- Key business requirements
- KPIs
- Organizational change impacts (see Chapter 10 for how these are used during organizational change management activities)
- Organization structure in SAP
- Process scope and SAP S/4HANA conversion impact by scope item
- Process flow diagrams for scope items
- Systems (to be replaced or interfaced with)
- Master data used
- Summary of main delta requirements

During design, the team drills down into the detail and in some cases defines specific configuration activities and values. This additional information is recorded in the configuration requirements. It should be possible to do the configuration changes to the development system at the beginning of the realize phase.

New functional specifications are written to define any new WRICEFs. Some old functional specifications may need to be updated to address the system conversion impact on custom code. In some cases, depending on partner contracts and when estimates are required, functional specifications are prepared in the realize phase. How the WRICEF will be technically delivered is defined in the technical specification in the realize phase.

The old SAP ERP solution may have custom developments that were delivered by SAP Innovation Services. The approach for these should have been determined earlier in the discover and prepare phases.

The project team needs to maximize the value of the SAP Fiori apps that provide an enhanced UX in SAP S/4HANA. SAP recommends that a UX lead works across the LoB teams. UX-specific working sessions are required after the fit-to-standard workshops. The lead can define, estimate, and prioritize UI configuration requirements.

A process to look at UX requirements is shown in Figure 8.11. The UX lead will decide how to use the following:

- Theming, branding, and personalization
- UI enhancements (with key user tools) and UI extensibility (with SAP Web IDE)
- SAP Screen Personas for classic non-SAP Fiori apps; SAP GUI for HTML and Web Dynpro for ABAP
- New SAP Fiori apps

The UX lead will drive the definition and update of business user roles, as well as design the SAP Fiori launchpad experience and SAP Fiori tile setup. In some cases, low-fidelity UX mock-ups may be produced.

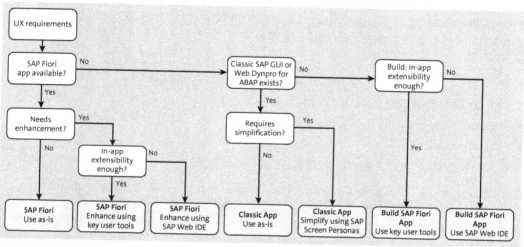

Figure 8.11 Design Options for UX Requirements

Further Resources

Refer to the Roadmap Viewer for details about how SAP can support UX work in the project.

Review and Customer Sign-Off

The project architects review and adjust the end-to-end design. SAP offers services that will make recommendations on potential design improvements and check whether the design is appropriate. Companies with SAP Value Assurance can use the Design Evaluation service. If there is uncertainty about the design of complex processes or concerns about the robustness, operability, and sustainability of a process and solution design, premium engagements offer the Application Architecture Evaluation service.

The project obtains formal approval of the design by business and IT stakeholders toward the end of the explore phase and incorporates all the design documents produced. It's important that the stakeholders genuinely understand the documents. They should be written in clear business language with SAP terminology clearly explained. Successful demonstrations and workshops are the key to truly informed approval.

With the sign-off, all stakeholders agree that the design is complete, and the solution proposals for requirements are understood and accepted. Issues identified during acceptance need to be documented and classified.

The backlog is updated and now represents the backlog for the realize phase. If an agile approach is adopted, the updated backlog is the baseline for sprint planning in the realize phase.

Custom Code Impact

As part of the conversion to SAP S/4HANA, companies need to identify custom source code that must be adjusted (must-dos) and that should be adjusted (should-dos). Custom code underpins many of the operational WRICEFs. A first analysis of the custom code situation should have been done in the prepare phase already, as discussed in Section 8.3.1.

The first stage of work on custom code impact is to understand the process and tools to be used. In the preparation for system conversion, the goal is to scope the impact of the custom code with the built-in usage monitor (Transaction SUSG), to use the Custom Code Migration app to detect unused code, and to use SUM to automatically remove unused code. SAP S/4HANA checks for simplifications also will be made via the ABAP test cockpit.

> **Further Resources**
>
> You can find more details in the Custom Code Migration Guide for SAP S/4HANA on the SAP Help Portal. Note that the guide is updated for each release of SAP S/4HANA software.

During the next phase, the team will need to do application-specific follow-up activities, such as functional adaptation of custom code, including the use of Transactions SPDD and SPAU to adjust the dictionary objects and custom code, respectively.

Most companies find that they can deprecate a significant amount of custom code that is no longer operational. The next stage is to create a list of custom objects that are candidates for adjustment. This should include the following:

- Modifications affected by upgrade or EHP installation
- Custom code affected by the database change to SAP HANA

- Custom code affected by the change of the simplified data model coming with SAP S/4HANA
- Custom code affected by the simplification of business processes and applications coming with SAP S/4HANA

A documented worklist of custom objects that are subject for adjustment is stored centrally—for example, in SAP Solution Manager. Some items on this list may be eliminated when design decisions are made to replace old WRICEFs with new standard features.

There is a growing area of simplified and optimized solutions with which SAP has completely changed how to process data. Here, a simple adjustment within a custom program may fall short. Instead, companies should proceed as follows:

- Companies can consider using SAP's new way of processing data and go to the SAP standard. This kind of transformation can be supported by SAP.
- Companies can think about a complete redesign of custom code in this space, leveraging the new business functionality offered by SAP.

You should also analyze all custom objects from the list and prioritize based on business criticality and urgency. The result is a documented and prioritized list of custom code objects that need to be adjusted. This also includes custom code objects that should be reimplemented on SAP BTP (e.g., SAP Fiori UIs).

SAP Solution Manager can help estimate the technical work. The upgrade/change impact analysis as part of the Custom Development Management Cockpit (CDMC) provides a way to estimate and manage the technical adjustment effort for release upgrades. The Scope and Effort Analyzer (SEA) in SAP Solution Manager estimates the technical adjustment effort caused by EHP installations.

Service Components

SAP can assist through the Custom Code Impact Analysis service component.

Data Volume Design

After the fit-to-standard analysis and design are complete, it's time to move on to data volume design. Data volume design concerns what data is stored where and for how long (i.e., defining the residence and retention time). If data deletion (deleting out-of-date records) and data archiving (transferring data to an alternative storage medium) weren't operational in the old SAP ERP solution, refer to Chapter 7 for new implementations.

The data volume design used in the old SAP ERP solution must be updated to do the following:

- Reduce overall data volume in large SAP ERP solutions prior to conversion.
- Reflect changes in the underlying data model.
- Consider new "data aging" solutions that are enabled by the SAP HANA database.

With data aging, an SAP HANA database allows data to be divided into current/hot data (stored in main memory) and historical/cold data (primarily stored on disk).

The following impacts must be considered:

- In large systems, deletion and archiving may be required in the existing SAP ERP solution before system conversion is done.
- There are quick wins in deleting or reorganizing temporary or basis table data in the existing SAP ERP solution.
- It's best to archive transaction data of deactivated company codes.
- In large systems, transparency is gained into open business documents that can't be archived. Open business documents that fail the archiving checks are likely to fail the conversion checks.
- Due to the changes in the finance data model, reloading accounting data that has been archived with some archiving objects is no longer possible after system conversion.
- Custom code changes may be required to access archived or historical (cold) data.
- Due to changes in the data model, existing archiving strategies must be checked and adapted.
- There may be benefits to incorporating data aging into the existing design.

The revised design defines infrastructure (e.g., content servers), use of data aging and operation, sequencing and monitoring of data archiving, and data deletion jobs.

Service Components

SAP offers the Data Volume Design service to assist through SAP Value Assurance.

Technical Architecture and Infrastructure Design

For on-premise SAP S/4HANA, a target technical architecture and infrastructure is defined in a technical design document. The technical architects review the existing design and create a new design focusing on the changes required for SAP S/4HANA.

SAP S/4HANA Cloud, Private Edition

For SAP S/4HANA Cloud, private edition, many aspects of this are managed by SAP. This includes topics like security of the environment, operations of the data center, and other services covered by your subscription contract.

The approach in the explore phase is as follows:

1. **Discover technical boundary conditions**

   These include technical solutions required, size and purpose of nonproduction systems, data center strategy, system availability requirements, service-level agreements (SLAs) for planned and unplanned downtime, high availability (HA), and disaster recovery (DR).

2. **Update the technical solution map**

   Update the detail information on each technical component—for example, deployment model, nonfunctional requirements, integration requirements, minimum releases, and release dependencies.

3. **Decide on integration with cloud applications**

   If there are new cloud applications in scope, define an integration considering the available bandwidth, peak times, availability requirements, and recovery procedures.

4. **Select hardware and perform hardware sizing**

   Work with the hardware supplier and undertake hardware sizing.

5. **Develop a virtualization strategy**

   Determine how a virtualization platform will fit into the design.

6. **Design a network**

   Consider changes to the data center interconnectivity, network zones and LAN/WAN bandwidth, and latency.

7. **Prepare testing**

   Review and revise existing test cases for flexibility, workload management, HA, DR, backup, and restore.

8. **Document the technical design**

   The revised technical design is developed and documented in a series of workshops. This includes technical components, scalability, load-balancing, backup, HA, DR, architecture, infrastructure, deployment plan and data center, and third-party integration.

The SAP Activate roadmap provides accelerators such as white papers, checklists, and a Technical Solution Map template and Technical Design Document template.

Service Components

SAP can assist on-premise customers through the Technical Platform Definition service component and the Advanced Sizing service component.

Integration Design

The purpose of this activity is to revise and renew the architecture and design required for interfaces between all systems. This activity is executed in close cooperation with the work on new interfaces in the WRICEF list and design. It should cover any new integration scenarios, including any new SAP cloud solutions.

The interface architecture identifies all the systems- and interfaces-to-be. Build on the interface register produced in the prepare phase to list the middleware technology, protocol type, frequency, and directions of communication of each interface.

After the architecture and scope are agreed upon, the existing integration design document is revised, or a new one is produced. The following aspects should be covered for each integration aspect or interface:

- Short description of the integration aspect
- General business requirements (e.g., frequency and required fields)
- Impact of system conversion
- IT systems interfaced to SAP S/4HANA
- Identification of integration requirements (referencing the requirement backlog)
- Solution for requirements (middleware, field mapping, or configuration)
- Important customizing
- Developments
- Organizational aspects
- Process quantification (i.e., expected data volume)

Functional specifications for any new interfaces between SAP and non-SAP systems are produced during the explore or realize phases, depending on the milestone definitions of the project.

The SAP middleware solutions to manage the operation of end-to-end integration processes are either SAP Process Integration (on-premise) or SAP Integration Suite. You can find APIs and prepackaged integrations online on SAP API Business Hub.

Service Components

SAP offers the Integration Validation service to assist companies using SAP Value Assurance and premium engagement.

Analytics Design

The project should evaluate the strategic and business value of the new analytics solutions available for SAP S/4HANA. The explore phase should build on the work already done during the discover and prepare phases to complete an analytics architecture, landscape, and design. The following SAP solutions may be considered:

- **SAP S/4HANA embedded analytics**
  This includes LoB-specific prebuilt solutions and comprehensive real-time reports produced based on SAP HANA CDS views.

- **SAP BW and SAP BW/4HANA**
  SAP's data warehousing solutions for SAP and non-SAP data.
- **SAP Analytics Cloud**
  Cloud-based analytics solution that can operate across all SAP on-premise and SAP cloud solutions, SAP BW/4HANA, and non-SAP solutions.
- **SAP Digital Boardroom**
  An add-on to SAP Analytics Cloud to provide real-time analysis for C-level leadership.
- **SAP BusinessObjects Business Intelligence**
  On-premise alternative to SAP Analytics Cloud.

Analytics design covers business intelligence (e.g., reports, tables, charts, graphs, and geographic analysis), predictive analytics, and planning requirements.

SAP BW/4HANA has its own separate SAP Activate roadmap that covers system conversion scenarios. If SAP BW or SAP BW/4HANA are part of the old landscape, an assessment should be done of the business benefits of moving some use cases to SAP S/4HANA embedded analytics. Some of the operational aggregates in SAP BW will no longer be required, and extracts and reports can be decommissioned.

SAP Business Explorer tools are no longer available or supported with SAP BW/4HANA. Companies moving to SAP BW/4HANA from SAP BW will need to transition their SAP Business Process Explorer reports and applications to the SAP BusinessObjects suite or SAP Analytics Cloud. SAP Analytics Cloud has its own separate SAP Activate roadmap.

The impact on the standard and custom SAP BW data sources and SAP BW extractors must be analyzed. Many standard extractors will continue to work with SAP S/4HANA, but some aren't on the allowlist. The design must address how this is resolved.

Analytics workshops are conducted for LoB-specific processes and requirements. A fit-to-standard analysis and design is performed for existing and new business requirements. The design should document which existing analytics use cases remain unchanged, are updated, or are replaced altogether.

Analytics design guidelines are produced that define the following:

- When and how to use the different analytics solutions
- When to use the different connection types between the solutions
- Data modeling guidelines
- User access and security concepts

Service Components

SAP can assist through SAP Value Assurance with the Analytics Design service component.

Security Design

The purpose of security design is to consider the impact of the SAP S/4HANA conversion on security and user management design. The security topics include infrastructure, network, operating system, database, and frontend access. User management covers roles, authorizations, user maintenance, and segregation of duties.

> **SAP S/4HANA Cloud, Private Edition**
>
> A move to SAP S/4HANA Cloud, private edition will involve a new approach and new responsibilities for security governed by standardized processes. In addition, some services will be provided by SAP or a hyperscaler operating your environment as part of the subscription services. Refer to SAP Trust Center for details on the security, cloud operations, data center details and agreements. You can access SAP Trust Center at *https://www.sap.com/about/trust-center.html*.

For on-premise SAP S/4HANA, security activities are prioritized (mandatory/recommended/optional) to create a detailed security roadmap for the implementation of changes in the realize phase and beyond. The required security topics are as follows:

- Planning SAP HANA security following the SAP HANA Security Guide
- Defining communication security
- Defining authentication mechanisms

There are also topics that are recommended but may not be required or prioritized by all companies:

- Planning the implementation of single sign-on (SSO)
- Defining processes for SAP auditing, logging, and monitoring
- Planning the security of the IT infrastructure
- RFC connections and gateway security
- Patching SAP Security Notes
- Custom code security

Regardless of the whether SAP S/4HANA is on-premise or in a private cloud, business roles and authorizations are impacted by the move to SAP S/4HANA. An upgrade of the authorization concept is required, leading to changes in backend Transaction PFCG roles and authorizations. These roles must be aligned with the design of the SAP Fiori launchpad. Many old transactions will be replaced by SAP Fiori apps either because the old transaction is deprecated or because the business decides to adopt a new alternative SAP Fiori app.

Segregation of duties is the assignment of steps in a process to different people to avoid fraud through individuals having excessive control. The management of access risks is supported by SAP Access Control, which is part of SAP governance, risk, and compliance solutions.

Service Components

SAP can assist through SAP Value Assurance with the Security Design service component.

Test Planning

The purpose of this critical deliverable is two-fold: (1) to manage the quality of the solution and to minimize issues during and after the go-live, and (2) to streamline the multiple system conversions that will be done during the project. A risk-based approach should be used to define test planning. The test strategy document covers the following topics:

- **Project testing**

  Use project testing objectives and assumptions, with a focus on areas of the solution that have changed or are new.

- **Test scope**

  Use regression tests from the old SAP ERP solution and the design to define the scope. The result is a revised list of test cases and test scripts focusing on the business-critical and frequently used business processes.

- **Types of testing**

  Select test cycles, including regression testing done after each system conversion, unit testing, business process (string) testing, integration testing, performance testing, and user acceptance testing (UAT).

- **Testing approach**

  Define how the different test types relate to each other, (e.g., a successful unit test is a prerequisite for doing a string test).

- **Testing deliverables**

  Describe the test processes per project phase, test environment, and test data.

- **Testing tools**

  Determine which tools will be used to perform different tests.

- **Test automation**

  Decide whether automation will be used and evaluate and select the appropriate tools.

- **Defect management**

  Describe how defects will be documented.

- **Roles and responsibilities**

  This includes the test lead and the responsibilities of individual project team members.

Detailed test planning should be done to define the timing, duration, criteria, dependencies, and resources for each of the test cycles.

You may use SAP Solution Manager as the central platform for test management of SAP-centric solutions. It can be used in combination with other test solutions if the company has other standards or tools.

Service Components

SAP can assist through SAP Value Assurance with the Test Planning service component.

Development Conversion

Before work starts in the realize phase, the development environment needs to be set up. The prerequisites are that the migration approach has been validated in the sandbox environment, a detailed migration plan is in place, and the hardware is ready.

The setup of the development system can be delayed to the middle of the realize phase to reduce the duration of parallel work with a product support track. This requires transports to be enabled from the sandbox to the development system.

A copy of the old development system is made for business-as-usual production support while the project runs. An end-to-end system conversion is done of the old development system. Use the cookbook developed when converting the sandbox and the Conversion Guide for SAP S/4HANA. Depending on the configuration of the transport landscape, there may be a need to perform multiple iterations of the sandbox and development system conversion to solidify and finalize the cutover plan. Executing test migrations will validate the end state of the conversion, as well as provide the figures for expected system downtime.

SAP S/4HANA Cloud, Private Edition

There are some extra considerations to move the development system to SAP S/4HANA Cloud, private edition. For example, as we stated earlier in our discussion about sandbox conversion, customers that have a subscription without a dedicated sandbox system will run system conversion initially in the quality system, then subsequently refresh the quality system and run the development system conversion.

Ideally, there will be a soft freeze to minimize production support changes during the project. Take care to properly retrofit changes performed in the production support landscape to the new development system to ensure the latest business requirements are accounted for. Depending on the changes, those retrofit activities may require special attention because transports between classic SAP ERP and SAP S/4HANA may cause inconsistencies.

Service Components

SAP can provision the development environment for on-premise customers through the Platform Execution Enablement service component.

End User Learning and Change Impact Analysis

During the explore phase, the training requirements for key users and end users are analyzed and documented. A learning needs analysis identifies the skill levels, knowledge gaps, and training requirements. Based on the analysis, a training strategy and plan is designed. See Chapter 10 for more information.

After the fit-to-standard workshops are complete, a change impact analysis is done. An OCM expert will usually join the project team. They will gather the organizational and technical changes identified in the workshops and refine these through comparing the business processes and solutions as is and to be. See Chapter 10 for more information.

Operations Impact Evaluation

An operations impact evaluation is undertaken. With the introduction of a new solution like SAP S/4HANA, the current IT support framework will change.

SAP S/4HANA Cloud, Private Edition

The change is larger if SAP S/4HANA Cloud, private edition is selected as some roles will be provided by the hyperscaler and some need to be covered by the company's IT organization.

The deliverables from the explore phase, such as the technical design document and design documents, are important sources of information on what needs to be supported by IT after the new solution is live and how.

The aim is to identify new operational activities, modifications to existing activities, and activities that can be retired. All the relevant support areas need to be analyzed: roles and skills, processes/procedures, operations documentation, and enabling support tools. Then a roadmap is defined that includes the key activities for IT to fill the gaps and prepare the future IT support framework. This will include establishing resources; setting up tools; documenting procedures, knowledge transfer, and operations cutover; and retiring parts of the old framework.

Service Components

SAP can support this task with the Operations Impact Evaluation service component.

SAP Solution Manager in the Explore Phase

SAP recommends the use of SAP Solution Manager in all phases of a system conversion project. Ideally, SAP Solution Manager will already be in place with the old ERP solution. Some companies and partners have their own standards for project tools and choose not to use some of the features listed here.

During the explore phase, SAP Solution Manager can be used for the following:

- **Custom code worklist**
  This prioritized list of custom objects and code must and should be adapted or reworked.

- **Process management**
  Business processes and process diagrams are created for the solution.

- **Document management**
  Project documents, such as design documents and WRICEF specifications, are stored with document versioning.

- **Requirements**
  The backlog of business requirements is transferred from a Microsoft Excel spreadsheet into SAP Solution Manager. This allows configuration and developments done in the realize phase to be linked back to specific requirements.

- **Project management**
  The project deliverables and tasks can be managed and tracked in SAP Solution Manager, which contains the SAP Activate roadmap content.

- **Change and release management**
  Configuration requirements are allocated to releases with full change control.

This sets a foundation for managing the build, test, and deployment in SAP Solution Manager during the realize phase. The approach to using SAP Solution Manager is agreed upon and documented in an SAP Solution Manager standards document.

8.3.3   Realize Your Requirements

In the realize phase, simplification item changes and new requirements are implemented based on the design. Existing custom code is adjusted. A conversion of the quality assurance system is done and then used for testing. We'll walk through the realize phase for a system conversion project in this section.

Phase Overview

During the realize phase, a series of cycles are used to incrementally test, extend, and validate the system environment based on the business scenarios and process requirements defined during the explore phase. Existing custom code is adjusted. A new or changed scope is implemented using configuration, extensions, integration, and analytics.

The main outputs of the realize phase in a system conversion include the following:

- Custom code is adjusted and tested.
- Updates are made to configuration and configuration documentation.
- Technical specifications, test cases, and custom code are created for new WRICEFs.
- Infrastructure, integration, security, and operational procedures are updated and tested.
- Quality assurance and production environments are migrated and converted to SAP S/4HANA.
- Data aging, data archiving, and data deletion are ready.
- Tests, including UAT, are complete based on a test plan, test cases, and test scripts.
- Support operations framework and procedures are ready.
- The cutover process is planned, and conversions of the production system are rehearsed.

The realize phase must be planned in detail, with dependencies coming together in the plan for testing. Carefully defined entry and exit criteria must be transparent to the whole team to ensure that the workstreams remain coordinated. The plan must be frequently updated to reflect progress and changes in scope and timescales.

The LoB teams (e.g., finance or manufacturing) from the explore phase continue to operate through the realize phase.

This section on the realize phase is organized into topics that appear in the roadmap. The use of SAP Solution Manager during the realize phase is covered in the last section.

Configuration

Most of the old configuration will continue to work unchanged in SAP S/4HANA. The purpose of this activity is to change the existing configuration according to the design defined and agreed upon during the explore phase. Some of this work will be driven by the SAP S/4HANA simplification items. Configuration is done in the development environment, and steps are executed in cycles (or agile sprints; see Chapter 6, Section 6.3.2). A configuration guideline should be available to document the approach and define the standards to be used.

Each configuration cycle consists of the following stages:

1. **Handover session**
   Handover occurs from the design team to the configuration team.
2. **Perform configuration**
   Configure settings in the development system by LoB and end-to-end process.
3. **Unit test**
   Test the newly configured functions.

4. **String test**
   Test the end-to-end process or solution impacted by the configuration change.

5. **Solution walkthrough**
   Present the new capability to the project team.

6. **Bug fixing**
   Resolve issues identified in the unit test, string test, and solution walkthrough.

7. **Documentation**
   Document the finalized configuration.

Much of the configuration is done using the Implementation Guide (IMG) in Transaction SPRO. SAP Fiori apps are configured using adaptation at runtime. Configuration of integration between SAP products and configuration of analytics are covered later.

The following sections cover the sequential stages of configuration.

Handover Session

Handover is done from the design team (in charge of the design documents) to the configuration team. The configuration team may be offshore or split across multiple physical locations. This is a good time to check the completeness and detail of the documentation.

Perform Configuration

Configuration changes are made in the converted SAP S/4HANA development system, and all changes are recorded in transport requests. These will be used later to transfer configuration from the development system into the converted quality assurance and converted production system. Configuration is also done to retrofit any changes from the business-as-usual production support landscape.

Most of the configuration is done using IMG in Transaction SPRO. The team should follow the configuration standards that govern the naming and numbering of new configuration records.

Configuration of the SAP Fiori UI is done with UI adaptation at runtime. You can move, rename, and remove sections, groups, and fields. You can also combine fields or add standard fields or custom fields. Classic non-SAP Fiori apps (SAP GUI for HTML and Web Dynpro for ABAP) can be configured using SAP Screen Personas.

Unit Test

The objective of this task is to properly unit test the new and changed functions in the development system, as well as log and fix issues. The unit test is owned by just one of the LoB teams.

String Test

A test is done for an end-to-end process by stringing together unit tests. The string test will often cross multiple LoB teams. Tests may be done in the development or quality assurance systems.

The focus should be on SAP processes and functionality. This can include standard integration between SAP products, for example, SAP S/4HANA and SAP Ariba. Testing of WRICEF objects and interfaces with non-SAP systems is done during integration testing. Test execution and results are documented, and issues are logged and fixed.

Solution Walkthrough

The aim of this task is to present any new and changed solution capability and business process to business process owners in the LoB teams via live demonstration. Their early feedback is incorporated into the solution. If open questions can't be resolved within the project, the business process owner takes the queries into the business for resolution. Changes to the scope or design must be managed through the change request process (see Chapter 6, Section 6.3.2).

Bug Fixing

Issues and bugs identified during tests and the solution walkthrough should be resolved directly within the current build cycle or logged in the project issue list. The string test should be repeated to check that changes haven't produced any unwanted side effects.

Documentation

The LoB teams document the configuration settings and impacts on the design including the reason for each decision.

Product Enhancements

In system conversion, product enhancement covers the adjustment of existing custom code and the development of new custom code for the WRICEFs defined during the explore phase. The following sections cover the product enhancement activities during the realize phase.

Adjust Affected Existing Custom Code

Make sure your developers have the required skill set to adjust your custom code for SAP S/4HANA. Refer to the Custom Code Migration Guide for SAP S/4HANA in the SAP Help Portal. There are also multiple options for developer training.

Use the prioritized list of custom objects requiring adjustment from the explore phase. Adjust custom code objects in the converted development system. Alternatively, custom code work can be done in the sandbox and transported to the development system later.

For standard known issues that don't require a change of the application logic, SAP provides a constantly growing list of quick fixes that can be triggered from the ABAP test cockpit. Quick fixes automatically adapt your custom code to minimize your adjustment efforts. All changes are logged in transport requests. Transport your changes to the quality assurance system after it has been converted to SAP S/4HANA. Test your changes, perform the corrections in development, and transport to quality assurance again.

Work with SAP to make custom developments delivered by SAP Innovation Services work with SAP S/4HANA. Alternatively, they may be replaced by new SAP solutions.

Take care to retrofit changes performed in the production support landscape to the new SAP S/4HANA development system to ensure the latest business requirements are accounted for.

> **Service Components**
> SAP provides support through the Custom Code Remediation service component.

Select Development Technologies

Before developing new code in SAP S/4HANA, developers should be aware of the latest technical options available—for example, using extensibility apps within SAP S/4HANA or side-by-side extensibility with SAP Extension Suite.

Extensibility apps provide a more readily maintainable alternative to classic extensibility for a growing list of objects and enhancements. This includes adapting SAP Fiori UIs, adding custom fields, adding application logic, and creating reports, email templates, and forms.

SAP Extension Suite allows development to be done in parallel with the SAP S/4HANA implementation to keep the core clean and make software upgrades faster. It also allows the team to consume the latest technology platform for innovation use cases such as mobile, machine learning, big data, and the Internet of Things (IoT).

Developers should also be aware of the latest best practices associated with the newest techniques. Where possible, these approaches should be considered before classic extensibility such as ABAP business add-ins (BAdIs) and user exits. As always, modifications outside stable enhancement points should always be avoided. The golden rule for modern extensibility technologies in the cloud can also be applied on-premise. Update your development guidelines and standards, and put in place rules and reviews to check that new approaches are adopted and the development quality is managed.

Technical Design

Detailed technical specifications are produced for all new WRICEFs based on the functional specifications prepared earlier. The technical specifications include details such as the entry point in the system, enhancement logic, process flow diagram, data model, and required authorizations. Template documents are available in the Roadmap Viewer. Unit test case documents are prepared. All documents are reviewed by the application design team to check that they fit with the evolving design.

Develop and Test WRICEF Objects

The developers build, unit test, and document the new WRICEFs. After development is complete, the WRICEFs are tested and retested by the application design team until all issues are resolved.

Enhancements may be required to UIs if requirements can't be met through configuration alone. Examples include the following:

- Enhancements through SAP Fiori extension points
- Backend extensions—for example, the addition of new custom fields
- Full-screen modifications
- Development of new SAP Fiori apps

> **Service Components**
>
> SAP Value Assurance offers the Technical Performance Optimization service component for WRICEFs.

Custom Developments

It's recommended to manage development requirements that are critical or exceed a certain threshold as custom developments. These are typically managed as small, standalone agile projects. The functional specification, technical specification, development, and testing are managed through agile sprints. Customers should strongly consider implementing the Solution Standardization Board (SSB) governance we discussed in Chapter 2, Section 2.4 to ensure alignment with the golden rules for implementation of SAP S/4HANA and with the Extensibility Guide.

SAP Innovation Services can develop one-of-a-kind solutions through company-specific custom developments. Using SAP maximizes supportability and operability.

Data Volume Management

Data volume management is configured based on the design from the explore phase. This includes data aging and processes to delete and archive data.

In data aging, an SAP HANA database allows data to be divided into current/hot data (stored in main memory) and historical/cold data (primarily stored on disk). Data aging is available for the following objects:

- Finance documents
- Unified journal entry

- Material documents
- Purchase orders
- Sales documents
- Deliveries
- Sales invoices
- Application logs
- IDocs
- Change documents
- Workflow documents

Further Resources

Refer to the SAP Help Portal for documentation on how to do the configuration (design time) and test the solution (runtime).

Set Up Infrastructure and Security

For an on-premise project, the technical infrastructure is adjusted as defined in the technical design document produced in the explore phase.

SAP S/4HANA Cloud, Private Edition

In SAP S/4HANA Cloud, private edition, new solutions and procedures are adopted, and elements of the work are defined and executed by SAP or a hyperscaler partner.

The IT infrastructure setup work includes the following:

- Server hardware, operating system, and virtualization platform
- Storage solution—that is, the physical setup of the storage infrastructure usually done by the storage supplier
- Integration of any components into the IT environment—for example, integration into the network and backup solution
- HA, DR, and backup

The security solution is implemented, including the following:

- User management, including roles, authorizations, and user maintenance
- Infrastructure and network security
- Operating system and database security
- Frontend access and authentication

The team must execute infrastructure tests based on the test cases and test plan. This will measure the performance against the defined KPIs to ensure the infrastructure operates within the boundary conditions of the business. The team resolves, documents, and retests issues and defects. Tests should include the following scenarios:

- Performance as issues may require changes to the functional design in addition to infrastructure changes
- Flexibility procedures (e.g., by moving the system load to other hosts, adding instances, or changing instances)
- HA
- DR
- Backup and restore
- Infrastructure security

Service Components

SAP can also assist with on-premise implementations through SAP Value Assurance with the Technical Feasibility Check, Business Process Performance Optimization, Technical Performance Optimization, and Volume Test Optimization service components. These may lead to changes in the functional design, configuration, and tuning for optimum performance, elimination of bottlenecks, and SAP Fiori–specific performance improvements.

Integration Implementation and Validation

Changes to the integration design defined in the explore phase are implemented. This activity should be executed in close cooperation with the configuration and product enhancement activities.

SAP recommends the Integration Validation service to mitigate risk based on the use of SAP Value Assurance services. The aim is to ensure technical readiness of the entire solution for go-live. It includes analysis of critical business processes and interfaces validating scalability, performance, data consistency, and exception management. A comprehensive monthly status of technical go-live readiness for core business processes is recommended. It includes these aspects:

- **Data consistency**
  In distributed solution landscapes, the consistency of the data across software systems must be subject to checks and validations. This requires transactional security, and all integration queues and interfaces must be monitored.
- **Business process monitoring and exception management**
  There must be 100% transparency into the status and completion of business processes. The flow of documents must be monitored.

- **Performance and scalability**
  The response time for critical transactions and runtime for batch jobs should meet business requirements. Adequate load-balancing must be in place.

> **Service Components**
> SAP recommend the use of the following services through SAP Value Assurance: Integration Validation, Interface Management, and Technical Integration Check. These tried-and-tested processes provide the project with access to lessons learned from hundreds of other live SAP implementations. See the Roadmap Viewer for more details.

Analytics Configuration

The analytics solutions are changed and implemented based on the design and guidelines documented in the explore phase. The scope may cover analytics, predictive analytics, and planning requirements. The design will typically be based on embedded analytics in SAP S/4HANA and SAP Analytics Cloud to define the UX for analytics and planning. SAP BW/4HANA provides a data warehouse for structured and unstructured data from SAP on-premise, SAP cloud, and third-party solutions. Parts of the existing solution (e.g., SAP BW, SAP BW/4HANA, and SAP BusinessObjects Business Intelligence) may need to be changed or superseded altogether.

Examples of the activities to be undertaken in SAP S/4HANA include the following:

- Configure the SAP Fiori launchpad.
- Perform the technical set up of SAP S/4HANA CDS views and SAP S/4HANA embedded analytical apps based on CDS views.
- Customize prebuilt SAP S/4HANA embedded analytics.
- Create custom CDS views for custom SAP S/4HANA embedded analytics.

Examples of the activities to be undertaken in SAP Analytics Cloud include the following:

- Configure general settings such as the import functionality, database connector, and cloud connector.
- Import and enable prebuilt content for SAP Analytics Cloud.
- Configure the underlying SAP Analytics Cloud data models, planning models, and predictive models.
- Set up a live data connection between SAP Analytics Cloud and SAP S/4HANA and SAP BW/4HANA to enable analytics without persistent data in the cloud.
- Import data into the data models and perform data preparation for analytics with persistent data in the cloud.
- Configure SAP Analytics Cloud stories for reports, tables, charts, graphs, and geographic analysis.

Further Resources

Refer to the SAP Analytics Cloud and SAP BW/4HANA SAP Activate roadmaps in the Roadmap Viewer for more details.

Service Components

SAP Services and Solutions can provide consulting enablement or implementation support for SAP Analytics Cloud and SAP Digital Boardroom.

Testing

During testing, the test strategy and test plan produced in the explore phase are put into action. Figure 8.12 provides an overview of the testing approach that illustrates what systems are used and the sequence of test cycles. You can also refer to Chapter 5, Section 5.5, for more information on testing.

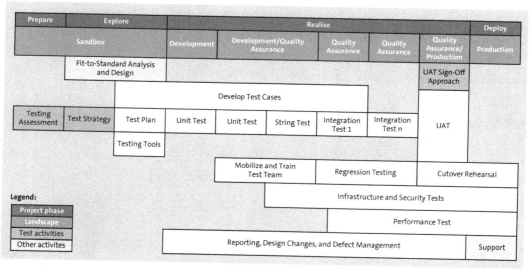

Figure 8.12 Overview of Testing Approach

Test cases and test scripts are created and updated. Testing tools are checked, and the testing teams are trained. A combination of manual testing and automated testing is used. The scope and source of the required test data is agreed upon. The details of the approval procedure for UAT are finalized, and the test plan is turned into a detailed schedule of activity.

During all test execution, defects are formally logged for traceability, fixes are applied and transported, and the process is retested until the issue is resolved. Errors can hide in the variants of processes, so ensure that test scripts mix these up well (e.g., a foreign currency order with batch management). All the different workstreams come together in the test process.

The following tests are available:

- **Integration tests**
  Integration testing is performed to verify proper execution of the entire application, including all WRICEFs, integration between SAP solutions, and interfaces to external applications. Integration testing is conducted in the quality assurance system. Integration testing is approved after all tests have passed.

- **Regression tests**
  During integration tests, many fixes are transported into the quality assurance system. Later fixes may break processes that had already passed their tests. To mitigate risk, regression tests are executed alongside the cutover rehearsals. The scope and approach are similar to integration testing. The quality assurance system is monitored as if it were production, as this will provide an indication of end state operations. For example, errors in the system log, which may not be noticed by testers, could cause instability in the production system.

- **UAT**
  UAT provides formal approval from actual users that the solution works as specified and meets the business requirements. The scope and approach are similar to integration testing.

Convert Quality Assurance

Before integration starts, the quality assurance environment needs to be set up. An end-to-end system conversion of the old quality assurance system is done. Use the cookbook developed when converting the development system and the Conversion Guide for SAP S/4HANA.

Operations Implementation

Changes to the support operations are implemented following the operations roadmap defined in the explore phase. The following areas are covered:

- **Detailed operations**
  The changes to the support framework are implemented. This is often managed through detailed IT change requests.

- **Roles and responsibilities**
  Changes to resources and their roles and responsibilities are implemented.

- **Support processes and procedures**
  Changed IT support processes are documented and tested. This includes incident management, problem management, access management, change management, test management, job management, and system recovery.

- **Operations support tools**
  Tools are adjusted or newly set up.

- **Operations documentation**
  An operations handbook is produced, and all documentation is updated and stored in a central repository.

- **Knowledge transfer**
  The IT support resources prepare to run the new solution. Knowledge transfer is done through a combination of activities, including formal training, self-study, shadowing, and on-the-job training.

Cutover Preparation

The conversion of the production system requires a clearly defined cutover plan and will typically be controlled by a cutover manager. The cutover plan documents the end-to-end activities of the cutover, from the steps leading up to the event through to the end of the conversion. Tasks commonly found in a cutover plan include the following:

- Prerequisite steps for the production conversion
- Ramp-down activities (e.g., batch jobs and interfaces)
- Preconversion validation reports
- End user lockout
- Technical migration and business data conversion
- Postconversion changes (e.g., transports and parameter changes)
- Technical postconversion validation reports that check for business data consistency
- Business-driven system validation and comparison of the pre- and postconversion reports
- Go/no-go decision
- Ramp-up activities
- User unlock

The cutover plan doesn't detail the technical conversion to the level that is captured in the cookbook. It's common to highlight specific tasks from the cookbook within the cutover plan to ensure the process is on schedule. The cutover plan should also include a contingency plan to revert the changes in the event there is a no-go decision.

Prepare Training and Organizational Change Management Alignment

Training material is created for end users. SAP recommends the SAP Enable Now tool (see Chapter 10, Section 10.5) for creating the training material, supporting translations, and developing e-learning. It can be used for SAP and non-SAP applications. Possible training documents include the following:

- **Course concept**
  Goal and structure of each training event

- **Training manual**
  Instructions for the trainers

- **Work instructions**
  Step-by-step explanations of each process and transaction

- **Exercises**
  Instructions and data for hands-on use of the solution

- **Simulations**
  Recorded walkthroughs of processes and transactions with guidance

- **E-learning**
  Self-learning for less complex topics

- **Web-based training**
  Alternative to classroom training that provides communication with the trainer via video, chat, and phone

Organizational change impacts were identified in the explore phase and help drive OCM activities. During the realize phase, these are reassessed with a focus on changes in the project scope, design, and assumptions. In particular, the alignment of OCM with the test and cutover processes is checked. See Chapter 10 for more information.

SAP Solution Manager in the Realize Phase

During the realize phase, SAP Solution Manager can be used for the following:

- **Custom code worklist**
  This prioritized list of custom objects and code must and should be adapted or reworked.

- **Document management**
  Project documents, such as configuration documentation, technical specifications, and test results, are stored and linked back to requirements.

- **Configuration**
  The IMG configuration activities used are logged against processes and requirements.

- **Project management**
  The project deliverables and tasks can be managed and tracked.

- **Change management**
  Configuration and developments in SAP S/4HANA are recorded in an SAP S/4HANA transport request. These transport requests can be linked to SAP Solution Manager change documents.

- **Manage transports into quality assurance system**
  SAP Solution Manager change documents are used to trigger transports from the development system to the quality assurance system.

8.3.4   Deploy Your Solution

During the deploy phase, the solution, supporting tools, and processes are made ready for the SAP S/4HANA production go-live. We'll walk through the tasks in the deploy phase for a system conversion deployment project in this section.

Phase Overview

Final go-live rehearsals are executed. This phase includes a go or no-go decision and ensures that the organization is ready to run in the converted environment.

The primary activities of the deploy phase in a system conversion project include the following:

- End user learning and organizational change readiness
- Finalize testing
- Operation and infrastructure readiness
- Dress rehearsal
- Convert production
- System go-live and hypercare support
- Handover to support organization

End User Learning and Organizational Change Readiness

In the deploy phase, the OCM activities ensure that all relevant stakeholders are ready to go live. Monitoring of OCM activities, including the communication plan, is crucial to ensure end user adoption. See Chapter 10 for more information.

The learning plan developed in the previous phases is delivered. The training is necessary to ensure that end users are prepared for the new solution. The steps may include the following:

- Finalize a detailed training schedule.
- Deliver end user training.
- Collect training evaluations feedback.
- Perform people readiness assessment.

After the go-live, it's vital to ensure that end users have adopted the solution and that knowledge resources remain maintained.

Finalize Testing

The testing activities initiated in the realize phase are finalized. The following testing activities must be closed and confirmed before cutover to production:

- Integration validation
- Infrastructure and security tests
- Performance tests

Operation and Infrastructure Readiness

The technical infrastructure must be ready. Ensure the operations and support organization is prepared to run the converted solution. The activity provides a defined support approach for monitoring and measuring the day-to-day support operations. The following topics need to be covered:

- Roles and responsibilities
- Support processes, governance, and procedures
- Operations support tools and documentation
- Knowledge transfer

> **Service Components**
>
> SAP can support this activity with the Operations Readiness service component. It includes a status review of the IT operations changes defined during the operations impact evaluation. Ideally, the check is performed a couple of weeks before go-live.

Dress Rehearsal

Before performing the conversion of production, it's important to rehearse the process end to end in a test system. The rehearsal is intended to confirm the ownership, sequence, and duration of the conversion activities. The cookbook produced when converting the development system and quality assurance system is updated. There may be a need to postpone the go-live date if significant changes and critical items are raised as a result of this rehearsal. The cutover schedule is likely to be complex with many dependencies and owners from IT and business. Therefore, communication plays a crucial role in ensuring a successful production conversion.

Convert Production

The existing SAP ERP production system is converted to SAP S/4HANA during the cutover.

The main activities in production conversion are as follows:

- Request a restore point of the production system prior to the final conversion process.
- Execute the conversion of the production system following the cookbook developed during the rehearsals.
- Capture any variances to the plan along with decision makers who approved the change.
- The cutover managers should proactively notify task owners of upcoming tasks to ensure their availability.
- Regularly communicate the project status to stakeholders.
- Test and validate the system.
- Complete all required documentation for regulatory purposes.
- Obtain system sign-off.

Service Components

SAP offers the production conversion as part of the Platform Execution service. The service provides a variety of support packages that are highly standardized, cost-effective, and scalable.

System Go-Live and Hypercare Support

The system go-live is the final milestone of a successful SAP S/4HANA conversion project. The solution is now running live in the production environment, and the hypercare period follows to ensure seamless adoption of the new system.

Hypercare is the period that comes directly after the go-live. Its purpose is to support questions and issues that might arise. During this period, predefined checks will be executed daily to closely monitor adoption of the solution. It's essential to verify how the system behaves and improve system performance if needed.

The main activities in the hypercare period should include the following:

- Monitor resource consumption
- Analyze workload
- Perform system health check
- Perform sizing verification
- Monitor security

Handover to Support Organization

After the hypercare phase ends, it's crucial to fully enable the regular support organization to safely and securely operate the new SAP system. The following topics are covered:

- Finalizing system documentation
- Completing operational procedures as part of the operations handbook
- Checking the customer support organization
- Resolving and closing open issues
- Performing the handover from the project team to operations

8.3.5   Run Your Solution

The final phase of the SAP Activate methodology is the run phase. After the successful completion of the system conversion project, companies and project teams further optimize the operability of the new SAP S/4HANA solution. In this open-ended phase, the operations team must ensure that the system is running as intended. This phase also supports the continuous adoption of the solution by new users.

The main topics in the run phase include the following:

- Ongoing system operations
- Continuous OCM
- Continuous end user learning activities
- Continuous improvement and innovation
- System upgrade

System Conversion versus New Implementation

With the conversion project completed, the run phase is the same for both a new implementation and a system conversion. The key deliverables that we'll discuss in this section don't differ from Chapter 7, Section 7.2.7 and Section 7.3.7.

Ongoing System Operations

For on-premise SAP S/4HANA, it's essential to perform routine actions to ensure that the system is running as expected—for example, to maintain the systems in a functioning and operating condition, guaranteeing systems availability and required performance levels. With the project end, the company's support organization is responsible for operating the new solution, encompassing IT support people, processes, and tools.

The support organization should continuously improve and optimize the IT operations. This may include implementing automation and shifting from reactive to proactive approaches.

SAP MaxAttention

SAP has a large set of offerings for SAP MaxAttention customers for safe and efficient operations. For example, SAP can configure application operations in your environment and train your IT support experts in using the tools. If you want SAP to execute IT operational tasks, then SAP application management services can help you.

Continuous Organizational Change Management

The purpose of this activity is to continue the OCM tasks after go-live to ensure continuous solution adoption by relevant stakeholder groups. The change management team regularly measures end user adoption and plans and implements OCM activities by leveraging lessons learned. See Chapter 10 for more information.

Continuous End User Learning Activities

In the run phase, it's good practice to monitor the users after the training has been completed and regularly update the training materials to ensure they stay relevant. Processes must be in place to enable new users and upskill current users. Based on many years of experience with global software deployments, the SAP Training and Adoption organization has developed a continuous learning framework with clearly defined steps and training activities.

Further Resources

For more information on implementing the continuous learning framework from SAP, visit *www.sap.com/training*.

Continuous Improvement and Innovation

To support the business and end users, IT maintenance processes must be set in place to continuously improve the solution. This requires periodic updates by implementing Feature and Support Packs in order to bring the latest software updates from SAP into the solution. A planning cycle involving business and IT should identify innovations to be deployed.

> **Service Components**
>
> SAP offers various services to support the improvement and innovation cycle: business transformation services, business process improvement, and planning and execution of SAP maintenance.

SAP S/4HANA provides visibility into planned innovations in the SAP S/4HANA product roadmap, which is available at *www.sap.com/roadmaps*. The roadmap describes how the product capabilities are planned to progress over time. It provides information on recent innovations, planned innovations, and a summary of the future direction for the product.

System Upgrade

Companies that want to implement significant business change should revisit the overall strategy developed when moving to SAP S/4HANA. This may drive an upgrade focused on business change. Upgrades focused on technical goals should be planned in parallel. Technical upgrades keep the SAP system current by implementing corrections and selected innovations.

An upgrade is managed as a project. The upgrade process, including tools, phases, and activities, is covered as a separate roadmap in the SAP Activate Roadmap Viewer. A first check of the upgrade readiness of SAP S/4HANA is usually performed before the new upgrade project starts. This will reveal what administration activities must be done before the upgrade can start. The maintenance planner can be used to plan the change event.

SAP Solution Manager in the Run Phase

The following components of SAP Solution Manager can be used to operate and upgrade the SAP S/4HANA solution:

- **Application Operations**
  Provides central monitoring, alerting, analytics, and administration of SAP solutions.

- **Business Process Operations**

  Supports the productive operation of the core business processes across the SAP S/4HANA system and component.

- **Change Control Management**

  Controls change in system landscapes in a comprehensive workflow.

- **IT Service Management**

  Provides central message Management and processing.

- **Landscape Management**

  Provides information on IT landscapes as a basis for landscape operation and change planning of SAP-centric solutions. Helps companies to best manage and use the existing landscape and evolve it through new installations, support package and EHP updates, and system upgrades.

8.4   Selective Data Transition

Selective data transition is an alternative to the new implementation or system conversion approach and is relevant for companies moving from an existing SAP ERP solution to SAP S/4HANA. We recommend reading Chapter 7 on new implementations and Section 8.3 in this chapter on system conversions first because this section only describes the differences between those approaches and this one. As its name implies, this approach involves transferring data from one or more existing SAP ERP solutions to a new SAP S/4HANA solution. The transfer is done by SAP using specialized tools and services. There are some partners with their own tools and services. The data selectively transferred can include the following:

- ABAP repository of objects and developments
- Configuration (Customizing) data
- Master data
- Transaction data (historical closed items and open items)

There are two common approaches for the target system creation within selective data transition: shell conversion and mix and match. In *shell conversion*, a shell copy of a production system is made without master data and transaction data and is converted to SAP S/4HANA. In *mix and match*, a new SAP S/4HANA install is created, and then elements of the configuration and ABAP repository are transported or manually transferred. Both scenarios require data migration to follow, including master data, balances, and open items. A comparison of the approaches is shown in Table 8.1.

Criteria	System Conversion	Selective Data Transition		New Implementation
		Shell Conversion	Mix and Match	
Process reengineering	◔ Simplification items adopted during project; innovations usually done after conversion	◑ Org. structure changes; possible process changes in some areas	◕ Extensive changes in several areas, including org. structure changes	● Fundamental process redesign, including organizational restructuring
Data cleansing	◔ Optional archiving prior to the project; data inconsistencies to be fixed	◑ Selection of active data; cleansing on the fly is possible.	◕ Selection of active data; cleansing on the fly is possible	● New data construction—fully clean for new processes
Data transformation	◑ Only mandatory changes are adopted	◕ Structural and field mappings are possible	◕ Structural and field mappings are possible	● New data construction—fully clean for new processes
Phased go-live	○ Full system conversion, no phased approach possible	● Fully supported (per company code, ideally)	● Fully supported (per company code, ideally)	● Fully supported (per company code, ideally)
Historical data	● Full transactional history converted	● For example, per time slice, functional area, or org. unit	● For example, per time slice, functional area, or org. unit	○ Only master data and open items
System split or consolidation	○	● For either split or consolidation scenarios	● For either split or consolidation scenarios	● For either split or consolidation scenarios

Table 8.1 Comparison of Implementation Approaches

The data is moved using Data Management and Landscape Transformation (DMLT) software and related services. For more than 10 years, DMLT tools and services have provided well-established solutions for organizational changes, acquisitions, divestitures, or harmonization of SAP landscapes. The software provides highly automated processes that move large amounts of data between SAP instances quickly. Similar software and services are provided by third-party vendors but fall outside of SAP's support arrangements.

Selective data transition should be considered when organizations need to do the following:

- Go live in phases (e.g., by country or business unit)
- Reduce the risk of a big bang go-live
- Split or merge existing SAP ERP instances
- Leave behind large amounts of old data—for example, to reduce the duration of system conversions and cutovers
- Reduce reimplementation effort by reusing elements of the solution while redesigning others

The split and consolidation of SAP ERP instances is a large topic in its own right and won't be covered in detail in this book. Instead, this section focuses on how selective data transition can be used to phase go-lives and accelerate projects. This may be required in SAP ERP solutions with large data volumes or with many users in multiple countries.

The starting point is to create a parallel SAP S/4HANA sandbox or development system. A new clean install of SAP S/4HANA can be used (mix-and-match approach). Alternatively, you can use DMLT tools to create a shell copy of an existing SAP ERP system (shell conversion). The shell contains the ABAP repository and configuration data without master data or transaction data. A system conversion is done to turn this into an SAP S/4HANA instance. The conversion process is simpler and faster without the master data and transaction data, and certain simplification items can be more easily implemented without business data.

For selective data migration of master and transaction data, DMLT tools are used. If no historical transactions are required, and only open transaction items are needed, the SAP S/4HANA migration cockpit (direct transfer scenario) may be simpler. DMLT allows a time slice of historical transaction data to be migrated.

Let's consider an example project scenario using shell conversion. This assumes a two-stage project. The first stage is a technical transition followed by a second stage to implement business transformation innovations.

Let's walk through the phases of the first (technical) stage, which is led by a technical team:

- **Prepare phase**
  In the prepare phase of a selective data transition using shell conversion, you perform the following activities:
  - Engage DMLT or a partner to advise you on the approach. This may lead to preparation work in the existing SAP ERP system.
  - Analyze DMLT source system functionality—for example, using business process improvement in SAP Solution Manager.
  - Analyze the existing landscape using SAP Readiness Check for SAP S/4HANA and Process Discovery for SAP S/4HANA transformation.
  - Execute SAP S/4HANA preparation activities in the existing SAP ERP solution; for example, archive data to reduce the data footprint and remove unwanted custom code and configuration. In addition, perform customer-vendor integration (CVI) to make the business partner the lead object.

- **Explore phase**
  In the explore phase of selective data transition using shell conversion, you perform the following activities:
  - Create a new SAP S/4HANA sandbox system. Create a shell copy using a recent copy of a production SAP ERP instance.
  - Perform an SAP S/4HANA system conversion of the shell system.
  - Make configuration changes required to execute explore workshops.
  - Conduct fit-to-standard analysis and design, focusing on mandatory SAP S/4HANA simplification items.

- **Realize phase**
  In the realize phase of selective data transition using shell conversion, you perform the following activities:
  - Set up data migration tools and environment.
  - Create a new SAP S/4HANA development system using a shell copy of the sandbox system.
  - Set up a production support track for ongoing maintenance of the live solution.
  - Make configuration changes required for simplification items.
  - Adapt ABAP code for SAP S/4HANA.
  - Implement any changes required for integration and analytics solutions.
  - Execute multiple data migration test cycles using DMLT in the sandbox.
  - Set up a quality assurance system and production system with a copy of the SAP S/4HANA development shell without master data and transaction data.

- Test selective migration of master data and transaction data in the quality assurance system.
- Set up SAP Information Lifecycle Management (SAP ILM) and a retention warehouse to move old data into a low-cost infrastructure.
- Run integration and UAT.

■ **Deploy phase**

In the deploy phase of selective data transition using shell conversion, you perform the following activities:

- Rehearse the cutover.
- Migrate master data and, if required, historical transaction data into the production system.
- Cut over to the production system.
- Migrate open transaction item data and master data that has changed since the last migration cycle.

After the technical transition stage is complete, a second project stage can be kicked off to implement business transformation innovations (e.g., adoption of SAP Fiori apps). The second stage is led by the business.

This approach is flexible and can be adjusted depending on your organization's requirements. For example:

■ The first go-live could include the business transformation scope in addition to the technical conversion.

■ SAP S/4HANA preparation activities could be done in the sandbox rather than the existing SAP ERP solution.

■ In the explore phase, you might jump straight to a development system instead of using a sandbox. (The sandbox is still required later to do the test cycles of data migration).

■ During the technical transition, configuration and ABAP code adaption could be done in the sandbox system and then could be moved to the development system. This can reduce the duration of the production support track.

■ Multiple sequential go-lives could occur, with master and transaction data migrated as required (e.g., by country and company code).

■ You can selectively transfer business data and master data from multiple source SAP ERP systems. A prerequisite for working with multiple source systems is that the ABAP repository and configuration are compatible. Harmonization work is required in the prepare phase.

■ You can use the SAP S/4HANA migration cockpit only for selective data migration (excluding historic transactions), which can provide a more application-focused approach when compared to the technical migration involved in DMLT services. Less harmonization work may be required.

- The old production system may be decommissioned to a dormant status to access historic data and archived data.

The following DMLT scenarios may be relevant in selective data transition. Scenarios 1 and 2 are used in our previous example.

1. **Create shell system**
   Create a copy of a system without master and transaction data, which includes configuration (Customizing) and the ABAP repository.

2. **Company code transfer**
   Transfer data related to one company code from a source SAP ERP 6.0 system to a single client in the target SAP S/4HANA system. The scope can include master data and transaction data only or configuration (Customizing) with or without master data. This can include custom tables. Because data is merged at a client level, organization structure mapping may be required.

3. **Client transfer**
   Transfer configuration (Customizing), master data, and transaction data from a source system and client to a target SAP S/4HANA system. Where there is more than one source system, a client merge is possible.

4. **System merge**
   Combine master data and transaction data from two or more clients from different SAP ERP source systems into a target SAP ERP system. Configuration data isn't included. This is suitable for single and multiclient production systems.

In scenarios 2 to 4 with multiple source SAP ERP systems, the ABAP repository and configuration of the source systems must be compatible. These approaches require manual harmonization work in the source systems and target development system. Analysis tools that compare the source systems can identify the harmonization work required. The transformation can include data model conversion, Unicode conversion, and database changes to SAP HANA in one step. The project can take several months. Multiple test cycles are required in a dedicated sandbox system. SAP uses the test cycles to finalize configuration and generate programs to do the transfer.

Service Components

SAP offers the Data Migration Execution service to deliver DMLT solutions for SAP S/4HANA.

8.5   Summary

This chapter described how to transition from an existing SAP ERP solution to a new on-premise SAP S/4HANA or SAP S/4HANA Cloud, private edition solution following the SAP Activate methodology through the discover, prepare, explore, realize, and deploy phases. We've seen that three approaches can be used:

- New implementation, for existing SAP customers that want to start again and reimplement. This is covered in Chapter 7.
- System conversion, for existing SAP customers that want to convert to SAP S/4HANA with a big bang go-live.
- Selective data transition, for existing SAP customers that want to convert to SAP S/4HANA in phases or split or merge their existing SAP ERP instances.

Now that we've covered both cloud and on-premise deployment, we're left with a final option: hybrid. We'll discuss hybrid deployments in the next chapter, including the available business scenarios that organizations can use to maximize their existing technology investment while transitioning their business processes to the cloud.

Chapter 9
Deploying Hybrid System Landscapes

In this chapter, we will look into how SAP S/4HANA Cloud can be used to run two-tier deployment landscapes, examine various recommended deployment types, and deep dive into a few important end-to-end business processes available with such two-tier deployments of SAP S/4HANA Cloud.

Organizations across the globe are in the midst of a major transformation. Digital technologies are forcing them to reimagine their business models, business processes, and how they can create more value for their customers. As a result, many are opening sales offices in new regions and growing existing sales and distribution operations, acquiring new companies to either consolidate their position in existing market segments or expand into new areas, and setting up new joint ventures and centralized shared services for certain back-office functions (like HR, procurement, and travel management) to obtain efficiencies of scale and synergies from acquisitions.

From an IT perspective, the best approach for these subsidiaries is to standardize via an integrated business solution that meets their functional requirements and is less expensive to deploy, easier to change, and simpler to manage. Yet these systems should also satisfy corporate requirements, which typically include regulatory transparency, visibility into operational metrics, use of centralized business processes, and key data roll-up.

In today's competitive world, in which globalization is the mantra and organizations are expanding in order to grow, new markets are opening up and thus creating new opportunities for organizations. Each organization must decide how to run its business so that it remains competitive and meets customer needs faster than its competition. To achieve this, it needs to simplify its processes and get into new ventures through mergers and acquisitions.

To ensure efficiency, simplify processes, and drive innovations, organizations are moving away from complex processes and integrations and from the practice of maintaining disparate IT landscapes from different IT vendors. As shown in Figure 9.1, a complex IT landscape with complex integration doesn't help organizations standardize. In general, companies expect predelivered integrations from a software provider not only to accelerate the adoption journey but also to make it easier to maintain a system throughout its lifecycle.

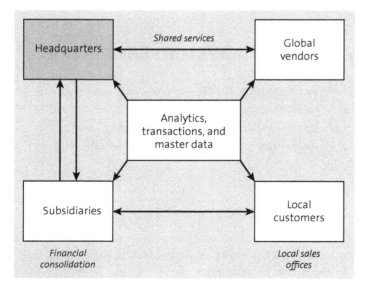

Figure 9.1 Complex IT Landscape

In this setup, data and processes are streaming through many different applications, vendors, and locations. Such high IT complexity results in misaligned business processes, inconsistent data models, and uncommon user experiences, which increases operational costs and reduces operational efficiency. Another result is limited governance and compliance across subsidiaries, which increases the risk for organizations.

Companies have the option to reimagine business processes by extracting simplified processes from complex ones and using simple and standardized integrations. For new acquisitions, an organization needs simple solutions, a faster way of onboarding them to the mainstream ERP system, and the ability to innovate fast with simple integration.

The answer to all these issues is a two-tier ERP setup. In this chapter, we'll explain this two-tier ERP setup and master data, walk through key deployment scenarios, explore integration accelerators, and discuss analytics options.

9.1   What Is a Two-Tier ERP Setup?

The hybrid ERP setup is shown in Figure 9.2; in the SAP world, this is known as a *two-tier ERP setup*. In this scenario, the complex processes continue to run in their proven on-premise applications, shown in the top half of Figure 9.2; meanwhile, simplified and standard processes shift into a cloud-based ERP system, shown in the bottom half of Figure 9.2, for business functions or subsidiaries.

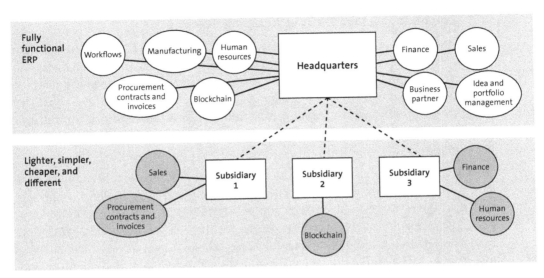

Figure 9.2 Two-Tier ERP

A two-tier ERP setup can be deployed in the following ways, as shown in Figure 9.3:

- Headquarters and subsidiaries
- Central services
- Ecosystem

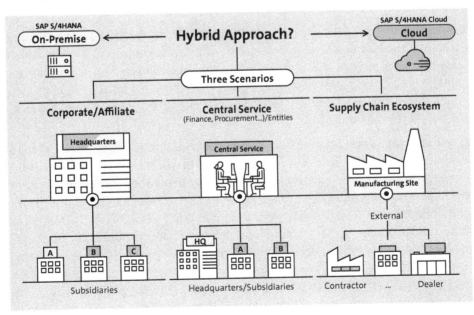

Figure 9.3 Deployment Possibilities

We'll look into these options in detail in subsequent sections.

9.1.1 Corporate Headquarters and Subsidiary Setup

The headquarters and subsidiaries setup is most applicable when organizations are growing inorganically by expanding into different geographies through mergers and acquisitions; in this scenario, if subsidiaries are not integrated with the headquarters' ERP system, then the organization cannot reap true growth benefits in this competitive world. Consequently, these expanding organizations need to integrate all subsidiaries rapidly and affordably to achieve real-time global visibility and efficiency in their business processes.

SAP's software as a service (SaaS) solution for two-tier ERP deployment provides standard integration scenarios between the headquarters and subsidiaries through SAP S/4HANA Cloud for the subsidiaries and on-premise SAP S/4HANA, SAP S/4HANA Cloud, private edition, or a non-SAP system for the headquarters. This hybrid ERP model between a headquarters and its subsidiaries helps organizations safeguard their investments while equipping global subsidiaries with more agile and flexible cloud-based software.

Subsidiaries require a degree of agility to meet their markets' needs quickly and innovate at their own pace; consequently, they need their own ERP systems to control their own destinies. Having a cloud ERP system means subsidiaries don't have to worry about infrastructure, hardware, and IT management.

9.1.2 Central Services Setup

To remain competitive in the current market, organizations need to start reimagining and reexamining their business processes. Part of this procedure is to identify which business processes are complex and which can run on a shared setup. Organizations can think of different business models in which certain business functions can be seen as profit centers or shared services—which brings us to the topic of line of business (LoB) functions in the cloud.

Imagine that a global organization has multiple ERP systems in different geographical locations, or even a single instance of an ERP system in which multicounty operations are carried out. For example, a global organization in the automobile industry might have operations in multiple countries with different business models and different business strategies to meet the customer requirements. If you take the procurement as a central service, the local entity will follow its own terms and conditions, but headquarters will have standard guidelines that might not be followed at local subsidiaries. Such an organization would have a complex architecture and complex business processes. If the organization has all the legal entities from different geographies in a single instance, then the processes that were defined initially will be forced on subsidiaries in a new market, and it may no longer be possible for such subsidiaries to change their processes to add a local flavor; unfortunately, this can restrict the growth of the organization and limit innovation.

Certain business units like localized subsidiaries may need to modify pricing models to meet their specific market requirements, but if they've inherited old pricing models, then they can't change them because it will impact all other business; hence, they have to work within certain boundaries. So there is a need to reimagine the business processes, but it can't be done because of the limitations built over a period of time. This situation can result in high costs for IT maintenance for running operations.

Cloud ERP systems have opened the possibility of looking at business functions differently. Organizations that are struggling to reimagine their business functions can make use of cloud solutions; for example, the organization in our hypothetical situation could shift its entire finance function to a cloud-based ERP system.

With two-tier ERP systems, the cloud solution can be integrated easily with on-premise systems without losing control. Organizations can think of using shared services to manage their finance functions separately to control their costs. Thus, cloud ERP and a two-tier ERP setup open immense possibilities for organizations to reimagine and redesign their business processes, which will result in great benefits and remaining competitive.

The example of moving the finance functions to the cloud for a global organization applies to nonglobal/local organizations as well. For example, IT services are normally central business functions that serve the entire organization and its LoBs. Organizations can reimagine their business functions to see IT as a profit center as well or outsource IT by taking it to the cloud without losing control. IT business functions can still carry out their business processes, can innovate at a faster speed to make their processes efficient, and can even apply new innovations by contracting IT services from third parties.

9.1.3   Supply Chain Ecosystem

An *ecosystem* is a closed environment in which entities are both interdependent and connected. A classic example is the case of the automotive dealers for an automobile company.

Some organizations don't require a headquarters and subsidiaries setup but still want to adopt cloud systems and have a two-tier ERP setup.

Let's again take the example of an organization in the automobile industry, in which the organization deals with multiple small vendors or dealers; each vendor and dealer operates its own disconnected systems. In this situation, the organization doesn't currently have visibility across its entire supply chain. Some companies aspire to build networks of their small vendors or dealers by encouraging everyone to implement a cloud solution that can be easily connected to the organization's ERP system. Here, the dealers that sell the organization's finished goods will place orders with the organization, and the organization will issue the finished goods to the dealers. In such cases, if the dealers are on a cloud solution connected to the organization's ERP system, then the organization itself will have visibility into dealers' stocks of finished goods and can subsequently better plan future manufacturing of its finished goods. On the other hand, if the dealers place orders in the cloud solution to fill end customer requests for the finished goods, then a sales order can be created automatically in the organization's ERP system, which will be considered a demand for manufacturing planning. Thus, in the connected network, the organization will get complete visibility across the entire supply chain.

Similarly, an organization could connect its ERP system to vendors running a cloud solution, which would result in collaborative manufacturing with its suppliers. An organization can also track the stages of manufacturing, as well as the inventory of raw materials available from its suppliers. Such visibility at the suppliers' end gives organizations the power to have accurate materials planning, thus reducing the cost of carrying inventory; now they can know how much raw materials to order for the day's production.

These are the points of view organizations can consider if they want visibility across the supply chain; a two-tier ERP system from SAP will help organizations achieve this goal.

In an IT context, a strong cloud ecosystem provides businesses with an easy way to find and purchase business applications and accordingly reimagine their business processes for changing business needs. Strong cloud ecosystems can host applications from various vendors. A single app store enables access to a catalog of different vendors' software and services that are already validated and checked for various threats. This helps safeguard data and keeps the customer purchase prices for business applications optimal.

Companies can validate the cloud ecosystems in this changing business environment, which will help them to arrive at new business models to serve their customers more efficiently and more competitively. For example, a company that manufactures compressors can launch a new product, compression as a service, on cloud infrastructure alongside its main business selling compressors. The best applications for this new service line are already in the ecosystem.

For another example, companies can serve their customers by having their sales offices running in the cloud, while their main business of manufacturing products at their manufacturing centers or headquarters will continue to run in their legacy ERP systems. It is now possible for organizations to analyze patterns across various entities and use machine learning technologies to infer and arrive at business-critical decisions. With cloud ERP systems, new technologies like artificial intelligence (AI) are arriving every quarter, which allows organizations to continuously innovate with their data to become more efficient and competitive.

It's also important to have a great ecosystem of software partners that provide various services in the cloud ecosystem. Partners should ensure that costs are not high for the customers and that their applications are built to scale with the business and have regular updates. The partners also should provide functionality that meets business requirements, as well as provide enough flexibility within the applications to meet the required business needs. The true essence of a cloud ecosystem is the collective set of capabilities from multiple partners and third parties enabling their services in the cloud ecosystem, developed depending on each other and helping to generate best practices and new business models.

Thus, a cloud ecosystem will help organizations to grow in this competitive world by changing business models per the requirements of the market.

Further Resources

Refer to the white paper titled *Two-Tier ERP Deployment for SAP S/4HANA Cloud: A Practical Guide for Senior Leadership*, available at *http://s-prs.co/v546319*.

9.2   Move Options

In this section, we look at move options that will help customers transition from an existing landscape to a two-tier ERP landscape.

Essentially, this boils down to two ways to transition for existing SAP ERP customers:

1. **Monolith-to-federated landscape**

   Many customers want to embrace the SaaS world by using two-tier ERP as vehicle to get into the cloud world. For example, large organizations have chosen to implement SAP S/4HANA Cloud in one of their standard subsidiaries. That means existing on-premise SAP ERP systems can be still connected to cloud solutions so that customers have a phased approach to transition into the SaaS world. A two-tier ERP setup gives companies a way to leverage the best of both the on-premise and cloud worlds while planning to embrace the SaaS world in the future, as shown in Figure 9.4.

2. **Federated-to-federated landscape**

   We see in many large enterprises the existence of multiple ERP instances to take care of various entities worldwide; for them, it's a matter of mapping systems to the cloud and then planning the move.

   A federated-to-federated landscape is applicable when organizations plan to transition to a public cloud solution by deploying multiple cloud ERP instances in a distributed manner. To better illustrate, let's take the headquarters-subsidiaries setup as an example deployment option for this move option. However, this will work too for other variants of deployment: corporate subsidiary, central services, and supply chain ecosystem setup. Figure 9.5 shows the move option from a highly federated landscape leaning toward on-premise to a federated landscape, which is a more hybrid option with a mix of cloud and on-premise.

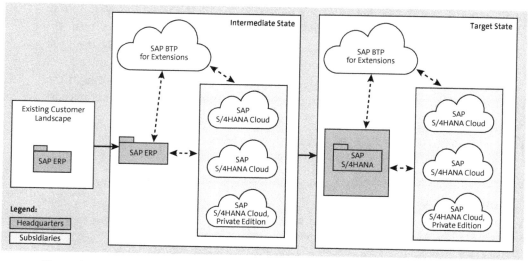

Figure 9.4 Monolith-to-Federated Landscape

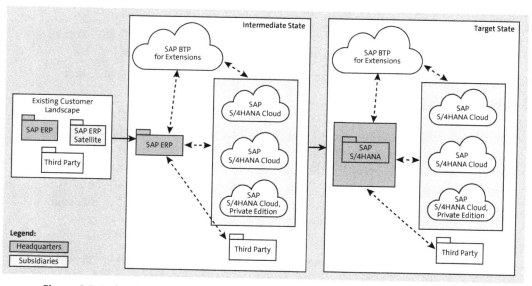

Figure 9.5 Federated-to-Federated Landscape

Many existing SAP ERP customers run a single monolith ERP instance. Such a landscape inhibits the freedom for smaller, nimble entities in their conglomerate to innovate at a pace faster than headquarters/corporate entities.

For such landscapes, it's ideal to move subsidiaries to the cloud as a first step before considering moving their headquarters to the cloud or to on-premise SAP S/4HANA.

A two-tier ERP setup provides standard end-to-end business processes between subsidiaries running SAP S/4HANA cloud and the headquarters running on-premise ERP. This ensures that subsidiaries moving to the cloud get to consume innovation faster, stay standard, and be nimble, and yet do not lose the flexibility demanded by corporate leadership or headquarters to have better visibility into and control of subsidiaries.

The extensions are developed on SAP Business Technology Platform (SAP BTP) so that it remains decoupled and is not affected by upgrade cycles/innovation cycles effected with SAP S/4HANA Cloud. Once the intermediate state is achieved, the SAP ERP system at the headquarters can transformed to SAP S/4HANA Cloud (public or private cloud) or on-premise SAP S/4HANA.

If a company has a federated landscape, a similar approach as that for the monolith to federated landscape setup applies. In addition, the integration between SAP ERP systems and third-party systems needs to be working after the upgrade. To ensure the integration works with upgrades, it is advisable to use allowlisted objects.

9.3   Master Data

In any two-tier ERP deployment, master data plays an important role. The need to create and manage master data centrally is vital. In this section, we will cover how business partners, product masters, and some financial master data elements can be managed centrally in a two-tier ERP deployment with SAP S/4HANA Cloud. Then we'll discuss the recommended replication options for managing master data in a two-tier ERP deployment.

Master data can be classified as global master data or local master data. *Global master data* is the component of master data that needs to be consistent between the headquarters and subsidiaries. For example, in the context of business partners (i.e., customers or suppliers), the global master data can include names, contact numbers, and so on. Similarly, for product masters, the master data can include product names, general item categories, and so on.

Local master data is the master data component that is different across the headquarters and subsidiaries. The most common example is the sales area–specific data for business partners in which you specify parameters such as the delivering plant, delivery priority, and so on. Similarly, for a product master, this can be plant-specific data.

SAP recommends a few deployment options in which centrally maintained master data can be made available to a subsidiary cloud system running SAP S/4HANA Cloud. Let's look at each one now.

In the first scenario, a subsidiary runs SAP S/4HANA Cloud; meanwhile, its headquarters runs the SAP Master Data Governance (SAP MDG) master data management tool alongside SAP S/4HANA or SAP ERP. In this case, replication is handled through the data replication framework (DRF).

In the second scenario, the subsidiary runs SAP S/4HANA Cloud, but its headquarters does not run SAP MDG alongside SAP S/4HANA or SAP ERP. In this case, either data replication is handled through the DRF, or data movement happens via allowlisted APIs.

The data replication/movement mechanism is dependent on what master data element is made available to a subsidiary running SAP S/4HANA Cloud. For example, in case of master data for the business partner and product master, real-time replication can be achieved using the DRF, whereas for financials master data like the cost center, replication can be achieved using allowlisted APIs.

Let's take a closer look at the DRF, followed by allowlisted APIs.

9.3.1   Data Replication Framework

The DRF is used to replicate master data elements from the SAP MDG hub system (as shown in Figure 9.6) or directly from SAP S/4HANA or SAP ERP without SAP MDG to target connected systems (as shown in Figure 9.7). In both cases, SAP S/4HANA Cloud is the target system.

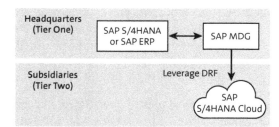

Figure 9.6 Data Replication Framework with SAP MDG

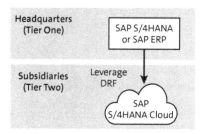

Figure 9.7 Data Replication Framework without SAP MDG

Further Resources

For more information on data replication, visit *http://s-prs.co/v546318*.

Using the DRF offers the following advantages:

- One-time setup
- Real-time replication support
- Monitor loads and control reloads
- Delta replication support

The following core master data elements are supported using this approach:

- Business partner
- Product master

System Setup

For setting up replication via the DRF, two communication scenarios are of interest on the SAP S/4HANA Cloud system:

- SAP_COM_0008
- SAP_COM_0009

The following are the most important steps to take in the SAP S/4HANA Cloud system:

1. Create a communication user.
2. Maintain communication systems pointing to a host SAP S/4HANA or SAP ERP system.
3. Maintain communication arrangements for inbound and outbound services.
4. Enable SAP Application Interface Framework to monitor inbound and outbound message flows.

Further Resources

For more additional information on detailed setup instructions, refer to the setup guide *Setting Up Integration of SAP S/4HANA Cloud to SAP Master Data Governance (1RO)* at *https://rapid.sap.com/bp/#/scopeitems/1RO*.

Field and Value Mappings

In two-tier ERP setups, company codes are commonly set up one way in the headquarters system and another way in the subsidiary systems. This necessitates field mapping, which in SAP S/4HANA Cloud is done using the Cross-System Company Codes configuration app. To maintain a company code mapping, first create a list of global company codes, and then assign those global company codes to local company codes.

> **Further Resources**
>
> For more details, refer to the following apps in SAP S/4HANA Cloud:
>
> - Configure Cross-Company Code
> - Cross-Company Assign

Similar to a company code, other system-internal codes can correspond to code lists in the external system. You can use value mapping to synchronize these. Run the two SAP Fiori apps highlighted in Figure 9.8, **Maintain Value Mapping** and **Assign Code Lists to Elements and Systems**, to accomplish this.

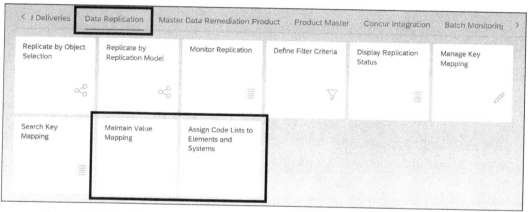

Figure 9.8 Value Mapping in Data Replication

> **Business Partner Replication**
>
> Consider the following pointers for business partner replication via the DRF:
>
> - If the business partner number being replicated centrally already exists in your SAP S/4HANA Cloud system, then that number is updated.
> - If the business partner number being replicated centrally does not exist in your SAP S/4HANA Cloud system, then a new business partner with the same number is created with the same account grouping as in the source system.
> - If the account group does not match, you need to enable a flexible account group; otherwise, the system will produce an error.

9.3.2   API-Based Replication

SAP S/4HANA Cloud also provides allowlisted APIs to propagate master data changes to a subsidiary running SAP S/4HANA Cloud. For example, let's consider the Profit Center: Create, Update, Delete API. This inbound service enables you to create, update, and delete profit center master data through Simple Object Access Protocol (SOAP) messages. The allowlisted API can be used to propagate changes from a source system into the target SAP S/4HANA Cloud system.

Compared to the DRF approach, the API-based approach can be used to handle many more master data elements centrally; all we need is a allowlisted API on SAP S/4HANA Cloud. Handling master data changes via allowlisted APIs also provides the added advantage of enriching data before propagating it into target subsidiary systems.

> **Further Resources**
>
> For a complete listing of all available allowlisted APIs, refer to the SAP API Business Hub for SAP S/4HANA Cloud at *https://api.sap.com*.

SAP recommends two tools for data enrichment via middleware:

1. SAP Process Orchestration
2. The Cloud Integration capability on SAP Integration Suite

Let's look at each one now.

SAP Process Orchestration

SAP Process Orchestration is on-premise, installable middleware that supports application-to-application (A2A) and business-to-business (B2B) integration. It can integrate a variety of applications and supports custom-developed interface adapters.

As shown in Figure 9.9, the master data changes in the source or hub system can be propagated to SAP S/4HANA Cloud, with support for data transformation, manipulation, and enrichment through the modeled process flows in SAP Process Orchestration.

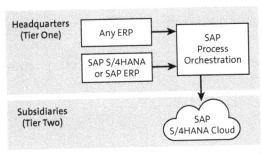

Figure 9.9 Transformation with SAP Process Orchestration

Cloud Integration

The Cloud Integration capability is cloud-based middleware available as part of SAP Integration Suite on SAP BTP that makes cloud-based integration simple and easy to consume. It offers out-of-the-box connectivity across cloud and on-premise solutions using prepackaged content and supports custom adapter software development kits (SDKs).

As shown in Figure 9.10, in a two-tier ERP deployment, the Cloud Integration capability comes in handy for transforming, enriching, and manipulating data before it is propagated to a system running SAP S/4HANA Cloud. This is helpful, for example, to enrich profit center master data with additional custom fields or handle mappings between two systems.

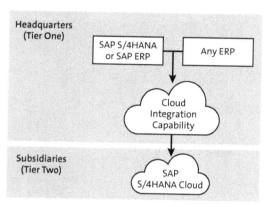

Figure 9.10 Transformation with Cloud Integration

Now that we've discussed master data in a two-tier ERP setup, let's turn our attention to how SAP S/4HANA Cloud accomplishes processes specific to two-tier ERP systems in LoBs like finance, sales, services, procurement, manufacturing, and sustainability.

9.4   Finance

Finance is a core function for every company because every organization's success and sustainability largely depend on efficient management of its finances.

In this section, you see key finance scenario highlights in a two-tier ERP system with SAP S/4HANA Cloud running at subsidiary companies.

9.4.1   Financial Planning

Financial planning involves determining the capital required across a business to meet its strategic goals and objectives for a given period. Financial plan data is created for different dimensions: cost centers, market segments, functional areas, and much more.

For companies working in a two-tier ERP deployment model, consolidated financial planning for the entire corporate group is performed in one of two ways. In a *top-down approach*, financial planning is done at the headquarters for the entire business and then cascaded to the subsidiaries. On the other hand, in a *bottom-up approach*, the subsidiaries provide a financial plan proposal to the headquarters, and the headquarters then consolidates the same for all the subsidiaries for group-level financial planning.

Two-tier ERP financial planning is a common practice for organizations with the following goals:

- Mobilizing cash from different subsidiaries so that the requisite finances are made available at any given time
- Identifying the revenue-generating areas in a business and assisting in investing accordingly
- Giving headquarters absolute transparency into financial processes, thanks to real-time visibility into the financial and consolidation activities at subsidiaries
- Reducing forecasting errors and the effort involved in collecting data from multiple sources

SAP provides the following options for financial planning in a two-tier ERP setup:

- Integrated financial planning using SAP Analytics Cloud
- Group reporting planning using SAP Analytics Cloud
- Financial planning and analysis with SAP Analytics Cloud
- Planning using SAP Business Planning and Consolidation (SAP BPC)

Let's look at all these options now.

Integrated Financial Planning Using SAP Analytics Cloud

Headquarters and subsidiary companies on SAP S/4HANA, both on-premise and in the cloud, can use integrated financial planning for profit and loss (P&L) and balance sheet planning in SAP Analytics Cloud, as shown in Figure 9.11. SAP Analytics Cloud is fully integrated and allows the import of actual data from SAP S/4HANA Cloud, SAP S/4HANA, SAP SuccessFactors, and SAP Integrated Business Planning (SAP IBP). It comes with predefined business content with demo data and supports planning on actual data from different connected systems with integrations in financial planning processes, including the cost center, product cost, sales and profitability, investments, P&L, balance sheets, and cash flow planning. The different planning areas seamlessly integrate; for example, the consensus demand plan quantity from SAP IBP flows into sales quantity planning, workforce planning from SAP SuccessFactors flows into cost center planning, cost center planning provides the activity cost rates for product cost planning, and product cost planning provides the product cost rates for the cost of goods sold calculation within profitability planning. In the end, a complete plan P&L, balance sheet, and cash flow statement are derived.

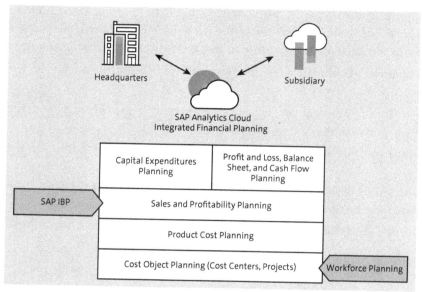

Figure 9.11 Integrated Financial Planning Using SAP Analytics Cloud

The plan values can be transferred back to planning table ACDOCP, and this plan data is available in analytical reports for comparison with the actuals like Cost Center – Plan/Actuals, Cost Center – Plan/Actuals YTD, Internal Order – Plan/Actuals, and Internal Order – Plan/Actuals YTD. Activity cost rates and planned statistical key figures can also be exported back. The plan data from table ACDOCP can be consolidated into group reporting table ACDOCU.

The *simulation cockpit* in an analytical application within the integrated financial planning package in SAP Analytics Cloud allows you to perform what-if simulations for integrated financial planning processes based on changes to drivers, such as sales quantity, raw material prices or personnel expenses. It enables three types of simulations:

1. *Raw material price simulation* allows you to simulate the impact of changes in raw material price on product cost, profitability, and P&L planning.

2. *Expense simulation* allows you to simulate the impact of changes in cost center expenses to product cost, profitability, P&L, and cash flow planning.

3. *Sales simulation* allows you to simulate the impact of changes in sales prices and quantity planning to product cost, profitability, P&L, and cash flow planning.

Scope Item

The required SAP S/4HANA Cloud scope item for integrated financial planning is 4RC, and for import connection setup with SAP Analytics Cloud it's 1YB.

The required communication arrangement is SAP_COM_0087—SAP Analytics Cloud.

Group Reporting Planning Using SAP Analytics Cloud

Subsidiary companies on SAP or non-SAP systems can send actual financial data to the headquarters on SAP S/4HANA Cloud or on-premise. The headquarters then can perform the consolidation and group reporting, as shown in Figure 9.12. This actual data can then be sent to SAP Analytics Cloud for group reporting planning. Group reporting planning in SAP Analytics Cloud is based on the SAP S/4HANA data model and is fully integrated with it. Planning administrators can prepopulate planning screens based on past actual data.

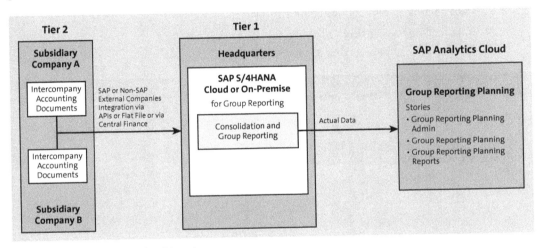

Figure 9.12 Group Reporting Planning

Group reporting planning allows the headquarters to plan the P&L and balance sheet at the group level based on the group reporting dimensions such as the consolidation unit, functional area, financial statement item, and partner consolidation units in SAP Analytics Cloud.

The group reporting planning for SAP S/4HANA business content in SAP Analytics Cloud comes with prebuilt packages including a model, stories, and data actions, as shown in Figure 9.13.

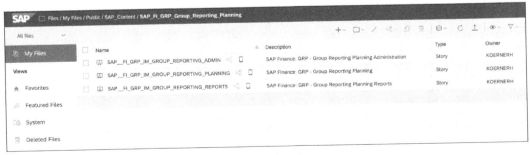

Figure 9.13 Prebuilt Packages for Group Reporting Planning

The group reporting planning story allows the planner to perform planning by editing last year's actual amounts and carrying forward the balance sheet. Figure 9.14 shows different views for group reporting planning. The details options include the following:

- **P&L Planning w/Hierarchy**
  Plan P&L statement.

- **P&L Planning by Partner**
  Plan P&L statement by partner.

- **Balance Sheet—Changing**
  Plan balance sheet (changing amount).

- **Balance Sheet—Closing**
  Plan balance sheet (closing amount).

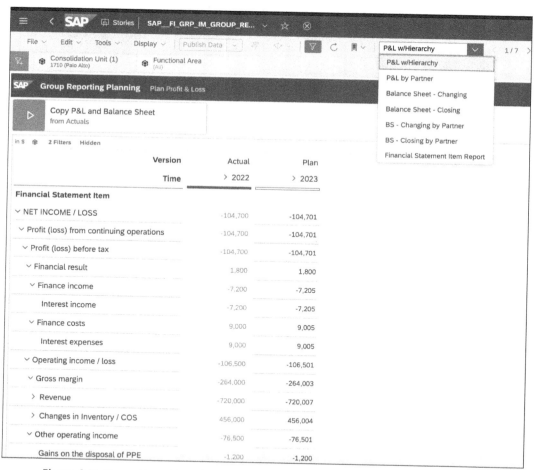

Figure 9.14 Group Reporting Planning

- **BS—Planning by Partner**
  Plan balance sheet (changing amount by partner).

- **BS—Closing by Partner**
  Plan balance sheet (closing amount by partner).

- **Financial Statement Item Report**
  View financial statement item report.

- **Copy Actual Amounts to Plan**
  Allows you to copy last year's actual net income and balance sheet amounts to a plan version as a starting point for planning. Ensure that you first delete all P&L and balance sheet plan amounts.

- **Calculate Balance Sheet Changing**
  Allows you to carry forward balance amounts to the next periods after manual changes to the changing balance amounts and performs calculations for cash balance and accumulated depreciation/amortization.

- **Calculate Balance Sheet Closing**
  Allows you to carry forward balance amounts to the next periods after manual changes to the closing balance amounts and performs calculations for cash balance and accumulated depreciation/amortization.

Group reporting reports, as shown in Figure 9.15, allow the planner to analyze the P&L and balance sheet based on consolidation unit, partner consolidation unit, and functional area. The different reports available for group reporting planning are as follows:

- **Profit & Loss**
  View P&L statement.

- **FS Item Report**
  View P&L statement and balance sheet with financial statement item details.

- **FS Item Report by Trans Type**
  View P&L statement and balance sheet by transaction type.

- **P&L by FuncArea**
  View P&L by functional area.

Scope Item

The required SAP S/4HANA Cloud scope item for group reporting planning on SAP Analytics Cloud is 5PU.

The required communication arrangement needed is SAP_COM_0087—SAP Analytics Cloud.

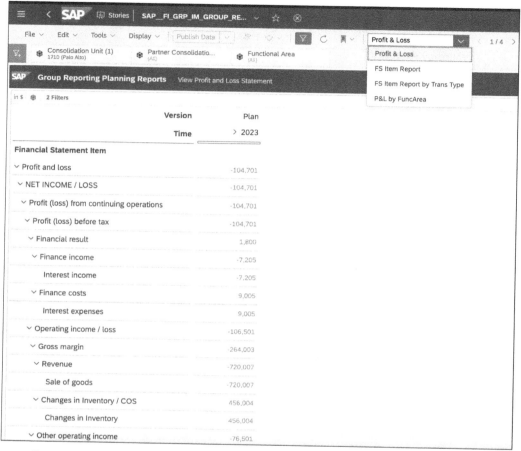

Figure 9.15 Group Reporting Reports

Financial Planning and Analysis with SAP Analytics Cloud

SAP S/4HANA offers financial planning and analysis in SAP Analytics Cloud based on SAP S/4HANA financial structures. A headquarters on SAP S/4HANA (on-premise) and subsidiaries on SAP S/4HANA Cloud can connect to SAP Analytics Cloud as a centralized planning tool. The solution includes a model, reports, dashboards, and a preconfigured integration process. The solution includes financial planning and analysis for P&Ls (including cost center and profit center planning), balance sheets, and cash flow. The multicurrency solution includes a set of financial analysis reports to enable variance analysis, trend analysis, year-over-year reporting, and financial statement analysis.

Scope Item

The required SAP S/4HANA Cloud scope item for SAP Analytics Cloud is 2EB. Refer to SAP Best Practices Explorer for more details on this scope item.

Planning Using SAP Business Planning Consolidation

In this approach, the headquarters is running on-premise SAP S/4HANA with SAP BPC, and the subsidiary is running SAP S/4HANA Cloud. The headquarters can trigger the group-level financial planning for the entire business and share the plan data with the subsidiaries, as shown in Figure 9.16. SAP BPC optimized for SAP S/4HANA provides the embedded modeling option. Actuals are sourced from table ACDOCA and plan data is stored in table ACDOCP. Companies who need to support business requirements on an existing on-premise installation for regulatory, policy, or complex requirements can continue using SAP BPC for planning. A hybrid solution where SAP Analytics Cloud serves as a frontend on top of SAP BPC is also possible. Architectural elegance is the area where SAP Analytics Cloud excels over all the SAP BPC variants and beats SAP BPC in every aspect. Functionalities that are now spread over the different products variants of SAP BPC are being unified in one cloud product, SAP Analytics Cloud, and it offers ease of use, plus a fully integrated and very strong reporting and dashboarding toolset. SAP Analytics Cloud also integrates with other data sources, like SAP Success-Factors, Salesforce, and SAP IBP.

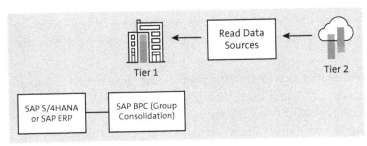

Figure 9.16 Planning Using SAP BPC

Further Resources

For detailed insights on planning in SAP BPC, see *https://www.sap.com/products/bpc.html*. For details on planning in SAP Analytics Cloud, see *https://www.sap.com/products/cloud-analytics.html*.

Plan Data Retraction

Plan data retraction from SAP Analytics Cloud to SAP S/4HANA Cloud is possible via a flat file. In all three approaches for financial planning with SAP Analytics Cloud, financial planning data can be imported into subsidiaries running SAP S/4HANA Cloud via ready-to-use CSV-formatted Microsoft Excel templates that are delivered as part of the SAP Best Practices content. Currently, the following planning dimensions can be imported into SAP S/4HANA Cloud:

- Profit center planning
- Functional area planning
- Market segment planning
- Internal order planning

- P&L planning
- Balance sheet planning
- Cost center planning

Scope Item

The required SAP S/4HANA Cloud scope item is 1HB. Refer to SAP Best Practices Explorer for more details on this scope item.

Before you can upload plan data into SAP S/4HANA Cloud, first confirm that all organizational unit and master data mentioned for planning already exists in the SAP S/4HANA Cloud system. Then check whether any plan data has previously been uploaded in the system. This can be verified using the Plan vs. Actual app, available for each of the planning dimensions (e.g., cost center, profit center, market segment, etc.). If no plan data exists in the system for any combination of these characteristics, then the plan data can be imported directly. But if plan data *does* already exist in the system for any of these characteristics, the Plan vs. Actual app displays the affected values and assumes that the existing plan data should be completely replaced by the new plan data upload.

After all the prerequisites are met, you can import the plan data into the system using the Upload Financial Data app. This app checks whether the values in the source file are valid. If not, the system returns a list of error messages. If all values are valid, the app checks all categories, ledgers, company codes, fiscal years, and posting periods.

To upload the plan data, click on the **Browse** button and select the plan data file. The plan data then will be successfully imported into the SAP S/4HANA Cloud subsidiary. You can now compare the current actual data with the imported plan data in the Plan vs. Actual app for each of the planning dimensions and even export the report result to a Microsoft Excel document. This can be used by the headquarters as a basis for planning for future periods.

9.4.2   Advanced Financial Closing

The existing traditional financial closing process has huge potential for optimization. Customers can now streamline and optimize the financial closing process with SAP S/4HANA for advanced financial closing.

Advanced financial closing on SAP BTP can seamlessly be integrated with heterogeneous systems landscapes. It supports the planning, execution, monitoring, and analysis with workflow-supported processes of period-end closing tasks for all entities (i.e., typically the headquarters and all subsidiaries) of a corporation, as shown in Figure 9.17.

Customers benefit from the standardized process, faster closing cycle, high-quality compliant results, end-to-end monitoring through embedded analytics, situation handling, automation using SAP Intelligent Robotic Process Automation (SAP Intelligent RPA), and transparency across all subsidiaries and headquarters companies.

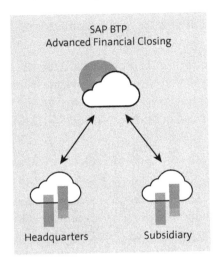

Figure 9.17 Advanced Financial Closing

Customers get many SAP Fiori–based apps for advanced financial closing on SAP BTP. Figure 9.18 shows the SAP S/4HANA for advanced financial closing dashboard.

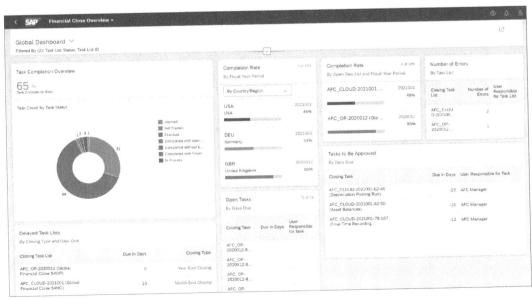

Figure 9.18 Advanced Financial Closing Dashboard

An accountant manager can use the Financial Close Overview app, which gives the overall closing task completion count and completion rate for the subsidiary and headquarters companies on SAP S/4HANA Cloud and on-premise SAP S/4HANA. He or she can further navigate to the closing tasks with errors to review the details and understand the dependencies of the task and impact on delays. Automatic or manual email notifications can be sent to the processing users, notifying them about an error or a delay in the task.

The processing user logs into advanced financial closing to get the overview of the closing tasks in his or her list and processes them. He or she can seamlessly navigate from advanced financial closing on SAP BTP to connected subsidiary systems on SAP S/4HANA Cloud and the headquarters system, typically an on-premise SAP S/4HANA system, with a single click of the **Process** button.

The processing of tasks can be automated for completion by using SAP Intelligent RPA.

Advanced financial closing provides out-of-the-box integration for companies with deployment needs for SAP ERP, SAP S/4HANA, SAP S/4HANA Cloud, and also Central Finance scenarios. Users can plug in advanced financial closing as a modular ERP extension in SAP BTP to further optimize the closing process. Also, the Cloud Integration Automation service, part of SAP BTP, makes the adoption of advanced financial closing easy for customers.

> **Scope Item**
>
> The required SAP S/4HANA Cloud scope item for advanced financial closing is 4HG, and the relevant communication scenario is SAP_COM_0566. Refer to SAP Best Practices Explorer for more details of this scope item.

9.4.3   Intercompany Reconciliation Automation

The traditional process of intercompany reconciliation (ICR) is tedious and labor-intensive. Subsidiaries traditionally required a lot of communication to resolve discrepancies, and at the headquarters it was difficult to reconcile due to large volumes of data taking a much longer time for group closing.

These drawbacks of the traditional approach are overcome with the advanced intercompany matching and reconciliation (ICMR) solution available with SAP S/4HANA Cloud or on-premise, which offers predefined rules for auto matching. Users can also get intercompany accounting document auto-matching proposals using the intelligent machine learning ICR service on SAP BTP. These innovations provide automation and modernization and increase matching accuracy and transparency among headquarters subsidiary companies, streamlining the local closing to corporate closing and speeding up the entity closing to group closing process.

As shown in Figure 9.19, subsidiary companies on SAP or non-SAP systems can send the intercompany accounting documents to headquarters running on SAP S/4HANA Cloud or on-premise through file upload or API or via the Central Finance solution. Within the headquarters, the intercompany documents will be first matched by predefined rules, and the remaining unmatched documents can be sent to the intelligent ICR service on SAP BTP, which will do the line-item matching and reason code assignment and will send the matched documents proposal back to the headquarters system.

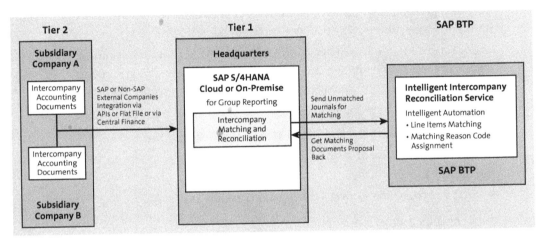

Figure 9.19 Intelligent ICR

Prerequisites for intelligent ICR include the following:

- **Provision ICR service on SAP BTP**
  As a prerequisite and one-time activity, provisioning of the ICR service is required on SAP BTP.
- **Schedule machine learning training job**
  A minimum of three months past data in the system is recommended to schedule the training job.

Scope Items

The required SAP S/4HANA Cloud scope items for intercompany reconciliation automation are 4LG and 40Y. The relevant communication scenarios for the setup are SAP_COM_0553 and SAP_COM_0377. Refer to SAP Best Practices Explorer for more details on these scope items.

9.4.4 Financial Consolidation

Financial consolidation is a process in which the financials of different legal entities—perhaps organizational subsets operating in different sectors and/or countries but belonging to one parent entity—are combined and reported centrally. The central reporting takes care of combining assets, revenues, and expenses of the parent and sublegal entities on the parent's balance sheet, giving shareholders, investors, and customers a complete overview of the company's financial health. This is not just a pure number aggregation; it needs to be mindful of established principles, accounting standards, and legal and regulatory compliance guidelines.

In a two-tier ERP setup, financial consolidation at the headquarters is an absolute need. Depending on the flexibility and complexity of an organization's operations worldwide, ownership pattern, and legal rules, its consolidation requirements can vary.

SAP S/4HANA Cloud provides many options for enabling financial consolidation:

- SAP BPC with SAP S/4HANA Cloud as a data source
- Statutory consolidation with SAP S/4HANA Cloud
- Central Finance
- Enabling consolidation via a third-party consolidation stack

Let's consider each of these options.

SAP BPC with SAP S/4HANA Cloud as a Data Source

SAP S/4HANA Cloud provides capabilities to connect seamlessly with SAP BPC running on SAP Business Warehouse (SAP BW), as shown in Figure 9.20.

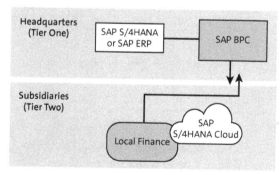

Figure 9.20 SAP BPC Connectivity with SAP S/4HANA Cloud

In this setup, the headquarters is running SAP S/4HANA or SAP ERP, SAP BW 7.40 or higher, and SAP BPC 10.x or later; meanwhile, the subsidiary runs SAP S/4HANA Cloud. This landscape option enables customers to leverage their existing investments in SAP BPC.

A technical prerequisite for this setup is integration from SAP BW to SAP S/4HANA Cloud. A source system needs to be created in SAP BW using the operational data provisioning (ODP) framework to transfer financial data relevant for consolidation from the subsidiary running SAP S/4HANA Cloud to SAP BPC at headquarters. The transfer of financial data happens via SOAP web services on an HTTPS protocol. The service center facilitates the activation of data sources available with scope item 1VG on the SAP S/4HANA Cloud side. Note that the data sources need to be created manually in SAP BW because replication happens via SOAP web services, which do not replicate metadata.

The following major data sources are available for extraction; more will be added based on customer feedback:

- Activity type
- Business area
- Chart of accounts
- Controlling area
- Company and company code
- Order number
- Cost center
- Transaction type
- Profit center and hierarchy
- Project details
- Country
- Customer group and number
- Distribution channel
- Division and segment
- Functional area
- General ledger account number and hierarchy
- Material number and group
- Plant
- Sales organization
- Work breakdown structure (WBS) element

Once this financial data is extracted into SAP BW and then into SAP BPC models, it's business as usual in the SAP BPC consolidation layer—in other words, executing data loads, working with models for consolidation (reporting and nonreporting), and maintaining consolidation logic.

Statutory Consolidation with SAP S/4HANA Cloud

SAP S/4HANA Cloud also comes with built-in consolidation capabilities mainly for legal/statutory purposes. This option is targeted for companies that currently do not have any consolidation layer investments and need quick, template-based functionality for International Financial Reporting Standards (IFRS)-based consolidation.

In the landscape shown in Figure 9.21, the consolidation engine is already part of SAP S/4HANA Cloud; it can also integrate with external subsidiary systems via flexible uploads and a powerful data management tool for validating data and maintaining data integrity.

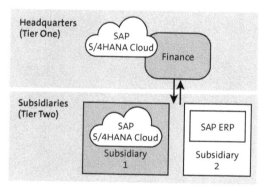

Figure 9.21 Cloud-Based Statutory Consolidation

Scope Items

The required SAP S/4HANA Cloud scope item is 1SG; the data extraction from external system scope item is 2U6, the data from group reporting data collection scope item is 287; and the multiple group currency scope item is 4VB. Refer to SAP Best Practices Explorer for more details on these scope items.

The SAP S/4HANA Cloud statutory consolidation functionality is an ideal fit for organizations with the following goals:

- Moving accounting to the cloud
- Accessing consolidation functionalities in addition to local accounting
- Consolidating subsidiaries that are running ERP solutions from multiple vendors

This statutory consolidation provides the following capabilities:

- **Master data**
  SAP S/4HANA Cloud provides predelivered consolidation units and group structures, along with a consolidation chart of accounts. The group can contain many subgroups to reflect the organization's structure. A rich collection of master data maintenance apps and self-service configuration apps is also available.

- **Data collection**
  A mechanism to collect financial data from local accounting systems and from non-SAP systems is available. The data collection and consolidation can be controlled from a central monitoring app. All subsidiaries of a corporate group can be shown with their processing status in a clear hierarchical view.

- **Data preparation**
  SAP S/4HANA Cloud can check the consistency of financial data via validation rules and currency translation to group currency. Built-in translation rules for applying the average rate, closing rate, and historical rate are available.

- **Consolidation**
  The Consolidation Monitor app is the key to executing rich, rule-based consolidation. This automatically eliminates intercompany transactions between subsidiaries.

  You can easily control which positions of the financial statements should be eliminated against each other. Any elimination rule generates a fully adjustable journal entry. For example, the following typical elimination steps are available out of the box with SAP S/4HANA Cloud:

  - Accounts payables/accounts receivables
  - Operational income/expenses
  - Financial income/expenses
  - Dividends
  - Reporting

- **Reporting**
  SAP S/4HANA Cloud comes with a rich set of preconfigured, consolidation-related reports to cover core reporting needs and data analysis. The following are some of the available reporting and analysis apps in this space:

  - Journal Entries List
  - Consolidated Income Statement and Balance Sheet
  - Balance Sheet by Consolidation Units and Subgroups
  - Statement of Comprehensive Income
  - Cash Flow Statement
  - Currency Translation Difference Analysis

  In addition to these predelivered apps, there is support for complex reporting requirements through on-the-fly reporting rules.

Central Finance

SAP S/4HANA Cloud can connect seamlessly with Central Finance deployed at headquarters.

Central Finance is an SAP S/4HANA deployment model in which customers connect multiple ERP systems in their group entities into a central SAP S/4HANA Finance system with real-time replication; the result is a central, unified financial reporting view. This deployment is preferred if real-time speed and agility are key to an organization's digital transformation. It is considered nondisruptive because the source systems are untouched and financial postings are replicated in real time via the SAP Landscape Transformation Replication Server, as shown in Figure 9.22.

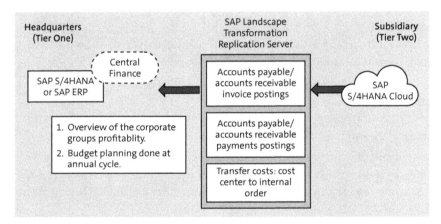

Figure 9.22 Central Finance Connectivity with SAP S/4HANA Cloud

SAP BPC optimized for SAP S/4HANA is the business planning and consolidation functionality implemented on premise as part of SAP S/4HANA.

In a two-tier ERP setup, it's common to see companies run SAP BPC optimized on the on-premise SAP S/4HANA instance because they seek to leverage real-time planning and consolidation capability at the headquarters and want to integrate subsidiary systems directly with their real-time planning and consolidation instance. Therefore, when SAP S/4HANA Cloud connects to on-premise SAP S/4HANA, it eliminates the need for extract, transform, and load (ETL) processes and the need for a separate planning and consolidation system. SAP BPC optimized for SAP S/4HANA comes with many predefined planning models for easy and faster adoption of planning templates, like cost center planning, profit center planning, P&L planning, balance sheet planning, and functional area and WIP planning. Once set up, it provides for replication of financial transaction data from SAP S/4HANA Cloud to SAP S/4HANA Central Finance 1610 FPS 02 or later.

The connectivity mechanism is SAP Landscape Transformation Replication Server (Data Migration Server [DMIS] support package 13 or later) via the cloud connector. Because it uses the same mechanism used to connect in the on-premise world, adding financial details of a subsidiary running SAP S/4HANA Cloud is nondisruptive.

Scope Item

The required SAP S/4HANA Cloud scope item is 1W4. The communication scenarios provided for integration are SAP_COM_0083 and SAP_COM_0200. Refer to SAP Best Practices Explorer for more details on this scope item. For a detailed setup guide, refer to the setup instructions in scope item 1W4.

Third-Party Consolidation Stack via APIs

SAP S/4HANA Cloud provides a rich and open set of APIs that enable third-party consolidation stacks to read financial data relevant for consolidation from SAP S/4HANA Cloud for further processing.

As shown in Figure 9.23, if the headquarters runs a non-SAP ERP solution, then financial measures relevant for consolidation can be retrieved via allowlisted APIs.

The following APIs are core for this deployment:

- Read Trail Balance
- Read Journal Entry Items
- Read Accounting Document

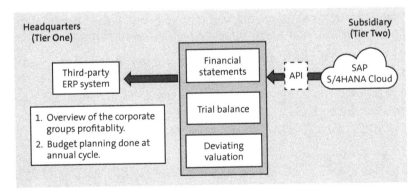

Figure 9.23 Read Financial Measures via Allowlisted APIs

Further Resources

Refer to the SAP API Business Hub at *https://api.sap.com* for details of these APIs and their structures and to learn how to access a sandbox environment.

9.4.5   Centralized Payments

Account receivables is one of the most critical processes for any business. Efficient receivables management reduces financial risks, enables healthy cash flow, and improves daily sales outstanding metrics.

However, today's receivables departments face many challenges when it comes to their invoicing and payments process. For example, one common task for receivables accountants is to match incoming payments with open invoices in the system. This can turn into a tedious task due to the huge volume of documents posted, partial payments, missing information, and much more.

To overcome this, SAP recommends a few different options, which we'll discuss in the following sections.

Centralized Customer Payments

Customers can deploy a centralized customer portal for electronic billing and payment processing across an entire business. This portal is attractive to SAP customers with the following goals:

- Standardized payment process across headquarters and subsidiaries
- Immediate access to transactional details like customer master data and invoice copies
- Reduction in time spent on day-to-day customer inquiries and accounting and settlement errors
- Faster processing of payments and deductions

The outcome is that customers can access invoices created at either the headquarters or subsidiaries through the customer portal, which is deployed on SAP BTP.

In a two-tier ERP scenario in which the headquarters is running on-premise SAP S/4HANA or SAP ERP and a subsidiary is running SAP S/4HANA Cloud, SAP S/4HANA Cloud—along with the SAP digital payments add-on—facilitates a centralized customer payment solution for both units. Figure 9.24 shows how a typical customer portal delivered by SAP and deployed on SAP BTP might be set up.

> **Scope Item**
>
> The required SAP S/4HANA Cloud scope item for customer payments is 1S2. The communication scenario provided for integration is SAP_COM_0216. Refer to SAP Best Practices Explorer for more details on this scope item.

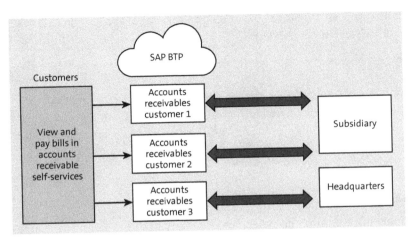

Figure 9.24 Centralized Customer Payments

Central Payment Factory

In this scenario, SAP S/4HANA Cloud or on-premise can work as a central payment factory for subsidiary companies on SAP or non-SAP systems, as shown in Figure 9.25. The headquarters can monitor and approve the payments for subsidiary companies with SAP S/4HANA for advanced payment management. It streamlines the end-to-end payment process across the corporate group and provides central monitoring of payments, central cash-position reporting, and the ability to handle and convert various payment output formats with high volumes of data.

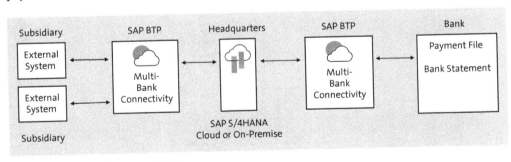

Figure 9.25 Central Payment Factory

The Manage Bank Messages app allows the headquarters to view the bank messages and payment files received from subsidiary companies. The headquarters can click on **View Payload** to view the payment file from subsidiaries. These payment items are processed automatically or can be processed manually. After processing, the payment items are visible in the Monitor Payments app. This SAP Fiori app gives the status of the payment batches and individual payments at different processing stages. The headquarters can approve or reject the payment items received from the payment file from subsidiary companies with the Approve Bank Payments app. To approve the payment batch, the payment specialist role must be assigned to the final approver; otherwise, the approval will fail with an error message.

Scope Items

The required SAP S/4HANA Cloud scope items for central payment factory are 4MT, J77, J78, and 16R. The communication scenarios provided for integration are SAP_COM_0648, SAP_COM_0649, and SAP_COM_0654. Refer to SAP Best Practices Explorer for more details on these scope items.

9.4.6 Supplier Financing

In the supplier financing scenario, the subsidiary company in the role of a buyer organizes factoring for the headquarters company as its supplier. The subsidiary as a buyer has a contract with a factor and a few important suppliers. The factor takes over receivables of the headquarters company and finances these receivables in advance. This is also known as reverse factoring.

Figure 9.26 shows detailed supplier financing steps involving the headquarters and subsidiary companies. As a first step, the subsidiary company, which is the buyer, receives the invoices from the headquarters via APIs and then executes the payment run for vCard payment and sends the instructions to the bank. The bank sends the payment and notification to the headquarters and notifies the subsidiary of the vCard usage. The subsidiary can then reconcile the vCard usage, identify invoices not paid, and pay the vCard balance via a normal payment run to the bank.

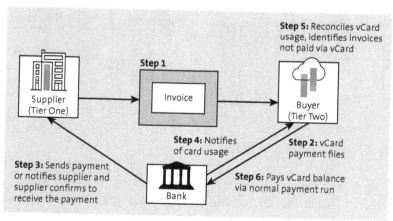

Figure 9.26 Steps in Supplier Financing in a Two-Tier ERP Setup

Supplier financing gives access to financing conditions that headquarters may not be able to receive directly, lowers financing costs, reduces days sales outstanding, improves days payables outstanding, improves cash flow, and optimizes working capital.

9.4.7 Cash Visibility of Subsidiary at Headquarters

In a typical headquarters-subsidiaries relationship, the headquarters would need visibility and control for decision-making. The headquarters would need visibility into the subsidiary operations and cash position for group level reporting. The headquarters needs to ensure that subsidiaries have access to liquidity for their day-to-day activities and that there is no impact on subsidiary operations.

With this scenario, the cash manager at headquarters gets cash visibility into subsidiary companies and can provide the reporting of the cash position for the entire enterprise. As shown in Figure 9.27, the cash specialists at subsidiaries perform daily banking duties related to disbursement and receivable accounts, including cash transfers, cash pooling, and approvals. A cash manager can then provide reporting of the cash position to headquarters with comprehensive information including opening and closing balance. With cash visibility, the headquarters can know the cash position at subsidiaries and allocate funds as needed.

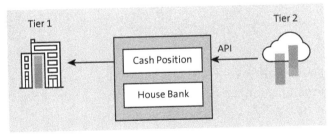

Figure 9.27 Cash Flow Visibility

With advanced cash operations, the headquarters gets a consistent view of the actual cash position, as well as the short- and mid-term cash forecasts. A comparison view between the actual and forecasted cash flow is available with drilldown features for the detailed transactions and rich dimensions for the analysis.

The headquarters can perform the following key process flows for the group:

- Perform and track bank transfers
- Approve and monitor bank payments

- Monitor bank statement processing status
- Check cash reports (e.g., Check Cash Position, Check Cash Flow Items, Cash Flow Analyzer, Cash Flow Comparison)

As a result of these process flows, organizations can achieve these business benefits at the group level:

- Analyze cash position with finest granularity drilldown.
- Forecast the liquidity trend and analyze the actual cash flows with rich dimensions (planning level, general ledger account, planning group) in cash reports such as Check Cash Flow Items and Cash Flow Analyzer.
- Use advanced capabilities of the Cash Flow Analyzer report with bank account group view and liquidity item hierarchy view.
- Compare the forecast snapshots made in the history with the actual cash flows.
- Facilitate cash operations such as making bank transfers, tracking transfer statuses, approving payments (bank communication management [BCM] integration), and monitoring payments.
- Monitor the status of bank statement import processing easily.

> **Scope Item**
>
> The required SAP S/4HANA Cloud scope item for advanced cash operations is J78. The communication scenario provided for integration is SAP_COM_0654. Refer to SAP Best Practices Explorer for more details on this scope item.

9.4.8   Treasury Integration

Treasury functions are a business priority for many customers who are planning a finance-focused cloud transformation. In the following sections, we'll cover two key integration scenarios for the treasury.

Treasury Payment Requests

In many cases, treasury functions are shared with the headquarters and subsidiaries in a typical shared/central services–style deployment in a hybrid cloud scenario. This integration scenario enables you to generate and fill payment requests triggered in the treasury risk management (TRM) functionality in the SAP S/4HANA Cloud system in your central financial accounting component.

The central accounting component can be either SAP S/4HANA Cloud or SAP ERP, as depicted in Figure 9.28. This scenario fulfills the requirements for deploying treasury and risk management in SAP S/4HANA Cloud while keeping the payment in an existing (shadow) central financial accounting system. In such cases, the treasury and risk management functionality in SAP S/4HANA Cloud can trigger the payment request creation or cancellation through IDocs. Requests are then generated in an SAP S/4HANA or SAP ERP system.

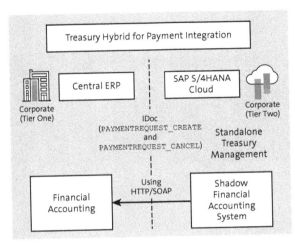

Figure 9.28 Overview of Treasury Payment Request Integration

This capability helps ensure there is a central treasury function for the whole enterprise.

Scope Item

SAP_COMM_0442 is the new communication scenario required for this setup. The required SAP S/4HANA Cloud scope item is 3NA.

The cloud connector is a prerequisite for this scenario. The communication scenario required for the cloud connector integration is SAP_COM_0200.

Note

Payment requests can be monitored in the Application Link Enabling (ALE) status monitor for the following IDoc types:

- PAYMENTREQUEST_CREATE
- PAYMENTREQUEST_CANCEL

Treasury Workstation Cash Integration

Treasury workstation cash integration, as shown in Figure 9.29, makes it possible for the treasury workstation, usually at the headquarters, to receive the cash flow data from any remote systems of the subsidiaries. This data is incorporated into the various cash reports (e.g., Cash Position, Check Cash Flow Items, and Cash Flow Analyzer) for the cash disposition analysis.

The headquarters can receive a more comprehensive and accurate cash disposition analysis at the group level, with consistent house bank and account master data between the headquarters and the subsidiaries.

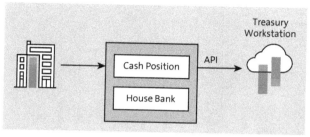

Figure 9.29 Treasury Workstation Integration

The process steps involved are as follows:

1. Send the cash flows into the treasury workstation.

2. Release the cash flows.

3. Check the cash flows.

4. Replicate the house bank and account data from on-premise SAP S/4HANA to SAP S/4HANA Cloud or vice versa.

5. Monitor the replication.

Scope Item

The required SAP S/4HANA Cloud scope item for treasury workstation cash integration is 34P. The communication scenarios provided for integration are SAP_COM_0278 and SAP_COM_0279. Refer to SAP Best Practices Explorer for more details on this scope item.

9.4.9   Global Trade

SAP Global Trade Services (SAP GTS) helps companies better manage global trade operations, ensure ongoing trade compliance, and optimize the cross-border supply chain. The solution delivers automation and comprehensive functionality to speed trade functions and maximize performance. With direct integration throughout the supply chain, customers can expect reduced costs, fewer trade penalties and fines, and faster customs clearance, both outbound and inbound. The system for SAP GTS lets you automate your global trade transactions, manage large numbers of business partners and documents, and ensure that your company always complies with constantly changing international legal regulations.

This solution supports your global trade activities with the tools you need to participate in the modernized systems and electronic means of communication used by government agencies and customs authorities. SAP GTS helps you avoid costly delays and financial risks involved with imports and exports, enabling you to react to international business opportunities quickly. The headquarters on SAP S/4HANA (on-premise) with existing SAP GTS can integrate with subsidiary companies on SAP S/4HANA Cloud to utilize existing rules in SAP GTS for trade being managed for subsidiaries on SAP S/4HANA Cloud, as shown in Figure 9.30.

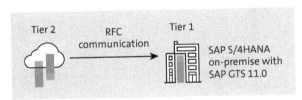

Figure 9.30 SAP GTS Integration

The headquarters can leverage the existing investment in SAP GTS for a subsidiary business being managed in SAP S/4HANA Cloud. They can use the existing SAP GTS infrastructure for a best-of-breed deployment of an international trade solution with minimal new configuration. The key process steps involved are as follows:

1. Integrate the global trade component.
2. Contact expert configuration for activation and definition of the infrastructure.
3. Synchronize the master data.

> **Scope Item**
> The required SAP S/4HANA Cloud scope item for transfer of primary master data for SAP GTS integration is 1WA. The communication scenarios provided for integration is SAP_COM_0084. Refer to SAP Best Practices Explorer for more details on this scope item.

9.4.10 Central Finance Compliance Management

Financial processes generate many documents on a daily basis. With the SAP Financial Compliance Management solution on SAP BTP, the compliance manager defines controls and procedures to monitor financial operation processes and detect anomalies that may cause financial loss when connected to the SAP S/4HANA Cloud or on-premise systems. Thus, the business benefits from reduced manual activities and automated checking and monitoring of financial processes. In this scenario, the headquarters and subsidiary companies can connect to the SAP Financial Compliance Management solution on SAP BTP for continuous monitoring and automating the detection of anomalies causing financial losses, as shown in Figure 9.31.

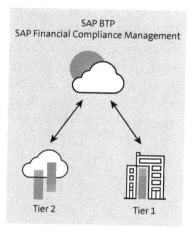

Figure 9.31 Finance Compliance Management

The compliance manager defines the controls and procedures to monitor financial operation processes and detect anomalies when connected to the SAP S/4HANA Cloud and on-premise systems.

Figure 9.32 shows the process steps flow associated with SAP Financial Compliance Management in a two-tier ERP setup.

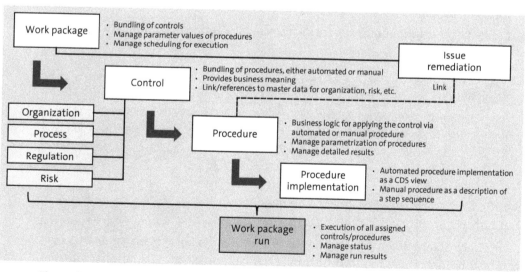

Figure 9.32 Process Flow

The key process steps involved are as follows:

1. Create automated procedures.

2. Create controls.

3. Create and run work packages.

4. Run automated procedures.

5. Display the automated procedure run results.

6. Perform issue remediation.

Scope Items

The required SAP S/4HANA Cloud scope items for central financial compliance are 3KY and J58. The communication scenarios provided for integration are SAP_COM_0734 and SAP_COM_0645. Refer to SAP Best Practices Explorer for more details on these scope items.

9.4.11   Central Privacy Governance

In this scenario, shown in Figure 9.33, SAP Privacy Governance on SAP BTP works as a central system for automatically detecting the privacy risk for personal information and privacy anomalies in a two-tier ERP landscape for headquarters and subsidiary companies on SAP S/4HANA Cloud or on-premise.

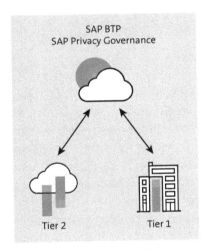

Figure 9.33 SAP Privacy Governance

SAP Privacy Governance comes with predelivered use cases to quick-start the business, covering information lifecycle management policies and retention rules for objects in procurement, sales, finance, and human resources. A typical use case is detection of a sales order with an elapsed retention period. Personal data in SAP applications must be protected according to the data protection laws and regulations. This is achieved by blocking and deleting data according to residence and retention rules. Residence rules are set to define the amount of time for which data can stay in the database, after which it is archived. Retention rules are defined to store the archive files for a set amount of time, after which they can be destroyed.

The key process steps involved are as follows:

1. Build automated procedures.
2. Build manual procedures.
3. Document regulation, policy, and control objectives.
4. Build risk, run an assessment, and mitigate risks.
5. Build controls.
6. Create and run work packages.
7. Run automated procedures.
8. Display automated procedure run results.
9. Report issues.
10. Assign and execute a remediation plan.
11. Run a report in the dashboard.

Scope Items

The required SAP S/4HANA Cloud scope items for central privacy governance are 3KX and 1KA. Refer to SAP Best Practices Explorer for more details on these scope items.

9.4.12   Intelligent Real Estate

SAP Intelligent Real Estate enables end-to-end real estate business processes between the headquarters and subsidiary companies running on on-premise SAP S/4HANA or an SAP S/4HANA Cloud system with a single source of truth for master data on SAP Cloud for Real Estate, which runs on SAP BTP, as shown in Figure 9.34. SAP Intelligent Real Estate supports all key future focus topics, including space management, remote work, sustainability, cloud, and analytics. The headquarters and subsidiary companies can manage buildings and space better for commercial and corporate requirements, can make intelligent leasing decisions with a comprehensive contract management solution from SAP S/4HANA Cloud and on-premise systems, and can analyze building efficiency with embedded analytics for detailed analysis of costs, revenues, and capacity utilization. They also get to enhance SAP BTP (which allows partner add-ons and contributions) with external innovations.

Headquarters and subsidiary companies get to leverage SAP Fiori apps on SAP S/4HANA Cloud and on-premise for usage and occupancy management, which supports business scenarios such as external lease-out, internal occupancy, and intercompany lease-out of spaces. They get embedded analytics in dashboards, making leasing more transparent and helping to make intelligent leasing decisions.

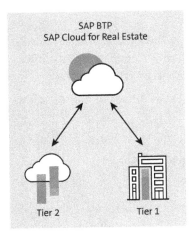

Figure 9.34 Headquarters and Subsidiary Leasing with SAP Intelligent Real Estate

Scope Items
The required SAP S/4HANA Cloud scope items for SAP Intelligent Real Estate are 5VX, 5VY, 5VZ, 5WO, 5YU, 5YW, and 5YV. The communication scenarios provided for integration are SAP_COM_0092, SAP_COM_0697, SAP_COM_0393, SAP_COM_0647, and SAP_COM_0472. Refer to SAP Best Practices Explorer for more details on these scope items.

9.5   Sales

A rapidly changing business environment often poses challenges to a business. Many organizations are exploring the issues posed by inorganic growth specifically from mergers and acquisitions for meeting the market demand and gaining competitive advantage. For a business, managing the upstream and downstream stakeholders in an endeavor to gain a competitive advantage has become more complex. Sales activities will become even more important in the scattered environment in which the different entities within a business use different system landscapes.

In this section, we'll look at two-tier ERP business processes in sales and how a business can overcome the accompanying challenges with SAP S/4HANA Cloud. We'll start with two-tier ERP sales, examining sales from a local sales office, drop shipments, and returns handling with an eye on both the current challenges and the processes with SAP S/4HANA Cloud.

9.5.1   Subsidiary as a Local Sales Office

In a setup in which a subsidiary is established as a local sales office, managing sales operations independently requires starting the sales activities, independently fulfilling customers' requirements, and handling subsequent processes such as returns.

A business might choose to set up a subsidiary as a local sales office if it has the following business objectives:

- Capturing a market that is strategically important
- Lowering the financial expenditures by bringing in business model optimization
- Targeting certain geographic regions for its products

Figure 9.35 represents the sales process from an independent subsidiary. This process usually begins when a customer approaches the sales office for quotations. Alternatively, a salesperson may identify an opportunity through the marketing campaign and directly approach a customer in their region to provide insights about the new products the company offers that might be of interest to the customer. As shown in Figure 9.35, the headquarters has visibility into the process of converting an opportunity into sales order fulfillment, even if it doesn't manage the sales directly.

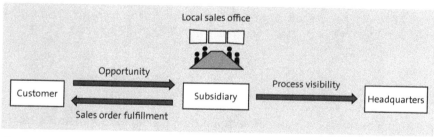

Figure 9.35 Sell from Local Sales Office

Communication between subsidiaries and headquarters is a key challenge for independent sales subsidiaries. The headquarters depends on manual communication channels for visibility of the process and for the overall performance of subsidiary; such access is even more critical if a business has multiple subsidiaries that collectively affect its overall performance.

Let's examine the two-tier ERP deployment model with either SAP ERP or on-premise SAP S/4HANA implemented at the headquarters and SAP S/4HANA Cloud implemented at the subsidiary. As highlighted in Figure 9.36, a salesperson converts the predecessor documents from sales activities like quotations to a sales order. The subsidiary confirms whether it can deliver the product on the date requested by the customer. It then performs follow-up actions like shipping and billing activities to complete the order-to-cash process.

This setup takes care of all the processes independently, from an inquiry to order fulfill-ment. With SAP S/4HANA Cloud, SAP offers best practices for the sales process via scope item BD9 with allowlisted APIs (SOAP or OData) and CDS views, which the head-quarters can consume to get required and critical information. This will help headquar-ters closely monitor all the phases of the order-to-cash process, from inquiry to billing to payment from customers.

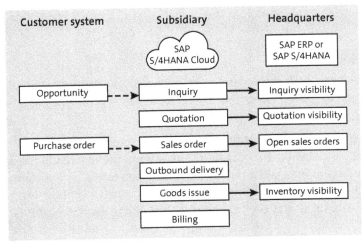

Figure 9.36 Sell from Local Sales Office with SAP S/4HANA Cloud

SAP has published four allowlisted APIs for integrating with SAP S/4HANA Cloud for these points:

- `API_SALES_QUOTATION_SRV` and `API_SALES_INQUIRY_SRV` for leads and opportunities
- `API_SALES_ORDER_SRV` for sales orders and their statuses
- `API_MATERIAL_STOCK_SRV` for inventory position

Further Resources

SAP has envisioned essential APIs for other critical information—specifically, customer credit details and customer account balances—that are under consideration for future releases. For more information on required APIs, visit *https://api.sap.com*.

9.5.2   Drop Shipping

Drop shipping is a supply chain management technique in which the retailer does not keep goods in its own stock but instead transfers customer orders and shipment details to the manufacturer or wholesaler. In the drop shipping process, a subsidiary does not hold or manage the inventory but instead requests that headquarters replenish the inventory directly to the customer. This is the case for a dependent subsidiary setup in the two-tier ERP system.

In principle, two drop-shipping models are possible, depending on a business' deployment model:

1. Drop shipping from headquarters
2. Drop shipping from subsidiary

Let's look at each of these in detail.

Drop Shipping from Headquarters

This scenario is applicable for a business that has a subsidiary as a sales office that does not manage the inventory. In this scenario, the subsidiary depends on the headquarters for inventory replenishment.

In this process, a customer approaches the subsidiary for the required product. As highlighted in Figure 9.37, the subsidiary will pass on the requirements to headquarters because the subsidiary does not manage the inventory. The headquarters will perform the delivery of the product directly to the end customer and create the billing document for the subsidiary. The subsidiary then creates the final billing document for the end customer.

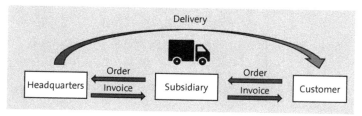

Figure 9.37 Drop Shipping from Headquarters

From a business perspective, real-time collaboration between the headquarters and its subsidiaries is required to realize this drop-shipping process. From an IT perspective, this requires enormous manual effort to integrate the software in such a way as to avoid the need for manual intervention. The following are common challenges with this setup:

- A lot of manual interaction due to more data entry points
- Limited or lacking information on the goods movement between and the subsidiary
- Enormous effort needed to establish the integration between the headquarters and the subsidiary

With SAP S/4HANA Cloud, SAP offers prepackaged integration content with SAP Best Practices scope items. These result in seamless integration, reduced implementation time, and end-to-end business coverage.

There are two variants of the drop shipping process from headquarters that come into play, depending on business requirements:

1. Drop shipping without advanced shipping notification (ASN)

2. Drop shipping with ASN

Figure 9.38 illustrates the end-to-end business process view of drop-shipping from headquarters when SAP S/4HANA Cloud is implemented at a subsidiary. Depending on whether the company is drop shipping with or without an ASN, several integration points are required in SAP S/4HANA Cloud, and these are marked with solid arrow lines:

- **Outbound service for sending purchase order**
  This is one of the critical integration points through which the requirements from a customer are transferred to the headquarters. In this process, the third-party sales order is created manually based on the customer's requirements via the customer's purchase order. On saving the sales order, a purchase requisition will be generated; this is converted into a purchase order in SAP S/4HANA Cloud. Once the purchase order is generated, it needs to be communicated to headquarters as a sales order to automatically capture mandatory information such as product details, required quantity, requested delivery date, and ship-to party information.

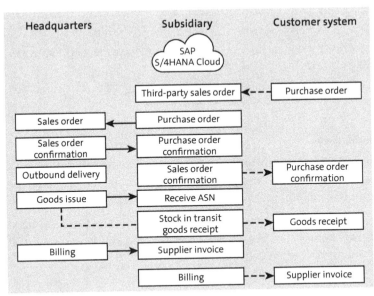

Figure 9.38 Drop Shipping from Headquarters with SAP S/4HANA Cloud

- **Inbound service for receiving order confirmation**
  Once the sales order is created at the headquarters, the headquarters performs an inventory availability check for the requested delivery date from the customer. The result needs to be communicated back to the subsidiary so that the subsidiary can

communicate it to the end customer. The **Purchase Order Confirmation** tab of SAP S/4HANA Cloud is updated with the details of the confirmed quantity.

- **Outbound service for sending purchase order**
  This is one of the critical integration points through which the requirements from a customer are transferred to headquarters. In this process, the third-party sales order is created manually based on the customer's requirements via the customer's purchase order. On saving the sales order, a purchase requisition will be generated; this is converted into a purchase order in SAP S/4HANA Cloud. Once the purchase order is generated, it needs to be communicated to headquarters as a sales order to automatically capture mandatory information such as product details, required quantity, requested delivery date, and ship-to party information.

- **Inbound service for creating supplier invoice**
  This is the last critical integration point required to capture the account payables information in SAP S/4HANA Cloud. The subsidiary gets the supplier invoice created automatically through the integration once the billing document is generated at headquarters for the subsidiary. This integration saves massive effort and takes significantly less time than creating the supplier invoice document manually for the end user.

Scope Item

The required SAP S/4HANA Cloud scope item is 2EJ. Refer to SAP Best Practices Explorer for more details on this scope item.

The communication scenario provided for integration is SAP_COM_0224.

Drop Shipping from Subsidiary

This scenario is applicable when the subsidiary acts as a manufacturing unit and/or a warehouse that manages the inventory. In this case, the headquarters depends on the subsidiary for inventory replenishment.

Figure 9.39 shows the business process flow between headquarters and the subsidiary. In this process, a customer approaches the headquarters for the product required and provides the quantity and the expected delivery date.

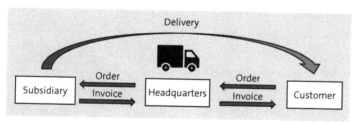

Figure 9.39 Drop Shipping from Subsidiary

Headquarters will pass on the requirements to the subsidiary because the headquarters does not manage the inventory. The subsidiary performs the delivery of the product directly to the customer and creates the billing document against the headquarters. The headquarters then creates the final billing document for the end customer.

Businesses whose headquarters handle fulfillment encounter similar challenges as businesses whose subsidiaries handle fulfillment.

Figure 9.40 illustrates the end-to-end business process view of drop shipping from the subsidiary when SAP S/4HANA Cloud is implemented there. Depending on whether the company is drop shipping with or without an ASN, several integration points are required in SAP S/4HANA Cloud; these are marked with solid arrow lines:

- **Inbound service for creating a sales order**
  This is one of the critical integration points through which the requirements from the customer are transferred from the headquarters. In this process, a sales order is generated based on the customer requirements via the purchase order at headquarters.

- **Outbound service for sales order confirmation**
  An availability check is performed during the sales order creation at the subsidiary with SAP S/4HANA Cloud. The availability check helps confirm availability of the quantities of a product needed to send to a customer by the requested delivery date. This information needs to be communicated to the headquarters so that the headquarters can communicate it to the end customer.

- **Outbound service for delivery request**
  This integration is required if a business is implementing a drop shipping process with an ASN. In this process, once the outbound delivery is generated and the goods dispatched from the subsidiary, delivery details must be sent to headquarters. The ASN is generated at headquarters and contains the details of the quantities dispatched.

- **Outbound service for billing document**
  This is the last critical integration point, in which the billing document is sent to headquarters to automate the creation of the supplier invoice. Once the billing document is generated at the subsidiary with SAP S/4HANA Cloud, it is communicated to headquarters as a supplier invoice. This integration saves massive effort and takes significantly less time than creating this document manually from the end user.

Scope Item

The required SAP S/4HANA Cloud scope item is 2EL. Refer to SAP Best Practices Explorer for more details on this scope item.

The communication scenario provided for integration is SAP_COM_0223.

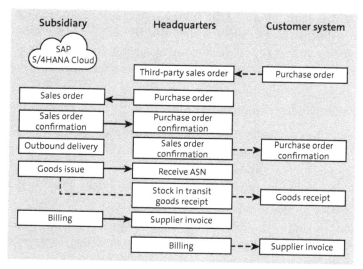

Figure 9.40 Drop Shipping from Subsidiary with SAP S/4HANA Cloud

To support the integration functions for both drop shipping from headquarters and drop shipping from a subsidiary, a business will need to perform certain prerequisite steps. For more information on these prerequisites, consult Section 9.3 on master data and Section 9.10 on integration between the subsidiary and the headquarters.

Note that SAP S/4HANA Cloud also offers allowlisted APIs and CDS views to help fulfill the headquarters' reporting/analytical needs; these APIs and views can be consumed to make customized reports.

9.5.3   Returns Handling

In the previous sections, process details have been provided for sell-from-stock and drop shipping scenarios. In both scenarios, after the product is sold, the customer may return it for various reasons. Returns processing will become perilous if a business does not have a proper channel of communication for capturing the return information and communicating as necessary with headquarters for making certain decisions.

Returns processing is classified based on the scenarios provided in the previous sections: either returns for sales from local sales offices or returns from drop shipments.

Returns processing for sales from local sales offices is applicable when a customer returns the product to a subsidiary sales office that manages all its operations as an independent subsidiary. Figure 9.41 shows the returns process to an *independent* subsidiary; note that system integration gives headquarters visibility into the returns process.

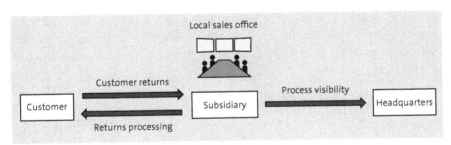

Figure 9.41 Returns Processing for Local Sales Office

This process begins when a customer wants to return the product to the subsidiary. The return can be initiated through a customer return note or through manual information. From here, two options are possible, depending on the company's returns practices: either a returns order is created and processed alone, or a follow-on process occurs in which a credit memo is created or a product is replaced. Let's look at each:

- **Returns sales order without follow-on functions**
  Once the return order is generated, the subsidiary will perform shipping activities like creation of delivery and goods receipt once the goods have physically arrived. As soon as the goods receipt is performed, the subsidiary can decide whether the product is to be sent back to the supplier or scrapped. As a final step, a billing document is created. To map this business requirement, SAP S/4HANA Cloud offers scope item BDD as a part of its SAP Best Practices content.

- **Returns sales order with follow-on functions**
  In this process, the subsidiary may initiate the quality check once the customer returns the product physically. A quality inspection also may be carried out at the customer premises. Once the return order is generated, the subsidiary will perform shipping activities like creation of delivery and the goods receipt. The subsidiary decides whether the product is to be replaced or refunded based on various factors. Accordingly, a sales order is generated for a free-of-charge product for replacement or a credit memo is created for a refund. To map this requirement, SAP S/4HANA Cloud offers scope item BKP as a part of its SAP Best Practices content.

In both scenarios with SAP S/4HANA Cloud at the subsidiary, SAP has published two allowlisted APIs for integrating with SAP S/4HANA Cloud for the following points:

1. `API_CUSTOMER_RETURN_SRV` for information on customer returns order
2. `API_CUSTOMER_RETURNS_DELIVERY_SRV` for information on customer returns delivery

Returns handling for other scenarios like drop shipping is anticipated in future product releases.

So far, the existing sales scenarios have been largely applicable to all kinds of businesses; however, there is always a chance of variations. Based on customer adaptation and requirements, SAP will release more scenarios or variants in later product releases of SAP S/4HANA Cloud.

9.6   Services

Never has technological advancement offered more innovation and transformation opportunities for the services industry. Systems integrations allow firms to grow revenue without increasing or modifying their entire business process. There are increased opportunities in manufacturing for companies to streamline the merger activities between their subsidiaries or retail channels for the betterment of services with digital technologies.

A company's revenue will stem from not only sale of products but also customer-specific solutions that transform the business and differentiate it from their peers in the marketplace. These solutions include value-added services, predictive analytics, proactive maintenance, and more.

In this section, we will look at two-tier ERP business processes in services and how a business can build new processes with the integration of an existing landscape into SAP S/4HANA Cloud. We'll start with two-tier service order management, repair order integration, and sales installation processes, with an eye on both the current challenges and the processes in SAP S/4HANA Cloud.

9.6.1   Service Order Management

Service order management is used to manage the end-to-end lifecycle of service requests. Service requests are generally raised for customer queries in terms of servicing or repair of products purchased.

Drop shipping is a supply chain management technique in which the retailer does not keep goods or service in its own stock but instead transfers customer orders and shipment details to the manufacturer or service provider. This drop shipping concept applies to both sales and services capabilities, as you will see in the following sections.

Service or repair of products are generally outsourced by the headquarters to a subsidiary. In service order management, similar to drop shipping (as discussed in Section 9.5.2), a setup exists between the headquarters and subsidiary wherein the headquarters does not manage service operations such as installation, but instead requests that a subsidiary carries out the activities at a customer location directly. This is the case for a dependent subsidiary setup in the two-tier ERP system.

Figure 9.42 shows service order management from an independent subsidiary. The process starts when the customer places an order at the headquarters for services. The internal sales representative at the headquarters creates the customer's sales order. The headquarters will contact the service provider, depending on the service to be provided. The headquarters has visibility into the process of converting a customer requirement into a service opportunity, even if it doesn't manage the services directly.

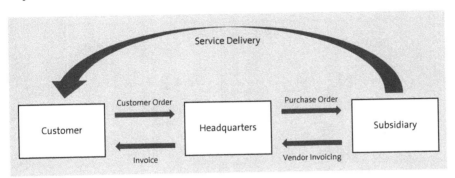

Figure 9.42 Service Order Management

Communications between subsidiaries and the headquarters need to be seamless for independent service subsidiaries. A subsidiary depends on manual communication channels for visibility of the process and for the overall performance of headquarters; such access is even more critical if a business has multiple subsidiaries that collectively affect its overall performance.

Let's examine the two-tier ERP deployment model with either SAP ERP or on-premise SAP S/4HANA implemented at the headquarters and SAP S/4HANA Cloud implemented at the subsidiary. As highlighted in Figure 9.43, the process begins with a salesperson interaction with the customer and continues as follows:

1. A sales order is created in the headquarters with a material that generates the purchase requisition. A purchase order is created against the purchase requisition.

2. The purchase is approved, and an Electronic Data Interchange (EDI)–based approach is used to automatically transfer the purchase order information for the creation of a service order at the subsidiary.

3. A service manager receives the automatically generated service order at the subsidiary with sold-to, ship-to, bill-to, and pay-to information coming from the headquarters. The ship-to information contains details of the end customer.

4. The service order is confirmed, and the EDI-based approach is used to confirm the purchase order at the headquarters for receipt of details.

5. A service technician in the subsidiary delivers the service required to the customer and confirms the service order.

6. Based on the service delivered and confirmation, the purchaser at the headquarters posts the service entry sheet.

7. A vendor invoice or billing document is created at the subsidiary and billed to the headquarters; consequently, a corresponding supplier invoice is created automatically at the headquarters.

8. The headquarters raises an invoice against the initial sales order.

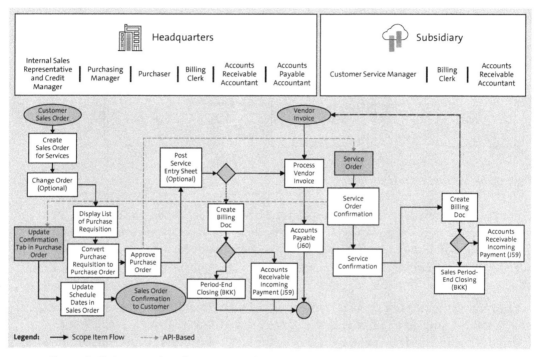

Figure 9.43 Process Flow for Service Order Integration with SAP S/4HANA Cloud

Advantages of the service order management setup between the headquarters and its subsidiary include the following:

- Real-time collaboration
- Minimal to zero manual information leakage
- One-time effort for system set up of EDI-based communication
- Allows headquarters to focus on manufacturing and the subsidiary to take up service operations
- Captures a market that is strategically important
- Lowers the financial expenditures by bringing in business model optimization

With SAP S/4HANA Cloud, SAP offers prepackaged integration content with SAP Best Practices scope items. Let's take a look at the available integration points for service order management:

- **Inbound service for receiving order confirmation**
  Once the sales order is created at the headquarters, a purchase requisition and purchase order are created. The result needs to be communicated back to the subsidiary so that the subsidiary can communicate it to the end customer. The **Purchase Order Confirmation** tab of SAP S/4HANA Cloud is updated with the details of the service order.

- **Outbound service for sending purchase order**
  This is one of the critical integration points through which the requirements from a customer are transferred to the headquarters. In this process, the third-party sales order is created manually based on the customer's requirements via the customer's purchase order. On saving the sales order, a purchase requisition will be generated; this is converted into a purchase order in SAP S/4HANA Cloud. Once the purchase order is generated, it needs to be communicated to headquarters as a sales order to automatically capture mandatory information such as product details, required quantity, requested delivery date, and ship-to party information.

- **Inbound service for creating supplier invoice**
  This is the last critical integration point required to capture the accounts payable information in SAP S/4HANA Cloud. The subsidiary gets the supplier invoice created automatically through the integration once the billing document is generated at the headquarters for the subsidiary. This integration saves massive effort and takes significantly less time than creating the supplier invoice document manually for the end user.

Scope Items

The required SAP S/4HANA Cloud scope items are 3D2 and 2EL. Refer to SAP Best Practices Explorer for more details on these scope items.

The communication scenario provided for integration is SAP_COM_0224.

9.6.2 Repair Order Integration

A repair order is a sales document for recording all the business processes that are involved in processing faulty goods that a customer sends in for repair.

The headquarters employs resellers/retailers/service providers as a channel through which a product can be delivered to the end customer. Customers reach out to the same channels if they need to repair a product they purchased. Subsidiaries help customers access the product warranty coverage and amount of repair through in-house repairs. Quality checks ensure that the repair is needed and determines if spare parts are to be added or replaced. These spare parts are procured from the headquarters.

Figure 9.44 represents the repair order integration from an independent subsidiary. The process starts with a customer walking into a retailer store or reaching out to a service provider/reseller with a product complaint. A subsidiary receives the customer material and places it under the customer stock. A customer service representative performs a precheck and assesses the repair. A repair order is created with parts to be procured from the headquarters.

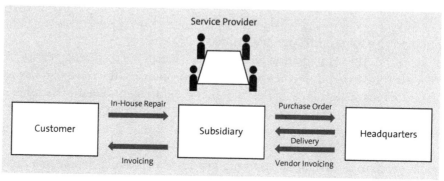

Figure 9.44 Repair Order Integration

Let's examine the two-tier ERP deployment model with either SAP ERP or on-premise SAP S/4HANA implemented at headquarters and SAP S/4HANA Cloud implemented at the subsidiary. As highlighted in Figure 9.45, the process begins with a service representative interaction with the customer and continues as follows:

1. A product is received from the customer through post goods movement and placed under the customer stock.

2. An in-house repair is created for the customer with the product and serial number details.

3. A preform precheck is done as part of the quality inspection and is confirmed.

4. A repair order is created from the in-house repair with a product that generates the purchase requisition. A purchase order is created with the vendor as the headquarters against the purchase requisition.

5. The EDI output type in the purchase order is used to send the details to SAP BTP.

6. In SAP BTP (specifically, the Cloud Integration capability), using standard artifacts, an integration flow (iFlow) is built that creates a sales order in the on-premise SAP S/4HANA system with a purchase order reference document.

7. The sales order triggers an EDI output for confirmation of receipt.

8. Delivery creation (post goods issue) from the on-premise SAP S/4HANA system is done for shipping the procured product to the subsidiary. In the subsidiary system (SAP S/4HANA Cloud), an inbound delivery is created against the purchase order and receipt of the material for repair is taken.

9. The repair confirmation is done against the repair order and goods issue for delivery of product to the customer.

10. A vendor invoice or billing document is created at the subsidiary and billed to the headquarters; consequently, a corresponding supplier invoice is created automatically at the headquarters.

11. The headquarters raises an invoice against the initial sales order.

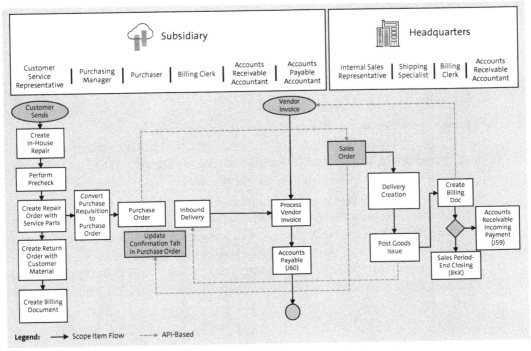

Figure 9.45 Process Flow for Repair Order Integration with SAP S/4HANA Cloud

Advantages of the repair order integration subsidiary and its headquarters are as follows:

- Minimal to zero manual information leakage
- One-time effort for system set up of EDI based communication
- Allows a subsidiary to procure spare parts from headquarters
- Increased customer satisfaction

With SAP S/4HANA Cloud, SAP offers prepackaged integration content with SAP Best Practices scope items.

Scope Items

The required SAP S/4HANA Cloud scope items are 3XK and 2EJ. Refer to SAP Best Practices Explorer for more details on these scope items.

The communication scenario provided for integration is SAP_COM_0223.

Let's take a look at the available integration points for services (which are very similar to service order management):

- **Outbound service for sending purchase order**
  This is one of the critical integration points through which the requirements from a subsidiary are transferred to the headquarters. In this process, the repair order is created from the in-house repair object after the precheck. After saving, a purchase requisition is generated; this is converted into a purchase order in SAP S/4HANA Cloud through a background processing job. Once the purchase order is generated, it needs to be communicated to headquarters for sales order creation to automatically capture mandatory information such as product details, required quantity, and requested delivery date.

- **Inbound service for receiving order confirmation**
  Once the sales order is created at the headquarters, the result needs to be communicated back to the subsidiary. The **Purchase Order Confirmation** tab of SAP S/4HANA Cloud is updated with the details of the service order.

- **Inbound service for creating supplier invoice**
  This is the last critical integration point required to capture the account payables information in SAP S/4HANA Cloud. The subsidiary gets the supplier invoice created automatically through the integration once the billing document is generated at headquarters for the subsidiary. This integration saves massive effort and takes significantly less time than creating the supplier invoice document manually for the end user.

9.6.3   Sales and Installation

When a customer requires a product along with installation, this is known as the sales and installation process. In SAP S/4HANA Cloud, sales and installation is referred to collectively as *solution order management*, which represents an end-to-end process that spans from creating a solution order to delivering products, one-time services, long-running services, and subscriptions. This includes integration with invoicing and controlling.

Subsidiary core business processes include services and installation activities. With the sales and installation process, a setup exists between the headquarters and subsidiaries wherein the headquarters does not manage service operations such as installation; instead, subsidiaries procure the materials from headquarters and carry out the activities at a customer location directly. This is the case for a dependent subsidiary setup in the two-tier ERP system.

In a setup in which a subsidiary is established as a local sales and service office, it receives a customer's request to manage the service activities at the customer location and gets the materials from headquarters.

Figure 9.46 represents the sales and installation process from an independent subsidiary. The process starts when the customer places an order at the subsidiary for product and service. The internal sales representative at the subsidiary creates the customer's order. The headquarters ships the material to the subsidiary, which takes care of installation at the customer location.

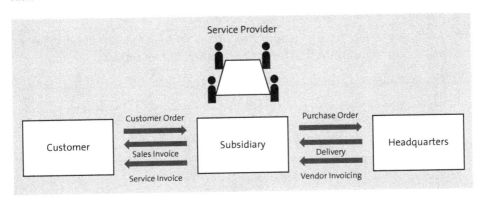

Figure 9.46 Sales and Installation Process

Let's examine the two-tier ERP deployment model with either SAP ERP or on-premise SAP S/4HANA implemented at the headquarters and SAP S/4HANA Cloud implemented at the subsidiary. As highlighted in Figure 9.47, the process begins with a salesperson interacting with the customer and continues as follows:

1. A service representative creates a solution order with the product required and service (installation) as additional line items.

2. The sales item in the solution order is released, which creates a sales order containing the product that generates the purchase requisition. The purchase order is created with the vendor as the headquarters against the purchase requisition.

3. The EDI output type in the purchase order is used to send the details to SAP BTP.

4. In SAP BTP (specifically, the Cloud Integration capability), using standard artifacts, an iFlow is built that creates a sales order in an on-premise SAP S/4HANA system with a purchase order reference document.

5. The sales order triggers an EDI output for confirmation of receipt.

6. Delivery creation (post goods issue) from the on-premise SAP S/4HANA system is done for shipping the procured product to the subsidiary. In the subsidiary system (SAP S/4HANA Cloud), the inbound delivery is created against the purchase order for receipt of product.

7. The service item in the solution order is released, which creates a service order that is replicated to field service management (FSM).

8. A service technician is assigned to the service request with details of the installation, containing product and customer information.

9. Service order confirmation is done in FSM and replicated to the SAP S/4HANA Cloud system at the subsidiary.

10. A vendor invoice or billing document is created at the subsidiary and billed to the headquarters; consequently, a corresponding supplier invoice is created automatically at the headquarters.

11. The headquarters raises an invoice against the initial sales order.

12. With a solution order, there is an option to bill the sales and service items together or separately, depending on the customer's requirement or request.

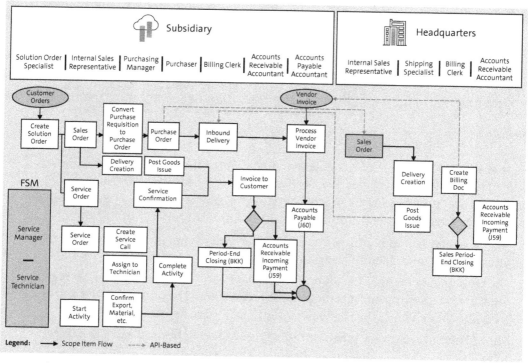

Figure 9.47 Process Flow for Sales and Installation Process with SAP S/4HANA Cloud

Advantages of the sales and installation process between a subsidiary and its headquarters are as follows:

- Minimal to zero manual information leakage
- One-time effort for system set up of EDI based communication
- Allows headquarters to have another channel of sales through a service provider
- One-order framework for customers with a solution order and single invoice creation option
- Increased customer satisfaction

So far, the service scenarios have been largely applicable to service-centric processes that are widely expanding; however, there is always a chance of variations. Based on customer adaptation and requirements, SAP will release more scenarios or variants in later product releases of SAP S/4HANA Cloud.

Scope Items

The required SAP S/4HANA Cloud scope items are 5GT, 49X, and 2EJ. Refer to SAP Best Practices Explorer for more details on these scope items.

The communication scenario provided for integration is SAP_COM_0223.

9.7 Procurement

Let's now turn our attention to the procurement business processes, their challenges, and how a business can overcome the challenges with SAP S/4HANA Cloud in a two-tier ERP deployment.

In a headquarters and subsidiary model, the headquarters often lacks visibility into procurement activities at connected subsidiaries in real time. That means the central headquarters is unable to plan, guide, and control procurement spend at subsidiaries.

Deployed in a two-tier ERP model, SAP S/4HANA Cloud helps businesses streamline procurement processes for both a headquarters and its subsidiaries, thereby improving compliance. To optimize procurement processes in a standard headquarters-subsidiaries setup, let's examine the following four scenarios to streamline procurement operations using SAP S/4HANA Cloud:

1. Procurement handled directly by subsidiary with process visibility provided for headquarters
2. Centralized purchasing from headquarters for subsidiaries
3. Centralized contracting from headquarters for subsidiaries
4. Centralized scheduling agreements from headquarters

We'll consider each one now.

9.7.1 Procurement Handled Directly by Subsidiary

In this deployment scenario, the subsidiary is modeled to run like an independent entity with an efficient purchasing organization that has a strong presence in a geographical location. The subsidiary is equipped to run its own procurement operations and manage local inventory. Supplier management and evaluation, source of supply management, and contract management are handled locally by the subsidiary.

Figure 9.48 shows the end-to-end business process view of independent procurement operations at a subsidiary with necessary procurement visibility available for the headquarters. With SAP S/4HANA Cloud implemented at a subsidiary, the headquarters also prefers that purchasing operations be independently carried out by the subsidiary for operational ease and cost effectiveness. Predelivered reporting content makes sure that headquarters reporting requirements are managed with ease.

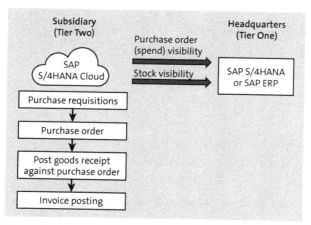

Figure 9.48 Independent Procurement Unit

The process typically starts with the creation of purchase requisitions at the subsidiary. Based on the material requirements planning (MRP) configuration, the SAP S/4HANA Cloud system can trigger purchase requisitions automatically, but these can also be created manually in the system.

As a next step, the purchaser converts purchase requisitions to purchase orders in the system. Based on the business requirements, a purchase order can be sent for required approvals. The vendor is informed about the requirement to supply the goods and services per agreed-upon terms and conditions.

SAP S/4HANA Cloud offers allowlisted APIs and CDS views to meet headquarters' reporting/analytical needs; these can be consumed to make customized reports. SAP has published the following allowlisted APIs to realize this two-tier ERP scenario:

- API_SALES_ORDER_SRV to integrate external applications with sales order processing
- API_MATERIAL_STOCK_SRV to retrieve material stock information
- API_PURCHASEORDER_PROCESS_SRV to create and update purchase orders with the data

9.7.2   Centralized Procurement at Headquarters

In a centralized purchasing setup, all purchasing activities are designed to flow through headquarters. This is attractive for organizations that aim to do the following:

- Leverage purchasing volumes as a means to reduce the cost of their operations
- Improve transparency at subsidiaries previously running decentralized local processes
- Migrate existing procurement systems to an efficient central purchasing setup

Centralized purchasing has become an integral building block of the SAP S/4HANA Cloud two-tier ERP procurement setup. Strategic procurement tasks such as supplier management benefit from both the transparency and the ability to initiate strategic activities from a single digital procurement control center. The central purchasing scenario of SAP S/4HANA Cloud gives a single point of access and visibility to purchasing documents like purchase requisitions and purchase orders from the connected subsidiary systems.

In this setup, the subsidiary's system can be an ERP system (such as SAP ERP 6.0 with EHP 6.0 or later *or* cloud or on-premise SAP S/4HANA). In such a landscape, central purchasers manage global purchases in SAP S/4HANA, meaning that they organize purchase requisitions and purchase orders centrally without having to navigate to multiple connected systems. Business process mapping enables overall visibility of purchase requisitions and purchase orders that are created across various plants at various geographical locations.

Figure 9.49 shows the end-to-end business process view of central purchasing with both subsidiaries and headquarters. First, all unsourced purchase requisitions are sent to headquarters for consolidation. Consolidation is handled at the SAP S/4HANA central purchase organization to leverage the benefits of purchasing volumes. Responsibility management gives an organization more flexibility for its approval processes. This feature is provided to display the attributes of purchase requisition items on the list page. It can facilitate centralized approval based on business requirements.

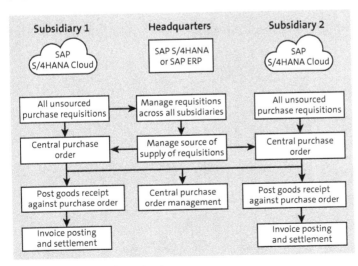

Figure 9.49 Central Purchasing

Managing the source of supply of all requisitions is another key function managed at the headquarters. A source of supply defines how or where a product is procured. This includes many other checks that are carried out: the vendor must not be deleted, an info record must exist, and so on.

A purchase order can be triggered from any system. However, central purchase order management is handled at the headquarters. An SAP Fiori app (Approve Purchase Orders) for the approval and flexible workflow framework in the headquarters' central SAP S/4HANA system facilitates the approval process for central purchase documents either at subsidiaries or at the headquarters, subject to business requirements. Purchasers can use a central processing feature on the list page of the central system to block or unblock the automatic creation of purchase orders in the connected systems. They can edit the purchase requisitions/purchase order items that are created in the central system or those that have been extracted from the connected system.

Follow-on purchasing activities like goods receipt against the purchase order and invoice posting and settlement are handled at subsidiaries locally.

For extracting both purchase orders and purchase requisitions in the central SAP S/4HANA system from connected subsidiary systems, administrators can schedule an application job in the central system. Two standard templates are delivered with SAP S/4HANA:

- Import Purchase Orders from Connected Systems
- Import Purchase Requisitions from Connected Systems

For extraction of purchase orders from different connected subsidiaries to the central system, there are two possible scenarios:

1. Initial load of all the documents
2. Delta load of required documents

Users can access the following filters to perform extraction:

- Connected system
- Document type
- Material group
- Plant
- Item category
- Purchasing organizations
- Purchasing group
- Processing status
- Creation indicator

Detailed extraction-related logs are displayed after successful completion. There is an option to perform a sanity check before the extraction job is scheduled.

9.7.3 Centralized Contracting from Headquarters

Centralized contract management is used to negotiate a global, long-term agreement between an organization and a supplier for the supply of materials or the performance of services within a certain period per predefined terms and conditions. This is common practice for organizations with the following goals:

- Streamlined contracting process across headquarters and subsidiaries
- Lowered costs and better conditions based on scaled purchasing activities across multiple subsidiaries
- Compliance with complex regulations across subsidiaries

Figure 9.50 shows the end-to-end business process view of the procurement process at a subsidiary using central contracting from headquarters. In our example, the headquarters is running SAP S/4HANA and the subsidiary is running SAP S/4HANA Cloud.

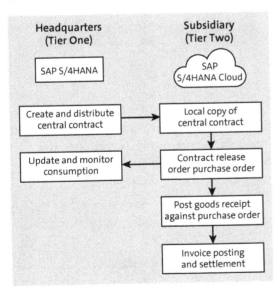

Figure 9.50 Central Contract

Once negotiated at headquarters, the central contract is created at headquarters and then distributed to the relevant subsidiaries. Operational purchasing activities like goods receipt against a purchase order and invoice posting and settlement are handled at subsidiaries locally. Users can select the type of central contract from the available options (i.e., quantity contract or value contract). The system also enforces that users add valid values in case of mandatory requirements.

Central contracts are associated to a central purchasing group, central purchasing organization, and company code for reporting purposes. To monitor usage on an ongoing basis, users can add a target value; this is mandatory when the contract is a value contract, but optional when the contract is a quantity contract. Creation of an item for lean services is possible for a free-text service.

The **Distribution** tab helps users maintain key combinations of company code, purchasing organization, currency, and plant. For central contracts, there are two distribution types: percentage and quantity.

To create a central contract pricing schema, the following master data in the SAP S/4HANA central system should be present in the subsidiary system:

- Material master data
- Supplier
- Condition types
- Pricing schema
- Incoterms
- Payment terms
- Document types
- Unit of measures
- Currency
- Tax code

Users can access the Job Schedule Import of Catalog Data app to extract the master data from different subsidiary systems into the central system. Modification of distributed contract information is possible before the distributed contract is created in the connected subsidiary system from the central purchase contract. The MM_PUR_S4_CCTR_MOD_DISTR_CTR business add-in (BAdI) can be used to modify this information.

After the central contract has been put into effect, follow-on purchasing activities like the goods receipt against the purchase order and invoice posting and settlement are handled at the subsidiary locally.

Consumption at each subsidiary is updated back to headquarters. The central on-premise SAP S/4HANA purchase system helps monitor contract consumption and renewal of expiring contracts across all subsidiaries on a real-time basis.

Organizations have the flexibility to distribute the entire quantity of the central contract to each of the connected purchasing organizations by creating local contracts in the connected systems. This also means that each system might correspond to 100 percent of the target quantity with reference to the central contract, totaling more than

100 percent of the target quantity. For example, if there are four connected systems in procurement landscape, users could allocate each of them 100 percent of the target quantity, meaning the sum of the distribution would be 400 percent of the target quantity of the central contract.

Global purchasers at the headquarters can now monitor the contract consumption and contract usage of connected systems in their central SAP S/4HANA system. This transparency helps users take the right action at the right time to ensure business runs smoothly, such as renewing a contract that is close to 100 percent consumption.

Two key analytical reports are available:

1. **Monitor Central Purchase Contract Items**
   View the details of the central purchase contract items or contextual information related to a material.
2. **Central Purchase Contract Consumption**
   Measure the consumption percentage of central purchase contracts from the previous year to date.

9.7.4   Centralized Scheduling Agreements from Headquarters

In a business environment, when there is an established source of supply, creating and managing purchase orders might become a very tedious task. To manage purchase activity over the long run, a scheduling agreement may be required.

A *centralized scheduling agreement* is a long-term agreement between a vendor and an ordering party for a predefined material or service that is procured on predetermined dates over a given time. Creating such agreements is common practice for organizations with the following goals:

- A streamlined business process across the headquarters and subsidiaries
- Monitoring of long-term agreements across connected systems

Figure 9.51 illustrates the end-to-end business process view of procurement at a subsidiary using centralized scheduling agreements from the headquarters.

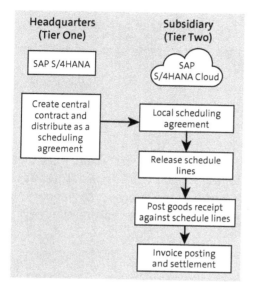

Figure 9.51 Centralized Scheduling Agreements

In the central buyer's SAP S/4HANA system at the headquarters, a central contract is created and then distributed across various connected subsidiary systems. The scheduling agreement outline agreement type is distributed to subsidiaries. Scheduling agreements both with and without release information (document types LP and LPA, respectively) are enabled. Scheduling agreements are not editable in the connected subsidiary systems, but schedule lines can be added manually in such systems.

The Schedule Import of Release Orders scheduling job can be used to extract the release information for scheduling agreements from the connected systems to update consumption.

Follow-on purchasing activities like goods receipt against a purchase order and invoice posting and settlement are handled locally at the subsidiary.

Scope Item

The required SAP S/4HANA Cloud scope item is 2ME. Refer to SAP Best Practices Explorer for more details on this scope item.

The communication scenario provided for integration is SAP_COM_0200.

9.8 Manufacturing

With recent changes in technology and digitization, the world has drastically changed; for manufacturers, the digital world has opened immense possibilities and new markets. Manufacturers want to reach their customers faster and exploit digitization without losing their competitive edge; acquisitions and mergers have become the fastest modes of reaching out to customers in new and emerging markets. With each acquisition, an organization can extend its LoBs while maintaining the core at its headquarters. To leverage the advantages of such a model, organizations are always on the lookout to simplify the processes at and get complete visibility into subsidiaries.

SAP S/4HANA Cloud's two-tier ERP capabilities target this market need, which not only helps organizations have smoother and faster mergers and acquisitions thanks to simplifying the integration between headquarters and subsidiaries but also helps organizations reduce their costs. With SAP's two-tier ERP approach, organizations can now have integrated processes running between their subsidiaries and headquarters and can have complete visibility into their subsidiaries without affecting the flexibility and freedom of the same.

In this section, we will cover how integrated manufacturing processes can be executed in a two-tier ERP mode, thus allowing organizations to utilize the core capabilities of subsidiaries and become competitive in a true sense. We'll discuss the following manufacturing scenarios:

- The subsidiary as a production unit and internal supplier to headquarters
- The subsidiary as the materials manager for a headquarters' assembly processes
- How SAP S/4HANA Cloud integrates with manufacturing execution systems

9.8.1 Production at Subsidiaries

When it comes to two-tier ERP deployment for manufacturing, one of the most common use cases occurs when a headquarters has settled and matured the main production line for the final finished goods, but its subsidiaries manufacture the required components or subassemblies. This model is commonly seen in many industry sectors, such as the automobile and pharmaceutical industries, in which the component manufacturing unit will be the subsidiary supplying units to the original equipment manufacturers (OEMs)—in other words, the headquarters.

In this two-tier ERP deployment, the headquarters will be running an on-premise ERP system (either SAP ERP or SAP S/4HANA) and the subsidiary runs SAP S/4HANA Cloud. In such deployment models, organizations will expect seamless technical integration between the headquarters and the subsidiary to support an integrated business process.

In this manufacturing scenario, master data becomes the critical factor; in this case, the most important master data elements are the material master and the business partners. As a prerequisite, master data should be in sync between the subsidiary and the headquarters. In this two-tier ERP scenario, the headquarters plays the role of master data guardian and maintains the sanctity of the data; the carefully maintained master data should be replicated from the headquarters to subsidiaries. (For SAP S/4HANA Cloud master data replication best practices, see scope item 1RO.) You can leverage several master data replication approaches, such as the DRF or API-based approaches.

Another school of thought says that subsidiaries can have their own master data that may not be available at headquarters; in such cases the subsidiaries are still allowed to create their own master data.

In this section, we will focus on the approach in which master data is replicated from the headquarters to subsidiaries. First, IDocs are used to send the master data from the headquarters (running on either SAP ERP or on-premise SAP S/4HANA) to the subsidiary (running on SAP S/4HANA Cloud). On the receiving side, the appropriate API needs to be enabled with proper communication arrangements.

Make sure configurations like RFC connections between the source and target system and the partner profile configuration are in place. For customer masters, use standard DEBMAS and material master MATMAS IDocs message types.

The first step is to trigger the outbound IDoc. As a starting point, the on-premise system will send master data through outbound IDocs. The outbound IDocs will be sent to the Cloud Integration capability, in which master data will be checked for mapping in iFlows; otherwise, using the communication scenarios, the master data will be created in SAP S/4HANA Cloud.

In this scenario, the headquarters starts with the demand management by creating planned independent requirements, either manually or by generating the forecast for finished product. Based on this, the headquarters runs MRP to create a procurement plan for finished goods, which is procured from the subsidiary location. As a result, purchase requisitions are generated. On approval, the purchase requisition will be converted to a purchase order with the vendor as the subsidiary. (Note that the purchase requisition/purchase order is an optional process.) At headquarters, the planners can analyze and evaluate the capacity load situation in subsidiary location by using two-tier ERP analytics. Planners can also manually create the purchase order directly without using the MRP run.

As shown in Figure 9.52, after issuing the purchase order from the headquarters on the subsidiary, the corresponding sales order will be created automatically at the subsidiary. A document reference in the sales order and purchase order will help link the demand and the supply: the sales order will reflect the customer purchase order number, and the purchase order will show the reference document number under the **Confirmation** tab.

If an available-to-promise (ATP) check is activated at a subsidiary, then the SAP S/4HANA Cloud system will perform the availability check and propose the delivery schedule back to headquarters. The delivery date is updated in the purchase order issued from headquarters.

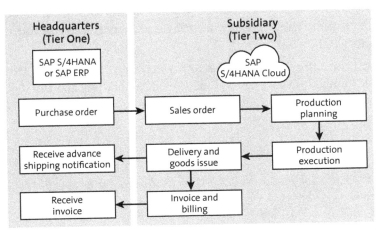

Figure 9.52 Subsidiary as Production Unit and Internal Supplier to Headquarters

At the subsidiary, the sales order becomes the primary demand. Subsequently, the MRP is run to fulfill the demands received from headquarters. This will generate the planned orders and purchase requisitions for produced and procured items (raw materials). These planned orders and purchase requisitions are converted into production orders and purchase orders.

Next, the production order must be released and confirmed. Headquarters can receive the update on the production bookings from the subsidiary through the two-tier ERP analytics report. Headquarters can also get a report on the production performance of the subsidiary location, scrap generated during the production process, raw material inventory levels, and an overview of any deviation from the raw material consumption.

Once the stock is available, the shipping specialist will review the sales order, and an outbound delivery is created against the sales order. This outbound delivery from the subsidiary will automatically create the ASN for the inbound delivery at the headquarters against the purchase order. This is the next level of integration provided by the two-tier ERP approach, in which the purchase order at the headquarters will be updated with inbound deliveries from the subsidiary.

Subsequently, at the headquarters, the goods receipt will be made against the inbound delivery.

Finally, the billing document will be generated at the subsidiary and a supplier invoice created at the headquarters. This will create the accounts payable liability to the subsidiary at headquarters.

This is the third level of integration with the headquarters provided by SAP's two-tier ERP approach. Now the headquarters will make the payment to the subsidiary, in the same way as clearing its vendors' liability. This will settle the accounts receivable transaction from headquarters at the subsidiary.

For manufacturers with complex processes, this SAP S/4HANA Cloud two-tier ERP deployment model facilitates close collaboration between headquarters and the subsidiary via integrated processes and visibility, easy maintenance of master data, and reduced manual effort.

Scope Item

The required SAP S/4HANA Cloud scope item is 21T. Refer to SAP Best Practices Explorer for more details on this scope item.

9.8.2   Assembly at Subsidiaries with Components Provided by Headquarters

With two-tier ERP for manufacturing, another use case occurs when a subsidiary manages assembly for the headquarters using components provided by the headquarters. In today's competitive world, many organizations outsource small assemblies to their subsidiaries, which have expertise in particular areas. (In the previous scenario, the subsidiary only prepared the components and subassemblies, not the entire assemblies.)

In the automobile industry, for example, the assembly of a wire harness requires expertise and specialized equipment; many automobile manufacturers prefer that their sophisticated subsidiaries handle this rather than their headquarters. In this scenario, the headquarters will supply the component to the subsidiary against the subcontracting purchase order.

In a two-tier ERP context, the subsidiary (which runs on SAP S/4HANA Cloud) has expertise in particular products and supplies these products to the headquarters (which runs on either SAP ERP or SAP S/4HANA). Let's see in detail how the subsidiary manages assembly for headquarters with components provided by headquarters.

As a prerequisite, the master data between headquarters and the subsidiary should be in sync. In general, master data will be created in the headquarters and shared across subsidiaries.

Figure 9.53 explains how the materials are handled by the subsidiary to make assemblies for the headquarters. The process starts when a purchase order is created at the headquarters. As part of integration in a two-tier ERP setup, an automatic sales order will be created at the subsidiary system with reference to the purchase order from the headquarters. If prices are within the limits, then an automatic order confirmation will be sent back to the headquarters and the information will be updated in the **Confirmation** tab of the purchase order. In a two-tier ERP system, purchase order to sales order automation supports change and delete processes also.

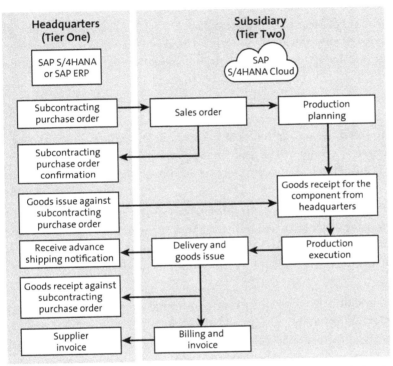

Figure 9.53 Managing Materials at Subsidiary to Manage Assembly for Headquarters

At the subsidiary, the demand fulfilment process starts with the MRP run for the demand, which comes in the form of sales orders from headquarters. The planned orders for the assemblies and the purchase requisitions for the components will be generated from the MRP run at the subsidiary. The purchase requisition for the components will be converted to purchase orders with zero value because these components are provided by the headquarters for assembly processing. The components, which will be received by the subsidiary from the headquarters, will be part of the books of account of the headquarters; the subsidiary will be the custodian, and these components' inventory will not hit the books of account of the subsidiary. The components requirements information will be communicated to headquarters manually via email or over the phone.

The headquarters will already have the bill of materials (BOM) for the subassembly and the components required for it. The headquarters will then issue the components against the subcontracting purchase order on the subsidiary and communicate the same to the subsidiary manually via email or over the phone.

A goods receipt will be posted for the components at the subsidiary with zero price against the purchase order created at the subsidiary with the headquarters as the supplier. Once received, these components will create inventory in the subsidiary system and will not hit the books of account of the subsidiary. From the headquarters' point of view, the components inventory will still show in its books of account, and though the components are physically at the subsidiary, the headquarters has visibility of the components.

Once components are available at a subsidiary, the production process starts with the conversion of a planned order to production. Components will be staged for the production order; then the order will be released to carry out the real production. Once production is complete, the order will be confirmed against produced quantities, along with scrap if there is any. Finally, a goods receipt will be posted against the production order.

The shipping specialist will start the order fulfilment process by creating an outbound delivery against the sales order once assembly is ready. The warehouse clerk will pick the order and post goods issue against the outbound delivery. Once goods issue is posted, an automatic ASN will be sent to headquarters under the two-tier ERP approach.

At headquarters, an inbound delivery will be created automatically and will be updated in the **Purchase Order Confirmation** tab. This will be helpful for goods receipt planning. Once goods are received from a subsidiary, the warehouse clerk will post the goods receipt against the inbound delivery at headquarters against the purchase order.

At the subsidiary, the billing clerk will create a billing document against the outbound delivery. Once the billing document is posted, an automatic invoice will be sent to the headquarters for payment. The headquarters will review the subsidiary's invoice and release payment.

Scope Item

The required SAP S/4HANA Cloud scope item is 2WL. Refer to SAP Best Practices Explorer for more details on this scope item.

To summarize, for manufacturers with sophisticated processes, this two-tier ERP deployment option provides a highly scalable, cost-effective business model that addresses the global requirements locally and can be deployed quickly.

9.8.3   Integration with Manufacturing Execution Systems

The main purpose of a manufacturing execution system (MES) is to monitor, track, and report the manufacturing process from the beginning stages of the process through the finished product level, recording the work in progress. An MES also helps enhance production efficiency and increase adoption of Industry 4.0 concepts.

As part of two-tier ERP deployment, a subsidiary using SAP S/4HANA Cloud will leverage the headquarters' MES to monitor and control the production process at the subsidiary.

Figure 9.54 shows the end-to-end manufacturing process at the subsidiary location that shares the headquarters' MES. As a prerequisite step before MES integration with SAP S/4HANA Cloud, master data and transaction data should in replicated in the MES. MES systems often require the following master data and transaction data:

- Material master
- Work center
- Routing
- Production order
- Goods movement

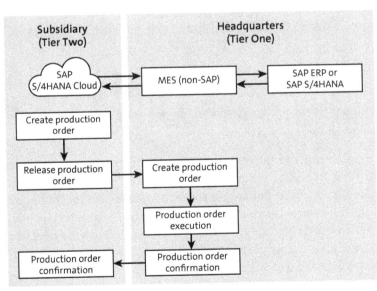

Figure 9.54 Supplier Subsidiary's Integration with MES

Through the DRF, you can replicate master data and transaction data via IDocs. You can also refer to the master data handling approaches from Section 9.3.

The manufacturing cycle starts with demand management. In this process, the production planner will have a forecast from the sales team or a concrete sales order from a customer for the finished goods. Now the sales plan needs to be synced with the production plan.

The next step is to create the production plan. Production planning is the core step of the end-to-end manufacturing process. Based on this production plan, subsequent steps are decided, and the planner will schedule the MRP. MRP will perform the net requirement calculation for the complete BOM structure and check whether the requirements are covered by the existing stock. If not, it will create the procurement proposals. Based on the procurement type, planned orders for produced items and purchase requisitions for procured items will be generated. The production planner will evaluate the MRP results and convert the planned order to a production order. The production supervisor will release the production order. This will release not only the production order header but also the operations.

This step is the handshake between the "top-floor" system (here, SAP S/4HANA Cloud) and the "shop-floor" system (here, the MES). So far, the focus has been on the top-floor system; now, let's turn our attention to the shop floor.

The MES system will get only production orders with the released status; the released production orders are replicated in the MES system. Use communication scenario SAP_COM_0156 to integrate a manufacturing execution system through ALE IDocs, BAPIs, and OData calls. This communication scenario can do the following:

- Replicate product orders from SAP S/4HANA Cloud to a client's outbound IDocs
- Replicate planned orders from SAP S/4HANA Cloud to a client's outbound IDocs
- Replicate work centers from SAP S/4HANA Cloud to a client's outbound IDocs
- Replicate routings from SAP S/4HANA Cloud to a client's outbound IDocs
- Carry out confirmation in a make-to-stock scenario for inbound RFCs
- Confirm production scrap for inbound RFCs

On receiving the production order in the MES system, the shop order is generated in the MES system. Once this is released, a unique shop floor control (SFC) number will be generated. This SFC number can have a quantity of one or greater than one based on the material being built. The production operator will pick the SFC and start the build, using a production operator dashboard. Once the SFC build is completed, the operator completes the SFC and records any nonconformity. The completion of the SFC will trigger a production order confirmation in SAP S/4HANA Cloud.

The production order confirmation in the subsidiary's SAP S/4HANA Cloud system will also include the production yield, raw material consumption, scrap, and rework quantities, along with confirmation of the start and finish date and time. This will result in the production of the finished goods, which will update the inventory and the financials.

This scenario illustrates how the two-tier ERP approach helps connect the SAP S/4HANA Cloud system at the subsidiary with the MES at the headquarters.

9.8.4 Just-in-Time Calls

One of the most common and frequently used scenarios in the automotive supplier and component manufacturing industry is just-in-time (JIT) supply to customer from stock. In this scenario, the supplier delivers components to the manufacturer in a JIT fashion. This scenario is a classic example of two-tier ERP deployment in an ecosystem deployment model.

Many automotive suppliers face the following challenges:

- Inherent complexity of multilevel suppliers and contractors
- Demand plan visibility
- Maintaining optimal inventory levels
- Inaccurate forecast of demand
- Inability to manage complete supply chain in an automated and efficient way

One of the major expectations from OEM is that suppliers need to manage delivery of components at the right time, in the right quantity, in the right sequence, and at the right place: JIT.

Figure 9.55 shows the sample deployment architecture for JIT call integration with supplier systems (automotive suppliers). As you can see, the JIT call from OEM gets passed through a middleware layer to the supplier system for the fulfillment.

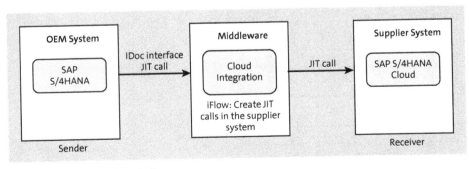

Figure 9.55 Just in Time Calls

Two important master data objects to consider in this scenario are as follows:

- Supply area
- Control cycle

These Kanban-specific master data objects need to be maintained apart from the regular master data like material master, business partner, and sales and purchasing scheduling agreements.

The overall process flow can be summarized as follows:

1. Manage master data.
2. Manage sales scheduling agreements.
3. Process delivery schedules.
4. Process customer JIT calls.
5. Process outbound deliveries.
6. Process billing.

Scope Item

Scope item 2EM takes care of JIT supply to customer from stock.

The communication arrangement SAP_COM_0168 in SAP S/4 HANA Cloud automates the process flow shown in Figure 9.56. The diagram provides a more detailed view of the process flow between the OEM (customer) and the supplier, from creation of the original JIT call through supplier creation of outbound deliveries to goods picking and issue to invoicing the OEM. The customer side shows the process steps on the OEM side of receiving the delivery and processing the invoice payment.

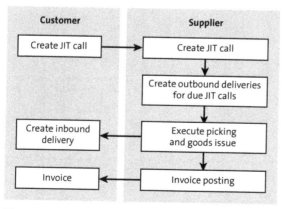

Figure 9.56 JIT Process Flow

9.8.5 pMRP with Scheduling Agreements

This two-tier ERP scenario covers the process of medium-term planning with predictive material and resource planning (pMRP), as shown in Figure 9.57. A business use case example is where the headquarters running on SAP S/4HANA manufactures the final assembly and the subsidiary running on SAP S/4HANA Cloud supplies a key subassembly as part of the final product.

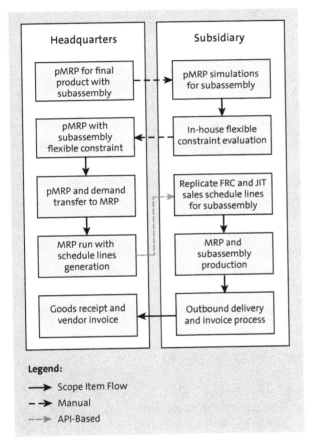

Figure 9.57 pMRP Process Flow

Using this scenario's capabilities, the headquarters and subsidiary can share details of targets and constraints for a quantity per period bucket through collaborative planning. Headquarters initiates the planning process through pMRP. The constraint quantity received from the subsidiary for the subassembly is considered at the headquarters to arrive at the final plan to manufacture the final product.

Business benefits include the following:

- Capability to create simulations at both the headquarters and subsidiary, considering types of flexible constraints, enabling you to plan effectively with resource-based simulations

- Joint planning between the headquarters and subsidiaries to arrive at a consensus plan for the final product and subassembly

- Operative planning with forecast-based schedules for the subsidiary to initiate material resource planning

The headquarters initiates a planning process through pMRP and shares a subassembly plan with the subsidiary. It receives a flexible constraint quantity as an output of simulation at the subsidiary. The finalized plan for the final product, along with subassembly quantities, forms the demand for MRP. Purchasing scheduling agreements are updated with forecast delivery schedules and JIT schedule lines, and goods receipts are posted at the headquarters. Later, the invoice is generated at the subsidiary and sent to the headquarters.

At the subsidiary, the pMRP simulation helps you plan early for subassemblies to communicate with the headquarters. In-house production proposals are generated when MRP is run at the subsidiary. An outbound delivery is created, and posting the goods issue for the delivery allows you to generate an invoice for sharing with the headquarters. In summary, this establishes synergy at the time of operative planning with forecast-based schedules for the subsidiary to plan in advance and quickly respond to JIT schedule lines from the headquarters, thus helping manage lean inventory and production.

9.9   Supply Chain Transportation Management

Typically, large enterprises are involved in transportation management operations, with the headquarters organization taking care of transportation planning activities for the transportation requirements generated at the subsidiaries. Let's consider a business case example using an on-premise SAP S/4HANA system at the headquarters, which needs to function as a planning system to receive demand generated through freight units. The freight units are triggered from sales orders in SAP S/4HANA Cloud and need to be replicated to the on-premise SAP S/4HANA system for further planning.

From the on-premise SAP S/4HANA system, the transportation planner is responsible for creating a freight order and assigns the freight unit received from SAP S/4HANA Cloud. The transportation planner also assigns a carrier to the freight order as the responsible party to execute the transportation of the goods. The freight orders created in the on-premise SAP S/4HANA system are replicated back to SAP S/4HANA Cloud for completing the subsequent steps, including freight order monitoring.

Business benefits include the following:

- Support transportation execution and monitoring in SAP S/4HANA Cloud and transportation planning in on-premise SAP S/4HANA
- Reduce freight costs with early transportation planning capabilities based on freight orders
- Get fewer delivery changes during logistics execution with late delivery creation based on the transportation plan

As shown in Figure 9.58, a sales order is created, triggering creation of the freight units as transportation requirements. Created freight units can be displayed in the document flow in the sales order. The freight units are replicated to the on-premise SAP S/4HANA system. The freight order is created for the selected freight units with the assignment of a carrier. The freight order created in the on-premise system is replicated into the SAP S/4HANA Cloud system. Subsequent process steps as described in scope item 3EP can be used to execute an end-to-end process: for example, delivery processing, monitoring execution of freight orders, accrual posting, billing and supplier invoicing, and so on.

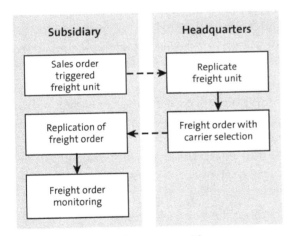

Figure 9.58 Supply Chain Process Flow

The following integration patterns are used:

- **Replicate freight unit from SAP S/4HANA Cloud to SAP S/4HANA**
  This is an outbound asynchronous SOAP-based API. Standard outbound interface `/SCMTMS/CO_CPX_TOR_GN_RQ_OUT` can be leveraged to create freight units.

- **Replicate freight order from SAP S/4HANA to SAP S/4HANA Cloud**
  This is an inbound asynchronous SOAP-based API. Standard inbound interface `/SCMTMS/II_CPX_TOR_GN_RQ_IN` can be leveraged to create the freight order from a freight unit.

Scope Items

The required SAP S/4HANA Cloud scope items are 3EP and 4OZ. The communication scenarios required for this integration are shown in Table 9.1.

Communication Arrangement ID	Name
SAP_COM_0008	Business partner integration
SAP_COM_0009	Product integration
SAP_COM_0425	Location integration
SAP_COM_0414	Transactional data (freight units and freight orders)

Table 9.1 Communication Scenarios for Supply Chain Transportation

9.10   Integration

In a two-tier ERP setup with SAP S/4HANA Cloud, integration plays an important role in an organization's digital transformation. On their journey to adopt innovations in the cloud, customers increasingly extend and integrate their existing on-premise applications into the cloud. In this section, we will cover available integration approaches, monitoring, and accelerators that can be managed in a two-tier ERP deployment with SAP S/4HANA Cloud.

Integration has become a key enabler for the digital transformation of organizations. Therefore, one goal of the future SAP integration strategy is to increase the simplicity of integration between SAP applications by aligning their processes and related data models, including the publication of APIs. The target is to simplify new integration solutions, especially for LoB cloud integration scenarios, and to further deepen integrations between SAP applications over time.

Enterprise architects defining the integration strategy in their company's system landscape usually try to find the best possible way to provide integration guidance across multiple teams, projects, and system integrators. For them, it is important to look for the most suitable integration technologies to approach new integration domains. Integration is a critical component of two-tier ERP solution. As shown in Figure 9.59, SAP S/4HANA Cloud can be integrated with both on-premise and cloud solutions from SAP and third-party providers.

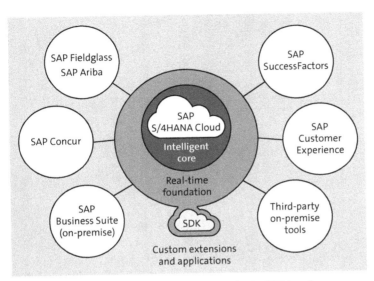

Figure 9.59 SAP S/4HANA Cloud Integrated into SAP Landscape

9.10.1   Integration Approaches

SAP recommends two connectivity options to integrate a two-tier ERP setup with SAP S/4HANA Cloud:

1. **Cloud Integration**
   This cloud-based integration platform is hosted by SAP Integration Suite; it is a process and data integration middleware tool in a secure and reliable environment.

2. **SAP Process Orchestration**
   This on-premise middleware platform is installed in the customer landscape; it designs, models, executes, and monitors business processes by ensuring connectivity to multiple business/technical systems and applications (SAP and non-SAP).

These connectivity landscapes are illustrated in Figure 9.60. Factors to consider when determining the best connectivity option include the dominant system landscape, the availability of prepackaged content, go-live timelines, and the total cost of ownership. For example, standard content is available for the Cloud Integration capability, which reduces the total cost of implementation; in contrast, a custom interface needs to be built for SAP Process Integration or SAP Process Orchestration, which can extend the implementation process.

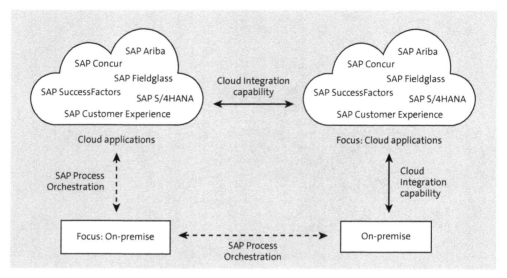

Figure 9.60 Two-Tier ERP Integration Approaches

Together, these integration approaches can support prepackaged integrations, template-based integrations, and allowlisted API-based integrations.

Let's look at each integration approach:

- **Prepackaged integration**
  For a seamless two-tier ERP integration with SAP S/4HANA Cloud, SAP has provided prepackaged integration content called iFlows, which are designed for the Cloud Integration capability. Think of them as bundles of ready-to-implement content that help reduce the total cost of implementation.

- **Template-based integration**
  Although the predefined, prepackaged integration scenarios cover many use cases, sometimes customers find that a standard scenario does not meet their requirements (e.g., a need to map an enhanced API). When this happens, customers can extend and adjust the standard content per their requirements by using the extensibility and self-service configuration features provided with SAP S/4HANA Cloud. This template-based approach can save a lot of time and effort because customers can adjust the content as needed based on a stable foundation of predefined and preconfigured content. For example, a customer can map a change in the drop shipping process.

- **Allowlisted API-based integration**
  When standard integration content is not available for a two-tier ERP integration, customers can use approved (allowlisted) APIs to build custom scenarios.

  APIs are predefined services used to interact with SAP S/4HANA Cloud and other SAP cloud products. In the case of SAP S/4HANA Cloud, they help integrate two-tier ERP business scenarios via Cloud Integration, enabling customers to securely expand and extend digital apps to other systems. They come in two variants:

- **OData protocol**
This is a data access protocol used to query and update data and to trigger business logic. It has been designed to provide standard create, read, update, and delete (CRUD) access via HTTP(S) and synchronous request with response.

- **SOAP protocol**
This is a protocol for exchanging information in distributed environments.

SAP API Business Hub is a centralized location for the allowlisted APIs used in SAP S/4HANA Cloud. You can access SAP API Business Hub at *https://api.sap.com*.

APIs are organized per inbound and outbound scenarios. *Inbound* refers to message processing from a remote system (in many cases, located in the customer landscape) to SAP S/4HANA Cloud. *Outbound* refers to message processing from SAP S/4HANA Cloud to a remote system.

Once you've selected an API in SAP API Business Hub for the required business scenario, you then need to find the communication scenario ID from the API details; create the respective communication arrangement and assign the communication system and communication user; and configure the inbound and outbound services by providing the host and port details of the receiver system. These steps are outlined in Figure 9.61.

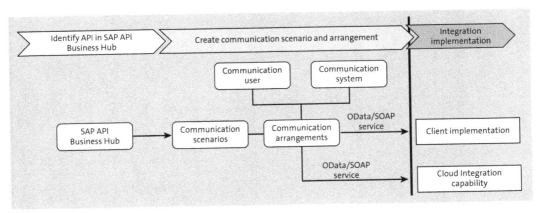

Figure 9.61 Consumption of Allowlisted API

9.10.2   Monitoring and Extensibility

Integration scenarios designed for two-tier ERP business scenarios need to be monitored and their errors handled. SAP Application Interface Framework enables you to monitor interfaces and their data messages and execute error handling in SAP S/4HANA Cloud. Because it displays errors or successful messages and shows the reason for the message failure, SAP Application Interface Framework monitoring saves time in daily work and increases efficiency in monitoring and error handling.

Figure 9.62 shows the message dashboard, which displays the number of errors and successful messages; Figure 9.63 shows the reasons for message failures.

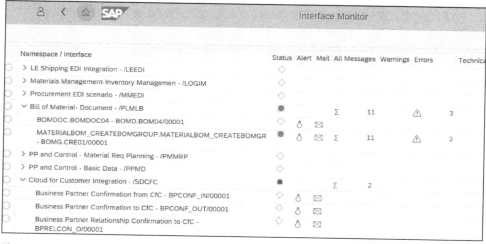

Figure 9.62 Error Monitoring in SAP Application Interface Framework

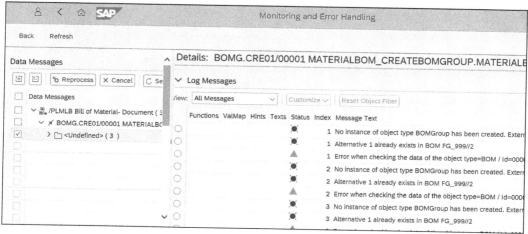

Figure 9.63 Error Handling in SAP Application Interface Framework

SAP S/4HANA Cloud also supports EDI capabilities—outbound or inbound services that can be configured by output parameter determination for event-based processing. EDIs need to be handled using the Cloud Integration middleware to build integration flows and mappings. This will enable consumption of existing EDIs for communication with the headquarters' on-premise systems. You can further enhance EDI services using the extensibility functionality in SAP S/4HANA Cloud.

9.11   Sustainability Product Footprint Management

The headquarters and subsidiary companies can connect to SAP Product Footprint Management on SAP BTP, which can act as a central system to calculate product footprints for products (see Figure 9.64). SAP Product Footprint Management is an SAP cloud-native application to calculate product footprints periodically and at scale considering the entire product lifecycle. It enables business users to replicate business activity and master data from the headquarters and subsidiary companies on SAP S/4HANA or SAP S/4HANA Cloud and map them with emission factors to calculate the product footprints based on a specified set of plants and time ranges. The calculated footprints can be integrated back, which enables companies to optimize their processes and make smart purchasing decisions to minimize greenhouse gas emissions.

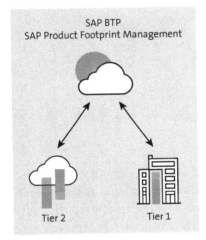

Figure 9.64 SAP Product Footprint Management

Now let's see the different phases involved in product footprint management, as shown in Figure 9.65:

❶ **Data acquisition**
As a first step, the headquarters and subsidiary companies on SAP S/4HANA and cloud systems are integrated with the SAP Product Footprint Management solution on SAP BTP for acquiring the existing business data and structures. First, SAP Product Footprint Management acquires product, business partner, material flow, and cost estimate info as primary data. There is a vast reuse of existing logic from inventory management and costing structures for calculation of footprints for purchased products and manufactured products. New APIs for data acquisition will support SAP S/4HANA customers on former releases, as well as SAP ERP customers in a two-tier ERP landscape.

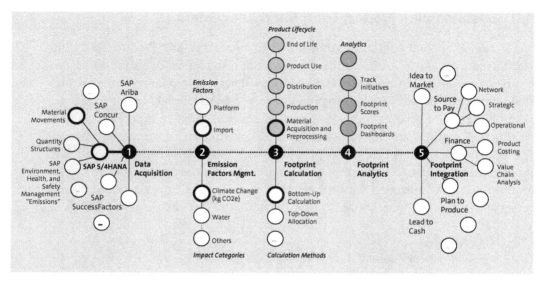

Figure 9.65 SAP Product Footprint Management Phases

❷ Emission factors management

Emission factors management helps customers upload the sustainability content from external data providers.

❸ Footprint calculation

The data acquired from source headquarters and subsidiary systems is mapped with the emission factors uploaded from external data providers with the help of preconfigured mapping templates for purchased products and manufactured products, and the climate change footprints are calculated. The calculation is achieved with the Calculate Footprints app. The footprint calculation can be executed on demand for the period, or the sustainability business support specialist can trigger only delta calculations from the previous iteration. Test runs can be triggered to validate the calculated footprints and analyze for any errors. The Monitor Footprints app allows monitoring of the footprint calculations. The sustainability specialist can analyze the footprint results and can give guidance for optimization.

❹ Footprint analytics

SAP Product Footprint Management can be integrated with SAP Sustainability Control Tower through APIs to analyze product footprints and gain new insights via holistic steering and reporting based on financial and environmental, social, and governance (ESG) indicators. This gives automated, timely, and auditable ESG reporting for a variety of regulations, standards, and ratings. SAP Product Footprint Management analytics dashboards are available as predelivered content on SAP Analytics Cloud, which gives footprint analytics for the purchased materials, supplier inflow analytics, supplier inflow heatmap, inventory analysis, inventory heatmap, and inventory table view.

❺ Footprint integration

The footprints can be published back from the SAP Product Footprint Management solution to the source headquarters and subsidiary systems on SAP S/4HANA Cloud and on-premise, and business users can analyze them in the View Product Footprints app. Business users like the inventory analyst can also find the footprints integrated in their regular SAP Fiori apps like Purchase Requisition and Stock—Multiple Materials and can make informed sourcing decisions to optimize and minimize the climate change impact.

These are the first use cases for purchased materials and manufactured materials, and there is more in the roadmap covering the footprint calculations at scale for the entire product lifecycle for disclosure and internal product optimization.

> **Scope Item**
>
> The required scope item for SAP S/4HANA Cloud integration with SAP Product Footprint Management is 5IM. Refer to SAP Best Practices Explorer for more details on this scope item.

9.12   Analytics and Reporting

Analytics is information resulting from the semantic analysis of data presented in a meaningful pattern. Using analytics, companies can gain fast and accurate insights into their business and implement new processes and applications based on those insights.

A growing number of organizations are looking for public cloud analytics solutions that can be implemented quickly without the need for manual upgrades and migrations. Similarly, analytics in a two-tier ERP deployment is an important consideration while deploying subsidiary ERP solutions. If pockets of analytics solutions remain in silos, then a company can't see the complete picture, thereby inhibiting the ability of the group organization to spot opportunities for growth and potential savings that can be obtained either due to overlap in operations or inefficient processes.

It is important that a decision-making chief analytics officer (CAO) or another C-suite executive has ownership of analytics across all groups' concerns and ties it in to the groups' visions and corporate priorities. Business benefits of central analytics include streamlined processes between headquarters and subsidiaries for better planning and reporting, ability of the headquarters to have visibility into subsidiaries' expenses and revenue, and process centralization.

In a two-tier ERP setup, analytics data integration is made possible in the following ways:

- **Data extraction**

  Data extraction is the process of retrieving data out of (usually unstructured or poorly structured) data sources for further data processing or data storage (i.e., data migration). This provides cross-system analytics with historical and near-real-time reporting capabilities.

- **Data replication**

  Data replication involves exchanges of data among source and target systems that are involved in an operational cross-system analytics scenario (i.e., data copy).

- **Virtual data access**

  In virtual data access, the data still resides in the source system and only the required data is read when needed. Virtual access can work in real time and be bidirectional, but it works best for lower volumes of data.

In this section, we'll discuss two-tier ERP analytics options that depend on these data integration methods.

9.12.1   Analytics via SAP Business Warehouse Tools

Figure 9.66 shows the most commonly used approach, in which SAP BW and SAP BPC are the central analytical systems deployed at the headquarters. This relies on the data extraction approach we discussed earlier. SAP BW will be used as a single source of truth for consolidated reporting across all subsidiaries in the landscape. The data from all the subsidiaries running SAP S/4HANA Cloud will be extracted to SAP BW. The staging and transformation for this scenario needs to be handled as a custom development on the SAP BW side.

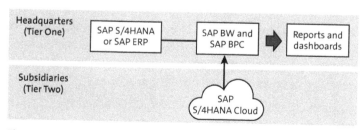

Figure 9.66 Analytics with SAP BW and SAP BPC

This approach is common when an organization has the following requirements:

- Optimization of existing investments in SAP BW and SAP BPC installations
- Delta and full data loads
- Change pointer support
- Data transformation required at a staging layer

There is one variant to this approach. As shown in Figure 9.67, it's possible that the headquarters might run SAP BW/4HANA and SAP BPC. (SAP BW/4HANA is an implementation of SAP BW running on SAP HANA, itself the database underlying SAP S/4HANA Cloud). In this case, the extraction from SAP S/4HANA Cloud would be handled via CDS-based ODP extraction into SAP BW/4HANA.

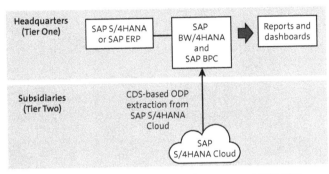

Figure 9.67 Analytics with SAP BW/4HANA and SAP BPC

9.12.2   Central Analytics on SAP BTP

SAP BTP, the platform as a service (PaaS) offering from SAP, is best positioned for developing custom analytical reporting. It provides many embedded analytical services, like streaming analytics or persisting data from external systems via data replication or remote access.

In the context of a two-tier ERP setup, SAP BTP is ably positioned to collate data from multiple systems to perform central analytics and reporting. It sits between the headquarters' on-premise system and subsidiaries' cloud systems, as shown in Figure 9.68.

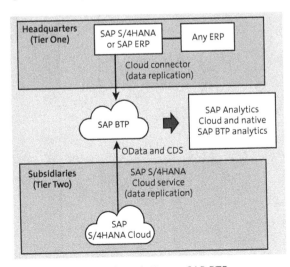

Figure 9.68 Central Analytics on SAP BTP

For on-premise SAP S/4HANA, SAP HANA smart data integration (SDI) is the recommended way to connect. As a prerequisite, SDI agents need to be installed on-premise. Then SDI can perform delta database replication based on transaction logs with custom logic.

For SAP S/4HANA Cloud, you can use the Replicate CDS Views app to replicate CDS views from SAP S/4HANA Cloud to SAP BTP. Use communication scenario SAP_COM_0048 or an OData API for this data replication.

This approach is recommended when an organization seeks to do the following:

- Leverage PaaS investments
- Leverage cloud SDK investments on SAP BTP
- Enhance partner analytical offerings by leveraging side-by-side extensibility on SAP BTP

9.12.3   Central Analytics on SAP Analytics Cloud

Let's take analytics via SAP BTP one step further with analytics via SAP Analytics Cloud, a tool built on SAP BTP. From planning predictive analytics to creating compelling data visualizations and from exploring data analytics to gaining smart insights along with data transformation, SAP Analytics Cloud has become the recommended solution for end-to-end business analytics in the cloud.

In a two-tier ERP deployment, as shown in Figure 9.69, the headquarters and subsidiary systems' data can be combined in SAP Analytics Cloud for planning (planning models for data-driven budgeting and forecasting), collaboration (access-controlled alignment across plants/segments/business entities), and forecasting (machine learning–driven forecasting).

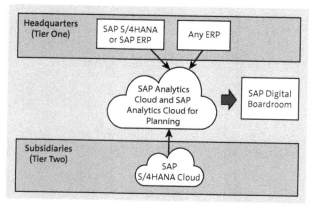

Figure 9.69 Analytics on SAP Analytics Cloud

This approach is recommended when an organization seeks to do the following:

- Execute a cloud-first business intelligence strategy
- Use SAP Digital Boardroom to give C-level executives more contextual information
- Use predefined libraries in SAP Analytics Cloud rather than the SDK approach of SAP BTP
- Develop ad hoc insights by slicing and dicing data

9.12.4 Ad Hoc Custom Reporting

One final analytics reporting method is known as the Z-code approach. Through this method, ad hoc custom reports are developed on the headquarters' on-premise SAP S/4HANA or SAP ERP system. Then, allowlisted APIs and CDS views on SAP S/4HANA Cloud can be used to read required data from subsidiaries running SAP S/4HANA Cloud.

Figure 9.70 shows this deployment: here, the headquarters runs SAP S/4HANA or SAP ERP and subsidiaries run SAP S/4HANA Cloud. The connectivity to SAP S/4HANA Cloud is enacted via the cloud connector.

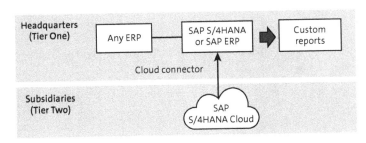

Figure 9.70 Ad Hoc Custom Reporting

This approach is recommended when an organization seeks to do the following:

- Create ad hoc reports
- Limit additional investments in analytical tools

9.13 Accelerators

An *accelerator* is predefined integration content delivered for two-tier ERP integration with SAP S/4HANA Cloud. If a standard integration for a specific business scenario is not available, SAP provides accelerators that can be deployed in customer landscapes.

Let's discuss a few of the most important accelerators delivered and their setup steps.

9.13.1   Download Accelerators

Various accelerators are available for two-tier ERP integration. Follow these steps to download various two-tier ERP accelerators:

1. Open SAP Best Practices Explorer at *https://rapid.sap.com/bp/*.
2. Select the SAP S/4HANA solution package, as shown in Figure 9.71.
3. Select the **SAP Best Practices for SAP S/4HANA Cloud** solution package.

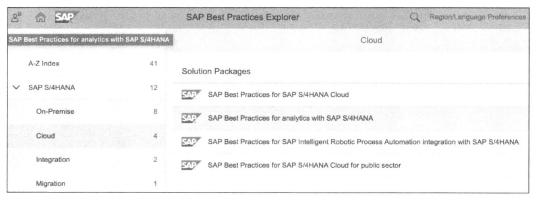

Figure 9.71 SAP Best Practices Explorer

4. In the **Scope Item Groups** dropdown, select **SAP S/4HANA Cloud for Hybrid Deployment (2-Tier ERP)**, as shown in Figure 9.72.

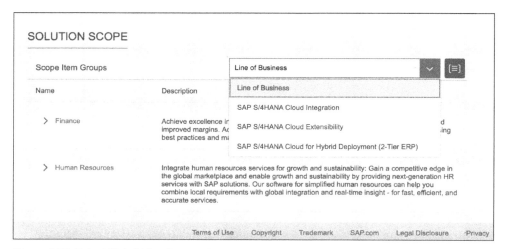

Figure 9.72 Select Hybrid Deployment

5. Select **2-Tier ERP Assets (User Guides, Templates, Etc.)**, as shown in Figure 9.73. This will trigger a download of all accelerators delivered with two-tier ERP.

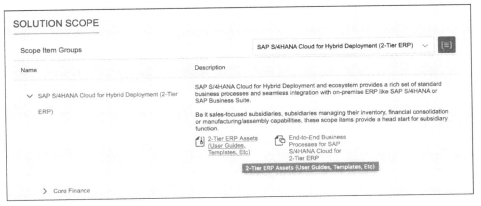

Figure 9.73 Two-Tier ERP Accelerator Download

9.13.2   Master Data Handling with SAP BTP Workflows

This accelerator provides the details of central master data handling of business partners using SAP BTP.

In a two-tier ERP scenario, a subsidiary (which runs SAP S/4HANA Cloud) wants to create a business partner (with the vendor role) for a local vendor. Because master data creation is performed at the headquarters (which runs on-premise), the subsidiary doesn't have the authorization to create a business partner.

Using a business partner workflow process, the subsidiary requests the creation of a business partner at headquarters. Once approved, the business partner is created in the headquarters—and then is replicated to the subsidiary.

Scope Item
Configurations and setup instructions mentioned in scope item 1R0 are mandatory for setting up the accelerator.

9.13.3   Finance Master Data Replication

A dedicated two-tier ERP accelerator to replicate cost center and profit center master data from the headquarters running SAP ERP or on-premise SAP S/4HANA to subsidiaries running SAP S/4HANA Cloud is provided.

Accelerator Download
You can download the two-tier ERP accelerator package from the SAP Best Practices Explorer as shown earlier and rename the file called "2Tier_FIN_Master_Data_Integration.dat" to "2Tier_FIN_Master_Data_Integration.zip" before importing it into Cloud Integration.

> **Communication Scenario**
>
> The communication scenario used for replication is SAP_COM_0179.

The outgoing IDocs (COSMAS01 and PRCMAS02) need to be processed and converted to cost center/profit center master data.

For the profit center, an iFlow is available; an example is shown in Figure 9.74.

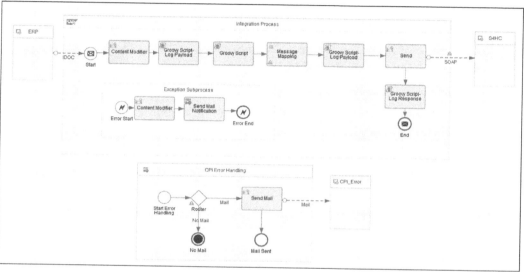

Figure 9.74 Profit Center iFlow: Two-Tier Accelerator

The message monitoring capability in the Cloud Integration capability can be used for error handling and for monitoring error/success messages.

9.13.4   Purchase Order to Sales Order Automation

Let's look at another common scenario in a two-tier ERP model, in which an organization sells from stock at a subsidiary with drop-shipping from the headquarters. In this setup, the subsidiary acts as a mere sales office with a sales presence; the delivery of the material is the responsibility of the headquarters. A purchase order from the subsidiary is converted into a sales order at the headquarters in this scenario, called PO2SO.

The Purchase Order – Sales Order Automation accelerator for SAP S/4HANA Cloud will provide the PO2SO integration, whereby the purchase order created at the subsidiary (running SAP S/4HANA Cloud) will be converted to a sales order at the headquarters (running on-premise SAP S/4HANA or SAP ERP).

9.13.5 Billing Document-Supplier Invoice Automation

In a situation in which products are sold by the headquarters to a subsidiary, one key step is for the headquarters to send a billing document, which is converted at the subsidiary into a supplier invoice.

The Billing Document – Supplier Invoice Automation accelerator for SAP S/4HANA Cloud enables the billing document created at the headquarters (running on-premise SAP S/4HANA or SAP ERP) to be converted to a supplier invoice at the subsidiary (running SAP S/4HANA Cloud).

Communication Scenario

The communication scenario used for supplier invoice create is SAP_COM_0057.

9.13.6 Business Partner Replication Using Cloud Integration

With SAP S/4HANA Cloud, the Business Partner Replication Using Cloud Integration accelerator was released. The integration of on-premise SAP S/4HANA with SAP S/4HANA Cloud supports a direct replication of master data without any middleware (scope item 1RO). But because a variety of customers needed middleware for their interfaces as per their security policies, this accelerator was introduced. This helps to replicate business partners from on-premise SAP S/4HANA to SAP S/4HANA Cloud using Cloud Integration.

This accelerator reduces the implementation timeline drastically and offers master data harmonization across the entire enterprise. It can be easily enhanced based on customer-specific requirements and offers troubleshooting via SAP Application Interface Framework, which is available in SAP S/4HANA Cloud.

Configuration and setup for this accelerator is available as part of the two-tier ERP assets in the SAP Best Practices Explorer.

9.14 Summary

In this chapter, we introduced the concept of two-tier ERP deployment with SAP S/4HANA Cloud and recommended deployment options in such hybrid deployments, and we did a deep dive into various end-to-end business processes, starting with master data and continuing through finance, sales, services, procurement, manufacturing, and sustainability. Toward the end, we touched upon integration approaches and central analytics supported in two-tier landscapes.

The next chapter will introduce the organizational change management and enablement topics that are critical for both the project team and for driving the adoption and use of SAP S/4HANA in your organization.

Chapter 10
Organizational Change Management

Organizational change management (OCM) is a collective term used to prepare and support organizations in making necessary changes across people, processes, technologies, and culture. In the context of deploying SAP S/4HANA with SAP Activate, well-executed OCM is crucial for user adoption and continuous business value creation.

10

Digital transformation journeys will look different from one organization to another. They may turn out more demanding than previous business application implementations as they require rethinking and reconfiguring of not only many business processes but also people's roles, mindsets, and behaviors. Organizational change management (OCM), an enterprise discipline of people management, seeks to address challenges companies face as they transition to cloud solutions. This chapter highlights how OCM is applied through the SAP Activate methodology and introduces new accelerators, roles, and steps for the setup of a Customer Center of Expertise (Customer COE) for the run phase. You'll become familiar with new learning concepts that focus on not only the needs of the project team but also end user training through peer learning and self-enablement. We'll also discuss SAP Enable Now, an online tool used to create, maintain, and customize learning material for end user adoption.

10.1 OCM and Digital Transformation

As organizations move toward cloud-based products with more standardized business processes and frequent update cycles for continuous innovation, OCM is fundamental to achieving successful solution adoption and a smooth transition for the business. From the inception of the project, you want the organization to orient itself toward embracing necessary change and for respective measures to take hold and sprout a growth mindset. In the build-up to the run phase, the people in the organization will become competent, self-assured, even happy to embrace continuous change. These outcomes might be achieved easier when you connect the implementation project with a larger transformation program and relate that program to the overarching purpose, vision, and mission of the organization. OCM provides the framework to support organizations adopting innovation at a high frequency while fostering development among individuals and teams.

507

SAP Activate places OCM at the center of the methodology, and it provides OCM best practices and tools to help drive change management practices within the project. It suggests managing OCM activities through online live working tools such as Microsoft Office 365, video- and audio-conferencing platforms, or team collaboration services like MURAL. By adopting sound OCM practices, people in the organization might experience the following:

- Less resistance to using the new system and its standardized processes, reducing adoption risks and the cost of risk mitigation

- User mindset changes toward faster adoption of new solutions, which leads to faster return on investment, maximizes solution utilization, and consistently reaches higher levels of value realization

- Smoother onboarding and eventual handover from the project to supporting entities

10.2   OCM Activities in SAP Activate

OCM activities, tasks, and accelerators are located within the solution adoption workstream of SAP Activate for both SAP S/4HANA and SAP S/4HANA Cloud. The workstream guides you through the SAP Activate roadmap, as shown in Figure 10.1.

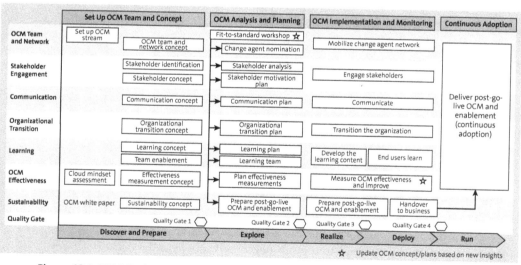

Figure 10.1 OCM Tasks in SAP Activate Roadmap

The OCM journey can be mapped to four key tasks:

1. **Setup of the OCM team and development of first concepts across multiple change dimensions**
   The activities in this task begin with establishing a common understanding of a

cloud mindset followed by a thorough analysis of adoption risk factors with suggestions for specific risk mitigation. The outcome will be considered for budgeting OCM measures in parallel with the implementation project.

2. **OCM analysis and planning**
The fit-to-standard workshops will impact processes, technologies, and people. That impact will be thoroughly analyzed, and its implications will be addressed with respective plans across the change dimensions.

3. **OCM implementation and monitoring**
Plans defined in the previous task will be applied. Their implementation success will be monitored closely. Plans will be refined continuously, with input from employees frequently solicited. Learning content will have to be adapted to a company's needs. Where required, new content may have to be created. End user training on the new content begins. OCM practices are progressively embedded into the normal day-to-day business operations.

4. **Continuous adoption**
The entire organization takes over responsibility for enablement for frequent innovations and organizational change.

Continuous Adoption

SAP S/4HANA subscription customers welcome frequent product updates. Implementing innovations often and quickly is part of their growth mindset. They embrace continuous operational improvements and automate their business processes wherever sensible. Adoption-oriented customers look forward to using innovations published in the SAP product roadmap (*https://roadmaps.sap.com/welcome*) and implement useful new features (see the **What's New** section on the SAP Help Portal at *http://s-prs.co/ v546308*).

Quality gates form an integral part of the SAP Activate methodology. They include checks for the OCM workstream.

In the following sections, we'll explore key OCM activities that occur over the lifecycle of a project using SAP Activate.

10.2.1 Discover

During this phase, a sober analysis of expected business benefits and value drivers will be conducted based on functional scope, regional and industry coverage, and complete solution adoption. The Digital Discovery Assessment tool looks at functional, regional, and industry coverage. The organization's propensity for sound adoption is determined with the Cloud Mindset Assessment. The assessment identifies risk levels depending on scope complexity and organizational readiness to embrace the character and level of expected change. For higher risks, the mitigation suggestion typically points to higher investments into OCM services, packaged content, or learning. Organizations that want to set themselves up for sustained adoption success recognize the need for this investment of people's time and energy.

The results of the assessment should be promoted among internal stakeholders to create broad awareness of the organization's need for a dedicated OCM program with its related topics.

Cloud Mindset

The more eagerly an organization intends to adopt cloud-based ERP, the more intensely it might need to shift its mindset. SAP states that there are six components to a cloud mindset:

1. Embracing ready-made business processes
2. Agility in deploying processes
3. Readiness to adopt frequent innovations coming with periodic product updates
4. Integrating and extending based on stable public interfaces
5. Digital transformation vision supported by employees
6. Users engaging in new ways of working

This new growth mindset includes higher levels of collaboration, self-organization, self-learning, and openness to experimentation and to automation wherever deemed sensible. Learn more about adopting a cloud mindset at *http://s-prs.co/v546309*.

10.2.2   Prepare

This phase marks the start of an implementation project, during which the project team is enabled to include the OCM workstream, the OCM team gets assembled, and OCM concepts are set out. The OCM project team is announced across the official company's networks and the OCM project plan is broadly defined and communicated to the main stakeholders.

Note that the OCM concepts to be developed and networks to be established by the OCM project team are unique to each organization. SAP Activate accelerators merely provide a framework and questionnaires facilitating this set of activities. Further note how SAP Activate distinguishes *concepts* from *plans*. Concepts raise all relevant questions and frame the space for planning to take over and address those questions in detail after the change impact analysis. In collaboration with the MURAL team, SAP provides for OCM workshop templates to develop these concepts and plans. Check out MURAL templates for organizational change management and fit-to-standard at *https://app.mural.co*.

Let's walk through some key OCM activities that occur during this stage:

- Careful consideration must be given to the setup of the OCM workstream at this stage. OCM team members will be identified and onboarded with clear roles and responsibilities, and these people should be assigned as dedicated resources to the project. Some backfilling of positions in business and IT may be required.

- Stakeholders who can affect or influence the success of the project will be identified and grouped accordingly (management, end users, etc.). Appropriate procedures should be thought of to manage the groups effectively and ensure they are onboard and aware of all key decisions expected from them.

- The OCM plan will not be completely successful without the full buy-in of the digital transformation ambassadors, or change agents. If engaged properly, change agents are a powerful influencing force providing invaluable support to the OCM team, evangelizing the merits of the solution, and channeling user feedback and concerns back to the project team.

- The communication approach (content, style, and model) is conceived during this phase, together with the planning, implementation, and monitoring of all communication activities necessary for the project.

- A first draft to prepare for the change impact analysis to be executed in the explore phase needs to be developed here. Change impact analysis workshops identify the changes expected by stakeholder groups—that is, what impact the change will have on skills, business processes, technologies, and the culture within the organization.

- An analysis of the appropriate learning needs for end user training throughout the transformation process will be conceived (see Section 10.4). SAP S/4HANA Cloud content may be revised to incorporate additional learning material and support adoption of a cloud mindset where advised. Tools to create learning and enablement content will be procured and installed at this time.

- Measurements are defined to assess the effectiveness of organizational change activities with key performance indicators (KPIs) or objectives and key results (OKR) in place to indicate progress on the transformation journey.

10.2.3 Explore

The concepts outlined during the previous phase for stakeholder management, communication, efficacy measurement, and sustaining solution adoption will now need to be carved out in detail for each stakeholder group, following careful analysis of the expected changes and their impact.

Change Impact Analysis

OCM workstreams are tasked with conducting a change impact analysis to determine appropriate change management measures that meet stakeholder requirements and support the transition to new ways of working. Consider the change impact analysis the centerpiece of OCM in the project; together with a well-executed fit-to-standard workshop, it is pivotal for a successful implementation. The change impact analysis can be integrated into each fit-to-standard workshop or scheduled separately. *Pro tip:* Schedule both types of workshops as close to each other as possible, ideally within the same work week. This way, change impact anxiety will have no time to build up.

The analysis will follow three steps:

1. Identify all the changes per business area.
2. Name all the stakeholder groups that are impacted by the changes.
3. Define the implications of each change impact to the teams and individuals.

Once impacts are outlined, their implications will be planned for—namely, organizational transition activities like, for example, changing job descriptions, change network–related activities like the number of agents per stakeholder group, other stakeholder group engagements, communications, or learning and skill-building activities.

Fit-to-Standard Instead of Blueprinting

Traditional implementation methodologies may have promoted blueprinting, an as-is analysis followed by a "to-be" definition of the desired future state of the organization. Actual functional capabilities of the business software were then compared to that future state in fit-gap analyses. Gaps often had to be filled with extensive custom code. Analyses and gap fillers were time-consuming. Extensive custom code led to difficulties in upgrading and prevented timely innovation adoption. These methodologies are no longer promoted. Even for on-premise implementations, methodologies now recommend a cloud mindset for as much standardization as possible, with agile implementation cycles and rapid adoption of innovation—in other words, fit-to-standard.

We discussed the fit-to-standard approach that embodies the cloud mindset in Chapter 2, Section 2.1 and again in Chapter 5, Section 5.1. If you're interested in understanding the purpose, flow, and mechanics of fit-to-standard workshops, review these chapters and sections in more detail before proceeding.

Learning Needs Analysis

During the explore phase, the end user learning strategy will be defined, with users directly accessing the SAP Best Practices learning methodology. In addition, a learning team is assembled to create and deliver easily consumable learning material to end users. The more the organization adopts standardized business processes, the less learning material will have to be custom made and the sooner end user learning can start, mostly based on readily available standard content. We'll go into more details in Section 10.4.

Planning the appropriate communication channels and methods is critical to ensure the right message is delivered to the business at the right time. All major communication tasks and milestones should be aligned with the project plan. In addition, all communication activities, including delivery dates, purpose, content, and key messages, are assigned to individuals responsible for the review and preparedness of the communication plan.

During the change impact analysis, the OCM team assesses the implications of the changes to understand what needs to be done to help stakeholders accept the project and the program goals. The team should evaluate stakeholders' influence and perceptions of the project and potential barriers to acceptance. This analysis will feed into the categorization of stakeholders into individual or stakeholder groups and form the basis for a review and refinement of the stakeholder strategy.

Organizational transition planning helps to provide a framework that establishes all the change management tasks that will become part of the business-as-usual activities during the run phase and beyond.

The ability to measure the effectiveness of specific OCM activities will be planned for each key activity described in this section. The plan incorporates measurements for communication effectiveness, stakeholder engagement, and learning and organizational transition effectiveness. Each OCM activity will have assigned a defined timeline, method, responsibilities, and improvement process for each measurement.

10.2.4   Realize, Deploy, and Run

OCM activities across these phases are focused on the execution and monitoring of the change management plans defined in the explore phase. Also in these phases, learning content needs to be amended or developed and trainers equipped to lead enablement sessions for end users where self-enablement alone might not be sufficient. Section 10.5 illustrates a contemporary way to enable end users.

Digital transformation ambassadors or change agents will be invited to participate in a kickoff workshop, where they will begin to assume their roles. Workshop attendees will gain a clear understanding of activities, responsibilities, timelines, and milestones.

Similarly, stakeholder engagement plans defined in the prior phase are executed, and executive management buy-in of the strategy is obtained.

Communication material is created and channeled to the right addressees at the right time as per the communication plan. In execution of the organizational transition plan, OCM activities support the shift to new ways of thinking and working. Characteristic of those new ways is the relentless quest for process simplification and automation, and the anticipation of innovations that become available with periodic software updates.

Throughout the realize, deploy, and run phases, the effectiveness of all OCM measures will be reviewed often and methodically. Formal and informal feedback is collected, via pulse surveys, management interviews, or peer-to-peer review. This feedback, which covers all aspects of the OCM plan (communications, learning plan, stakeholder engagement, and organizational business processes transition) will prompt adjustments as needed. Small adjustments as part of a regular activity to fine-tune OCM activities are typically easier to digest by the teams affected than big changes on exceptional occasions. Familiarizing employees with a pattern of frequent small changes to which they contribute or provide feedback may support solution adoption throughout the run phase.

Mentoring Eases the Digital Transformation Process for Employees

Employees are encouraged to seek mentoring or coaching during a digital transformation process. This practice promotes a more open, collaborative, and creative environment with management and peers and it creates the opportunity for self-development, higher agility, and acceptance of changes.

As the project prepares to deploy the solution, preparations begin for the setup of a continuous change management practice within the organization to facilitate continuous OCM. The new practice will provide support for user roles and responsibilities and define an approach each for communication, stakeholder management, organizational transition, learning, effectiveness measurement, and continuous improvement. Before transitioning into the run phase, OCM responsibilities and activities are to be handed over from the implementation project to the practice embedded in the business. Organizations that already have a Customer COE in place may benefit from expanding its capabilities to OCM for cloud or hybrid IT landscapes and assume the role of this practice. Where no such Customer COE is in place yet, you may want to consider establishing one. Section 10.3 will introduce the concepts, roles, and benefits of Customer COEs.

10.3   Transition to the Customer Center of Expertise

This section focuses on the concept of the Customer COE and addresses how a company should adapt and reconfigure its support model, service offerings, processes, and roles and responsibilities required with a hybrid of SAP solutions.

A Customer COE is a team of experts drawn from across an organization tasked with maximizing the return on a company's business software investment. This is achieved by optimizing business processes, IT applications, and resources, as well as by applying continuous innovation and improvement.

A company's investment in SAP may consist of several solutions. With the move to the cloud, a company may have a mix of on-premise and cloud solutions. A Customer COE should be put in place regardless of the company's landscape, system complexity, or integration needs. The Customer COE should focus on increasing the business value of the solutions while meeting the needs of the business. This is accomplished by designing organizational and operational excellence, adopting effective governance, and developing the appropriate talent/skills—all while lowering costs.

10.3.1   Organizational Readiness in the Customer Center of Expertise

OCM played a vital role in preparing and transitioning the organization to the new ways of working. Transition planning occurs in the prepare phase of the project, as we saw in Section 10.2.2.

Continuous change management supports an organization's ability to continually improve organizational efficiencies through expanded use of the solution and adoption of the new system functionality.

Reskilling IT resources and businesspeople is therefore an essential element in ensuring that the Customer COE has the right skills and resources available as part of the transformation.

To help drive innovation, IT departments will be required to develop new skills and roles within the organization focused on continuous improvement practices. This change in focus impacts both business and IT employees to support the digital transformation and requires an early transformation of employees.

Typically, highly technical and detail-focused IT professionals will gain a deeper understanding of the business goals and vision; similarly, strategic business professionals will understand the more technical intricacies of a cloud ERP system and know how to use the full capabilities of the solution to obtain the full return on investment.

10.3.2   Capabilities Framework

SAP has defined a Customer COE capability framework that will drive effectiveness through business value and efficiency by focusing on delivering best-in-class services.

The framework consists of the following:

- Strategy
- SAP architecture and innovation
- Organization and governance
- Processes, tools, and standards
- People and skills and digital change

Figure 10.2 shows a holistic approach to safeguarding your investments in SAP software.

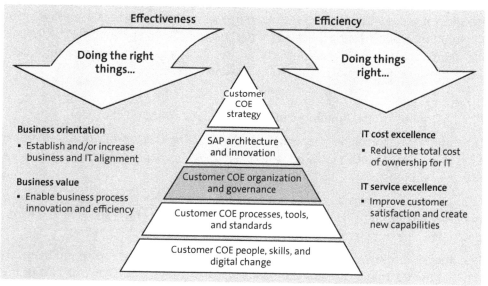

Figure 10.2 Customer COE Capability Framework

Companies should establish a support model that allows for innovation of the SAP solutions and processes to realize the entire value of their investment. The Customer COE forms crucial links among the business, SAP solutions, and the IT department to achieve the company's goals and performance objectives. It requires exceptional end-to-end solution orchestration underpinned with system availability, performance and security goals, and dynamic business innovation.

To achieve the appropriate end-to-end solution orchestration, the Customer COE needs to do the following:

- Implement standardized end-to-end operation processes flexible enough to react to fast-changing business needs.
- Balance the need to implement automated and proactive processes with having manual and reactive processes, according to a risk-based assessment and value to business.
- Define KPIs that will support a continuous improvement mindset, ensuring state-of-the-art IT that is ready for new challenges.
- Maintain knowledge of the latest innovation by maintaining a close connection to experts from the SAP ecosystem (internal and external skills).

For organizations with hybrid SAP solutions that include SAP S/4HANA Cloud, the Customer COE capability framework should be reviewed and revised to reflect the business objectives set out with the SAP S/4HANA Cloud implementation. An adjustment of the strategy, governance model, and IT processes will be required due to the standardization and automation that comes with SAP S/4HANA Cloud.

10.3.3   Roadmap for Organizational Readiness

A company's transition from the project to the deployment and setup of the Customer COE begins during the discover phase. The speed of transition to the new model depends on the maturity of the existing Customer COE. It's important to understand at the start what needs to change, who will be impacted, and the path to getting to an effective business organization that supports governance of the future digitalization of the business.

Let's walk through some key activities for the Customer COE for each phase:

- **Discover**
  During this phase, you identify the business value and benefits, as well as define the adoption strategy and roadmap. You should leverage the Customer COE capability framework to drive initial discussion and ensure a common understanding of the Customer COE organization model to manage all SAP-related topics. For a Customer COE, some key recommendations are as follows:
  - Identify and onboard business owners and digital business analysts to support the SAP S/4HANA Cloud implementation and future operations.
  - Determine the business scope and the number of planned end users to perform an initial identification of Customer COE roles that might be affected with the implementation of SAP S/4HANA Cloud.

- **Prepare**
  During the prepare phase, it's recommended that you conduct a workshop to focus on the company-specific scope for the Customer COE, roles, and a high-level definition of innovation services. The workshop helps the organization focus on decisions such as what to deliver with internal versus external resources, nominating Customer COE leadership roles, and creating a project plan for your Customer COE establishment or transformation based on your current and strategic organization's needs.

- **Explore**
  Key activities that facilitate the setup of the Customer COE include the following:
  - Provide clarity on the future operation of the Customer COE and its post-go-live capabilities to enable management to identify and plan for internal and external resources.
  - Provide ongoing guidance to employees earmarked for the Customer COE on roles and responsibilities throughout the implementation project and the post-go-live.

10

- Identify tools and standards for IT service and operations management that need to be leveraged or established for future Customer COE support and operations.

- **Realize**

  Key activities to facilitate the setup of the Customer COE include the following:

  - Define what success looks like for an SAP S/4HANA Cloud implementation post-go-live and in daily business operations.

  - Define the right business KPIs to drive and guide continuous business improvement.

  - Adapt existing service-level agreements (SLAs) and prepare the internal service desk accordingly. This includes adapting to new categorizations of incidents and service requests, along with the related communication with their SAP counterparts.

  - Train the business on testing and other relevant tasks to support SAP release cycles.

- **Deploy**

  During the deploy phase, it's recommended that you implement the defined processes and tools, prepare key users to train the end user community, and support an efficient business operation after go-live.

- **Run**

  During the run phase, it's recommended that business and IT resources work together under the Customer COE model to establish normal business operations with increased focus on business optimization, innovation, and digitalization and with a lower total cost of ownership (TCO).

10.3.4   New Roles with SAP S/4HANA Cloud

SAP S/4HANA Cloud will require new skills to support digital transformation. Roles and responsibilities within the business and IT teams will be impacted and therefore provide the opportunity to reskill current operations staff to support the new digital strategy. Being able to actively engage in an online community like SAP's, which is available at *community.sap.com*, is an essential skill for all existing roles to stay current, find answers to common questions and get tips on known challenges. The following new roles will also need to be introduced in order to successfully run the organization:

- **Digital business analyst**

  The role of the digital business analyst is the biggest change in business roles. It evolved from a traditional business analyst role to a key player in developing prototypes driving the digitalization of business. The digital business analyst works closely with business architects in IT.

  Companies with a digital transformation office may not be required to differentiate between the roles of digital business analyst and business architect. Both roles leverage business digitalization to create business value.

■ **Cloud business architect**
The cloud business architect may traditionally come from an SAP S/4HANA solution architect role. Reskilling or upskilling may be required to serve in a cross-functional cloud architect capacity to ensure technical feasibility and realization of current and planned business requirements.

■ **Prototyper/user experience (UX) developer**
The prototyper may come from the traditional ABAP development role and is only required for companies with a need for extensions (either using in-app extensibility capabilities in SAP S/4HANA Cloud or SAP Business Technology Platform (SAP BTP) for side-by-side extensibility). Employees in this role should be enabled to guide users toward simple and effective business solutions.

■ **Data scientist**
With the development of big data, the Internet of Things (IoT), and other technologies, the role of a data scientist is highly desirable in a Customer COE. Traditional developers can be reskilled with mathematical and algorithm knowledge and machine learning tools to perform this role.

■ **Change agent**
A leader focused on change management promotes and enables change to happen and is an essential part of a Customer COE. People in this role should have good understanding of business culture, be experienced in business disciplines that are impacted by the change, and be comfortable in working through uncertainty.

Figure 10.3 provides a comparison of Customer COE roles found in an SAP S/4HANA environment and the change required with SAP S/4HANA Cloud.

The increased granularity of role descriptions provides the visibility required to map and transition each employee role. It's important to note that there is no direct relation between the role description and the full-time equivalent (FTE) required in the target Customer COE, so several roles can be combined into a single job position. For example, companies replacing their traditional ERP with SAP S/4HANA Cloud or implementing a hybrid two-tier ERP setup will significantly reduce the need for Basis experts or database administrators. In addition, some roles, like enterprise architect or developer, might not warrant staffing with FTEs in all organizations. One FTE might need to play multiple roles. Outsourcing, ad hoc service acquisition, or subscription to respective services may also deserve consideration.

Companies with the hybrid solution that includes SAP S/4HANA Cloud should note that traditional operational roles are supported by SAP under the SAP S/4HANA Cloud subscription model. A good example is that the role of the traditional SAP basis expert tasks and the application management (for more complex changes) now form a part of the periodic releases. Many maintenance tasks for data—for example, creating a new purchase group or a new cost center—will be performed in the business by authorized personas.

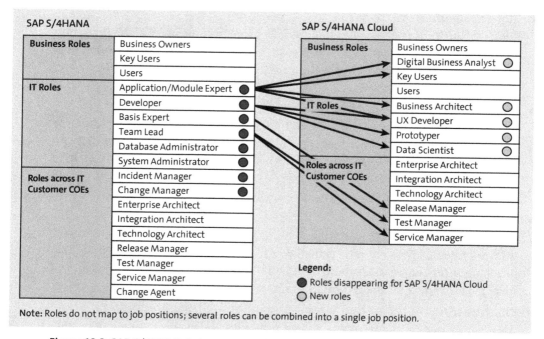

SAP S/4HANA

Business Roles	Business Owners
	Key Users
	Users
IT Roles	Application/Module Expert ●
	Developer ●
	Basis Expert ●
	Team Lead ●
	Database Administrator ●
	System Administrator ●
Roles across IT Customer COEs	Incident Manager ●
	Change Manager ●
	Enterprise Architect
	Integration Architect
	Technology Architect
	Release Manager
	Test Manager
	Service Manager
	Change Agent

SAP S/4HANA Cloud

Business Roles	Business Owners
	Digital Business Analyst ○
	Key Users
	Users
IT Roles	Business Architect ○
	UX Developer ○
	Prototyper ○
	Data Scientist ○
Roles across IT Customer COEs	Enterprise Architect
	Integration Architect
	Technology Architect
	Release Manager
	Test Manager
	Service Manager

Legend:
● Roles disappearing for SAP S/4HANA Cloud
○ New roles

Note: Roles do not map to job positions; several roles can be combined into a single job position.

Figure 10.3 SAP S/4HANA Roles versus Roles Required with SAP S/4HANA Cloud

Line of business (LoB) experts with strong knowledge of discrete business processes may transfer from the IT organization to the business organization, thereby strengthening the business's native IT solution skills.

To define a successful support model, companies are required to define and assign new roles and responsibilities to employees or third parties and adjust existing support practices. A collaboration governance model between business, IT, and other stakeholders of your SAP solution should be defined at the start of the project in the discover phase.

It's important to define the new governance model at the start of the SAP S/4HANA Cloud journey. Don't wait until the deploy or run phases to prepare your organization!

10.4   Team Enablement and Self-Enablement

Learning about SAP S/4HANA products and self-enablement on the applications do not have to wait for the implementation project to begin. In fact, SAP provides for a number of ways for the project team and future users to experience SAP S/4HANA early on: a free trial system with predefined business processes, free massive open online courses (MOOCs), product documentation, and a card game to determine project scope by business scenarios.

During discover, representatives of customer LoBs and the presales team are asked to determine the business processes to be in scope of an implementation. To mitigate the risk of this activity becoming another series of tedious meetings, customers may consider taking advantage of a virtual discovery card game available among the accelerators of SAP Activate in the Roadmap Viewer at *http://s-prs.co/v546310*.

Playing through the business scenarios is a highly engaging learning experience that delivers outcomes like the Digital Discovery Assessment in just a few hours. A free trial system access is available to anyone at any time (we discussed the access to trial environment in Chapter 7, Section 7.1.2 for public cloud, Section 7.2.2 for private cloud, and Section 7.2.3 for on-premise). Future users and key users might want to explore "their" business processes, familiarize themselves with the user experience of SAP Fiori apps, and touch on the benefits of embedded analytics, as well as intelligent automation of processes. In addition, business and technical users can access SAP Help Portal resources online at *https://help.sap.com*. This provides detailed product documentation and step-by-step tutorials for how to use the functionality. An additional useful resource is openSAP, which offers free courses with a wealth of SAP S/4HANA content. Users can access openSAP at *https://open.sap.com* and sign up for any available or planned courses.

Figure 10.4 shows an example of one of the learning journeys for SAP S/4HANA Cloud project team enablement specific to SAP Activate. The journey directs learners to the SAP Learning Hub at *https://learninghub.sap.com* and to other resources such as blogs or e-learning courses. One of the first steps on this journey is to join the SAP S/4HANA Cloud implementation learning room, where you can access a range of materials providing information about implementation approaches, methodologies, and tools. Companies with access to the starter system also can use the key learning assets inside the SAP S/4HANA Cloud application in the My Learning app.

Once in the prepare phase, the project team needs to learn further aspects of the SAP S/4HANA Cloud solution and the SAP Activate methodology. They will continue using the self-service channels and content as discussed previously and add project- and role-specific topics as per the SAP Learning Hub's learning journeys. Beyond functional and role-oriented knowledge, the team needs to learn about collaboration and alignment across LoBs. Typical implementation or application questions may have already been answered in the SAP S/4HANA Cloud customer community, mentioned in Section 10.3.4. Or you can add your inquiry at *https://community.sap.com/topics/s4hana-cloud*. SAP partners can ask expert-level questions in the SAP S/4HANA Cloud Expertise Services community at *https://expertiseservices.s4hanacloud.community.sap/home*.

SAP recommends that all project team members have access to the SAP Support Portal, where the project team can communicate directly with SAP support. The end user details for accessing the SAP Support Portal enable each company to access the SAP

Best Practices and SAP Roadmap Viewer applications and be recognized as a customer, thus getting access to additional documents and accelerators useful during the implementation project.

Figure 10.4 SAP S/4HANA Cloud Learning Journey

10.5   Enablement Content Development with SAP Enable Now

SAP has developed an end-to-end solution to collaboratively create, manage, and deliver all building blocks for intelligent user assistance. SAP Enable Now consists of formal training, informal learning, and on-the-job performance support. Formal training is via traditional instructor-led trainings and online courses. Informal learning comprises the self-directed learning and sharing knowledge located in the Info Center. The SAP Enable Now Info Center is a content library where users can find everything related to SAP Enable Now, such as links, tips, and product trainings, as well as free content and templates to use in their own projects. Figure 10.5 shows one of the screens in the SAP Enable Now Info Center. Informal learning reduces support tickets, improves communication efforts, and allows for the proactive enablement of every user. On-the-job performance support is provided by the web assistant embedded in SAP S/4HANA.

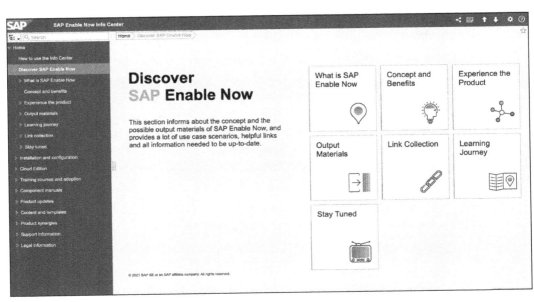

Figure 10.5 SAP Enable Now Info Center

SAP Enable Now improves end user adoption organically and accelerates learning with contextually relevant, timely, and proactive enablement content, directly from within the solution itself. Training simulation and test script creation are available by adding video, animations, or detailed and fully interactive software simulations with just a few keystrokes.

With SAP Enable Now, you can innovate with a focus on business solutions and processes that span several products relevant to your LoBs, customers, and entire industries. You can increase productivity of your workforce by starting in the learning classroom, create online courses quickly, provide a knowledge portal for explorative learning, and deliver in-app performance support. In addition, you can grow your competitive advantage by maximizing the value of your employees by using unique, customized, and cost-efficient training for faster time to competence.

> **Further Resources**
> You can learn more about SAP Enable Now in the SAP Enable Now Info Corner at *http://s-prs.co/v546311*.

10.6   Summary

This chapter provided an overview of the OCM activities mentioned in the six phases of SAP Activate. OCM should be fully embedded in your project and should also be sustainable across the organization. A key component of OCM activities is the monitoring

523

and measurement of all OCM activities throughout each phase of SAP Activate to ensure project success across all areas of the implementation.

In addition to OCM, the company team enablement and self-enablement sections of this chapter discussed the different training offerings from SAP to ensure the success of your SAP project. Team training material, self-learnings, and SAP learning journeys are mission-critical for every member of the project teams. There is a wide variety of materials offered in the SAP Learning Hub to accommodate different types of learners across the globe. Learning journeys, e-books, and SAP Live Access are just a few of the platforms offered to the company's teams and individual users for enablement on the new SAP system.

In the next chapter, you'll learn about the SAP Activate methodology for other SAP products, such as SAP SuccessFactors and SAP Analytics Cloud.

Chapter 11

SAP Activate for Other SAP Products

*We've discussed how SAP Activate is used in the context of an
SAP S/4HANA project, but SAP Activate provides coverage of other
SAP products as well. We'll introduce those products in this chapter and
show you assets that you can use in implementation of products such
as SAP SuccessFactors and SAP Analytics Cloud or while upgrading your
SAP S/4HANA solution.*

This book has provided detailed information about the use of SAP Activate in the context of deploying the SAP S/4HANA solution in your organization. This chapter will focus on introducing other "flavors" of SAP Activate for SAP solutions across a wide range of cloud and on-premise products. We'll focus on four key examples of SAP Activate, and we'll share links for each to the implementation roadmaps currently available and SAP Best Practices packages (where available) that you can use in your next project.

The SAP Activate methodology assets are available in SAP Activate Roadmap Viewer, and the SAP Best Practices assets can be accessed in SAP Best Practices Explorer (refer to Chapter 3). We'll introduce a few flavors of SAP Activate content for other products in this text in more detail and then provide a list of all currently available SAP Activate methodology packages that companies and partners can access.

11.1 SAP Activate for SAP SuccessFactors

SAP Activate provides comprehensive coverage of the SAP SuccessFactors solution, with assets for planning and managing the project in the form of a dedicated SAP Activate methodology for SAP SuccessFactors, which is available in the Roadmap Viewer via the main page at *http://s-prs.co/v502741*. Once there, click on the **Explore All Roadmaps** button, then select the **Cloud Specific Methodology**. Finally, click on **SAP Activate Methodology for SAP SuccessFactors** in the list of available roadmaps. The main page of the methodology for SAP SuccessFactors is shown in Figure 11.1.

The methodology follows the same six phases we defined in Chapter 2 of this book, but the content inside the guidance is specific to the deployment of the SAP SuccessFactors solution.

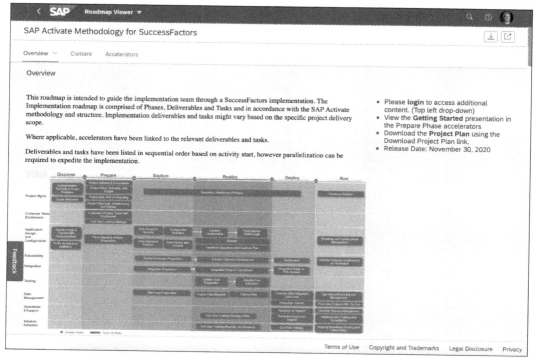

Figure 11.1 SAP Activate Methodology for SAP SuccessFactors

To complement the methodology, SAP has also released several packages of SAP Best Practices content for SAP SuccessFactors. At the time of writing, the following packages are available for SAP SuccessFactors in SAP Best Practices Explorer:

- SAP Best Practices for SAP SuccessFactors Performance & Goals
- SAP Best Practices for SuccessFactors Employee Central
- SAP Best Practices for SuccessFactors Compensation
- SAP Best Practices for SAP SuccessFactors Succession & Development
- SAP SuccessFactors Talent Management Suite Integration to SAP ERP HCM Rapid-Deployment Solution
- SAP Best Practices for SAP SuccessFactors Employee Central Payroll
- SAP Best Practices for SAP SuccessFactors Recruiting
- SAP Best Practices for SAP SuccessFactors Learning
- SAP Best Practices for SAP SuccessFactors Onboarding
- SAP Best Practices for SAP SuccessFactors People Analytics
- SAP Best Practices for SAP SuccessFactors Employee Central integration
- SAP Best Practices for SAP SuccessFactors Workforce Planning

You can find these packages in SAP Best Practices Explorer by following these steps:

1. Go to SAP Best Practices Explorer at *https://rapid.sap.com/bp/#/*.

2. Select the **Complete Portfolio** tile.

3. Select **Cloud · People** in the left navigation panel.

The list of available SAP Best Practices for SAP SuccessFactors will be displayed on the right side of the screen. From there, you can navigate to a specific package and its contents, as shown in Figure 11.2.

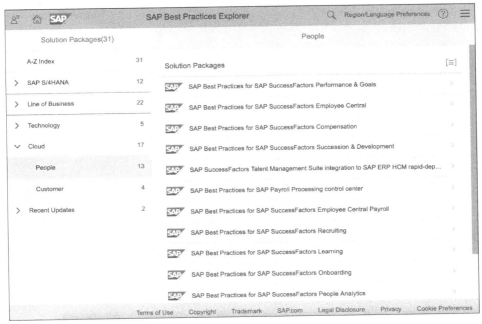

Figure 11.2 SAP Best Practices Packages for SAP SuccessFactors

SAP Best Practices for SAP SuccessFactors provide the same navigation structure we explained in Chapter 2. The key assets that are provided in the package are delivered inside the scope items as the following documents:

- Process flow
- Configuration guide
- Configuration workbooks
- Test scripts

SAP Best Practices for SAP SuccessFactors cover a wide range of country-specific configurations that you can select on the main page of each package using the selection box below **Version** on the screen. And just like any other package, you can download the content of SAP Best Practices for SAP SuccessFactors using the **Download** link at the top-right corner on the main page in each package.

11.2   SAP Activate for the Intelligent Enterprise

This SAP Activate roadmap has a special role: it has been used to prototype and deliver implementation methodology guidance that spans multiple distinct SAP products in order to support end-to-end business scenarios that go beyond one product—for example, the hire-to-retire or source-to-pay business scenarios. Companies implementing multiple SAP products need SAP Activate to support the scope of their projects, and that is why this methodology roadmap exists, to provide the right content for such situations. This roadmap, like all other SAP Activate methodology roadmaps, continues to evolve and bring new content to users. As of the time of writing, SAP has added SAP Concur to SAP Activate for the intelligent enterprise to expand the existing coverage that includes SAP SuccessFactors, SAP S/4HANA Cloud, and SAP Fieldglass.

You can access this methodology content in SAP Activate Roadmap Viewer via the main page at *http://s-prs.co/v502741*. Once there, click on the **Explore All Roadmaps** button, then select the **Cloud-Specific Methodology** tab. Finally, click on **SAP Activate Methodology for Intelligent Enterprise** in the list of available roadmaps. To browse the detailed guidance, you can select **Content** tab at the top of the page and then select the appropriate filter selection on the left side of the screen in the **More** section. You can filter the content by specific business scenario, by a selection of products, or by a combination of the two. Figure 11.3 shows an example of filtering all SAP Activate content relevant for the hire-to-retire business scenario.

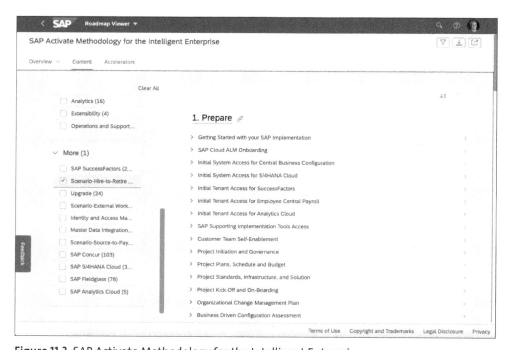

Figure 11.3 SAP Activate Methodology for the Intelligent Enterprise

The navigation in the methodology content is the same as for all the other roadmaps, and the guidance includes details specific to all covered solutions, including solution-specific accelerators. SAP continues to evolve this methodology content and add coverage for additional business scenarios and solutions.

11.3   SAP Activate for SAP Analytics Cloud

SAP Analytics Cloud is a popular choice for analytics solutions for companies running SAP systems. This new solution provides companies with an elastic cloud environment to support their analytics requirements. For companies implementing SAP Analytics Cloud, SAP provides guidance via the SAP Activate methodology in the Roadmap Viewer, which you can access via *http://s-prs.co/v502741*. Once there, click on the **Explore All Roadmaps** button, then select the **Cloud-Specific Methodology** tab. Finally, click on **SAP Activate Methodology for SAP Analytics Cloud** in the list of available roadmaps. See Figure 11.4 for an overview of the content provided in this methodology roadmap. The methodology will guide you through specific steps that help your team access the trial environment, enables your team using the predelivered self-guided enablement materials, helps prepare prototypes of the analytics views, and assists with other key activities.

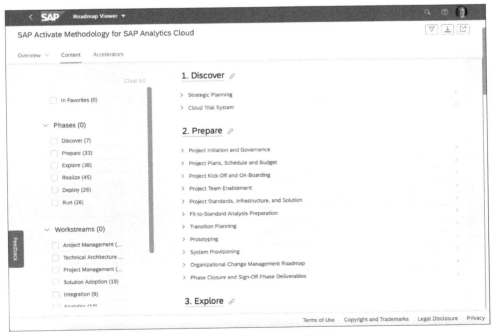

Figure 11.4 SAP Activate Methodology for SAP Analytics Cloud

SAP Best Practices also offers content for SAP Analytics Cloud in the package focused on using this solution for human resources (HR) analytics. The package can be found in SAP Best Practices Explorer at *http://s-prs.co/v502742*. The package provides users with HR Analytics with SAP Analytics Cloud scope item (41E), which contains the following assets (see Figure 11.5):

- Test script
- Building blocks
  - Model Configuration for HR Analytics with SAP Analytics Cloud (43S) and configuration guide
  - Story Guide for HR Analytics with SAP Analytics Cloud (43T) and configuration guide

You can use these assets to set up connectivity between your SAP Analytics Cloud and SAP SuccessFactors solutions for your HR analytics needs.

Figure 11.5 Assets Available in HR Analytics with SAP Best Practices for SAP Analytics Cloud Package

The configuration guides provide detailed guidance on how to configure these SAP Best Practices, including the setup of the model and the definition of the story in the SAP Analytics Cloud environment (e.g., the HR Analytics from SAP Analytics Cloud [43S] building block).

11.4   SAP Activate for SAP S/4HANA Upgrade and Product Integration

The last methodology roadmap we want to introduce in this chapter is for planning and conducting an upgrade from one release of SAP S/4HANA to a newer or latest release of the product. This upgrade roadmap also provides information about implementation of additional capabilities that are embedded in the SAP S/4HANA solution. Customers upgrading to a new release of SAP S/4HANA usually want to add new capabilities into their solution, so this roadmap covers both the functional upgrade and implementation of additional capabilities. The following selections can be made in the roadmap to select a company-specific scenario:

- Upgrade with functional enhancements
- Implementation of SAP Transportation Management (SAP TM)
- Implementation of SAP Extended Warehouse Management (SAP EWM)
- Implementation of SAP S/4HANA service
- Implementation of production planning and detailed scheduling (PP-DS) for SAP S/4HANA
- Implementation of advanced available-to-promise (ATP) for SAP S/4HANA

Users of this methodology can access it in the Roadmap Viewer via *http://s-prs.co/v502741*. Once there, click on the **Explore All Roadmaps** button, then select the **On-Premise-Specific Methodology** tab. Finally, click on **SAP S/4HANA Upgrade and Product Integration Roadmap** in the list of available roadmaps.

To select the specific scenario, you'll need to continue navigating as follows:

1. Select the **Content** tab on the screen shown in Figure 11.6.
2. Scroll down to see the **More** option in the selection of filtering options on the left side, as shown in Figure 11.7. Select the desired option, and the roadmap content will adjust based on your selection.

The filtering process is similar to the one we explained in when discussing SAP Activate for the intelligent enterprise in Section 11.2.

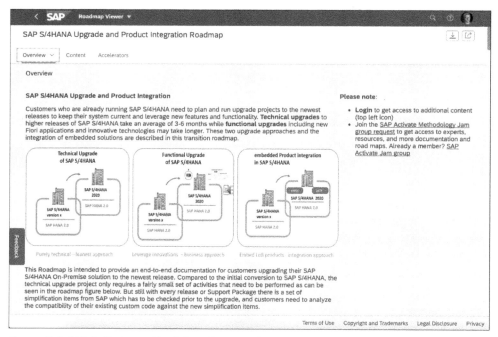

Figure 11.6 SAP Activate Methodology for SAP S/4HANA Upgrade and Product Integration

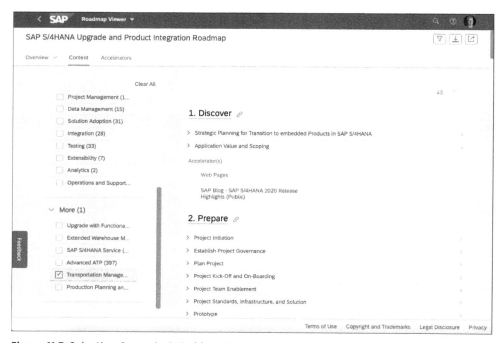

Figure 11.7 Selecting Scenario Suitable to Your Scope

11.5   Additional SAP Activate Methodology Roadmaps

We've introduced four examples of SAP Activate assets that are available to use in projects that include other SAP solutions, products, and end-to-end business scenarios. You can always find the latest content of the SAP Activate methodology in the SAP Activate Roadmap Viewer. As of the time of writing (winter 2022), the following methodology roadmaps are available to SAP customers and partners:

- **Cloud-specific roadmaps**
  - SAP Activate Methodology for SAP S/4HANA Cloud
  - SAP Activate Methodology for RISE with SAP S/4HANA Cloud, Private Edition
  - SAP Activate Methodology for SAP S/4HANA Cloud Three-System Landscape
  - SAP Activate Methodology for SAP SuccessFactors
  - SAP Activate Methodology for SAP Service Cloud Roadmap
  - SAP Activate Methodology for SAP Service Data Warehouse Cloud
  - SAP Activate Methodology for Intelligent Spend Management Roadmap
  - SAP Activate Methodology for SAP Analytics Cloud
  - SAP Activate Methodology for Intelligent Enterprise
  - SAP Activate Methodology for SAP Sales Cloud
- **On-premise-specific methodology roadmaps**
  - SAP Activate Methodology for Transition to SAP S/4HANA
  - SAP Activate Methodology for Transition to SAP BW/4HANA
  - SAP Activate Methodology for SAP S/4HANA Central Finance
- **Upgrade methodology**
  - SAP Activate for Upgrade of SAP S/4HANA Cloud Three-System Landscape
  - SAP S/4HANA Upgrade and Product Integration Roadmap
- **General methodology roadmaps**
  - SAP Activate Methodology for New Cloud Implementations (Public Cloud—General)
  - SAP Activate Methodology for SAP Business Suite and On-Premise—Agile and Waterfall

You can find all these assets in the Roadmap Viewer at *http://s-prs.co/v502741.*

11.6   Summary

This chapter provided an overview of the available SAP Activate methodology and SAP Best Practices assets. Four examples were selected to show you the various assets that you can use in your next implementation or upgrade project. We recommend that you regularly check the SAP Activate Roadmap Viewer and SAP Best Practices Explorer for new content as SAP continues to add to the portfolio of available assets. You should also consider following the SAP Activate community on SAP Community to keep up to date on any new additions or updates to existing content (*https://community.sap.com/topics/activate*).

Appendix A
SAP Activate Certification Preparation

In this appendix, we offer practice questions and answers to test your understanding of SAP Activate and to prepare for the certification exam. Note that these questions are based on the information presented to you in this book, information available to readers in SAP Activate tools (e.g., Roadmap Viewer and SAP Best Practices Explorer), and on the SAP Activate community at SAP Community.

We recommend that you also consider taking SAP-recommended courses to prepare for the SAP Activate certification exam. Details of the certification exam are available on the SAP Training website at *http://s-prs.co/v502748*.

In this chapter, we'll present all the questions in Section A.2 and the correct answers with explanations in Section A.3. Both sections use the same hierarchy to allow you to find answers to questions at your convenience. Users of this book are highly encouraged to follow the SAP Activate community for additional information about strategies shared by users of SAP Activate to prepare for the certification exam. You can also post your questions in the community to engage directly with the SAP Activate team at SAP and other SAP Activate experts.

A.1 Exam Structure

The certification exam questions are structured into the following categories (the number in brackets indicates the number of practice questions in each category):

- SAP Activate Overview (5)
- SAP Activate Elements (5)
- Workstreams Overview (5)
- Transition Path "New Implementation SAP S/4HANA Cloud" (6)
- Transition Path "New Implementation SAP S/4HANA On-Premise" (6)
- Agile Project Planning (5)
- Agile Project Delivery (5)
- SAP Activate Methodology Access—Distribute (1)
- Transition Path "System Conversion to SAP S/4HANA" (3)
- Transition Path "Selective Data Transition to SAP S/4HANA" (3)

Each category is assigned a relative percentage weight in the exam that provides insight into the number of questions from this category that you can expect in the exam (see the SAP Training website for a detailed breakdown of the certification exam in Figure A.1).

Topic Areas

Please see below the list of topics that may be covered within this certification and the courses that cover them. Its accuracy does not constitute a legitimate claim; SAP reserves the right to update the exam content (topics, items, weighting) at any time.

Agile Project Delivery	> 12% ⌄
SAP Activate Overview	> 12% ⌄
SAP Activate Elements	> 12% ⌄
Workstreams Overview	> 12% ⌄
Agile Project Planning	8% - 12% ⌄
Transition Path "New Implementation SAP S/4HANA Cloud"	8% - 12% ⌄
Transition Path "System Conversion"	< 8% ⌄
Transition Path "Selective Data Transition"	< 8% ⌄
Transition Path "New Implementation SAP S/4HANA On Premise"	< 8% ⌄

Figure A.1 Structure of SAP Certified Associate: SAP Activate Project Manager Exam

A.2   Practice Questions

This section will present the practice questions in the same categories that SAP uses for the certification exam. We'll follow the sequence of categories presented in the list in the previous section.

These practice questions will help you evaluate your understanding of the topics covered in this book. The questions shown are similar in nature to those found on the certification examination. Although none of these questions will be found on the exam itself, they will allow you to review your knowledge of the subject. Select the correct answers, then check the completeness of your answers in Section A.3. Remember that on the exam you must select *all* correct answers and *only* correct answers to receive credit for the question.

A.2.1   SAP Activate Overview

This section focuses on the definition of the SAP Activate approach and examines your knowledge in this area. You can find answers to the questions with explanations in Section A.3.1.

1. Which statement best defines SAP Activate? (Select one correct answer.)

☐   A. SAP Activate is a methodology for implementation and upgrades of SAP
     S/4HANA software.

☐   B. SAP Activate provides users with prescriptive guidance, ready-to-use business
     processes, and tools for implementation and upgrades.

☐   C. SAP Activate provides tools for SAP customers who are implementing the SAP
     S/4HANA product in their organizations.

2. When was SAP Activate introduced to the market? (Select two correct answers.)

☐   A. SAPPHIRE 2015

☐   B. When SAP shipped SAP R/3 4.0C

☐   C. In early 2020

☐   D. Along with the introduction of SAP S/4HANA

3. What are the components included in SAP Activate? (Select two correct answers.)

☐   A. Methodology

☐   B. SAP Best Practices

☐   C. SAP NetWeaver

☐   D. Consulting services from SAP Services and Support

4. Which tool can you use to get answers to your questions about SAP Activate from
    experts? (Select one correct answer.)

☐   A. SAP Activate community on *sap.com*

☐   B. SAP Solution Manager

☐   C. SAP Best Practices Explorer

☐   D. Digital Discovery Assessment tool

5. Where can you access the SAP Activate methodology? (Select one correct answer.)

☐   A. SAP Best Practices Explorer

☐   B. SAP Activate community

☐   C. Roadmap Viewer

☐   D. Implementation Guide (IMG)

6. Where can you download SAP Activate accelerators for project management? (Select one correct answer.)

☐ A. Roadmap Viewer

☐ B. SAP Solution Manager

☐ C. SAP Best Practices Explorer

☐ D. Digital Discovery Assessment tool

A.2.2 SAP Activate Elements

This section focuses on your understanding of the SAP Activate elements and examines your knowledge in this area. You can find answers to the questions with explanations in Section A.3.2.

1. What other components are used in SAP Activate to set up the initial system/landscape for SAP S/4HANA implementation? (Select one correct answer.)

☐ A. SAP Best Practices

☐ B. Enterprise management layer for SAP S/4HANA

☐ C. Qualified SAP partner packages

☐ D. All of the above

2. What are the hierarchy levels of the SAP Activate methodology? (Select three correct answers.)

☐ A. Program

☐ B. Project

☐ C. Phase

☐ D. Task

☐ E. Deliverable

3. What does the SAP Best Practices for SAP S/4HANA Cloud package deliver? (Select three correct answers.)

☐ A. Standard operating procedures (SOPs)

☐ B. Preconfiguration

☐ C. Business process flows

☐ D. Building block documentation

☐ E. Test scripts

4. What capabilities does SAP Solution Manager offer for users of SAP Activate? (Select two correct answers.)

- ☐ A. Ability to run business process automation
- ☐ B. Ability to load the complete SAP Activate methodology content into the tool
- ☐ C. Ability to create a work breakdown structure (WBS) based on the SAP Activate methodology
- ☐ D. Ability to download SAP Best Practices and use the content for business process modeling
- ☐ E. Ability to automatically mark completed activities in a project schedule based on the progress of work

5. What configuration capabilities in the SAP S/4HANA solution can users access to configure the software to the company's needs? (Select two correct answers.)

- ☐ A. IMG
- ☐ B. SAP configuration cockpit (SCCP)
- ☐ C. SAP setup framework (SSF)
- ☐ D. Self-Service Configuration UIs (SSCUIs)

A.2.3   Workstreams Overview

This section focuses on your understanding of fundamentals of the SAP Activate methodology workstreams and examines your knowledge in this area. You can find answers to the questions with explanations in Section A.3.3.

1. What options for transition to SAP S/4HANA from SAP ERP are supported by the SAP Activate methodology? (Select three correct answers.)

- ☐ A. New implementation
- ☐ B. System conversion
- ☐ C. Data center lift
- ☐ D. Selective data transition
- ☐ E. Upgrade

2. Which of the following statements are included in the SAP Activate principles? (Select two correct answers.)

- ☐ A. Confirm solution fit
- ☐ B. Start with SAP Best Practices
- ☐ C. Confirm backlog with sponsor
- ☐ D. Use SAP Solution Manager

3. Which techniques does SAP Activate use to confirm solution fit and define delta requirements? (Select one correct answer.)

    ☐   A. Fit-to-standard
    ☐   B. Blueprinting
    ☐   C. Backlog
    ☐   D. Fit-gap

4. Which key templates/accelerators can the project manager use to explain how the project will be managed from time, quality, and risk perspectives? (Select one correct answer.)

    ☐   A. Project Management Plan Template
    ☐   B. Project Schedule Template
    ☐   C. Project Scope Statement
    ☐   D. Fit-to-Standard Overview Presentation

5. What technologies are delivered with SAP S/4HANA applications? (Select two correct answers.)

    ☐   A. SAP HANA
    ☐   B. SAP Fiori
    ☐   C. SAP SuccessFactors
    ☐   D. SAP Concur

A.2.4   Transition Path "New Implementation SAP S/4HANA Cloud"

This section focuses on your understanding of SAP Activate for implementation of SAP S/4HANA Cloud solutions and examines your knowledge in this area. You can find answers to the questions with explanations in Section A.3.4.

1. Which system is used for fit-to-standard workshops in SAP S/4HANA Cloud? (Select one correct answer.)

    ☐   A. Development
    ☐   B. Starter
    ☐   C. Test
    ☐   D. Production

2. In which workstream will you find organizational change management (OCM) assets? (Select one correct answer.)

☐   A. Project management

☐   B. Solution adoption

☐   C. Technical solution management

☐   D. Data management

3. Which working environment can project teams use to structure their work around SAP Activate tasks, access SAP Best Practices documentation (including business process diagrams) in one place, and run their projects? (Select one correct answer.)

☐   A. SAP Activate community

☐   B. Roadmap Viewer

☐   C. SAP Best Practices Explorer

☐   D. SAP Cloud ALM

4. Which asset in the SAP Activate methodology provides project managers with a checklist of items that have to be completed in each phase? (Select one correct answer.)

☐   A. List of SSCUIs

☐   B. Quality gate checklist

☐   C. Project management plans

☐   D. Sign-off template

5. Which of the following items are part of the five golden rules for implementation of SAP S/4HANA Cloud, private edition? (Select two correct answers.)

☐   A. Use preconfigured processes

☐   B. Inform stakeholders about new functionality

☐   C. Review the operations process before go-live

☐   D. Ensure transparency on deviations

6. In which tool can you access test script documents for SAP S/4HANA Cloud? (Select one correct answer.)

☐   A. Roadmap Viewer

☐   B. IMG

☐   C. SAP Best Practices Explorer

☐   D. SAP Activate community

A.2.5   Transition Path "New Implementation SAP S/4HANA On-Premise"

This section focuses on your understanding of SAP Activate for on-premise implementations of SAP S/4HANA solutions and examines your knowledge in this area. You can find answers to the questions with explanations in Section A.3.5.

1. Which tools can you use to prepare for transition to SAP S/4HANA? (Select two correct answers.)

   ☐   A. SAP Transformation Navigator

   ☐   B. IMG

   ☐   C. SAP Readiness Check for SAP S/4HANA

   ☐   D. Transport management system (TMS)

2. Where will the project team access SAP Best Practices documentation and adjust business process models for delivered preconfiguration? (Select one correct answer.)

   ☐   A. Roadmap Viewer

   ☐   B. SAP Activate community

   ☐   C. SAP Solution Manager

   ☐   D. Process Discovery report

3. What is the sequence of workshops in the explore phase for SAP S/4HANA implementation? (Select one correct answer.)

   ☐   A. Prepare system, conduct fit-to-standard, perform delta design

   ☐   B. Perform delta design, prepare system, conduct fit-to-standard

   ☐   C. Prepare system, perform delta design, conduct fit-to-standard

4. Which of the following items are outputs of the realize phase of a new SAP S/4HANA implementation project? (Select two correct answers.)

   ☐   A. Configuration and configuration documentation

   ☐   B. Cutover to production

   ☐   C. Landscape sizing

   ☐   D. Support operations framework and procedures

   ☐   E. Project scope statement

5.   Which types of testing are recommended by SAP Activate to be used during the realize phase to test configuration and custom code? (Select two correct answers.)

☐   A. Unit testing
☐   B. Peer testing
☐   C. Integration testing
☐   D. Change management testing

6.   What can project teams do with SAP Best Practices content in SAP Solution Manager? (Select two correct answers.)

☐   A. Access test script documents
☐   B. Adjust business process models
☐   C. Import legacy data
☐   D. Automatically update scoping information

A.2.6   Agile Project Planning

This section focuses on examining your understanding of the agile approach in SAP Activate—specifically, the planning activities in the context of your project. You can find answers to the questions with explanations in Section A.3.6.

1.   Which new roles are introduced in SAP Activate with the use of the agile approach? (Select two correct answers.)

☐   A. Scrum master
☐   B. Product owner
☐   C. Agile train master
☐   D. Backlog manager

2.   How frequently does the agile project team plan? (Select one correct answer.)

☐   A. Every iteration/sprint
☐   B. Only after fit-to-standard
☐   C. At the beginning of the project
☐   D. Once for each release

3.   Who estimates the effort needed for each backlog item? (Select one correct answer.)

☐   A. Scrum master
☐   B. Product owner

☐   C. Team

☐   D. Project manager

4.   Who sets the priority of the backlog item? (Select one correct answer.)

☐   A. Scrum master

☐   B. Product owner

☐   C. Team

☐   D. Project manager

5.   What artifacts and data points will be used during release and sprint planning? (Select three correct answers.)

☐   A. Backlog

☐   B. Retrospective

☐   C. Sprint duration

☐   D. Team size and capacity

☐   E. Burn-down chart

A.2.7   Agile Project Delivery

This section focuses on examining your understanding of the agile approach in SAP Activate—specifically, the executing and closing activities in your project. You can find answers to the questions with explanations in Section A.3.7.

1.   What agile practices do agile teams use to continuously improve? (Select one correct answer.)

☐   A. Backlog grooming

☐   B. Retrospective

☐   C. Sprint planning

☐   D. Daily standup

2.   How does the project team continuously align and communicate progress? (Select one correct answer.)

☐   A. During daily standup

☐   B. Making work visible

☐   C. Tracking progress in burn-down chart

☐   D. All of the above

3. Which key artifact gets updated every sprint? (Select one correct answer.)

☐ A. Backlog

☐ B. Project schedule

☐ C. Management plans

☐ D. Scope document

4. Who signs off on the completion of backlog items during the sprint demo? (Select one correct answer.)

☐ A. Project manager

☐ B. Scrum master

☐ C. Team

☐ D. Product owner

5. What is the purpose of the daily standup meeting? (Select two correct answers.)

☐ A. Communicate progress

☐ B. Identify blockers

☐ C. Update status report

☐ D. Debrief project sponsor

A.2.8   System Conversion to SAP S/4HANA

This section focuses on examining your understanding of using SAP Activate for system conversion to SAP S/4HANA. You can find answers to the questions with explanations in Section A.3.8.

1. Which of the following steps are part of the planning system conversion? (Select three correct answers.)

☐ A. Perform blueprinting workshops

☐ B. Clarify custom code adaption

☐ C. Perform data volume planning

☐ D. Define cutover approach

2. Where do you find list functions that have changed from SAP ERP to SAP S/4HANA? (Select one correct answer.)

☐ A. SAP API Business Hub

☐ B. Simplification list

☐   C. SAP Solution Manager solution documentation

☐   D. IMG

3.   Which solution supports the system conversion approach from SAP ERP? (Select one correct answer.)

☐   A. SAP SuccessFactors

☐   B. SAP Fieldglass

☐   C. SAP S/4HANA

☐   D. SAP Concur

A.2.9   Selective Data Transition to SAP S/4HANA

This section focuses on examining your understanding of using SAP Activate for selective data transition to SAP S/4HANA. You can find answers to the questions with explanations in Section A.3.9.

1.   Which objects can be transitioned to the SAP S/4HANA system during the selective data transition approach? (Select one correct answer.)

☐   A. ABAP repository objects (e.g., custom code)

☐   B. Transactional data

☐   C. Master data

☐   D. All of the above

2.   Which tools are used during the selective data transition to move data from the SAP ERP system to the SAP S/4HANA system? (Select one correct answer.)

☐   A. SAP Solution Manager

☐   B. SAP Best Practices Explorer

☐   C. Data Management and Landscape Transformation (DMLT)

☐   D. SAP Transport Management (SAP TM) system

3.   What are the common approaches to selective data transition? (Select two correct answers.)

☐   A. Conversion

☐   B. Mix and match

☐   C. New installation

☐   D. Shell conversion

A.3 Practice Question Answers and Explanations

In this section, we'll provide the answers to the practice questions. We'll also provide short explanations for each answer and sometimes refer to more details in the book.

A.3.1 SAP Activate Overview

This section provides correct answers and explanations (where necessary) to the questions listed in Section A.2.1.

1. Correct answer: **B**

   Answer **B** touches best on all the aspects of SAP Activate (methodology, ready-to-run business processes, and tools/applications for configuration and extensibility). **A** focuses too heavily on just one aspect of implementation—the methodology—and also only on the SAP S/4HANA solution, while SAP Activate is available for a range of SAP solutions. **C** only considers the tools and doesn't highlight the availability of preconfigured processes and prescriptive methodology.

2. Correct answers: **A, D**

   Both **A** and **D** are correct as SAP Activate was first introduced at SAPPHIRE 2015 along with the release of SAP S/4HANA.

3. Correct answers: **A, B**

   SAP Activate includes prescriptive guided methodology, preconfigured processes delivered in SAP Best Practices, and tools/applications for configuration, extensibility, data migration, and testing.

4. Correct answer: **A**

   The SAP Activate community provides SAP customers, partners, and interested parties with access to the experts that designed SAP Activate and use it in their implementation projects. You can find blog posts, ask questions, and engage with SAP Activate experts from both SAP and the broader community.

5. Correct answer: **C**

   The full version of the SAP Activate methodology can be accessed in the Roadmap Viewer using your computer, tablet, or mobile device. The Roadmap Viewer provides you with access to all available SAP Activate methodology roadmaps, phases, deliverables, tasks, and accelerators.

6. Correct answer: **A**

   The Roadmap Viewer provides users with access to a complete set of accelerators delivered within the SAP Activate methodology. All users can access and download accelerators such as project scope documents, WBSs, and project management plans. Note that access to accelerators is based on access level; users are recommended to log on to the tool using their SAP IDs to get access to all available materials.

A.3.2   SAP Activate Elements

This section provides correct answers and explanations (where necessary) to the questions listed in Section A.2.2.

1. Correct answer: **D**

    During the implementation of SAP S/4HANA software on premise or in a hosted setup, the project team can deploy the initial preconfiguration from either SAP-offered content and services (e.g., SAP Best Practices and the enterprise management layer for SAP S/4HANA), which we outlined in Chapter 4, or preconfigurations delivered in packages from SAP partners that are qualified for use on the SAP S/4HANA system.

2. Correct answers: **C, D, E**

    The SAP Activate methodology hierarchy levels are phase → deliverable → task, which is the structure of the SAP Activate methodology roadmap in the Roadmap Viewer. Note that in some environments, such as SAP Cloud ALM, the deliverable level may not be shown.

3. Correct answers: **B, C, E**

    The SAP Best Practices package for SAP S/4HANA Cloud provides users with access to preconfigured processes, business process documentation, business process flows, and test scripts that provide a detailed, step-by-step description of how to execute the business processes in the system.

4. Correct answers: **C, D**

    Of the listed answers, SAP Solution Manager allows users to upload the project WBS into the tool to manage the project using the cProjects functionality (not the full content of the SAP Activate methodology) and download/access the SAP Best Practices documentation in the tool. Users can adjust both the WBS and business process documentation and process flows.

5. Correct answers: **A, D**

    SAP S/4HANA software provides configuration capabilities through the IMG in Transaction SPRO for SAP S/4HANA and SAP S/4HANA Cloud, private edition. If you implement SAP S/4HANA Cloud, you'll use SSCUIs to configure your solution.

A.3.3   Workstreams Overview

This section provides correct answers and explanations (where necessary) to the questions listed in Section A.2.3.

1. Correct answers: **A, B, D**

    The three available strategies for transition to SAP S/4HANA from an SAP ERP solution are the new implementation, system conversion, and selective data transition. There is no upgrade option because SAP S/4HANA is a different product from SAP ERP. *Data center lift* is a made-up term.

2. Correct answers: **A, B**

   SAP Activate principles are discussed in Chapter 2 of this book and are as follows:

   - Start with SAP Best Practices
   - Confirm solution fit
   - Modular, scalable, and agile
   - Cloud ready
   - Premium engagement ready
   - Quality built-in

3. Correct answer: **A**

   SAP Activate uses fit-to-standard to confirm solution fit and identify the delta requirements for customer solution. We've discussed the approach in Chapter 2. The term *blueprint* is used by the ASAP methodology that was used to implement previous versions of the SAP ERP solution; SAP Activate today offers support for SAP ERP using the fit-gap approach.

4. Correct answer: **A**

   The Project Management Plan Template provides project managers with a structured way to document the management plans for all knowledge areas of the Project Management Institute's Project Management Body of Knowledge (*PMBOK Guide*), including time management, quality management, and risk management.

5. Correct answers: **A, B**

   The SAP S/4HANA application is built on top of the SAP HANA in-memory database and provides a modern user experience powered by SAP Fiori. The two other answers, SAP SuccessFactors and SAP Concur, are additional SAP products that aren't delivered with SAP S/4HANA; however, they can be integrated with SAP S/4HANA.

A.3.4   Transition Path "New Implementation SAP S/4HANA Cloud"

This section provides correct answers and explanations (where necessary) to the questions listed in Section A.2.4.

1. Correct answer: **B**

   SAP S/4HANA Cloud has four systems in the landscape. The starter system is provisioned first. The development system, test system, and production system are only provisioned after fit-to-standard workshops are completed.

2. Correct answer: **B**

   The SAP Activate methodology provides the OCM deliverables and tasks in the solution adoption workstream, where users can find adoption activities including end-user training, OCM, and value management.

3. Correct answer: **D**

   SAP Cloud ALM provides users with access to SAP Activate tasks, via which the project team can keep track of their progress. Users can access the SAP Best Practices documentation in the same environment in SAP Cloud ALM. The other tools mentioned in answers **B** and **C** don't provide combined access and aren't environments for teamwork, only for viewing the content. The SAP Activate community is a community space that doesn't contain SAP Activate tasks and SAP Best Practices process documentation.

4. Correct answer: **B**

   The quality gate checklist provides project managers with the list of key deliverables that need to be completed in the phase. The SSCUI list provides a complete list of SSCUIs in SAP S/4HANA Cloud. The project management plans detail the management plans for all project management knowledge areas (e.g., risk management, quality management, time management, etc.), and the sign-off template provides a template for formal sign-off that needs to be adjusted for each sign-off event.

5. Correct answers: **A, D**

   The five golden rules for implementation of SAP S/4HANA Cloud, private edition are as follows:

   - Foster a cloud mindset by adhering to fit-to-standard and agile deployment as detailed in SAP Activate.
   - Use preconfigured solutions with predefined processes and use the SAP Fiori UX.
   - Use modern integration technologies.
   - Use modern extension technologies.
   - Ensure transparency on deviations.

6. Correct answer: **C**

   SAP Best Practices provide you with test script documents that SAP customers and partners can access in SAP Best Practices Explorer after they have authenticated themselves and thus are recognized as partners or customers.

A.3.5   Transition Path "New Implementation SAP S/4HANA On-Premise"

This section provides correct answers and explanations (where necessary) to the questions listed in Section A.2.5.

1. Correct answers: **A, C**

   SAP customers can use the SAP Transformation Navigator to plan their transition journey to the SAP S/4HANA solution by following the step-by-step process to create a value-based business case and desired end-state product map. In addition,

SAP customers can use the SAP Readiness Check for SAP S/4HANA tool to assess their existing environment in order to understand the impact of simplification on SAP S/4HANA, custom code scope, add-ons, and so on.

2. Correct answer: **C**

    Out of the listed tools, only SAP Solution Manager allows users to access the SAP Best Practices documentation (after it has been imported) and modify the predelivered business process models in the modeling functionality in SAP Solution Manager.

3. Correct answer: **A**

    During the explore phase, the project team will first prepare the system for fit-to-standard analysis workshops by adjusting the master data and organizational structure and implementing the quick-win configuration that can be shown during the workshops. After the system has been prepared, the project team will proceed to fit-to-standard workshops to confirm the fit of the standard processes and to capture delta requirements. After that, the project teams proceed to delta design workshops to design the resolution of design delta requirements and gaps. These workshops can happen on different schedules for each area, such as finance, procurement, logistics, and so on; however, they follow the same pattern of preparing the system, conducting fit-to-standard sessions, and designing for delta requirements and gaps.

4. Correct answers: **A, D**

    During the realize phase, a lot of work is done on configuration, developer extensibility, key-user extensibility, integration, testing, and so on. **A** and **D** reflect the work that is done in the realize phase. The cutover to production (**B**) is done in the deploy phase, and the landscape sizing (**C**) and project scope statement (**E**) are done in earlier phases of the project.

5. Correct answers: **A, C**

    SAP Activate recommends the following types of testing during the realize phase:

    -   Unit testing to confirm that configuration or custom code works as required per the requirement definition
    -   String testing to start testing data flows between integrated business functions
    -   End-to-end integration test to confirm the integrated solution works
    -   Data migration testing
    -   User acceptance testing to expose selected end users to the new functionality and uncover issues the project team might have missed
    -   Performance and load testing to stress test the application for specific use cases, such as a storm test for a utility company or inclement weather test for an airline

6. Correct answers: **A, B**

   SAP Solution Manager provides users access to SAP Best Practices documentation, including the ability to access and download test script documents. In addition, users can view and edit the predelivered business process flows inside the SAP Solution Manager tool.

A.3.6   Agile Project Planning

This section provides correct answers and explanations (where necessary) to the questions listed in Section A.2.6.

1. Correct answers: **A, B**

   The SAP Activate methodology follows the Scrum agile approach that introduces the following agile roles:

   – Scrum master

   – Team

   – Product owner

2. Correct answer: **A**

   Planning in agile projects occurs on multiple levels. In the SAP implementation project context, the planning activities occur when the project is planned in the prepare phase; then, in each subsequent phase, project plans are detailed, and the agile project team plans each sprint/iteration during the regular agile cycle. Sprint planning is part of every sprint/cycle.

3. Correct answer: **C**

   The effort estimation for each backlog item is up to the experts in the project team. It's not the role of Scrum master or product owner.

4. Correct answer: **B**

   Prioritization of backlog items is the responsibility of the product owner in the agile project. The product owner should use a value-based prioritization framework to assess the benefits of each backlog item and properly prioritize them in the project.

5. Correct answers: **A, C, D**

   During planning, the project team uses the backlog (**A**) to understand the prioritized backlog items and to make the commitment. This sets the scope of work for the sprint. The second variable in planning each sprint is to know the fixed duration of the sprint (**C**). The last variable is to know the size of the team and, most importantly, the capacity of the team (**D**) to do the work that is being planned.

A.3.7   Agile Project Delivery

This section provides correct answers and explanations (where necessary) to the questions listed in Section A.2.7.

1. Correct answer: **B**

   In each sprint, the agile project team will use a retrospective meeting to identify the improvement opportunities by asking a series of questions, such as the following:

   – What do we want to keep?
   – What do we want to change in the next sprint?
   – What do we want to stop doing?

   Out of each retrospective, the project team decides on one or a few improvement steps that are then implemented for the next sprint to continuously improve the process.

2. Correct answer: **D**

   All the listed practices are used by project teams to align the resources and communicate progress both inside the team and to project stakeholders. The agile approach is based on radical transparency, which helps everybody understand the plans, current status, and what needs to be done to achieve the goal set for the sprint or release.

3. Correct answer: **A**

   Of the listed artifacts, only the backlog is typically updated each sprint, even if it's to indicate that some backlog items have been completed. The backlog is a living document in agile projects. The other listed artifacts are typically updated less frequently.

4. Correct answer: **D**

   The product owner is responsible for reviewing and approving that the backlog items have been delivered and that they meet the definition of done.

5. Correct answers: **A, B**

   Agile teams perform daily standup meetings to communicate progress to the rest of the team and to identify blockers that may be preventing them from progressing in work on specific backlog items. During the standup, each team member addresses the following questions:

   – What have I done since our last meeting?
   – What do I plan to do until the next meeting?
   – What blockers am I facing?

   Some teams may add additional questions to gauge the confidence of the project team in their ability to deliver committed backlog items.

A.3.8   System Conversion to SAP S/4HANA

This section provides correct answers and explanations (where necessary) to the questions listed in Section A.2.8.

1. Correct answers: **B, C, D**
   SAP Activate doesn't prescribe any blueprinting workshops. The other three steps are part of the planning system conversion, as we described in Chapter 8 of this book. Refer to Chapter 8, Section 8.3 for an overview of all the planning and execution steps.

2. Correct answer: **B**
   SAP provides detailed information about new, updated, and changed functions in SAP S/4HANA in the simplification list.

3. Correct answer: **C**
   Of the listed solutions, only SAP S/4HANA software supports the system conversion from previous versions of SAP ERP software. The other solutions listed don't support the system conversion approach.

A.3.9   Selective Data Transition to SAP S/4HANA

This section provides correct answers and explanations (where necessary) to the questions listed in Section A.2.9.

1. Correct answer: **D**
   All of the listed items can be transitioned during the selective data transition approach.

2. Correct answer: **C**
   During the selective data transition, data is moved using the DMLT software and related services. For more than 10 years, DMLT tools have provided well-established solutions for organizational changes, acquisitions, divestitures, or harmonization of SAP landscapes. The software provides highly automated processes that move large amounts of data between SAP instances quickly. Refer to Chapter 8, Section 8.4.

3. Correct answers: **B, D**
   There are two approaches for selective data transition: shell conversion and mix and match. In shell conversion, a shell copy of a production system is made without master and transaction data, and this is converted to SAP S/4HANA. In mix and match, a new SAP S/4HANA install is created, and then elements of the configuration and ABAP repository are transported or manually transferred.

Appendix B
The Authors

Sven Denecken is the chief operating officer (COO) of SAP S/4HANA and head of product. In his role as COO, Sven is responsible for business operations, developing the organization and its people, controlling, and communications for the SAP S/4HANA unit. In his role as head of product success, Sven ensures that the SAP S/4HANA product portfolio is aligned with market and customer requirements and drives thought leadership. Sven's many years of experience working with customers and partners, together with an extensive network that includes the SAP field organization and industry analysts, enable the SAP S/4HANA development teams to respond quickly to changing markets and ultimately provide solutions that help customers gain a competitive advantage.

In coinnovation projects with customers, Sven and his team discover key trends and next practices in the use of new technologies to ensure the evolution of both products and content.

As a member of SAP's executive leadership and by closely cooperating with teams, Sven supports the strategy of SAP's solutions and its alignment with customers, SAP's field organization, and the ecosystem.

You can connect with Sven at *www.linkedin.com/in/sdenecken/en*.

Jan Musil is the SAP Activate chief product owner at SAP. Jan leads a team of experienced product managers who design, build, and maintain SAP Activate, the innovation adoption framework that guides SAP customers and partners in their deployment of SAP solutions, including SAP S/4HANA, SAP SuccessFactors, SAP Ariba, SAP Analytics Cloud, and more. Jan and his team ensure that the SAP Activate content is continuously updated to stay in step with product capabilities and the latest practices for deployment of SAP solutions. This is done in close alignment with product engineering experts, field consultants, customers, and partners.

Since the start of his career, Jan has held roles in SAP product engineering, quality management, customer support, project management, and service operations in the United States, Germany, and Czech Republic.

Jan is passionate about the innovation of SAP solution deployment strategies, especially in the areas of agile implementation, cloud deployment, reuse of standard software packages, structured quality approach, program management, and value management.

Jan is a frequent speaker at SAP and industry events, has coauthored books about SAP Activate, and has contributed to books about SAP Solution Manager, project management, and several other industry publications.

You can connect with Jan at *www.linkedin.com/in/musiljan/*.

Srivatsan Santhanam has been with SAP Labs, India, since 2004 and is the head of the SAP Concur engineering product unit in SAP Labs India. He has nearly two decades of industry experience and is one of the early pioneers and thought leaders in the hybrid cloud/two-tier ERP with SAP S/4HANA Cloud product space.

Srivatsan has six US patents to his credit and many more in a filed state. He is a regular blogger and a coauthor of an SAP PRESS E-Bite, *SAP S/4HANA Cloud for Two-Tier ERP Landscapes*. He is an alumnus of the Indian Institute of Management-Ahmedabad and has a master's degree in data science from IIIT Bangalore.

Srivatsan is a regular speaker at many SAP, technology, and innovation events worldwide.

You can connect with Srivatsan at *www.linkedin.com/in/srivatsansanthanam/*.

B.1   Contributors

Vital Anderhub is a member of the product management team for SAP's operations platforms. His tasks involve solution management and knowledge management for SAP Solution Manager, SAP Focused Run, and SAP Cloud ALM.

Swati Balani is a product manager from the SAP S/4HANA product success, coinnovation, and content team at SAP Labs India and is the finance SME for the two-tier ERP product space with SAP S/4HANA Cloud. She has built several two-tier ERP scenarios and assets with intelligent technologies, including machine learning, sustainability, and analytics with SAP Analytics Cloud, covering finance, enterprise risk and compliance, and real estate. These scenarios illustrate how customers can drive incremental cloud transformation with SAP S/4HANA Cloud by leveraging SAP Business Technology Platform for business transformation as a service.

Lauren Bettuzzi has been a product specialist for SAP Activate since 2016. Her focus is on improving the customer's end-to-end experience during implementations. For the application design and configuration and analytics workstreams, specifically for SAP S/4HANA Cloud implementations, her expertise is in providing detailed implementation methodologies. She has three years of experience in cross-continental projects within SAP and with SAP partners.

Jitendra Bhandari is a senior product manager in the product engineering board area with a focus on SAP S/4HANA Cloud and the SAP Activate methodology. Jit has tremendous full lifecycle implementation knowledge in R/2, R/3, and SAP ERP, with a focus on logistics modules of SAP. Jit has been a part of the SAP Activate team since 2019 and mainly focuses on the integration and extensibility workstreams, including artificial intelligence. Jit has worked with SAP applications for more than 26 years, from both functional and technical perspectives.

Janko Budzisch is the chief product owner for SAP's operations platforms for SAP Solution Manager, SAP Focused Run, and SAP Cloud ALM. His main task is to drive the strategic direction of these product lines with input from customers, partners, and SAP's internal stakeholders. His mission is to provide SAP customers and SAP-centric service providers with the most suitable operations platforms to support their transformation into intelligent enterprises.

Bob Byrne is a senior product manager in the product engineering board area. His focus is on SAP S/4HANA Cloud and the SAP Activate methodology—specifically, the SAP Activate implementation methodology for SAP S/4HANA and two workstreams, customer team enablement and solution adoption. Bob has been with SAP for 15 years.

Dan Ciecko is a senior product manager for SAP Activate Methodology based out of Chicago, Illinois. Dan joined SAP in 1997 and has spent most of his career as a platinum consultant implementing various SAP products. Through this experience, he learned the mechanics of software implementations of both on-premise and cloud environments and how to efficiently bring quality and value to customers. Dan now works on the strategic direction of the SAP Activate Methodology. In addition, he owns the SAP S/4HANA Cloud and the intelligent enterprise implementation roadmaps.

Irene Dennehy is a postgraduate in business innovation and communications who joined SAP S/4HANA Cloud Expertise Services in the role of operations specialist in January 2020. Passionate about change management, she connects teams and individuals, supporting embracing challenges with a growth mindset. Before joining SAP, Irene managed operations and projects in partner companies such as EY (Ernst & Young), Compaq/HP, and Oracle, and she worked in startups and event management in Ireland, Italy, Switzerland, and Portugal, her native country. Fluent in four languages, Irene believes that listening, understanding, and respecting diverse cultures creates the perfect environment for achieving successful outcomes with true team excellence.

Christina Galbreath is a product manager within SAP Activate. She has been with the solution discovery team for five years and leads the content publication process for SAP Best Practices with a focus on SAP S/4HANA and SAP S/4HANA Cloud solutions. In addition, she manages the administration, maintenance, and feature requirements for all publishing tools.

Amin Hoque is an enterprise architect working with customers in the United Kingdom. He joined SAP in 2001 and has worked within SAP's consulting and development organizations. As a product manager, he drove the development of the configuration solution for SAP S/4HANA Cloud. In global consulting, he worked on the project implementation approach for SAP Best Practices. Amin has successfully implemented SAP solutions in many vertical sectors, including consumer goods, utilities, manufacturing, and retail. His roles have included solution architect, project manager, implementation consultant, trainer, and developer. Amin regularly posts SAP blogs. You can connect with him at *www.linkedin.com/in/amin-hoque-uk*.

Ying Huang is a product expert for SAP S/4HANA. Her journey of SAP solutions started with SAP R/3 3.1H. She has both consulting and industry experience implementing and running SAP solutions, including SAP's master data, analytics, and reporting solutions. She has extensive business knowledge in the areas of supply chain, sales operation planning, project portfolio planning, and management for IM&C. Her focus for SAP Activate is on the software lifecycle events, operations and support workstreams, and Customer COE topics of SAP S/4HANA Cloud.

Adnette Kamugisha joined SAP in 2013. She is a product manager for SAP Activate in the SAP S/4HANA organization in North America. Before joining the product management team, she worked with services portfolio management within the SAP Digital Business Services group. In the SAP Activate Methodology team, Adnette works on the technical architecture and infrastructure content to guide customers during system provisioning. She also works closely with various stakeholders to support the deployment experience of other SAP solutions.

Lisa Kouch has worked at SAP for more than 20 years, holding roles in consulting, SAP IT, and global project management office (PMO). She now works with the SAP Activate team as a senior product manager. She is the responsible for the project management content and serves as the build lead for the SAP Activate for SAP S/4HANA Cloud three-system landscape, the SAP Activate methodology for SAP SuccessFactors, and the SAP Activate methodology for SAP Service Cloud roadmap. She is also the PSCC lead for objectives and key results. Outside of work, she enjoys reading and spending time with her family.

Anil Kumar K.R. is a product manager for the SAP S/4HANA product success, coinnovation, and content team at SAP Labs India and is the sales and service SME for the two-tier ERP product space with SAP S/4HANA Cloud. He has helped to build two-tier ERP service assets that envision business scenarios from an end-to-end perspective. He has demonstrated thought leadership in understanding market requirements in the two-tier ERP space.

Shiva Kumar H.S. is a product manager from the SAP Concur engineering Unit in SAP Labs India. As a product expert, he has been supporting customers and partners to increase their adoption of two-tier ERP with SAP S/4HANA Cloud. He is also a thought leader in the hybrid cloud and two-tier ERP product space.

Prasanth P. Menon is a product manager from the SAP S/4HANA product success, coinnovation, and content team at SAP Labs India and is the SME who takes care of technology topics for the two-tier ERP product space with SAP S/4HANA Cloud. He helped the two-tier ERP team with integration and all technical setup related to data replication and extensibility.

Andreas Muno works in the SAP S/4HANA Cloud expertise services team on solution adoption, organizational change management, cloud mindset, and other cross topics. A trained economist, patented innovator, and startup cofounder, he has over 20 years of SAP experience in consulting and developing business software in Europe and as an industry solution and product manager in the US, with a variety of focus areas from public services, supplier relationship management, mobile applications, business process modeling and optimization, records management, and best practices to integrated business scenarios with SAP S/4HANA Cloud and its extension capabilities. More recently, he dialed in on the human factor in cloud software adoption success, enabling SAP's partners to bring about excellent outcomes at their joint customers, strengthening ecosystem relationships, and mentoring and coaching colleagues to become the best they can imagine.

Kelsey Lapczynski is a product specialist within SAP Activate. She has been with the SAP Activate team since 2017 and leads the testing workstream across multiple implementation roadmaps, with a focus on SAP S/4HANA and SAP S/4HANA Cloud solutions. In addition, she manages the SAP Activate community, where she supports customers and partners on their implementation journeys.

Petra Ohlinger works in SAP's product engineering organization, responsible for building product content for SAP S/4HANA to help SAP customers succeed locally and globally. With 30-plus years of experience in the areas of financial accounting and localization, Petra worked as a consultant for SAP in Germany, the US, and France, mainly on international projects, before she focused on building templates (SAP Best Practices, SAP Model Company for Multinational Corporations, and now the enterprise management layer for SAP S/4HANA).

Michelle Otun is a principal consultant based in the United Kingdom working on the SAP S/4HANA Cloud portfolio and services. She joined SAP in 2017, having previously worked across a variety of industries and consulting firms and successfully completed many large-scale SAP implementations. Michelle has worked on several internal initiatives since joining SAP and currently leads organizational change management for SAP S/4HANA Cloud.

Reshmi Paul is a product specialist for SAP S/4HANA based in Walldorf, Germany. She joined SAP in 2015 as a working student and later joined SAP Hybris. In 2017, she joined the product management team as a product associate. She completed her education at the University of Mannheim.

Jagmohan Singh Chawla has worked in application lifecycle management for more than 15 years. He is currently a chief solution expert in SAP Cloud ALM in the areas of project and task management. He also has experience working with system implementation partners and is passionate about tools and methodologies.

Christian Vogler is a product expert for SAP S/4HANA based in Walldorf, Germany. He joined SAP in 2011 from a partner company and has worked in presales and enablement for SAP Environment, Health, and Safety Management. In 2011 and 2012, he was the regional lead for the SAP Sustainability Performance Management solution for Asia Pacific, India, and Japan. In 2015, Christian joined the SAP S/4HANA team, where he provides a library of key assets, including the roadmap, customer-facing presentations, and solutions in detail. He also provides direct support for key deals or key accounts, including solution demonstrations.

Index

Q

- Learn about the SAP Activate certification test structure and how to prepare
- Review the key topics covered in each portion of your exam
- Test your knowledge with practice questions and answers

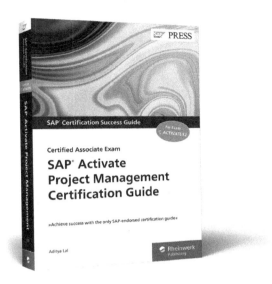

Aditya Lal

SAP Activate Project Management Certification Guide

Certified Associate Exam

Preparing for your SAP Activate project management exam? Make the grade with this certification study guide for C_ACTIVATE12! From agile project planning and delivery to new implementations and system conversions, this guide will review the technical and functional knowledge you need to pass with flying colors. Explore test methodology, key concepts for each topic area, and practice questions and answers. Your path to SAP Activate certification begins here!

530 pages, pub. 01/2021
E-Book: $74.99 | **Print:** $79.95 | **Bundle:** $89.99

www.sap-press.com/5194

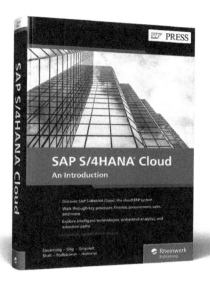

- Discover SAP S/4HANA Cloud, the cloud ERP system

- Walk through key processes: finance, procurement, sales, and more

- Explore intelligent technologies, embedded analytics, and adoption paths

Thomas Saueressig, Jan Gilg, Uwe Grigoleit, Arpan Shah, Almer Podbicanin, Marcus Homann

SAP S/4HANA Cloud

An Introduction

SAP S/4HANA Cloud has a lot to offer—see what's possible! Explore core functionality like finance, logistics, and reporting with embedded analytics. Learn how SAP S/4HANA Cloud impacts your users and how it can be extended, integrated, and adopted by your organization. Get information on the latest intelligent technologies and see how SAP S/4HANA Cloud can help unify and streamline your business. A bold new world awaits in the cloud!

approx. 465 pages, 2nd edition, avail. 05/2022
E-Book: $74.99 | **Print:** $79.95 | **Bundle:** $89.99

www.sap-press.com/5457

- Learn what SAP S/4HANA offers your company
- Explore key business processes and system architecture
- Consider your deployment options and implementation paths

Devraj Bardhan, Axel Baumgartl, Nga-Sze Choi, Mark Dudgeon, Piotr Górecki, Asidhara Lahiri, Bert Meijerink, Andrew Worsley-Tonks

SAP S/4HANA

An Introduction

Interested in what SAP S/4HANA has to offer? Find out with this big-picture guide! Take a tour of SAP S/4HANA functionality for your key lines of business: finance, manufacturing, supply chain, sales, and more. Preview SAP S/4HANA's architecture, and discover your options for reporting, extensions, and adoption. With insights into the latest intelligent technologies, this is your all-in-one SAP S/4HANA starting point!

648 pages, 4th edition, pub. 03/2021
E-Book: $69.99 | **Print:** $79.95 | **Bundle:** $89.99

www.sap-press.com/5232

- Your guide to SAP S/4HANA migration and implementation projects

- Planning, preparation, implementation: find the information you need for each project phase

- Get detailed instructions for brownfield and greenfield scenarios

Frank Densborn, Frank Finkbohner, Jochen Freudenberg, Martina Höft, Kim Mathäß, Boris Rubarth

Migrating to SAP S/4HANA

The best-selling book on SAP S/4HANA migration is back! Dive into this complete guide to SAP S/4HANA migrations paths, processes, and tools. Start with the basics: explore prerequisites for migration and learn about the on-premise, cloud, and hybrid operating models. Then get to know each migration path: brownfield, greenfield, or selective data transition. Understand the steps you'll take as you plan, prepare, and perform your migration, for any implementation path you choose. Your SAP S/4HANA migration starts today!

606 pages, 2nd edition, pub. 03/2021
E-Book: $79.99 | **Print:** $89.95 | **Bundle:** $99.99

www.sap-press.com/5279

Interested in reading more?

Please visit our website for all new book
and e-book releases from SAP PRESS.

www.sap-press.com